NATION STATE BY ACCIDENT

Nation State by Accident

The Politicization of Ethnic Groups and the Ethnicization of Politics: Bosnia, India, Pakistan

CARSTEN WIELAND

MANOHAR
2006

Revised and enlarged edition of *Nationalstaat wider Willen: Die Politisierung von Ethnien und die Ethnisierung der Politik, Bosnien, Indien, Pakistan*, Campus Verlag GmbH, Frankfurt am Main, Germany, 2000.

First English edition 2006

ISBN 81-7304-624-7

Published by
Ajay Kumar Jain for
Manohar Publishers & Distributors
4753/23 Ansari Road, Daryaganj
New Delhi 110 002

Printed at
Lordson Publishers Pvt Ltd
Delhi 110 007

Distributed in South Asia by
FOUNDATION
BOOKS
4381/4, Ansari Road
Daryaganj, New Delhi 110 002
and its branches at Mumbai, Hyderabad,
Bangalore, Chennai, Kolkata

For
SHIRANI

Contents

Preface to the [illegible]

Preface to the English Edition

Nearly five years have passed since the first edition of this book was published in German. In a human being's life this is not much time; by academic standards it's even less. But a lot has happened since then. Many people speak of a 'new era', a 'watershed moment' or even a new chapter of modern history when they refer to the events of 11 September 2001.

When on that day the planes as living bombs, filled with passengers and fuel, crashed into the towers of the World Trade Center in New York City and into the Pentagon in Washington, D.C., I felt, as many others did, that something has happened which could challenge the fabric of international relations. At this moment, though, I didn't have much time to reflect. What I had to do was pack my suitcase and rush to the next airport where I was lucky to get one of the few available seats on the flights to the North American continent. The German Press Agency (DPA) sent me to Washington as a correspondent to support our exhausted colleagues there.

After I had gained some distance from these events, I wondered if my studies about 'ethnicity' and 'ethnic conflicts' had now become less relevant or even obsolete. Everybody talked and wrote about terrorism and Islamic fundamentalism. The bloodshed in Bosnia, Rwanda and other conflicts in the world had been forgotten.

At a first glance it seems that when this book was first published in 2000, a decade of international politics that had been seen in 'paradigm of ethnicity' was coming to an end. Most international crises and debates revolved around this issue after the old patterns of confrontation of the Cold War in the 'paradigm of nation-states' had vanished. Maybe then, with 11 September a new paradigm emerged that we could call the 'paradigm of terrorism'? As in the case of 'ethnicity', the term 'terrorism' has never been clearly defined, and still it was swiftly used to cover a multitude of events and contexts, rightly and wrongly.[1]

'Terrorism' has become a catch-all term with fading contours since 11 September. Particularly the lines between resistance and terrorism have been blurred, which had its strongest impact on the power relations in the Middle East. Hezbollah leader Sheikh Hassan Nasrallah is certainly right when he says: 'Defining terrorism is one of the most difficult problems in the world today.'[2]

Does all this mean that we can turn away from 'ethnicity' and focus on 'terrorism' and Islamic fundamentalism as a driving force in international politics? Not at all, since at a second glance the claim that a change of paradigm has taken place looks exaggerated. For many who have written about globalization in recent years, both 'ethnicity' and the new scope, the new quality, and the new motives of international terrorism—which entails the aspects of cultural parochialism like Islamic fundamentalism—are two sides of the same coin.[3]

Therefore the real change of paradigm took place with the fall of the Berlin wall on 9 November 1989—on 11/9—not with Bin Laden's attacks against the US in 2001—on 9/11. The forces of ethno-nationalism, Islamic fundamentalism and international terrorism have, above all, one thing in common: They ignore the classic level of conflicts and conflict resolution—the state or, as most would say, the nation state.

There are many other common features, too. The ideological programmes of both ethno-nationalism and religious fundamentalism are remarkably shallow. Answers seem to be easy, goals are clear. Good and bad, friend and enemy are quickly and clearly defined. The election programmes of ethno-national parties in Bosnia-Herzegovina, for example, were always thinner than those of their smaller liberal or social democratic counterparts. Like with religious fundamentalists, ethno-nationalists mostly don't give a detailed and constructive elaboration on how the society and the state should look like, on how social and economic progress can be achieved. If one takes 'the nation state' or 'the Islamic state' away, nothing much is left.

Both ideologies suffer from reductionism and absolutism. Reductionism of political concepts and world views. Absolutism in violence and 'moral' legitimacy. Nationalism, especially in its integral form, has often been described as a religion of modern times or the substitute of religion. This makes both even more comparable.

Both ideologies entail a higher readiness to use blunt force in order to reach a goal, which has contributed to an increase in barbarism and civilian victims during these 'new wars' in comparison to conventional state warfare. The asymmetry of combatants—ethno-national activists against the state, religious fundamentalists against states—and of their political rationalities has lifted the limits of violence and blurred the line between times of war and peace.[4]

So-called ethnic conflicts have claimed millions of civilian lives after the end of the Cold War (more than 200,000 in Bosnia alone between 1992 and 1995, and about 800,000 in Rwanda in 1994), and the number of victims of terrorism motivated by religious fanaticism tends to be higher than the number claimed by terrorism of other ideologies.[5]

'Ethnicity' and 'terrorism' have also formed alliances at times, although rarely 'ethnicity' and religious fundamentalism. Pakistan is such a case. The country has come into existence through the concept of Muslim ethno-nationalism, and has developed in the direction of Islamic fundamentalism, after its ethno-national project had been fulfilled. This also bore the Taliban movement that took over neighbouring Afghanistan and, in turn, harboured and trained the terrorists who launched the attacks of 11 September. Taliban supporters also tried to forge together ethno-nationalism and Islamic fundamentalism in Bosnia-Herzegovina. However, even though the physical existence of many Bosnian Muslims (Bosnjaks) was threatened during the war in 1992-5, a radical Islamization of Bosnian society didn't take place. Strong traditions of a more moderate, and partly even secular, Islam of European descent were able to act as countervailing forces.

It was already after 11/9 not after 9/11, that the world has been witnessing a dangerous erosion of common codes of conduct and an attrition of international law. The old conventions of warfare have lost their cogency and normative power in the new contexts.

Ernst-Otto Czempiel draws a dialectic connection between ethno-national civil wars and militant Islamic fundamentalism: 'War ... has largely disappeared from the international system, and violence in form of civil wars has intruded the states. From there, however, it now comes back into the international system in the form of terrorism.'[6] Taking it one step further one could say: in the 'paradigm of ethnicity' the state is undermined from 'below', and in the 'paradigm of terrorism' it is attacked from 'above' (while the operational structures of terrorism consist of supra-state and sub-state elements at the same time). But both attack the state.

Also, the socio-political contexts of and recruitment strategies in 'ethnic conflicts' and Islamic fundamentalism show similarities. The activists appeal to poorer and less educated masses as their political constituency. The leaders themselves, however, mostly stem from urban, well-educated middle classes, and often even intellectual milieus. Although the ideologies are strongly and necessarily nurtured from *cultural* and *religious* or *quasi-religious* sources, they strive for exclusive *political* aims. Therefore, attempts to fight them on the political level only are not all too promising.

Reactions and military responses to the two phenomena have been very different though. Whereas when facing 'ethnic conflict' international actors have shown a great degree of confusion, hesitation, and, if at all, preferred soft approaches like UN peace-keeping missions (that often failed like in Srebrenica or Rwanda), the answers to international acts of terrorism after 9/11 have been purely military, strong, decisive, and paucilateral.[7] They have also been widely criticized as over-reactions and collective punishments, particularly the wars against Afghanistan and Iraq. Given the fact that 'ethnic conflicts' so far have claimed a multitude of lives in comparison to even the most atrocious terrorist attacks, this is surprising. Maybe not so much at a second glance: The victims of 'ethnic conflicts' are citizens of the troubled countries only, the conflict is territorially limited (apart from the refugee problem). The victims of terrorism are mostly citizens of Western countries, and the conflict is potentially ubiquitous.

The predominantly Anglo-American war against Iraq in March and April 2003 was a direct consequence of 9/11 at least according to the initiators of that war. But what has happened in Iraq since then is the ethnicization of politics, a familiar phenomenon that reminds us of the darkest chapters of ethno-national politics and controversial 'conflict solution' in Bosnia, Lebanon, and in colonial times with the partition of India and Pakistan (which left behind a still simmering ethno-national conflict in Kashmir). These were and are all solutions within the 'paradigm of ethnicity'.

The Iraqi Governing Council that was established by the Americans after the war was composed, of all possibilities, according to an 'ethnic'/religious ratio instead of one featuring social forces like trade unions, women, peasants, communists, liberals, conservatives, and maybe regional representatives. This misconception has helped to reinforce primordial and parochial alignments. There was no room for trans- or supra-'ethnic' political forces to take hold, and no room for a civil society to develop.

After a war like in Iraq, after a complete regime collapse, followed by occupation quasi colonization, and a comprehensive international mandate for political and economic reconstruction (through the controversial UN Resolution 1483, May 2003) there was enough of a political vacuum to set the points in a new direction towards a civil-democratic state. Of course, religious and other primordial elements would have pushed into politics, especially after decades of unjust distribution of resources and political power. But when, if not after such a war, is there a chance to at least try to escape the 'paradigm of ethnicity'? This opportunity was definitely missed. Considering the post-war situation in Iraq, this is an irreparable damage whose consequences will be long felt.

The 'paradigm of ethnicity' works in vicious circles, it is self-perpetuating, re-enforcing, and tends to create a political chain reaction. In Iraq, grievances that one group felt underrepresented vis-a-vis the other, bloody suicide attacks against Shi'a pilgrims and clerics, clashes between Shi'a and Sunni gangs, between Arabs and Kurds, became part of this logic. According to observers, there was even talk of building a wall through the northern city of Kirkuk along ethnic lines. This reminds one of ideas in Sarajevo during the early 1990s. In post-war Iraq more and more Arabs were moving away from Kurdish areas to the south. A state of their own was the final goal for ethno-nationalist Kurds.[8] The chain reaction had also reached neighbouring Syria in mid March 2004 with bloody riots between Kurdish activists and security forces in several cities.

The situation in Afghanistan after 9/11 has not led to a satisfactory outcome either. Warlords and 'ethnic' factionalism have ruled daily life before and after the US bombings of October 2001, interrupted by a somewhat more stable period under the Taliban. Due to the lack of a sweeping political concept after the war, Afghanistan is again being ruled according to the 'paradigm of ethnicity'. The country is a patchwork of different fiefdoms along 'ethnic' cleavages and still a hideout for Al-Qaida terrorists.

These examples show that the phenomena of 'ethnic conflict' and 'international terrorism' after 9/11 rather develop hand in hand than replace each other. The world is caught up in a vicious circle: an unstable society and polity torn apart between ethno-national activists is a fertile operating ground for Islamic fundamentalists and terrorists. And countries that are alleged to support terrorism are bombed and administered into 'ethnic conflict'.

The rise of primordialism, the political polarization of populations, the weakening of existing state structures in troubled areas are common outcomes of ethno-nationalism and Islamic fundamentalist terrorism.

This developement was not unavoidable. Czempiel, for example, outlined the perspective of the 'world of societies' (*Gesellschaftswelt*) as opposed to the world of states (*Staatenwelt*) and ideological block confrontation.[9] The process of increasing emancipation, education, information, participation, and democratization characterize this new world that already began to take shape in the middle of the twentieth century under the cover of the states and burst open after 11/9. This world of societies also changed the means and the logic of foreign policy with the rising influence of transnational cooperations and non-governmental organizations. However, Czempiel recognizes and criticizes a setback in recent years with unilateralism and an emphasis on state sovereignty taking hold again.

When we look at the developments described in the discussion about ethno-nationalism and militant Islamic fundamentalism, it reminds less of what is typical of society (*Gesellschaft*) than of community (*Gemeinschaft*). In a world of communities, not societies, the focus is on primordial features, on descent, not on rational, flexible or even multiple identities. People are condemned to unchangeable 'ethnic' or religious ascriptions. In case of an 'ethnic conflict' or a terrorist attack this external ascription can mean life or death.

In philosophical terms this expresses the bankruptcy of humanism. Not only the unimpeachable moral value of human beings is increasingly ignored in the conflicts and conceptions that have dominated since 11/9 but also their moral equality regardless of religious conviction or descent as well as the freedom of individual choice. People are not judged according to what they think but on what they 'are' by birth. Policy actors focus on minority rights within the 'paradigm of ethnicity' instead of human rights that, if consequently applied, render collective rights superfluous. Groups or 'nations' are not defined on the basis of a common discourse, like the representatives of Enlightenment did, but on *a priori* ascriptions and assumptions. This is the eclipse of *ratio* in favour of *origio* in domestic and international politics.

The hopes in the first months and years after 11/9 have not been fulfilled. When the wall came down in Berlin, two new potential paradigms opened up. The first one was linked to humanist, all-encompassing idea of self-determination as well as ideals of democracy, international liberalism, multilateralism, and freedom. In the context of conflict solutions it means the promotion of a strong civil society, a civil-democratic understanding of the nation, and political institutions that reflect and respond to discursive and rational demands. The second possible paradigm entailed an even stronger *a priori* and objective classification of human-beings into ethno-national camps.

One was the *paradigm of humanism* and the other was the *paradigm of primordialism.* Without any doubt, the latter prevailed. The term primordialism comprises 'ethnicity' and religion in particular, and thus also religious fundamentalism. Therefore 'ethnicity' and Islamic fundamentalist terrorism could be called sub-paradigms of the paradigm of primordialism. In this context, research on 'ethnic conflicts' is as important as it was before 9/11.

The revival of primordialism as a political driving force after 11/9 does not mean, of course, that primordial concepts had been absent in politics during the 'paradigm of the nation-states'. In the case of the British separation of India ethno-nationalism has played a crucial role.

All in all, this book goes beyond the mere description of the case studies of Bosnia-Herzegovina and India/Pakistan. It offers conclusions regarding the nature of future conflicts, and tries to deconstruct the notion of big blocks as coherent actors, such as 'ethnic groups', ethno-nations, civilizations or cultures, and the like.

The first edition of the book has triggered debates in particular on the definition of ethnic groups, since scholars still struggle to come to grips with the terms ethnicity and nation. I have offered a new reading of the terms 'ethnicity' and ethno-nation, and I'm still convinced that they hold valid explanatory power for a systematic approach beyond the case studies.

For the arguments mentioned above, there was no need to revise the central theses of the book, even though recent world events suggested the emergence of new global trends. Nevertheless, this edition has been substantially enlarged and brought up to date in view of the changes since the beginning of the new millennium. During repeated trips to Bosnia I could conduct and incorporate new interviews with politicians, historians, and journalists, some of whom I had last met during the war.

Apart from my deep gratitude to various scholars and journalists expressed in the preface of the first edition, I would like to mention once again Prof. Dr Dietmar Rothermund, the reputed German expert on South Asia, who made it possible for this book to be published in English by Manohar, New Delhi. I also thank Inter Nationes, Bonn, for their financial contribution to the translation costs, as well as Vijay Chabra and Rosy Singh who supported me in the heavy task of translation.

Damascus
April 2004 CARSTEN WIELAND

NOTES

1. A good guideline for the history and the multiple definitions of terrorism is Bruce Hoffman, *Inside Terrorism*, London, 1998; *Terrorismus: Der unerklärte Krieg*, Frankfurt/M, German (2nd) edition, 2001.
2. Interview with the author, Beirut, 20 February 2004.
3. For example, Benjamin R. Barber, *Jihad versus McWorld: How Globalisation and Tribalism are Reshaping the World*, New York, 1996 (2nd edn.); Thomas L. Friedman, *The Lexus and the Olive Tree: Understanding Globalisation*, New York, 2nd edn., 2000.
4. Herfried Münkler, *Die neuen Kriege*, München, 2002, pp. 57ff.
5. Hoffman (2001), p. 121.
6. Ernst-Otto Czempiel, *Weltpolitik im Umbruch*, München, 2002, p. 39.
7. I would like to introduce this term here as standing between unilateral and multilateral. It means a 'coalition of the few' and thus also expresses insufficiency (according to its Latin connotation), different from the word plurilateral that is sometimes used in international law in context of WTO negotiations and procedures (which simply means: 'several' states).
8. Pierre-Jean Luizard, a French expert on Iraq, in an interview with the author, Beirut, 19 February 2004.
9. Czempiel (2002), pp. 15ff.

Preface to the German Edition

It was on the plane from New Delhi to Berlin when the idea of a comparative study of nation-building in the Balkans and the Indian subcontinent was born. I had just completed my studies in India and was returning to Humboldt University, Berlin. My experiences as a journalist in the besieged city of Sarajevo in November 1994 and as a correspondent in India in 1996 and 1997 had triggered my curiosity into what lay behind the political tensions in these conflict-ridden societies. My observations gradually developed into great scepticism vis-à-vis the conventional news reporting found in the media and in popular political and historical assumptions. Why did the Muslims end up in a state of their 'own' without the majority of them wanting one? Why did outsiders speak of an ethnic conflict while many of those involved in it denied its existence? Why did Muslims fight against Muslims?

For the enquiry into these and many other issues I received the greatest conceivable support, personally and professionally, from Prof. Dr Günter Schödl at Humboldt University, Berlin. His extraordinary interest and engagement in this project gave me the courage and strength to carry out a study of this dimension. His personal interest when I was pursuing my master's thesis and his support as a supervisor during my subsequent Ph.D. dissertation deserve my highest respect and gratitude. In addition, he has given me valuable insights into the nationalisms of south-eastern Europe. I am also highly indebted to my co-supervisor Prof. Dr Peter Heine, who encouraged me with his pragmatism and gave me important references concerning the political development of Islam. I would also like to thank Prof. Dr Dietmar Rothermund of the University of Heidelberg for his spontaneous professional support and guidance as an expert in the field, and for his valuable suggestions.

An important partner in the discussions on the Indian history of ideas was K.N. Panikkar of the Jawaharlal Nehru University, New Delhi. He has earned my high respect for his personal endeavours and his tireless efforts in creating enlightenment against the ethno-nationalistic currents in his country. To his colleague, M.K. Palat, I owe many insights into the nature of British colonial rule, and to Uma Singh I owe insights into the political contradictions attendant upon the birth of Pakistan.

In Bosnia I could always count on the help and expertise of the journalist Zdravko Ljubas, whose eyewitness accounts have enriched this book. The methods of comparative politics I owe to Prof. Herbert Kitschelt of Duke University. Also after my studies in the United States in 1995-6 he made valuable suggestions to improve my work.

I sincerely thank all participants in this dialogue who cannot be mentioned here individually. Of course, I take full responsibility for any misinterpretations, exaggerations, or omissions.

This work was submitted as a Ph.D. dissertation to the Humboldt University, Berlin, under the deanship of the ethnologist Prof. Dr Wolfgang Kaschuba. The defence took place on 14 December 1999.

Berlin CARSTEN WIELAND
December 1999

Introduction

> Ah! If only I had found one person more in you
> for whom it was sufficient to be a human being![1]
>
> *Nathan the Wise to the Templar*

In a bar in the centre of the besieged city of Sarajevo in November 1994 two young journalists, both in their early twenties, are sitting in front of me. Sanela is fashionably dressed and her lips are painted violet in this grey city. 'I am Muslim', she says, 'but religion is a private matter. I can still drink beer and wear short skirts. I am only Muslim because my name is Muslim.' Zdravko agrees. He is a Croat, just because he was born Catholic. But religion hardly plays a role in his life. 'The young people are indifferent to religion', he claims, 'only the politicians don't want to understand this.'[2] The heavy rumbling of exploding grenades can be heard coming from the mountains. The loudspeakers are blaring music by the pop band Unlimited. Yet borders are suddenly everywhere. They are life threatening, and they strangulate Sarajevo more and more. Sanela and Zdravko are shaking their heads. Some years ago they used to meet friends who are now on the other side of the border and are fighting against them and the city.

Change of scene: Kalam, a picturesque mountain village in the Swat valley in north-western Pakistan, a stone's throw from the embattled Line of Control dividing the disputed Kashmir region. Two aspiring businessmen are strolling up to me. They come from the pulsating city of Lahore, both are in their early twenties, and a bit dumpy. 'We are sick and tired of the partition [of India and Pakistan]!' curses Shumail. 'This is just a war between governments.' His friend, Gohar, adds: 'Why can't it be like in West and East Germany where the people come together? After all, we watch the same Indian films and look up to the Indian film stars. For centuries we have lived together. Even today, in India there are more Muslims than in Pakistan. It was the British who divided us.' Both men have no faith in the Pakistani politicians. They describe themselves as not particularly religious. Even their politicians had nothing really to do with Islam, they figure. 'Our country is in the hands of corrupt feudal lords,' says Shumail and turns his arm over the sunny mountains towards the direction of Islamabad.[3] But not all people think like them. Others want to strengthen the borders or create new ones. On some stones in the Swat valley someone had scrawled in white Urdu script: 'We want the Sha'riat' or even: 'For an independent Swat.'

Both scenes are chance encounters from two strife-torn countries which are the subjects of this book. The episodes described above already say a lot about the political problems in Bosnia-Herzegovina and Pakistan. They even anticipate important interpretative approaches. But for a much more banal reason they have become an important impetus for the case studies. Both times I met young people who are not really bothered about the religious or 'ethnic' criteria ascribed to them. The youngsters condemn the politics of confrontation practised by their politicians who appeal to these very criteria in order to legitimize their acts. The more I delved into the history of Bosnia-Herzegovina, India, and Pakistan, the clearer it became to me that these young people are not the only ones who think like this. Why then do we have separation, borders, war? Why huge waves of refugees and 'ethnic' expulsions? Moreover, if one studies the behaviour of the key leaders of the groups among the Muslim populations in both countries, one comes to a baffling conclusion. The majority of them did not want a state of their 'own' for a long time, had never wanted it, nor do they want it even today, and yet they ended up with one. This requires an explanation—if one does not want to simply settle things with the peculiar but not quite inapt remark of the creator of Pakistan, Mohammed Ali Jinnah: It had been him alone who carved out Pakistan for the Muslims, with the help of his secretary and his typewriter.[4]

Geographically, Bosnia-Herzegovina, and India-Pakistan are situated far apart. Yet they share many parallels and, above all, the above-mentioned contradictions. Hence this book, through a comparative study, explores the Muslim nation-building up to the crucial turning point in the state-building of Pakistan in 1947 and to the temporary turning point in Bosnia-Herzegovina after the Dayton Agreement of 1995 and partly beyond. In the case of India the time frame discussed stretches beyond the creation of the state of Pakistan and explores the politics and ideology of the country until the end of the 1990s.

The study has been undertaken during a time when Bosnia-Herzegovina and Pakistan are increasingly being referred to in a single breath. Particularly after the Bosnian war, references can be found in footnotes and illustrative examples about the similar fate of 'the Muslims' in both cases.[5] However, I am not aware of any comprehensive work that compares, *per se*, the Muslim nation-building in Bosnia-Herzegovina and in Pakistan. A further indication that clear-cut parallels suggest themselves is apparent from the contemporary choice of words with reference to the developments in both countries. When the British colonial masters left India, they described the plan of their departure as Balkan Plan.[6] Similarly, the notion of the Pakistanization of Bosnia-Herzegovina circulates today.[7]

METHODOLOGY

As the title of the book suggests, in both cases there occurs a *politicization of 'ethnic groups'* and an *ethnicization of politics*. There is more to it than just a play of words. First, this is the political programme of an 'ethnically' moulded nationalism. Second, these words sketch the sequence of the developments at whose end stands what most call ethnic conflicts or—in a more advanced stage—separatism. At the same time, the title makes it clear that both phenomena are closely related and both influence each other.

This means in concrete terms: (1) People with varied (real or imagined) features regarding their descent and personal attributes, which they simultaneously share with many others (like religion, language, customs, etc.), are addressed via these very features by spokesmen with political aims who incite them to a *group-specific* behaviour which would otherwise be out of question (the politicization of 'ethnic groups'). (2) In turn, this behaviour changes the political scenario and the political outputs (the ethnicization of politics).

In case (1) certain factors influence the group which, for the sake of simplification, is called an 'ethnic group' at this point.[8] The 'ethnic group', dependent on these factors, can hence be referred to as a *dependent variable*. It is transformed under the effect of independent variables. The questions can thus be put as follows: What are the ingredients required to construct 'ethnic groups' and to politically activate them? What is the impact of social elites, foreign power relations, political factors, etc., on the formation of 'ethnic groups', ethno-nations, and finally ethno-national states? In case (2) the 'ethnic group' is a self-explanatory factor in itself, an *independent variable*. Political contents, the constellation of political parties, and finally maps are independent variables. They come to be so because the 'ethnic' principle ultimately determines the political agenda to a great extent.

As an example, the use of 'ethnic group' as an independent and a dependent variable means: by way of mobilizing previously unconnected discontents, 'ethnicity' can give a helping hand to the start of a particular conflict. And the other way round as well: 'ethnicity' is, in some cases, a response of marginalized groups to the disintegration of political and economic ruling structures and the attempt of this group to improve its economic and political situation by the way of cultural mobilisation.[9] Anthony Smith describes the various approaches that can arise from the twofold use of 'ethnicity' as a dependent and an independent variable:

> On the one hand, the politics of ethnicity and nationalism can mean the impact of politics on ethnicity and national identity. This in turn can signify either the uses of ethnicity and nationalism in the power struggles of leaders and parties, leading to a micro-analysis of ethnic politics; or the processes by which states create ethnic groups and nations and their conflicts, producing macro-analysis of national formation.
>
> On the other hand, one can analyse the impact of ethnicity and nationalism on politics. This in turn can signify either the ways in which ethnic groups and nationalist movements seek their political goals, again leading to a micro-analysis of the politics of ethnic nationalists; or the role of culture and ethnicity in creating states and influencing state systems, producing a macro-analysis of state and interstate formation.[10]

The dovetailing of a politicization of 'ethnicity' and an 'ethnicization' of politics often makes it difficult to demarcate the two aspects.[11] Sometimes it is like getting embroiled in the controversy of the hen and the egg: did the politicians come first, shake the 'ethnic groups' into action, and thus instrumentalize them? Or were there quasi-natural 'ethnic' interests which were reflected in the political scenario right from the beginning (without any massive mobilization)? The answer must be solomonic: there is no either-or but a both-and. The case studies highlight how and by which influences 'ethnic groups' are constructed. They also show the following: Once 'ethnic groups' are politicized and mobilized, they influence the political disputes decisively. At this juncture there is a third aspect that co-relates both aspects: as the politicization of 'ethnic groups' was in progress, external factors entered the scene and promoted or discouraged the influence of the 'ethnic' paradigm on the political outcomes—and so the causal circle goes on. Both aspects are equally important for comparing the case studies. The double use of 'ethnicity' as a dependent and an independent variable makes it easier to look at the connections. It also contributes to defining more closely the factor 'ethnicity' and to making it operationable. This method raises the explanatory power in the comparison of both case studies.

In this work the term 'ethnicity' is therefore understood as primarily functional. Apart from the variable approach it is helpful to define the content of 'ethnicity' not as a historical-individual phenomenon but rather as a situative-structural concept of action. Only in this way can it be simultaneously and suitably applied to the Balkans and the Indian subcontinent in a comparative study.

Systematic approaches of this type allow us to reasonably curtail the purely descriptive elements in the case studies,[12] and to keep us from slipping into a historical 'examplism'.[13] The comparative method forces us to set priorities and carefully select phenomena, events, actors, and institutions. This is always a balancing act, particularly in view of the risk of isolating the case studies from their historical setting and thus trimming them for the sake of comparison. At least this book makes a serious attempt to credibly verify arguments drawn from the historical context, and at the same time systemize them effectively.

For this reason the investigation stands at the intersection of several disciplines in the humanities. On the one hand, the study aspires to meet the demands of a historical study. To an equal extent, it falls back on theories and methods of comparative political science. This is necessary because of the many problematic terms, the individual elements of comparison (like the party system), and the claims of presenting convincing results that go beyond the case studies. In addition, the study draws on the tools and approaches of sociology and ethnology.

Since two vast multidimensional cases are being handled here, it must also be clearly outlined what this book does *not* strive to achieve. It does not claim to offer a complete chronological presentation of the recent history of India and the Balkans—not even with reference to the respective evolution of 'the Muslims'. Similarly, it cannot go into the psychological factors, as to *why* people tend to accept ethnic attributes as criteria of action. Rather the study seeks to highlight *how* these attributes are politically instrumentalized and with what consequences.

The comparison is conceptualized in a way that takes into consideration phenomenal as well as functional elements. This means that, on the one hand, there are *equal phenomena* that play a *comparable role* (as the formation of Muslim cultural movements and parties as the forerunners of a Muslim national identity). On the other hand, *diverse phenomena* also play a role that have a *comparable function* (like British colonial rule and the international community as catalytics for a territorial solution to the ethno-national conflicts or the function of myths). Anyone who compares will encounter differences, of course. They are singled out and systematically analysed in this study. This also implies that *equal phenomena* can have *diverse effects* (as did the different approaches of the main Muslim figures, Izetbegovic and Jinnah, in the final and decisive phase of nation-building).

CONTENTS

In the first part of the book, 'ethnicity' mostly appears as a dependent variable. This part explores those features that were singled out in order to mark off 'ethnic groups' from one another in Bosnia-Herzegovina and India. Religion being the main means of contrast in both cases, the presentation begins with the entry of Islam into these areas. Then come those factors which lead to a sharpening of 'ethnic' differences, such as the making of historical myths, the standardization of languages, the instrumentalization of banal conflicts, the homogenization and the progressively increasing claims of neighbouring 'ethnic groups', the influence of occupying powers, etc. Particularly noteworthy about the Muslim nation-building is a gap between the demands of the Muslim ethno-national leaders and the Muslim population. This is also apparent in the interpretations of Islam. Some Muslims were less interested in Muslim nationalism than in the teachings of Islam.

The second part of the book deals with the advanced stage of Muslim nation-building which culminated in state building in India and which could conceivably end with state-building in Bosnia-Herzegovina as well. In this phase, the ethno-national leaders of 'the Muslims' increasingly set the tone ('ethnicity' as an independent variable). The main Muslim actors, Alija Izetbegovic (1925-2003) in Bosnia-Herzegovina and Mohammed Ali Jinnah (1876-1948) in India, are compared and contrasted above all with respect to their political motives, their concepts of the nation, and their attitudes towards Islam. An important aspect of this work comprises the alternatives to ethno-national block-building and its encrustation into statehood. The Muslim nation-building and the radicalization of the conflicts were not historically determined, much less so was the result of a Muslim state. This is why a look at the alternatives is imperative. They are reflected in the attitudes of a large part of the Balkan and Indian populations and in political counter projects. External catalytics, however, worked in favour of an ethno-national state-building—above all British colonial rule and its downfall, as well as the federation of Yugoslavia and the international actors as mediators in the Bosnian war.

Finally, the actual results of Muslim nation-building will be highlighted. The realities in Pakistan must be measured according to the self-made standards for a Muslim homeland. Whether a part of Bosnia-Herzegovina will develop in the same direction remains an open question after the Bosnian war.

LITERATURE

The literature and, above all, the status of the source materials for the study of Bosnia-Herzegovina and India are partly very different. In the case of Bosnia, in particular, because of its topicality quotations from the salient players are available mostly from the hands of journalists. In contrast, for India there are many collections of documents available, including speeches and resolutions of party conferences which have been used and interpreted as academic references for a long time. This proviso must be conceded, although the study attemps to even out the eventual imbalance in the source materials by using publications from the main Bosnian actors. Another difference is that the Indian case concentrates to a much greater extent on personalities. This becomes obvious in the approaches as well, particularly those found in the older monographs. Historians devoted a lot of attention to the charismatic trio Jinnah-Nehru-Gandhi. Often this emphasis bordered on personality cults.[14] All the same, it is true that these individuals did have an extra-ordinarily strong influence on their people, something that cannot be observed to the same degree in Bosnia-Herzegovina. This legitimizes also an eventual shift of balance in the literature.

TERMINOLOGY

The study deals with events that involved unimaginable horrors, and whose roots and motives often remain unclear to the current political players—also and particularly so to journalists. Hence, this study will not take over popular minimizations and will avoid generalizations. Terms like ethnic cleansing, which were created during the Bosnian war, are excluded from this writing. Instead, ethnic expulsions and, in extreme cases, ethnic extinctions are used. Similarly, terms such as *the Muslims*, *the Serbs*, *the Croats*, *the Hindus*, etc., have no place here. For example, how can one justify speaking of a Hindu-Muslim conflict without a billion people smashing each others' heads every day? If these groups appear in the study at all, it is only to describe the ethno-national paradigm and to re-enact it theoretically, and even then they appear in quotation marks. Otherwise, it is spokesmen, activists, politicians, landlords, traders, workers, etc. who act. This also makes sense methodologically. As mentioned earlier, the book will show that 'the Muslims' and their political action group(s) do not overlap in various fields but are, in fact, often poles apart. Besides, the use of collective terms veils the mechanisms and triggers of conflicts. It would be imprudent to take over 'ethnic' labels which themselves execute an important function politically and historically. For an outside observer[15] it would be fatal to accept a certain paradigm from the start which is, at the same time, the object of analysis, thereby legitimizing it—particularly when it can bring about such bloody consequences.

NOTES

1. Lessing (1779, rpt 1987), p. 50. Gotthold Ephraim Lessing (1729-81).
2. Sanela Hadzihasanovic and Zdravko Ljubas in a conversation with the author in Sarajevo (10 November 1994).
3. Shumail Saiqol and Gohar-e-Shafiq in a conversation with the author in Kalam (25 December 1996). Shumail referred to the Pakistan government of Prime Minister Nawaz Sharif.
4. Collins and Lapierre (1976), p. 240; Hoodbhoy, Nayyar and Nayyar, in: M.A. Khan (1985), p. 169.
5. For example, in: Steindorff (1997), in: *SOEM*; Thomas/Friman (1996); A.S. Ahmed (1997). In an overview of the development of Muslim states, Lapidus (1988) alludes to the parallels between the Balkans and India in more detail.

6. See Chapter V.5.2.3. 'Ethnic' Labels and Enclosures in India.
7. Anis Bajrektarevic in an interview with the author (26 March 1998). He points out that Bosnia-Herzegovina is falling apart into ever smaller fragments: Herzeg-Bosna, 'West-Srpska' (Banja Luka), 'East-Srpska' (Pale), the 'Muslim' area. Similarly, the British colonial empire fragmented into Sri Lanka, Afghanistan, Burma, India, Pakistan, and Bangladesh. In both cases the separation took place in steps.
8. For a closer examination of these definitions, see Chapter I.2. 'What is an 'Ethnic Group?'
9. Esser (1988), in: *ZS*; and Bell, in: Glazer and Moynihan (1975) [quoted in Heckmann (1992), p. 33].
10. A. Smith (1996), in: *IA*, pp. 445-6.
11. For the problem of the correct use of dependent and independent variables, see: King, Keohane and Verba (1994), pp. 107ff.
12. For a discussion on the advantages and disadvantages of case-oriented and variable-oriented approaches, see: Ragin (1987), p. 53.
13. Heckmann (1992), p. 3.
14. Deconsecrating Gandhi, *The Economist* (29 August 1998).
15. Here I am following Kaschuba (1995), in: *EE*, pp. 123ff, who appeals to ethnologists to take the position of outside observers and warns them not to fall prey to the 'ethnic paradigm', thereby allowing the instrumentalization of their studies.

I. The Delicate Trio of Ethnicity, Nation, and State

A man like you does not stay
where the accident of birth has thrown him; or if he stays,
he stays out of insight, reasons, choice of the better.[1]

Sultan Saladin to Nathan

The enlightened German author Lessing pleaded that the accident of birth be relativized through contemplation. Nathan the Wise succeeded, most human beings failed. In the case studies taken up here, the principle of descent has gained strong *political relevance*, too. The accident of birth has become a political instrument to which human beings are subject and object at the same time.

The study deals with political processes in which the position of human beings in society has become more and more detached from social, economic, and individual principles, and instead has been narrowed down to the *ascription* to a postulated community of common ancestry. So what have to be explained first are the technical terms which serve as the criteria of ascription and which describe the processes built on these criteria. But then one quickly ends up on theoretically slippery ground in a highly complex and topical field of research. The abundance of literature on this subject makes rigorous restrictions necessary. The intention is not to include all academic debates and their variants but rather to place the terms in an important framework and to finally determine suitable definitions for this study.

1. WHAT IS AN ETHNIC GROUP?

[The term ethnic] is a completely unsuitable collective name for any really exact analysis.[2]

Max Weber

Even if this term ethnic appears to be suspect and fuzzy to Weber and many others, it has become *qua nomina* a central component of political confrontation. So it must have been made 'suitable' in one way or the other. This also means that the term ethnic group must possibly be differentiated from other macro-sociological categories like a purely religious or language community or a class (in the economic sense).

In response to this, Ganzer emphasises that an ethnic similiarity of people must always include elements of both *a community of descent and culture.*[3] If one of them is left out, then other categories will take over. Although Ganzer thus represents the primordial approach, this idea serves as a point of departure or an ideal case for all who want to deal with ethnicity,[4] either academically or politically. There will be more discussion on the tricky term 'culture' later in the study. In the context mentioned just now, it can be understood as a collective term for primordial and situational *pre-political* features. Besides, it is certain that an ethnic group is defined by inner coherence as well as by external demarcation.[5] This minimum definition should suffice for the time being until we arrive at a more precise one. The theoretical approaches differ, above all, on the question whether more emphasis should be laid on the principle of descent or on external phenomena like 'culture'. In the following sections the approaches are presented as ideal types and in a coarse-grained pattern.

1.1. The Primordial Approach (also: tribalistic[6])

The primordial approach has both a theoretical and a practical aspect. On the level of theory, the representatives of this approach assume that ethnic groups—however they be defined—present a 'social reality' *a priori* that was discovered by academics only later.[7] In practice, this means: primordial factors like race, language, religion, colour of skin, traditions (from clothing to cooking recipes), and/or the sense of belonging to an area—defined in a diffuse way, not in terms of state boundaries—influence the people by way of and since their birth. As a result, those who share these factors are effectively bound to each other. They constitute a clear-cut group with a fixed identity. No member can escape the ascription of ethnicity; it occurs 'from above' and is *objective.* Changing sides is impossible, and attempts to do so are considered as only 'fooling around'.[8] Hence, ethnic groups are clear-cut and solid social units. This concept allows us to consider ethnic groups as input-givers in comparative political science. They influence and explain processes. They can, therefore, be introduced as *independent variables*.

Interestingly, the term 'tribe' is hardly used anymore in the humanities. Instead, it has often been equated with the 'tribalistic' concept of ethnicity. The relatively new term of ethnicity is supposed to bring together under one label phenomena such as 'problems of minority groups' in the 'First World' and 'tribalism' in the 'Third World'.[9]

But a normative aspect plays a role here, too. In South Africa, for example, the use of the word *tribe* has been abandoned since the end of apartheid in 1994 because it is considered to be politically incorrect. 'Tribe' has a negative connotation, evoking images of bare feet, machetes, and thatched roofs. A baffled South African journalist once asked me why Europeans spoke of ethnic groups in the case of the Balkans and of tribes in the case of Africa, although the people in Bosnia smash each others heads like primitive tribal warriors.[10] However, there are some Anglophone journalists who do use the term *tribe* with barely concealed contempt when they report about the Balkans.[11] Köstlin supports this provocative choice of words because the ethnic paradigm is directed against the European Enlightenment, and is thus anti-modern and regressive. In this manner 'the own folk cultures are understood as tribal societies within high culture societies'.[12] In a malicious undertone Weithmann also speaks of tribe, clan, joint family, kinship and blood vendetta, of backwoods, country bumpkins, and tribalism with reference to the Balkans.[13] In a vein, Burg and Shoup speak of Bosnia as a 'society of "mountain men"'.[14]

An extreme form of primordialism is the racist approach. It played a role in the case of British colonial rulers and Hindu nationalists.[15] In this case, too, the terms are fluid. Particularly when reading old documents one gets the impression that by race the authors actually mean a form of ethnicity. All in all, the racist element *qua verbo* or *qua idea* is much more strongly articulated in India than in the Balkans.

1.2. The Situative Approach
(also: constructivist, instrumentalist[16])

Here, a real common descent retreats into the background or is completely discarded. In an extreme case, an ethnic group is just what it considers itself to be or is what it is perceived to be from the outside.

Therefore, Kaschuba describes an ethnic group as a 'fictive reality', as an (highly effective) 'ideal'.[17] Others speak of a 'world of perception', a 'structure of relevance' that competes with other symbol systems.[18] The reason why people invoke common features—real or imagined ones—depends on the social, political, or economic situation and is *by no means unavoidable.*[19] According to the needs certain features are selected which serve to create a 'we group' in order to compete against other alliances. So one can almost speak of 'interest groups'.[20] They have a social function. As per this view, ethnic groups are primarily a product of external influences, and hence constitute a *dependent variable.*[21]

Because of their situative dependency, ethnic groups or the boundaries of ethnic groups undergo constant transformation. The members themselves can define their participation to a large extent. Thus, the ethnic ascription is rather *subjective,* or, as A. Cohen puts it: 'People can think themselves into difference.'[22]

An important exception can be found in Elwert's view. Although to him the ethnic group is a (European) construct and a 'strategic group', he sees no space for subjective ascription. The concept of ethnicity itself was 'invented' *a posteriori* by academics. It was no natural principle of organization; rather the colonizers had imposed it on the natives against their will, thereby substituting socio-professional, generational, neighbourhood-related, etc. principles of order.[23] Also, Huntington holds this ascription, which he calls tribalism, to be a modern product.[24] Clues in support of this hypothesis can be found in the Indian case.[25]

For the majority of the constructivists, however, *belief* in things in common is the decisive factor, as J.S. Mill[26] and Max Weber[27] have already determined, in order to detach the vague term ethnicity from the sphere of value. Most scholars today agree with this view. So Sabrina Ramet defines an ethnic group with reference to the Bosnian Muslims as 'a group of people who *believe* that they constitute a primary cultural unit and who *believe* that they have common cultural interests.'[28] Brass makes the same argument in the Indian case.[29]

What creates this belief or what strengthens it is a controversial topic. The constructivists follow different approaches here. Some highlight the role of elites and symbols which construct a feeling of ethnic togetherness quasi from above.[30] Others concentrate on the impact of political institutions[31] or economic disparities.[32] Again, others bring in the individual, his or her decisions and preferences.[33] One group of constructivists also attempt to explain the behaviour of ethnic groups with the help of game theory models, on the basis of the rational, self-centred action of human beings (game theory, rational-choice approach).[34]

Critique

The primordial approach has the following shortcomings. It nails down ethnic groups in a deterministic way. It does not allow a change in the primordial factors, and so it is unable to explain why some ethnic groups disappear, new ones emerge, and others assimilate or prevail. Another unanswered question is why some primordial characteristics are more significant than others as demarcation factors. The primoridal approach cannot explain either why ethnic groups sometimes face each other in a cooperative and sometimes in a hostile way.

The situative approach must face one problem above all: the fact that it neglects or denies the principle of descent makes it difficult to demarcate ethnicity from other social categories. This approach gets into explanatory trouble when the question arises: why do the masses become so easily mobilized by appeals to their descent and culture? So the ethnic group must dispose of additional resources that other interest groups do not have. Constructivists are also unable to explain why some ethnic groups stubbornly hold on, and why people are ready to sacrifice their lives for their goals.[35] It is, above all, the rational choice representatives who fail at this point.[36]

Both approaches in their pure form offer two simplified views with respect to so-called 'ethnic conflicts'. The 'primordial hate school' over-emphasizes historical constellations which allegedly keep coming up again and again. The Bosnian conflict is often interpreted in this way.[37] On the other side, there are those who follow the approach of the 'lost paradise'. They point to the peaceful co-existence of different ethnic groups and deny the role of primordial factors as the cause of conflict. From their point of view, it is primarily the elites who are responsible for the violence.[38]

1.3. The Situative-Primordial Approach

Because of this dilemma many recent scholars have come to the conclusion that the best way out of this ideological impasse is to bring the two approaches together.[39] With some writers one can even observe a shift from pure constructivism towards compromise. This applies to Brass, who develops his theories on ethnicity in the Indian setting. In 1974 he only spoke of elites who create symbols in order to influence the masses, but in 1991 he took note of primordial factors from which symbols must be drawn: '[E]lites and counter-elites within ethnic groups *select aspects of the group's culture*, attach *new value and meaning* to them, and use them as symbols to mobilize the group, to defend its interests, and to compete with other groups.'[40] Freitag, who investigates the Indian cow-protection movement, also arrives at a similar conclusion. She indicates further that the new meaning of symbols can deviate essentially from their original meaning.[41]

In other words, most advocates of the situative-primordial approach assume that ethnicity has not existed at all times but that it is created and invented. In this process, however, 'old material' is used selectively. This is particularly obvious when the past—selectively interpreted and appropriated—is packaged and sold as 'common' history. Within this approach there are, of course, nuances as to whether more of the old elements or the new features of an ethnic group are to be highlighted. Brass clearly tends to the instrumentalist side, whereas A. Smith stresses the effectiveness and obstinate persistence of ethnic arrangements and postulates. He criticizes the instrumentalists who, in his view, paid too little attention to this factor.[42]

The situative-primordial approach allows us to use and analyse ethnicity as both an independent *and* a dependent variable. From this approach new debates emerge. The famous question—are ethnic groups something old or are they new—appears in a new light when one applies social modernization as an independent variable to ethnicity as a dependent variable. At this point there are two lines of argumentation:

(1) Some think that ethnic groups wear out in the process of modernization and dissolve into other collectivities. To supporters of this view it does not matter if ethnic groups are viewed as *a priori* primordial or as *invented* realities. Here primordialists and constructivists can sit in one boat. This is one of the rare cases in which constructivists use ethnicity as an independent variable.[43] Typical in this context are the functionalist and the Marxist approaches. The first assumes that new units take shape which meet the functional demands of modernity (form follows function). The liberals think along the same lines, too. For once they are in harmony with the Marxists here.[44]

The Marxists find that it is mainly the economic cleavages that are the 'natural', 'real' and, at the same time, modern divisions. Ethnic cleavages are, on the other hand, the result of a 'false consciousness' spread by the bourgeoisie and instrumentalized for the sake of its capitalist interests. In the process of the determinist development of historical materialism, these outdated ethnic disparities disappear.[45] Tito and Nehru were also convinced of this. Both underestimated the 'obsolete' forces and thus, in the end, both had to make grave political concessions to them.[46]

(2) Others hold that ethnicity as a principle of order was not weakened but rather strengthened through modernity. Some say that modern conditions have actually made it possible and enabled it to develop as a social and political force.[47] This implies that ethnic groups constantly change through these modern influences. Therefore, supporters of this line of reasoning are called pluralists. In this argumentation the constructivist element obviously prevails. As a special case—if not completely deviating from it but supplementing it—Gellner should be mentioned. Nation-building through a highly developed form of social organization helps primordial factors (mainly language) to gain new value.[48]

It is even more difficult to summarize the different branches of arguments when including a third feature: ethnic ascription. The situative-primordial approach understandably allows some scope for the interpretation of subjective *and* objective elements. On the one hand, the ethnic group may be a club for members with common interests which the individual joins for situative reasons. On the other hand, the created ethnic principles of order can exert such a pressure that the individual finds it hard to escape them, and if he does, he has to suffer serious social disadvantages (high opt-out costs). The parallels between the primordial/objective and the situative/subjective hold true within the 'camps' of the situative-primordial approach as well.

1.4. Table of the Ideal Types

It has become clear by now how diverse the approaches and definitions of ethnicity are, and at what different conclusions the authors arrive. There is a strained relationship between the features of subjective/objective ascription, dependent/independent variables, and the common classification of the primordial/situative. *Table (a)* gives an overview of

TABLE (A): THE STRAINED RELATIONSHIP BETWEEN THE DIFFERENT APPROACHES THAT TRY TO DEFINE THE TERM ETHNIC GROUP (IDEAL TYPES)

approaches (↓) allow the possible statements (→)	subjective ascription	objective ascription	ethnic group as dependent variable	ethnic group as independent variable	ethnic group strengthened/ created through modernization	ethnic group weakened through modernization
primordial	–	+	–	+	–***	+
situative	+	–*	+	–	+	–**
primordial-situative	+	+	+	+	+	+

Notes: + = typical/often * = *exception*: Elwert
– = untypical/rare ** = *exception*: Marxists, Functionalists, Hobsbawm
*** = *exception*: Gellner

the above discussion. Although it shows only the ideal types, important exceptions are also pointed out.

2. WHAT IS AN 'ETHNIC GROUP'?

Some may suspect the letting off of smoke bombs, others may criticize the splitting of hairs when such an old term like ethnicity is re-introduced into the discussion, enclosed in quotation marks. Yet it plays a central role in the understanding of both case studies and nation-building in general. The previous chapter showed the difficulties in clearly defining ethnicity. The dilemma is this: if the term is used in a broad way, it loses its contours but it could gain in comparative explanatory power. If it is used in a narrow way, it gains focus but it loses the possibilities of comparison, or the phenomenon is not covered any more, and too many exceptions must be made. Thus the term loses its methodological punch as well.

In my opinion the confusion about the term ethnicity has transcended the boundaries of what is academically bearable. It is too fuzzy and, above all, unsuitable for further debates on the term 'nation'. The aspects of ancestry, of tradition in the pure sense, of a more or less direct 'passing on' of specific forms of life, and of the narrow social interrelations of people perish in the current revival of the so-called ethnic paradigm.

The primordial aspect of origin is diluted although it is essential to differentiate the term ethnicity from other social groups. In other words, the diversity of primordial aspects which comprise an ethnic group is pulped into what serves the cause of political mobilization. The early leading scholar of the history of society (*Gesellschaftsgeschichte*), Hans-Ulrich Wehler already pointed to this 'deformation' and 'homogenization' of traditions in his critique of modernization theory.[49] Now the following questions arise: does one still want to speak of traditions, of tribes, etc. in the multi-dimensional primordial sense? Can one still do it? Must one do it any more at all?

Those who want to do this will have problems at least when they use the word ethnicity. Phadnis, for example, considers the term 'unscientific'. Its usage can be justified only because it somehow covers the complexity of the problem and because there is no alternative.[50] Thapar thinks similarly. Nowadays the term *tribe*, in the sense of ethnicity, is too highly politicized and interpreted too broadly. In her view it is applied to describe different social and economic, even biological and racial, units. She suggests an alternative: instead of ethnicity one should rather adopt the more narrow principle of *lineage* which also includes other aspects such as social status and economic resources.[51] Marriage adds a pinch of situative elements, too. Yet the concept remains more transparent and operational for the needs of the social sciences. At the same time it is obvious that nations can hardly be created on the basis of such lineages.

Thus we face a dilemma. On the one hand, ethnic features in the traditional sense are operational only at the cost of their deformation, indeed to the extent of their complete distortion. On the other hand, the whole world speaks of 'ethnic conflicts'. How are academics supposed to reply? They must do two things: first, expose the fraud and second, at the same time, operate with the *politically* relevant terms on which the fraud existentially depends. Otherwise it cannot be exposed. Both must be thought of together, otherwise there is a danger of uncoupling the academic debate from the political realities.

Many respected scholars have already dealt with the apparent fraud. For example, Hobsbawn and Ranger described the selective exploitation of the past and its polishing as the *invention of tradition*.[52] This is the controversial material from which finally arises the *imagined community*, as Anderson coined it.[53] The first part of this book deals mainly with this process.

The second problem has been tackled less well. Among academics and, above all, among journalists there is a terminological confusion about and/or a lack of distance from the terms which spills over from the political sphere, particularly with reference to ethnicity and 'ethnic conflict'. In the following section I will explain why I do not want to employ the phrase ethnic group (without quotation marks) in connection with nation-building, and why I still continue to use 'ethnic group' (with quotation marks).

The Concept

First, the definition. The concept of 'ethnicity' is founded on the principle of picking *one* primordial feature that serves or should serve as a means of contrast against 'the other' (the primary feature).[54] It is, however, too weak to politically mobilize the people who share this feature against 'the others'. In order to still make this happen, other primordial components (secondary features) are gathered around the central feature. They are bent accordingly for this purpose, over-emphasized, or constructed ex post. So the concentric concept of 'ethnicity' has an epicentre, around which the contrast is brewed with the help of later and additional attributes ('ethnicentre'). This process is not only a technique of selection for strengthening a group but is also a pre-selection for the one-sided alignment of the group for the sake of its indispensible self-definition.[55] In this way, the target group or constituency is created in the first place.

The 'Ethnicentre' Religion

In both the case studies described in this book, religion is the primary feature of contrast. For this reason the churches and the religious leaders in the Balkans and in India play such an influential political role.[56] The followers of Islam were depicted as an 'ethnic group' demarcating them from the other 'ethnic groups' whose fundamental component of contrast was their confession as well.[57] One technique of intensifying the contrast is the attempt to make the linguistic element overlap with the religious one. Standardization of the language, particularly of the script, and language conflicts follow.[58] Other examples are the over-emphasis on and the new interpretation of customs such as the killing of cows and the protest against this practice in India.[59] Dress serves the same purpose. Jinnah changed his attire in order to postulate a 'Muslim' unity. An indispensable component is the selective reconstruction of history and the generation of myths. In Bosnia-Herzegovina as well as in India this served and still serves the purpose of concocting for each religion its 'own' history—and with it a 'community of common destiny' (*Schicksalsgemeinschaft*).[60] This is supposed to anchor solidarity beyond pure faith and also to connect religion with the principles of origin and territory.

The concept of 'ethnicity' is also applicable to other constellations. The 'ethnicentre' need not always be religion. Also, language can be a point of departure for further contrast (as in the land of the Basques or in Quebec). But religion as the primary means of contrast occurs more often than other factors. '[T]here are few multireligious ethnic groups and their relative scarcity suggests that religion is the root of ethnic differentiation or that religious distinctiveness is a key to ethnic saliency', Enloe notes. Yet this influence can vanish:

> [Religious] resources are most valuable for ethnic groups only in the earliest stages of communal political development. [...] [E]thnic groups will inevitably outgrow their dependence on religious resources. Or, if they do not, then they risk deflation of their political potential and even their capacity to survive as a distinct group.[61]

In the Balkans and in India a rivalry took place between the spokesmen of the 'ethnic groups' to strengthen the religious resources of mobilization with the help of other primordial features, and thus to avoid any appropriation by 'the others'. The concept of 'ethnicity' also implies that the opponents confront each other on an equal level. This means that both have the same main feature as the means of contrast which they cultivate further during the contest.

'Ethnicity' Versus Ethnicity

There are several reasons why I would like to hold on to the phrase ethnic group (both with and without quotation marks). The first is for methodological reasons. Those who describe themselves as spokesmen of 'ethnic groups' use this very term and claim that it *is* all about actual ethnic groups (without quotation marks). This is essential, in order to understand (a) the nature of so-called 'ethnic conflicts' and, (b) why such conflicts can break out in the first place at all.

Falling back on the ethnic principle has a specific advantage which references to other social categories cannot offer. It appeals to resources that are available *a priori* and *in persona* and that do not need to be put together through political discourse and strenuous consensus-building. An opinion-building exercise with frictional losses is not necessary. This explains why in the absence of democratic political discourse the use of the 'ethnic' paradigm helps to achieve a lead in mass mobilization (as in the first free elections in post-communist Yugoslavia or under colonial rule in India). Ethnic-primordial features are harbours at which political projects can easily dock their ships.[62] This is also the phenomenon that Izetbegovic probably had in mind when he said: 'When you call on a public debate on democracy, some hundred intellectuals will come. When it is about nationalism, you will get tens of thousands of all social layers into the street.'[63]

The second reason why at least the *ideal* of ethnicity must be maintained is that it is necessary to differentiate it from 'ethnicity'. This is particularly important in the Indian context. There the ethnic concept hindered and still hinders the realization of the 'ethnic' one. The 'ethnic' concept is built around the epicentre religion. For example, a Muslim from Punjab has less in common with his co-religionist from Bengal than he does with a Hindu or a Sikh from his home town. A range of languages, customs, even different sects within the same religion up to syncretisms cross-cut in all possible variations and tremendously weaken the postulated main feature religion—indeed to such an extent that it takes great effort to construct and mobilize the notion of Muslim 'ethnicity', and even then it is important to remember that it broke apart after the foundation of the Pakistani state. Against this background this book contrasts regional ethnic groups with the Muslim 'ethnic group'. Finally, the concept of Muslim 'ethnicity' has become the *state ideology* in Pakistan, whereas the very existence of regional ethnic groups contradicts it.

This terminological gambit solves another problem which bothers most of the scholars who work on India. Manor notes with surprise that many analysts tend to avoid the otherwise popular term ethnicity with reference to India. He explains the reason behind their predicament on the basis of a list of different cross-cutting meanings of ethnicity on the subcontinent: (1) religion: above all, Hindus, Muslims, and Sikhs; (2) language: at least nine main languages and countless others;

(3) classified 'tribes' outside Hindu society (scheduled tribes); (4) 'tribes' (racially distinct tribes): in the Himalayas and in the mountains of the North-East; (5) 'Aryans' and 'Dravidians': north-south divide along the dispersal areas of the ancient Indo-European and Dravidian languages.[64] Having said this, Manor concludes, quite optimistically: '[T]he complexity of Indian society tends to prevent tension and conflict from building along a single fault-line in ways that might threaten national unity and the democratic process'.[65]

The chaos is perfect in the case of the Balkans, too. Sundhaussen summarizes:

> Slovenes and Croats belong to the same (Roman Catholic) denomination. However, they differ in their scripts. Croats and Serbs use the same (Croato-Serbian or Serbo-Croatian) script. However, they belong to different denominations. The Bosnian Muslims differ from their contemporaries (Serbs and Croats) in denomination only, whereas they differ from other Muslims in Yugoslavia (e.g. from the Albanians) in both language and origin. The Macedonians share with the Serbs the same Orthodox denomination. However, they have had their own script since the end of World War II. And insofar as the Montenegrians want to define themselves as a nation, they need in addition to language and faith (which they share with the Serbs) at least a further mark of distinction in order to underpin their autonomy (e.g. different historic traditions and social forms of organization).[66]

In other words, the phenomenon of ethnicity in such a complex diversity and in such a variety of cross-cutting cleavages is not good for purposes of political conflict or nation-building, unlike the systematically fine-tuned concept of 'ethnicity'. In the case of the latter, it also becomes possible to employ a diverse terminology for the Indian case without a loss of meaning: 'ethnic group' means the same as community in the specific Indian sense. In the case of Pakistan, the phenomena *ethnic groups* and *Muslim community* work against each other.

The purpose of the above reflections is to make the concept of 'ethnicity' ideologically operational, geographically independent, and semantically stable for further analysis:

(1) In terms of content it is clearly defined. It does not depend on a real—not even on an alleged—reflection of primordial factors but rather on their weighting and their combination. Before each analysis the 'ethnicentre' and the contrast boosters must be determined. At the

same time, the concept accepts primordial features, particularly that of origin, as an *indispensable tool* of analysis.

(2) In this way, the concept becomes manageable and flexible and thus applicable to different cases without losing its explanatory power.

(3) The selection of a main feature implies that 'ethnicity' as a *concept of action* is itself constructed and is already an *instrument* available for further purposes. It is not a description of the state of real and static conditions. The transition from the 'ethnic group' to the ethno-nation (see below) can now proceed without any ruptures.

2.1. Crumbling Components

Looking at the transition from 'ethnic group' to 'ethnic' nation-building, Reiter's sharp critique of primordial features which are used as components for nation-building cannot be ignored here. First of all, he makes an essential distinction which is also adopted in this book, if not in strict terminological terms then at least in the wider content. He defines *class* (Klasse) as a number of people with the same or similar features (e.g. religion, etc.). These features can be subjective or objective. On the other hand, a *group* is a manageable and temporary community formed to pursue common actions and common interests. It has functional but no real value.[67] So in the course of this study I will speak of *action groups* in contrast to (*postulated*) *large groups*.

Reiter thoroughly takes apart each class feature. According to him, *religion* is indeed a collective idea and has a social framework of reference. Its great disadvantage is that:

> It is private and not public, it is not concealable, because of which there is, strictly speaking, only one single object of classification at a time—and that is the classifier himself, since he is the only one who can know to which religion he belongs. The occupation of such a class with other individuals or groups can only be done on speculation.[68]

Hence, religion is not reliable. Opportunism is possible. Only external cultural acts can be judged, not faith itself. This study will show how these very cultural acts can be mixed or combined beyond recognition. One aspect of this is the debate on religious conversions and the motives behind them. They can be of a quite situative kind (e.g. because of tax advantages). Hence, as a class feature, religion is a shaky candidate.

Much less can it be seen as a group aim. Groups form alliances for social and political power struggles. With reference to the exodus of the Serbs in 1690,[69] Reiter points out: 'There was a group aim—it was not dear God—it was based on individual goals that were very much common to all: to save one's skin.'[70] It was a bond of common purpose, a front to repel the others. The same is true of the refugees in present-day Bosnia-Herzegovina or of those living abroad.

Furthermore, Reiter calls *culture* 'the most imprecise of all principles of classification'. It 'is as a classifying feature not only completely useless; in this function it is, beyond this, mendacious to the core'. For a long time many comparatists have rejected the term 'culture' as an all-or-nothing concept. Also, Gellner calls culture an 'elusive concept'[71] and defines it provisionally as 'a system of ideas and signs and associations and ways of behaving and communicating'.[72] For his purposes Gellner introduces language as a cultural feature (which again makes it difficult to demarcate language from culture as Reiter does).

Reiter is not only concerned about the lack of explanatory power of the concept of 'culture' but also about substantial distortions in this idea which have their own consequences: 'Hence it is imputed that the farmer Schmittke has the same culture as some Mister district court councillor'.[73] Reiter asks: What is German in Goethe and Beethoven, what is Bulgarian in Kyrillus and Methodius?[74] Only Goethe could have been proud of himself 'for it was he after all who wrote Faust, he and no one else. Nobody helped him, above all no nation [...].[75] Hence, if one uses 'culture' as an independent variable, then one must make assumptions *a priori* which are not sufficiently founded. Then the whole outcome becomes vague, too, or one must make do with a very limited statement. For '[t]he culture, which is allegedly the property of a nation, turns out very soon, even without looking at it more closely, as the preferred object of only a fraction of the population [...].'[76] Reiter consolidates his argument with reference to the term of 'cultural assets':

> These are the products of the richer social layers, whereas one is either not familiar with those of the poorer ones because they have perhaps not survived the onslaught of time due to bad material, or because they paled beside the others on account of their low artistic and handicraft quality, and no one took any further interest in them.

—except ethnologists who speak of them in a somewhat derogatory tone as 'popular culture'.[77]

The following chapters describing the case studies deal directly with this problem. They treat 'culture'—if at all—with reference to the Great Tradition (the masses) and the Little Tradition (the elites). Despite a remaining lack of precision, this has the systematic advantage that the threads of the Little Tradition can be spun directly to political activists in the nation-building process. This makes it easier to draw a contrast between the action group and the category of contrast of the large group. The case studies support Reiter's view that 'culture' is no good as a class feature, and for group-building even less. From this observation the urgent recommendation emerges *not* to use 'culture' as an independent variable. This criticism applies particularly to Huntington's thesis of the 'clash of civilizations' (Kampf der Kulturen),[78] and, in the case of Bosnia-Herzegovina, to the theses that the constant changing of political powers and the rule of 'alien cultures' (West—East, Habsburg—Ottoman, Occident—Orient) had a direct influence on Muslim nation-building.[79]

In contrast to 'culture', Reiter rejects *historical consciousness* as a class feature from the outset. It is only when an action group has been first created that it can operate with it. Therefore, between the groups there arises a kind of 'classification bickering' about which history, which honour, etc. falls to whose share. This observation corresponds with the findings of this study. It is only after the homogenization of a group has begun, for example on a religious basis, that a suitable history is tinkered accordingly.

Reiter considers *language* as the only logical class feature. In his view, it is also well suited for group-building.[80] But the following case studies provide evidence in support of the opposite conclusion. First, language is not necessarily a group-comprising class feature. Instead, only the literate people and the leaders used *part* of the language which serves as a means of demarcation; in our examples it was the script. Second, language failed completely in the process of group-building (above all, due to these reasons) before and after the partition of India and Pakistan.

Despite the 'desecration' of these ethno-national components, the influence they have attained through their politicization must not be underestimated.

3. WHAT IS A NATION?

> Nation and nationalism belong to the 1001 topics on which no two scholars can ever agree.[81]
>
> *Imanuel Geiss*

This statement does not really raise hopes that more clarity can be provided with the concept of the nation compared to the concept of ethnicity. The Roman author Tacitus used *natio* in the sense of a tribe or a community of common descent in the same sense as the Greek word *ethnos*.[82] Scholars today agree that nation and ethnicity differ in some way. But they are divided on how this difference operates.

Two minimal features can be mentioned at the outset. The nation is, in the first place, a *political* term. This means that it contains a minimum degree of collective capacity of action, of articulation of interests, of (cultural and/or political) institutionalization, and of the idea of territory, or the aspiration for it. All aspects that were discussed with reference to ethnic groups can play a role for this term as well. However, *situative* elements are clearly in the forefront. In contrast to earlier historians the majority today considers nation as a thoroughly modern concept.[83] Nevertheless, in most recent times some authors note that the term 'nation' already occured in the Middle Ages as a (still controversial) framework of order and reference. However, they concede, that the modern phenomenon of nationalism has given this term a new and decisive boost since the French Revolution.[84]

There is little point in listing the various definitions of a nation because none has really made a breakthrough. Instead, the politically relevant differences should be emphasized here which also prominently influenced the events in the case studies.

To some, the idea of territory is the focus of a nation.[85] But it is rarely explained what 'territory' is actually supposed to mean. A. Smith, for example, relates ethnicity with a specific and fixed territory. He defines 'ethnic community (or 'éthnie') as a named human population of alleged common ancestry, shared memories, and elements of common culture with a link to a *specific territory* and a measure of solidarity'.[86] Dipankar Gupta goes even further. He relates ethnicity not only with the claim to territory but also to sovereignty.[87] Reiter, on the other hand, rejects this. He says that territory has nothing to do systematically with the ethnic principle. It became significant only when other factors of nation-building had already taken effect.[88] Also, Deutsch holds the idea of territory to be a political projection: 'No person can be born at more than one spot on the map. The actual place of his birth has the size of a bed or a room, not the size of a country.'[89]

Hence, the following differentiation is plausible, and will play an important role in this study: because according to the concepts of ethnicity more than in any other ideology, persons *per se* are in the limelight as carriers of certain characteristics, and because these persons have to be accommodated somewhere, spatial arrangements inevitably play a role. The geographical structure of the living space often gives rise to certain characteristics of a people which are, after all, described as ethnic (e.g. customs, clothing, etc.). For this purpose, the Latin basis of the word 'territory', i.e. *terra* seems appropriate—ground, earth, or perhaps here a strip of land or region. It is not an object of intellectual projection and it has no sharp contours. It is quite different from the concept of nation, in which land becomes a component of ideology and politics as such. Then boundaries gain significance as protecting a 'cultural heritage' or even as enclosing a 'holy land'. However, they do not have to be drawn *de facto*. Particularly in the case of ethno-nationalism they can at first play only a symbolic and imaginary role (different from that of a 'nation state'). Hence, A. Smith speaks of 'historical territory' with reference to the nation.[90]

Keeping these stumbling blocks in mind, it is helpful to say at the outset what a nation is *not*: (a) It is not a state. (b) It is neither *a priori* the population of a state.[91] In other words: '[T]he nation [can] very much exist without the own state, a state without a unified nation.'[92] This is an important observation. For it breaks with the alleged determinism that a nation must (a) strive for a state in order to be a nation, or (b) a nation must always be thought together with a 'nation state'.

By no means is this aim in Bosnia-Herzegovina and India always in sight. The Bosnian Muslims are sometimes described as a 'denominational nation' (*Konfessionsnation*) only, just because they do not strive for their own statehood. This also makes methodological sense. Those who think in terms of this historical determinism try to find the historical obstacles that stand in the way of an ethno-national state-building programme in the first place. Thus they run the danger of taking over the ethno-national paradigm and of legitimizing ethno-nationalism with terms such as 'the delayed nation'.[93] An equation of nation and state has carelessly taken root, and it is explosive up to the spheres of international law.[94]

Most authors completely lose sight of the civil-democratic version. This happens not only because some of them confuse the project with its consequences but also because the nature of the project is reduced to a *single* possible origin. For the 'nation' is mostly understood as '[the] highest form of ethnic group'[95] or as 'an 'ethnic' group which seeks to advance its interests through organized political action'.[96] This explains the widespread use of 'nationality' in the sense of 'ethnic' descent instead of a purely legal citizenship.

Gellner has weakened the ethnic principle, quite usefully, with his interpretation of the development of the nation as a form of 'high culture'. According to him, it is a standardized, formalized, and codified form of life supported by a single written language:

> The agrarian age of mankind is a period in which some can read and most cannot, and the industrial age is one in which all can and must read. In the agrarian age, literate high-cultures co-exist with illiterate low or folk cultures. During the period of transition between the two ages, some erstwhile low cultures become new high cultures; and on occasion a new high culture can be invented, re-created by political will and cultural engineering, based on elements drawn from a distant past, and reassembled to create something in effect quite new [...].[97]

The problem is only that *not* all must be able to read in order to be nationalists. Particularly in the Indian language conflict, it became clear that people were drawn into it who did not understand what it was all about. Most of them could not even read the script which triggered the conflict in the first place. Still it was used in as a distinguishing feature of nation-building (as a postulated category of identity of the large group).[98] Also, in the Balkans the language conflict revolved and still revolves mainly around what is on paper. Admittedly, today this is not any more altogether contradictory given the relatively high rate of literacy. But one thing becomes clear: Gellner's concept placed a great deal of emphasis on the industrialized states in which nation-building and technical development went hand in hand.

A further criticism of Gellner comes from India, not quite accidentally. Making language the main criterion of nation-building, he denies the possibility, or at least the plausibility, of multilingual states (or nations in the popular sense of the term).[99] This applies to India in particular which has to deal with this contradiction in praxis. Therefore, when looking at problems in such states, many point to Gellner's approach.[100] However, the opposite perspective must be allowed, too: why do linguistically heterogeneous states like India or Canada exist and exist successfully for many decades? Above all, why do religious cleavages in India appear to have more explosive potential than linguistic divisions?

Gellner could not completely resolve the tension between primordial features and nation-building. Structural approaches, therefore, also emphasize different factors. Anderson argues that the social construction of groups has fundamentally changed with nation-building. He describes the development of national groups in contrast to, say, religious ones as follows: 'The fundamental conceptions about [early] 'social groups' were centripetal and hierarchical, rather than boundary-oriented and horizontal'.[101] Only the transition from the dynastic to the national principle has made it possible at all 'to think' the nation.[102] According to Anderson, the tools of modernization were, above all, capitalism, the print media, and the Reformation respectively Enlightenment in Europe. These social innovations brought about a change of consciousness. Here he gets closer to Gellner. The colonial powers, according to Anderson, tried to impose this new consciousness from above with the catalytics of nation-building' 'Census, Map, Museum'.[103] He refers to India in particular. But there are also many examples of this in Bosnia-Herzegovina. Anderson's approach remains equally restricted to the European 'western' area too. This makes sense when one considers nations as modern products that were exported from the West. Yet it runs the danger of not covering all phenomena outside Europe which also bear the label of nation-building.

Emerson refers to this aspect. Already in 1960 he investigated the conditions under which colonies became independent. In his definitions of the nation he distances himself from the primordial approaches. According to him, the term 'nation' is a merely functional association which is territorially bound and temporary. He regards the glue that holds the nation together with diffused feelings:

> The nation is a community of people who feel that they belong together in the double sense that they share deeply significant elements of a common heritage and that they have a common destiny for the future. In the contemporary

world the nation is for great portions of mankind the community with which men most intensely and most unconditionally identify themselves, even to the extent of being prepared to lay down their lives for it, however deeply they may differ among themselves on other issues.[104]

After Emerson has shed light on all such cases worldwide, he is puzzled by the diversity of the phenomena. That is why he formulates, with Salomonic wisdom, the following observation: 'The simplest statement that can be made about a nation is that it is a body of people who feel that they are a nation; and it may be that when all the fine-spun analysis is concluded this will be the ultimate statement as well.' Particularly with reference to the Indian subcontinent he arrives at a constructivist minimal definition: 'The case of Pakistan came close to sustaining the theory that a nation is whatever can get away with establishing its claim to being one [...]'[105] This statement convinces in two ways: (a) Interests must be (effectively) articulated (*active* aspect). Thereby it remains completely open how these interests are rationalized. (b) On the other hand, external authorities must in some way or the other accept or honour the presented claims. One who 'gets away' with something must also 'get through' with it somewhere (*passive* aspect).

Weber has looked at both of these aspects. According to him, the term 'nation' implies 'that it *imposes* on certain groups of people a specific notion of solidarity vis-à-vis others'.[106] In this very general definition the supplement 'specific' suggests features that other interest groups lack.

In this study both aspects—active and passive—play an important role. Particularly in the case of a possible state-building (that Emerson strongly implies) both factors are interrelated. Therefore, it is a good idea to refer to them *separately*. Many authors do not do so. Seton-Watson, for example, speaks already in terms of a nation if 'a significant number of people in a community consider themselves to form a nation, or behave as if they formed one'.[107] Also, Gellner deals only with the active internal aspect. Recognition takes place only among the members of the nation themselves: 'Two men are of the same nation if and only if they *recognize* each other as belonging to the same nation.'[108]

Such approaches ignore the passive external aspect that becomes particularly evident in Yugoslavia. There, this aspect was at least as strong as the active part of the Muslim spokesmen, if not stronger.[109] The creation of the 'Muslim nation' by decree had domestic political reasons and revalorized the status of the Muslims vis-à-vis the Serbs and the Croats in the state fabric of Yugoslavia. This, in turn, gave a boost to a Muslim national consciousness.

This reciprocal relation is essential. The motivation comes from both inside and outside. But who gets motivated? In any case, it must be more than just a handful of thinkers. Against this background Alter provides a suitable formula: 'The nation is the politically mobilized people.'[110] The Indian poet and philosopher Tagore defined it similarly: '[The nation] is the appearance of a whole people as an organized power.'[111] But these definitions have their own problems. Apart from the fact that they consider only the active aspect, they also create a new need for clarification, namely for the word 'people' (*Volk*). The understanding of this term determines to a great extent what is understood by the term 'nation'. Therefore, the term 'nation' shall now be divided into three ideal types.

3.1. The Subjective Nation Concept
(political, liberal, civil, democratic, situative, voluntary, etatist, republican, 'élective', 'French')

Each person is a member of a nation because he or she wants to be so. The nation is an open society, a 'community by choice'.[112] The people (*Volk*) are the electorate. The most well-known advocate of this position is the French historian Ernest Renan who said: '*L'existence d'une nation est . . . un plébiscite de tous les jours.*'[113] It must prove itself every day anew and is therefore transitory. Renan brushes aside primordial and territorial determinisms: 'The human being is neither a slave of his race, his language, his religion nor of the course of the rivers or the direction of mountain ranges.'[114]

The French Revolution is taken as the starting point of this nation concept. In 1789, Sieyès, in his famous speech on the 'Third Estate', defined a nation as '[a] society that lives under a common law and is represented by one and the same legislative assembly'.[115] In this sense, Kant understood his republican concept, too: individuals associate themselves in a state by free will with a self-determined constitution and government.[116] A postulated, common ancestry of a people as a quasi 'common parental tribe' has only 'intellectual and legal significance' but not a real one.[117] So Kant's definition of the state lacks any reference to descent: 'A state (*civitas*) is a union of an aggregate of men under rightful laws.'[118]

All in all, three things are outstanding in the situative nation concept: (1) First, a state exists. Within its boundaries a nation forms itself (*state into nation*). (2) In this *state-nation* all citizens have equal rights, irrespective of descent, religion, etc. This is enshrined in a constitution that speaks of citizens (*citoyens*) and does not list 'nations', 'nationalities', etc (3) Ideally, the law of citizenship is the *ius soli.* The fact that a person was born in the territory of the nation makes him a citizen and a member of the nation, not his family decent. The title United *Nations* also addresses this interpretation in pure legal terms (although the different concepts of nation in this context lead to confusion).[119]

Alternatives to the 'Plebiscite'
(only: situative, voluntary)

Nehru also followed a constructivist approach to nation-building in principle: 'What a nation is is difficult to define. Possibly the essential characteristic of national consciousness is a sense of belonging together and of together facing the rest of mankind.'[120] But he thus steps away somewhat from the plebiscite element and replaces it with a diffused feeling of belonging together. For Nehru, people occupied the primary position and territory was secondary.[121] The external aspect is interesting. Being different from the ethnic group which deals with familiar and direct neighbours, the concept of nation opens up larger dimensions. Other, bigger national units become the reference points (confrontational) or, as with Nehru, mankind (co-operative).

Deutsch introduced a new angle into the discussion. He does not fall back on political and plebiscitary elements but turns to communication. In this sense he defines *Volk* as 'an extensive all-purpose communication network of people. It is an agglomeration of individuals who can bridge distances by communicating with each other quickly and effectively, and on diverse topics and circumstances.'[122]

At first glance this approach seems very plausible. But it fails exactly in the case of so-called 'ethnic conflicts'. It is not applicable to the case studies of Bosnia-Herzegovina and India. On the one hand, it does not explain why *despite* moderate communication violent nationalisms break out. The former E.U. administrator for Mostar, Hans Koschnik, said in the Balkan context: 'In the history of this rugged region there were very few connections from village to village. The settlements of the central Balkan region were always small islands [. . .].'[123] On the other hand, it remains unexplained why people live side by side, develop close lines of communications, and yet let themselves be incited against each other by demagogues from far away.[124] The colourful, neighbourly mixture of people of different religions, languages, and customs in the Balkans and in India is the best example of this.

Deutsch could counter that, after all, he had taken into consideration that communication was stronger within a *cultural* society than on its peripheries.[125] Only because of this it could overcome long distances. But with this remark he introduces the problematic term 'culture' and thus distances himself from the purely situative principle. As Weber states, although with some reservations: 'The "ethnic" faith in togetherness is very often, but not always, a barrier for 'communities with social intercourse.'[126] Deutsch's argument becomes circular: culture as a criterion of social solidarity eases communication, which in turn strengthens solidarity. Then the so-called *speech communities* are in the final analysis *cultural communities* whatever these may be. Confusingly enough, a common language is also supposed to be a part of culture. But in the case of Bosnia-Herzegovina and India it becomes clear that—in its standardized form—it can divide rather than unify. This is the case when 'cultural' and political factors influence the standardized languages which are stronger than the binding force of the spoken language.

Jürgen Habermas follows a different approach. For him, citizenship in the legal sense and an association of people (*Volksgenossenschaft*) in the normative sense are equally coupled with a subjective confirmation of the individual. Habermas links the profession for a nation to the efficiency of the welfare state. This is the substitute for the emotional and ideological glue from the times of nationalism, as he terms it. Civil rights must pay off: 'My suspicion is that a liberal political culture can hold together multi-cultural societies only if democratic citizenship pays in terms not only of liberal and political rights, but of social and cultural rights as well.'[127] This means that if the nation can no longer 'buy' its citizens, they will turn their backs on it. According to Habermas, the increasing exchange of information in modern complex societies does not necessarily mean that, at the same time, 'an inter-subjectively shared world' emerges. Hence, the citizens need more than communication; they need social and economic incentives. With this point he has mitigated Deutsch's model. Habermas' approach, however, cannot solve the problem that people let themselves be fobbed off with less welfare and still continue to strongly identify with 'their' nation, and that others are less nationalistic despite receiving major social benefits. Here he encounters a similar circular problem like Deutsch. Admittedly, Habermas based his model specifically on modern and complex states. But even here it remains an open question whether the citizens of the different EU states would identify with the European level as soon as it is assigned the competences for welfare. It looks like Habermas' idea is less an explanatory model than a goal—or rather also a practical, institutional approach designed to defeat the nation state:

> In view of both the growing pluralism inside national societies and the global problems that national governments face from the outside, the nation state can no longer provide an appropriate frame for the maintenance of democratic citizenship within the foreseeable future.[128]

Summing up, one may say that the subjective nation concept has to come to grips with inconsistencies, and it does not exist at all in its pure plebiscitary form. It is a highly constructivist approach. It functions only on the essential condition that a solid state apparatus is already in existence. Hence Deutsch simply speaks of the nation as a 'people in possession of a state'.[129] This says everything and nothing, because the decisive component is, of course, the people, about whom nothing is said. The subjective nation concept denies the people a common ancestry alongwith any kind of ethnic basis. Correspondingly, this concept has little significance in Muslim nation-building. In the case studies it appears only as a contrasting programme of the Congress to Jinnah's Muslim nation concept, and with the small, trans-'ethnic' alternative parties in Bosnia-Herzegovina.

3.2. Two Objective Nation Concepts (cultural, deterministic, 'German')

They differ from the subjective concept in the sense that they embed the member of a nation *a priori* into a series of preconditions. Depending on the types of these conditions, the concept is consequently or only tendentially objective. The latter's preconditions do not have a consequent and primordially ethnic character. They cannot be heard or seen with a human being. Instead, they are themselves the objects of constant construction. The member of a nation has several possibilities of a subjective ascription. However, they shrink to the extent that situative factors are subject to a quasi primordial encrustation.[130]

The best example of such a construction is the postulate of a 'common' history. It changes to the extent that it moves forward, that new myths are generated and accepted in the 'national' consciousness, and that discussions and differences of opinion can flare up regarding its interpretation. Every member of the nation ideally participates in this process. Objective factors like language or religion are different. They cannot be changed.[131] It is necessary to make these fine distinctions since there are many thinkers who advocate a political nation concept, on the one hand, but still fall into objective criteria without being ethno-nationalists, on the other.

Both objective concepts have the following features in common: (1) First comes the nation and then the state (*nation into state*) (2) It is mainly a cultural nation (*Kulturnation*)[132] because it provides a diffuse feeling of togetherness on the basis of objective criteria like descent, language, religion, customs and/or history (the factors vary according to the concept). Ideally, a cultural homogenization takes place. (3) When the nation achieves statehood, its constitution will not speak of 'citizens' but of dominant 'nations', 'nationalities', and 'national minorities'. (4) The right of citizenship ideally is the *ius sanguinis*, in particular in the consequent version. People of the 'same blood' are members *a priori*, no matter where they were born and how they think.

A people (*Volk*) is hence not an electorate but a people that is characterized *a priori* through postulated common aspects which lie beyond the formation of political will. As a political ideology this concept leads to an ethno-national state, as it is defined below. The objective nation concept originated with the Romantic intellectuals and the national movements in Germany in the eighteenth and particularly the nineteenth centuries.

In India the term nation embodies this meaning when—and *only* when—it is used with reference to Iqbal's and Jinnah's Two-Nation Theory. It refers to Hindus and Muslims as separate 'nations' on the basis of their religion. As a counter concept there is 'Indian nationalism' which has the opposite meaning, namely a civil-democratic character.

The above-mentioned deception with ethnicity is therefore, of course, also a swindling with the cultural and 'ethnic' nation concept. As Weber points out:

Nationality' shares with 'people' in the popular 'ethnic' sense at least normally the vague idea that at the root of the feeling that is seen as 'common' must lie a community of common descent, although, in the reality of things, human beings who consider themselves fellow nationals are not only sometimes but rather often further apart from each other with respect to descent than those who ascribe themselves to different and hostile nationalities.[133]

According to Weber, this applies particularly to Serbs and Croats. Nationalist spokesmen often had a different nationality than those on whose behalf they claim to speak:

'Nation' is a term which, if clearly at all can by no means be defined according to the empirical qualities of those ascribed to it. [...] That 'national' belonging does not have to be based on a real community of blood goes entirely without saying; everywhere it is extremely radical 'nationalists' in particular who are of alien origin.[134]

In the Balkans the most notorious example is the 'Bosnian-Serb' warmonger, Radovan Karadzic, who stems from Montenegro.

Sulzbach also supports Weber: 'A nation is a group of human beings who are united by a common error with regard to their descent and a common dislike for their neighbours.'[135] In this sense Karl Popper ridiculed Hegel's absolutist nation concept: the nation is 'an amount of people held together by a common misunderstanding with reference to their history.'[136]

3.2.1. *The Tendentially Objective Concept* (additionally: 'moral')

It emphasizes, above all, 'common' historic events, that is—following the concept of 'ethnicity'—secondary features. Almost all authors and politicians take up such elements. Even Renan, beyond his famous quote on plebiscite, spoke of the nation as a 'soul' with a 'rich heritage of memories', a 'collective heritage of glory and remorse'.[137] Sièyes also got caught up in a web of contradictions because he considered the nation, on the one hand, as a community of civil rights, but as an *a priori* existing and thereby pre-legal and pre-political fact on the other.

Thus, he suggested a given 'unified will' of the French nation *à la* Rousseau. The finding of a politically institutionalized consensus *a posteriori* thus appeared unnecessary, which had grave consequences for the political culture of France.[138]

Also, in England, where the political scenario was different, the tendentially objective concept dominated the debate. J.S. Mill, who otherwise also advocated a clear-cut voluntaristic approach, wrote:

> But the strongest of all [causes of common feeling] is identity of political antecedents; the possession of national history, and consequent community of recollections; collective pride and humiliation, pleasure and regret, connected with the same incidents of the past.[139]

Nations that 'feel' subjugated are linked as much as possible to an ancient 'common' past with political demands of self-determination. From such fairy tales arises the 'Paradigm of the Sleeping Beauty'.[140] A 'nation' has been slumbering since the 'deepest' past and is waiting to be kissed back to life by a prince charming. Possibly a cunning witch had put her into this deep sleep. The villain is quickly identified. In the Balkans it was the 'peoples' dungeons' (*Völkerkerker*) like the Ottoman Empire or Yugoslavia, and in India it was the British colonizers. The younger the nation is, the older must be its vulcanizing history.[141] Nehru and Gandhi liked to play this card in order to mobilize the Indian freedom movement. The more they wanted to agitate the people, the more they took to a personified nation concept. Nehru evoked elements like the 'majestic soul' of India which defies all adversities. His speech on India's 'tryst with destiny' delivered before the Constituent Assembly on 15 August 1947 has become legendary:

> Long years ago we made a tryst with destiny, and now the time comes when we shall redeem our pledge. . . . At the stroke of the midnight hour, while the world sleeps, India will awake to life and freedom. A moment comes, which comes but rarely in history, when we step out from the old to the new, when an age ends, and when the soul of a nation, long suppressed, finds utterance. . . .[142]

3.2.2. *The Consequently Objective Concept: The Ethno-nation* (additionally: organic, ethnic)

All features of the tendentially objective concept are valid here, too. But the human being is already nationally predestined merely by virtue of his most personal characteristics, by his very nature. He cannot change his skin and is thus, by being who he is, the indispensible carrier and the most important political resource of this concept. 'Everyone remains what he 'is', even if he has a 'false' national consciousness'.[143] At the same time the nation itself takes a substantial shape.

Reiter calls this 'internalized personality' of a group a substitute for the lost acquaintance of human beings among each other.[144] Using the terms of Tönnies it can be said: the ethno-nationalists want to transform a *society* into a *community*. A purely 'ideal, mechanical' link of otherwise separated people is substituted by the bond of 'real and organic life', an apriorical 'unity of will'. Tönnies describes the contrast between society and community as follows: 'Society is the public, is the world. In the community of his own one is bound right from birth, with all weal and woe. One goes into society like into alien lands.' And in the society no activities take place, 'which can be traced from a unity that exists *a priori* and necessarily'.[145]

The organic nation concept[146] originated, above all, from the German philosopher of history, Johann Gottfried von Herder (1744-1803).[147] For him, the people (*Volk*) is 'both a plant of nature and a family'. '[T]he most natural state is hence also *one* people with *one* national character'.[148] We will later refer to the reception of Herder's concept and its political consequences in the Balkans and in India.[149] The Indian philosopher, Sri Aurobindo (1872-1950), for example, took over Herder's concept in order to contrast it with the state, which he saw only as a 'soulless machine'.[150] This organic idea even had a lot of influence on thinkers who did *not* advocate the primordial-ethnic nation concept. Gandhi warned against the division of the country as 'a vivisection of the living flesh of India'.[151] Even Nehru spoke in his polemic of the 'glorious beauty of the flesh' of India.[152]

The consequently primordial character of the objective concept becomes evident in the components which comprise the 'people's spirit' (*Volksgeist*). With Herder language comes up as the basis of nation building: one language = one nation.[153] Language must be able to develop freely as a divine gift. But Herder himself did not yet relate any national political demands with it. They arose later in radical forms when Herder's language nationalism and the idea of the nation state were brought together. For this reason some say that Herder's ideas were actually misused.[154]

A people was for Herder one who had an *original* language. But in Bosnia-Herzegovina and in India Herder's belief was turned upside down. The primary feature was not language but religion. In these cases Herder served as a plea to create a language community ex post which was supposed to overlap with the idea of a religiously founded nation. But the concept is the same. Religion is—in the minds of ethno-nationalists—a consequently primordial category, too.

In this context, the term 'denominational nation' (*Konfessions-nation*)[155] comes up, above all with reference to the Muslims in Bosnia-Herzegovina. It is mostly used to highlight the traditionally religious character of this large group or class (Reiter), which rather undercuts the potency of political claims. But the word 'nation' hints at the fact that it represents more than a primarily religiously defined ethnic group. It implies at least that the group can be mobilized politically through the detour of religion.

The concept of the ethno-nation stands in close relation to the concept of 'ethnicity' introduced above. This means: (1) It includes all possible—real, deformed, or alleged—primordial features as components. (2) It also offers space for the important factor of a constructed history, which, by definition, is a component of both objective nation concepts.[156] (3) It refers to a *special* group which contrasts itself with other politicized groups by means of the additional resource—the inescapable principle of 'common' ancestry. In this sense the ethno-nation also contains the idea of a primary distinguishing feature ('ethnicenter') and several secondary components.

3.2.3. *The Real Power of the Unreal*

The success of the concept of 'ethnicity' in its politicized manifestation of the ethno-nation is not easy to explain, particularly when the ethnic paradigm is defined situatively to the core, as many do it today. Certainly, and first of all, it has a clearly situative character. But, as mentioned earlier, it could not survive without the primordial resources at least in the initial phase of mobilization. Hence, the heretical question must be permitted: from what point on, if at all, can something constructive be considered as primordial? Does not the constant proclamation of 'ethnic' differences at some time become a self-fulfilling prophecy if it is underpinned by corresponding cultural, political, and institutional engineering? Do expulsion, torture, and war in India and Bosnia-Herzegovina not deepen the 'ethnic' cleavages, and are they not as real and 'available' as primordial features?

At this point, Kaschuba's definition of an effective 'fictive reality' fits in. Deutsch also takes on this phenomenon:

> Subjective attitudes [...] turn into objective facts when they are shared by many people for some length of time—although they may prove no less short lived and fragile as many tangible facts may turn out to be.[157]

Given this, the question comes up: should 'ethnicity' not be considered primarily as an independent variable from some point on? And if yes, when?

On the one hand, there is the really serious danger that one accepts too readily constructed features as primordial, thus legitimizing the ethno-national paradigm and the related political projects. On the other hand, a loss of perception could set in, reducing explanatory power in the social sciences and history, if one ignores the factor of a quasi-primordial availability of 'ethnic' resources. It remains a tightrope walk.

Politicians would do good not to accept primordial or quasi-primordial factors as a basis of their political action.[158] For academics, however, a look at such a possibility must be allowed. But then it becomes important to concede to the 'ethnic' principle at least the same level of flexibility and transitoriness as to (other) primordial features. The case studies in this book anyway support the thesis that the concept of 'ethnicity' is very fragile and short-lived. Ethno-nationalism can indeed produce a strong homogenizing effect and accomplish substantial political changes. But in the case of Pakistan particularly it becomes clear that the last consequence of ethno-nationalism, the 'nation state'—undoubtedly its biggest 'success'—is at the same time the reason for its failure. Among the Bosnian Serbs a similar phenomenon can be observed. 'The Bosnian Muslims', however, are still engaged in a phase of homogenization in which the concept of 'ethnicity' gains significance as an independent variable.

As mentioned above, A. Smith most vociferously advocates such a dual viewpoint of 'ethnicity' as a dependent and an independent variable at the same time. This is why he criticizes the normative-situative approaches which suggest that ethno-nationalism had an 'almost pathological character', as Anderson puts it.[159] A. Smith holds it to be unsuitable and superficial to try to fight national myths with counter-myths of the 'evil nation'. This, he says, ignores the long-lasting power of primordial factors on which the ethno-nation is built and which influence political developments.[160] However, A. Smith is firmly convinced of the functional value of the national (i.e. here the ethno-national) concept that proves efficient, 'socially functional', and solid in the world order of states.[161]

This study supports the thesis of a strong influence of primordial or postulated primordial elements. In this respect it follows A. Smith. However, it does not accept the idea that the ethno-national paradigm is solid and indispensable. On the contrary, it becomes less and less practicable the more powerfully the 'ethnicentres' are used for state-building (Pakistan). It loses its power of cohesion the longer the final success of the concept—the ethno-national state—exists without other state-supporting ideologies or concepts of everyday politics being able to establish themselves.

4. WHAT IS NATIONALISM?

The term nationalism can be found for the first time in the works of Herder (1774).[162] So right from the start it got an ethno-national touch. In fact, it is mostly used in this sense. But first a systematic view of the phenomenon will be given without any normative analysis. For now, the following minimal definition serves this purpose: nationalism is a political concept of action (ideology) whose goal is directed towards state-building, and at the same time it is a dynamic-practical principle with the phenomena of a growing, political mobilization, and an increasing level of political organization for achieving this goal. The interpretation of the state's people (*Staatsvolk*) decides if it is a civic-democratic nationalism or an ethno-nationalism.

In both cases social action plays a role—often to an extent which had never existed before.[163] Emerson gives nationalism the credit of having promoted democratic structures. Large sections of the population, which earlier stayed at home, now come out into the streets.[164] Such movements are supported by a great deal of 'solidarity'.[165] Hechter defines the level of solidarity with the degree to which the members of a group 'comply with corporate rules in the absence of compensation [...].'[166] This is an essential definition with reference to nationalism because the struggle often demands great sacrifices and provides an idealistic compensation only. Anderson concludes: 'The whole point of the nation is that it is interestless. Just for that reason, it can ask for sacrifices.'[167] Social and economic theories cannot explain '[the] attachment that peoples feel for the inventions of their imaginations – or [...] why people are ready to die for these inventions.'[168] Horowitz applies this to the so-called 'ethnic conflicts' as a whole, whose 'emotions' could not be grasped through rational theories.[169] A. Smith agrees: no rational choice approach could explain why it is possible that people fight for entirely hopeless causes. This phenomenon, he says, should not be ignored with regard to nationalism, otherwise the special character of such movements is systematically suppressed.[170] Deutsch traces the origin of such a delusion on the part of individuals to a cognitive vicious circle:

> A nationalist prefers giving attention to the transmission and communication of those news which contain specifically national symbols, or that originate from a specifically national source, or that is composed in the specifically national code of language or culture. [...] The feedback information about the consequences of his own actual behaviour gets superimposed and suppressed. Hence, extreme nationalism leads to an *epistemological catastrophe.* Emaciation and paralysis of the cognitive faculties are the consequences.[171]

Rogowski contradicts. For him nationalism is 'the product of value-maximizing [...] behaviour' and is 'based almost always on an accurate appraisal of self-interest and social reality (that is, rarely a consequence of hysteria or delusion)'.[172]

Is nationalism now rational or irrational? We can get closer to the answer only when we classify the phenomenon into different functions and contents (see below). It is certain that such movements can generate an astonishing amount of solidarity. This is because each person believes that here lies his or her maximum personal interest. Depending on the type of nationalism, the unique resource of primordial anchors is of great use. In this context Tarrow points to the interrelationship between the elites and their followers:

> [L]eaders can only create a social movement when they tap more deep-rooted feelings of solidarity or identity. This is almost certainly why nationalism and ethnicity—based on real or 'imagined' ties—or religion—based on common devotion—have been more reliable bases of movement organization in the past than social class.[173]

The real or imagined group features serve to recruit fellow combatants whose individual input is again decisive for the success: '[T]he greater the average proportion of each member's private resources contributed to collective ends, the greater the solidarity of the group', says Hechter.[174]

One could add: the stake of each person increases in proportion to his or her personal sacrifices. This has an escalating effect which militant nationalists often trigger deliberately. According to Tarrow, 'crowds acquire an identity through attacks on an "other"'.[175] Pogroms, rapes, and torture in Bosnia-Herzegovina and India did not occur coincidently at the height of nationalistic tensions. They contributed significantly to the mobilization of broader layers of the population.[176]

4.1. The Double Face of Nationalism

In the case of nationalism one encounters the same problem as with ethnicity and nation. The phenomenon is so diverse that no consistent typification or definition has been able to prevail. Nationalisms exist under the most diverse conditions, in various places, at different times, supported and influenced by numerous internal and external factors. For these reasons Schödl considers this phenomenon a 'non-theorizable' process.[177] With regard to eastern and south-eastern Europe he points to an important double dimension of nationalism. It has a substantial, and, above all, an organizational and functional side:

> Nationalism can be [...] a certain element of an autonomous-emancipatory nation-building as well as a manipulative technique of rule. Its form, effect, and mass appeal depend less on the content and consistency of the symbols that create meaning; more important in this sense is probably the make-up of the consciousness of a society that is *simultaneously* striving for self-determination and new self-identity, for mobilization *and* consolidation.[178]

Most analysts agree that in terms of content nationalism has little to offer. Ideologically, it drills through wafer-thin boards. Besides it is contradictory and illogical.[179] Perhaps it is nothing more than a 'collective, social prejudice'.[180] But it works. It mobilizes social resources, creates the political capacity to act, and often, but not always, it also creates a state.

But this does not happen in a day. With reference to small nations in eastern Europe, Hroch has divided the process which national movements undertake into three phases. In phase A, based on its own interests, only an academic circle of elites deals with the factors that are relevant for nation-building (standard language, folk customs, folk songs, history, religion, etc.). In phase B the intellectuals launch a deliberate agitation in order to create a 'national consciousness' among the population. Phase C is the period of the masses. The social structure of nationalism expands until it ideally involves all layers of society. This phase comes to an end when the nation is 'completely formed' and 'all deficits of a complete national existence are eliminated'. In the ideal case, this is the foundation of a state.[181]

This theory is a useful model. Hobsbawm also discusses the three phases.[182] He particularly emphasizes the fact that 'national consciousness' develops unevenly within social groups and, he adds, also in different regions of a country. Till now this aspect has been neglected. The role of elites in nation-building, and their gradual influence on a wide social spectrum and on the hinterland is significant in both case studies. The regional factor is even crucial in the Indian case.

However, Hroch's three-phase model does not hold true for all case studies. In Bosnia-Herzegovina, for example, phase B was skipped or only touched upon briefly. In India it lasted somewhat longer. But in both cases a more or less broad approval of ethno-national concepts was achieved, however, just 'at the last second', at the peak of the crisis. In Pakistan it ebbed away soon after. In both cases there can be no talk of a national movement with a mass basis—and *yet* statehood was the result. This indicates that other factors were also active as the midwives at the birth of nationalism. In addition, Hroch's approach falls prey to historical determinism. Schödl criticizes him for lumping together a variety of politico-historical processes. 'Deviationists' like the states of eastern and south-eastern Europe were not granted an independent development but just a 'delayed' one.[183] In their cases, however, Schödl observes an own path of development which cannot be squeezed into the modernization approach of 'Western' nationalisms.

Even further, says Schödl, east European nationalism experienced a transformation, changing from being an *instrument* of modernization to a *substitute* for modernization, even as a substitute for politics, and an end in itself.[184] This destructive and growth-inhibiting function results from a paradox, as Berend and Ránki argue:

> [I]n the West the bourgeois national state was born of the advancement of bourgeois civilization; in the East it was rather the failings, the contradictions, and the impediments of this development which fostered nationalism and strengthened independent national endeavours.[185]

On the one hand, modernization and the entry of capitalism have provided the minimal requirements for national ambitions in eastern and south-eastern Europe. On the other hand, the relative backwardness of these regions was the main cause for the growth of nationalistic feelings, according to Berend and Ránki.

Also, for Horowitz the concept of relative backwardness vis-à-vis 'ethnic' competitors is an important potential area for conflict.[186] This study will show that some of the elements of eastern European nation-building can also be found in India and the Pakistan movement. All in all, the British introduced modernization in the Indian subcontinent in the Western style. Thus the relative backwardness of the country and the exploitation by the colonizers became all the more visible. Besides, in many places there was an economic and social gap between the religious groups.

Von Beyme, however, cites some examples from eastern and south-eastern Europe where this theory of deprivation fails. The Baltic states as well as Slovenia and Croatia were the more prosperous areas that opted for separatism.[187] Also, the Indian case offers counter arguments: the very regions of north India where the Muslim upper class had maintained a powerful position also harboured the hot-beds of the separatist Muslim League.

Such contradictory observations provoke the double-edged question that has already appeared in the discussion on ethnicity in a similar form: is nationalism a vehicle for social modernization, as Gellner describes it?[188] Or is modernization a vehicle for nationalism? Unfortunately, this exciting debate cannot be followed in detail here. But the examination of nationalism, once as an independent and once as a dependent variable, helps to narrow down this phenomenon and makes it suitable for the case studies. So two aspects are in the forefront of the discussion: (1) What are the functions of nationalism? and: (2) What are the contents of nationalism?

4.1.1. *Function*

4.1.1.1. EMANCIPATORY NATIONALISM (Risorgimento nationalism, liberal nationalism, reform nationalism)[189]

Emancipatory nationaism is a means to an end and it aims at the liberation from political and social subjugation. In this process 'nationally conscious' peoples emancipate themselves from a multi-national system of rule (eastern Europe), or new classes of society do so within an existing dynastic state structure (western Europe). Representatives of this type of nationalism emphasize the right of every nation—including the right of each member—to autonomous development. Individual freedom and national independence are closely related here. The subjugated people join hands against the oppressors. Herder and his idea of a quasi organic and free development of every nation strongly influenced this notion.

Whereas Risorgimento nationalism as a type is mainly applied to Europe, reform nationalism is, above all, a phenomenon of the colonized, already existing states. But both proclaim a national (re-)birth. The movements in the colonies targeted the cultural influence of the colonizers and their political patronage. For this purpose, they speeded up the process of cultural homogenization and social reform based on the Western model despite the confrontation with the European colonial power. This process of modernization was itself a basic precondition for the rise of nationalism, i.e. for the political mobilization against the colonizers.[190] The protagonists of reform nationalism came from the traditional, state service classes.

The Indian independence movement had such an emancipatory character. The elite came from the upper class and had received British education. With growing national consciousness there was also an increasing homogenization of society and religions. Moreover, Nehru was a socialist modernist who wanted to break with the traditions of his society (in contrast to Gandhi).[191] The Congress party wanted to free the 'Indian nation', and it clearly targeted the British as its opponent. The Muslim League, on the contrary, strove to emancipate itself from 'the Hindus' as it feared that Muslims would have to live under their 'foreign rule' after the departure of the British. Jinnah's main argument was a *political* self-determination for 'the Muslims'. Two emancipatory claims, based on two completely different nation concepts, got into a muddle and turned out to be incompatible. Therefore, particularly in the case of India, it is important to systematically differentiate between the functions and contents of nationalism. Indian nationalism was potentially integrative, while Muslim nationalism was secessionist. Yet both strove for political emancipation.

4.1.1.2. INTEGRAL NATIONALISM (reactionary, aggressive-expansionist, extremist, militant, mystic)

Integral nationalism is an end in itself in the way in which Schödl has described it (see above). The nation is an absolute value to which the individual has to submit completely. Nationalism becomes a mystic cult, a substitute for religion. It has no secular intentions like, for example, the modernization of society. This form of nationalism is possible only in a world of already established nation states in which the so-called 'delayed nations'[192] make a dash to overtake the others. This is particularly evident in the Balkans. The nationalist founding myths like the battle on Kosovo Polje (field of the black birds) give the nation a quasi sacral character. In the absence of political or economic aims, the Serbian Academy of Sciences in 1986 instead came up with the old claim that Serbia were everywhere where Serbs lived. The war mongers Karadzic and Mladic extended this claim to include all areas where Serb graves lie.[193] This explains the angry outbursts of the Bosnian-Serb commander Mladic against Holbrooke, the US special envoy, who felt that statements such as the following were extremely irrational: 'We will not give up even an inch of our *sanctified* Serbian land.'[194]

On the Indian side, it was mainly Aurobindo who attributed a sacred value to the nation. Unlike in the Balkans, for Aurobindo nationalism was a god-given religion. But the political consequences were the same. With reference to Bengali nationalism he said: 'Whatever there may be in some minds, it is not, at the heart of it, a political self-interest that we are pursuing. It is a religion by which we are trying to realize God in the nation, in our fellow-countrymen'.[195] In this sense, nationalism can well be described as irrational.

The troubled Indo-Pakistan relationship has put brakes on the process of development and modernization in both countries and indeed in the whole region, including supranational organizations (like the SAARC[196]). Their nationalisms are purely an end in themselves. Dutt notes this with a sense of resignation: 'The Indo-Pakistan relationship is a complex mix of national prejudices, inflated psyche, injured ego and plain rivalry.'[197] Pakistan's nuclear tests in 1998 are part of this. They were conducted although the country plunged into a grave economic crisis as a consequence.[198] In an interview, the then prime minister, Nawaz Sharif, admitted openly: 'The pressure was irresistible at home.

It was mounting on the government every day, every hour. The outside world is not aware of the emotional feelings of the people of this region.'[199]

These examples show how closely integral nationalism's great potential to mobilize people is linked to the primordial anchors of ethno-nationalism.

4.1.2. *Content*

The classification here is directly based on the systematic reflections on the term 'nation'.

4.1.2.1. CIVIL-DEMOCRATIC NATIONALISM (secular, 'political')

Civic-democratic nationalism is based on the civil-democratic ideal of the nation. Emphasis lies on the function and form of the state. This type of nationalism has an integrative effect because it ideally comes into being through a plebiscitary element (content), and because it often redeems emancipatory claims at the same time (function). A society (not a community!) based on equality accompanies the created state. Hutchinson calls this phenomenon 'political nationalism' in contrast to 'cultural nationalism'.[200] A precondition for this nationalism is the *overcoming* of possible ethnic or even 'ethnic' differences.[201]

In our case studies this political nationalism plays a role as the ideology of the Indian freedom or independence movement. In this sense—and only in this sense—the word nationalism is applied in the Indian context and usage. This nationalism is secular, trans-'ethnic', and integrative. The member of the nation is 'the Indian'. He or she defines himself or herself through a feeling of common belonging with regard to the common state, and through the already existing state territory in which he or she lives.

4.1.2.2. ETHNO-NATIONALISM OR COMMUNALISM ('cultural')

Ethno-nationalism or communalism is based on an organic, 'ethnic' ideal of the nation. This nationalism does not fall back on the state as an integrating factor. Rather state is the consequence of a preceding process of 'ethnic' and parallel cultural homogenization of a people as a community (not a society!).

This term is derived from the concept of 'ethnicity' and the ideology of the ethno-nation. So all definitions above are valid here, too. In the case studies described here, the 'ethnicentre' and thus the focus of agitation is religion. In this sense, the specific Indian expression *communalism* can be used in contrast to *nationalism*. The mixing up of the two terms and their lack of clarity has troubled many authors.[202] Thapar gives a suitable and widely accepted definition of the term communalism which covers all the aspects of ethno-nationalism defined here:

> Communalism in the Indian sense therefore is a consciousness which draws on a supposed religious identity and uses this as the basis for an ideology. It then demands political allegiance to a religious community and supports a programme of political action designed to further the interests of that religious community. Such an ideology is of recent origin but uses history to justify the notion that the community (as defined in recent history) and therefore the communal identity have existed since the early past. Because the identity is linked to religion, it can lead to the redefinition of the particular religion [...].[203]

Similarly, Bipan Chandra writes: '[C]ommunalism is the belief that because a group of people follow a particular religion they have, as a result, common social, political and economic interests', which differ from community to community and in addition are incompatible.[204] Engineer defines communalism primarily as a 'misuse of religion by vested interests'.[205] Dixit emphasizes the decision-making role of political actors: 'It is only when a deliberate choice is made by a community to initiate political demands on the basis of religio-cultural differences that communal awareness turns into communalism in the form of a political doctrine'.[206] K.N. Panikkar uses the term in the same sense.[207]

These definitions share with Hutchinson's 'cultural nationalism' the idea that an own state does not *necessarily* have to be a direct goal of action. What makes the term communalism so suitable is the original meaning of a community, that is, a small, closely knit social unit with a neighbourly life companionship, that is directly vulnerable during ethno-national conflicts, when communities attack each other, break down, and, in extreme cases, 'un-mix'. This process is very well reflected in the actual structure of settlement and conflict in the Balkans and in India.

But until now I have found only one author who applies the term communalism to describe the conditions in the Balkans, and probably not by coincidence in a Pakistani periodical.[208]

As Thapar hints, this phenomenon hides a paradox: the more religious features serve the cause of political contrast, the more they dilute their original content. This happened in Bosnia-Herzegovina and Pakistan. Religion was used as a 'motivating force'[209] for political purposes. At first, cultural-religious interests were in the forefront, but soon a political action group developed that moved further and further away from the religious guidelines.

Brass points out that, from the primordial viewpoint, a Pakistan movement (just like the Zionist movement of the Jews) was the most improbable possibility of all because a 'nation state' did not at all fit into the concept of the traditional, religious leaders.[210] Alavi writes: 'The irony of the argument that Pakistan was founded on religious ideology lies in the fact that practically every Muslim group and organization in the Indian subcontinent that was specifically religious—Islamic—was hostile to Jinnah and the Muslim League, and strongly opposed to the Pakistan movement.'[211] This contradiction arose because the 'Muslim' ideology became secularized. Describing the years after 1912 Burke writes: 'A new generation was coming to power on a *national* rather than *religious* concept of the Indian Muslim community, emphasizing the collective political aspect of Muslim loyalties rather than the individual vocations of Muslim believers.'[212] This uneasy relationship between traditional Islam, pan-Islam, and nationalism can also be observed in India and Bosnia-Herzegovina. Gellner remarks: 'Nowadays, to be a Bosnian Muslim you need not believe that there is no God but God and that Mohamed is his Prophet, but *you do need to have lost that faith.*'[213] So in general one can conclude with Linz: '[P]rimordialism might be the original source of nationalism, but ultimately nationalism's political implications are *incompatible with primordialism.*'[214]

A quotation of Radovan Karadzic also shows to what extent religion and ethno-nationalism had distanced themselves from one another in the Balkans. He expressed his happiness about the good cooperation that he had received from his ethno-nationalist opponent (partner?) on the Bosnian-Croatian side, Mate Boban. Together with him Karadzic hatched plans to divide Bosnia-Herzegovina. Karadzic observed about

Boban: 'He was more Croat than Catholic. His idea was to concentrate the Croat population in one part of Bosnia, so that they could protect their ethnicity and not Catholicism.'[215] The original main point of contrast, the ethnicentre religion, had meanwhile become undesirable and irritating. Someone who is still looking for a real difference and seeking a 'sense' in the confrontations should give up at this point.

Two important observations emerge from the discrepancy between the primordial feature, religion, and the political demands derived from it:

Ethno-nationalists are Not Fundamentalists

The divergence of religious principles and religious-political demands prohibits the equation of ethno-nationalists and (religious) fundamentalists. This is an important observation because the ethnicentre, religion, somehow tempts to brand the opponents as fundamentalists, in the Balkans as well as in India. This far-reaching confusion has also spread in the press and in academic discourse. Above all, Serb and Croatian alarmism towards the Bosnian Muslims counts as a malicious misinterpretation of this kind.[216] In the Indian context, Bipan Chandra points out that communalists pursue political interests that go beyond religion. They attack other communities. In contrast, fundamentalists mostly target their own community in order to transform it in accordance with their strict religious sense (although this impression has changed in the global perspective, especially after 11 September 2001).[217] By contrast, ethno-nationalists are often the least devout ones of all. This ideology can go along with secularism or even atheism, as in Bosnia-Herzegovina.

Islamic fundamentalists or Islamists fall back on the original revelations of the Koran, and partly to post-Koranic legally relevant utterances which are attributed to the Prophet Muhammad (*hadiths*).[218] Generally, they take the all-Islamic *umma* as a reference point, and reject the 'nation state' as something post-Islamic and Western.[219] They are interested in the condition of society at the micro-level, not necessarily in the political framework at the macro-level. Islamists rarely have a political concept. Their actions are rarely goal-oriented and, therefore, although causing physical and political damage, they are less succesful in the long run. This is still true after the terror attacks on

11 September 2001. There is nowhere a coherent political vision from the side of Islamic fundamentalists (except perhaps a particular social order which, however, is highly disputed among Muslims and even Muslim conservatives themselves). The secular and controversial Syrian philosopher, Sadiq Al-Azm, even holds that with the 11 September attacks the Islamic fundamentalists have passed their peak—just because of the lack of further political concepts and the lack of a popular following.[220]

One of the rare instances where Muslim ethno-nationalism and Islamic fundamentalism have historically merged is in Pakistan. Here the latter is supposed to make up for the flaws of the former, as described in the case study in more detail.[221] Nevertheless, both ideologies can rarely be found in one and the same person without major contradictions. This does not exclude a rising trend of Islamists jumping on the bandwagon of Muslim ethno-nationalism, using this chance pragmatically to spread their ideology. This is what they tried in Bosnia, for example, but with sobering success.

Action Group and Large Group Diverge

Ethno-nationalism is caught up in an internal contradiction between the category of contrast of the large group and the aims of the action group which appeals to that very category. This implies: (a) Religion as a primordial anchor and a political means of recruitment loses its original purpose (and contents in the first place). (b) Members of the class feature can then serve as a political constituency in a limited sense only. Thus a large gap emerges between the action group and the class feature (in Reiter's sense).

Such a discrepancy can emerge not only through dogmatic-religious moments as the case studies show. Also, the economic and social interests of the action group mostly differ fundamentally from the (other) members of the postulated large group. Hence there is no such thing as a 'community of will' which this nationalism postulates. This carries all the more weight as ethno-nationalists—precisely because of this essential (mis-)judgement—do not take any political and institutional precautions for balancing interests, as it is indispensable in the civic-democratic concept.

4.2. Table of Nationalisms

TABLE (B): THE DUAL CHARACTER OF NATIONALISM (IDEAL TYPES)

Nationalisms according to function (→) and content (↓)	emancipatory	integral
civic-democratic (in India: *nationalism*)	Indian freedom movement (Nehru/Gandhi)	—
ethno-national (in India: *communalism*)	Pakistan movement (Jinnah)	Balkan nationalisms,* today's Pakistani and Hindu nationalisms

Note: * Mainly after the First World War. The early Balkan nationalisms in the Ottoman and the Habsburg empires also had emancipatory traits, even if there was no specific claim for reform or modernization.

5. WHAT IS A 'NATION STATE'?

Nationalism as an ideology and as an organized political movement strives for the overlapping of nation and state in the nation state. On this basis it can again be differentiated between a civil-democratic and an ethno-national version.

5.1. Nation *State* and *Nation* State

The nation state springs from the French experience. It came into being through the process of a civil-democratic nation-building, as described above. The emphasis lies on the 'state'. Therefore, the term state nation (*Staatsnation*) has also been adopted. This makes more sense because the connotation of the nation state has shifted clearly in favour of the ethno-national version, the *nation* state. In the history of ideas this corresponds to the German understanding in which all members of a 'cultural nation' (*Kulturnation*) are supposed to live in their own state boundaries. In other words, a cultural people (*Kulturvolk*), territory, and executive power are supposed to belong under one hub. This is exactly how the Balkan, Pakistani, and Hindu ethno-nationalists saw it and continue to see it.

If this ideal is not achieved, ethno-nations often see themselves as *homelands* for the scattered fellow nationals in the 'diaspora'.[222] Others speak of sponsor-nations[223] or 'external centers'.[224] Depending on how virulent the ethno-nationalism is, the spokesmen of the homeland more or less vigorously engage for political rights of the 'ethnic' minority of 'their' kin in alien lands. This often leads to high tensions, particularly when the homeland is of very recent origin itself and is possibly not recognized as a nation by its neighbours, or when this is done only grudgingly. In Yugoslavia, since the elevation of the Muslims to a nation, the Bosnian Muslim ethno-nationalists have considered themselves as a homeland for their fellow believers in the Serb Sandshak region, in Macedonia, and in Kosovo. Today, some Albanians in Macedonia and Kosovo locate their homeland in Albania. Macedonia has begun to view itself in the same way for 'ethnic' Macedonians in Bulgaria and Greece. Both countries, however, deny that they are Macedonians in the first place.[225] Others assign the homeland role to Turkey for 'the Bosnian Muslims' in continuation of the Ottoman tradition.[226] Serbia and Croatia have been throwing their weight around as homelands for 'the' Bosnian Serbs and Croats since the nineteenth century. Thus, they sandwich 'the' Bosnian Muslims. Pakistan draws a great part of its legitimization as a state from the claim of being a homeland for all Indian Muslims. But the fact that still more Muslims lived in India and continue to do so and that the Bengali Muslims became independent offer counter evidence to these ideological contortions. The confusion over the homeland and territorial irritations are a prelude to the conflict which is created by a combination of both nation state concepts.

5.1.1. *The Murderous Mixture*

[A]ll men are entitled to present themselves in the society of others by virtue of their right of common possession of the earth's surface. Since the earth is a globe, they cannot disperse over an infinite area, but must necessarily tolerate one another's company. And *no-one originally has any greater right than anyone else to occupy any particular portion of the earth.*' (Immanuel Kant)[227]

Kant's humanist, cosmopolitan idea is doomed to failure when the concepts of *nation* state and *state* nation are pursued simultaneously, for this leads to murder and manslaughter, as Sundhaussen describes in the case of the Balkans.[228] In this region the postulated 'historical rights' of ethno-nations formed an unholy alliance with the modern right of self-determination on the basis of the state nation:

According to opportunity, the nationalists either referred to 'historical rights', in case the disputed area had meanwhile ('unlawfully') been settled by members of another ethnic group or to self-determination, in case their own nation had expanded beyond the medieval state boundaries (and whose members now lived in an area to which other nations claimed 'historical rights').[229]

Kaplan speaks of the 'law of the Balkans': 'Each nation demands a revision of the boundaries back to the drawing of the time of its greatest expansion.'[230] Also, the reform-oriented Serb prime minister Zoran Djinjic identifies the 'eternal tension between state and nation' the reason for the instability in the Balkans:

It was always the question who founds a nation state at the expense of the others, and afterwards one waited for the next war in order to annul it again. [...] Always when someone in the world declares war on someone else, we start a war. And the question is: why? Because always accounts from the past remained open, and because one always waited for a world crisis in order to settle these accounts.[231]

The intensity of the fight over territory is linked to the supposed 'holiness' of the land on which the 'wrong' people allegedly live, as for example in Kosovo. The ethno-national law of purity applied to heterogeneous states allows only two solutions: (1) The state boundaries must be carved out in accordance with the 'ethnic' settlement, or (2) the 'ethnic' settlements must be 'adapted' to the state boundaries. The latter leads to 'ethnic' expulsions, and, in its most gruesome form, 'ethnic' extermination campaigns, as they are all too familiar in the Balkans.

It is a fact that the 'ethnic' map has been simplified after the creation of 'nation states'. But it is still sufficiently complicated, particularly in the Balkans and on the Indian subcontinent. In the Bosnian war the goal of 'homogeneous' populations has been pursued with ruthless consistency, and to a large extent it has been achieved.[232] In India the combination of both nation state concepts was less 'successful'. Indeed, the British plan to divide the subcontinent was called the 'Balkan Plan' on purpose; ethno-national confrontations and expulsions did not lag behind the Balkan 'example'. After partition two heterogeneous states came in to being. A shift in the ethnicentre from religion to language in Pakistan made the self-proclaimed Muslim 'nation state' split into two. In India, as in other former colonies, both nation concepts collide because a state is created first (often with arbitrary boundaries), and within it a 'delayed' ethno-nation develops, or several ones do.[233] If several ethno-nations emerge at the same time, the colonial state becomes a strait-jacket, secessions occur, and populations 'un-mix'.

These phenomena, once again, justify sticking to the term 'ethnicity'. No social or political category can substitute this term. For its essential ideological resource is the primordial anchor of the 'right' human being *itself.* Because of his ancestry he cannot and must not escape his skin; besides he requires living space. Land then becomes scarce and, in principle, undistributable if with each 'right' person, his house, and his soil is associated a piece of political and state-constitutional territory *and* if the 'right' person lives together with the 'wrong' person for whom the same claim is raised. This 'politics of blood and soil' has become particularly notorious in the political deadlock in Israel and Palestine.[234]

5.2. The Unfulfilled Ideal

As the reader might have noticed, the term 'nation state' has not been spared the quotation marks either because a real nation state is virtually non-existent. According to estimates, only about 4 per cent of the world's population lives in such an entity, and without Japan the figure is only 1 per cent.[235] Connor counts just seven 'homogeneous' states which do not have any boundary conflicts.[236] In spite of this, we allegedly live in the 'age of the nation state'. Where does this contradiction come from? It shows that those who talk about it have taken over the ethno-national paradigm —and this is the vast majority of historians, politicians, journalists, etc. As Rizman argues: '[T]he whole international order with its powers and privileges operates under this false or rather self-constructed ideological assumption.'[237]

The 'nation state' is no more than an ideal goal of ethno-national ambitions. According to Alter, '[t]he term nation state therefore does not refer to reality but to a *political programme*'.[238] In this sense it is used in this study, too. Alter recommends:

> From today's perspective it would be more adequate to speak of an age of sovereign states which, in their overwhelming majority, are trying to legitimize

themselves with recourse to the principle of the nation state[239] and to the right of self-determination.[240]

6. NATION AND ISLAM: A CONTRADICTORY ALLIANCE

Where God commands . . . I am a Muslim first, a Muslim second and a Muslim last and nothing but a Muslim. . . . But where India is concerned, where the welfare of India is concerned, I am an Indian first, an Indian second, and an Indian last and nothing but an Indian . . . I belong to two circles of equal size but which are not concentric. One is India and the other is the Muslim world . . . we belong to these circles . . . and we can leave neither.[241]

Muhammad Ali, leader of the Indian Khilafat movement, appropriately summed up the schizophrenic identity of the Indian Muslims shortly before his death. The gap between the action group and the category of contrast religion cannot escape notice. Is the general structure of ethno-national movements the reason, or is it because Islam is particularly 'unsuitable' for nation-building? This question is the point of departure for an extensive debate which can only be touched upon here.

Two factors seem to make it conceptually difficult to combine nation and Islam: (1) The assertion that in Islam a separation of church and state, of sacred and secular, is (a) dogmatically, and (b) practically impossible; and (2) the Islamic idea of a community of all Islamic believers (*umma*) which transcends state structures and which considers the pilgrim city of Mecca the religious heart of the world.[242]

6.1. The Dogma of Indivisibility

A differentiation of dogma and praxis is important here. The dogmatic claim to consider religion, society, and the state apparatus as one unit is widely propagated by Islamic and Western scholars alike. It is mostly founded on the principle: *al-Islam din wa daula* (Islam is religion and political power).[243] However, this principle has also been deconstructed as lacking any historical precedent as well as any cogent arguments in the sources of Islamic revelation or law.[244]

Without going too deeply into the dogmatic arguments, it can be stated that this dogma of indivisibility is pursued particularly rigidly by those who follow a programme of everyday politics. Accordingly, Javid

Iqbal, the son of the father of the Pakistan idea, Muhammad Iqbal, describes Islam as a 'form of life [...] which, apart from the purely religious aspect, also incorporates social, political, legal, economic, military, ethical, literary, artistic, mystic, philosophical and also scientific aspects [...]'. This statement strongly reminds of the construction plan of 'ethnicity' with the ethnicentre religion. In this sense Iqbal continues: 'From this it follows that one should not view and understand Islam as a religion only but also as a mental attitude, a way of thinking and living, a form of culture or civilization—because all this is what Islam means in its totality to the Pakistani. . . .'[245] Thus he cites the actual purpose of his exposition: an ideological justification of the existence of the state of Pakistan.

This point raises contradictions with respect to a possible special role of Islam in relation to nation-building: (a) Iqbal uses the Islamic teachings selectively. On the one hand, he emphasizes the merging of the religion with state and society. On the other hand, he ignores the idea of an all-Islamic *umma*, as demanded by the orthodox *ulema*. (b) As the Balkan example shows, other religions are also suited for the purpose of 'ethnic' demarcation. The Orthodox and the Catholic churches have endorsed this development even more strongly than the Bosnian Islamic scholars.[246]

If Iqbal were correct, an Islamic 'culture' could have developed only poorly or not at all under 'foreign rule'. In the teachings of Islam this is expressed in the notion of *dar al harb* (land of war). This means that where ever Muslims live as a majority an *Islamic* (not secularly Muslim) rule should emerge to create *dar al salam* (land of peace). This point is delicate because it brings up the question of minorities of other faiths. It is aggravated in combination with ethno-nationalism. Since in its genesis a clearly demarcated territory gains importance, the problem has finally to be solved by constitutional law. If Muslims are the majority, the society is structured according to Islamic rules. Moderate Islamic scholars like the expelled former Iranian prime minister, Bani Sadr, point to the special protection of minorities enshrined in the Koran: 'Non-Muslims are entitled to hold other religious beliefs, political ideologies or opinions. [...] [I]n their good, just and pious works and deeds they are to be helped and assisted.'[247] But this is not compatible with a strictly civic-democratic principle either. For—apart from restricting the concept to the minorities who adhere to a modern *codified religion*[248] —normative assumptions are made *a priori* (pious works, etc.) which do not depend on political consensus finding. Besides, people are classified differently according to their faith. But at the same time this idea of an Islamic constitution is no good for ethno-nationalism either which pre-supposes *a priori* a 'unity of will', and this does not exist because of different ideologies and faiths.

More straightforward is the concept put forward by radical theologians: Muslims are not supposed to live under foreign rule at all. With this some Islamic scholars underpinned the Two-Nation Theory in India. The paradox is, however, that a purely religious-dogmatic argumentation wants to substantiate the political or 'ethnic' programme of the Two-Nation Theory, thereby neglecting the claim of the *umma*.[249] Consequently, in India there were prominent Muslims who came up with plausible dogmatic counter arguments.[250]

These contradictions contain the same dynamite as the dangerous mix of civil-democratic nationalism and ethno-nationalism described above. This is also what the Bosnian President, Alija Izetbegovic, had to experience. During the ethno-national conflict his Islamic writings gained new meaning. In particular the claim that wherever Muslims are in a majority they should rule over themselves provoked the ethno-national rivalry into action. When, so to speak, the territory of Yugoslavia had shrunk to the area of Bosnia-Herzegovina, and when suddenly the Muslims found themselves in a majority, this no longer remained a purely academic exercise.[251] On the other hand, when someone (like Jinnah) strives to square the circle by suddenly demanding a secular, civil-democratic state structure and society after having caused the ethno-national foundation of a state based on Islam, he confuses a great part of his followers and puts the ethno-national legitimacy of that state at risk. By doing this, he reveals that it was not Islam that was the basis and motive of creating the state but political reasons.[252] Here again the gap between the action group and the category of identity of the large group is obvious.

Many assumptions in the Islamic doctrine gain new relevance through the national paradigm. This is something that Islam shares with the principles of other religions, all of which originated in a traditional, pre-national setting. Islam is particularly challenged in so far as its dogmatic claims aspire more vigorously the above-mentioned harmony of religion and political structure. But often it is just the situative political motivation that decides when and how these dogmas are demanded and kept.

E. Ahmed points to this issue. He topples the dogma of indivisibility from its pedestal and claims that, in most cases, Muslim rulers did not establish Islamic rule themselves. During eleven out of fourteen 'Islamic' centuries Islam and the state had been two pairs of shoes: 'A fusion of religion and political power was and remains an ideal in the Muslim tradition.'[253] Cultural, political, scientific, etc. advancements are the *collective* achievements of Christians, Jews, Hindus, and others alike (in strong contrast to Iqbal's views).

With respect to the lack of unity between religion and state, the orthodox *ulema* support E. Ahmed's view, albeit regretfully. They hold that state power and religion had parted ways after the reign of the fourth caliph in 650. The reasons were that the rulers themselves were not pious; secular laws and governance dominated; the 'Islamic world' was split into different political units.[254] The last point directly addresses the dogmatic contradiction between pan-Islam and statehood.

6.2. 'Nation State' Against *Umma*?

The French Marshal Lyautey described the Islamic world as a gigantic drum whose vibrations on the one side could be felt immediately at the other side.[255] This image arises mainly out of the paranoia of Western colonial rulers who feared a strong opponent. But the political cleavages do not run along such straight lines at all. Here, too, is a yawning gap between theory and praxis.

The classic Islamic scholar Ibn Khaldun defined three pillars on which the Islamic state should be erected: (a) group feeling (*asabiyah*), (b) a ruling structure with leaders, and (c) a large community that is based on the common religion (*umma*).[256] There is no mention of 'ethnic groups', territory, or boundaries. The state defines itself mainly through the imposition of justice and the defence of Islam. The 'nation state' does not fit into the traditional Islamic concept.[257] This is why the subject of how to deal with this modern, Western phenomenon is so controversial among Islamic thinkers. Four main dogmatic currents can be observed:[258]

(1) *Islamism without nationalism.* This conservative school emphasizes

the strict Islamic principle of equality beyond ethnic differences. For the Saudi-Arabian theologian Bashmil, the main representative of this position, nationalism contradicts the teaching of the Koran, 'how the Prophet connected a Muslim negro with a Muslim Arab but not an Arab Muslim with a member of the most noble Arabic tribe, the Quraish, as long as they were still heathens'.[259] Sura XLIX, 13 also expresses the supra- or trans-'ethnic' principle in Islam:

> O mankind! We have created you from a male and a female, and made you into nations [peoples][260] and tribes that you may know one another. Verily, the most honourable of you in the Sight of Allah is that (believer) who has *At-Taqwa* [= who is the most pious]. . . .[261]

The highest, and above all, the most important level of ascription is the *umma* with its symbolic centre at the Ka'aba in Mecca. This was also recognized by the most important Muslim antagonist of Jinnah, the Indian Islamic scholar, Maulana Abul-Ala-Maududi. He was a strong opponent of the Two-Nation Theory:

> [T]here is no scope for any kind of distinction on the basis of nationality or race or geography or class for those people who accept the principles of Islam. Its ultimate vision is a world state in which the chains of racial and national prejudices are broken. . . . Where there is nationalism, there Islam can never blossom, and where there is Islam, there is no room for nationalism.[262]

(2) *Islamism above nationalism.* The 'modern conservatives' (Schimmel) seek a relative absorption of nationalism through Islam. Still they make ethnic distinctions. Many Arabs, for example, think that they can be especially proud of Islam because their land was allowed to be the cradle of the Koran and because they shared its language.[263] On the other hand, the Turks also point to the extent of *their* contribution to Islam in history.

(3) *Nationalism above Islamism.* In this current, ethno-national aspects gain an upper hand. For some representatives like the Egyptian Sati Husri the most important component of a nation is not religion but history and language. Husri, who was influenced by the ideas of Fichte and Herder, historically established the notion of pan-Arabism. According to him, all Arabic countries formed a nation.[264] On the other hand, some Egyptians take pride in their 'national history' and

in their 'indissoluble' connections to Europe as opposed to their fellow believers in Kuwait, for example. This notion can be integrated into the scheme of a tendentially-objective nationalism, as described above.

(4) *Nationalism without Islamism* (ethno-nationalism). Here the religious feature loses its dogmatic meaning. The religious attribute turns into the ethnicentre, the religious content into a (sometimes even undesirable) matter of secondary importance. The only thing which remains 'Muslim' is the nationality. The members of the nation can be even secular in character. The typical example is the 'Muslim nation' which was pro-exclaimed under Tito in Yugoslavia. According to, socialist ideology, the term nation could not be associated with religion at all (although the creation of this 'nation' awakened pan-Islamic ambitions among some Bosnian Muslims, both dogmatically and ideologically). Also, Jinnah's arguments for a 'Muslim nation' and his rule as the head of state had less to do with issues of faith than with political goals.

In particular, the first and the last approaches clash. Tensions have been present in Bosnia-Herzegovina and in India/Pakistan all the time. Rashid writes in relation to India:

> Territorial nationalism with its roots in 18th century Europe has very little to do with the concept of the *umma* prescribed by Islam. Over time, however, the derived had become the inherent, and a large number of Indian Muslims responded to the call for Pakistan without any sense of unease over this apparent inconsistency.[265]

With an increase in these tensions it seems that 'ethnicity' mixed with religion plus contrast boosters offers the only possibility of creating a 'Muslim nation'. Therefore, Rashid holds: 'Islam is a necessary but not a sufficient basis for the autonomous Muslim state.'[266] Also, Tibi says that it is true that Islam provokes a strong 'psycho-social' bond among Muslims but its political impact on nation-building is meagre.[267] Ruthven agrees and stresses that legal pluralism in Islam prevented, to a large extent, the appropriation of religion by ethno-nationalism:

> The impact of Islam upon society was [...] paradoxical: while proclaiming its hostility to kinship solidarity, it also mutilated against the emergence of alternative sources of allegiance. Neither city nor monarchy, nation nor 'people'—or their representatives—were endowed with the kind of legitimacy that could enable

them to alter the divine law or introduce new laws that could bind the community unconditionally.[268]

Since religion did not provide any reliable political binding force, Muhammad Iqbal passionately insisted on an economically viable and a cultural (in this sense: ethnic) unit as a foundation for Pakistan as a state. However, this hope remained unfulfilled.

Gellner arrives at a different conclusion altogether. For him Islam is the best raw material for nationalism. On the one hand, Islamic folk culture is 'sub-ethnic', 'sub-political', and tribal. On the other hand, there is the *umma* which is 'trans-political', 'trans-ethnic', and is not bound to any state. It had represented a 'high culture' already in pre-national times, which only needed to be 'recalled' and installed nationally. 'Islamic society was ever ideally prepared, by an accident of history, for this development. It possessed within itself both a high and a low culture'.[269] The case studies of Bosnia-Herzegovina and India, however, do not support this very abstract theory. The pan-Islamic notion of an *umma* functioned rather as a brake-block than as a catalytic for 'ethnic' nation-building. At least it created an additional cleavage among the Muslims.

However, it cannot be ruled out that Muslim ethno-nationalism gets hooked up with an Islamic conservatism or even fundamentalism. This is happening in Pakistan at the moment.[270] This has less to do with Tibi's controversial thesis that the Islamic world is caught up in a cultural crisis of meaning because of its technological backwardness vis-à-vis the West.[271] It does not give an answer, for example, why Islamic movements of modernization like that of the Islamic ideologue Al-Afghani or the Aligarh movement in India did not succeed in the long run. The Pakistani turn towards Islamic conservatism lies more in a historically and individually conditioned and ethno-national state crisis of meaning. It is thoroughly political and ideological and has nothing to do with a diffuse notion of Orient-Occident duality or any 'cultural' phenomenon. In Bosnia-Herzegovina, for example, the *ulema* plays a contrary role. It is progressive and resists fundamentalist currents, on the one hand, and ethno-nationalist ambitions of Muslim spokesmen, on the other—even and just after the war.[272]

At this point two types of pan-Islam must be differentiated. One is traditional and emerges from the purely dogmatic idea of the *umma* as a religious community. The other one has political-ideological traits, which include the pan-Islamic movements as they are described in the case studies (Khilafat movement in India, Young Muslims in Bosnia-Herzegovina). The latter type builds on the former. Dogmatic pan-Islam is hardly compatible with the concept of a nation state. In contrast, the political type often takes a detour via the nation state in order to articulate itself. Bodansky emphasizes the differences between the Sunni and Shia interpretations at this point: whereas Sunnis more easily follow the pragmatic road towards the *umma* via the nation states, most Shiites consider the nation state as an un-Islamic entity and do not regard it as a valid vehicle for the propagation of Islam (therefore it is both the right and duty of a Shia ruler in Iran to support all Islamist revolutions beyond his borders).[273]

The important point is this: pan-Islamic movements tell us less about the religious state of mind of 'the Muslims' in general than about the individual, political circumstances of the state in which they take root.

This becomes clear after the abolition of the Caliphate by Atatürk in 1924. The resulting Khilafat movement in India emerged because of specific domestic political reasons and reveals a lot about the *Indian* Muslims, and not about the Muslims in the rest of the world.[274] Why did not other religious brothers get together in that year and defend the Caliphate to the same extent? Where were the Bosnian Muslims? Almost all of them are Sunnis, too. Geographically, they are much closer to the Bosporus, and historically they are much more closely linked to it than South Asians. Purely dogmatic explanations are bound to fail.

The origins of the political-ideological pan-Islam can thus be explained in ethno-national contexts because it falls back on organizational patterns of the 'nation state'. In this sense, Izetbegovic spoke of an Islamic belt from Morocco to Indonesia and sees Pakistan as a model for Muslims all over the world.[275] Pakistani ideologues see it the same way, of course. Even Jinnah himself, at the end of his life, spoke about a 'united front' of Islamic states with Pakistan as the pivot, however, with sobering success.[276]

Self-evidently, the Organization of Islamic Countries (OIC) is founded on the principle of 'nation states', too. However, this does not mean that the pan-Islamic spokesmen necessarily identify with nationalism. For example, Abd al-Rahman Azzam, the architect of the first international Islamic organization, the Arabic League, says: '[I]n its modern form, nationalism (secular) is a new evil, and racism is worse still'.[277] But the Arab League and the OIC are children of the national paradigm. Schulze holds that it is only with the development of a secularized nation concept through nationalist ideologies that the *umma* has freed itself from the strait-jacket of the nation state as a 'supra-state', and thus offer a new possibility of collective identification to Islamic intellectuals. In the nineteenth century the terms 'nation' (*watan*) and 'congregation' (*umma*) were still interchangeable for Islamic intellectuals.[278] Accordingly, the logical order of creation is: first nation, then *umma*. As this background makes clear, this approach has a *political* and not a *dogmatic* explanatory purpose.

But it would be surprising if the term nation were better clarified in the Islamic world than it is in the 'Western' schools of thought. Tibi writes, for example, that the Arabic translation of 'nation' is '*umma*' itself.[279] Gellner sees it the same way, as mentioned above. According to this view, the national paradigm has completely absorbed the dogmatic, pre-political, and supra-ethnic connotation. It is true that the supra-national pilgrimage to Mecca contradicts this. But Tibi's and Gellner's approach have explanatory power for the scope of actions and ideas of the domestic and foreign policies of Muslim states. For the hypotheses cited above do not necessarily mean that the notion of *umma* excludes nationalisms in Muslim states. It just has a tendency to hamper nation-building, particularly in the early stages.

An example that makes one forget the *umma* and which reveals the rift between Muslims was the dogmatic *and* political conflict between Shia Iran and Sunni Afghanistan in the time of the Taliban. Another instance is the Gulf war in 1991, the notorious dissensions among the mainly Islamic OPEC states, the contrasting stands of Arab states in the war against Iraq in 2003, and their conflicting attitudes towards the Palestinians. This is why Caesar holds that the dogma of the *umma* is retreating into ever smaller and national circles.[280] Given this tendency, it appears puzzling that Tibi contradicts himself elsewhere and describes the *umma* as a large 'we-group' of 1.2 billion people, equal to an 'ethnic group', whose members could be called into action simultaneously.[281]

This shows that the difficulty of differentiating *umma* and nation does not only lie in the diversity of the term nation but also in the term *umma* itself. Lewis gives four different connotations of the word: *umma* can have an ethnic (Lewis) character (e.g. the Arabic *umma*); a religious one (the Koran speaks of an *umma* of Christians); a moral one (the

Koran mentions the *umma* of good and bad people); and an ideological one (those who do something right and those who do something wrong).[282]

It becomes even more difficult with the appearance of another term in connection with Islam and nation. In Turkish 'nation' is translated as *millet*.[283] *Millet* is a phenomenon that first appeared under pre-national Islamic rule. It is an autonomous religious community—albeit pre-state and manageable in its size—with its own laws in social, cultural, and partly in economic life. The spiritual leaders played a dominant role in the *millets*. Islamic power structures like the Ottoman empire granted religious minorities their own *millets*. There they could develop freely and—as the modern meaning of the word suggests—develop a 'national consciousness'. The *millet* was strongly based on religious features. In this way 'ethnic groups' and finally ethno-nations originated in the Balkans. This etymological approach is quite plausible.

Now the confusion is perfect. It is neither clear what 'nation' means in Islam nor how this modern form of organization goes together with Islamic teachings. Different scholars have different opinions. Therefore, Schimmel states.

> Since there is no such thing as one high spiritual authority in Islam comparable to that of the Pope, all these different doctrines can co-exist. Islam has drawn the boundaries of its tolerance so widely that any person is accepted as a Muslim who accepts the words of the creed, testifies the unity of God and the position of Muhammad. Hence, within a certain frame, ever new attempts to re-interpret the doctrines can be undertaken.[284]

Dogmatic flexibility must remain the smallest common denominator here. For this study and its theses this means: The appeal to 'Islam' in the process of nation-building occurs in a specific context each time, and this is mainly characterized by political interests. Islam shares this fate with other religions, that however, might be more apt for nationalism from the very beginning. The alliance between Islam and nationalism remains particularly contradictory because the notion of the *umma* as a pan-Islamic factor—in its traditional-dogmatic as well as in its political-ideological form—can counteract the process of nation-building. At least, it creates tensions or delays in this process, as in Bosnia-Herzegovina and India.

7. OPPORTUNITY MAKES STATES

Why do ethno-national state projects so often win against the competition? In order to answer this question it makes sense to recall two theses proposed till now: (1) During the ethno-national nation-building process a gap arises between the ethno-national action group and the category of 'ethnicity'. (2) Ethno-national action groups have the advantage against trans-'ethnic' alternatives in that they can mobilize political resources unbeatably quickly through primordial resources.

However, the last point alone cannot sufficiently explain the process of state-building in the case studies. Why do all these contradictions not lead to a burst of the predetermined breaking point between the action group and the large group? Why can an ethno-national state-building come to be even if *not* all members of a nation support this project (as in India and Bosnia) or/and if even the ethno-national action group itself does not completely back it (as in Bosnia)?

Here it is necessary to look outside. External factors have already been mentioned in connection with the term 'nation'. A nation must be recognized as such from the outside. Its political demands must be directed against someone, and at least be noticed outside its borders. If these demands are ignored, they often cease to exist.[285] If they are promoted, they sometimes achieve more than their supporters themselves had ever considered possible. The creation of a state is, after all, not a child's play. It is a risky venture, often the action of last resort, the final step of the escalation of political events.[286] Despite their advantage in mobilizing people the ethno-nationalists have to make an immense political effort to realize the last stage of their project. This was particularly obvious in Pakistan.

But who or what is the external point of reference? Nehru called it 'mankind' in the humanistic sense. US President Woodrow Wilson (1856-1924) used a rather vague moral category, too.[287] But the normative approach is of little help here; it veils the real actors. The external reference points of the case studies can be named precisely: British colonial power in India and the 'international state community' in Bosnia-Herzegovina, that is, those states which exercised influence with their foreign policy, including international organizations like the European Community (EC), later the European Union (EU), and the United Nations.[288] They created a favourable political climate in which ethno-national state projects could flourish.

7.1. The Confusion Between State and Nation

While discussing the 'nation state' it has become clear that its ethno-national connotation mostly prevails. In this respect, the cases of India and Bosnia-Herzegovina have a common background concerning the history of ideas, independent of the different points of reference in practice. The independence of India, Pakistan, and the former Yugoslav states took place in the age of the ethno-national paradigm. This means that the building of ethno-national states made sense in some form or the other—to the (internal) demand-raisers as well as to the (external) addressees, even when the latter did not always like the idea from the beginning. At least the costs of secession appeared to be lower than the advantages of an alternative solution. In this sense Hobsbawm criticizes that 'the states of the European Union in the beginning of the 1990s are equally involved in the destruction of Yugoslavia as Tito's heirs'.[289] Also, Horowitz points out that the success of secessionist movements always depends on the level of international backing, although he rather thinks of military support.[290] In the case studies described here the external influences are much more subtle and based on ideology.

The first factor is the careless equation of nation and state. This began at the time of the League of Nations and continued up to the founding of the United Nations. Article 4 of the UN Charter reads: 'Membership of the United *Nations* is open to all other peace-loving *states* [...].'[291] The Universal Declaration of Human Rights considers itself as a standard for 'all *peoples* and all *nations*'.[292] It applies to all, irrespective of 'race, colour, sex, language, religion, political or other opinion, *national* or social origin, property, birth or other status'.[293] Hence, the members are states but somehow nations as well, as the name of the club already suggests; or maybe even peoples (*Völker*) as in the German term *Völkerbund* (League of Nations)? And nations are probably peoples who have achieved something higher, like statehood? What does *states* mean, then? What about the peoples who are not nations, and the nations that are not states, and the states that are not nations (that is, 96 per cent of the population in the non-nation states of this world)? The UN Charter does not give any answer to all this.[294] Perhaps this would not be a problem if nation were not understood in the ethno-national sense with all its consequences. Also, Dann points to a 'remarkable ethnicization of the understanding of nation' which raises many questions.[295]

Part of it is the Sleeping-Beauty view of world history. The idea of nations which are 'left behind' and others which are fully awakened was elevated to a political principle by the father of the idea of the League of Nations, Woodrow Wilson, by means of the right of self-determination (even if this was not consequently implemented). At the end of World War I and thus with the collapse of the large 'multi-national' empires, he said in Paris:

> [The Versailles Treaty] is much more than a treaty of peace with Germany. It liberates great peoples who have never before been able to find the way to liberty. [...] It [...] substitutes a new order in which backward nations . . . shall no more be subjected to the domination and exploitation of a stronger nation. . . . It recognizes the inalienable rights of nationality.[296]

At the same time he saw himself and his assembled fellow heads of state not as representatives of their governments but of their peoples.[297]

Originally, the right of self-determination served the colonies to make life difficult for the colonial rulers. In this context it had a liberal-emancipatory character. The UN General Assembly in particular stood for this principle. In this panel the 'Western' states were and continue to be in a minority. In the 1950s they observed, rather sullenly, that the Human Rights Commission laid on the table propositions such as: '[S]lavery exists where an alien people hold power over the destiny of a people.'[298] The opposite of slavery in this sense meant, of course, state sovereignty, including a membership offer to the club on the East River in New York City. What this means in connection with the ethno-national concept is described by Lepsius: 'The modern nation politicizes the ethnic-cultural entities of the peoples through the idea of sovereignty of the people which elevates the peoples to politically constituted, independent subjects of history, to nations.'[299]

But although the United Nations advanced the principle of self-determination, it is still disputed today whether it has meanwhile become a sueable right. For some it has remained a purely *political* principle—an 'ideological weapon'—without significance in international *law*.[300] Others say that today the right of self-determination is binding as a norm of international law.[301] The latter view has gained ground particularly after the war in Kosovo in 1999.

But if one follows this opinion, a new dilemma occurs. Scholars of international law are no less at a loss when it comes to defining terms like 'peoples', 'minority', 'nation', etc., than their colleagues from ethnology, history, and political science. There are no generally accepted definitions, just some fundamental assumptions.[302] So who or what are the 'peoples' who are supposed to be the carrier of this right which, by the way, is not granted to 'minorities'? When do 'minorities' become 'peoples' and when do they become 'nations'?

Democracy becomes a headache if nobody explains who the 'self' actually is that determines itself or is supposed to do so. As far back as 1793 the French general Carnot warned: 'If . . . any community whatever had the right to proclaim its will and separate from the main body under the influence of rebels, etc., every country, every town, every village, every farmstead might declare itself independent.'[303] The connection of the liberal-emancipatory approach from colonial times with the realistic-institutional approach opens the Pandora's box, leading to a potential infinite political disintegration.[304] Mayall counts, for example, 8,000 ethnic groups in the world, taking language and culture as the basis.[305] This provides 'enormous potential for growth in the membership in the General Assembly', as Moynihan states with a twinkle in his eye.[306]

Inconsistency is, therefore, necessary in dealing with the right of self-determination. In turn, the infinite political and legal contradictions in granting ethno-national wishes for sovereignty lead Thomas to conclude that it is almost always better to solve problems within the existing state boundaries, irrespective of how they may have come to be. The tragic consequences in the case of Yugoslavia underline the truth behind this statement.[307]

So the big problem is not only the 'self' in the determination but also the fusion with its democratic articulation. Consider that the existing government claims that it represents the people, and thus the people determines itself. The ethno-nationalists claim the opposite; the people were not a (one and only) nation, and 'their' nation wanted a state for itself. If an election takes place in which the secessionists clearly win, the international community cannot contradict this outcome at least in theory, since it accepts simultaneously the right of self-determination and democracy as central values. The 'majority trap' thus snaps shut. The same happened during the disintegration of Yugoslavia.[308] Along with this formal aspect there was also sympathy for ethno-national projects, particularly the ones of Slovenia and Croatia which were mainly viewed from the emancipatory angle. But no Western politician ever questioned the national self-understanding of these young states or consistently and promptly demanded minority rights in practice. The fact that Tudjman's Croatia came into existence through a reactionary, consequent-objective type of nationalism remained (almost) under impetus wraps. The confusion between state and nation provided additional impetus for the declaration of independence.

Democracy in connection with political self-determination played a role in India, too. The politically liberal British introduced democratic institutions step by step which were tailored in line with the ethno-national paradigm. Thus they created a favourable starting point for ethno-national spokesmen and their ambitions for a state of their 'own'. As the election outcomes strengthened the position of the (potentially) secessionist Muslim League, the counter arguments melted away.[309] The sword of self-determination had hung over the colonial rulers since the League of Nations, and simultaneously the equation of state and nation took political shape.

7.2. The Sweetest Fruits Hang at the Top

World politics works on the basis of three fundamental assumptions: (1) States are the dominant and sovereign actors in the arena of so-called inter*national* relations.[310] (2) States hold the monopoly of power. (3) Conflicts and interventions are fought and settled at the state levels.[311] For these reasons Sulzbach provides the formal minimum definition: 'A "nation" is [...] a group of people who demand an own state because of its sovereignty vis-à-vis other states.'[312] State sovereignty is the highest goal; the ideological motivation is secondary.

In the case of assumption (1) the ethno-national paradigm entails all the contradictions mentioned above. A national banner at the flag post in front of the UN headquarters in New York City, a seat in the General Assembly and in the Security Council by rotation, close to the pulse of world politics—all this raises the spirits of ethno-national spokesmen. The desire for official recognition at the highest level in the international arena as an end in itself is a motive that should not be underestimated. Indian and Pakistani politicians pressed the buttons for the atomic tests since they felt neglected by the international actors, the magazine *Newsweek* suggested.[313] Also, Slovenia and Croatia gained recognition first, and, second, a free hand for negotiations about a EU membership.[314] Unshared prosperity is a further motivation for independent statehood. So both young states do not have to feed the economically weaker regions in eastern Yugoslavia any longer. In this context Mayall and Simpson argue:

> The state is often a valued prize in the competition between opposing ethnic and/or religious groups. The winners gain monopoly access to the outside world and the ability, therefore, to extract a rent from foreign governments, or private investors, during the process of modernization. [...] In other words, both the heterogeneous nature of post-colonial society and the international environment provide a fertile soil in which separatism and secession can propagate and flourish.[315]

Finally, the desire to gain a voice in the resolution of international conflicts is another incentive to become independent. In the extreme case, the assumption that only state representatives should have a place at the negotiation table (also because they have the monopoly of power), together with the confusion of state and nation, led to the fact that self-proclaimed, ethno-national leaders like Radovan Karadzic were courted on equal footing with other heads of state. So Karadzic was traded far above his constitutional value in the market place of international relations.[316] This very assumption makes any intervention in intra-state conflicts—so-called civil wars—a very delicate matter in international law.

The international state community faces problems in responding to each new challenge of this kind, as during the disintegration of Yugoslavia and in the Kosovo conflict. The German foreign minister at that time, Hans-Dietrich Genscher, thought he had found a clever way out of the Yugoslav dilemma and hatched a plan to simply elevate the conflicting parties to subjects of international law. This happened with the recognition of the Yugoslav republics as states. But no second step was taken to resolve the problems. So they escalated in a new constellation.

Once the ethno-national actors break through the barrier of 'foreign rule' and achieve the highest level of sovereignty, they have new avenues to power. This does not mean that the conflicts with their opponents are over. They often continue, but this time at the state level. In integral nationalism the new resources are used as ammunition against the neighbouring state which is now the enemy. The highest and 'most noble' symbol of power in this paradigm is considered the possession of atomic bombs.

Nevertheless, it is too simple to presume that the incentives of the world order alone encourage ethno-national elites to break out of the state systems. In many states there are domestic conflicts of this type which do not lead to secession but whose impact can be cushioned.[317] This is why the external factors are to be regarded as only *one* variable among many others.

However, these external factors should not be underestimated. In recent times politicians and scholars of international law have become more and more aware of their disruptive power within existing state bodies. Specialists in international law often use this observation to launch a fundamental critique of absolute state sovereignty as it was postulated by classic international law. Louis Henkin, for example, considers the term sovereignty superfluous and normatively overloaded. It is only the glamour associated with it that provoked unities to break free from partly well-functioning associations.[318]

In particular, the catastrophe in the Balkans in the 1990s gave an impetus to a new thinking in this field. Some scholars of international law suggest the introduction of a 'buffer' between the concepts of democracy and state-building: the 'inner right of self-determination'. This means that states should be organized in a way that the minorities can determine themselves *within* the state. This would make the 'external (or offensive) right of self-determination' obsolete—which is the creation of a sovereign state on ethno-national principles. This also means a reconciliation between the principle of existing state sovereignty (including territorial integrity) and the demand for self-determination. In other words, The principle of absolute state sovereignty is weakened because a specific form of domestic organization becomes a precondition for the acceptance of the state in international law.[319]

The CSCE (today OSCE)[320] took the first step in this direction after the end of the Cold War. Its members from opposing political camps professed—formally—a community of values. They accepted peoples' sovereignty, democracy, and constitutionality as principles of domestic organization. Stronger and practical significance obtained the Badinter Commission which was set up by the EC just before the break-up of Yugoslavia. It made the protection of minorities a precondition for recognizing the Yugoslav republics as independent states. It is another story that the politicians ignored the demands of the commission to a large extent. Still, it meant an upgrading of the inner right of self-determination in the theory of international law, and at the same time, a qualification of state sovereignty. This becomes even more obvious in the CSCE's behaviour after the collapse of Yugoslavia. The Conference changed its mode of decision making from unanimity to 'consensus minus one'. The 'one' in this case was rump-Yugoslavia.[321] Finally, with its bombardment of Serbia in 1999 NATO placed human rights in Kosovo (and perhaps also the right of self-determination of the Albanian population) over the state sovereignty of rest-Yugoslavia. After the bombardment of Iraq in 1991 with certain qualifications—this was the second case in which military force was used to protect a minority against the will of a sovereign state—but without giving this minority any prospect of having a state of its own! This aspect is particularly important because it is exactly what the international players did not take into consideration during the disintegration of Yugoslavia in 1991. It seems that only the resulting chain reaction of ethno-nationalisms gradually brought about a shift in thinking in favour of the inner right of self-determination, but in many respects it was already too late.

7.3. A Pearl Without Market Value

Those political forces which served as the direct political reference points in the case studies thought and worked within the ethno-national state paradigm. The United Kingdom of colonial times was deeply imprisoned in this mindset. And the present EU states have not yet been able to overcome it. Each country followed its own foreign policy in the Yugoslav conflict, not to mention non-EU states, the United States and Russia. This had a strong effect on the problems in India and Bosnia-Herzegovina. Right from the beginning the international actors accepted the ethnic concept on which the spokesmen constructed the contrasts. The British assumed that Hindus and Muslims were two irreconcilable 'nations', even 'races'. Similarly, the 'western' state community saw the quarrels in the Balkans as a product of 'age old ethnic hatred'.[322]

Their concepts of solution looked accordingly: All external players treated 'ethnic groups' as an independent variable without further scrutiny. This did not leave any conceptual leeway or negotiating plane for representatives of multi- and trans-'ethnic' policies. It was practical and handy to assign a spokesman to each ethno-nation. In this way, Jinnah became the mouthpiece of 'the Muslims', Karadzic the leader of 'the Bosnian Serbs' and so on. But none of them had sufficient democratic legitimization. This pulled the rug from under the feet of other (also Muslim) parties which wanted to keep India as one country. The colonial British even worked intentionally against multi-'ethnic' forces in Punjab. The plans for the division of Bosnia-Herzegovina along 'ethnic' lines made it difficult for multi- and trans- 'ethnic' parties to make their mark as alternatives. So Rizman states: 'There are few rewards, if any, for those policy makers who really care for ethnic harmony or for that matter for those who are trying to correct historical injustices towards less privileged ethnic groups.'[323]

Another thing which favoured the ethno-nationalists is, as mentioned above, that they are (almost) not dependent on political consensus building. They can fall back on a more easily accessible constituency when they exclusively cater for their target group. An external political environment like the one just described facilitates their task even further.

For this reason Gordana Knezevic, a journalist with the daily Bosnian newspaper *Oslobodenje*, wrote in the context of the impeding war in Bosnia-Herzegovina, with a note of resignation:

> This is not a civil war. This is the war against civilians. Sarajevo is a multi-cultural, muti-ethnical, multi-religious city. It has its own tradition, one might say the cult of respecting the other peoples believes [*sic*] more than their own. That was a real pearl of [the] Balkan. But the trouble with this pearl is that it can't be traded. It does not have any market value. Nobody is to fight for it. It has only human value. The battle for human values might be real in some Steven Spielberg film, but not in nowedays [*sic*] Europe.[324]

8. POLITICAL INSTITUTIONS AND ETHNO-NATIONAL CONFLICTS

Many authors have pondered on how this pearl can regain its market value. They ask: How can ethno-national conflicts (which they mostly call ethnic) can be dampened within societies that are cast into states? How can political cleavages, which go beyond the 'ethnic' ones, gain importance? And how can trans- and multi- 'ethnic' actors gain more political resources (again)?

Their approaches are based on a change in political institutions. As independent variables they are supposed to influence the behaviour of the people, and thus also of the 'ethnic' groups as dependent variables.

This is an assumption which already Hegel shared: 'The political mind, patriotism as a whole [...] and the wanting which has turned into habit is only the result of the institutions which exist in the state [...].'[325]

In Horowitz' blunt words the institutional approach means that 'ties of blood' need not necessarily lead to 'rivers of blood'.[326] Therein lies the vague hope of the OSCE to reconstruct, in the long run, *one* functioning society in the whole state of Bosnia-Herzegovina through democratic institutions.

Three terms have already appeared several times and should now be explained more clearly: *Multi-'ethnic'* means that several 'ethnic groups' are integrated in this concept with equal status. *Supra-'ethnic'* points to a plane of reference which, politically and institutionally, stands above the one on which ethno-national conflicts are fought (this is how the earlier Yugoslavia understood itself or in certain cases supranational organizations). *Trans-'ethnic'* concepts search for solutions beyond ethno-national paradigms. They do not consider 'ethnic groups' as political variables (especially not as independent ones).

8.1. Recipes for a Functioning Society

The interrelation of institutions and 'ethnic' cleavages already occupied the mind of John Stuart Mill. He held the opinion: When democratic institutions and different 'national structures of consciousness' develop at the same time, a democratic state system is condemned to failure. *Before* democracy comes in, the society of an existing state must homogenize and develop a 'harmony of feeling'. This could happen under a despotic government which does not give preferential treatment to any 'nationality', as he calls it.[327] The Indian case supplies illustrative material for Mill's thesis: Did the British prematurely allow parties and introduce elections? Was this the reason why the two proclaimed ethno-nations could develop apart? There are hints for this.[328] Also in relation to Yugoslavia one could claim that democratization set in too early and, above all, too suddenly.[329] But still, this thesis is problematic. For in its last consequence it means that democracy and ethno-nationally heterogeneous states could never co-exist. But as mentioned earlier, 96 per cent of the human beings live in such states, and more and more of them are democracies.[330]

However, Mill's thoughts went into the right direction. The manner in which conflicts are institutionally settled decides to a large extent which meaning falls to ethno-national activists. Gurr makes the following observations: 'Communal identities that are given institutional form and substantial resources tend to persist; identities denied lead to political mobilization; identities ignored usually weaken, but can be activated by new leaders responding to threats to group identity and status.'[331] Old democracies can deal well with 'ethnic' cleavages, he holds. In a *process* of democratization, however, such contrasts often become virulent.[332] Horowitz calls the very instant of state independence 'watershed moments' for ethno-national conflicts.[333] Both observations play a role in the case studies. They are not all too far from Mill's stand. But no author describes the mechanisms which strengthen ethno-national projects in such times of radical upheaval. At this point it makes sense to point again to the thesis of an inherent advantage of mobilization which ethno-national spokesmen have vis-à-vis other political currents.

In India and, more so, in Bosnia-Herzegovina it can be observed how the boundaries of political parties have come closer to the boundaries of the 'ethnic groups'. Once this advanced level of politicization of 'ethnic groups' is reached, it is difficult to hold against it with democratic structures. Horowitz writes: 'Once ethnic politics begins in earnest, each party, recognizing that it cannot count on defections from members of the other ethnic group, has the incentive to solidify the support of its own group.'[334] The spokeman of the Bosnian foreign ministry, Amer Kapetanovic, expresses the problem in simple terms with regard to the Bosnian Muslims who have tended to break out of the 'ethnic' party system: 'But as long as the Bosnian Serbs and Croats vote for their ethnic parties, the Muslims will think: We would be stupid if we did not vote for our ethnic party, too.'[335] And so the vicious circle goes on.

In other words, the politically exclusive friend-foe-scheme of Carl Schmitt applies seamlessly and without exception to ethno-national constellations.[336] The political consituency becomes unmovable and depends on the number of 'right' human beings (provided that they vote in the 'right' way). Because of this and because of the narrow interests which the parties follow, support and coalitions beyond ethno-national party boundaries are theoretically impossible (they still occur at times, as in Bosnia-Herzegovina in 1990, although this is extremely rare).[337] This cripples the state and has an escalating effect.

In his analysis of solidarity within groups, Hechter comes to the conclusion: '[T]he only groups that can attain lasting solidarity are those that produce excludable goods.'[338] The ethno-national parties are essentially dependent on such exclusivity. 'Take away communal ideology [from communal parties], or make them abandon it, and nothing is left of them. The group or the party disintegrates', writes Bipan Chandra.[339] Such parties mobilize their constituencies exclusively through ethno-national contents. In this way they inflame incessantly ethno-national tensions and distributive struggles. Multi- and trans-'ethnic' parties are crushed between the millstones. No one gives them their vote any more.

In such situations it is easily forgotten that ethno-national cleavages are only *one* type of many other social contrasts of interests. Arend Lijphart observed dominant cleavages in 22 democracies from 1945 to 1980 on the basis of the following issues (in the order of their frequency of occurrence and in Lijphart's terminology): socio-economic, religiously based, cultural-ethnic, city versus countryside, regime support, foreign policy, and postmaterialism.[340]

Different institutional arrangements influence to what extent imagined or real 'ethnic' interests can penetrate party politics. Despite different designations they can be divided into three categories of ideal types:

(1) In an '*ethnocracy*' or 'ethnic democracy' the domination of one 'ethnic group' is established constitutionally from the beginning.[341] The concept is based on the idea of an 'ethnic'—in the extreme case an organic—understanding of nation (the fundamental rights for the non-dominant 'ethnic groups' vary accordingly). Such types of constitutions are common in the Balkans, particularly in Croatia and Serbia, and also in Pakistan. Political liberties are granted, but the 'losing' 'ethnic group' or 'nation' has a lesser claim on the state, and shows less loyalty to it as well.

(2) The *federal-corporatistic model* (*consociational model*) starts similarly from the basic assumption that 'ethnic' interests face each other more or less irreconcilably. With this consensus model they are supposed to be counter-balanced as well as possible.[342] The model is based on compromises and on the vertical and horizontal distribution of power. Proportional representation ensures that all sections of the pluralistic society are reflected as precisely as possible in the political party spectrum. This model avoids everything that could promote the political

domination of any group. Majority rule and the two-party system (the 'Westminster model') are, in this view, fatal for already 'split' societies. Rather, autonomy rights and, if necessary, even veto rights for individual groups are provided for. The most famous advocate of this multi-'ethnic' model as a solution to the problems of 'ethnically' pluralistic societies is Lijphart.[343]

(3) The *liberal concept* ignores the classification of human beings into 'ethnic groups'.[344] Individual human rights, not the rights of 'nations', 'nationalities', etc., have priority. The principle of civil society rules, and the nationality is the citizenship. The unifying force is not descent but basic political convictions, values, and institutions. The state structure is preferably unitary, since there is no need to take into consideration any special interests *a priori*. This model clearly follows the civil-democratic nation concept and is trans-'ethnic'. Stanovcic supports this approach for the Balkans: 'Minority problems can be solved only in an atmosphere in which the individual is more highly regarded than the state.'[345] And the state means in the Balkans—not only but mainly—the ethno-nation.

8.2. Discussion and Critique

The debates about the best solution beyond a secessionist option continue among scholars and politicians and are far from resolved. In this vein all conceivable mixed forms and sub-varieties are presented as classifications and/or as political propositions.[346] Some authors do well in taking into consideration the different types of ethno-national conflicts, their causes the 'ethnic' population structure (among others the fact how closely the 'opposing' groups live to each other), and the stages of 'ethnic consciousness' of the conflicting groups.[347] Others reflect on *how* an 'ethnic group' can or should 'survive', for example, culturally or also politically.[348]

But the opinions also differ fundamentally. Smooha and Hanf do not find Lijphart's consensus model convincing and instead suggest the liberal approach. But they contradict themselves when they say at the same time that liberal governments have a better chance of survival if they grant the 'ethnic' minorities 'material and symbolic' gains. If these are concrete concessions, then this concept has clearly adopted certain multi-'ethnic' features.[349] Others like Horowitz say that Lijphart's proposition did not take root in reality in a cogent way.[350] Some years later, however, Lijphart triumphed with reference to South Africa: in its new constitution he saw his model realized in an exemplary way.[351] Again, others concede that Lijphart's consociational model did take root in practice but that it caused more harm than good. Wilkinson argues that after Nehru, since the 1960s, India has become more and more consociational with regard to the Muslims (as it was during the colonial period), while the level of ethnic violence in the country has increased. He comes to a very critical conclusion which is backed by the findings of this work, too:

> Consociational agreements have several weaknesses—most importantly the institutionalization and freezing of ethnic identities that are by nature multidimensional and oppositional—that seem to identify rather than moderate ethnic violence. Consociational power sharing may have a role to play during transitions from authoritarian rule, when dominant ethnic groups want guarantees that will minimize their short-term losses. Those seeking to resolve conflict in new democracies in Africa, Eastern Europe, and the former Soviet Union, however, would do well to look elsewhere for permanent solutions.[352]

Horowitz also dissociates himself from Lijphart and gives a series of practical instructions on how a government could dampen 'ethnic' conflicts instead. These are: (1) The competences of institutions should be scattered in such a way that no single one of them can serve as the reference point of 'ethnic' interests alone. (2) As a diversionary manoeuvre he recommends to keep intra-'ethnic' conflicts boiling. (3) Changes in details like the mode of election can provide incentives to inter-'ethnic' cooperation. (4) The government should try to shift distributive struggles and conflicts of interests to other levels and cleavages than 'ethnic' ones. (5) If (economic, social, etc.) differences between the 'ethnic groups' can be cleared up, the danger of an 'ethnic' conflict is reduced. But how all this is supposed to be realized in practice remains an open question.[353]

Suggestions for conflict solution are accompanied by approaches based on the history of ideas. Sundhaussen feels it would have been more fortunate for the Balkans if people had taken the French nation concept as a basis and *then* grafted the German element of federalism onto it. This is the only way to achieve peace in this region, he holds.[354] The irony is that it was just the 'Western' states which supported the inverted principle with their policies in the Balkans in the 1990s. In the light of this the chances of success for the OSCE observers appear to be rather dim, even if they try their best by mulling over political science books and follow an institutional patchwork approach.

Here a fundamental critique comes in which concedes to institutions a limited influence only. Representatives of this approach focus on 'culture' as an independent variable.[355] According to them, values, convictions, and habits are stubborn—so much that they can long outlive institutional changes. Inglehart writes:

> People live in the past far more than they realize. [...] Few people invent concepts. It's vastly easier to take prefabricated ones from the available stock, based on experiences interpreted earlier by members of one's society. [...] Thus one orients one's life by following old road maps.[356]

The international protectorate in Bosnia-Herzegovina is facing this challenge. The problem is the same as in the discussion on the real power of the unreal. From what time on can situative features ('cultural', historical, political, etc., influences) be viewed as quasi 'primordial', that is, can they be regarded as so stubborn and sluggish to become independent variables? If one follows this approach, the task of an international protectorate in Bosnia-Herzegovina should be to create new 'worlds of experience' whose impressions gradually build on trans-'ethnic' alternatives and become encrusted as new realities.

In this context Flere addresses the problem of political culture. He finds that people in the former Yugoslav republics repose great faith in authority.[357] This comes from a search for orientation after the collapse of the country. According to him, the people are still not able to develop faith in democratic institutions. Such approaches qualify the hammer-blow hypothesis of programmed 'ethnic' hatred. Rizman, on the other hand, concentrates on elites. When they misuse their role—and often enough their charisma—in order to stir up ethno-national conflicts, no theory, no matter how polished it may be, can help to resolve the conflict.[358]

In this sense Brass criticizes Horowitz's thesis that 'ethnic groups' as a matter of principle feel an antipathy against each other, particularly when one suffers from relative backwardness (real or imaginary) vis-à-vis the other. Also, Manor since the Bosnian war considers Horowitz' claim to be refuted that the roots of 'ethnic conflicts' in Asia and Africa went deeper than in Europe, and that hence the consensus model was less useful there.[359] Brass calls such theses 'too general' and 'too psychological'.[360] With reference to the supposed importance of relative backwardness, he cites India as a counter example. There a separatist movement brews in a region (north India) in which the Muslims were just *not* discriminated against. Brass and Manor point to a crucial point. A fundamental critique of multi-'ethnic' approaches is therefore necessary.

8.3. Playing the Witch Against the Devil?

Those who construct multi-'ethnic' arrangements *specifically* for fighting ethno-national conflicts accept the ethnic paradigm *a priori* and subordinate other political issues.[361] They assume from the beginning that they deal with 'ethnic conflicts' (although most of them do not or cannot provide any clear definition, as explained above). Under certain circumstances they thereby legitimize the claims of ethno-nationalist actors.

Lipschutz and Crawford make an exception here: '"Ethnic" and "sectarian" conflicts are not caused by ethnicity or religion. Such conflicts occur when a country's "social contract" comes under pressure from both internal and external forces.'[362] However, most of the institutional approaches described above display a methodical circularity: ethno-national conflicts are supposed to be defused in the same paradigm in which they manifest themselves. Other shortcomings are as follows:

(1) All these approaches must start at an imaginary, temporal point zero at which the institutions are to be constructed. This snapshot fades out at historical causes and long-term developments.

(2) The approaches suffer from their formality. They assume that ethno-national conflicts can be settled by purely institutional arrangements. Social actors and factors which are outside political institutions and party politics are ignored. Among these are education (or better yet *re-education* as in post-war Germany) and the so-called democratic-civil society with its non-governmental organizations. The very macro level on which the political confrontation has occurred is now supposed to be turned 180 degrees in order to produce the opposite effect. But the societal micro-level and cultural factors—the hotbeds and docking stations of ethno-nationalism—are not considered.

(3) There are also shortcomings at the political macro level itself, although they depend a lot on the respective concept. Pure multi-

'ethnic' arrangements have the great disadvantage that they do not grant trans-'ethnic' parties any room from the beginning and deprive them of resources. Ethno-national competitive thinking is perpetuated and re-institutionalized. Exactly this happened in Bosnia-Herzegovina.

(4) In order to leave the level of the conflicts, one may go in two directions: there is not only the way down to the social micro level but also the step upwards to the supra-'ethnic' and supra-national level. Yet this option is still hardly acknowledged. The dampening effect of the European Union on regional and ethno-national conflicts even beyond its present borders is highly underestimated. It is no coincidence that Scottish, Catalan, and north Italian 'regionalists' or 'nationalists' (the boundary between them is often fluid) are often at the same time also enthusiastic supporters of European integration. On the other hand, many heads of state find it easier to upgrade regions if 'nation state' borders are no more a reflection of the Schmittian friend-foe dichotomy. In this way the British Prime Minister Tony Blair followed a two-fold strategy and granted Scotland, Wales, and finally Northern Ireland more autonomy, and at the same time led Great Britain closer to the EU. The old demand to create a Committee of Regions as a second chamber next to the European Parliament has also been raised with this idea in mind.

Another indirect effect of the EU is that the mere prospect of becoming part of the club helps in solving problems that have been in a deadlock at the national level for many years, like the tug-of-war between Turkey and Greece over Cyprus.

Also, politicians in the Balkans expect a lot from a supra-national level of identification and politics. The separation of Montenegro from Serbia seems to many less explosive in the broad context of European integration where national borders lose their relevance in view of economic priorities. Serbia's assasinated reformist Prime Minister Zoran Djinjic attempted to do exactly that. According to his own account, he tried to shift the focus from the nation to the economy, and thus even saw the separatist ambitions of Montenegro in a much more relaxed manner than his ethno-nationalist predecessors.[363] Domestically, however, he had a difficult stand given his liberal views in this society during transition.

Another well-known Serb opposition figure to the Milosevic regime,

Vesna Pesic, pleaded for a shift of priorities as well. A future existed only with reference to the civil-democratic nation concept and an integration into the EU which 'depoliticized' the states and turned them into regions, she told me in Mexico-City where she was posted as the Yugoslav ambassador. There will never be peace with the blood-oriented 'ethnic' concept, she said, and Bosnia will fall apart if its leaders insisted on pursuing it.[364]

Also quite telling are the preferences of the political parties in Macedonia. For example, in October 1998 all parties favoured EU membership—and not only for economic reasons. Whether moderate or ethno-nationalist Macedonians and Albanians, they all saw a possibility of breaking out of the ethno-national vicious circle. 'We hope that the national element will go out of fashion with the abolition of boundaries in Europe', the president of the Liberal-Democratic Party (LDP), Angelka Peeva, told me.[365] Yet this option is still in the distant future, and so is the hope that SAARC would at some point overcome its paralysis and develop supranational structures in South Asia.

Nonetheless the fundamental critique of the institutional approaches presented above needs to be qualified. In historical retrospective political institutions did actually provoke ethno-national conflicts. Good examples are the state structure of Yugoslavia and the separate electorates for Muslims in colonial India. Logically reversed, this means that institutions of the same political level should also be able to revoke these developments. To this extent the approach of the critics is quite understandable and makes sense. It plays a significant role in this study at any rate. But this *alone* does not do justice to the concept of 'ethnicity' just because it differs from that of other social groups. It draws its resources *not only* from the given political sphere. In a reverse conclusion this means that political institutions *alone* cannot counteract ethno-national conflicts, not even when it was these very institutions which provided the arena for the confrontation in the first place.

For these reasons the following comparison takes a number of factors into consideration: components which contribute to the construction of an 'ethnic group' ('ethnicity' as a dependent variable), on the one hand, and results which come up with the advanced politicization of 'ethnic groups' ('ethnicity' as an independent variable), on the other hand.

9. TELEGRAMME

9.1. Definitions

The basic definitions for this study can be boiled down to simple formulae which are built on one another.

Ethnic Group

A group of people whose descent can be considered as 'common' in relation to its societal value. Customs, language, religion, etc., are additional group features. The primordial elements are diffuse and exist in different strengths. They do not have to occur all at once. The borders around the ethnic groups are tendentially fluid. Cross-cutting cleavages and syncretisms are possible. Each ethnic group is unique in its historic setting.

Religion + x = 'ethnic group'

X can be: language, history, symbols, customs, etc. These secondary features are all added, overevaluated, or constructed ex post in order to strengthen the primary feature religion (ethnicentre) against the opposing group which is constructed in the same way. 'Ethnic group' is a situative concept of contrast. It is not individually and historically embedded. The borders of 'ethnic groups' are tendentially sharp and impermeable.

In other cases, the formula can be: language + x = 'ethnic group' or other combinations.

'Ethnic group' + x = ethno-nation (or community in the Indian context)

X are: political, social, and economic ambitions, striving for self-determination, and *possibly* a state whose borders should overlap with the borders of the 'ethnic group'. The x factors include political dynamics and a degree of organization. The ethno-nation is, at the same time, the object to which ethno-nationalists appeal. They are active as a political action group. As spokesmen of the 'ethnic group' they mobilize their resources (which are: religion + x) and achieve *political* results. It is not necessary and even impossible that all members of the 'ethnic group' are mobilized. There is always a discrepancy between those who share the group features and those who act.

The term 'ethnic conflict' therefore should be called correctly ethno-national conflict.

Nation

Ethno-nation *or* civic-democratic nation = German *or* French nation concept = objective *or* subjective assignment of 'ethnic' features.

Ethno-nationalism/communalism

Ideology and political phenomenon on an ethno-national basis.

'Nation state'

The state according to the construction plan of the ethno-national *or* civic-democratic nation concept.

Here, however, this is mostly used in the sense of: Final success and the almost unreachable ideal of a state in the ethno-national paradigm. The correct term would be ethno-national state. The term 'nation state' is still used in this work because it is applied in this way by ethno-national activists. It is, however, more of a political programme than a historical and political reality.

NOTES

1. Lessing (1987), p. 69 [1779].
2. Weber (1921), p. 242.
3. Ganzer (1990), in: *Soc.*, p. 4.
4. The term was coined by Glaxer/Moynihan (1975), The term ethnic has been circulating in German literature only since 1989 [Scheffler, in: Seewann (1995), p. 9]
5. See A. Cohen (1985).
6. Representatives of the primordial approach are, for example: Shils (1957), Geertz (1963, etc.); Isaacs (1975); van den Berghe (1975, etc.); Gellner with his linguistic approach (1964, 1983); Ganzer (1990), in: *Soc*; Robinson (1993) with reference to India; Weithmann (1995) with reference to the Balkans.
7. Heckmann (1992), p. 30.
8. Ganzer (1990), in: *Soc*, p. 14.
9. Heine and Stipek (1984), p. 15. For the universality of the term 'ethnicity' see also: Scheffler, in: Seewann (1955), p. 10.

10. The conversation took place in the editorial office of the newspaper *The Argus* in Cape Town in March 1995.
11. For example: 'Tribalism Revisited', in: *The Economist* (21 December 1991) on the conflict in the Balkans and the 'constant hate' against one's neighbours. See also: Moynihan (1993), pp. 16ff.
12. Koestlin (1995), in: *EE*, p. 19.
13. Weithmann (1997).
14. Burg and Shoup (1999), p. 18.
15. See Chapter III.1.1.2. 'The Myths from the Indus Valley'.
16. Supporters of this approach are, for example: Deutsch (1966, etc.); Barth (1969); Young (1976); Francis (1976); Horowitz (1985); Brass (1974); A. Cohen (1974, 1985); Patterson, in: Glazer and Moynihan (1975); Okamura (1981), in: *ERS*; Banton (1977, 1983, 1995, in: *ABS*) ; Olzak (1992); Reiterer, in: Seewann (1992); Thapar (1992); K.N. Panikkar (1997); Engineer (1987; 1995b, etc.); Phadnis (1990); Köstlin (1995), in: *EE*; Kaschuba (1995), in: *EE*; Habermas, in: Taylor (1993).
17. Kaschuba (1997), in: *EF*, pp. 502, 508.
18. Reiterer, in: Seewann (1992), p. 38. He uses the terms from Berger and Luckmann (1969) and Schütz (1982).
19. Brass (1974), pp. 119-20, above all, protests against the alleged unavoidability of ethnic group-building with reference to India. Manor (1996), in: *IA*, pp. 459-60 supports his position.
20. Kratochwil (1996), p. 24.
21. Obviously, the ethnic group explained in terms of an interest group can also be used as an independent variable when its influences on other factors are explored. Here, as mentioned before, the differences are sketched out only in an ideal-typical manner. See also the situative-primordial approach.
22. A. Cohen (1985), p. 118.
23. Elwert (1989), in: *KZSS*. There is also a similar argument by Kreile (1997), in: *APuZ* and Oommen (1995).
24. Huntington (1968), p. 38. A similar argument can be found in Heine and Stipek (1984), pp. 15-16.
25. This is also the view of Oommen (1995), p. 224. See Chapter IV.1.2.2. 'India Through British Glasses'.
26. Mill often speaks of 'feeling of nationality' (Mill (1991), p. 427 [1861]). He gives the term 'nationality' ethnic-situative connotation.
27. Weber speaks of an 'artificial' creation of an ethnic faith in commonness' (Weber (1921), p. 237). For a discussion on ethnicity and Max Weber, see: Stone (1995), in: *ABS*.
28. S. Ramet (1990), in: *SSJ*, p. 2 (italics added).
29. Brass (1991), p. 70.
30. This approach is followed for example by Brass (1974); A. Cohen (1985); Haller, in: Devetak, Flere and Seewann (1993).
31. This is done for example by Lijphart (1977); Horowitz (1985); Coakley (1992),

in: *IPSR*; Smooha/Hanf, in: A. Smith (1992); Stanovcic (1992), in: *IPSR* with completely different results. For more see Chapter I.8. 'Political Institutions and Ethno-national Conflicts'.

32. Sekelj (1993) has successfully applied this approach to the Yugoslav example. See also: P. Ramet (1984).
33. For example: Lal (1995), in: *ABS*.
34. See for example Banton (1977, 1995); Bates and Weingast (1995); Varshney (1995).
35. For a topical critique of the approaches, see: A. Smith (1966), in: *IA*, pp. 445-7.
36. For this critique, see, among others: A. Smith (1995), p. 40. Chapter I.4. 'What is Nationalism?' deals with this issue in detail. For the fundamental shortcomings of this approach, see: Elster (1989), pp. 30ff. There is also a discussion on the basic postulates of rational choice and its opposing approaches which seek to explain human acts. From the Indian side for views regarding game theory and its alternatives, see: Johari (1982), pp. 148ff.
37. For more on the subject, see Chapter V.1. 'The Cage Breaks Open'.
38. For a discussion on these two approaches, see: L. Cohen (1997), in: *NP*.
39. The main advocate is A. Smith (1992, 1995, 1996, in: *IA*, etc). This approach is also followed by: McKay and Lewis (1982), in: *ERS*; Hackstein and Orywal, in: Schweizer, Schweizer and Kokot (1993); Kreile (1997), in: *APuZ*; Heckmann, in: Seewann (1992).
40. Brass (1991), p. 75 (original italics).
41. Freitag (1989), p. 198.
42. A. Smith (1996), in: *IA*, pp. 445ff and (1996), pp. 29ff.
43. Advocates of this postulate are, for example, the primordialist Geertz (1963, 1971) and the constructivists Hobsbawm and Ranger (1983); Hobsbawm (1990). For the Marxist approach, see: Solomons and Back (1995), in: *ABS*; K.N. Panikkar (1990, 1991, 1997). For a discussion, see: S. Ramet (1990), in: *SSJ*. But Ramet (like many authors) leaves out the possible constructivist element of this approach.
44. Gellner (1994), pp. 34ff points out that Marxists and liberals have been trapped in the same error: they have underestimated the strength of ethno-nationalism.
45. For a discussion on Marxism and ethnicity respectively nation, see: Solomon and Back (1995), in: *ABS*; Gellner (1994), pp. 1ff, 34ff, specially pp. 37-8.
46. More on Tito's concept of nation: Tito (1946) and Tito, in: Alter (1994), pp. 223-4.

    More on Nehru's concept of nation: Nehru (1946b) and in this study in Chapter V.4.2.1. 'The Alternatives to Jinnah'.
47. The most well-known advocate of this thesis is Kohn (1969). The same opinions can be found in variations in: Shoup (1969), in: *PC*; Bertsch (1973), in: *PC*; Young (1976); Elwert (1989), in: *KZSS*; Anderson (1991); Heckmann, in: Seewann (1992); Reiterer, in: Seewann (1992); Habermas, in: Taylor (1993). Some debates are well presented by P. Ramet (1984) who refers to Yugoslavia.

Also, Deutsch (1961), in *APSR*, 1966) with his theory of communication can be included in this approach (see also Chapter I.3.1. 'The Subjective Nation Concept').

48. Gellner (1983). Gellner is firmly *against* the postulate of the 'awakening' of nations. He follows the constructivist approach of a new form of organization. Yet he proceeds from primordial elements (language, literature) as independent variables which are used in the process of nation-building. This is the reason why he sharply criticizes Kant who allegedly followed an 'anaemic' approach, ignoring all traditions. With Kant's concept there would never be a nation-building, says Gellner (Gellner 1983, pp. 130-2). Kedourie disagrees with this stand. He holds that nationalism is a further development of the Kantian principle of self-determination (without Kant having intended it). See: Kedourie (1993).
49. Wehler (1975), pp. 20ff.
50. Phadnis (1990), p. 241.
51. Thapar (1992), p. 117.
52. Hobsbawm and Ranger (1983). The same idea was also articulated by Gellner (1964), p. 58.
53. Anderson (1991).
54. In very rare cases there can also be several primary features where religion and language overlap to a great extent, in case of the Sinhalese and Tamils in Sri Lanka. Both factors are used as primary means of contrast. But this does not play any role in the further definition of 'ethnic group'. Its structure remains the same.
55. Horowitz (1985), pp. 41-2 probably comes closest to this concept. He points out that a specific feature is taken out to demarcate one ethnic group (which he uses without quotation marks) from the other. When several ethnic groups are involved, different features for different interactions between the groups are picked out. Therefore, the features equally belong to the interaction as to the group itself. However, Horowitz (a) does not have any epicentric concept of 'ethnicity', and (b) he defines his term of ethnicity as absolutely situative and does not contrast it with connotations such as 'tribe' or ethnic group (without quotation marks in our sense here).
56. For more on the role of the churches with reference to Balkan nationalism, see: L. Cohen (1997), in: *NP*; Okey, in: Kerr (1992); Ocvirk, in: Devetak, Flere and Seewann (1993); Golitzin, in: Thomas and Friman (1996) (typical view of an Orthodox priest); Schissel, in: Thomas Friman (1996).
57. Heine and Stipek (1984), p. 133 point out that such an over-contrasting of religious differences can also happen within the same religion. Then different dogmatic interpretations are highlighted, as in Nigeria. This phenomenon can be observed when further cleavages exist that lie beyond religion (in Nigeria, for example, the oppressors against the oppressed).
58. See Chapter IV.3. 'The "Ethnicization" of Language'.

59. See Chapter IV.1.2.3. 'From the Village God to *Hindutva*' and Chapter IV. 2.2.2. 'The "Cow Trade" and the Caliphate'.
60. The term was coined by the Austrian social democrat Otto Bauer (1908).
61. Enloe, in: Sugar (1980), p. 359. See also: S. Ramet (1990), in: *SSJ*, p. 8.
62. Gosztoni (1993), in: *OE*, 7/1993, pp. 630ff presents a similar thesis. He further points out the great self-dynamics of such mobilizations whose escalation is difficult to control even by those who started them.
63. Quoted in Beyme (1994), p. 127.
64. Manor (1996), in: *IA*, pp. 460-1.
65. Manor (1996), in: *IA*, p. 465.
66. Sundhaussen (1993), p. 12.
67. Reiter (1984), p. 206.
68. Reiter (1984), p. 178.
69. Tens of thousands of Serbs fled from the Ottoman troops from north Albania to southern Hungary. They were led by the Patriarch Arsenije III. Crnojevic (1693-1706). More in: Hoesch (1995), p. 107.
70. Reiter (1984), p. 184.
71. Gellner (1983), p. 43.
72. Gellner (1983), p. 7.
73. Reiter (1984), p. 192.
74. In the ninth century both monks standardized a language in the monastery of Ohrid (in present-day Macedonia) which Bulgarians claim to be Bulgarian and Macedonians to be Macedonian. For the instrumentalization of the monks and for the quarrel of Macedonia with its neighbours, see among others Wieland (1997), in: *SOE*.
75. Reiter (1984), p. 193.
76. Reiter (1984), p. 194.
77. Reiter (1984), p. 203.
78. Huntington (1996) and (1993), in: *FA*. He is supported by Tibi, in: Volle and Wagner (1994). For a critique in this sense see: Wieland, in: Jonach (1998).
79. See the arguments of Dzaja in Chapter IV.4.1.1. 'The Cultural Entrepreneurs in Bosnia-Herzegovina'.
80. Details on Reiter's line of argument in Chapter IV.3. 'The "Ethnicization" of Language'.
81. Geiss, in: Schlegel (1994), p. 12.
82. Geiss, in: Schlegel (1994), p. 13.
83. A summary of the historians' positions and the development of the term nation can be found in A. Smith, in: A. Smith (1992), pp. 58ff.
84. See: Schulze (1999), pp. 117ff and Münkler, Grünberger and Mayer (1998). Hardtwig (1994) even endows the 'nation' of the fifteenth and the sixteenth with modern elements such as national myths, an estate-encompassing culture, etc. Also, Armstrong (1983) places 'nation' in premodern times.
85. For example, in Emerson (1960) with reference to the emancipation of the colonies.

86. A. Smith (1996), in: *IA*, p. 447 (italics added).
87. Gupta (1997), p. 6.
88. Reiter (1984), p. 346.
89. Deutsch (1966), p. 18.
90. A. Smith (1996), in: *IA*, p. 447.
91. Conner, in: A. Smith (1992), p. 48.
92. Alter (1985), p. 17.
93. Schödl also protests against the uncritical acceptance of the determinism of modernization, in: Winkler and Kaelble (1993).
94. See Chapter I.7.1. 'The Confusion of State and Nation'.
95. Moynihan (1993), p. 5.
96. S. Ramet (1990), in: *SSJ*, pp. 2-3.
97. Gellner (1983), p. 77.
98. Hobsbawm also points to this gap between the action group and the category of identity of the large group. In 1789 the French language was the essential component of the French nation. But only half of the French spoke French, and only 12 to 13 per cent spoke it correctly [Hobsbawm (1990), p. 60]. In this way, Gellner's approach has its limitations even in the industrialized nations.
99. Oommen (1995), p. 216.
100. Hall, in: Hall (1998), p. 15.
101. Anderson (1991), p. 15.
102. Anderson (1991), p. 22.
103. Anderson (1991), p. 163.
104. Emerson (1960), p. 95.
105. Emerson (1960), p. 92.
106. Weber (1921), p. 528 (original italics).
107. Seton-Watson (1977), p. 5.
108. Gellner (1983), p. 7 (original italics).
109. See Chapter IV.6.1.2. 'Nation Via Decree'.
110. Alter (1985), p. 16.
111. Tagore (1921), quoted in: Alter (1994), p. 53 (own translation).
112. Sundhaussen, in: Elvert (1997), p. 79.
113. Renan (1882), quoted in Alter (1985), p. 19 (own translation).
114. Quoted in Alter (1994), p. 46 (own translation).
115. Emmanuel Joseph Sieyès (1748-1836). Quoted in Alter (1994), p. 37 (own translation).
116. 'A *republican constitution* is founded upon three principles: firstly, the principle of *freedom* for all members of a society (as men); secondly, the principle of the *dependence* of everyone upon a single common legislation (as subjects); and thirdly the principle of legal *equality* for everyone (as citizens). It is the only constitution which can be derived from the idea of an original contract, upon which all rightful legislation of a people must be founded' [Kant: *Perpetual Peace*, in: Reiss (1991), pp. 99-100, original italics; orig. 1795]; see

also Kant: *Idea For a Universal History With a Cosmopolitan Purpose* (1784). Kedourie (1993), pp. 47-50 contrasts the Kantian republican concept with the organic concept of Fichte and Herder.

117. Kant (1990), p. 206 (*Metaphysic of Morals* (*Metaphysik der Sitten*) orig. 1797) (own translation). See also: Kant: *Metaphysic of Morals*, in: Reiss (1991), p. 164.
118. Kant: *Metaphysic of Morals*, in: Reiss (1991), p. 138; orig. 1797.
119. See Chapter I.7 'The Confusion of State and Nation'.
120. Nehru (1946a), p. 392.
121. There is a nice little anecdote about Nehru addressing a gathering of farmers: 'They raised the slogan *Bharat Mata ki jai* ('Victory for Mother India'). Jawaharlal requested silence. They became quiet. Then he asked them: 'Who is Mother India? What does it mean to you?' First they were rendered speechless. [...] Nehru insisted on an answer, and so some of the large crowd of farmers touched the earth on which they were sitting and murmured: 'Here she is. This is Mother India!' Nehru listened to their answers for a while. Then he interrupted them and said: 'No, you are mistaken. It's not the earth that is Mother India. It is *you*, all of you together, *you* are India.' They applauded him for a long while' [T. Ali (1985), p. 70, own translation].
122. Deutsch (1972a). Quoted in Deutsch, in: Alter (1994), p. 63 (own translation).
123. Hans Koschnik in an interview, 'The Balkans need time for peace' (Der Balkan braucht Zeit für Frieden), in: *Das Beste* (February 1998) (own translation). See also: Weithmann, in: Weithmann (1994), p. 8.
124. A similar criticism is expressed by Behschnitt (1980), p. 19.
125. Deutsch (1966), p. 38.
126. Weber (1921), p. 238.
127. Habermas, in: Balakrishnan (1996), p. 290.
128. Habermas, in: Balakrishnan (1996), p. 293.
129. Deutsch (1972a), quoted in Deutsch, in: Alter (1994), p. 63 (own translation).
130. More in Chapter I.3.2.3. 'The Real Power of the Unreal'.
131. With the reservations expressed by Reiter.
132. The difference between state nation (*Staatsnation*) and cultural nation (*Kulturnation*) was first drawn by Friedrich Meinecke (1917). (See also: Meinecke, in: Alter (1994), pp. 49ff). It has come to stay in academic discourse but it remains controversial. Thus Sundhaussen criticizes it in: Elvert (1997) saying the term is misleading. Culture and politics could not be separated. Reiter's reservations and my own doubts regarding this term have already been mentioned. But it is this very confusion, the fuzzy and the inexact, the mixing with situative and political elements which makes up a cultural nation. Against this background the shortcomings of the term rather support its use in the context of the nation.
133. Weber (1921), p. 242 (own translation).
134. Weber (1921), p. 528 (own translation).
135. Sulzbach (1969), p. 12 (own translation).

136. Quoted in Seewann, in: Seewann (1995), p. 7 (own translation).
137. Renan, in: Alter (1994), pp. 45-6 (own translation).
138. For this contradiction see a.o.: Preuß, in: Preuß (1994); Pasquino, in: Furet (1989), pp. 314ff.
139. Mill (1991), p. 427.
140. See: Emerson (1960), p. 91; Sundhaussen, in: Elvert (1997), p. 84.
141. See: Hobsbawon and Ranger (1983).
142. Jawaharlal Nehru before the Indian Constituent Assembly, New Delhi (14 August 1947). Quoted in Collins and Lapierre (1976), p. [before the foreword] and p. 251.
143. Sundhaussen, in: Elvert (1997), p. 84 (own translation).
144. Reiter (1984), p. 433.
145. Tönnies (1972), pp. 3, 40 [1887] (orig. italics; own translation).
146. Already Kohn (1955, 1967) made the distinction between a western, voluntaristic principle and an eastern, organic principle. See also: Rösel (1995), in: *PG*, pp. 118ff.
147. For Herder's theories, see: Herder (1965). With special reference to nation-building among the Slavs: Birke, in: Hubatsch (1950); Sundhaussen (1973); Ziegengeist and Graßhof (1978).
148. Herder (1965), quoted in Herder, in: Alter (1994), p. 189.
149. See, among others, Chapter IV.1.2.3. 'From the Village God to *Hindutva*', and Chapter IV. 3. 'The "Ethnicization" of Language'.
150. Appadorai (1992), p. 224 on Aurobindo's concepts, pp. 219ff, and Mehta (1996), pp. 187ff, Karan Singh (1963).
151. Sankhdher, in: Grover and Arora, Vol. I (1997b), p. 62. Gandhi's concept presents an exception that is difficult to classify. He dialectically connects the primordial features of both Muslim and Hindu, and places them on the higher level of an organic Indian nation. More on Gandhi's philosophy in: Mehta (1996), pp. 217ff; Rothermund (1997), pp. 495ff; Parekh (1989b). Nehru's drift towards an organic nation concept belongs here, too.
152. Nehru (1946b), quoted in Alter (1994), p. 271.
153. On language nationalism see also: Fishman (1972); Reiter, in Grothusen (1974); Giles and Bernard (1979).
154. Sulzbach (1969), p. 56; Sundhaussen, in: Elvert (1997).
155. Turczynski (1976). He warns not to overrate Herder's language nationalism at the expense of the religious factor. See also: Okey, in: Kerr (1992), p. 56.
156. Mayall and Simpson hold that colonies are often not able to fall back on the resources of a 'common' national history for political mobilization. This is why only the consequently objective features remain which deepen 'ethnic' cleavages [Mayall and Simpson, in: A. Smith (1992), p. 10].
157. Deutsch, in: Torsvik (1981), p. 52.
158. For more see Chapter I.8. 'Political Institutions and Ethno-national Conflicts', particularly 8.2. 'Discussion and Criticism' also Chapter 'Résumé'.

159. Anderson (1991), p. 141.
160. A. Smith, in: A. Smith (1992), pp. 73-4. See also: A. Smith (1995), pp. 40ff.
161. A. Smith (1995), p. 153.
162. Alter (1994), p. 18.
163. On the theory of social movements and their classification, see: Tarrow (1994).
164. Emerson (1960), p. 213.
165. On the principle of solidarity see, above all, Emile Durkheim's landmark writings. Here Durkheim (1951), p. 159.
166. Hechter (1987), p. 39.
167. Anderson (1991), p. 144.
168. Anderson (1991), p. 141.
169. Horowitz (1985), pp. 131-4.
170. A. Smith (1995), p. 40.
171. Deutsch, in: Winkler (1985), p. 51 (italics added; own translation).
172. Rogowski, in: Tiryakian and Rogowski (1985), p. 87.
173. Tarrow (1994), p. 5.
174. Hechter (1987), pp. 18, 168.
175. Tarrow (1994), p. 5.
176. See Chapter V.3.3. 'Tactics of Terror'.
177. Schödl, in: Winkler and Kaelble (1993), p. 131.
178. Schödl, in: Hösch and Seewann (1991), p. 87 (orig. italics; own translation). See also: Schödl, in: Winkler and Kaelble (1993).
179. See, for example, Schödl, in: Winkler and Kaelble (1993), p. 133; Smith (1995), p. 148.
180. Schödl, in: Winkler and Kaelble, p. 133.
181. Hroch, in: Kocka (1988), pp. 339ff; Hroch, in: Schieder (1971); Hroch (1985); Hroch (1968).
182. Hobsbawm (1990), p. 12.
183. Schödl, in: Hösch and Seewann, p. 89, Schödl (1990), pp. 6-7; Schödl, in: Winkler and Kaelble (1993), pp. 129, 134.
184. Schödl, in: Winkler and Kaelble (1993), pp. 146, 151, 155.
185. Berend and Ránki (1982), p. 9. They further differentiate between three different types of development for eastern Europe: the Austrian-Bohemian, the Russian-Polish-Hungarian, and the Balkan.
186. Horowitz (1985).
187. Beyme (1994), pp. 126-7.
188. Gellner (1983).
189. The classification and the following elaborations are based mainly on Alter (1985), pp. 33ff. However, 'Risorgimento nationalism' and 'reform nationalism', which basically have a similar character, were clubbed together here.
190. Huntington (1968), pp. 265ff. He explains it in the case of Pakistan.
191. For categorizing Nehru, see also: Hutchinson, in: A. Smith (1992), p. 103.
192. The term was coined by Helmuth Plessner with reference to Germany. See: Alter (1985), p. 46.

193. This is a phrase already used by the Cetnik leader Draza Mihailovic in the Second World War [see: Malcolm (1966), p. 179].
194. Holbrooke (1998), p. 239 (italics added).
195. Appadorai (1992), p. 239.
196. South Asian Association for Regional Cooperation. It was established in 1985 with the aim of fostering economic cooperation among the member states. Because of the nationalist attitudes of the countries involved it has remained a paper tiger until today. It is, above all, the Indo-Pakistani dualism which cripples the SAARC.
197. Dutt (1997), pp. 183-4.
198. See Chapter VI.2. 'Pakistan: In search of the nation'.
199. 'Madam, I Was Hurt Very Much', interview with Nawaz Sharif, *Time* (8 June 1998).
200. Hutchinson (1978), in: *ERS*, pp. 122ff; Hutchinson, in: A. Smith (1992), pp. 101ff.
201. Heine and Stipek (1984), p. 15.
202. Dumont (1970b) says, somewhat perplexed: 'Communalism . . . gets the edge of meaning through the parallelism with the other term: it is something like nationalism' [quoted in Pandey (1990), p. 1].
203. Thapar (1992), p. 61.
204. B. Chandra (1987), pp. 1ff.
205. Engineer, in: Grover and Arora, Vol. 1 (1997a), p. 6.
206. Dixit (1974), p. 1.
207. K.N. Panikkar (1997), p. 67.
208. Karpat (1997), in: *IS*, p. 332. The *Islamic Studies* is published by the Central Institute of Islamic Research in Karachi.
209. Weiss, in: Weiss (1986), p. 5. See also: Wilder, in: A.M. Syed (1995), p. 32.
210. Brass (1991), p. 73.
211. Alavi, in: Weiss (1986), p. 21.
212. Burke, in: Burke and Lapidus (1988), p. 8. See also: Lapidus (1988), pp. 738, 744, 888; Weiss, in: Weiss (1986), p. 5.
213. Gellner (1983), p. 72 (italics added).
214. Linz, in: Tiryakian and Rogowski (1985), p. 205 (italics added).
215. Silber and Little (1995), p. 341.
216. See, above all, Chapter V.4.1.1. 'Izetbegovic'.
217. B. Chandra, in: Grover and Arora, Vol. II (1997a), pp. 332-3.
218. For a classification of the different streams of Islamists as well as their distinction from Islamic modernists, see: Ruthven (2000), pp. 290ff. For a good overview, see also: Steinbach (1993).
219. For more details, see Chapter I.6. 'Nation and Islam: a Contradictory Alliance'.
220. In a talk with the author in Berlin on 11 July 2002, Al-Azm underlined his view by comparing Muslim fundamentalists with other extremist terrorist movements (like the leftist '*Rote Armee Fraktion*' in Germany or the group of

Islamic radicals who took siege of the Great Mosque in Mecca in 1979 as a protest against the 'un-Islamic' Saudi rulers) which died out shortly after their main attacks because they lacked both a following among the people and clear-cut political aims. However, I think that the thesis of a lack of popular following is debatable and is not comparable to Western terrorist movements like the RAF. Also, Bodanski (2001), p. 2 sees the failure of Western terrorists in their social isolation in contrast to the Islamists, who side with the impoverished and politically frustrated masses. For the lack of a coherent political vision of the Islamists, see also: Ruthven (2000), p. 370.

221. See Chapter VI.2.2. 'Pakistan: In Search of Nation'.
222. The homeland concept and its consequences in present-day Europe have been very well described by Brubaker (1996). See also: Connor, in: Sheffer (1986).
223. Malcolm (1996), p. 148.
224. Turczynski (1976); Dzaja (1994), p. 46.
225. For the problem of Macedonia as a homeland in relation to the current Macedonian understanding of the nation, see: Wieland (1997), in: *SOE*.
226. Akadül and Vaner (1994), in: *ER*. For the role of Turkey as a regional player, see also: Axt (1992), in: *SOE*.
227. Kant: *Perpetual Peace*, in: Reiss (1991), p. 106; orig. 1795 (italics added).
228. For a combination of both concepts see: Sundhaussen, in: Elvert (1997); Sundhaussen (1993), p. 27. Also: Stingl, in: Gumpel and Schönfeld (1986), pp. 83ff; Geiss, in: Schlegel (1994), p. 26.
229. Sundhaussen, in: Elvert (1997), p. 85.
230. Kaplan (1993), pp. 88, 302.
231. Djinjic (2002), in: *SOEM*, p. 29 (own translation).
232. See Chapter VI.2.1. 'Bosnia-Herzegovina: in Search of the State'.
233. For this argument see: Smith (1992), p. 7.
234. For a view on the strongly territorialized ethno-nationalism of the Zionists see: Zimmermann (1996); Treffer (1995). For an excellent and systematic view of the Zionist appropriation of land see Diner (1980) and Diner, in: Benz and Graml (1998).
235. Rizman, in Devetak, Flere and Seewann (1993), p. 304. However, Sharma, in: *JEWS* (1996) qualifies the common image of homogeneous Japan and counts about 5 million people as 'ethnic minorities' out of a population of 125 million (1990).
236. Connor (1985), p. vii. See also: Moynihan (1993), p. 72.
237. Rizman, in Devetak, Flere and Seewann (1993), p. 304.
238. Alter (1985), p. 123 (own translation, italics added).
239. In the sense used here: ethno-national state principle.
240. Alter (1985), p. 113.
241. Muhammad Ali in a speech during the London Round Table Conference

in 1930. Quoted in Freitag, in: Burke and Lapidus (1988), p. 115. For Muhammad Ali's search of identity see also: Hasan, in: Hasan (1998), pp. 57ff.

242. As background, see: T. Nagel (1981).
243. Khoury, Hagemann and Heine (1991), pp. 614, 685.
244. This remarkable and deviating minority approach has been taken by: Jung (2002), in: *ApuZ*, pp. 31ff.
245. Iqbal, in: Italiaander (1987), p. 121. Javid Iqbal (*1924) was a delegate for Pakistan in the UN General Assembly in the early 1960s and works as a lawyer in the Supreme Court in Islamabad.
246. Apart from historical reasons Ocvirk also mentions dogmatic-structural ones. According to him, the Orthodox church is most suitable for nationalism. It is strongly bound to the folk group or 'ethnic group', and with it to the ethno-nation. Also, the Catholic church relates to ethnic features but rather pre-national ones. Its missionaries often brought literacy with them. The Protestant church, on the other hand, is more interested in the individual. Islam has exercised, from the very beginning, a supra-'ethnic' and universal claim through the *umma* [Ocvirk, in: Devetak, Flere and Seewann (1993), pp. 223-4]. He could have added that Hinduism is the least suited for nation-building, and yet it is successfully used for this purpose.
247. Bani-Sadr (undated), p. 24. See also: Heine and Stipek (1984), p. 19.
248. Followers of traditional religions who happened to fall under Islamic rule had only the choice of conversion, slavery, or death [see: Heine and Stipek (1984), p. 19].
249. Schulze (1994), p. 150.
250. One example is the Muslim Congress president, Abul Kalam Azad. See Chapter IV.6.2. 'Delhi or Mecca?'.
251. See Chapter V.4.1.1. 'Izetbegovic'.
252. See Chapter V.4.1.2. 'Jinnah'.
253. E. Ahmed, in: M.A. Khan (1985), p. 19. He traces the separation of religion and state rule back to the year 945. At that time the Buwayhid prince Muiz al-Dawla Ahmad marched into the capital of Baghdad. Thus he ended the rule of the caliphe Abbasid who combined the secular and sacred power of the Islamic 'nation' (E. Ahmed).
254. E. Ahmed, in: M.A. Khan (1985), pp. 18-19. For the history of Islam in general, and the history of the caliphes in particular, see the standard work by Halm (1988). For a short overview, see Antes (1991b).
255. Nanda (1989), p. 104.
256. Weiss, in: Weiss (1986), p. 2. The theological texts can be read in English in: Khaldun (1958).
257. See also: Tibi (1987).
258. In (1) and (2) the classification is based on Schimmel, in: Italiaander (1987), pp. 48-9 (3) and (4) are different from Schimmel in both content and concept.

259. Quoted in Schimmel, in: Italiaander (1987), p. 48.
260. The translation 'nation' is inappropriate here. A word with a pre-national connotation like 'peoples' would be correct because in the original Arabic text the word *sh'ab* (people) is used.
261. Quoted in Koran (1994), p. 803. See also: Heine and Stipek (1984), p. 18.
262. Quoted in Wilder, in: M.A. Syed (1995), p. 34.
263. Schimmel, in: Italiaander (1987), p. 49. See also: Heine and Stipek (1984), p. 19. Ethnic prejudices against black Muslims, Berbers, and Turks have existed since the Middle Ages.
264. For the nationalist ideology of Sati Husri, see: Tibi (1971), pp. 103ff.
265. Rashid, in: M.A. Khan (1985), p. 72.
266. Rashid, in: M.A. Khan (1985), p. 78.
267. Tibi (1987), p. xxi.
268. Ruthven (2000), p. 355, see also p. 142.
269. Gellner (1983), p. 76.
270. See Chapter VI.2.2. 'Pakistan: In Search of the Nation'.
271. Tibi (1991).
272. See Chapter VI.2.1. 'Bosnia-Herzegovina: In Search of the Nation'.
273. Bodansky (2001), p. 34.
274. See Chapter III.2.2.2. 'The "Cow Deal" and the Caliphate'.
275. Izetbegovic (1970), p. 49. See Chapter V.4.1.1. 'Izetbegovic'.
276. Sekhan, in: Grover and Arora, Vol. II (1997), p. 235.
277. Caesar, in: Banac, Ackermann and Szporluk (1981), p. 438.
278. Schulze (1990), p. 446. For further background on Islam in the world of 'nation states', see: Rosenthal (1965); Piscatori (1986).
279. Tibi, in: Schlegel (1994), p. 154.
280. Caesar, in: Banac, Ackermann and Szporluk (1981), p. 445.
281. Tibi, in: Volle and Wagner (1994), p. 106. Thus he supports Huntington's thesis of a 'clash of cultures'.
282. Lewis (1988), p. 32. See also: Antes (1991a), p. 39.
283. See Chapter III.3. 'The Ottoman *Millet* as a National Forge?'.
284. Schimmel, in: Italiaander (1987), p. 49.
285. See Chapter I.8.1. 'Recipes for a Functioning Society'.
286. See also: Mayall and Simpson, in: A. Smith (1992), p. 8.
287. For Wilson's ideas see the collection of sources by Padover (1942).
288. Naturally, Tito's Yugoslavia was an effective reference point, too. But since we talk about the phenomenon of state building here, this factor as a preliminary stage is being ignored for the moment.
289. 'Die neuen Nationalismen', Eric J. Hobsbawm, in: *Die Zeit* (6 May 1999; own translation).
290. Horowitz (1985), p. 272.
291. Charter I (1993), p. 6 (italics added).
292. Universal Declaration . . . (1983), p. 6 (italics added).

293. Universal Declaration . . . (1993), p. 7 (italics added).
294. See also: Moynihan (1993), pp. 4-5, 71.
295. Dann (1996), p. 29.
296. Padover (1942), p. 105.
297. Padover (1942), p. 100.
298. Emerson (1960), p. 302. For more on the uneasy relationship between the right of self-determination and colonial politics see also: Paech (1998), in: *APuZ*.
299. Quoted in Reiterer, in: Seewann (1992), p. 37 [Lepsius (1990)].
300. Devetak, in: Devetak, Flere and Seewann (1993), p. 26. See also: Alter (1985), p. 96; Emerson (1960), p. 303; Fraenkel (1994), p. 107.
301. Heintze (1994), p. 21; Tomuschat (1989), p. 996; Kimminich (1997), p. 117.
302. See: Heintze (1994), pp. 41ff, 187-8; Kimminich (1997), p. 114; Paech (1998), in: *APuZ*, pp. 19, 22.
303. Lazare Carnot (1753-1823) was also a member of the French National Assembly during the Revolution (quoted according to: Emerson (1960), p. 299).
304. For the rare 'liberal-realistic consensus' see: Mayall and Simpson, in: A. Smith (1992), pp. 6-8.
305. Mayall (1991). See also: Thomas, in: Thomas and Friman (1996), p. 204.
306. Moynihan (1993), p. 72.
307. Thomas, in: Thomas and Friman (1996). He cites numerous examples from all over the world to show how much state recognition is influenced by situative, political arbitrariness, when one speaks of secession and when not, etc. He deals intensively with the Balkans and India/Pakistan/Bangladesh.
308. See: Ivanov (1994), in: *SOE*; Sterbling (1996), in: *SOE*.
309. This argument is to be understood formally only. In Chapter V.2.2. 'Elections in India in 1946' it becomes clear that the election was not a referendum on an independent Pakistan.
310. Here nation and state are equated, too. But the terminology keeps both options open (civic-democratic or ethno-national).
311. See: Mickey and Albion, in: Devetak, Flere and Seewann (1993), p. 63.
312. Sulzbach (1969), p. 12.
313. 'An Explosion of Indian Self-Esteem', Russell Watson, and, 'We are a Nuclear Power', Interview with the Indian prime minister Vajpayee, in: *Newsweek* (25 May 1998), and: 'Out of Pandora's Box', Michael Elliott, in: *Newsweek* (8 June 1998).
314. See also: Remington, in: Thomas and Friman (1996), p. 234.
315. Mayall and Simpson, in: A. Smith (1992), pp. 7-8.
316. See Chapter V.5.1. 'The Ethno-national Card: Upgraded by the West'.
317. For the concepts see Chapter I.8. 'Political Institutions and Ethno-national Conflicts'.

318. Henkin, in: Macdonald (1993). For the deconstruction of the notion of sovereignty from the point of view of international law see, for example, Laski's theses in: Hebeisen (1995); Camilleri, in: Walker and Mendlovitz (1990). Kimminich (1997), pp. 90ff describes the change from state sovereignty to state permeability, which is the porosity of the state at multiple levels in the age of globalization. Sieyès had already criticized the over-emphasis of sovereignty, which can be found in the very clear and systematic work of Dock (1972) [1900].
319. For the inner right of self-determination see among others: Heintze (1994), pp. 84ff, 153ff.
320. Since 1995 the OSCE (Organization for Security and Cooperation in Europe) monitors the compliance with the Dayton Agreement in Bosnia-Herzegovina.
321. Steinberg, in: Damrosch (1993), p. 57.
322. See Chapter V.5. 'The Poker of the External Powers'.
323. Rizman, in: Devetak, Flere and Seewann (1993), p. 305.
324. 'Why Bosnia Should be Saved', Gordana Knezevic, in: *Why* (April 1992), p. 6.
325. Hegel (1970), pp. 401 § 268 (orig. 1821). Georg Wilhelm Friedrich Hegel (1770-1831) (own translation).
326. 'Even in the most severely divided society, ties of blood do not lead ineluctably to rivers of blood' [Horowitz (1985), p. 684].
327. Mill (1991), p. 434 (original 1861).
328. See Chapter IV.5. 'The Majority Trap in India' and Chapter V.2.2. 'Elections in India in 1946'.
329. See Chapter V.2.1. 'Elections in Bosnia-Herzegovina in 1990'.
330. For this contradiction see: Mayall and Simpson, in: A. Smith (1992), p. 6; Rizman, in: Devetak, Flere and Seewann (1993), p. 304.
331. Gurr (1993), in: *IPSR*, pp. 162-3.
332. Lake follows the same approach (1995), in: *PB*, p. 3.
333. Horowitz (1985), p. 580.
334. Horowitz (1985), p. 318.
335. In an interview with the author in Sarajevo (24 June 2000).
336. Schmitt (1932).
337. For a theory of the ethno-national party scheme see among others: Horowitz (1985), pp. 298ff.
338. Hechter (1887), p. 39.
339. B. Chandra (1993), p. 155.
340. Lijphart (1984), p. 128. For the development and shifting of social cleavages see the landmark book of Inglehart (1990).
341. For these concepts see: Smooha and Hanf, in: A. Smith (1992), pp. 31-2; Heckmann (1992), pp. 211-14; Stanovcic (1992), in: *IPSR*, pp. 364-8.
342. For these concepts see: Smooha and Hanf, in: A. Smith (1992), pp. 32-3; Horowitz (1985), pp. 569ff; Heckmann (1992), pp. 217-19; Stanovcic (1992),

in: *IPSR*, pp. 368-9. For different models of democracy see: Lijphart (1984); Held (1987), among others pp. 186-214.

343. Lijphart (1984). For his consensus model see among others: pp. 23-30.
344. For these concepts see: Smooha/Hanf, in: A. Smith (1992), pp. 33-4; Heckmann (1992), pp. 214-17; Stanovcic (1992), in: *IPSR*, pp. 363-4.
345. Stanovcic (1992), in: *IPSR*, pp. 363-5.
346. For example, Coakley considers the consociational model as a centralized state in contrast to a federal one [Coakley (1992), in: *IPSR*, pp. 347ff].
347. Stanovcic (1992), in: *IPSR*, among others p. 360 does this with reference to Yugoslavia. Also Deutsch (1984), in: *IPSR*, pp. 125ff refers to this point. He comes to the conclusion that a spatial division of 'ethnic groups' is sometimes the best solution.
348. According to this, Coakley (1992), in: *IPSR*, pp. 343-5 classifies his scheme.
349. 'Liberal democracy in plural societies stands a better chance if it delivers material and symbolic gains to the minorities.' [Smooha and Hanf, in: A. Smith (1992), pp. 45-6].
350. Horowitz (1985), p. 576.
351. Lijphart, in: Reynolds (1994), pp. 222ff.
352. Wilkinson (2000), in: *AS*, p. 791.
353. Horowitz (1985), pp. 598-9.
354. Sundhaussen, in: Elvert (1997), p. 90.
355. Almond and Verba (1963, 1982); Inglehart (1990).
356. Inglehart (1990), p. 422.
357. Flere, in: Devetak, Flere and Seewannn (1993), pp. 259ff.
358. Rizman, in: Devetak, Flere and Seewannn (1993), p. 305.
359. Manor (1996), in: *IA*, p. 474.
360. Brass (1996a), p. 35.
361. With a similar approach Eriksen criticizes pluralistic theories of society in general [Eriksen (1993), in: *AP*, pp. 156-7; Bhambhri also refers to him: Bhambhri (1996), in: *SS*, p. 55]. See also Brass (1985b).
362. Lipschutz/Crawford (1995), in: *PB*, p. 1.
363. Djinjic (2002), in: *SOEM*.
364. In an interview with the author in Mexico City (5 April 2001).
365. In an interview with the author in Skopje (18 November 1997). See also: Wieland (1997), in: *SOE*, p. 710.

II. Hijacking History

The Nuclear Bombs, the Field of the Black Birds, and the Historical Cabinet of Mirrors

I believe that a nation is happy that has no history.[1]

M.K. Gandhi

Any nuclear clash between India and Pakistan
(may God forbid it) would, in part, be due to history.[2]

Rajmohan Gandhi

The less I know about the history of
the Balkans, the better I feel.[3]

Milan Panic

The view of history of the Serbs was their problem,
ours was to end the war.[4]

Richard Holbrooke

On the 28 May 1998, the ground underneath Baluchistan trembled. The shock waves of the nuclear explosion startled the entire world. Shortly afterwards, Nawaz Sharif, the prime minister of Pakistan, was sitting in front of the cameras—with a serious but proud expression on his face. His right fist clenched. Now and then he would lower it on to the desk in a composed manner. On his left stood the white-and-green flag of Pakistan, on his right, behind him, was Mohammed Ali Jinnah, in a picture frame. The founding father of Pakistan had to take the rap as the country detonated the first nuclear explosives in its history.

The newspaper *The Nation* reported proudly: the nuclear medium-range missiles—model 'Ghauri'—were ready for operation.[5] Ghauri, a Muslim conqueror from the thirteenth century, had defeated the Hindu ruler Prithviraj Chauhan. Thus, for the first time, he established 'Muslim rule' on the subcontinent, as many historians call it. The nuclear research centre near Islamabad is built like a mosque.

Conservative Muslim activists in particular had pushed Sharif to draw even with the Indians by carrying out their own tests.

Three weeks earlier, it was the Thar desert in Rajasthan that had trembled. The Hindu nationalist government of the Indian People's Party (BJP)[6] wanted to display strength—for 'Hindustan'. The Indian nuclear missile carries the name Prithvi.[7] It seems as if 'the Muslims' and 'the Hindus' were facing each other once again in a replay of their age-old enmity as 'their' rulers did at that time. US president Bill Clinton reacted with resignation: 'I cannot believe that the Indian subcontinent is starting the 21st century with the most terrible mistakes of the 20th century.'[8] However, the game of nuclear deterrence on the subcontinent differs from that of the Cold War. The ethno-nationalists in India and Pakistan may use the obsolete means of the twentieth century, but for their arguments they reach even more deeply into the historical box of tricks—going as far back as the Middle Ages.

Fanatical religious leaders on both sides fancy themselves on a historic mission. They exercise a decisive influence on the governments of India and Pakistan. The fundamentalist Hindu organization, the Vishva Hindu Parishad (VHP), which is close to the BJP, announced that it wanted to build a temple on the nuclear test site in Rajasthan. The house of god is supposed to be a 'Shakti Peeth', a place of cosmic energy. VHP president Ashok Singhal stated that the temple would symbolize the reassertion of India as a powerful nation. Shakti means 'energy'; it is also the name of a Hindu goddess. The Indian nuclear tests were also carried out under this code name.[9] Meanwhile, a patriotic pop music video entitled 'We are Indians' jubilated the nuclear tests. This was the BJP's idea. The five nuclear explosions echo in the song's background.[10]

This episode shows that: (1) In order to legitimize their *current* power-political ambitions, the rulers of India and Pakistan use specific *traditional* factors with mass appeal, like history, religion, and folklore. (2) Historical figures come to symbolize a view of history that suggests an aggressive thinking within the political camps. (3) Religious, political, and military antagonisms are blended together. The notion of a 'Hindu bomb' vis-à-vis an 'Islamic bomb' is brought forward by many protagonists and has been accepted, rather uncritically, by the world media (although the biggest irony is that the 'father' of the Indian bomb is a Muslim engineer, Avul Pakir Jainulabdeen Abdul Kalam, who later became the country's president, in July 2002, with the blessing of the BJP; the elevation of the nuclear scientist to the position of the head of state shows that this is a political rather than an ethno-national competition). (4) During the tests the most frequently occurring words in local newspapers were: 'nation', 'strength', 'pride'. Criticism of the nuclear tests on both sides of the border was restricted to a small circle of intellectual debates.[11] Even some members of the lowest strata of society shared this setting of priorities to amorphous ideological constructions. For example, a poor village doctor in the Indian village of Dasna, near Delhi, said: 'This nuclear test was about self-respect, and self-respect is more important than roads, electricity and water.'[12]

In this paradigm, Jinnah, who had a secular state of Pakistan in mind, becomes the godfather of an 'Islamic' bomb. Similarly, Hindu gods become the addressees of military pride and medieval rulers are transformed into heroes of a modern concept of nation born in the nineteenth century. Another grotesque comparison was brought forward by the radical VHP. In order to underline Muslim aggressiveness, it compared the alleged destruction of the alleged temple of the 'national' Hindu god Ram in Ayodhya in favour of a mosque built in the sixteenth century with the terrorist attacks on the World Trade Center in New York city on 11 September 2001.[13]

The same kind of propaganda technique is equally effective in the Balkans. On 28 June 1989 the Serb President Slobodan Milosevic melted down the history of over 600 years when he summoned hundreds of thousands of Serbs to the field of the black birds (Kosovo Polje). There street vendors sold posters of Milosevic, Jesus, and Prince Lazar,—the Serb military leader who was executed by the Ottomans in 1389, after a rather sluggish battle on the field of the black birds. Some historians doubt whether this battle took place at all.[14] But this does not matter. Milosevic had the bones of the prince carried throughout the country. His death was not to be in vain but, it was claimed, would strengthen Serbia, even centuries later. The Serb president felt that the time had come to wipe out the long-preserved memory of this humiliation. In the age of the nation state Kosovo became the 'holy heart' of Serbia with the blessings of the Orthodox church. And Serbia was supposed to be wherever Serbs lived.[15] This provided the impulse for 'Serb' territorial gains in a disintegrating Yugoslavia. The consequences turned out to be particularly drastic when Serb ideologues appropriated Muslims as Serbs.[16] But actually behind this drama was only the postsocialist reinforcement of Milosevic's power by other means.

These and many other examples show the simultaneousness of the unsimultaneous.[17] This is a core feature of the political myth as defined by Ernst Cassirer, the father of symbolic forms. Space, time, and numbers merge. Boundaries become blurred. The myth displays a muddled stratification of thought, not a chronology of events.[18] The following episode makes clear where this can lead to. A UN official recounted that he had accused a Serb officer of destroying the 'beautiful and ancient Old City' of a Bosnian town. The Serb replied: 'But we will build a new and more beautiful ancient Old City in its place.' [19]

The US journalist Robert Kaplan talks about the returning 'spirits' of the Balkans and considers the history of this region to be no more than a logical succession: 'Instead it jumps around and moves in a circle, and where history is perceived in this way, myths take root.'[20] However, history never repeats itself exactly. One could, therefore, compare the opposite of a linear construction of history with a *historical cabinet of mirrors*: no matter where a person looks and in which direction he moves, the omnipresence of a specific 'key event' will catch his eye—often distorted but inescapable.

National, mostly ethno-national, protagonists are responsible for creating a great deal of such mirrors. For these myths assume a *function*—a 'function of comprehending the world', as Cassirer calls it—which replaces the empirical reality: 'In the relation between myth and history, the former takes on the primary position and the latter becomes secondary and derived.'[21] The productive and creative force of the myth itself becomes the governing principle of action.

'The one who fills the memory, coins the terms and interprets the past', writes Dzaja on the Balkans, is the one who thinks that he will win the future in the struggle for political identity.[22] This is a crucial power resource in the political sphere which is marked by the ethno-national paradigm. To view history through the rearview mirror—and this in convenient sectors only—is an effective means of creating a common identity, a functional 'self-image'.[23] This imagined past, as K.N. Panikkar calls it, is subject to 'selective appropriation' for serving new goals.[24] Moreover, present events are derived monocausally from the (imagined) past and/or are compared with it uncritically.

So, according to one's *gusto*, the rearview mirror is focused to reflect the 'golden age' which befits the self-image of the respective group or its spokesmen. The selective appropriation of history leads to a separate perception of history and, under specific political circumstances, may serve as the means for dividing a society. For this purpose epics dig out from the oblivion "heroes of the past for new objectives".[25] For India this can be generalized with some exceptions: 'The Hindu tends to glorify in retrospect the Vedic age or the Gupta period of Indian History, the Muslim is brought up to look to the medieval period of Muslim dominance as the golden age'.[26] In the same way, Serb and Croatian writers nourish the idea of the Ottoman empire as the 'dark age'.[27] They often use the technique of *pars pro toto* (Ghauri = Islamic age, Prithvi = Hindu era, Jinnah = Islam, Lazar's sacrifice = Serb destiny, Kosovo = heart of Great Serbia, etc.). The parts as a symbol becomes the real influencing agent and can thus be put on a level with the whole.[28]

Politicians who legitimate their acts through such historical images (the battle on the field of the black birds as the war motive in the 1990s, the 'Muslim conquest' of India as a recurring motif on nuclear missiles) attain more than historical contortions. They often use myths for the 'moral re-armament of the nation'.[29] Moreover, they employ skilful tactics that help them to outwit thier political rivals, avoid difficult decisions and painstaking majority-building. Münkler observes that political actors, who suffer from a 'mythical narrowing of their field of vision', aim to achieve several goals:[30] (1) They reduce political complexity: 'Suddenly it is clear and undoubtable what has to be done'.[31] (2) They evade any later political evaluation. Their action is justified by the myth itself. (3) In case of failure they can thus get away without taking any political responsibility; they reduce the failure to a 'mythical disaster', and sometimes in this way create a new myth which fits into the picture.[32]

But a myth *must* also *fit* into the picture. This is an additional precondition which Cassirer mentions. The myth is not a 'conglomerate of arbitrary images and unrelated ideas' but can be grasped as a 'characteristic mental structure'. The individual mental recipient has a critical outlook:

> The single expression of mind is not accepted simply as what it is and as what it directly occurs to be, but it is confronted with the question to what extent it will stand the test of the experience of the totality and how it will survive vis-à-vis this totality. Only if it manages to withstand this question and this critical test, it will become part of the realm of reality, of the objective certainty.[33]

This is a process which is constantly subject to change. It is true that myths are created by intellectuals, that means 'from the top',[34] but they must also arrive 'at the bottom'. 'Symbols are coded signals,' writes Voigt, 'which can be understood only by the one who can decode the message'.[35] The signals are effective only if they reach 'the bottom'. And it is the effect of the myth—the intensity with which it is lived—which matters, and not so much the content, as Cassirer observes.[36]

In this way emotions can easily grow out of control and provoke new conflicts in the present. The following two examples show the actual power of the past, no matter how ancient the past is.

After the Croats had recaptured Eastern Slavonia, the local Serbs boycotted the schools in the autumn of 1997 for Croatian history books described them as aggressors of the war. Consequently, UN forces brokered a deal which suspended the teaching of recent history for five years.[37]

A controversy about school text books also broke out in India in 1977. Hindu nationalists accused, among others, the historians Romila Thapar and Bipan Chandra of omitting from their texts the claim that the 'Muslim invaders' were responsible for the outbreak of communal conflicts. Instead, the authors held Hindu nationalists like Tilak and Aurobindo responsible for the 'ethnic' alienation in the country.[38] The historians protested and referred to the secular order of Indian society. Their books could be published. But prime minister Morarji Desai joined hands with the Hindu nationalists on this issue, banned other trans-'ethnic' history books, and replaced them with books with a pro-Hindu bias.[39] Such incidents poisoned the social climate. The distorted historiography was directed against the Muslims in their own country and against Pakistan at the same time. The consequences are hard to come to terms with, believes the Indian professor of political science, Uma Singh, and she adds self-critically: 'Our history books have done maximum damage to the understanding of our neighbours.'[40]

These incidents show that the writing and teaching of history becomes a delicate matter, especially when nations derive a large part of their legitimacy from it. Certain myths can even become the focal points of nation-building. Consequently, their destruction threatens the entire state project. Münkler writes:

> Nations founded as nation-states can afford demythologizations, whereas in the case of nations which exist in lingual-cultural terms only and are simultaneously subject to assimilation policies, the demand for demythologization and rationalization is always tantamount to partisanship – one that is directed against the 'imagined community'.[41]

Since there are practically no nation states at all, myths have mostly a stabilizing effect. In case of ethno-nations which are not founded as nation states and whose 'ethnic groups' can be demarcated from others only with extreme difficulty, myths can become the decisive backbone for the legitimacy of statehood.

Thapar points out that myths may not only be static but also dynamic. In this form they serve to legitimize and to process changed social or political conditions.[42] Myths are meant to homogenize their target group. This may become necessary through an ideological challenge (like socialism or nationalism) or through the struggle for resources because of possible 'ethnic' rivalry.

So the most important instrument to mythologize nations is 'their' historiography. Satish Chandra writes that this is true especially in African and Asian states where nationalism is not the *result* of a long unifying historical process but rather the *means* to achieve such a unification. Therefore, in these countries historians enjoy much more respect than in the 'West'.[43] Accordingly, in this sense at least the Balkan states could be classified as Afro-Asiatic. In these countries historiography does not remain a pure academic act, but it becomes political. In this context Anthony Smith speaks of *ethno-history* or *ethnic mythistoire*:

> I mean not an objective historian's dispassionate enquiry into the past but the subjective view of later generations of a given cultural unit of population of the experience of their real or presumed forebears. That view is inseparable from what the historian and social scientist would term 'myth'.[44]

Renan had earlier identified a constitutive part of nation-building here:

> To forget the history, and even to get it wrong, are essential factors of nation building, and this is why the progress of historical studies is sometimes a danger for the nation.[45]

The following chapter provides examples of such a politically relevant historiography in relation to both case studies.

NOTES

1. Khilnani (1997), p. 164.
2. R. Gandhi (1987), preface. Son of M.K. Gandhi.
3. Panic was a moderate Serb prime minister till Slobodan Milosevic brought him down in 1992. Quote from: Owen (1996), p. 86.

4. Holbrooke to the British ambassador in Belgrade, Ivor Roberts, Roberts disapproved of the bomb attacks on the Serbs which he feared would lead the Serbs to see themselves as victims (31 August 1995) (Holbrooke (1998), p. 178).
5. See: 'Pakistan zündet fünf Atom-Sprengsätze', in: *Süddeutsche Zeitung* (29 May 1998).
6. Bharatiya Janata Party.
7. The Indians named their nuclear missiles after the elements, but simultaneously they also sought to commemorate the Hindu rulers with the same names. Their missiles are called Prithvi (earth), Agni (fire), and Sagarika (ocean). See: 'Aiming Missiles', in: *Economist* (9 May 1998).
8. 'Auch Pakistan testet Atomwaffen', in: *Der Tagesspiegel* (29 May 1998).
9. See: Gabriele Venzky: 'Atomares Wettrennen der Erzfeinde', in: *Der Tagesspiegel* (19 May 1998).
10. 'Atomtests besungen', in: *Der Tagesspiegel* (10 July 1998).
11. (Self-)critical opinions on the tests are published in a special edition of *Philosophy and Social Action*, 24 (1998): 3-4. In this issue the former head of the Indian navy, Admiral Ramdas, condemns the policy of his country.
12. Friedman (2000), p. 38.
13. 'After the Slaughter, What Hope?', in: *Economist* (9 March 2002), p. 56. For a discussion on how the destruction of the mosque allegedly located on the exact spot as 'Ram's birthplace' by a radical Hindu mob in 1992 is to be placed in India's political context, see Chapter VII 'Resumé'.
14. For example, the historian Sima Cirkovic has doubts about it ['Die schaurige Sage vom Amselfeld', Wolfgang Höpken, in: *Die Zeit* (12 March 1998)]. For more details on this legendary battle and its mythicization see Malcolm (1998); Lauer and Lehfeld (1995), pp. 139ff; Tomasevic, in: Vucinich/ Emmert (1989); for emphasis on current developments: Vickers (1998). Dreschner and Petrovic (1995) pp. 50ff describe the myth of the field of the black birds from Serb-transfigured point of view.
15. This old maxim was again called on the agenda by the Serb Academy of Sciences in 1986. For details on the theses of the Society, see: Krizan (1992), in: *OE*, pp. 123ff.
16. See Chapter IV.1.2.1. 'To Whom Does Bosnia Belong?'.
17. There is an excellent comparative overview of historical myths from all continents: 'Nations and Their Past: The Uses and Abuses of History', in: *Economist* (21 December 1996).
18. Cassirer, Vol. II (1924; 1994), pp. 82, 101, 103.
19. Bowman (1994), in: *BF*, p. 151.
20. Kaplan (1994), p. 88. The problems of this view are discussed in Chapter V.1. 'The Cage Breaks Open'.
21. Cassirer, Vol. II (1994), p. 8 [1924].

22. Dzaja (1994), p. 35. See also Lauer, in: Lauer and Lehfeld (1995), p. 110.
23. Thapar (1992a), p. 140.
24. K.N. Panikkar (1997), p. 73.
25. Thapar (1992a), p. 150.
26. Gore (1996), in: *SS*, p. 43. For the selective perception of history in India, see especially the works of Thapar and K.N. Panikkar.
27. For example, also the Bosnian writer Ivo Andric with his novels '*Die Brücke über die Drina*' (1962) and '*Omer-Pascha Latas*' (1983). For this, see also: Balic, in: *IS* (1997), p. 139.
28. Cassirer, Vol. II (1994), p. 65. See also: Dörner (1995), p. 27.
29. Münkler, in: Münkler and Sorch (1988), p. 55.
30. See: Münkler, in: Münkler and Storch (1988), pp. 68-9; Münkler, in: Frindte and Pätzold (1994), pp. 21-3.
31. Münkler, in: Frindte and Pätzold (1994), p. 23.
32. This applies, for example, to the Serb myths of sacrifice which received an impetus after the Bosnian war, which ended in disappointment for the Serb nationalists, particularly after the bombing of Kosovo. Many Serbs were convinced that the entire world had always been against them. They just had to defend themselves against suffering and injustice. For a debate on this topic, see the works of Colovic and his article: 'Die Rückkehr des Mittelalters in die Moderne', Ivan Colovic, in: *Die Zeit* (15 January 1998). Devetak argues in the same way as Münkler. However, instead of the myth, he argues that the plain stereotype of a hostile nation can be held responsible for social, political, and economic shortcomings. [Devetak, in: Seewann (1992), p. 56.]
33. Cassirer, Vol. II (1994), pp. 27-8.
34. Münkler, in: Frindte and Pätzold (1994), p. 25.
35. Voigt, in: Voigt (1989), p. 14.
36. Cassirer, Vol. II (1994), p. 8. See also: Lauer, in: Lauer and Lehfeld (1995), p. 109, who refers to Cassirer.
37. 'The Croatians are coming', in: *Economist* (10 January 1998).
38. Among other books, was *Communalism and the Writing of Indian History* edited by Romila Thapar, Harbans Mukhia and Bipan Chandra (1969). In this work I rely to a large extent on the conclusions of these renowned historians, and on many of their publications, including recent ones. I especially rely on Thapar and Chandra. Other books featuring in this 'textbook controversy' were *Medieval India* by Romila Thapar, *Modern India* by Bipan Chandra, and *Freedom Struggle* by A. Tripathi, Barun De, and Bipan Chandra. Jaffrelot (1996), pp. 287-8 describes the controversy.
39. Among these are books of the Hindu historian R.C. Majumdar.
40. In a discussion with the author in New Delhi (16 September 1996).
41. Münkler, in: Frindte and Pätzold (1994), pp. 23-4.

42. Thapar (1992a), p. 142
43. S. Chandra, (1996), p. 13.
44. Smith (1995), p. 63.
45. Renan (1882), pp. 7-8, see also: Hobsbawm (1990), p. 12. Translation by the author.

III. Nation or No Nation?

1. THE ADVENT OF ISLAM

Islamization gained historiographic significance in modern times because (a) Islam mutated into a criterion of 'ethnic' demarcation, and (b) this criterion was exploited for ethno-national projects. The questions about the 'ethnic substrate' of Muslims are particularly tricky, for instance: Where do they 'actually' come from? Who are they 'really'? And how did conversions to Islam take place?

Other researchers have already drawn comparisons to both cases described. One of them is Lapidus who observes: 'The history of Islam in India most closely resembles that of the Balkans': (a) A conquest brings Islamic religion into the area. (b) The Islamic ruling class holds a political appeal for non-Muslim elites, farmers, and workers. (c) The building of new cities is conducive to conversions and trade. (d) Mass conversions and forced conversions are extremely rare. Lapidus stresses that the latter applies to the entire Islamic world. Conversion means accepting a different faith, different rituals, and a different political loyalty. However, it does not necessarily change the habits of individuals in their everyday life.[1]

Yet some historical myths in the Balkans and in India portray this reality differently. They support a thinking divided into ethno-national camps. This was—consciously or unconsciously—reproduced by many local and foreign historians. In the present chapter an attempt is made to expose the errors into which communal historiography fell with regard to the descent of predominantly Sunni Muslims in Bosnia-Herzegovina and India.[2]

1.1. More Than Just Religion?

1.1.1. *The Bogomil Myth and Conversions in Bosnia-Herzegovina*

Long before the final conquest of Bosnia (1463) and Herzegovina (1482) by the Ottomans' Muslims lived in these lands. The earliest traces of their existence date back to the year 895. At the time Islamic nomads emigrated from Asia as mercenaries employed by Hungarian kings. In the eleventh and thirteenth centuries Hungarian Muslims (Ismailites) inhabited Bosnia-Herzegovina in compact settlements. Also, Bosnians who served in Moorish Spain, Arab seamen, and Turkish immigrants (Kalisians) brought Islam into the country.[3] However, it is only after the rise of the Ottoman Empire that one can speak of an Islamization of Bosnia-Herzegovina. The circumstances and the role of the Bosnian church (so far mostly called 'Bogomil') have provided ample material for historical and political debates.[4]

It is no coincidence that the Bogomil myth experienced a boost whenever the *Zeitgeist* suggested upgrading Bosnian Muslims as an ethno-nation—against the ethno-national competition which viewed 'the Muslims' as Serbs, Croats, or Turks. This is especially true during the Austro-Hungarian period of Bosnia-Herzegovina (from 1900 onwards) and later in Tito's Yugoslavia (from the 1960s onwards).

The myth is based on the presumption that Muslims in present-day Bosnia-Herzegovina can trace their descent directly from the Bosnian nobility of the Middle Ages, and that it had already established its identity through a church of its own—through 'Bogomilism'.[5] Thus it was able to protect itself from the appropriating attempts of the Orthodox Church and, above all, the Franciscans, who traditionally considered Bosnia-Herzegovina as the area of their missionary activities.[6] After the final Ottoman conquest of Bosnia-Herzegovina, so the myth goes, the Bosnian nobility willingly and unanimously converted to Islam. Since the majority of the Bosnian population consisted of Bogomils as well, they were also converted *en masse.* In this way they paved the way for the consolidation of the Ottoman Empire. Simultaneously, they rose to the status of a political ruling class as well as to a socially and taxwise priviledged class in Bosnia-Herzegovina.[7]

This version of events was propagated particularly by the communist Yugoslav and Muslim historian Atif Purivata (1928-2001). He wanted to prove that the Bogomils formed the 'nucleus of Muslim nation-building'.[8] His arguments came at a time when, in 1968, the Bosnian-Muslims in Yugoslavia were granted the suffix 'in the national sense', and, when, in 1971, their status as a 'nation' was embodied in the constitution.[9] Purivata was convinced that 'the overall socio-economic and particularly the cultural and political development of Moslems has affirmed them as a separate ethnic identity.'[10] The thesis that today's Muslims have descended directly from the Bogomil nobility replaces the Islamic faith as the only criterion of identity.[11] Instead, the Bosnian Muslims were seen to be coming from an own age-old Bosnian culture. This is why, according to Purivata, the Muslims have to be strictly contrasted with the Turks, with whom they share the same religion only.[12]

Against the Bogomil thesis, and especially against its postulated automatism, the new research brings the following arguments to bear:

(1) It is quite right that the Bosnian church had its own identity. At least it withstood the hierarchies of the Catholic and Orthodox Churches outside Bosnia-Herzegovina. The country was not yet rigidly classified in terms of denominations.[13] However, at the time of the Ottoman conquest the Bosnian church was already in decay.[14] It was not a state church either. Therefore, the existence of a widespread 'Bogomil' upper strata is doubtful. The Bosnian *beys*[15] had various origins: (a) only partly from the Bosnian nobility; (b) from the *Knabenlese*, a practice whereby little boys were taken away from their parents at an early age and raised forcibly in Islamic schools; (c) from officials from Asia Minor, who were allotted land in Bosnia-Herzegovina; and (d) from immigrants of different origins, like Hungarians, Croats, Slavonians, Dalmatians, and Serbs.[16]

(2) In addition, the so-called 'Bogomil treason' (the Bogomils had let the Ottomans into the country) turned out to be a 'Bosnian stab-in-the back legend', as Dzaja argues convincingly.[17] A papal legate was at a loss for an explanation because of the defeat inflicted by the Sultan, and therefore he manipulated his report.[18]

(3) The Bosnian state in general had begun to decay. Even before the Ottoman conquest the kingdom had to pay tribute to the Sultan.[19] The country's feudal structure was fragmented and its protagonists caught in strife. The Bosnian rulers often called upon the Sultan to intervene in their affairs as mediator and protector.[20] That is why the conquest came quite easily to the Ottomans.

(4) Members of *all* religious sects converted to Islam, not 'Bogomils' alone.[21] Most of the 'new Muslims' were therefore old established Bosnians. Islamic believers did not emigrate to Bosnia-Herzegovina in large numbers. This also refutes the thesis (often used by Serb nationalists) that Bosnian Muslims were in fact Turks. Even though the

leading Muslim clerics comprised Turks, Albanians, Tatars, Arabian Sunnites, and others, their number decreased consistently after the fifteenth century.[22]

(5) There were no conversions *en masse* and hardly any under coercion (except for the *Knabenlese*). Conversions took place step by step and in different ways.[23] Members of the political and military upper class were more willing to embrace Islam than the rest of the population. For many Islamization had, first of all, just a 'declaratory character'.[24] This means that they at best adopted a Muslim name. Many also had pragmatic reasons for their conversions, for example, because the church was farther away than the mosque or because they hoped to win liberation from slavery, tax benefits, or high posts. Islamization progressed more rapidly in growing cities than in rural areas. The deepening of Islamic tradition, however, took many generations. Meanwhile, Muslims continued to pray in churches and kiss holy Christian symbols.[25] This is why Fine speaks of the 'acceptance' of Islam rather than 'conversion', as the lifestyles of the people remained by and large unchanged. [26]

Even Purivata had softened his stand on this issue when I talked to him in June 2000. About one year before his death he acknowledged the research by Srecko Dzaja and Smail Balic. Today, he said, no scholar supports the Bogomil thesis in its pure version any more. Purivata suggested as a compromise that 'we could say: *Most* Bogomils accepted Islam. . . . Also Orthodox and Croats did.' (Surprisingly, he did not even want to exclude the possibility of a multi-religious 'nation' in Bosnia in the future, which deviated substantially from his previous standpoint. He said: 'In Bosnia, religion, ethnicity and nation are the same in some way. [. . .] But a nation with different religions . . . —may be some day we will have this here, too. Who knows?' He also held that the 'political feeling' in Bosnia has been stronger than the 'religious feeling', which concurs again more with his previous views.)[27]

The latest research also questions whether the Bosnian church was affiliated to the Bogomil monastic order from Bulgaria at all. This was particularly what the Croatian historian Franjo Racki had claimed (in articles of 1869/70).[28] By the way, the Bosnians themselves called each other *Krstjani* (Christians).[29] Now whether the Bosnians were partly Bogomils or whether they followed an 'archaic monastic church'[30] or whether they displayed Catholic traits[31] does not in any way affect the above arguments.

From today's point of view it is much more interesting—and typical— that Racki's theory had two *contemporary* rivals. One was represented by the Serb author Petranovic, who believed that the Bosnian church was in fact an apostate Serbian Orthodox church. On the other hand, Catholic writers were convinced that the Bosnian church was indeed a branch of the Catholic church.[32] What this is supposed to mean in the context of religion-based nation-building is clear: the Bosnian Muslims are supposed to be either 'Serbs' or 'Croats'.

The Bogomil thesis is in fact a dual myth which the latest research claims to have refuted. First, the Bosnian 'Bogomil' nobility did not convert to Islam 'as one man' followed by the entire population. Second, the members of the medieval Bosnian church were not Bogomils at all. The whole argument boils down to this: The Bosnian church was one—but only *one*—factor which left its mark on the Islamization of Bosnia-Herzegovina. The Bogomil myth is a 'historically unsustainable attempt' to construct a Muslim nation-building similar to that of the Serbs and Croats.[33] The statement that 'the Ottoman occupation encountered an already established people of Bosnians [...]',[34] which continued unhindered, must therefore be placed in the realm of ethno-national legends. Rather the Ottomanization represented an institutional break for Bosnia.[35]

The refutation of the Bogomil myth means that: 'The Muslims' in Bosnia-Herzegovina do not have a longer ethnic and social continuity than their neighbours.[36] The retrospective ethno-national attempts of appropriation of the Bosnian church (from which side ever) aim at revealing primordial factors that establish, categorize, and instrumentalize 'the Bosnian Muslims' as an 'ethnic group'.

1.1.2. *The Myths from the Indus Valley*

Similar to developments in Bosnia-Herzegovina, the lines of arguments adopted by Indian ethno-nationalists date back to the dim and distant past. In their case, not even the Middle Ages are enough. Some Hindu nationalists like to refer to a phenomenon around 1500 BC: an Indo-Germanic tribe named 'Aryan' allegedly emigrated from Central Asia to northern India (and another branch of the tribe went to Europe). It defeated the high civilization of the Indus valley and formed the ruling class in the northern part of the subcontinent.

What makes this theory so delicate? First, it is probably wrong. Second, nationalists use 'history' here also to endow a religious group with 'ethnic' characteristics—in this case even racial-biological traits. Both the Aryan and the Bogomil myths have this in common

The Hindu nationalists of the early twentieth century, especially Savarkar, Golwalkar, Tilak, and Aurobindo, looked for a definition of 'Hinduism' (Hindutva).[37] In order not to propagate hollow words they had to formulate a Hindu identity which as such did not yet exist. Their argument was: the true Hindus are the Aryans, the highest 'race' of India which had laid the foundations of Hindu religion and culture. The fairer-skinned, upper-caste Hindus are their direct descendants. This turns all others into strangers, especially the later 'immigrants' like Muslims and Christians. Hindus, however, had their 'Holy Land'—India. [38]

Thus, not only was a stark contrast created between 'pure' Hindus and what was seen as the largest group of Muslim competitors but 'the Muslims' also got the status of outsiders, a claim that was underpinned with arguments which went far beyond religion. In the struggle among ethno-national ideologues in the first half of the twentieth century the Aryan myth particularly enjoyed great topicality.

The Hindu nationalists got support for their arguments largely from European scholars of the nineteenth century, like Friedrich Max Müller and even Ernest Renan. Since Müller[39] the idea that the Aryans were a separate, biological race rapidly gained acceptance, for he carelessly put language and race on the same level in his research.[40] Soon this concept was instrumentalized politically. With Joseph Arthur (Count of Gobineau), the composer and author Richard Wagner, and his son-in-law, Houston Stewart Chamberlain, the concept escalated into a north-Teutonic, racist superiority saga. [41]

The Aryan myth proved to be applicable in multiple ways. Till today some Hindus burst with pride at the idea of a 'common' Indo-European heritage, often in harmony with a sympathy towards Hitler, the ally against colonialist Britain. The myth also suited the upper-caste Hindu elite who wanted to curry favour with the colonialists with the same arguments.[42] Thus they made a point against the Muslim elite at the same time. The Aryan myth has become common knowledge to such an extent that it is also used by people who have no Hindu nationalist sympathies. Reference to the immigration thesis can also be found in Nehru's *Discovery of India*.[43]

Only the latest research has raised plausible doubts about the Aryan thesis. According to these scholars, the biological aspect in particular is not tenable. Satish Chandra and Romila Thapar claim, among other things, that the term 'Aryan' ('Aryan' means 'the noble' in Sanskrit) was a self-given name. It referred to a culture which was composed of various religions and races.[44] Thus the authors suggest that in the Indus valley a slow transformation took place among the local population, from which emerged the Aryan culture. This version contrasts with the theory of Aryan immigration or conquest. A conciliatory position is that the Aryans did immigrate but then mingled with the population of the Indus valley.[45]

We cannot go into the details of this debate here. However, it is interesting that archaeologists, on the basis of their findings in the antique settlements of Harappa and Mohenjodaro, consider an Aryan immigration as disproven, whereas the linguists are more inclined towards the migration thesis. As evidence they present the close relation of the old Indian standard language Sanskrit to Persian and the European family of languages.[46]

Especially those Indian historians who deal with the modern ethno-national polemics in their country reject the migration theory.[47] They hold the opinion that archaeological findings tell a lot more than linguistic theories and religious texts (like the Vedas). According to them, language can spread without conquest, too. Thapar even suggests that the term 'Aryan' should be abandoned altogether. In her view it has been politically appropriated to an excessive degree. Indeed, the Aryan myth today has mainly become an instrument of propaganda of Hindu nationalists to exclude Indian Muslims from a common, cultural heritage and to even brand them as a separate race altogether.

This is also done through exactly opposite tactics. Some Hindu nationalists *negate* the immigration thesis in order to enhance the status of Hinduism while derogating all other religions. They argue in the following way. The immigration thesis is an invention of Western, secular, and leftist intellectuals. They place Hinduism and Islam on the same level. 'The Muslims' (and the British or Christians) immigrated to the land—and is this supposed to be the case with 'Hindu Aryans' as well? With such an assumption one robs Hinduism of its characteristic Indianness which sets it apart from the other, 'foreign' religions. According to these Hindu nationalists, Hinduism was not forced onto the native people of India (the Dravidians) like the other religions. Instead, it constituted the Indian culture *a priori* and *per se.* Hindu nationalism is nothing else but Indian nationalism. And if the Aryans did migrate at all, it was from India to all parts of the world where Indo-European languages are spoken today.[48]

In whatever way people juggle with the myth of the 'Aryans', they serve to degrade 'the Muslims' as a cultural antibody in an allegedly pure 'Hindu nation'. In this respect the myth of the Aryans differs from the Bogomil myth: Ethno-national Muslims of Bosnia-Herzegovina employed it *themselves* in order to demarcate themselves from others. But the *function* of both myths remains the same.

The Indus valley, however, also serves Pakistani ideologues to distinguish *themselves* from Hindus. Thus, they want to derive the foundation of Pakistan from 'ethnic' features as a 'logical' consequence of history. Official history books of the country legitimize the existence of West Pakistan on the basis of the separate civilization of Mohenjodaro. They argue that it has always been closer to the Sumerians and Babylonians than to the southern subcontinent. For East Pakistan, today's Bangladesh, they claim a separate tradition because Buddhism could endure there until the thirteenth century.[49] Some Pakistani authors, like the writer of a university textbook, speak of the *Indo-Pakistani* subcontinent in the boundaries from 1947 onwards—since the Aryan age.[50] An even more lively fantasy grabbed the imagination of Aitzaz Ahsan, former interior minister under Benazir Bhutto. He claimed that India and Pakistan had already been separate states in the pre-Aryan age, since 3000 BC![51]

The official history books of Pakistan trace the beginning of their state to more than a dozen different places and dates. To name a few:

- the early Stone Age
- the civilization of Mohenjodaro and Harappa
- the birth of Islam on the Arabian Peninsula
- the first invasion of Muslim soldiers in Sindh in the eighth century
- 'Pakistan' in the thirteenth century comprising the whole of northern India, Bengal, and stretching up to central India.[52]

Also, the founder of the state, Jinnah himself, rode on the wave of myths, spiced them up with Muslim self-pity, in order to mobilize the masses: 'Pakistan has been there for centuries, it is there today, and it will remain till the end of the world. It was taken away from us; we have only to take it back.'[53]

Jinnah and others also put forward moral arguments. The formation of Pakistan had been a 'blessing' in order to fight the 'unethical caste-system' of the 'idol-worshipping' Hindus.[54] It is also said that the 'Indo-Muslim' or 'Hindustani' culture of the Middle Ages was, in principle, Islamic. Hence, Pakistan is the natural heir of this tradition.[55] Again, other Muslims claim exactly the opposite. They boast about being actually 'foreigners' and thus 'pure' Muslims, although the stream of immigration had dried up centuries ago.[56] In this way they add fuel to the Aryan myth.

Supporters of the Two-Nation Theory *on both sides* go back very far in history in order to justify their stands. Merely religious differences do not seem convincing enough to them. Their intention is to construct 'ethnic' contrasts using all possible 'old material' by re-interpretation of history. Some Hindu nationalists and a few Muslim nationalists carry this exercise as far as to racial theories.

Comparative view

Both examples bring to light the historiographic constructions on which ethno-nationalists fall back in order to sharpen the contrasting feature religion, which they need as a resource of mobilization. Around it they tinker 'ethnic' differences to make their ideology more plausible. In Pakistan this ritual of re-interpretation is primarily important because a major part of the country's state ideology is based on it.[57]

Academic debates are underway to clear the mists of confusion and get a more proper picture of history. The task here can only be to properly understand the reasoning and to assess its plausibility. However, in the future ethno-nationalists will not be interested in academic findings either. Remnants of human bones serve as the ultimate evidence to refute their legends of descent and race. Researchers have a clear message here both for Bosnia and India: 'Ethnic', geographic, and linguistic sub-divisions do not match with the anthropological data.

Excavated skulls of West, East, and South Slavs do not differ. Divergences among South Slavs are minimal. They result from different assimilation processes of pre-Slavic groups.[58] Also, in the Indus valley findings of human bones contradict the thesis of a possible break around 1500 BC— that means the time when the Aryans are supposed to have immigrated. Besides all that, the alleged Brahman 'Aryan descendents' in south India have more biological similarities (e.g. small build, dark skin) to their lower-caste neighbours than to their 'Aryan' caste-fellows from the north.[59]

So the differences between the 'ethnic groups' are not the work of nature but of human beings. Self-created cultural factors in the widest sense are used for the purpose of demarcation. At a more advanced stage, as we shall soon see, political and economic criteria are added (like the competition over political and economic resources). The arguments deviate more and more from the claim of any basic differences, and hence it becomes necessary to explain the fundamental and uncompromising hostility with which members of the 'ethnic groups' faced each other armed with the belief of being worlds apart.

1.2. Who Became a Muslim? Who Was a Muslim?

1.2.1. *The Social Structure of Muslims in Early Bosnia-Herzegovina*

The refutation of the Bogomil myth undercuts the idea that the entire aristocracy comprising the big landowners of Bosnia-Herzegovina can look back to a long continuity in their history and lineage. Indeed, it seems obvious to assume that all landowners converted to Islam in order to safeguard their assets.[60] This led to another myth which says that all Christian nobles converted to Islam collectively. But this belief was invalidated in the 1930s, however without ever losing its appeal entirely.[61]

All in all, the thesis of religious conversion as a strategy to safeguard one's assets appears too general. Malcolm writes: 'It is not true that one had to be a Muslim in order to become rich in the Ottoman Empire.'[62] He gives examples such as the Christian *spahis*[63] who could manage without Islam and yet remained prosperous. There were indeed legal differences among the religious groups, such as that Christians had to pay a special tax. Muslims, in turn, paid the obligatory alms tax (*zakat*). So Malcolm argues that financial advantages could not have been the *only* reason to change one's religion.[64] Rather, as the Ottomans continued to rule, political and social advantages became more and more noticeable. Malcom himself qualifies his above assertion: 'But it is true, that, after the early sixteenth century at least, it was necessary to be a Muslim in order to have a career in the structure of the Ottoman state itself.'[65]

Since the sixteenth century an increasing number of people converted to Islam. In cities Islamization took place most visibly. Many Muslims were therefore a product of urban society. They practised trade and handicraft together with a small minority of self-employed Christians and Jews. It was mostly because of them that Sarajevo became a prosperous city in the seventeenth century. In principle, the Ottoman authorities gave the cities a free hand in pursuing their economic life. Dubrovik could hold on to its independence for a long time. Its port was an important trade centre. The ships sailed regularly up to Goa in India.[66]

A change occurred also in the rural areas. Towards the nineteenth century the fifteeth-century-cleavage between *bey* and subject increasingly gave way to the cleavage between rich Muslims and poor Christians and between poor but somewhat better-off Muslims. A new law of succession helped the prosperous Muslims. In 1594 the Sultan issued a decree which granted the Islamic landowners the right to leave their land to members of their own family.[67] Because of this, landed property became more and more concentrated in the hands of certain families who, at the same time, were strongly bound to their soil.

When Bosnia-Herzegovina came under Austro-Hungarian administration in 1878, 6,000 Muslim *beys* ruled more than 85,000 serfs (*kmets*). Out of these labourers two-thirds followed Orthodox beliefs and one-third were Catholics. In addition, there were some 77,000 free Muslim peasants.[68] In terms of property, the Christian population, on average, was clearly at a disadvantage against the Muslims.[69] This situation was aggravated in the Austro-Hungarian period and continued, with some exceptions, till recent times.[70]

The longer the Ottomans ruled, the more evident became the political, social, and economic advantages for the Muslim population. This led to the emergence of a Muslim upper class, which mainly relied on the ownership of land. It established contacts with the fast growing cities, where also mostly Muslims represented the upper class. This turned out to become important, particularly in the Austro-Hungarian period, when the Muslims became more politically active.

1.2.2. *Conversions and the Social Structure in Early India*

There may have already been Muslim settlements in south-west India in the early Islamic period. But the year AD 711 is considered to be the actual start of Islamic influence on the subcontinent. In that year Arab troops under the leadership of Muhammad ibn al-Qasim occupied the southern Indus valley. In line with the teachings of the Koran, he recognized the local Hindus and Buddhists as 'protégés'.

In modern historiography the eleventh century is seen as a turning point. The main protagonists were today's Pakistani heroes, who were revived by the naming of the country's nuclear missiles: Mahmud of Ghazni (reign 999-1030) and Muhammad of Ghur (twelfth century). Both came from present-day Afghanistan. Muhammad of Ghur is considered to be the founder of Turkish rule on the subcontinent.[71]

The debates revolve mainly around the Islamic elements that the rulers brought to the subcontinent. Many historians, especially the British, have called this period the beginning of 'Muslim rule'. Milestones are the Sultanate of Delhi (1206-1526) and the Mughal era, which lasted up to 1857 when the last Mughal emperor was deposed by the British after a revolt ('Great Mutiny'). But this generalization is misleading because:

(1) It is true that all emperors professed Islam (with varied degrees of passion). But they belonged to different royal families. They were dynastic and absolutist. They had drifted far away from the Islamic principle of equality. They did not represent 'Islam' en bloc.[72] The ruling class was a motley of ethnic groups. The only thing that held them together were the dynasties themselves.[73] The policies vis-à-vis religious minorities were of a varied nature. In particular, the great Mughal emperor Akbar (1556-1605) made efforts towards an active exchange of ideas among the different religions in his empire and even towards establishing a common religion, the 'divine faith' (*Din-e-ilahi*).[74] Some doubt whether he himself was still a 'Muslim'.

(2) The upper classes were by no means all Muslim. Above all, Akbar had Hindu ministers, officers, advisors, and civil servants. Almost all tax collectors (zamindars) had always been Hindus. Hindu princesses formed part of Akbar's harem. One of them gave birth to the first successor to his throne. Akbar even forbade Hindu girls to convert to Islam when they married Muslim men. Thereby he extended to Hindus the same protection enjoyed by Muslim families against their daughters marrying out of the faith.[75]

(3) The Muslim emperors fought wars against each other with the same bitterness and ferocity as they marched against the Rajputs.[76]

(4) The more the empire expanded, the more dependent the Muslim emperors became on the collaboration with the Hindu upper classes. The Rajputs continued to reign in their principalities. They also fought more often against each other than against their Muslim rivals.[77]

(5) Seen from 'above' one can hardly speak of a pure Muslim era. From 'below' the picture appears even more differentiated. The religion of the ruler did not simply trickle down to the population. This point needs closer examination.

Until the thirteenth century the word 'Muslim' was hardly used. Also, later people were judged primarily on the basis of their ethnic origin. They were either Turks (*Turushkas*) or Arabs (*Yavanas*). A distinction was made in terms of language groups, too. All speakers of a non-Aryan language were called *Mlecchas* (Turks, Arabs, Persians).[78] In many Indian languages the name *Turk* prevailed for 'Muslim'.[79] The same term was used for Bosnian Muslims as well.

Apart from their origin Muslims were nowhere near a homogeneous group either. Most of them were converted Hindus. But the strict caste system proved stronger than the new religion. Thus, a social ranking can be spotted among the Muslims, which was completely opposed to the principle of equality in Islam. From top to bottom: immigrant Muslims, converts from the upper castes, converts from the lower castes, and former untouchables (outcastes).[80] In addition, most Sunni rulers discriminated against the Shia minority.[81] Still today, Shias and Sunnis in Lucknow—the stronghold of the Shia minority in India—fight more often against each other than against Hindus.[82]

Forced conversions or proselytizations on the part of the rulers were extremely rare. Rather, it was mixed marriages that led to conversions.[83] Mystic Sufi sects played an important role in spreading Islam. In many respects, they appealed to Hindus because it reminded them of their own religious teachings. Ascetic ethics, the idea of the ephemerality of the material world, and mystical self-denial were closer to introspective Hinduism as it had developed since the early Middle Ages. Emperor Akbar also tried to use these syncretisms in his attempt at forging a common faith.[84]

Neo-Muslims continued to visit their village temples and worshipped local Hindu gods. Many performed marriage ceremonies according to

Hindu customs. They consulted Brahman pandits for fixing an appropriate date for the wedding. Studies confirm the existence of these practices until at least the 1920s.[85] Some Neo-Muslims continued to refrain from eating beef. Hindus, in turn, worshipped popular Islamic saints and adopted Muslim customs.[86] Such syncretisms exist even today.[87]

It is often difficult to differentiate between the 'true Muslims' and the 'true Hindus'. It is interesting that ethnic and religious characteristics crosscut or can be mutually exchanged, especially after multiple conversions and re-conversions. Dominique-Sila Khan observed a paradox in Rajasthan: those Muslims who clearly profess one of the current Islamic lines of thought (Sunnis or Shiites of Twelve Imams) show fewer characteristics of the old Islamic tradition from the Middle Ages (Ismailis) than those who call themselves 'Hindus' today.[88] At the end of her study Khan concludes:

> The various indigenous beliefs and practices conveniently labelled 'Hinduism' and the Ismaili branch of Shia Islam shared an astonishing capacity for absorption and integration of foreign elements without losing their coherence or their congenial qualities. Both were, by nature, encompassing and, for this very reason, flexible and tolerant.[89]

All in all, the popular views of religion could not be demarcated clearly. Traditional aspects dominated over religious cleavages. The religious groups were characterized more by internal differentiations than by their religious unity.[90]

Economic and social interdependencies also remained intact, no matter who had converted to which religion. Gore writes: 'Hindu and Muslim landlords and businessmen had generally more in common with each other than Hindu or Muslim patrons had with their co-religionist dependents.' Conflicts arose from clashes of economic interests, not from purely religious reasons. Since the majority of tax collectors and moneylenders were Hindus or Sikhs, a dislike towards them was rarely religiously motivated.[91] Mostly, it was the Muslim landlords who were involved in fights with them ('land wars'). This was, therefore, often interpreted as a religious conflict—although sometimes with partly good reason, as Bayly asserts. In rural clashes religious terminology was widely used. Bayly concludes:

> [T]he widely attested syncretism of rural religion, which received encouragement from the state in the course of the eighteenth century, by no means excluded the

possibility of communal conflict where lines of religious division happened to coincide with deep economic antagonisms.[92]

Even then, writes Bayly, the mentalities were variable, fragmented, and subject to economic conditions. Before 1860 there existed no universal communal identity in India. Jaffrelot endorses this assessment.[93]

The many voluntary conversions to Islam also contradict the idea of a communal identity. A direct reason to convert from a financial point of view did not exist either. Echoing Malcolm's argument for Bosnia-Herzegovina, Mukhia states that in the Indian case the special tax for non-Muslims (*jazia*) more or less levelled out the alms tax of the Muslims (*zakat*).[94] Some rulers (like Akbar) even abolished the *jazia* altogether. On the other hand, there were rulers like Alauddin Khalji (reign 1296-1316) who demanded heavy special taxes from Hindus and curtailed their privileges in a systematic manner. Also, Muslim landlords were more privileged than the big landowning Hindu castes. At times this provoked rivalries along religious cleavages.[95]

But the economic condition of the Muslims was itself very varied. In the northern and particularly in the north-western part of the country most Muslims could establish themselves as prosperous and influential landlords, and in cities as well-educated traders. In contrast, most Muslims in the north-east were simple peasants.[96] Against this background, Bipan Chandra writes: 'Social and economic history would have revealed that there was no Muslim rule under the sultans or the Mughals. All the Muslims did not form the ruling class. The Muslim masses were as poor and oppressed as the Hindu masses.' Furthermore: '[A]n upper class Muslim had far more in common culturally with an upper class Hindu than he had with a lower class Muslim. Or that a Punjabi Hindu stood closer culturally to a Punjabi Muslim than to a Bengali Hindu', and vice versa.[97] The term 'culture' is to be understood here in its ethnic sense. The regional differences include characteristics like descent, customs, traditions, language, and clothing.

Dixit, however, contradicts this by drawing attention to an important detail. She states: '[T]he medieval Indian society had three very distinct cultures: culture of the Muslim elite, culture of the Hindu elite, and culture of the masses.'[98] The two elites tried hard to distinguish themselves from each other (in terms of customs, clothing, etc.). Equally clearly they distinguished themselves from the masses, no matter to which religion they belonged. The masses—the next-door neighbours of whichever faith—were culturally not alien to each other. The elites, in comparison, lived in an 'artificially created cultural world.'[99] This created conflicts of a cultural-religious nature. On the contrary, Yogendra Singh believes that the 'Little Tradition' (i.e. popular customs) did interact with the 'Great Tradition' of the elite.[100]

However, both authors share the observation that the 'Great Tradition' displays a more clearly outlined cultural and religious profile. If one wants to spin this argument further, it is possible to discover social carriers of an 'ethnic' contrast as early as in the late Middle Ages, which delivered the substrate for the modern ethno-nationalists. However, the question remains why and under what conditions the elites drifted apart, and how these minorities of both religions could assert themselves *politically* and *ideologically* against the syncretized masses.

Just as in the case of the dynasties, also in traditional societies the religious identities were in a complete jumble. In India one can clearly see the cross-cuttings of the different ethnic and religious cleavages. This is to provoke the greatest contradictions in the Two-Nation Theory on which the state of Pakistan was to base its legitimization.

Comparative view

Conversions in Bosnia-Herzegovina and India were mostly the result of a gradual acceptance of Islam by the population. Proselytizations and the use of force were rare. Obviously, it is not possible to discern the motivation of each individual ex post. In both cases data are missing on the amount of taxes levied on Muslims and non-Muslims. Only this could have revealed any possible economic pressure for conversion. It is certain that Islam as such became attractive for Christians in Bosnia-Herzegovina, and for low-caste Hindus and outcastes in India—and not just because of economic reasons.

Despite these arguments it can be possibly generalized that by conversion most people hoped to raise their social status, for in case of doubt it was more lucrative to be a Muslim under a Muslim ruler. In course of time Muslims in Bosnia-Herzegovina clearly formed the prosperous class of landlords; and more and more landlords turned Muslims. In India, in contrast, an economic classification of 'the Muslims' turns out to be quite differentiated. Yet another difference is important: Muslims in Bosnia-Herzegovina became the majority; in

India they remained a minority. This will play an important role in the demand for an own state.

In both countries followers of different faiths lived next door to each other. They also shared local rites and customs. Especially in India, strong syncretisms can be observed. As far as Bosnia-Herzegovina is concerned, the opinions are divided. Algar asserts that Bosnian Muslims were not inclined to syncretisms at all though they lived closely together with Christians.[101] Steindorff, in contrast, speaks of 'numerous syncretisms' in the daily lives of all three religious groups.[102] His definition, however, boils down to merely respecting the faith of the other (when Muslims during Ramadan offer food to their Christian guest, or when the groups celebrate religious festivals together). But an actual fusion of customs, as it took and continues to take place in India, cannot be observed in Bosnia-Herzegovina.

2. BROTHERS OR OCCUPANTS?

2.1. The Ottomans and Bosnian Self-consciousness

The above discussions may provoke the rash conclusion that: '[D]uring Turkish rule, belonging to the Moslem religion meant holding a privileged social position; as a result of this the Bosnian Moslems thought of Turkish authority as their own.[103]

The following data could support this thesis. After the Austro-Hungarian annexation of Bosnia-Herzegovina, many Muslims emigrated to Turkey (from 1878-1910: 300,000, from 1910-35: 100,000). So the observation seems likely that: 'The bond of religion proved to be stronger than that of ethnic origin.'[104] From a religious point of view the Ottomans were in any case less suspect to Bosnian Muslims as an occupation force than the Catholic Habsburgers. With exceptions, Islam had become the most important identity feature of the Bosnian Muslims ('denominational nation' or *Konfessionsnation*), especially as a demarcator against constant attempts at proselytizing and appropriation by the Franciscans and the Orthodox.

Nevertheless, this thesis appears too simple. Miedlig differentiates: On the one hand, the identity of Bosnian Muslims was supranational. It oriented itself towards the pan-Islamic *umma* and naturally looked towards the East for guidance. On the other hand, it remained Bosnian-regionalistic up to the nineteenth century.[105] The regional identity is emphasized by those authors who try to locate the early stages of Muslim nation-building as far as possible into the past. Among them is the above-mentioned historian Purivata.

The following statements are important for taking a differentiated view:

(1) 'The Bosnian Muslims' do not display 'ethnic' or even 'national' features just because they followed the same religion as the Ottomans, and thus a different one than their neighbours. Malcolm, Pinson, Miedlig, and others repeatedly point out that Bosnian society was still anchored in traditional structures. The hesitant Islamization is just one example of this. Other cleavages like city-countryside or landlord-peasant were often (still) more prominent than religious ones.

(2) 'The Bosnian Muslims'—it means here, as so often, the Muslim 'culture-forming'[106] upper class ('Great Tradition')—showed an inherent self-assurance, *even though* they followed the same religion as the Ottomans. This happened not only through the well-proven method of demarcation against the other religions but also against the Ottomans themselves.

For this view there are several indications. Birnbaum takes the above-mentioned inheritance decree of the Sultan in 1594 to pin down an independent development of the Bosnian nobility:

> It created the prerequisites for the emergence of a class of hereditary nobles unknown and, incidentally, not recognized elsewhere in the Ottoman Empire. The members of this local nobility that was now forming could therefore consider Bosnia their *inalienable homeland* [...].[107]

The Bosnian Muslim elites expressed their self-assurance, among other ways, by calling themselves 'Bosnjak'—and this exclusively in the Muslim sense. This happened from the seventeenth century onwards and became more and more common until into the nineteenth century, also as an external ascription.[108] It was in opposition to the name *Turci*, which was also common both as a self-given as well as an external ascription.[109] To distinguish themselves from their non-Muslim surroundings they simply called themselves 'Muslims', too.[110]

Some, however, laid great importance on the term 'Bosnjak' as a Bosnian anecdote shows. The sermons of an Istanbul *hatib*[111] regularly spoiled a Bosnian *spahi* the Friday mood, for the *hatib* mentioned only

Arabs and Azems (Persians and other non-Arabs) but never Bosnians. The *hatib* defended himself in front of the grim *spahi* by saying that by Azems he also meant Bosnians. However, the next time, the stubborn *hatib* did not deviate from his usual sermon, till the *spahi* put his hand on his sword. Then the intimidated *hatib* quickly added: '. . . vel Bosniakati'—'. . . and the Bosnians, too.'[112]

This tension was not confined to words only. The determination to achieve regional self-assertion led to serious rows among fellow believers. The Bosnian provincial rulers were very powerful thanks to a very regionally organized administrative structure.[113] Malcolm lists conflicts by the dozens between rebellious Bosnian *beys*, *kapetans*,[114] *ajans*,[115] and the Ottoman governors who now and then made their troops march in, as in 1813, 1827 and 1828 in Sarajevo, in 1814 in Mostar, and in 1820 in Mostar, Srebrenica, Banja Luka, and Derventa. Istanbul's attempts to centralize the administrative structure encountered stiff resistance.

The Bosnian-Muslim activists showed their defiance in another field as well. The Muslim elite developed a typical Bosnian conservatism out of its defensiveness against the non-Muslim neighbours *as well as* against the Ottoman rulers. On the one hand, it meant using the Arabic script—directed against its neighbours—'through which, for the first time in the written culture, dividing lines between the Serbian-Orthodox and the Croatian-Catholic ethnic groups were drawn and the hitherto common traditions in this respect were broken off', says Miedlig.[116] In addition, the Muslim scholars put up resistance against the Sultan at the Bosporus. Dogmatic differences cropped up between the fellow believers and came to the surface most clearly during the period of the *tanzimat* (reform) in the nineteenth century. The Bosnian *ulema* condemned the modernization of the social and political life as 'un-Islamic' and 'Western'. The clerics were annoyed in particular by the new legal equality of all citizens (i.e. also of non-Muslims). The *ulema* persisted in its orthodox Islamic traditionalism[117] which the ordinary Muslim population mostly followed.

In the light of this observation, the interpretations hardly seem credible that Bosnian Muslims considered the Ottoman rule as their own, or that the Bosnian nobility were the 'strongest supporters'[118] of the Ottomans. Rather regional interests played a greater role than religious ones.[119] The evaluation of this fact once again leads to completely contrasting statements in the literature. A part of the confusion can be attributed to the problem that authors use the terms 'ethnic' and 'national' differently, perhaps carelessly or retrospectively.

Pasic sees the identity of 'the Bosnian Muslims' as fully Ottoman and uses this as an opportunity to call them a 'special *ethnic* community'.[120] Ipsen, in contrast, sees in this a 'profound orientalizing of Bosnia' precisely the reason why Bosnia-Herzegovina persisted in a 'pre-national' stage.[121] Others, in turn, take the demarcation against the Ottomans to upgrade 'the Bosnian Muslims' as a group. Birnbaum says:

> Thus a separate Muslim *national* consciousness gradually emerged in the territory of B&H based on religious identification, specific cultural and social conditions, shared historic experience and economic factors, and nourished also by an increased suspicion against the Ottoman Empire and its intents in Bosnia.[122]

Again others see in this demarcation just the opposite. For instance, Miedlig writes:

> The rejection of the social and political modernization decreed by the Ottoman reformers at the same time also implied the prevention of the formation of 'ethnicity' [...] within their own *traditionally* perceived large group. Because of this fixed conservatism which was in the first place religious, further class-specific and characterized by a strongly regionalistic *anti-Turkish* self-consciousness, it could not consider itself as an 'ethnos' with the will to develop into a modern 'nation', unlike the Bosnian Serbs and Croats who were lucky in addition because they could fall back on their respective motherland. One stuck to the traditional pattern of the Islamic 'denominational nation' (*Konfessionsnation*) which was furthermore state supporting and ruling.[123]

According to my point of view Miedlig employed the terms 'ethnos' and 'nation' most appropriately and, going by the state of research, applied them aptly to the Bosnian Muslims before 1878. For an 'ethnic' or even 'national' consciousness of Bosnian Muslims seems questionable, especially in view of the social and economic backwardness of the country (therefore: 'traditional' group). Until into the second half of the nine-teenth century, Muslim and Orthodox peasants formed spontaneous alliances against landlords or tax collectors. Muslims, Christians, and Jews lived and worked together in the cities self-evidently and without any problems.[124] 'Ethnicity' existed neither in the objective nor in the subjective sense. Much less could such an ascription superimpose itself on other cleavages. The same was probably true of the majority of peasants of other beliefs. Accordingly, Malcolm concludes: '[B]asic causes of anger and unrest were economic rather than religious.'[125]

The classification of 'the Muslims' in Bosnia-Herzegovina is extremely difficult. They were Islamic but not in bondage to the Ottomans. They collaborated and rebelled. They were Bosnian but also oriental. Some were simply peasants, craftsmen, labourers—just like their neighbours of whichever faith.

Bosnian society was traditional, local, and regional. These factors competed with the religious bonds to Istanbul. Finally, a typical Bosnian conservatism emerged which was defensively directed against Christians on both sides *and* against the Ottomans. So one judgement can be placed in the realm of fables: the Ottoman period had been the 'Golden Age' of Bosnia-Herzegovina. Rather this selective appropriation of the past is the work of Bosnian Muslim nationalists of the twentieth century.

2.2. The Ottomans and Indian Self-consciousness

'Turkey is almost as much or as little the Fatherland of Indian Mussalmans as of the Turks themselves.'[126] These are the words of Muhammad Ali, leader of the Indian Khilafat movement of the 1920s. The proud utterances of 1914 were already part of his political agitation and reflect pan-Islamic intentions. Here two parallels between Bosnia-Herzegovina and India can be drawn:

(1) This attitude is typical of Muslim circles which recall their religious ties with the political centre of Istanbul. In both countries this can be observed more or less at the same time.

(2) The pan-Islamic nostalgia stands in contrast to the relationship between converted Muslim locals and the former invaders since the Middle Ages.

How Bosnian Muslims tried to demarcate themselves from the Ottomans has been explained above. They were more strongly exposed to a relatively well-organized Ottoman authority than the Indians. The centre of power at the Bosporus was nearer to the Bosnians. Their area was smaller. Despite impressive constructions the presence of the Ottomans was much less evident in Indian everyday life than in the Balkans. The Muslim elite in India of Turkish, Persian, and Arab descent was small and limited to warriors, teachers, and administrators.

There was no massive immigration. The existing social structure remained intact.[127]

However, at the court of the Mughals itself the number of foreign-born Muslims was high. Under Akbar (1556-1605) and Aurangzeb (1658-1707) they amounted to about 70 per cent.[128] A non-Indian descent was career-promoting to such an extent that many showed off with fictitious ancestors. One popular trick was marrying Kashmiri girls. Because of their fair skin, they and their progeny were to pass for Turks or Persians.[129]

From these examples one cannot infer a strong Muslim Indian self-consciousness. As described above, the caste system dictated the social hierarchy. Many cleavages ran through the Muslim population. Social status, syncretisms, regional customs, and languages prevented a general 'ethnic' consciousness of the Indian Muslims which could have been directed against the Ottomans. This was true both subjectively and objectively. Nobody at that time proclaimed an Indo-Muslim community. This came about only later.

A deliberate demarcation of Indian Muslims against the Ottoman and Arab ruling elite *cannot* be observed in India to the extent as in Bosnia. The society in India was, as in Bosnia, traditional, local, and regional. The influence of the Ottoman elite was restricted to the ruling dynasties.

3. THE OTTOMAN *MILLET* AS A NATIONAL FORGE?

3.1. Bosnia-Herzegovina

The Ottomans brought to Bosnia more than just a new religion. Their social and political institutions influenced life in the Balkans for almost 500 years. For the nation-building the system of *millets* is of particular importance.

During the Ottoman rule freedom of worship prevailed.[130] The religious minorities could also organize themselves quite independently—in their *millets*. The Arabic word *milla* means 'religion' or 'religious community'. Literally, *milla* stands for 'word' and thus it means a group that accepts a particular word or script as its guide.[131] In modern Turkish it took on the meaning of 'nation'.[132] This etymological transformation reflects a social and political development which the *millet* system could have triggered.

In the *millets* the religious leaders took over political tasks as well. They collected taxes and were the highest authorities of civil law. The *millet* financed church institutions, schools, and hospitals—and only its own.[133] This local self-government based on religion had far-reaching consequences:

(1) It increased the influence of the clergy. This applies to the minority *millets* as well as to the Muslim ones.[134] Suttner speaks of an 'extremely active but unreligious participation in the life of the parishes'. This means the secular consequences (e.g. sanctions in the case of tax offence) made it impossible even for non-believers to turn their backs on the church. 'For only the remaining within the social fabric of the parish ensured a continued legal security in the civic sense.'[135]

(2) The *millets* became the 'crystallization-cores for collective identities'.[136] They combined religion, lifestyle, community, 'ethnicity' and eventually ethno-nation.[137] (It must be said that in a *millet* various ethnic groups—regional or linguistic ones—could gather under the common religious hub.[138]) Because religion merged into ethno-nation in course of time, Muslims often called themselves *islamiki millet*. Otherwise the term *islamiki narod* (Islamic people) was rather common.[139] Babuna considers the *millets* to be a factor that was more formative for Muslims than for the other groups:

> In the case of the Bosnian Muslims, who were of South Slav origin like Serbs and Croats, religion represented the most important distinction from the other ethnic groups. For this reason, religion played the role of an important ethnic boundary between the three different ethnic groups.
>
> In addition to the basically anti-national character of the Islamic religion, the millet system, in which nationality and religion had blended, determined the ethnic and national development of the Bosnian Muslims more than it did in the case of Serbs and Croats.[140]

But the *millet* is considered an important factor for the other competing groups, too. Banac writes that: the *millet* 'was a great instrument for the spread of Serb national identity in the Western Balkans'.[141]

Riedel, on the contrary, lays emphasis on the possibility of cross-cutting identities in the traditional social structure of the *millets*. In this way, a Slav, Croat, Serb, etc. living in Bosnia could have converted to Islam and at the same time call himself either a Bosnian, Muslim, Croat, Serb, or Slav. Riedel states that 'the national affiliation becomes a bone of contention only when politicians declare it as something objectively measurable and demand exclusiveness'.[142] Only then the conditions are given that the identity features religion and ethnicity cannot cross-cut any more but (have to) overlap as religion and 'ethnicity'.

There are good reasons to consider the *millet* system as a formative factor for a *specific*, that is, strongly religiously oriented nation-building—as *one* factor. For this religious self-government, for instance, cannot sufficiently explain why the 'ethnic' and ultimately the ethno-national consciousness of the Orthodox and Catholics in Bosnia grew faster and stronger than that of the Muslims.

3.2. India

For the Muslims in India the concept of a minority *millet* was the only possibility. The idea came about not through an Ottoman state organization as in Bosnia-Herzegovina. Rather it helped Muslim thinkers to define 'their' community against the Hindu majority. The change of meaning of *millet,* as mentioned above, applies to the Indian case in exactly the same way as to the Bosnian one.

At the time of the Khilafat movement in the 1920s, the moderate Islamic organization Jamiat-i-Ulama-i-Hind sought the support of the Hindu-dominated Congress Party under Gandhi. In this context it used the concept of *millet* to define the Islamic community as an independent but *integrative* component of Indian society. It rooted its solidarity in the organization of an Islamic education system and in the spiritual leadership of the *ulema*. With this the organization did not imply any political independence, following the Ottoman tradition. In an independent India the Jamiat-i-Ulama-i-Hind could have imagined a predominantly non-Muslim government. The Muslim *millet* would have found its place there and administrated itself according to Islamic law (the Sharia).[143]

Only twenty years later the concept of *millet* was equated with a 'Muslim nation', which reveals the speedy politicization of the 'ethnic groups'. This definition can be found in the minutes of the Muslim League Party conference in Punjab (17 November 1942).[144] The source and the date leave no room for doubts. It implied a separate Muslim state—Pakistan.

Those who saw the Muslim nation in the tradition of the *millet* followed a strongly religiously connoted concept of nation in India as well. Not all Muslims, however, shared this interpretation—including Jinnah, who postulated Pakistan as a secular state and who did not want to know anything about the Sharia. Islamic vocabulary (words like *millet*) and symbolism only served the purpose of generating mass appeal. In contrast, the Jamiat-i-Ulama-i-Hind, with its traditional *millet* concept, opposed the partition of India till the very end. Thus the interpretation of *millet* developed along the existing inner Muslim cleavages.

Comparative view

The concept of *millet* in its traditional sense is politically *integrative*. It allows several communities with different forms of organization and views of religion to live in one state. The *millet* in its modern sense is *separatist*. Because of the elements that were brought in as a reason for political autonomy, the modern *millet* is a model of ethno-nationalism of a strongly religious nature. In Bosnia-Herzegovina as well as in India it has by and large adopted this meaning.

NOTES

1. Lapidus (1988), pp. 244, 247.
2. For a discussion on Islam in Bosnia-Herzegovina, see: Algar, in: *IS* (1997), p. 243; Poulton (1991), p. 41. For a discussion on Islam in India, see: Schimmel (1983).
3. Balic (1994), pp. 36, 83ff; Balic (1997), in: *IS*, pp. 138ff; Reuter (1992), in: *SOE*, p. 665.
4. For a thorough and lucid account in: Fine, see: Pinson (1996), pp. 11ff; Miedlig (1994), pp. 26ff; Höpken, in: Kappeler/Simon/Brunner (1989), pp. 18ff.
5. For a more detailed account on Bogomilism, refer to: Malcolm (1996), pp. 27ff; Dzaja (1978; 1984); Balic (1992), pp. 90ff; Bauer (1971); Fine (1975), whom Dzaja (1978), in: *MZB* criticizes, interprets the Bogomil myth as a 'nativistic movement' with socio-revolutionary character (see: Dzaja (1984), p. 221).
6. Alexander, in: Wolff and Hoensch (1987), p. 34.
7. The thesis postulated in such clear terms can be found particularly often in earlier treatises, for instance in: Ipsen, in: Markert (1954), pp. 29ff;

Stavrianos (1958), p. 63; Hadzijahic (1962), in: *SOF*, 192; Purivata, in: Blagojevic (1974); Bauer (1971), p. 28, but surprisingly also in more recent works, for instance in: Bell-Fialkoff (1999), p. 124; Mønnesmann (1997); Hösch (1995), p. 83; Reuter (1992), in: *SOE*, p. 665. Even the cor-respondent of the *Frankfurter Allgemeine Zeitung (FAZ)*, Viktor Meier, conjectures: 'Their close connection with Bogomilism was certainly an important cause of their easy conversion' [Meier, in: Schönfeld (1987), p. 127].

8. Höpken, in: Kappeler, Simon and Brunner (1989), p. 182.
9. For more see Chapter IV.6.1.2. 'Nation Via Decree: The Bosnian Speciality'.
10. Purivata, in: Blagojevic (1974), p. 307.
11. See also: Irwin (1984), in: *EEQ*, p. 445.
12. Purivata, in: Blagojevic (1974), p. 317.
13. See also: Steindorff (1997), in: *SOEM*, p. 279.
14. Dzaja (1984), pp. 28-9.
15. Muslim noble landlords (Turkish).
16. Dzaja (1978), p. 69. He refers to research conducted by V. Cubrilovic in 1935 (based on sources from the fifteenth century) which has been con-firmed today.
17. Dzaja (1984), p. 27.
18. Dzaja (1984), pp. 26ff exposed this manipulation through his research into the primary sources.
19. Miedlig (1994), p. 8; Balic (1992), p. 33.
20. Hondius (1968), pp. 43-4.
21. See in particular Malcolm (1996), p. 53; Dzaja (1978), pp. 69ff; Dzaja (1984), pp. 36ff; Birnbaum (1987), in: *WS*, pp. 14ff; Thomas, in: Thomas/Friman (1996), p. 19.
22. Miedlig (1994), p. 29.
23. This was first pointed out by the Bosnian researcher Nedim Filipovic. See in particular: Malcolm (1996), p. 52; Dzaja (1978), pp. 72ff; Balic (1992), pp. 90ff. Lapidus (1988), p. 309 refers to a census of 1520-30, according to which only 19 per cent of the population in the Balkans were Muslim. In Bosnia-Herzegovina it was 45 per cent. Everywhere most of the Muslims lived in cities.
24. Dzaja (1978), p. 84.
25. Malcolm (1996), p. 59.
26. Fine, in: Pinson (1996), p. 19. See also: Lapidus (1988), p. 309.
27. Purivata in an interview with the author in Sarajevo (27 June 2000). He stated that in the 1960s, he only had findings available from the Yugoslav author Aleksandar Soloviev.
28. For a more detailed discussion see: Malcolm (1996), pp. 27ff.
29. Dzaja, in: Weithmann (1994), p. 152.

30. Steindorff (1997), in: *SOEM*, p. 279. Malcolm (1996), pp. 27ff gives a detailed account of the doubts that exist in considering the church as 'Bogomil'. He himself, however, abstains from passing any judgement.
31. This is Fine's claim in: Pinson (1996), p. 8. However, he refers mostly to sources from Catholic Dubrovnik. Thus, he runs the risk of following the denominational (later: national) appropriation attempts from the Catholic side. This scepticism is particularly appropriate because the Franciscans in Bosnia-Herzegovina were notorious for acting in a particularly aggressive manner.
32. Malcolm (1996), pp. 28-9; S. Ramet (1990), in: *SSJ*, p. 5.
33. Höpken, in: Kappeler, Simon and Brunner (1989), p. 182; see also: Heywood, in: Pinson (1996), pp. 39ff; Calic (1996a), p. 29.
34. Hadzijahic (1962), in: *SOF*, p. 178.
35. Dzaja (1984), p. 40. By contrast, Reuter pleads for continuity. Since previously there were already some Muslims scattered in Bosnia-Herzegovina, 'for Bosnia the conquest of the Balkans by the Ottomans did not imply the beginning but the decisive intensification of the Islamization process' [Reuter (1992), in: *SOE*, p. 665]. Miedlig has an entirely different view. He considers the year 1463 to be a 'radical break with the economic, social and cultural development of the medieval Bosnia' [Miedlig (1994), p. 26].
36. Compare Dzaja (1984), p. 220.
37. See: Savarkar (1922), Golwalkar (1938). Both paved the way for the Hindu nationalist organization the Rashtriya Swayamsevak Sangh (RSS), from whose ranks emerged the murderer of M.K. Gandhi. For the 'Aryan' concepts of Tilak and Aurobindo see also: A. Smith (1996), in: *IA*, p. 456.
38. This argument has been particularly clearly disclosed and refuted by: Thapar (1975), (1992), (1996); Satish Chandra (1996); Jaffrelot (1996), pp. 26ff.

    With this thesis the Hindu nationalists got caught up in several contradictions: (1) If the Aryans are supposed to be 'natives', the thesis of immigration and conquest would become problematic. (2) The low-caste Hindus and outcastes as well as the Dravidians from Southern India are kept outside of the Hindu-'Aryan' concept. But at a time when questions of the political majority played an ever greater role, the Hindu nationalists needed this very large number of people as a potential force of mobilization against 'the Muslims'.
39. Müller (1859), (1861). For the Hindu nationalists' reference to Müller, his instrumentalization of ethno-national historiography, and the contradictions therein see: Rothermund (1986b), pp. 47ff.
40. For a critical appraisal, see Thapar (1996), pp. 15ff.
41. Kennedy, in: Erdosy (1997), pp. 35ff.
42. Thapar (1975), p. 12 (1996), p. 9.
43. Nehru (1946a), pp. 72ff.

44. Thapar (1975), p. 6, (1996), p. 24; Satish Chandra (1996), p. 33.
45. A good overview in: Flood (1996), pp. 31ff.
46. The dispute of the academic camps is very well documented in the anthology of Erdosy (1997). Of particular interest are essays by Erdosy, Kennedy, and Witzel. See also: Mallory (1989); Poliakov (1974); Renfrew (1987).
47. These include in particular: Thapar (1992a), (1996); Satish Chandra (1996); Chowdhury (1993); Biswas (1990).
48. Talageri (1993).
49. Satish Chandra, in: Grover and Arora (1997b), p. 83. Pakistani historians who justify the Two-Nation Theory with reference to the past are, for example, Mahmud Husain, I.H. Qureshi, S.M. Ikram, und Moinul Haq.
50. Jalal, in: *IJMES* (1995), p. 80.
51. Nayar, in: Grover and Arora, Vol. I (1997b), p. 33.
52. An amusing overview can be found in: Jalal (1995), in: *IJMES*, pp. 78ff.
53. Jinnah in a speech at the Aligarh University (10 March 1941). Kaushik/Kaushik, in: Grover and Arora, Vol. I (1997b), p. 44.
54. Jalal, in: *IJMES* (1995), p. 78.
55. Satish Chandra (1996), p. 45.
56. A.S. Ahmed (1997), p. 104.
57. A more detailed account in Chapter VI.2.1 'Pakistan: In Search of the Nation'.
58. Mikic, in: Bernhard and Kandler-Pálsson (1986), p. 339.
59. Kennedy, in: Erdosy (1997), pp. 60-1.
60. For instance in Bauer (1971), p. 17.
61. Malcolm (1996), p. 63.
62. Malcolm (1996), p. 65; Balic (1992), p. 99.
63. Horse-mounted feudal lords (Turkish).
64. Malcolm (1996), p. 65.
65. Malcolm (1996), p. 65.
66. Hondius (1968), p. 51.
67. Birnbaum (1987), in: *WS*, p. 19.
68. Reuter (1992), in: *SOE*, p. 666. See also: Reuter-Hendrichs (1988), pp. 9ff; P. Ramet, in: Kappeler, Simon and Bruniner (1989), pp. 107ff; Babuna (1996), p. 84; Castellan (1991), p. 353 mentions 6,000 to 7,000 *kmets* (serfs), and 85,000 beys; out of these three-fourths were Orthodox, one-fourth were Catholics, and only 'a few thousand' were Muslims. Wandruszka and Urbanitsch, Vol. 3 (1980), p. 666 mention three-fourths Orthodox *kmets.* Here one can also find more detailed statistics on the social structure with respect to religious ascription.
69. See also: Dzaja (1994), p. 41; Malcolm (1996), p. 94.

70. Milojevic, in: Devetak, Flere and Seewann (1993), pp. 146ff even claims that the war in Bosnia-Herzegovina in 1992-5 can be explained by the unequal distribution of income. The Muslims were able to extend their income even further under a favourable Yugoslav regime. Against this argument, however, it could be held that under Tito state and church were separated, and thereby the Muslim community as such lost valuable possessions (nationalization of *vakufs*). But all in all, the position of the Muslim nation (in the Yugoslav sense) improved indeed in course of Yugoslav history.
71. For an in-depth discussion on the medieval history of India and Islam see: Schimmel (1983); Sharma (1996); and V.A. Smith (1990).
72. Compare: Mukhia, in: Thapar, Mukhia and Chandra (1969), p. 25.
73. Lelyveld (1996), p. 25.
74. Y. Singh (1996), p. 69; Gore (1996), in: *SS*, p. 36. For a detailed account of Akbar's life and his reforms see: Athar (1996), in: *SS*, pp. 83ff.
75. Ruthven (2000), p. 272.
76. Rashid, in: M.A. Khan (1985), p. 73.
77. Dixit (1974), p. 133.
78. Thapar (1992a), p. 78; Thapar, in: Thapar, Mukhia and Chandra (1969), p. 8.
79. Schimmel (1983), p. 18.
80. Y. Singh (1996), p. 74; Gore (1996), in: *SS*, pp. 35ff; Roy, in: Oddie (1998), pp. 29ff; Sharma (1996), pp. 186ff.
81. Sharma (1996), p. 183.
82. Hasan (1997b), p. 8.
83. Schimmel (1983), p. 20.
84. Y. Singh (1996), p. 69; Schimmel (1983), pp. 8-9, 11-13; Sharma (1996), p. 197.
85. Dixit (1974), p. 20.
86. Y. Singh (1996), pp. 79-80; Dixit (1974), p. 5.
87. For examples from daily life, see: Hasan (1997b), pp. 34-5.
88. D.S. Khan (1997), p. 269. The so-called Nazari believers in Rajasthan were attached to various cults from the broad spectrum of Hindu traditions. In the thirteenth and fourteenth centuries missionaries came from Multan, the centre of the Ismaili branch of Shiites at that time. The Nazaris converted to Shiite Ismailism. When the central Islamic authority in Multan fell apart in the fifteenth century, the Nazaris were exposed to the influence of various religious groups and sects. With the arrival of religious sectarian thinking in recent times, the pressure on them increased to adopt either a Hindu, a Sunni or a 12-Imams Shia identity. Those who converted to Islam were forced to give up their earlier beliefs and practices. However,

those who came under the influence of local movements, and who call themselves 'Hindus' today, could retain their traditional heritage—which is strongly characterized by the Shia-Ismailism of the Middle Ages.

89. D.S. Khan (1997), p. 272.
90. See also: Brass (1974), pp. 122ff.
91. Gore (1996), in: *SS*, p. 35.
92. Bayly (1985), in: *MAS*, p. 193.
93. Jaffrelot (1996), p. 5.
94. Mukhia, in: Thapar, Mukhia and Chandra (1969), p. 34.
95. Bayly (1985), in: *MAS*, p. 192.
96. Seal (1971), p. 303; M.A. Khan (1985), p. 75.
97. B. Chandra, in: Thapar, Mukhia and Chandra (1969), pp. 52, 53.
98. Dixit (1974), p. 21.
99. Dixit (1974), p. 23.
100. Y. Singh (1996), pp. 13ff. For the different types of traditions, see also: Reiter (1984), p. 192. Also Rothermund (1965), p. 36 operates within these categories, which were coined by Redfield (1956).
101. Algar, in: *IS* (1997), p. 243.
102. Steindorff, in: *SOEM* (1997), p. 288.
103. Pasic (1971), in: *ISSJ*, p. 407.
104. Ipsen, in: Markert (1954), p. 30.
105. Miedlig (1994), p. 31.
106. Used in a limited sense and not without a headache, like Reiter (1984), p. 194. See Chapter I.2.1. 'Crumbling Components'.
107. Birnbaum (1987), in: *WS*, p. 19 (italics added).
108. Miedlig (1994), p. 31; Malcolm (1996), p. 148, Hadzijahic (1962), in: *SOF*, p. 192.
109. See example: Steindorff (1997), in: *SOEM*, p. 280; Banac, in: Pinson (1996), p. 133.
110. Clayer and Popovic, in: Hasan (1998), p. 406.
111. Muslim preacher.
112. Banac, in: Pinson (1996), p. 133. He refers to Salihagic (1940), p. 20.
113. Malcolm (1996), pp. 89ff and 119ff.
114. Military governor.
115. City and province governor.
116. Miedlig (1994), p. 32; see also: Dzambo (1985), pp. 23-5; Kind (1994), p. 55. For more on the developments of languages, see Chapter IV.3. 'The "Ethnicization" of Language'.
117. Miedlig (1994), p. 32.
118. Bauer (1971), p. 28.
119. Ivo Andric also describes the notorious Bosnian Muslim stubborness in his novel *Omer Pascha-Latas: Der Marschall des Sultans* (1983).

120. Pasic (1971), in: *ISSJ*, p. 408 (italics added).
121. Ipsen, in: Markert (1954), p. 30.
122. Birnbaum (1987), in: *WS*, p. 19 (italics added).
123. Miedlig (1994), pp. 32-3 (original italics).
124. Numerous examples in: Malcolm (1996), pp. 129ff.
125. Malcolm (1996), p. 130.
126. Dixit (1974), p. 67.
127. Lapidus (1988), p. 248.
128. A detailed list of elites in the court of the Mughuls with reference to descent and religion can be found in: Dixit (1974), pp. 13-15.
129. Dixit (1974), p. 15.
130. This applied at least to all monotheistic faiths, like to Christians and Jews. Non-Muslims, however, had to pay a special tax, as mentioned above.
131. Lewis (1988), pp. 38ff.
132. Riedel (1997), in: *SOE*, p. 559. See also: Lewis (1988), p. 41; Ursinus (1989), in: SOEF, pp. 195ff; Grunebaum (1984), pp. 87ff; Sugar (1977), p. 44; Lopasic (1981), in: *BSMESB*, p. 115.
133. For a background to the *millet* system, see also: Castellan (1991), pp. 118ff; Freidenreich (1971), pp. 14ff; Karpat (1997), in: *IS*, pp. 332ff; Karpat, in: Esman and Rabinovich (1988), pp. 35ff; Braude and Lewis (1982); Lewis, in: Michalski (1995), pp. 103ff; Wandruszka and Urbanitsch (1980), pp. 767-8.

    It was not until around the mid nineteenth century, during the Tanzimat, that the spiritual guidance of the *millets* was called into question. A new middle class demanded competences from the religious leaders. The state was centralized and acquired, among other things, a monopoly over legal and educational matters. For this see: Shaw and Shaw (1977), pp. 123-4. For the functions that laymen could take over in the *millets* from the 1860s see: Karpat (1997), in: *IS*, p. 344. Karpat finds that these laymen jobs further strengthened the 'ethnic' component of the *millets*.
134. At first, *millets* were only meant for minorities. Two *millets* were introduced under Mehement II from the very beginning (1453): the Orthodox and the Armenian. The Jewish *millet* was very active, too, although it was officially approved only in 1839. The Muslim *millet* was the only one that belonged to the bureaucratic elite and which took a high position. See: Babuna (1996), pp. 30ff, 138-9. Lewis, in: Michalski (1995), p. 104 lists four main *millets*: Muslims, Greeks, Armenians, and Jews.
135. Suttner (1997), in: *SOEM*, p. 7.
136. Calic (1996a), p. 27.
137. See also: Benbassa and Rodrigue (1993), p. 80: 'Le cemaat ou taife, appelé plus tard millet, ou communauté éthnico-religieuse, était la forme la plus

avancée d'un mode d'autogouvernement [...]. Il se rapprochait beaucoup de la "nation" qu'on connaissait en Europe, avec ses privilèges et ses restrictions.'

138. Lewis, in: Michalski (1995), p. 104.
139. Babuna (1996), pp. 32, 139.
140. Babuna (1996), p. 32.
141. Banac (1984), pp. 65-6.
142. Riedel (1997), in: *SOE*, p. 559.
143. Gilmartin, in: Burke and Lapidus (1988), p. 152.
144. Bakshi, Vol. II (1997), p. 207.

IV. The Politicization of the Muslims

In the early stage described so far, the terms 'ethnic' and 'national' make little sense to describe a group. The same is true for labels such as 'Serbs' and 'Croats' etc. The cleavage between Indian and Pakistani was meaningless in the first place, even through the popular historical rearview mirror. For the word Pakistan was artificially coined just a few years before the foundation of the state—and with this creation the tiresome problem of how to name the 'Muslims in the national sense', which has plagued the Bosnian Muslims until today, could be quickly taken off the agenda.

We are still in the pre-state phase of the Muslims in Bosnia-Herzegovina and India. Now starts the period of objective and exclusive ascription of people into different 'ethnic groups'. Everyone is born into a fixed framework. Nobody can (or is allowed to) change it. Gradually, more and more 'cultural' and 'political' connotations are added to religion.

1. CONSTRUCTING ETHNO-NATIONAL CAMPS

1.1. BOSNIA-HERZEGOVINA

1.1.1. *New Labels for Political Goals*

In the preceding chapters national classifications were avoided because, until the nineteenth century, the situation in Bosnia-Herzegovina can best be described in the words of Malcolm: '[W]hether the inhabitants of Bosnia were really Croat or really Serb it cannot be answered for two reasons: first, because we lack evidence, and secondly, because the question lacks meaning.'[1] Fine agrees with this statement, noting that it was only from 1878 onwards that the nationalists began to teach 'that if one is a Catholic, one is a Croat; if one is an Orthodox, one is a Serb. But in terms of the origins of these Bosnian Catholics and

Orthodox, this was nonsense.'[2] This is why it is equally meaningless as well as thoughtless to claim that the Muslims in Bosnia-Herzegovina 'were simply Serbs or Croats who [. . .] converted to Islam', as the BBC correspondents Silber and Little do.[3] Also, international mediators in the Bosnian war shared the same view.[4] Such statements are grist to the mills of Serb and Croatian ethno-nationalists because they encourage an ideological appropriation of 'the Muslims' as 'actual' Croats or Serbs. When the present-day Muslims became Muslims, the Orthodox called themselves Orthodox and not Serbs, and the Catholics called themselves Catholics and not Croats. Those who judge like Silber and Little confuse different stages of historical development. Since these very phases are decisive for the ideology of ethno-nationalists, a political judgement is automatically associated with such statements.

In such a thought pattern religious affiliation defines the nationality,[5] and vice versa. The following pages show how religion was increasingly interpreted in an exclusive way and stylized as a starting point of exclusive 'cultures' and 'history'. Besides, it becomes clear how ethno-nationalists linked and still link this with the demand for an exclusive territory.

Initially, it was nothing more than gross ideological patterns which had little to do with the reality of the Balkans—but which anticipated the development, in some way, as a self-fulfilling prophecy. The Serb and the Croatian nation-building processes were always further advanced than the one of the Bosnian Muslims.[6] The latter contributed least to 'ethnic' and, finally, ethno-national concepts.

1.1.2. *To Whom Does Bosnia Belong?*

> It is our misfortune that we are living between two aggressive Balkan states.[7]
>
> *Adil Zulfikarpasic*

In the middle of the nineteenth century both Christian churches experienced a boom in Bosnia-Herzegovina. The centre of the Ottoman Empire showed signs of decline. The churches in the provinces prospered. Orthodox and Catholics vied with each other for new followers. Some of them carried out not only religious but also political agitation. In Sarajevo during the 1860s, for instance, a teacher of an Orthodox school, Teofil Petranovic, summoned a group of people. They went from village to village and demanded that the peasants not call themselves 'Orthodox' any more but rather identify themselves as 'Serbs'. Similar things happened in Banja Luka and other places.[8] The Bosnian Muslim authorities were surprisingly tolerant towards these forms of agitation.

Thus, the 'ethnicization' of religion was given a free reign. The Orthodox Church in particular played an important role within Serb nationalism. The self-confidence of the clergy had risen tremendously since the Ottomans recognized the Serb patriarchy as independent in 1557. The Orthodox dignitaries called themselves 'holders of the Serb throne'. Serb Orthodox monks, who went on a pilgrimage to Russia in the seventeenth and eighteenth centuries, portrayed the whole southern Slavic area as 'Serb'.[9]

Serb ideologues did the same. The Serb representative of enlightenment, Dositej (1742-1811), spoke of the 'Slavo-Serb nation' which also included the Bosnian Muslims. He explained: 'One can change rites and belief but never tribe and language.'[10] These words formed the basis for the works of the famous author, Vuk Stefanovic Karadzic (1787-1864). Still today, Radovan Karadzic, the Serb warlord in Bosnia-Herzegovina, likes to refer to 'his ancestor' with regard to ideology and name.[11] In 1836 Vuk Karadzic coined the phrase which was rediscovered by Serb ethno-nationalists for the Bosnian war in 1992-5: 'Srbi svi i svuda' (all Serbs and Serbs everywhere). However, Karadzic meant it differently from what his supposed descendants interpret today. He detached Serbism from its religious exclusiveness. The Serb nation should instead define itself by a common language. This Serb-dominated pan-Slavism also included the Muslims (though not all Croats, and not even all Serbs in the sense of a national pan-Serbism).[12]

The Serb geographer Jovan Cvijic went as far as to describe Bosnia-Herzegovina as the 'core land' and the 'heart' of the Serb people. The law graduate and later diplomat Miroslav Spalajkovic wrote in his dissertation in 1899 that 'the most noble part of the Serb masses, that part whose blood remained purest from any foreign tinge', had its home in Bosnia-Herzegovina.[13]

Similar flattery came from the Croatian side. The ideologist of the great Croatian Law Party, Ante Starcevic (1825-96), saw the Bosnian-Muslim upper class as 'the oldest European and the purest Croatian nobility'.[14] Following the example of Karadzic, the Croatian linguist Ljudevit Gaj (1809-72) included parts of Bosnia-Herzegovina in the spacial image of a South Slavic ideology and justified it on the basis of the common language.[15] He himself contributed to a linguistic homogenization by turning from Kaykavian into Stokavian in his writings. Thus he strengthened 'Serbo-Croatian' as a written language (even if it continued to have different typefaces). In this way, Gaj deprived Croatian nationalism of any linguistic justification but he gave Serb, and, later, Croatian ethno-nationalists a pretext for their expansionism.[16]

Gaj and Croatian Illyrism[17] (later South Slavism) considered all Slavs as one people, including the Bosnian Muslims. The bishop of Zagreb and linguist Josip Strosmayer (1815-1905) and his friend, Father Franjo Racki, followed the same idea.[18] These concepts were essentially supranational. The US journalist and author Kaplan even calls Strosmayer a philanthropist in order to contrast him with the supporters of 'cruel' ethno-nationalism.[19]

The problem with the South Slavic movements was only that they radicalized in the course of time and, supported by political parties, degenerated into pan-Serbism or pan-Croatianism.[20] In this way the protagonists of an exclusive nationalism maintained an upper hand around the turn of the century. This made 'the Muslims' fall between all stools.

The appropriation of Bosnia-Herzegovina did not remain a subject of ideologues only but took shape in concrete territorial plans. In July 1876 Serbia and Montenegro declared war against the Ottoman Empire; before this they had made an arrangement that Serbia should annex Bosnia and Montenegro Herzegovina.

With the outbreak of World War I and the decline of the Habsburg Empire, the question 'to whom does Bosnia belong?' appeared on the agenda once again. Suggestions to incorporate Bosnia-Herzegovina into a Great Croatia came from conservative Catholic circles under Archbishop Stadler. The spokesmen of the Bosnian Muslims oscillated between advocating autonomy within Hungary and calling for a Yugoslav state.[21] Finally, through South Slav realpolitik the latter option came into being in 1918 under the name of 'Kingdom of the Serbs, Croats, and Slovenes' (S.H.S. Kingdom). From 1929 on, it was called 'Kingdom of Yugoslavia'. This description was paradoxical because, on the one hand, the state was not created on the basis of a federalist Yugoslav philosophy but rather under Serb domination.[22] On the other hand, the state was formed around the myth of a nation state, even though the majority of the South Slavs never regarded themselves as one people.[23]

The myth did not hold for long. During World War II Serb Cetniks and Croatian Ustasha groups settled old scores of previous wars. The fascist 'Independent State of Croatia' (NDH), which was dependent on Nazi Germany and under the rule of the Ustasha leader Ante Pavelic (1889-1959), comprised the western parts of Bosnia-Herzegovina. Pavelic, too, considered the Muslims as actual Croats: 'Croat national consciousness never was extinguished in the Muslim element of Bosnia, and after the departure of the Turks has resurfaced.'[24] Most Muslims were ready for cooperation with the Croats. Pavelic declared them pro forma as 'a formative people of the state' along with the Croats.[25] But Muslims increasingly looked for direct contact with the German occupants against the harassments of the Ustasha. They were also afraid of the Cetniks who were especially brutal with Muslims. The terror unleashed by both sides finally led many Muslims into the hands of Tito's partisans, even though this happened with inhibitions and hesitations.[26]

With the 'new edition' of Yugoslavia in 1944, the multi-'ethnic' Yugoslav constituent republic of Bosnia-Herzegovina came into being.[27] In this framework 'the Muslims' were granted the status of a 'nation' in 1968. No sooner than the 'multinational' state crumbled in 1991, that 'the Bosnian Muslims' saw themselves once again confronted with unchecked appropriation attempts by their ethno-national neighbours. The arguments were similar to those made a hundred years ago. Croatia's former president Franjo Tudjman also described Bosnia-Herzegovina as a 'core land'—as a Croatian one, of course:

> [L]arge parts of Croatia had been incorporated into Bosnia by the Turks. Furthermore Bosnia and Hercegovina were historically linked with Croatia and they together comprise an indivisible geographic and economic entity. Bosnia and Hercegovina occupy the central part of this whole[. . .].[28]

The Catholic and the Muslim populations in Bosnia-Herzegovina were 'for the most part ethnically identical'. It is a 'historical fact', he said, that 'the majority of the Moslems is in its ethnic character and speech incontrovertibly of Croatian origin'.[29] To his friends Tudjman confided that he did not really hate Serbs but Bosnian Muslims. In

May 1995 he told a British parliamentarian that he preferred Milosevic to Izetbegovic.[30]

Tudjman's national aims were consequent and blunt. During the Bosnian war, on the occasion of some peace negotiations, he sketched his vision of Bosnia-Herzegovina on a napkin: fifty-fifty between Serbs and Croats.[31] Tudjman's diabolic logic was: 'The one who wanted to destroy Yugoslavia could not spare the "little Yugoslavia" Bosnia-Herzegovina (since the coexistence of Serbs, Croats and Muslims there would have been used as an international counter argument for irredentist plans elsewhere).'[32]

Thus he shared the same ideological wavelength with his Serb counterpart Slobodan Milosevic. During the Bosnian wars the state-controlled Belgrade-based *Ponos Radio* (Radio Pride) continuously played old and new 'folk music'. Most songs contained political or war themes. Among them were also some which sang the praises of the Serb claim over Bosnia-Herzegovina.[33]

So Tudjman and Milosevic—the leaders of the large so-called homelands of the Bosnian Serbs and the Croats respectively—were in one boat as far as Bosnia-Herzegovina was concerned. Before the war, in March 1991, they had both met in Tito's former hunting lodge in Karadjordjevo and discussed the partition of Bosnia.[34] This was only a logical consequence of the exclusive and simultaneously expansive nationalism which the presidents of Croatia and Serbia advocated.

When Bosnia-Herzegovina declared its independence after a plebiscite in April 1992 (which the majority of the Bosnian Serbs boycotted) and for the first time in its history was recognized as a sovereign state, it could only mean an affront against the radical ethno-national concepts of Croatia and Serbia.

In the nineteenth century religion ceased to remain just a matter of individual faith. It became an 'ethnic' feature. The labels in Bosnia-Herzegovina were no more 'Orthodox' or 'Catholic' only but 'Serb' or 'Croatian', supported by the respective so-called homelands of Serbia and Croatia. Pan-Serb and pan-Croatian ideologues tried to appropriate the nationally 'abandoned' Muslims with primordial arguments. Both attempts to carve out a Yugoslav state came in the way of such efforts, at least officially. After the fall of Yugoslavia Bosnia-Herzegovina once again landed in the Serbo-Croatian clutches.

1.2. India

1.2.1. *To Whom Does India Belong?*

The objective ascription of 'ethnic groups' and their labeling increased rapidly in the nineteenth century in India, too. The ethno-national codification of 'the Muslims', on the one hand, and the growth of a subjective Muslim consciousness, on the other, were accompanied by two modern developments: (1) British historiography and (2) the standardization and nationalization of Hindudom (*Hindutva*).

Both influences led to the hardening of fronts separating human-beings of Muslim and Hindu faith. Above all, this gave significance to a new factor: territory. The question 'to whom does India belong?' was raised from between the lines and led to a new competitive mentality. The postulate of a homeland arose. Political and economic resources were increasingly considered in terms of the 'own' group.

Even though without state and borders, the Hindu nationalists, to a certain extent, played the role of Serb and Croatian nationalists for the Indian Muslims. Their propaganda of an ethno-national homogenization provoked reactions from Muslim ideologues. Many Muslims suffered an economic decline due to 'their' loss of political power at the hands of the British in 1857 (as many saw it afterwards) and fell into political lethargy. 'The Hindus' were a step ahead with social modernization.

Unlike in the later Bosnia-Herzegovina, there were no already formed nations or even 'nation states' which projected their ideology on the Muslims, and which wanted to or did exercise power over them. However, Muslims, Hindus and others passed through the identity forge of a foreign power. The British state authority did not possess any aggressive neighbouring territory but, instead, it had penetrated Indian social life to its very depths. Thus, the British formed an important reference point, especially for Muslim spokesmen.

1.2.2. *India Through British Spectacles*

> The [British] regimess attempt to catalogue everything, 'public' and 'personal', 'sacred' and 'profane', and to record for succeeding generations 'established' customs and 'normal' practice that had always had a great deal of fluidity built into it, reinforced such matters as [religious] procession routes, timing, musical accompaniment, and made issues out of questions that had not been the subject of such serious, or continuous, contention before.[35]

Pandey, and many others, criticize that the meticulous cataloguing of social data encrusted flexible traditions and strengthened the thinking in religious camps.[36]

Another speciality of the colonial masters was the population census. As in socialist Yugoslavia, it had the effect of a catalyst for ethnic self-ascription and confusion. The first census of 1872 worked with four sub-divisions: aboriginals, Aryans, mixed people, and Muslims. In 1881 mixed people and aboriginals were placed together. What is noteworthy is that Muslims were treated as a homogeneous group from the beginning. This was far from the reality, as described above. The British made sub-groups for Hindus only. One census headline read: 'Caste if Hindu, otherwise religion.'[37]

In 1901 British census officers began classifying castes and communities according to their ritual purity and to their respect among the local population. This resulted in the mushrooming of caste-based associations and movements. Everyone wanted to be superior and purer, and combined this with political claims.[38]

The East India Company codified 'Hindu Law' for the first time. Since it was derived from the Brahman tradition, it was thus equated with 'Hinduism' as such.[39] A uniform code of law was now available, operational, and therefore interpretable and manipulable.

Pandey speaks of a 'colonial obsession with ethnic and doctrinal signs'. She points out cases where this added fuel to ethno-national fights.[40] As Thursby writes:

> [The] combination of the British bureaucratic construction of record-keeping categories with the British orientalist reconstruction of Indian culture contributed to the making of an image of each of the two great communities which supplied an ideological framework for their self-understanding and for separate community mobilization.[41]

Lelyveld, too, summarizes the British approach with a critical eye:

> [T]he British analysis had a way of becoming self-fulfilling, by freezing identities, chopping off ambiguities, and eventually providing the mold for associational activities. In the context of British power old social designations took on new meanings. Would-be Indian politicians would have to declare whom they represented, and do so in terms the British could understand.[42]

The censi, which were carried out with a great deal of expenditure, also contributed to a better administration and to the perpetuation of colonial power, of course. From the eighteenth century onwards, Cohn writes, 'nation states came to be seen as the natural embodiment of history, territory and society. The establishment and maintenance of these nation-states depended upon determining, codifying, and re-presenting the past'.[43] This is what the British did in India.

British historians introduced the division into periods with religious and national labels: the 'Hindu period' (before the eleventh century), the 'Muslim period' (until 1857), and the 'British period'.[44] Two things are striking here: (1) These categories made it easier for the ethno-nationalist ideologues to fall back on the convenient notion of a 'Golden Age'. (2) The first two labels have originally a religious connotation, the last one a national one. Bipan Chandra cuttingly remarks: '[N]one of them describe the British rule as Christian rule even though the higher bureaucracy was Christian to a far greater extent than the higher nobility of the Mughuls was Muslim.'[45]

This classification was no coincidence. It was not only the result of a predominance of military and diplomatic history over social and economic history but it also reflected the British understanding of Hindus and Muslims as two separate cultures, 'ethnic groups', and nations.[46] The following quotations show how unbridgeable the alleged Hindu-Muslim differences seemed to them.

The Minister of Indian Affairs, Amery, said in the British House of Commons, on 14 August 1940: 'In religious and social outlook, in historic tradition and culture, the difference between [the Muslims] and their Hindu fellow countrymen goes as deep, if not deeper than any similar difference in Europe.' He referred to the Muslims as one 'body'.[47] He thereby ignored any ethnic differentiation among the people of the subcontinent since the Middle Ages. In 1930 the Indian Statutory Commission released the following text:

> It would be an utter misapprehension to suppose that Hindu-Muslim antagonism is analogous to the separation between religious denominations in contemporary Europe. Differences of race, a different system of law, and the absence of inter-marriage constitute a far more effective barrier. It is a basic opposition manifesting itself at every turn in social custom and economic competition, as well as in mutual religious antipathy.[48]

Such statements distort the historical reality. Besides, the comparison with Europe would be challenged by the ethno-nationalists of the

Balkans at least, who, with similar arguments, postulate a rift as deep as thinkable between themselves and their neighbours.

Many Indian and Pakistani historians adopted the British view. Even in standard academic works a confrontational historiography with religious labels can be found, as in Sharma's writings. The Indian historian looks for reasons why the Hindu kings of the Middle Ages did not unite against the 'Muslim threat':

> The primary cause of the weakness of India was that Rajput states were engaged in constant fighting against each other for power and glory and failed to unite themselves against a common enemy even in the greatest danger to their country, its culture and religion.[49]

Sharma's fellow Indian Nanda puts it even more pungently:

> The successive waves of Muslim invaders from the north-west, from Muhamad Bin Qasim to Mohamed Ghori, and finally to Babar, posed a challenge to Hinduism the like of which it had never faced before.[50]

The Pakistani A.S. Ahmed calls Hindus the 'traditional opponents' of Muslims.[51] The application ex post of modern European categories—like 'nation'—to pre-modern constellations is a product of British historiography. Sharma cites yet another example. He declares the Hindu king Shivaji (1627-80), who defied 'the Muslims', a 'nation-builder': 'By his own success he proved that they [the Hindus] could be their own masters and masters of their motherland. Shivaji created a nation and an independent Hindu state.'[52]

1.2.3. *From the Village God to* Hindutva

To universally define the 'Hindu religion' is as hopeless to nail pudding on the wall. Scores of theological and philosophical traditions, numerous rites, symbols, and divinities clearly distinguish 'Hinduism' from Islam and Christianity. There is no 'holy book' (only a series of 'holy writings' like the Vedas), no uniform codex of faith, no founder, no prophet, no church institution.[53] The name 'Hindus' was originally a foreign and collective description dating from the time of Alexander the Great used for all those people who lived beyond the Indus.

Two factors in particular prevented the emergence of a collective identity among Hindus: (1) The doctrine of inclusivism erases any difference between 'we' and 'them'. Therefore, it was possible to absorb many cultural and religious influences over the years (except Islam!) (2) The strict social hierarchy and internal differentiation separated the experiences of life far more effectively than the belief in a common faith could bind them together.[54]

Attempts to modernize Hinduism were always combined with the intention to universalize and centralize it. For this purpose reformers borrowed ideas from competing religions like Christianity and Islam. The development of Hinduism in the nineteenth and twentieth centuries took place in a field of tension, dominated by Western influence, colonial resentment, and an increasing wave of Indian secular nationalism.

The so-called Hindu Renaissance in Bengal at the beginning of the nineteenth century served as the stepping stone towards the reform of Hinduism. The social reformer Rammohun Roy (1772-1833) was the pioneer. This son of a Brahman received his education in a Muslim school, worked with the British East India Company for a while, and oriented himself to the ideals of the Protestant Reformation and the European Enlightenment. He condemned polytheism, child marriage, and the burning of widows (*sati*). His rational deism did not only blend elements of different religions but also strove to give Hinduism a uniform interpretation and educational ideal. Therefore, he recalled the 'real' teachings of the Upanishads and the Brahma Sutra.[55] Roy founded the reform society 'Brahmo Samaj' in which Keshab Chandra Sen (1838-84) and Debendranath Tagore (1817-1905), father of the poet and philosopher Rabindranath, carried on Roy's message. This social and religious reform movement was based primarily on three pillars:

(1) The revival of old Indian philosophy which, above all, European scholars like Müller had made accessible again. (2) The legacy of the French Revolution and the ideas of English philosophers like Bentham. (3) German thinkers like Goethe, Schelling, Fichte, Kant, and Herder. German ideas of 'people' (*Volk*), 'society', and 'nation' were well received. Herder's concept of society as an organic being had a particularly strong influence on philosophers and ideologists, as in the Balkans.[56]

A strand of Roy's thoughts resurfaced in the secular Indian national movement. Nevertheless, as K.N. Panikkar criticizes, the Hindu Renaissance laid the foundation stone for communalist thinking. Concepts of 'Hindu' and 'Muslim' traditions were constructed. Like the Koran for Islam, now the Vedas and the Upanishads served as prescriptive codes for universal rules and regulations for the Hindus. Syncretic traditions, like the Bhakti movement of the Middle Ages, became less influential, although they were frequently invoked during the Indian freedom movement.[57] Flood holds a similar view: '[W]ith the Brahmo Samaj, we have the beginnings of a sense of a Hindu national identity, albeit of a highly "deistic" and abstract kind [. . .].'[58]

The so-called Hindu nationalism took an entirely different track from the beginning. Its ideology is based on religious fanaticism and its thinking ran along ethno-national camps. The construction of a Hindu identity goes hand in hand with the idea of the nation state as well as with a nostalgia for a supposed 'Golden Age' before the 'Muslim invasion'. The demarcation against 'the other' (especially Muslims) throws the traditionally inclusive nature of Hinduism overboard.

K.N. Panikkar is right in establishing a connection between the initially contradictory approaches of the Hindu Renaissance and Hindu nationalism. What they have in common is the standardized interpretation of Hindu religion. Also, organizationally there is a central thread. The cultural organization the 'Arya Samaj' saw itself in the tradition of Roy's reformist ideas. However, it combined them with elements of an aggressive Hindu nationalism, also in reaction to the activities of Christian missionaries. One of its leaders even demanded the expulsion of all Muslims or their conversion to 'Aryanism'.[59] From their ranks emerged the founders of even more radical organizations like the right-wing Hindu party, the Hindu Mahasabha, and the cultural organization, the Rashtriya Swayamsevak Sangh (RSS), which is often classified as fascist. Its cadres support the nationalist Bharatiya Janata Party (BJP) which has been in power since April 1998. The murderer of M.K. Gandhi, Nathu Ram Godse, was also a member of the RSS (although in the subsequent official investigations the RSS as an organization was not brought into direct connection with this act).

The most radical and influential ideologue among the Hindu nationalists was Vinayak Damodar Savarkar (1883-1966).[60] He has already been mentioned in connection with the Aryan myth. As chairman of the Hindu Mahasabha, he fought against the secularly oriented Congress party and the Muslim League during the period before independence. His slogans 'Hinduize All Politics' and 'Militarize Hindudom' alienated all those Muslims who were interested in Indian politics.[61] He supported a kind of apartheid of Hindus and Muslims in everyday life (see the 'Hindu Swimming Pool Controversy' of 1942).[62] Savarkar, who was said to have not been particularly religious himself,[63] transformed the culture of the Brahmans into an 'ethnic' nationalism. He and his fellow agitators, like Golwalkar, took their ideas from European theories of nationalism, especially the 'German' concept of nation.[64] Savarkar welcomed the German invasion of the Czech Sudetenland in 1938. The Sudetens, he said, shared a 'common blood and common language' with the Germans.[65] In his view, the 'multi-national' state of Czechoslovakia was a miscarriage. Savarkar threatened that if the Hindus became strong enough, the Muslims in India could face the same destiny as the Jews did in Germany.[66]

The Hindu nationalists understood 'Hindustan' according to the German idea of the 'organic people's community' (*organische Volksgemeinschaft*). To Savarkar India was the 'holy land': 'A Hindu means a person who regards this land of Bharat Varsha, from the Indus to the Seas, as his Fatherland as well as his Holy-Land, that is the cradle of his religion.'[67] According to this view, the Hindus looked towards Delhi, and the Muslims towards Mecca.[68]

The use of religious symbols and political rituals helped the new concept of *Hindutva* gain national prominance. Local divinities were raised to the status of 'national' gods. In each village a temple for the 'Hindu nation' was supposed to be built.[69] Religious texts and pilgrimages became the instruments of nation-building. Mandelbaum writes:

> The Hindu epics and legends, in their manifold versions, teach that the stage for the gods was nothing less than the entire land and that the land remains one religious setting for those who dwell in it. That sense was and is continually confirmed through the common practice of pilgrimage.[70]

Such ceremonies were newly invented, revived, or linked with protests for political independence. The Hindu activist B.G. Tilak was the main driving force.[71] Festivals for Ganesh, the Hindu god with the elephant head, and Shivaji, the almost forgotten Hindu king, after whom even a Hindu nationalist regional party is named today (the Shiv Sena in Maharashtra),[72] served as fitting occasions. The worship of the cow grew into well-organized mass mobilizations, the so-called 'cow protection movements', at the end of the nineteenth century. Fanaticized mobs attacked Muslim butchers in order to save the 'Holy Mother Cow' from the butcher knives of the Muslims. These movements stood in direct connection with large-scale street riots between the ethno national camps (communal riots).[73]

The unpolitical and quasi amorphous form of Hinduism was turned completely upside down. Jaffrelot writes:

> The Hindu nationalist strategy of identity-building derives its paradoxical character from the fact that it simultaneously stigmatises and emulates the Other and eventually produces a Hindu nationalist identity which [. . .] has little to do with Hinduism. [. . .] The overall aim of their ideological project seems incongruous to the extent that it was directed towards building an ethnic nation by reducing to uniformity a society distinguished by extreme differentiation. [. . .] Hindutva nationalism and Hinduism share common features which belong almost entirely to Brahmanical culture. Its notion of ethnicity overlaps with 'Indian traditional xenology', a Brahmanical *Weltanschauung*—through what G. Pandey calls 'upper caste racism'.[74]

Refering to Anderson's terms, Thapar and K.N. Panikkar call the Hindu community an imagined community.[75] The Hindu nationalists carried out an 'ethnicization' (communalization) of politics after they had contributed to a great extent to the politicization of the 'ethnic groups' (communities). Shortly before the partition of the country in August 1947, Savarkar said: '[E]very political question in India is either religious or cultural and every religious and cultural question is political.'[76] Thus, the concept of *Hindutva* strove to imitate the fundamental features of Islam, according to which religion and politics cannot be separated—with the difference that the politicized Hindudom reflected a much stronger 'ethnical' component. The Hindu Mahasabha claimed that *Hindutva* was no religion but a 'nationality'.[77]

Even Gandhi confessed that for him politics and religion could not be separated: 'You cannot divide social, economic, political and purely religious work into watertight compartments. I do not know any religion apart from human activity.'[78] The posthumous Gandhi cult for the purpose of national integration disguises the distorted view of history to which also the 'Great Soul' (*Mahatma*) had succumbed. His philosophy and politics cannot be compared to those of the Hindu nationalists, of course, but there was a religious bias in him. He spoke in favour of the purity of religions and against mixed marriages.[79] He described Hindus and Muslims en bloc and in stereotypes. Here are three examples. The following quotation is from the time of the Khilafat movement in 1924:

> [T]he Mussulman, being generally in a minority, has as a class developed into a bully . . . the thirteen hundred years of imperialist expansion have made the Mussulmans fighters as a body. The Hindu has an old-age civilization. He is essentially non-violent. . . . The Hindus have become docile to the point of timidity or cowardice.[80]

Gandhi describes the Muslims as 'imperialists', i.e. as an alien body on the subcontinent. In this way he brings the factor of territory into the game. The next quotation also shows his objective generalization of the Muslims as a separate group, in defiance of all intentions of fraternization.

After the rebellion in Malabar in 1921 ('Moplah' rebellion) he condemned 'the Muslims' for violent acts, which were, of course, the work of a handful of Muslim rowdies. The cause of the uprising was economic in nature. A fight between landlords—mostly Hindu—and peasants—mostly Muslim. In 1918 the monsoon did not arrive. Since then food prices had shot up tremendously.[81] Gandhi, however, referred exclusively to the religious cleavage and spoke again as a Hindu in the ethno-national sense:

> A verbal disapproval by the Muhammedans of Moplah madness is no test of Musalman friendship. The Musalman must naturally feel that the shame and humiliation of the Moplah conduct about forcible conversions and looting. And they must work away so silently and effectively that such things might become impossible even on the part of the most fanatical among them.[82]

Towards the beginning of the twentieth century a creeping 'ethnicization' of the rhetoric can be observed, to which not only diehard ethno-nationalists succumbed. This had serious repercussions for the subjective perception of threat as seen by the Muslim spokesmen.

Gandhi's ideas on the reform of the educational system ('Wardha Education Scheme') also made a contribution to this development—a typical component of the nation-building process, as Gellner describes it. Gandhi advocated that non-violence and rural subsistence economy should be taught in schools. Self-pounded rice and the handlooms in classrooms mirrored Gandhi's ideals but did not appeal to most Muslims (and surely not to many Hindus either). Moreover, the Muslim League suspected that the Wardha project aimed at the sanskritization of the language and at the edging out of Arabic and Persian elements.[83]

The Congress added fuel to the fire by declaring the poem 'Vande Mataram' as the new national anthem. The poem's author was the

Bengali Hindu nationalist Bankim Chandra Chatterjee. He also incorporated it ex post into his novel *Anandamatha* (The Abbey of Bliss) in which he portrays the decline of 'Muslim rule' in the eighteenth century and describes 'the Muslims' as cowards and drunkards. He personifies 'Mother India' as a Hindu goddess. He discarded Urdu (which many Muslims spoke) as non-Indian.[84]

Such callous judgements gave rise to feelings of mistrust among many Muslims towards the Congress which claimed to be the voice of all Indians. Gandhi's strongly religious rhetoric fueled this sense of alienation among Indian Muslims. His knowledge of Indian history was 'highly abstract and simplified', as Parekh notes quite rightly.[85] Even poorer was his knowledge of the history of the Muslims in India. He consistently placed them in a Hindu context. He saw the Muslims only as former Hindus and regarded the 'Muslim' past of India as a 'historical aberration', an 'unfortunate episode', brought about by Hindu decadence. Nehru himself complained about his comrade at the spinning wheel: 'Even Gandhiji's phrases sometimes jarred upon me—thus his frequent reference to Rama Raj as a golden age which was to return.'[86]

Against this background of a more and more sharply defined and politicized Hindu ideology one has to look at the development of 'the Muslims' in the country. The Hindu symbolism employed by Gandhi and certain sections of the Congress (which Nehru recognized and strongly criticized)[87] supplied the ammunition for the ethno-nationalist spokesmen on the Muslim side even more than the polemics of radical Hindu nationalists. Jinnah, who was a member of the Congress till 1934, seized every opportunity to denounce exactly this: 'I have no hesitation in saying that it is Mr. Gandhi who is destroying the ideal with which the Congress was started. He is the one man responsible for turning the Congress into an instrument for the revival of Hinduism.'[88]

Since the nineteenth century religion had become more than just a private matter in India as well. It became an official category—clearly outlined and defined, unmovable. Further separating elements joined this pattern, like blood and soil. The racial worldview is striking among the Hindu nationalists. The rhetoric of the 'holy land' was directed against the Muslims in an aggressive way. Their homeland, they said, was on the Arabian peninsula and not on the Indian subcontinent. This rhetoric contributed to a great extent to the subjective perception of threat by the Muslim spokesmen.

Comparative view

The encrustation of 'ethnic' categories took place almost simultaneously in Bosnia-Herzegovina and India. This requires an explanation in view of the geographical distance and the cultural peculiarities of both countries. The combining element can be found in the history of ideas. In the Balkans and on the subcontinent mainly German, i.e. 'ethnically' oriented, theories of nationalism were received. Particularly noteworthy in this context is Herder. Also, the relationship to European racial theories shows how strongly thoughts and actions in both cases depended on the contemporary global ideological currents. During the time of the National Socialists in Germany racial theories gained a foothold in Bosnia-Herzegovina and in India, too, and influenced the argumentation of the ethno-national protagonists. Following this trend Bosnian Muslims tried to toady to Hitler claiming to be an own race (as 'Goths') in demarcation to the South Slavs.[89] And the Brahmans with their racial Aryan myth tried to not only exclude Muslims but also to gain the sympathy of the Europeans.

Also, apart from these extreme cases a gradual homogenization of the groups along religious lines can be observed. However, it is difficult to isolate one group as the initiator. There are, however, many hints that in both cases 'the Muslims' were primarily the objects of a collective, ideological homogenization by their counterparts.

Three things went hand in hand: (a) Religious membership became the *objective* 'ethnicum'. (b) The principle of territory gained importance. (c) Spokesmen of the 'lagging' group (here in each case 'the Muslims') ultimately resorted to the same means and developed a *defensive homogenization* within the same paradigm. It was, however, less pronounced (especially in the case of 'the Muslims' in Bosnia-Herzegovina) in comparison to their neighbours or fellow citizens.

2. THE 'ETHNICIZATION' OF CONFLICTS

The previous chapter investigated the influence of the history of ideas. Now the focus shall be on practical changes which brought about an encrustation of the 'ethnic' categories. There is a close interaction between the history of ideas and practice. Modern conditions like faster and mass effective communication, new means of transport, and economic progress set the practical stage for the development of the theories of nationalism in Europe. In Bosnia-Herzegovina and India these ideas came in before or simultaneously with practical modernization. Both the British and the Habsburgers left their mark in this respect.

The consequence of this combination of the history of ideas and of modernization was that ethno-national cleavages could be superimposed on the new emerging social and economic cleavages far more easily.

2.1. Bosnia-Herzegovina

2.1.1. *Masters and Missionaries*

Travellers in the seventeenth century were full of praise for the Bosnian Muslims. They were tolerant, polite, and educated, they said. There seem to have been few quarrels between *rayas*[90] and Muslim landlords, too. Malcolm observes that only external political influences led to the fanatization of certain sections of the Muslims in the nineteenth century.[91] They felt trapped and threatened; Serb revolts against Ottoman rule from 1804 onwards turned into anti-Muslim massacres and campaigns of forceful conversions. In 1815 a Serb state was founded with far-reaching autonomy, a prince, and a parliament. With its help the Serb clergy could better promote the Orthodox Christians, also outside the borders. Meanwhile, France had occupied Dalmatia. This gave a backing to the Catholics in Bosnia. The Christian merchant community in Sarajevo enjoyed special protection through the French, Prussian, and Austrian consulates.

A French traveller in 1808 observed the following with regard to the Muslims:

> This situation, by raising their fears, has rendered them ill-disposed towards everyone. It has inspired them with a fear of seeing their raya rebel; and to keep them in check, they have had recourse to barbarity.

In 1822 another French traveller got carried away and generalized: '[T]he Muslim takes his faith to the most extreme form of fanaticism.'[92]

Quarrels between Muslim and Christian clergymen increased. Petty reasons gained great importance, like the controversy over the height of a new cathedral's tower in Sarajevo in 1872.[93] But the main reasons were of financial nature. For example, in 1874 the harvest was destroyed. As a result, Christian peasants east of Mostar refused to pay their taxes. The tax collectors reacted brutally and the peasants fled into the mountains. Along the border to Montenegro the atmosphere was even more hostile against Muslims since the prince of Montenegro was a protégé of Moscow. He was said to plan the destabilization of Herzegovina by arms supplies.

Similar incidents took place in northern Bosnia. At the same time, more and more Christian missionaries poured into the country. The atmosphere was poisoned. Malcolm writes: 'The basic cause of popular discontent was agrarian; but this discontent was harnessed in some parts of Bosnia by members of the Orthodox population who had been in contact with Serbia, and who now publicly declared their loyalty to the Serbian state.'[94]

In these circumstances the education of the people played a decisive role. A Serb agitator confessed as late as 1907: 'In the countryside we still have very few followers because of the extremely low standard of education of our population.' The clergy, he complained, failed to show enough missionary zeal.[95] This statement explains two things: (1) A national identification requires an agitational network, which means the linkage of the hinterland with the urban hotbeds of national ideologies. (2) The agitator speaks of 'our' population, although he admits that there are few followers only. The *a priori* appropriation of people on the basis of their objective, i.e. externally dependent, 'ethnic' affiliation is a typical characteristic of 'ethnic' nation-building.

This can be clearly observed in the case of Serbs and Croats in the nineteenth century. But Muslims were also increasingly thrust into exclusively 'ethnic' categories. The time of religious peace in the 1860s under the tolerant Ottoman governor Topal Osman-Pasha was over. Serbia's attack against the Ottoman Empire in 1876 stirred up feelings of hatred among the Bosnian Muslim spokesmen against their Orthodox neighbours. The Ottoman Empire responded with harshness and brutality in turn. When Austria-Hungary took over the control of Bosnia-Herzegovina in 1878 some Muslims fled to Turkey out of fear of retaliation.[96]

Those who remained found themselves no longer in a leading position. They were faced with a 'foreign' Catholic government. According to the popular view, this 'cultural defensiveness' acted as a catalyst for the political and national development of the Muslims.[97] The use of gross categories like 'culture' and 'foreignness', however, should not lead to rash conclusions. A closer look reveals that all conflicts between 'ethnic groups' were based on concrete reasons where hard interests were at play.

2.1.2. Beys *and Peasants*

An issue constantly on the boil was the unresolved agrarian question. It had a double effect: (1) The economic backwardness of Bosnia-Herzegovina, based on the outdated and loss-incurring system of bonded labour (*kmet* system), blocked the modernization which was taking place in other parts of south-eastern Europe.[98] This prevented the formation of strong nation-building elites. In Bosnia-Herzegovina a rural Muslim ruling class did exist. However, it took no political shape which could have made it appear as a unity. (2) The conflict-ridden agrarian conditions[99] led to upheavals and protests all over again as in 1875, 1883, 1903, and 1908. Babuna writes: 'Also under the Austro-Hungarian administration the most important cause of political and national unrest was the agrarian issue.'[100] This continued until the early Yugoslavia. In particular the years 1918 to 1920 witnessed *kmet* revolts that led to violence against Muslims.[101]

The social structure of Bosnia-Herzegovina made it easier for ethno-national agitators to capitalize politically on the peasant protests, because, as mentioned earlier, the majority of the *kmets* were Orthodox, or, in other words, 'Serbs'.[102] The argument over compulsory taxes imposed on peasants quickly turned into the Serb demand for an autonomous state in Bosnia-Herzegovina in 1883. Thus, for the first time socio-economic, political, and ethno-national cleavages became blurred because many Muslim *beys* (in fact, the opponents of the *kmets*) came along and allied themselves with Serb nationalists against the unloved Habsburg administration. So it happened 'that, for the first time, Serb peasants and Muslim landlords took part in a rebellion together'.[103]

This politically motivated alliance of the moment is grotesque because Muslim *beys* did not only strongly defend the existing agrarian conditions but they later also wanted to limit the rights of the *kmets*—even going against the reform-oriented intentions of the Habsburgers. The *beys* strongly articulated their demands in the Muslim movement for autonomy at the turn of the century. Their aim was to safeguard their assets.[104] For along with autonomy the Ottoman Sharia law remained in force, and on this the *beys* based their property rights. This shows that the demand for 'ethnic' independence served only as window-dressing to conceal their underlying petty political interests. Babuna writes: 'The landowners, with their motto of religious autonomy, could mobilize other social classes for their own cause.'[105]

They skilfully intertwined their goals with religious demands and presented two memoranda to the government (in 1900 and 1901) under the slogan 'Islam in danger'. In the letters of protest, which, in fact, were *political* programmes, the signatories described themselves as an 'Islamic people' with a 400-year-old Islamic history.[106] In the protest memorandum against the Austro-Hungarian annexation in 1908 and in another letter in 1917 they refused the integration into a South Slavic state 'out of historical, cultural and social reasons'.[107] This shows that they gradually detached their Muslim identity from an exclusively religious focus, or, in other words, they 'ethnicized' it.

2.1.3. *Conversions and Overreactions*

The history of Bosnia-Herzegovina is full of big and small problems which initially did not have any 'ethnic' or 'national' origin at all. This mainly concerned religious questions. Since religion now had strong political importance, conversions became a delicate affair. This seems illogical because conversions from Islam to Christianity were relatively rare in Bosnia-Herzegovina, although the Muslims were separated state-wise and were far away from the Ottomans.[108] But still Muslim spokesmen demanded laws from the Austro-Hungarian administration which would impose restrictions on conversions. Because of Christian influence the *ulema* propagated the need to safeguard religious assets. Religious affiliation was not a personal decision any more but a collective good which needed to be defended. No longer could anyone change his or her confession quietly and without any hassles, even if it was a voluntary move.[109]

In such a tense situation the smallest incident could turn into a political issue. Simple love dramas and family disputes got a religious-political colour. This happened to a 16-year-old Muslim girl Fata Omanovic from Mostar in 1899.[110] After a quarrel with her parents she ran away to her Christian girl friend and became a convert. Muslim activists sold it as a case of abduction and forcible conversion. They complained about the lack of religious education among the Muslim population and the overall difficult position of Muslims in the country. Moreover, they used this opportunity to criticize the—in their view—bad administration of the *vakufs*.[111] The demands assumed bigger and bigger political proportions.

The Fata case united two rival Muslim opposition movements in Mostar at first. Ultimately, it forged a common Bosnian-Muslim movement for autonomy out of what used to be Herzegovinian separatist protests. There was, indeed, also an interaction with the strong Serb agitation in Mostar. But this shows that in a tense situation in the context of ethno-national cleavages, a single incident, which under normal circumstances would have simply been shrugged off, can trigger political actions.

The literature is too limited to state with certainty if the Bosnian Muslims became radicalized only because of external factors. However, there are strong indications in support of this argument. After all, the Orthodox and Catholic fanaticisms, the Serb and Croatian ethno-nationalisms respectively, provoked each other. 'Ethnic' demarcations against 'the other' grew stronger. In this atmosphere of growing mistrust and hostility Muslim activists pursued a policy of safeguarding their religious assets. Economic and social conflicts were exploited to achieve religious and political goals. But at the same time socio-economic, political, and ethno-national cleavages cross-cut each other.

2.2. India

As in Bosnia-Herzegovina, a growing sensitization towards actual or ostensible religious issues took place in India at the beginning of the twentieth century. Religious symbols and rituals gained political importance. Religious spokesmen exploited social conflicts to fight out their ethno-national camp battles.

2.2.1. *Waterpool and Weaver Strike*

In particular, two incidents, in Kanpur and Bombay, which had nothing to do with religion initially, can be regarded as galvanizing events for the politicization of 'the Indian Muslims'. Both events led to the recruitment of new Muslim spokesmen. They exploited the wave of outrage, enjoyed a large following, and retained their authority beyond the immediate occasions.

In 1913 a new street became the cause of unrest in Kanpur, in northern India.[112] The washing place of the mosque at the Macchli Bazaar was in its way. The British urban development officers wanted to clear the obstacle. Muslims, with whom they discussed the matter, gave their consent. They said that the washing place did not necessarily need to remain an integrated part of the mosque. Besides, it was anyway already desecrated because most of the people entered it with their shoes on.

Yet, after the washing place had been removed, it appeared to be holier than ever before. Two managers of the mosque protested, and more and more Muslims joined them. A new clique of leaders, who were recruited from among the protestors, took over the administration of the mosque. They used Islamic symbols in a political way. The agitators invoked the 'martyrdom of a part of the mosque' and the common heritage of Muslims, like Persian literature. They were successful. Door-to-door propaganda roused the community spirit. The number of angry people grew. They attacked the police and the Hindu temples.

Muslim agitators talked their followers into a common feeling of threat. Soon the agitation spread beyond the Kanpur site. 'National Muslim leaders' were brought into the city in order to deliver speeches and draw up memoranda. Even pan-Islamic feelings emerged. References to the Balkan wars and the dilemma of the Ottoman Empire entered the rhetoric of the Indian Muslims for the first time: '[W]hen hundreds of mosques have been destroyed in Macedonia [...] it is no wonder that a mosque is being demolished in India.'[113]

United by this 'common cause' Muslim workers from weaving mills and Muslims from the upper classes marched together. They forgot the differences in their customs and lifestyles. Freitag observes:

> Because issues of practice divided Muslim from Muslim—whereas symbolic language had the potential to unite them—practice became secondary to the language of community. In turn, activity in the public arena on behalf of the community became an important way of identifying who was a Muslim.[114]

In 1931 Kanpur became the site of unrest once again. Muslims were underrepresented in economic life and in the city administration.

This raised their feeling of discrimination. A small spark was enough to invoke talk of the 'martyrdom' of the Muslims. In that year Congress activists triggered the fights because they wanted to coerce all Hindus, and especially Muslims, to take part in a strike.

It was again a strike that was responsible for the outbreak of big trouble in the industrial city of Bombay (today Mumbai) in 1929.[115] Purely economic issues turned into communal riots. This is particularly striking because the Muslim population of the city was highly fragmented. The census of 1901 identified among Muslims 14 different ethnic backgrounds (also foreign ones like Arabs, Turks, and Egyptians), at least four different language groups, and several professional groups. Different Islamic practices created tensions, especially between Sunnis and Shiites. A Muslim ruling class had never existed in Bombay. Equally alien to the city was the concept of religious camps.

However, in 1929 everything changed. The owners of textile mills decided to cut salaries and sack employees. This led to several strikes. By the spring of 1929 the trade unions had organized themselves properly. This step proved especially threatening to the Pathans whom the industrialists engaged as strikebreakers. The Pathans came from the predominantly Muslim North West Frontier Province (NWFP, now in Pakistan). They did not let themselves be easily intimidated. In addition, they had already become quite unpopular as moneylenders, too.

Soon rumours spread that Pathans kidnapped children for human sacrifices. Many Pathans were assaulted brutally. The fact that Pathans (coincidently) were Muslims and were attacked by Hindu workers provoked Muslim activists into action from all over India. The feeling of being discriminated against and the lure of Muslim martyrdom once again served as rhetorical ammunition. At the same time, Muslims in Bombay reacted hypersensitively to the slightest provocation. They now felt offended by things which never had disturbed them earlier, for example, the music accompanying Hindu processions passing in front of mosques.[116] Such processions were regulated by a law of 1902, and there had never been protests against it. But Bombay had changed. The events from 1929 onwards replaced the cleavage of 'class' in favour of a thinking along ethno-national camps.

However, there are also counter examples where an agitation broke down because Muslim activists fell out with each other over dogmatic issues. This happened in Lahore in 1935. There the Sikh authorities tore down the Shahidganj Mosque which was under their administration.

As a consequence, Muslim groups launched a massive protest. The Urdu press added fuel to the fire. The groups of leaders varied and radicalized themselves. Finally, the *ulema* was sidestepped, and a leader was chosen from the countryside. But since he belonged to the mystical Sufi sect and was at home among the landowning class, there were divided opinions about him and hence the agitation broke down.[117]

2.2.2. *The 'Cow Deal' and the Caliphate*

Music in front of mosques, pig heads in mosques, cow heads in temples: these were the typical provocations leading to communal tensions.[118] As shown above, the use of old religious symbols with new meanings played an important role in mobilizing people. They were familiar also in the traditional sphere of the remotest villages, and thereby served as a link to a newly emerging community which was to define itself through religious membership.[119]

One of the most important symbols was the cow. Hindus worshipped it, and Muslims ate it. This had never been a problem so far—until 1887. In that year some Hindu activists founded the Cow Protection Society (*Gorakshini Sabha*). Under its direction supporters burned down slaughter houses or bought cows from Muslims for their release. Since it was the Muslims who slaughtered and ate cows, Hindu fury was directed against them (especially against the butchers), but it was also directed against the British who consumed the worshipped creature and who allowed its slaughter.[120]

So the movement was initially *not* based on the concept of ethno-national camps. Rather the cow protection movement is to be placed in the context of the modernization and homogenization of the Hindu religion. Yang writes:

> The sacred became generalized in many daily routines and living space itself became ritualized. Moreover, the issue of the cow touched the religious sensibilities of many Hindus deeply because it centered on their fundamental symbol as well as their 'sense of place'. In short, it related to a community's self-definition.[121]

The cow protection movements reached a peak in 1893. Technical progress and modern communication contributed to the rapid spread of the protests. For the first time, ideology made its way into the rural areas and determined the conflicts. Freitag summarizes the effects of the cow protection movements: (a) The activities brought cities and rural areas together. (b) The ideology united groups with varied interests among the Hindus. It even bridged the gap between landowners and tenants. (c) The existing structure of leading authorities in the villages could be used to mobilize supporters. (d) Mobilization mechanisms were developed and strengthened.[122]

In course of time, these movements clearly assumed the character of a struggle between ethno-national camps. Muslim activists, as a countermove, provoked Hindus by ritually slaughtering cows in the open marketplaces.

It is all the more surprising that political actors could make peace for a while. This shows that the thinking in ethno-national camps could not only be stirred up but also weakened; this means it could be controlled from above. What was the secret of this political-religious truce? The answer to this question lies in a very distant place—in Istanbul. And the issue had as little to do with the cow as faith had to do with the political demands of the camp activists.

Kemal Atatürk (1881-1938) had driven out the Greeks from Turkish soil during the second Balkan war and toppled the old Ottoman regime. He let himself be elected as the first president of a modern, secularly-oriented Turkey.[123] Under his administration the Turkish National Assembly abolished the Sultanate in 1923 and the title of the Caliph in 1924.

For (most) Sunnis the Caliph was the highest religious authority on earth.[124] The majority of Muslims in India are Sunnis. Their leaders were outraged at the measures taken by Atatürk. Yet it was not dogmatic reasons alone which played a role here. The Caliphate was for many a bulwark against Christian influence in the Balkans, even against the whole structure of European imperialism. Since for the Indians the British were the incarnation of imperialism, and since they were actively involved in the destruction of Ottoman rule as well, the so-called Indian Khilafat movement was particularly directed against them. Thus began the first all-India Muslim mass movement. Gandhi recognized this and climbed on the bandwagon. He made the Congress an ally of the pan-Islamic cause. He saw an opportunity to unite Hindus and Muslims against a common enemy and to deal the British a blow.[125] In this way, Gandhi attracted a large number of Muslims into his Non-Cooperation movement.

The Khilafat movement is interesting for two reasons. It gives an insight (a) into the manipulation of religious symbols by political elites, and (b) into the self-image of the Indian Muslims, respectively their spokesmen.

Point (a) has already been hinted at. The leaders of the Khilafat movement reached a compromise over the issue of the cow,—with the brothers Shaukat and Muhammad Ali, on the one side, and Gandhi, on the other. Hindus were asked to call off the cow protection movements. In turn, Muslims were asked not to slaughter cows in public any more. Some Muslims even followed the appeal not to kill cows altogether or to give up eating beef.[126]

Gandhi confessed:

I claim that with us both the Khilafat is the central fact, with Maulana Muhammad Ali because *it is his religion*, with me because, in laying down my life for the Khilafat, I ensure the safety of the cow, *that is my religion*, from the Mussalman knife.[127]

Many Hindus, but also Muslims, viewed the Khilafat movement with scepticism. Gandhi and the Alis, however, carried along the masses and turned the issue into a matter of national interest. Indeed, the clashes, which had been sparked off around the cow, ebbed away.

To examine point (b) one has to wade through a lot of contradictions. It came close to political and ideological acrobatics to turn the Khilafat movement into a campaign of Hindu-Muslim fraternization. Also, the anger at the loss of the Caliphate was a remarkable ideological construction in itself.

This becomes obvious with the question whether or not the Khilafat movement had a pan-Islamic character. On the one hand, it had a pan-*Islamic function*, indeed. The Indian Muslim leaders appealed to the pan-Islamic sentiments of the Indian Muslims, to which they reacted positively. Khilafat leader Muhammad Ali invoked the Turkish 'Motherland' of the Indian Muslims.[128] The political 'foreign rule', under which 'the Indian Muslims' lived made their spokesmen cling all the more to the distant Caliphat.[129] Ali claimed that this was the only level of identification for a Muslim and rejected any form of nationalism as un-Islamic.[130] After the fall of the last Mughul emperor, the Indian Muslims held the Friday prayer in the name of the Ottoman caliph. The Bosnian Muslims did the same, by the way.[131]

Another argument for the pan-Islamic theory is that in 1877-8 and

1897 Indian Muslims generated relief funds for their Turkish fellow believers when they were at war with Russia and Greece. The Balkan wars in 1912-13 and in 1921-2 evoked sympathy for the Turks, too. The Muslim Urdu press reported in detail about the events. The tenor of the articles was along the fixed lines of a 'Christian conspiracy' against Islam.[132]

A possible pan-Islamic sentiment in India taught the British quite some respect. This is why, during the Mutiny of 1857, they asked for an assurance from the Ottoman Sultan, who in fact called upon the Indian Muslims to be loyal to their colonial masters.[133] In 1914 the British assured the Indian Muslims that the war against the Ottoman Empire was not directed against the Caliph. The holy places would not be attacked.[134]

On the other hand, however, the Caliphate had only partially a pan-Islamic basis. The Arabs had long laid their claim to the office. They believed that only a representative of the Arabic Quresh tribe could be a true Caliph, not an Ottoman. They greeted the dissolution of the office with malicious glee. Caliph Abdul Hamid II (reign 1876-1909) was already experiencing poor support from the Muslims. He called upon Muslims all over the world to support him in containing Christianity, and was joined by the pan-Islamic ideologist Jamaluddin al-Afghani (1838-97). Yet it met with little response, also from the Muslims in India.[135]

The relationship between the caliphate and the Indian Muslims had always been strained. This makes the Khilafat movement all the more illogical. The Mughals, for instance, refused the authority of the caliphs in Istanbul and proclaimed themselves to be caliphs.[136] All the more surprising is the fact that in India also the Shiites supported the Khilafat movement, even though they did not approve of the caliphate in principle. The anti-British thrust covered up the dogmatic subtleties. Many Muslims in India felt as one group for the first time. Therefore, as Minault writes, this action promoted less pan-Islamism than a pan-Indian Islam.[137] Also, for the first time, they expressed their anger against the British occupiers in such an open way. This deepened the internal cleavages among the Muslims, for many advocated a continuing cooperation with the British.

Three of the distinguished Muslim ideologists, Syed Ahmed Khan (1817-98), Muhammad Iqbal (1875-1938), and Jinnah, condemned the Khilafat movement. Khan rejected the caliphate on dogmatic grounds. For him, Turks and Indian Muslims were no closer than 'earth and moon'.[138] For Iqbal, in contrast, the collaboration with the Congress went too far. He described the Khilafat movement as 'an act of foolishness' and as 'a surrender to the Hindus'.[139] Jinnah was annoyed at the influence of religious leaders and ideas in the mass movement. Besides, he belonged to a Shiite sect and was not very interested in the office of the caliphate. But his *political* arguments are extremely noteworthy. In the end it was *he* who later instrumentalized religion in the same way and, through his ethno-national slogans, carved out a new state in the subcontinent. However, at that time Jinnah found,

> that [Gandhi] had ruined politics in India by dragging up a lot of unwholesome elements in Indian life and giving them political prominence, *that it was a crime to mix up politics and religion the way he had done.*[140]

Mullahs, Jinnah said, had nothing to meddle in politics.[141] For these reasons, Jinnah and the entire Muslim League distanced themselves not only from Gandhi but also from the Congress which had got dragged into the movement. This growing estrangement between the two parties later became an important factor in the country's partition.

Indeed, Gandhi had exploited Muslim loyalties out of political intentions. His actual aim was India's independence—self-governance (*swaraj*). Gandhi told Muhammad Ali who was in prison in 1918:

> [M]y interest in your release is quite selfish. We have a common goal and I want to utilize your services to the uttermost, in order to reach that goal. In the proper solution of the Mahomedan question lies the realization of Swarajya.[142]

At the same time, Gandhi also instrumentalized Hindus. To them the Caliphate was a closed book. Even Gandhi had only a dim idea about Turkey and the Caliphate. Those Hindus who supported the Khilafat movement did so out of three reasons: (1) Finally, a wedge could be driven between 'the Muslims' and the British colonial power. (2) Many Muslims became integrated into Gandhi's independence movement. (3) The cow was protected.

For many Muslims, the event held bitter disappointments: (1) Turks themselves had abolished the Caliphate—not the imperialist European Christians. (2) At times, the Khilafat participants boycotted and gave up important government posts. Many Muslims lost economic and social influence. This affected them all the more, as in certain regions they lagged behind the Hindus anyway. (3) The protection of the cow was against Islamic law. Islamic spokesmen criticized their fellow believers for having surrendered to 'the Hindus' at a high price.[143]

The Khilafat movement broke apart in quarrels. A. Rashid concludes:

> [T]his coming together seemed to take place on the basis of a tactical rapprochement between the leadership of the two communities rather than as a result of a deeper and therefore more resilient ideological accomodation.[144]

After the event 'Hindus' and 'Muslims' faced each other more than ever as strictly demarcated camps. Both had homogenized, politicized, and radicalized, and were more strongly influenced by religious leaders. Accordingly, Jaffrelot finds that the origin of Hindu nationalism actually lies in the failure of the Khilafat movement.[145]

This provided Muslim ideologues with welcome arguments. The concept of 'nation' entered the debate, although still without any reference to territory. So Zulfiqar Ali concluded in 1929:

> [T]he separation of the Ali Brothers from Mahatma Gandhi is, in principle, the separation of the entire Muslim nation (*quawm*) from the Hindu nation, and is a practical manifestation of the reality (*haqiqat*) that the two are separate nations.[146]

Any type of incident could assume ethno-national dimensions. A common aspect is that familiar symbols (like the cow or the Caliphate) played an important role. The Khilafat episode reveals particularly well how strongly the use of these symbols—and their new significance—could be manoeuvred by religious and political spokesmen. The failure of the movement brings about the same consequence as the other examples. The thinking in religious camps became more encrusted and politicized. This paved the way for an 'ethnic' concept of nation which was now increasingly employed by Muslim ideologues.

Comparative view

In Bosnia and India in the late nineteenth and early twentieth centuries an increased sensitivity to religious issues can be observed. Boundaries became entrenched in areas where conversions had taken place and were still a part of everyday life. The more strongly religious affiliation was felt as a matter of contrast, the more important was in the eyes of the ideologues the safeguarding of religious assets.

The big question is: to what extent had these distinctions penetrated the people's consciousness? Since there are no 'analyses of consciousness', we depend on external indicators. Banal conflicts that acquired political dimensions lead to two observations: (1) The main cleavages did *not* run along religious ascriptions when the problems of everyday life had come up. (2) The outcome, however, often had the effect that the cleavages broke open along the lines of religious camps.

One reservation cannot be emphazised strongly enough: collected data are insufficient. No 'democratic will' can be attributed to individual conflicts. Those people who took part in such upheavals are always mentioned. All others were simply peasants, craftsmen, traders, or officers without any political agenda. Many people are apolitical. There were trouble spots but no extensive fire. Nevertheless, typical patterns can be derived from such examples showing how *more and more* people were dragged into such conflicts.

The following questions remain open for the moment: Do the religious cleavages after such conflicts last for long? Would they be immediately 'ready' and 'employable' at other occasions? Would they fade away under economic or social changes or through a contrary use of religious symbolism? The latter action took place during the Khilafat movement in India. There is no parallel in Bosnia-Herzegovina of such an instance of cooperation between the 'ethnic groups'—a quid pro quo from above in religious symbolism and ideological goals.

3. THE 'ETHNICIZATION' OF LANGUAGE

> It is indeed more difficult for a Palatine to understand a Saxon than it is for Serbs, Croats and Bosnians to understand one another. But if I say it there, each side will kill me. For they accuse each other: because you did not recognize our language, you did not recognize our poets, our culture either. There is something to it.[147]
>
> *Hans Koschnik*

To Serbs/Croats and Indians/Pakistanis the same principle applies: 'Intense nationalism everywhere has a tendency to take minor differences among peoples and magnify them into "epic proportions",' Thomas writes.[148] The more the conflicts between the groups intensified, the more the spokesmen polished 'their' language. Above all, they used the script as a means of demarcation. Hindi was written in Devanagari only, Urdu in Persian characters (from right to left), Croatian in Latin ones, and Serb in Cyrillic ones.

The 'Ethnicization' of language means that language is no longer only what people speak but the feature by which they are defined. Language becomes a fixed and important group feature used to demarcate one group from the other that (allegedly) speaks differently. It is loaded with historical, cultural, and political connotations. In the ideal case, at the end of this process a 'national language' emerges along with the state-building.

In such an ethno-national language conflict one motivation comes to light in particular: language becomes a symbol of (potential) dominance. It can be in close connection with the socio-economic interests of an elite, which was particularly the case in India. Against this background, Horowitz concludes:

> Language is therefore a potent issue because it accomplishes a double linkage. It links political claims to ownership with psychological demands for the affirmation of group worth, and it ties this aggregate matter of group status to outright careerism, thereby binding elite material interests to mass concerns.[149]

Just because language becomes a *political* problem, linguistics plays a secondary role. Its methodology it can only determine the difference or distance between languages but not their respective cultural and historical construction. This is why one speaks of *Abstandsprache* (language of distance) and *Ausbausprache* (language of construction). *Abstandsprachen* are distinguished through 'obvious', linguistic characteristics. By contrast, *Ausbausprachen* are 'a product of the linguistic acculturation of a society'.[150] They have grown historically and are primarily defined not through linguistic but through cultural characteristics.

In particular Herder and the German Romantics gave a boost to the concept of *Ausbausprache*. Herder believed that language and poetry reflected the natural spirit of a people (*Volk*). Language conveys world views to the following generations and thereby binds them into a social heritage. The concept had an explosive impact because Herder saw language as a constitutive factor of the organic community of a nation.[151] His (often misinterpreted) ideas encouraged the rise of language-oriented nationalism in the Balkans and in India.[152]

The role of language in nation-building is disputed. 'Language is simply ideal for the 'nation'', says Reiter, as it can be effectively used as a group-encompassing feature.[153] It is evident, it can be passed on, it is flexible and long lasting, and it lends a sense of history and emotional solidarity to a group. Sundhaussen disagrees that language can also be a problematic 'proof' of identity since it is often hard to categorize. Several idioms exist side by side at any one time, in addition colloquial language, mother tongue, liturgical language, business language, etc.[154] Unlike Reiter, Sundhaussen refers to the possibility of changing one's language.

Das Gupta associates language with political loyalty, too.[155] Nationalists then argue whether a change of language automatically implies a 'change of nation'. The problem is aggravated when languages are standardized *from above*. Their use for nation-building has a clearly exclusive character. Since the nineteenth century in the Balkans and the early twentieth century in India ethno-nationalists have created the paradigm according to which nation and language should overlap.

This stands in stark contrast to linguistic findings. For in the entire South Slavic area there are no distinct *Abstandsprachen* 'which were justified to take note of', writes Katicic.[156] Rather the normative grammars are twisted artificially in the pursuit of national projects.[157] Also, Hindi and Urdu are cast in the same mould. In their pronunciation there are hardly any differences. As in the case of the South Slavs, the quarrel revolves mainly around the script which has played an important role only since the beginning of the modern age.

Of course, ethno-nationalists see it differently. They either ignore the difference between *Abstandsprachen* and *Ausbausprachen* or they want to merge them. The former Croatian Vice-President Brozovic claims that as soon as different standardization processes take place, independent *Abstandsprachen* automatically come to be because 'the people' or 'the public opinion' wanted it this way. Referring to his country he writes: 'The simple fact that this is the language used by the Croatians makes it the Croatian language.' However, he does not analyse the reasons behind the emergence of different standardizations.[158]

On the other hand, Riedel draws the attention to the dangers of such an instrumentalization of *Ausbausprachen*:

> [E]very standard language [is] the result of a development process [...] which just cannot be derived as necessary with the help of linguistics. The formation of written languages is primarily a political act of will, and, therefore, an expression of political interests. [...] Insofar a linguistic nationalism, which, with its puristic programme, intends to keep off foreign cultural elements from a genetically

pure language, corresponds to an ethnically defined nation state. It is based as well on a purity requirement, namely on the purity of the ethnicum, respectively of the titular nation of a nation state.[159]

3.1. Bosnia-Herzegovina

> When someone speaks about languages in the Balkans, somewhere the knives are already being sharpened.[160]
>
> *Milovan Djilas*

3.1.1. *Setting the Points*

Similar to the 'ethnic' mix in the territory of Yugoslavia there has always existed an idiomatic confusion, too. The 'ethnicization' of languages makes this mixture particularly explosive.

The 'Serbo-Croatian' language is divided into three dialects: Stokavian, Kaykavian, and Cakavian.[161] The Croatian population speaks all three dialects in different regions. The Serbs speak Stokavian. However, Stokavian has three different pronunciations: Ekavian, Iyekavian, and Ikavian.[162] These subtleties sparked off the Serbo-Croatian language conflict in 1967.[163] And once again it was Bosnia-Herzegovina which got stuck between the fronts. The debate did not only boil down to the ethno-national demarcation between the Serbs and the Croats but also returned to the old question: 'to whom does Bosnia belong?'

Out of all the possibilities available the Serb linguistic reformer Vuk Karadzic picked out just the Iyekavian dialect as the 'purest', which was widely prevalent mainly in eastern Hercegovina. He wanted to raise it to the status of the standard Serb script with the argument that most of the people spoke and wrote it, that almost all folk songs were composed in this dialect, and that it was nearest to the old Slavic tongue.[164] For a short time in the second half of the nineteenth century there was the possibility that a *uniform* standard language for both Serbs and Croats might develop on its basis. The Illyrian-minded Croats, on their part, committed themselves to Stokavian as well, although most of them spoke Kaykavian. As a student in Graz, the Illyrian ideologist Gaj had read Karadzic's collections of folk songs, fairy tales, and proverbs with much enthusiasm.

However, strong ideological disagreements undermined this superficial harmony. Under no circumstances did the Croats want to be described on the basis of their language as 'actual' Serbs, as Karadzic did. The Serbs on their part, including Karadzic, did not want to be appropriated by Illyrism. Therein they saw the age-old attempt of the Catholic Church to expand to the east and to convert the lost 'Illyrian' sons. In terms of linguistics, both people were as close as never before. But they quickly looked for new lines of demarcations. First, they stuck to the national descriptions of 'Serbian' and 'Croatian' with regard to 'their' language, instead of 'Serbo-Croatian' or 'Croato-Serbian' or whatever. Second, the Serbs held on to their Cyrillic and the Croats to their Latin (Illyrian) script.

3.1.2. *The Contradictions*

Ironically, Karadzic's Iyekavian variant gained acceptance among the Croats and just *not* among the Serbs. The Serbs stuck to what they spoke, which is Ekavian.[165] As a consequence of Balkan language nationalism, this implied that Iyekavian was Croatian and Ekavian was Serb.

In Yugoslavia the communist ideologists tried, as so often before, to square the circle. Differences which proved insurmountable on the national-ideological level were to be defused by means of an everyday political compromise. The language regulation of Yugoslavia (agreement of Novi Sad in 1954) laid down: 'The national language of Serbs, Croats and Montenegrians is one single language'; the written language 'is uniform with two pronunciations, Iyekavian and Ekavian', which are of equal status.[166] This is how it was put on paper. In reality, most Serbs and Croats continued to consider their respective languages as different. The 'Serb' Ekavian dominated in everyday life. In 1967, with a declaration in favour of the 'Croatian' Iyekavian language, the Croatian counter movement, Matica Hrvatska (the Central Croatian Cultural and Publishing Society, founded 1842) provoked the biggest nationality conflict that Tito had experienced in his country until then, as mentioned above.

After the war, from 1991 onwards, the Serb and Croatian governments have tried once again to separate their languages, with increased enthusiasm. Serbs, who partly used the Latin script, now only write in Cyrillic. With Croats it is just the other way round.[167]

But to whom does Bosnia belong after all? If one follows Vuk

Karadzic, the Bosnians speak the purest 'Serb' (i.e. Iyekavian) and therefore they are Serbs. Also, without the help of Karadzic Serbs can argue similarly, even though they have opted for Ekavian themselves. The reason is that Stokavian as a whole came to Bosnia from the east in the middle of the fifteenth century. At that time, Stokavian-refugees immigrated seeking protection from the Ottomans.

However, now Iyekavian has worked its way up to the status of the *Croatian* standard language. Thus, according to the logic of the Croatian language-nationalists, the Muslims are Croats. Moreover, they could argue with Cakavian (i.e. the 'exclusive Croatian' dialect) which is also found in Bosnia-Herzegovina. So the question whether Cakavian or Stokavian forms the 'actual' substrate of the hotchpotch of dialects in Bosnia-Herzegovina immediately gets a political character.

On the other hand, it is not only Bosnian-Muslim nationalists who point out that *their* language, too, has characteristic features which are nowhere to be found left or right with their neighbours. Islamization entailed Turkish loan words and phonetic modifications.[168] Since the seventeenth century Catholic priests and writers inside and outside Bosnia-Herzegovina have described the language as 'Bosnian'.[169] Long before Karadzic they had described this dialect as the best and the purest. Muslim authors liked to cast it into the Persian script.

But Bosnian Muslims had not developed any vernacular writing culture of their own. Although in Yugoslav Bosnia-Herzegovina Iyekavian was promoted, the standardization of an 'own' language has lagged behind that of the Serbs and the Croats until today. The Muslim communists were not interested at all in a language of their own and placed their dialect in the overall Yugoslav context. In 1947 they wrote about themselves: 'Slav in origin and speaking the same language (Serb) as the Christians of that region [. . .]'.[170]

Bosnia-Herzegovina is once again a meeting point of different concepts. The Bosnian daily *Oslobodenje*, for example, uses both Latin and Cyrillic scripts. In recent times Bosnian Muslim (Bosnjak) nationalists have felt that they have a lot of catching up to do. They also want to give a national character to the language, and try to standardize Turkish loan words.[171] In the 1991 census 90 per cent of the 'Muslims in the national sense' described their language as 'Bosnian'.[172]

A peculiar spectacle of the grotesque results of the language quarrels could be seen during the peace negotiations in Dayton in 1995. There were six language channels available on the headphones—the first three for English, French, and Russian, the fourth for 'Bosnian', the fifth for 'Croatian', and the sixth for 'Serbian'. However, for the last three channels there was only *one* interpreter. Exactly the same translation could be heard on each.[173]

For the South Slavs it can be said in general: 'Their language and tradition survived best in those regions where they had formed a political organization already very early', mainly in Croatia and Serbia.[174] Just as in the ideological-political and territorial spheres, Muslims are confronted with appropriation attempts in the linguistic field, too. Again, their land is labelled by some as the 'core land', on which a nationally stabilized homeland falls back on and lays claim to at the same time. The Muslims themselves have nothing of their 'own' to counter with in this linguistic politics. However, this could change in the future.

3.2. India

3.2.1. *Setting the Points*

Even though there was talk of an 'idiomatic confusion' in the Balkans, the language scenario over there appears quite clear compared to the situation on the Indian subcontinent. Gross simplifications must therefore suffice in order to explain the ethno-national divergence of Hindi and Urdu.[175]

Both belong to the eastern branch of the Indo-Germanic family of languages. The 3,000-year-old holy texts of the Vedas reveal this. The Brahmans were the first ones to standardize their language. They saw the Vedic texts as being threatened by linguistic changes, and hence feared that their religious influence was also in danger. So they created the classic Sanskrit, with its first grammar from the fourth century BC. In this process not only the *etymological* ancestor of Hindu and Urdu, respectively Hindu-Urdu, appeared, but, as described above, the Brahmanical tradition also played an extremely important role in the formation of a modern, *political* 'Hindudom'.[176] With some imagination one could then equate Hindi with Hindu. The 'sanskritization' of Hindi became the strongest religious and political argument in favour of the division of Hindi and Urdu.

Sanskrit, which was loaded with religious connotations, played the same role in the emergence of Hindi as old Persian did for the development of Urdu. Perso-Arabic elements were already present in the broad regional spectrum of dialects of early Hindi-Urdu. Out of this amalgam Khari Boli developed between the twelfth and the seventeenth centuries as a linguistically more standardized form and a common basis for Hindi *and* Urdu. Particularly in the later Mughal period Persian influence made its way into Urdu more steadily. Persian and Sanskrit influences are therefore no critieria *a priori* for a linguistic Hindi-Urdu dichotomy.

From the seventeenth century, however, differences began to emerge between both branches. The term 'Zaban-e-Urdu' (language of the camp) came into being only at this time to designate the dialect in the region around Delhi. The Turkish word for 'camp' was used because Urdu was spoken in the camps and courts of the Muslim conquerors.[177] As a name of the later *Ausbausprache* it came up for the first time in 1776.[178] Hindu writers mostly used the Devanagari script and were inclined to sanskritize the vocabulary. Their Muslim colleagues mostly wrote in Perso-Arabic. But there were also many examples where these cleavages crosscut.[179]

It was the British who encouraged the encrustation of these differences.[180] In 1800 they founded the Fort William College in Calcutta where they promoted Indian literature in the style of academic purity—Hindi as free as possible of Persian loan words, and Urdu as strongly as possible Persian. The differences were strongly emphasized, even if they could be found only marginally in the abstract vocabulary and in the construction of sentences. In terms of grammar and basic vocabulary the languages are identical.[181] A regional hybrid (Hindustani) served as the colloquial language spoken by Hindus *as well as* Muslims in the northern provinces.

The linguistic developments mentioned here took place exclusively in the 'Great Tradition'—mainly among poets and writers. On top of this, the differences between both variants almost exclusively applied to the script only. But India was a society with an oral cultural tradition. So the Hindi-Urdu debate enjoyed an extremely limited mass appeal. Only the British influence and the printing technology gave this controversy a new platform altogether.[182]

Other developments also show the British influence as a factor in the Hindi-Urdu division. An important step was the dismissal of Persian as the official language in the northern provinces in 1837. It was replaced by English and Hindustani in the Perso-Arabic script (which was the same as Urdu). This triggered the first organized language protest by Hindu activists. They demanded the replacement of Urdu with Hindi in the Devanagari script. The colonial rulers finally yielded to this demand in 1881.[183] This had three consequences:

(1) The Hindu/Hindi—Urdu/Muslim cleavage was deepened and became politicized. (2) The Muslims felt discriminated against. Many of them were advocates or worked as recorders in government offices. Both in their professions and in recruitment they were now given a backseat vis-à-vis Hindus. (3) Urdu movements were founded and their supporters quarreled with Hindu activists. The latter felt encouraged by the British and made more and more demands, such as the introduction of compulsory Hindi lessons in schools. They argued that Urdu was a 'foreign' language and that Urdu texts contained 'indecent' material. Apart from this, Hindi and Urdu activists contributed to the homogenization of 'their' respective languages.

These linguistic fronts in the larger cultural battle greatly influenced the fights between the ethno-national camps towards the end of the nineteenth century and the beginning of the twentieth century. These cleavages were supported by the British, because since the end of the eighteenth century, they had started to regard Hindus and Muslims as separate races and (ethno-) nations, and language constituted a decisive element in their definitions. The strong influence of Herder on the British Orientalists is clearly seen here.[184]

The initiator of the Muslim Urdu movement was Syed Ahmad Khan. His arguments in support of Urdu were quite similar to those given by Bosnian-Muslim nationalists in favour of Bosnian. With an own language for all Indian Muslims he wanted to undermine pan-Islamic ambitions.[185] This is one reason why he had criticized the Khilafat movement. This displays the same identity crisis of the Muslims—between an 'ethnic' Islam and pan-Islam—as it existed in Bosnia-Herzegovina, too.

3.2.2. *The Contradictions*

At the peak of the ethno-national rivalries, till 1947, Herder's equation of 'language equals nation' had prevailed with the ideologues. The Hindu nationalist Savarkar claimed that Hindus were given 'their' language quasi in their cradle: '[T]hey began to babble it while they sucked the life-giving milk at their Mother's breast.'[186] 'Mother' with a capital 'M' is also to be understood as 'India' in the territorial sense. The highly stylized Sanskrit-Hindi assumed an ethno-national connotation. Even though most Hindus did not understand it, they had to be integrated at least politically. Thus Savarkar called for 'anti-Urdu weeks'. The linguistic preferences of a small educated elite were supposed to become a mass phenomenon. Savarkar threatened: 'Let no Hindu write, read or speak Urdu or use or learn the foreign and unscientific Urdu script [. . .].'[187]

Gandhi as always sought a compromise. He propagated the colloquial language of Hindustani as the national language which could be cast into both scripts without any problems. Nehru supported this idea. The Congress even introduced Hindustani as its working language in 1925. However, many members had a hard time using it. They were used to English. Also, Gandhi himself had great trouble learning Hindustani and Hindi; his mother tongue was Gujarati, and he otherwise preferred English, though he avoided the language of the colonial rulers for political reasons.

Jinnah's case was completely different. He spoke Urdu much worse than Gandhi spoke Hindi. He preferred to stick to English, which Gandhi held against him. Nevertheless, Urdu rose to the status of the national language of Pakistan, and sanskritized Hindi became the official language in India (besides English). Gandhi's Hindustani fell by the wayside. Both ethno-national camps had become mired in their linguistic trenches. Interestingly, however, not all Muslim spokesmen supported the Urdu movement. Some spoke in favour of the idea of Hindustani. In particular, the Islamic Deoband school and the Islamic organization Jamiat-ul-Ulema-i-Hind wanted to detach the Urdu movement from Muslim ethno-nationalism.

Urdu still fulfilled an important function in the ideology of a Muslim state. The language served as an anchor of identity for the new 'nation state'. So Liaqat Ali Khan declared in the constituent assembly of Pakistan:

> Pakistan is a Muslim country and it must have as its *lingua franca* the language of the Muslim nation. . . . Pakistan has been created because of the demand of a hundred million Muslims in this sub-continent and the language of a hundred million Muslims is Urdu. . . .[188]

Such talk was completely in contradiction of the facts. In the 1951 Census only 7.2 per cent of the Pakistanis indicated Urdu as their mother tongue. It is true that Urdu, Punjabi, and Sindhi have the same script and some common words. More than 54 per cent, however, spoke Bengali, a language quite different from the northern Indian languages.[189] This was also the biggest problem of the young state. The ruling Urdu elite feared that the Bengali-speaking East Pakistanis would establish stronger cultural bonds with the Indian West Bengalis than with the West Pakistanis 1,600 km. away. So apart from Herder's premise that language precedes nation-building, the promotion of Urdu also had a power-political aspect. The concern was that ethnic cleavages within Pakistan could break up the religiously-based 'ethnic' camps that gave the state its legitimacy in the first place.

And this is exactly what happened. Although, after strong protests by the Bengalis, Bengali was raised to the status of the second official language, and the head of state Ayub Khan (1958-69) toyed with the idea of a new, mixed national language similar to Gandhi's idea of Hindustani,[190] the Bengalis still saw themselves at a disadvantage against the Urdu elite, not least because of their language when it came to recruitment for government posts. The conflict between the western and the eastern parts of the country escalated. In 1971 East Pakistan split off as Bangladesh.[191]

In India, too, Hindi failed as a factor of national integration. Until today English often comes in handy as a communication bridge between Indians. In 1996, for the first time, an Indian prime minister took office who did not speak Hindi. H.D. Deve Gowda from the south Indian state of Karnataka earned grins and respect at the same time when, after taking a crash course in Hindi before his inauguration speech, he finally managed to struggle his way through the prepared text. Gowda tried hard to leave a positive impression on the largest language group of the country and to acknowledge Hindi as an integrative force of a modern and independent nation.

But in secular India Hindi has to struggle against several stigmas. It must free itself from its strong association with Brahmanical Hindudom. Only in this way it can it win a wider recognition from the Muslims. Besides, many south Indians view the Sanskrit language from the northern 'Hindi belt' with suspicion.[192]

Another contradiction after independence was, that the majority of

Urdu speakers stayed on the Indian side.[193] The cradle of Urdu culture remained in India although the Muslim middle class in Uttar Pradesh and Bihar—the main torchbearers of the Urdu movement—lost its political prominence.

The people in villages continue to speak their own dialects. Hindus may call their dialect Hindi and Muslims their dialect Urdu, but the outsider does not hear any great differences between them. They are sometimes much more evident between the dialects of the touchable and the untouchable castes than between Hindus and Muslims.[194]

An ethno-national labelling of languages did prevail. But in practice it found no expression. Pakistanis watch Hindi movies from Mumbai and sing their hit songs with pleasure. They do not need any subtitles. Sometimes mass culture reveals more than the painstaking work of linguists.

The Urdu movement arose from the agitation of the educated middle and upper classes in Uttar Pradesh and Bihar. Their activities got each other worked up in interaction with the counter objectives of Hindu nationalists. Both happened in the northern regions which today are also described as the 'Hindi belt'. The colonial influence of the British acted as a catalyst through the standardization of language and through varying concessions to Hindi and Urdu activists.

The following factors sealed the fate of Hindi and Urdu as separate standard languages: Herder's concept of nation, the homogenization and modernization of 'Hindu' and 'Muslim' cultures, communal rivalry, the desire for independence and, as a consequence, the modern urge for a 'national language'.

The two most highly formalized languages were forced into their respective religious camps. In turn, the religious difference was enriched with 'ethnic' factors. As A. Rashid rightly concludes:

> Thus the closing inwards of communities along the lines of Hindu and Muslim was increasingly a matter not just of religion but of language and culture as well. What had been different in the inherent ideology of the two communities thus assumes greater significance, and exclusivism emerged as a central factor on both sides.[195]

In reality ethnic, regional, linguistic, and religious cleavages crosscut in all conceivable forms.[196] In this way India is different from, for example, Sri Lanka, where religious and linguistic cleavages between

Sinhala-speaking Sinhalese/Buddhists and Tamil-speaking Tamils/Hindus overlap.[197]

To what extent the Hindi-Urdu controversy deepened the gulf between the ethno-national camps in India is controversial. Some point out that S.A. Khan's worldview of Hindu-Muslim antagonism was greatly influenced by this fight.[198] Others insist that S.A. Khan's concept of nation was based less on language than on religion, and that he viewed Hindus and Muslims as separate nations *before* the language conflict broke out.[199] Again others see language as an instrument in the hands of elites of both sides who pursued their own respective political, social, and economic interests.[200]

Comparative view

Most of the speakers of 'pure' Urdu live in the 'enemy's land' of India. Most of the speakers of 'pure' Serbian live in the 'enemy's land' of Bosnia-Herzegovina. This illogicality shows that in the cases described, language as an ethno-national component is not really convincing. Even in the best case scenario it raises contradictions. Yet it became effectively politicized and instrumentalized for ethno-national purposes, although not without great efforts of mobilization. The interests of an action group and of a postulated language community—i.e. the followers addressed—are hence not automatically congruent. This is why, for example, certain Muslims refused to support the Urdu movement.

In India the instrumentalization of language led to pragmatic approaches. Similar to the compromises made during the Khilafat movement, the suggestion of Hindustani was an attempt to hold back the ethno-national dynamics with ideological constructs of equal rank, although this time without any success.[201]

Similarly, the attempt of the Yugoslav communists failed to get the 'Serb' and 'Croatian' languages under one roof. Both competing script types were possible and were allowed: Cyrillic and Latin, like Devanagari and Persian with Hindi-Urdu/Hindustani. In Yugoslavia the binational title remained; in India the crosscutting of various ethnic cleavages prevented a national designation of languages.

The Hindi/Urdu and the Serbian/Croatian phenomena have the following in common: (1) Both were developed by the literati and only gradually enjoyed mass appeal among a still illiterate population. (2) Both were sub-dialects not only of a vertical minority (literati) but also of a horizontal one (regional reference). (3) Both differ almost exclusively in their scripts [which strengthens hypothesis number (1)]. (4) Both became an important instrument for the elites of an ethno-nationalism which was strongly based on religious features. (5) Both show an extremely inconsequent distribution with reference to this ideal.

According to Clyne's research, the rivalries between Serbian/Orthodox—Croatian/Catholic and Hindi/Hindu—Urdu/Muslim are the only known examples where scripts (are supposed to) overlap with religion.[202]

4. NATIONAL MIDWIVES FROM ABOVE

At the end of the nineteenth and the beginning of twentieth centuries, Muslims in Bosnia-Herzegovina and India lived under 'foreign' rule, Austria-Hungary and Great Britain. They had ousted the Ottomans and the Mughals respectively. In both cases the new masters were not ethno-national rivals but foreigners. Furthermore, they were from an economically, militarily, and politically more advanced and well-organized administrative state. They were confronted with a traditional local population.[203]

The Habsburgers and the British viewed 'the Muslims' as an 'ethnic', religious, national—and in the case of the British even racial—entity. This promoted the group consciousness of the Muslim elites. Foreign rule penetrated the political and social life and modernized it. Groups who wanted to express themselves had to do it within a given framework. The political system of the occupants was their plane of action and identification. In both cases the established institutions opened up new avenues of cultural homogenization and political representation. The respective rulers used these new forums in their interest. Just as the Habsburgers sought to play off the South Slavs against each other, the British tried to do the same with the Indians.

4.1. The Cultural Entrepreneurs

4.1.1. *Bosnia-Herzegovina*

The Austrian Finance Minister Benjamin Kállay was determined to turn the Bosnian Muslims into *one* people. From 1882 to 1903 he was governor in Bosnia-Herzegovina. His official acts started out exactly with the criteria which Gellner describes as typical of nation-building.

Kállay supported 'national' champions of culture: the press, like the Muslim newspaper *Bosnjak*;[204] literary societies; multi-confessional schools; symbols, like the Bosnian flag and the coat of arms by decree in 1889; the collection of Muslim folk songs; historical researches; and the foundation of a state museum in Sarajevo. The Kállay government officially introduced the term 'Bosnian language', despite the protests by Serb and Croatian nationalists.[205]

One of the most important new institutions was an independent Islamic authority for the Bosnian Muslims, the *reis-ul-ulema*[206] in Sarajevo, from 1882 onwards. For all of those who look for a 'clash of civilizations'-kind-of-pattern in the issue, this must be a disappointment. For it was *Christians* who invented, created, and posted new *Muslim* clerics and dignitaries. The Habsburg government thus expressed the hope for an independent national church policy as the Orthodox had already demonstrated. The invocation of the name of the caliph in Istanbul was banned from the Friday prayers.

The aim of Austria-Hungary was to weaken Serb and Croatian nationalisms. Kállay wanted to isolate the Bosnians from these influences and strengthen their own identity. They were, after all, the only ones without a homeland or a sponsor-nation. However, his success was limited to a few moderate urbane landowners. A *political* interest connected him with them: they had defended agrarian feudal rights since Turkish times. For Kállay, this meant stability, although it did hamper the overdue steps towards modernization in Bosnia-Herzegovina.[207]

With these *beys* Kállay wanted to revive the pre-Islamic traditions and peculiarities of 'the Bosnian Muslims'. The most famous and important among them was Mehemet Beg Kapetanovic (1839-1902), editor of *Bosnjak* and mayor of Sarajevo. He introduced the term 'Bosnjak' for someone who belonged to the Muslim upper class which, according to him, had not only religious but also many 'ethnic' features which went as far back as the Middle Ages.[208] Kapetanovic turned the tables and called Bosnia-Herzegovina a homeland. Serbs and Croats, he said, were 'actually' Bosnjaks, too.[209] But the Muslims occupied the first place.[210]

By the turn of the century it had become clear that Kállay's efforts were doomed to failure. Kapetanovic and his supporters stood quite alone in the end. The Muslims were not united among themselves.

This episode shows that the occupants encouraged the Muslim elite as the upholder of ethno-national ideologies, *although* it had a different 'cultural' identity. The gross pattern of a supposed 'cultural difference' is therefore inadequate to explain the slow and halting attempts at nation-building of the Bosnian Muslims. This shakes the foundations of Dzaja's Orient-Occident generalization.[211] Rather, more important reasons can be found in the lack of economic modernization; at a time of growing demand for goods, the *beys* missed the opportunity of becoming the leading economic class. Instead of investing their capital in factories, 'the landowners preferred to sell off their land to be able to procure industrial products from the monarchy', writes Babuna. Further barriers to modernization were the unresolved agrarian issue and the archaic educational system.[212]

4.1.2. India

The strong influence of the British on Indian culture has already been mentioned. In particular their historiography and the ways in which they dealt with Indian traditions and languages contributed to the communalization of the Indian public. Academia and the educational system played a major role. Here also Gellner's criteria of nation-building come in.

There were many British 'Benjamin Kállays' in India. The first one was William Jones (1746-94) who founded the Bengal Asiatic Society. It published writings on Indian culture, comparative studies of religions, linguistics, and the natural sciences. Above all, Jones started to compile a Hindu and a Muslim code of rights. A number of British publications on India followed.[213]

The promotion of a Muslim public was often associated with the concept of *divide et impera*. This becomes more evident later when the political scene and the negotiations about Pakistan are examined.[214] But this hypothesis is highly controversial. The question is: did the British divide the country by ruling it, or did they rule a divided country?[215]

Statements of British contemporaries contradict each other. Dufferin said the following in a newspaper interview in 1887:

> The diversity of races in India, and the presence of a powerful Mahomedan community, are undoubtedly circumstances favourable to the maintenance of our rule; but these circumstances we found and did not create, nor, had they

been non-existent, would we have been justified in establishing them by artificial means. It would have been a diabolical policy on the part of my Government to endeavour or emphasise or exacerbate race hatreds among the Queen's Indian subjects for a political object.[216]

A call of 1899 sounded quite different. 'We have maintained our power by playing off one part against the other, and we must continue to do so. . . . Do what you can, therefore, to prevent all having a common feeling.'[217]

Contradictory statements and expressions of will cannot be clarified here in detail. In any case, historians agree on the point that the university in Aligarh—the hotbed of Muslim ethno-nationalism—could not have unfolded its potential without British support. It was Syed Ahmed Khan who speeded up the foundation of the modern and independent 'Muhammadan Anglo-Oriental College' (later: the Aligarh Muslim University) in the 1870s. He was quite a unrepresentative Muslim, with modern, undogmatic views. Critics accused him of being a heretic (Jinnah also faced these allegations). Yet the British accepted the opinions of this man as those of 'the Muslim camp'.

Khan's All-India Muslim Educational Congress (1886, since 1890 Conference) was the first country-wide association of Indian Muslims. It had its origin in the north Indian Urdu movement. Khan realized that a cultural development of the Muslims was possible only *with* the British.[218] A modern and moderate Muslim Urdu-speaking elite grew up in Aligarh. From its ranks came the politicians of the Muslim League and the spokesmen of Pakistan. Therefore, Lelyveld concludes: 'Aligarh was not a school, it was a political symbol.'[219]

Khan's models for Aligarh were Oxford and Cambridge. The university stood as a counter example to the traditional Koran schools (*madrassas*). Khan wanted to redress the educational backlog of the Muslims vis-à-vis the Hindus, and thereby increase their competitiveness for important government posts. Ironically, in the early years, one-fifth of the students were Hindus, and Hindus from the Urdu-speaking elite also co-financed the project.[220] Another contradiction can be noticed here, which is important for the theory of nation-building: the Aligarh movement did *not* at all start in a region where 'the Muslims' were at a disadvantage (unlike, for example, in Bengal). On the contrary. In the United Provinces the 'heritage' of the Mughals had persisted in the most tenacious way.[221] There the Muslim Urdu-speaking elite assumed a dominant role and prevented the social upliftment of backward Hindus. Thus, the starting point of the Pakistan movement was not a place of Muslim discrimination—in contrast to its rhetoric and to the arguments of many history-writers.[222]

Comparative view

Gellner's factors of nation-building reappear in the policy of the occupants both in Bosnia-Herzegovina and in India. The Austrians and the British more or less provided the modern material for a homogenization of cultural traditions. In this way they promoted the thinking within ethno-national camps.

Both cases can be compared not only in ideological but also in organizational terms. The Bosnian Vakuf-Mearif movement played a role similar to the Muslim Conference in India. The organization initially had a cultural programme, namely Muslim education and religious self-governance.[223] However, unlike in India, it was directly opposed to the occupying power and spearheaded a movement for political autonomy at the end of the nineteenth century.

It was from the Vakuf-Mearif movement that the party of the Muslim People's Organization (MNO)[224] emerged in 1906. In exactly the same year, the Muslim League was founded as a party in India, that also had its origins in a cultural movement (of the Muslim Conference and the University in Aligarh). Both organizations became the main self-proclaimed mouthpieces of 'the Muslims'. However, they essentially safeguarded the economic interests of only a part of the community—those of the Muslim upper class, mostly landowners. The elite had nothing to do with the peasants of the same faith.[225] Action group and group feature clearly differ here. Besides, in both cases, the spokesmen played the tune of 'Muslim discrimination', although they were never affected by it themselves.

Yet another parallel: both were religiously moderate parties that promoted the worldview of a local—namely 'ethnic'—Islam against pan-Islamic streams.

5. THE FORMATION OF POLITICAL PARTIES

The phase of political representation of 'the Muslims' in Bosnia-Herzegovina and India began in 1906. At this point the Muslim People's

Organization as well as the Muslim League did not have the slightest intention of demanding Muslim statehood. Both parties took a stand on everyday problems and entered into political marriages of convenience. However, their relationship with the occupying power was not without problems.

5.1. Identity-splits in Bosnia-Herzegovina

At the end of Kállay's tenure Muslim-Habsburg relations were highly strained. To ease the pressure, the administration allowed the formation of political parties after his retirement in 1903. They reflected the tripartition of the Muslim intelligence. By 1919 five different Muslim parties came into being, which merged with each other or splintered off.[226] They represented the following interests (a) pro big landowners, loyal to Habsburg;[227] (b) anti big landowners, politically pro-Serb, religiously pan-Islamic (orientation towards Istanbul); (c) pro-Croatian, for a third—Croato-Muslim—pillar in the Austro-Hungarian Empire.

This spectrum yields three conclusions: (1) An independent Muslim politics does not exist, but there is a subordination to three external centres of power (Austria-Hungary, Croatia, Serbia). (2) There is no political Muslim ideology. (3) Social cleavages influence the interests which are exploited by activists of the three centres of power.[228]

Here it also becomes clear that cleavages crosscut instead of overlapping. So a pan-Islamic orientation in religious and 'ethnic' terms is hard to reconcile with a pro-Serb outlook. While (b) represents the lower strata, the upper class is divided in (a) and (c). They were thus *political* alliances which went against ethno-national factors.[229]

The pragmatism of the Muslim politicians paid off. In 1909 the demand of 'the Muslims' for religious autonomy was fulfilled. In 1910 the Muslim representatives officially accepted Austro-Hungarian rule and pledged their loyalty. In turn, Bosnia-Herzegovina got a constitution and a parliament (*sabor*), where the representatives of the MNO manoeuvred successfully by shifting alliances with Serb and Croatian parliamentarians. They were thus able to protect their agrarian privileges.[230] As parliamentarians who tipped the scales they distinguished themselves as a *political* Muslim action group.

From 1919 on the Yugoslav Muslim Organization (JMO)[231] was the largest representative of Muslim interests. In the elections it collected almost all 'Muslim' votes. However, out of 24 of its parliament members 15 declared themselves as Croats, two as Serbs, five as undecided, and one as Bosnian.[232] Their president, the crafty tactician Mehemet Spaho (1883-1939), represented, as usual, the interests of the big landowners, and once again he prevented land reforms.[233] Muslim pragmatism also manifested itself in a lead article of the JMO newspaper of 1920: '[It] recommended that Muslims should identify with whichever nation offered them the fairest chance of "economic development".'[234] Such an opportunistic approach was not only prevalent among Bosnian Muslims. Since the end of the nineteenth century a rapid change took place from one 'ethnic group' to the other. People even took along piggyback a new and fitting ethno-nationalism to the other side. This applied to all, whether they began their lives as Serbs, Croats, or Muslims, and to which ever 'ethnic group' they headed for afterwards.[235]

The Muslim spokesmen were particularly disunited. So they could hardly get enthusiastic about the idea of an 'own' state either. In any case, such a demand never came from the JMO at all, not even during the political vaccum after the first Balkan wars. As a protective shield against Serb and Croatian pressure, the party opted for the concept of South Slavism. (Others could also imagine autonomy within Hungary.)[236] The main aim of the JMO was: Bosnia should survive as an autonomous unit with Yugoslavia. The party programme stressed that there did exist Muslim nationalism but no national consciousness among the Muslims. It further emphasized that the national question did not belong to the sphere of politics but culture.[237] Obviously, the Bosnian Muslims were far away from Hroch's third stage of nation-building.

Instead, the Muslim politicians made their mark with their tactics of changing partners in the new 'Kingdom of Serbs, Croats, and Slovenes' and later in Yugoslavia, too. By 1941 there were nine Muslim parties. Most were pro-Serb, none pro-Croatian. Three parties—one pro *beys*, one pro peasants, one pro women—could survive only for a few months.[238] Ethno-national cleavages now became all the more conspicuous.

After Spaho's death in 1939, the Muslim politicians were edged out. The Serb government signed a treaty with the Croatian opposition, in which they both agreed to divide Bosnia-Herzegovina among themselves. A land reform by Belgrade deprived many Muslims of their economic basis.[239] Thus, the traditional privileges of property of many Muslims began to fade. This continued with the process of nationalization in the later Yugloslavia.[240] The Tito regime interrupted the development of democratic political parties. Conflicts were officially settled within the Communist Party. Their splitting up into organizations of the Yugoslav republics, however, gave at least an equally good forum to ethno-national conflicts.[241]

The Muslim identity splits on the individual as well as on the political level continued until the war in the 1990s. Caught between two aggressive ethno-nationalisms, some Muslim spokesmen again oscillated between the one or the other side, even though they were trying to strengthen their own ethno-nationalism at the same time. In a remarkable interview with a Slovenian newspaper in 1993, the Muslim hardliner and vice-president of the Federation, Ejup Ganic, suggested that 'the Muslims are Islamized Serbs, and the biggest mistake we made was at the beginning of the war when we concluded a military alliance with the Croats'. Later he amplified his remarks in an interview in Zagreb: 'We are related much more closely with the Serbs than with the Slovenes and the Croats. We speak a dialect that is more similar to Serbian than Croat. The same goes for mentality, habits, and customs.'[242] He hinted that the Muslim side were already involved in 'secret talks' with the Serbs.

5.2. The Majority Trap in India

Since the Mutiny of 1857 the British had passed a number of reforms which involved the Indian subjects—in careful steps—in the administration and judiciary.[243] The Indian National Congress was founded in 1885 to represent the interests of all Indians, or at least this is how it saw itself. From 1906 on the Muslim League challenged this claim more and more vigorously. It was encouraged by the British reforms of 1909, 1919, and 1935. They contributed decisively to the fact that a contest of interests could take place within the structures of political majorities. The reforms were also accompanied by decentralization. The most important change, however, was that the British introduced separate quotas and electorates—among others for 'the Muslims'. This triggered incentives to play the role of political spokesmen and to occupy other important posts. The struggle gained momentum with growing opposition against the colonial rulers and with the prospect of an independent India.

The British introduced the majority system as a novelty in the Indian subcontinent. With the quota system they violated the principles of their own liberal tradition.[244] Indeed, references to quotas can be found in old political texts of India which deal with consensus and balance.[245] But the new prospect of political representation through *one man–one vote* provided the argument with which Jinnah *mainly* legitimized the demand for Pakistan: the Muslims are threatened by a Hindu majority and would not get a say in a common democratic system. Syed Ahmed Khan was the first to express these apprehensions, in 1883: '[P]rinciples of simple elections cannot be satisfactorily worked because the larger nation will dominate the smaller one completely.'[246] This is remarkable because, still in 1927, the Liberal Jinnah had spoken out *against* separate electorates and in favour of a system of common representation.[247]

Some, mainly Indian, historians place a direct blame on this new election element for the partition of the country.[248] It is striking that the British gave 'the Muslims' special political guarantees. However, they cannot be necessarily accused of having aimed at a divide along religious camps *from the beginning*. For example, the Muslim League was founded three years *before* the introduction of quotas which made sense only with its existence. Besides, also economic and social cleavages, representatives of various social castes and institutions were considered in the quotas from 1909 on. But the Muslims were listed separately as the *only* religious group.[249] The endeavour of the British to divide *politically* is rooted in their fear of resistance. As early as 1899 George F. Hamilton gave a wise interpretation of the situation and an apt forecast, almost accurate to the year:

> I think the real danger to our rule in India, not now but say 50 years hence, is the gradual adoption and extension of western ideas of agitation and organisation, and, if we could break the educated Hindu party [Congress] into two sections holding widely different views, we should, by such a division, strengthen our position against the subtle and continuous attack which the spread of education must make upon our system of Government.[250]

In fact, in the beginning of the twentieth century a large number of parties mushroomed in India. Muslims were involved in several of them—in the Congress, in the Muslim League, and in other Islamic or liberal parties. Politically and dogmatically 'the Indian Muslims' were far from acting as one block. Various Islamic movements and legal schools were close to different political parties, or they abstained altogether.

Until shortly before the foundation of Pakistan, there was no organization which could be considered as the mouthpiece of all Muslims, even if the Muslim League claimed this role for itself. In the elections the 'Muslim' vote did not clearly go in favour of one political representative as it did in Bosnia-Herzegovina at the time of Spaho and the JMO.

The Muslim League itself never had a mass basis like the Congress. Only the urban middle class and, especially, Muslim landowners from the Muslim- minority provinces in the north supported it.[251] Money, status, and education determined the membership. The newspaper *Bengalee* wrote mockingly: '[T]he League and its branches are engineered mostly by Government pensioners or ex-officials, of gentlemen who are compelled to solicit Government assistance in their family or pecuniary difficulties.'[252] Muslim traders and businessmen joined the League only quite late.[253]

It was the only party to demand a Muslim state at all. However, the Muslim League's foundation programme still looked quite different. Three points stand out in particular: (a) Promoting Muslim loyalty towards the British government. (b) Safeguarding and extending the political interests of the Muslims in India. (c) Avoiding hostilities against other communites.[254]

After 1920 the party had sunk into insignificance. Frustrated, Jinnah left for London in 1931. But five years later he came back to lead the Muslim League to a decisive election. The Government of India Act of 1935 (or 'Communal Award') brought about a change. For the first time, Indian parties which gained the majority could appoint ministers in the provinces in order to share responsibility with the British.[255] At the same time, the provinces got more powers (decentralization) and 30 per cent of the adult population was entitled to vote.[256]

Various Muslim parties had fallen out with the Muslim League and competed separately. Others represented economic and social programmes and thus divided the support on which the League relied. This was done mainly by the National Agriculturalist Party (NAP). Its elite was the same as the elite of the Muslim League, namely big landowners, albeit Hindus *and* Muslims.[257] It was the Congress party which undoubtedly emerged as the India-wide winner of the elections in 1937.[258] The League could not form a government in any Muslim-majority province. In Punjab and Bengal Muslim regional parties, which cooperated with other communities, undercut the League. However, the Congress won only half of the 'Muslim constituencies'. It had run only in a small number of them in the first place. Inder Singh sums up the situation: 'The election results proved that neither the Congress nor the League could claim to represent Muslims.'[259]

What made the elections so meaningful was the aftermath. For the first time, there was a chance of bringing both camps together politically. The election manifestos of the Congress and the Muslim League were almost identical. They were ideal partners. Yet the Congress rejected the possibility of forming coalition governments with the Muslim League. Nehru cast to the winds a corresponding question from Jinnah in Bombay. He insisted that the Congress was the sole representative of Indian interests. There were only two parties: the Congress and the British.[260] Nehru lectured with an arrogance that embittered Jinnah:

> Why should I accept [. . .] [the League] as the representative of the Muslims of India when I know it represents a handful of Muslims at the top who deliberately seek refuge in the name of religion to avoid discussing mass problems. I have a certain measure of intelligence and I have studied political, economic, and social problems for a quarter of a century now . . . Am I to insult my intelligence by talking baby-talk of an age gone by? . . . Do you not say that this policy which the Muslim League has followed is a policy more injurious to the Muslims of India than anything that a majority could do would be?[261]

Jinnah responded:

> [T]he sole aim and object of the Congress is to annihilate every other organization in the country, and to set itself up as a fascist and authoritarian organization of the worst type.[262]

Jinnah saw Nehru's strict anti ethno-national approach only as a confirmation of his belief that 'democracy can only mean Hindu raj all over India'.[263] Jinnah intensified his camp agitation. Many historians consider the elections of 1937 as an important landmark on the way to Pakistan.[264] According to the ethno-national logic, with these elections 'the Muslims' came under the rule of 'the Hindus' for the first time in history.[265]

The tone between Gandhi, Nehru and Jinnah became increasingly rough. Personal animosities and vanities prevented substantial debates. The correspondence between the three leaders reads like a quarrel between peeved children. They quote their respective preceding insults and misunderstandings, and keep going round and round in a circle.[266] The political issues in the election campaigns narrowed down to independence and ethno-national proportional representation which became increasingly confined to the Congress and the Muslim League. The remaining parties all over India were marginalized.

It was the notorious elections of 1937 which made Jinnah redouble his efforts to get rid of his opponents. Just a year later he actually managed to achieve this, when the Muslim Unionists of Punjab, who cooperated with the Hindus, joined the Muslim League. The division of Punjab—and hence of India—had come one step closer.

Comparative view

The introduction of the political party system was a catalyst for the formation of *political* loyalty among the Muslims in Bosnia-Herzegovina and India, which took both place at the same time. Another thing in common is that Muslims were involved in different political parties representing opposing standpoints, and that they cooperated with opponents from the other ethno-national camp. In Bosnia-Herzegovina Muslim party members additionally ascribed themselves—or the whole kin—to a rival 'ethnic group', even in midst of the highest ethno-national tensions. This did not happen in India. The Muslims in the Congress and in the provincial governments merely denied the existence of any conflict of interest between the two communities.

Only in course of time could one political party gain the position of being as the main mouthpiece of 'the Muslims'. In both cases they predominantly advocated the interests of the big landowners and the urban bourgeoisie. They were pragmatic. For them it was a matter of political objectives, and not of religious dogmatism.

6. SPLIT BROTHERS

They called themselves 'brothers in faith'. But this did not mean at all that all Muslims shared the same opinion. In particular, their attitude towards Islam differed on dogmatic and ideological issues. Therefore, the main feature of their ethno-national demarcation was in no way as distinct as their spokesmen would have liked it to be.

6.1. Bosnia-Herzegovina

6.1.1. *Bosporus or Bosnia?*

With the abortion of the Kállay-Kapetanovic coalition, the formation of a national Muslim Bosniandom failed, too. This was—apparently paradoxically—closely connected to Islam. Most Muslims once again oriented themselves in accordance with their historical bonds with the Bosporus.[267] They often called themselves *Turcin* (Turks).[268] During Kállay's government a particularly conservative trend prevailed in Bosnia-Herzegovina. The clergy opposed compulsory education for girls and the introduction of the Cyrillic and Latin scripts in the Koran schools.[269] Now only a few Muslims were enthusiastic about an 'ethnic Bosniandom' which had earlier served as a demarcation against the Ottomans. This territorially-based identification lost its effectiveness against the growing Serb and Croatian demands anyway.[270]

After World War II the pan-Islamic current experienced a political boost. A small group which called itself Young Muslims (*Mladi Muslimani*) declared *jihad* against the communists.[271] In 1946 the communists had abolished Sharia law in Yugoslavia. In 1950 wearing a veil was made a punishable offence.[272] Officials closed down Koran schools and Muslim cultural centres and nationalized the *vakufs*. Finally, they appointed loyal Islamic heads.

The *Mladi Muslimani* used all this as an opportunity to demand a place for 'the Bosnian Muslims' in the worldwide *umma*. They explicitly saw their model in Pakistan—regardless of the fact that the Pakistani pan-Islamists, like the Jama'at-i-Islami, were *against* the founding of the state. But this contradiction did not bother them. They mixed pan-Islamic rhetoric with the demand for the autonomy of Bosnia-Herzegovina and considered Islam the basis of their national identity.[273] So they used pan-Islamism as an instrument for political, ethno-national demands. This ideology also had a certain mass appeal. In the war of Israel with Syria and Egypt in 1973 Muslims in Sarajevo came out on the streets and declared their solidarity with the Arab world (against Yugoslavia's officially proclaimed non-aligned approach). From the end of 1970s on, the mosques increasingly filled up, and more and more Bosnian Muslims undertook a pilgrimage to Mecca.[274]

In 1974 the Muslim historian Aziz Hadzihasanovic warned in the newspaper *Oslobodenje*: '[It is a] misconception that Muslim nationalism, unlike Serb and Croatian nationalism, was somehow naive, harmless, . . . on another political plane.'[275] One of the most vigorous critics of the political misuse of Islam was Hamdija Pozderac. He was the only Muslim member who served as the president of the Federation of Yugoslav Communists and as Vice-President of Yugoslavia. His criticism was based on the legitimate fear that pan-Islamic feelings could weaken Muslim national identity and serve to call the Serb and Croatian ethno-nationalists into action.[276]

The communists took a strong stand against the pan-Islamic movement. In 1983 some Young Muslims were put behind bars. Among them was a man, who until his death in 2003 symbolized the internal Muslim split between pan-Islamic and Bosnian national ideology, and whose importance no one could have guessed at that time: Alija Izetbegovic.

6.1.2. *Nation Via Decree: The Bosnian Specialty*

In addition to the pan-Islamism of some Muslims, the growing pressure exerted by Serb and Croatian ethno-nationalists also caused the communists a headache, too. Both things were closely connected. Pan-Islam undermined the 'ethnic' identity of 'the Muslims' vis-à-vis the competition. But a politically instrumentalized pan-Islam, like that of the Young Muslims, stood for ethno-nationalism. Tito neither could nor wanted to land himself with yet another one of these sorts. The others were bad enough.

So he decided to play a clever game and exploited another cleavage among the Muslims: their growing secularity. At this time, around 65 per cent of the 'socially engaged national Muslims' professed atheism. Only around 35 per cent held onto religious traditions.[277] By the end of the 1980s only 37 per cent of the 'Muslims' were still believers.[278] Most of the official posts were occupied by atheists.

Thus, the ex-Muslims increasingly lost their religious mark of distinction. Simultaneously, the self-assurance of a secular Muslim elite in Yugoslavia's culture and politics grew. It could not be ignored anymore. Tito saw the chance to strengthen this as a new contrasting feature of 'the Muslims' against the ethno-national rivals.

Bosnian-Muslim historians delivered the theoretical justification: '[T]he religious elements [are] losing their former significance and [are] giving way to other spiritual and material factors, not unlike the process characteristic of other Yugoslav peoples.'[279] To underpin their argument they revived the Bogomil myth[280] while Tito took care of the *political* upgrading. In 1968 the Muslims rose to an equal 'nation' in the state fabric of Yugoslavia.[281]

Until this moment, the usual statement through unofficial channels had been: 'Peoples' [= 'nations'] were those ethnic formations whose ethnic centre lay within the borders of Yugoslavia, whereas with 'nationalities' one assumed the centre to be outside Yugoslavia.'[282] So far, this homeland thesis had pushed off the Muslims into a pan-Islamism with Turkish orientation.

Now the situation changed. The constitutional upgrading of 'the Muslims' was supposed to drive a wedge between the Serb and Croatian claims to Bosnia-Herzegovina. The Yugoslav leadership (which initially had believed in unitarism) now wanted to replace the bipolar system with a balance-of-power system where no single entity would be allowed to dictate the agenda.[283] The new situation provided the Bosnian-Muslim politicians with greater access to institutions and with more bargaining power. Often they played the mediators between the republics and tipped the scales. Most negotiations had the character of everyday politics and not a religious or even an ethno-national one. This reminds of Spaho's time.

However, the upgrading created fresh problems.

(1) The new 'Muslim nation' received the name of the religious group, although their identification increasingly detached itself from religion. The Federation of Yugoslav Communists in any case wanted to focus on Islamic *culture* and strictly separate it from Islamic *religion*.[284] This caused some confusion whose consequences are evident even till today. 'The wrong name,' Balic says, 'has become the death trap for the Muslim Bosnians.'[285] The Bosnian historian Hadzijahic called in vain to upgrade the term 'Bosnian'. As early as 1945 he demanded that Serbs and Croats living in Bosnia-Herzegovina should also call themselves Bosnians (*Bosnjaks*) (just as Muslims in Serbia had to describe themselves as Serbs).[286] This opportunity was gone soon.

It took the war in the 1990s to give a new impetus to the tiresome name issue. In 1993 the 'All-Bosnjak Assembly' held the view that Bosnian Muslims, and Muslims alone, should be called *Bosnjaks* from now on.[287] In this way it wanted to revive the old connotation of the fifteenth century which had served to demarcate Bosnian Muslims from the 'Turks'. The historian Purivata justified this decision: 'The main reason is the feeling of being Bosnjak as one's citizenship, and as a political and regional feeling.' He also mentioned a sense of 'patriotism' which the Muslims expressed through this term. It was the Serbs and the Croats themselves who rejected this name at the beginning of the twentieth century, when it was offered to them as an all-comprising term for the inhabitants of Bosnia by the Habsburg governor Kállay. As a compromise Purivata suggested, in 2000, that the Muslims be called *Bosnjak*, and all citizens of Bosnia-Herzegovina be called *Bosanski*.[288] The term Bosnjak has become the usual term to refer to Bosnian Muslims.

The decision of the All-Bosnjak Assembly, which Izetbegovic initially opposed, has prevailed today. What it means, however, is just the opposite of Kállay's offer: it excludes all other population groups from Bosnia-Herzegovina in ethno-national terms.

(2) The arbitrary picking up of certain features for nation-building was indeed the prevalent trend in the Balkans. But in the intricate mess resulting from crosscutting cleavages such a step could not contribute to logical conclusions. So 'the Muslims' demarcated themselves from their Serb and Croatian neighbours as a 'nation', although they basically speak the same language. Moreover, many saw and still see themselves as the new homeland for, say, 'the Muslims' in the equally newly formed 'nation' of Macedonia, although they have almost nothing in common with them except faith. Understandably, the 'new' Slavic Macedonians were not enthusiatic about this. Also, Serb and Croatian nationalists complained about the 'artificial' nation and its 'pointless' proclamation.[289] Bosnian-Muslim intellectuals, on the other hand, mustered up their courage and demanded the official introduction of a 'Bosnian' language. A few even demanded that Bosnia-Herzegovina be renamed as a 'Muslim Republic'.[290] Höpken therefore points to the mixed character of this 'nation-building':

> [T]he upgrading of the Muslims to a nation—as much as it may appear as per ordre de mufti—[was] ultimately the result of a multi-variable process [...], in

which the plebiscitary component and the national-political creative will of a political elite came in equally. Therefore 'grown' and 'created' nation cannot be juxtaposed dichotomically.[291]

Among the Bosnian-Muslims three main currents prevailed which were actually mutually exclusive: (1) Believing Muslims, who regarded Islam 'less as a transcendent orientation than as a spiritual backbone of their specific *Bosnian* culture',[292] as 'the decisive history-building and cultural factor of their "ethnicity"'.[293] (2) Believing Muslims, who sympathized with pan-Islamism. (3) No longer believing Muslims. As 'modern' citizens they had 'grinded off' the religious foundation of their 'ethnos' in the socialist state.[294] There were, as demonstrated, several crosscuttings.

The pan-Islamic and secular powers weakened the ethno-national profile of 'the Bosnian Muslims'. While it was the traditional, religious recalling which, among other things, came in the way of nation-building during Kállay's times, it was the fading influence of religion among 'the Muslims' which initially had the same effect in Yugoslavia. For, in this way, the most characteristic feature which distinguished them from the neighbours was watered down. This did not really make an upgrading of 'the Muslims' against other peoples plausible. On the other hand, it did not come completely out of the blue either. Some Muslim intellectuals and activists upheld the paradigm of 'ethnic' demarcation in the same way as it was exemplified by their surroundings.

6.2. India: Delhi or Mecca?

The pan-Islamic rhetoric adopted by Jinnah from 1937 on had mainly two reasons: (1) There were strong ethno-regional differences and syncretisms among Muslims. So a common 'Islamic' idea and symbolism was necessary to mobilize the masses. (2) Jinnah sought the support of the *ulema*. Many members of the *ulema* thought in pan-Islamic patterns and rejected an independent statehood for Muslims.

Among these the orthodox Deoband School (since the mid 1880s) is particularly important. It was one of the most vehement opponents of British rule. Although in principle it considered India a religiously hostile country (*dar al harb*), it supported the idea of an all-Indian federation. In 1888 it had published a religious judgement (*fatwa*) in favour of an alliance between Hindus and Muslims.[295] An ethno-national state for Muslims was far from its philosophy. During the

Khilafat movement the Jamiat-i-Ulema-i-Hind emerged from among the Deobandis. It recommended a composite nationality of Hindus and Muslims, and engaged itself in the activities of the Congress.

The orthodox Jama'at-i-Islami, which was founded by Maulana Maududi in 1941, was also against a Muslim state. Like the Deobandis he aimed for an 'Islamic revival' and a recalling of Islamic values and morals. In this way, he believed, the conflict with the Hindus would be resolved automatically. For this the Muslims did not need an independent state. Since the foundating of Pakistan, however, this organization has become the driving force for an Islamization of the country.[296]

The above-mentioned Aligarh movement stood in stark dogmatic contrast to them. These Muslims with modern approaches and Western education supported a separation of religious and political life. They advocated the idea of a secular state. This was also Jinnah's idea.

Besides, there were other Islamic law schools and Sufi sects which were not particularly involved in politics. They were sometimes syncretic or ethnically oriented, were often in intense dogmatic conflict with each other, and hardly appeared on the stage of Muslim nation-building. However, they contributed to a sharp dogmatic split in the Muslim constituency.[297] The pan-Islamists did so, too. But when Pakistan was within reach, some of them, like certain sections of the Deobandis, the Jamiat, and the Jama'at climbed onto the bandwagon and demanded a Muslim homeland. In this way the pan-Islamists became divided, too. Some remained loyal to the Congress—the most eminent among them was Abul Kalam Azad (1888-1958). The Urdu poet, journalist, and philosopher even led the party as its president (1939-46). He was a friend of Gandhi and Nehru, and became the first minister of education in India after independence. He was pro-Khilafat and anti-British. Islam and Indian nationalism were no contradictions to him. He doubted that Islam was strong enough to unite all Muslims. His argument in favour of the co-existence of Hindus and Muslims was based on the teachings of the Koran. Hindus had never been aggressors against Muslims. Thus the Muslims should treat them like the former non-Muslims in Medina.[298]

Through the Congress Gandhi and Nehru had Muslim supporters in the population, too. For Gandhi Hinduism and Islam were two sides of the same coin. Syncretically-influenced Muslims favoured this interpretation. For Nehru religion was of secondary importance anyway.

Secularism had also influenced Western-educated Muslims. Some of them were interested in economic issues and leaned towards Marxism.[299]

Another seed of conflict was hidden within the Muslim community, namely the dogmatic differences between Sunnis and Shiites. The latter mostly rejected a Pakistani state. The president of the All Parties Shia Conference even wanted his supporters to be treated in the same way as the other minorities (Sikhs, Christians, Anglo-Indians), and demanded quotas for them, too.[300]

Among the Muslims dogmatic-religious and ideological-political cleavages crisscrossed each other. There were, prima facie, three main streams: (1) The pan-Islamically oriented Muslims from the tradition of the Khilafat movement. (2) Those who aimed at an *Indian*—that is, an 'ethnic'—Islam. (3) Those who cultivated syncretic customs.[301] Moreover, there were dogmatic and ideological differences between Sunnis and Shiites, and between believing and secular Muslims.

In addition to this, Muslim identity was wedged between various *political* concepts. The definition of the Indian and Muslim nations and the consequences for the future state fabric dominated the debates of the organized Muslims and divided them into the above-mentioned camps.

6.3. A Warning to the Distant Brothers

Muslims in Bosnia-Herzegovina and India had at least two points of contact: Pan-Islamic solidarity and a secular line of thinking. Both ideologies have global dimensions and, in fact, did *not* mutually exclude each other.

The principle of secularism was embodied in the most important leading figures of Yugoslavia and India: Tito and Nehru. They represented a moderate state socialism, non-alignment, and thus a new idealism of two states that were reduced to the playboard of the superpowers during World War II. Both men appreciated each other and worked together on an international level. Both had the same goal: they wanted to create and hold together a secular state, far from all kinds of ethno-nationalism. This principle formed the basis of their mutual respect.[302] The Muslims—in both states the ethno-national junior partners—played a very decisive role in their plans. The more they identified themselves with the secular state, the more stable appeared its future. In fact, many Muslims did support the ideas of Tito and Nehru.

Shortly after the founding of the socialist state of Yugoslavia, and shortly before the independence and partition of India, Muslims who were loyal to Tito composed a document which was printed and published in Bombay. In this paper the 'liberated Muslims of Yugoslavia' clearly rejected the secessionist policy of the Muslim League. They still hoped for a united India. Their pamphlet supported Nehru's and Gandhi's policy. The arguments drew upon the experience of atrocities inflicted on the 'ethnic groups' during World War II, from a Marxist view of history, and from the idealism of a new beginning in (a hoped for) ethno-national harmony. These were clear words indicating a new secular Muslim self-consciousness in Yugoslavia—arguments shared also by the Indian Muslims of the Freedom Movement.[303]

At first, the writers drew parallels between the fates of their countries. Both had to free themselves from their occupants—Yugoslavia as a 'colony of Anglo-French imperialism' and as Hitler's backyard and India as a British colony.[304] The position of Muslims among the other population groups is compared, too:

> Thus Muslims are to be found in many parts of Yugoslavia, as in many parts of India, speaking different languages, belonging to different nationalities, living in widely-separated areas; in Bosnia they are a majority while elsewhere they are a minority (as, for instance, [a] majority of Punjabis and Bengalis are Muslims by religion while in Tamilnad [*sic*] or Bombay they are a small minority).[305]

The authors wanted to show that except for a few details, Bosnian and Indian histories share incredible similarities. They link the comparison of their social and political past with a clear broadside against the leaders of the Muslim League:

> There were reactionary leaders and parties among the Yugoslav Muslims, who raised the cry "Islam is in danger". They sought to take advantage of the fact that the common Muslims of Yugoslavia were backward in education and wealth as compared with the Christians and Serbians [!], and to incite them against the Christians.[306]

The signatories criticized the earlier Muslim spokesmen in Bosnia-Herzegovina, like Mehemmet Spaho, and their collaboration with the ideologues of other 'ethnic' camps in the failed Yugoslavia before

World War II. Behind this lurks the undisguised call to strip Jinnah and his supporters—the Muslim big landowners and the educated bourgeosie—off their power.

[Moslem, Serb and Croat reactionary leaders] depicted their mutual conflicts as a struggle among the Moslems, Serbs and Croats, endeavouring to portray and identify their own interests, which had nothing in common with the fate and life of the people, with the people's interests. In this way, they inflamed religious hatred, sowed intolerance and chauvinism, put forth the slogan that Islam was in danger—all this with the aim of preventing raproachement of the Moslems and their brethren and their link-up with the general people's democratic movement headed by the working class.[307]

The message 'from the heart' of the Bosnian Muslims to their brothers in the subcontinent reads thus:

Unite all your forces against all those who stand in the way of your national liberation and in the way of the realization of a free and democratic Indian State, in the way of unification of all the democratic forces of India on the basis of equality, brotherhood and unity of the Moslems and Hindus.[308]

This unusual document provides an interesting insight into the self-definition of both Bosnian and Indian Muslim spokesmen of that time. What is noteworthy is that the authors define the cleavages in terms of *linguistic* criteria, not in religious terms. With regard to India they speak of 'national linguistic units' (like Bengal, Punjab, Sind, 'Pathan-land'), to whom 'freedom' and 'self-determination' must be granted after independence.[309] (Indeed, precisely such an Indian confederation was under discussion.) The Bosnian authors describe themselves as 'Serbian-speaking'.[310] Therefore, the question of a special autonomy arrangement did not arise at all.

Moreover, the text shows a clear rift between the 'Muslim' spokesmen from the time before and during the World War II and those who politically represented 'the Muslims' in Tito's Yugoslavia. The protagonists of a potential Muslim nation-building had changed completely. The new spokesmen were true representatives of Tito-Yugoslavism. No ambitions of a Muslim state-building were to be expected of them. They considered ethno-national conflicts as the product of reactionary and imperialistic foreign interference—and thus as obsolete for India as well.[311] On this point, too, they turned out to be greatly mistaken.

Comparative view

The confusing cleavages within the Muslims have to be sorted out for comparison. The following questions need to be addressed in this regard: why has there been no Muslim 'nation state' in Bosnia-Herzegovina till today? Why did the Muslim League have such a hard time gathering the Muslim masses behind its 'nation state' project which was developed only quite late in the game?

The answer appears paradoxical. On the one hand, it was the orthodox teachings which deterred them from demanding a 'nation-state', and, on the other hand, it was 'too little' of these teachings. In other words, pan-Islam in both cases, on the one hand, as well as secularism in Bosnia-Herzegovina and syncretism in India, on the other, weakened Islam as the 'ethnic' nation criterion which was supposed to provide the building material for a Muslim state.

7. HOW ADVANCED WAS THE NATION-BUILDING? (Discussion and Synopsis)

The multiple crosscutting cleavages among the Muslim communities in Bosnia-Herzegovina and India weakened their ethno-national endeavours and made them fall 'behind' in comparison with their neighbours. Nationalistic Serbs and Croats, on the one hand, and Hindu nationalists, on the other, went through a stronger process of homogenization and proclaimed their homeland. The Muslims had none, and nor were they so keen on proclaiming one.

However, despite the inherent weaknesses of Muslim ethno-nationalism, Muslims could establish themselves as a *(party)-political* action group.[312] This is not a contradiction, for: (1) A religious or 'ethnic' identification need not be reflected in the action patterns of the political protagonists. (2) A *political* action group, in turn, does not necessarily have to be a *national* one at the same time. This means that it does not have to be backed by a broad national movement or ideology which would function as its vehicle. Even less does it need to show any nation-*state* ambitions.

About (1): The most influential Muslim spokesmen in Bosnia-Herzegovina and India represented only a small part of the economic, political, and dogmatic interests of the people, who felt to be part of Islam.

Reiter also holds that it does not depend on the 'principles of classification' (like ethnicity, religion, language). Instead, action groups emerge from 'social or power-political aspirations'. He writes: 'Religion is not a group aim' but a class feature.[313] Similarly, Alavi writes: 'Private affirmation and practice of their faith did not necessarily bring Muslims together into a unified political group.'[314] Das Gupta argues along the same lines; citing the language dispute in India he describes how action groups make use of the mass media, a rational hierarchy of leaders, rational political arguments, and objectives, and, as a result, distance themselves from the language community (large group): '[These new groups] contributed significantly to [a] gradual dissociation from the traditional norms of primordial group formation and structure, and to the growth of modern political development.'[315] This speaks against the (exclusively) primordial or tribal theories which do not allow a politically motivated detachment from the category of identity.

About (2): In the cases described the primordial factor of religion plays the most important role as a demarcation criterion against the respective other 'ethnic group'. As shown, other distinctive features were constructed around it. For religion alone was not enough to unite the community in a way that it would have expressed a uniform 'ethnic' consciousness, and, above all, that it would have been capable of demanding common *political* objectives.

The action group had to build up connections with the large group. This took place through the instrumentalization of religious symbols, of linguistic features, of historiography, and of social conflicts, as the first part of this book has shown. But even this was achieved only to a limited extent. A broad national movement with state ambitions, as defined by Hroch's last phase, had emerged neither in Bosnia-Herzegovina nor in India. At most, the all-India struggle for independence can be defined as an emancipatory movement, especially due to the mass-oriented actions and Gandhi's mass appeal. The burning of imported clothes or the Salt March (1929) aimed at strengthening a national self-consciousness and suggest economic self-sufficiency.

Against this background the following contradiction between Reiter and Dzaja can be explained. Reiter calls the 'Mohammedan nation' in Bosnia-Herzegovina 'disfunctional' in contrast to the Pakistanis.[316] Dzaja, on the other hand, insists that, from 1878 on, the Bosnian Muslims 'have proved to be a compact political *action group* and were largely able to develop *an own identification pattern*.'[317]

Reiter speaks of 'nation' as a collective action group which, qua definitionem, aims at the foundation of an independent state. The success certifies a 'nation' that it 'functions'. Dzaja, by contrast, calls the action group 'political' (i.e. in terms of everyday politics). Both speak of different things.[318]

On the one hand, they are both right. Reiter's final analysis is correct. There is a Muslim state in Pakistan and no Muslim state in Bosnia-Herzegovina (as yet). Dzaja's observation is true: Muslim parties and interest groups influenced the policy of the country as independent variables.

On the other hand, both statements suffer from over-simplification. Reiter speaks of a *Muslim* nation in India. In the face of the many ethnic cleavages among the Muslims and the great number of Muslims who do *not* (want to) live in 'their' Pakistani homeland, this ascription is questionable. Pakistan is not the state of 'the Muslims' on the subcontinent. This is Pakistani propaganda. However, if Reiter restricts himself to the founding of a state *on religious pretexts*, and thus describes its upholders as a 'nation' (= collective action group), then his statement is technically correct.

Dzaja's statement invites criticism because he describes the political action group of the Muslims as a 'compact'. The cleavages within the political activists of the Bosnian Muslims do not permit this description. It is ironic that in Bosnia-Herzegovina not even the *political* action group could or would ascribe itself into uniform '*ethnic*' camps. In the newer Yugoslavia this phenomemon was supplemented by a 'Yugoslav identity' in the Muslim action group.

These subjective factors of 'ethnic' ascription prevented the emergence of an ethno-national movement with territorial ambitions, on the one hand. On the other hand, these circumstances suggest that not only were 'the Bosnian Muslims' denied the status of a nation but also that of an 'ethnic group'. Miedlig concludes: 'So one can [...] hardly speak of a uniform Bosnian-Hercegovinian 'ethnos', since the individual groups feel and reason their 'ethnicity' in a different way.'[319] He writes further:

> How little 'ethnos', let alone 'nation', played a role as an ideological-propagandistic development concept—not only in this traditional milieu but also with the 'progressive' cultural innovators—is also proved by the fact of [...] the 'openness' vis-à-vis the present, already matured South Slavic ethnic groups of the country.[320]

Höpken reaches a similar conclusion but he refers exclusively to the concept of 'nation'. For this, he writes, until World War II, the Muslims lacked the 'group integrative [...] preconditions' and a 'plebiscitary component'.[321] However, he sees indications of two competitive interpretations. One holds that the Muslims are not a nation in the modern sense like the Serbs and the Croats. The other one asserts that they are equally engaged in nation-building, although with pre-modern elements. He considers at least a part of the population as a 'pre- or proto-national [...] community of faith'.[322]

In a parallel development, in India syncretisms and the different definitions of nation created by Muslim politicians led to a similar phenomenon. The opinions of the Indian authors are also similar: 'There was no automatic and universal translation of the attribute of *Muslim by faith* or *Muslim by descent* to an automatic assertion of Muslim ethnic identity,' Alavi writes.[323]

Robinson concludes after his study of Muslims from UP, who were the forerunners of ethno-national activism and the staunchest supporters of Pakistan: '[B]y most standards applied to modern European nations, they were not [a separate nation]. They had no racial homogeneity, little common history and many conflicting interests [...] Being Muslim, of course, did not make them a nation.'[324] Emerson arrives at the same conclusion as well.[325] Robinson's assessment, however, again shows the confusion of terms. He uses 'nation' in the sense of 'ethnicity', although this corresponds to the usage of Indian ethno-nationalists.

Regarding the question whether Hindus and Muslims are two 'nations' or not, Brass comes to a draw. The answer depends on whether the emphasis is laid on the common aspects or on the differences. He finally attributes the *political relevance* of the differences to the available theory framework of the elites:

> From the point of view of social science theories of nationalism, what matters is that it cannot be maintained that either Hindus or Muslims constituted sufficiently solidary groups in the nineteenth century, bound together by conscious communal identifications uniting all classes, regions, and sects, with a common view of their past and that recognition of a common destiny which characterizes the modern nation. *The two religious communities did not constitute two nations in the ninteenth century, if only because the idea of nationalism had not yet entered the minds of the educated elites.*[326]

Similarly, Aziz points to the intentions of Syed Ahmed Khan. He did speak of differences between Hindus and Muslims but never of a territorial separation, for 'politics in the modern sense of the term had just begun'.[327]

For Brass the emphasis on the differences was a *conscious political choice* of the elites who were the heads of religious revival movements. They drew the attention of their followers from connecting symbols to mutually excluding ones. Robinson does not agree. For him the 'Islamic tradition' itself has an 'emotional power' which works equally on both the masses and the elites. He therefore regards the rational framework of decision making of the elites as limited. In contrast, Brass argues that different elites associate different *political* meanings with Islam.[328]

The findings from the case studies support Brass's view. In fact, various Muslim spokesmen interpreted Islam in different ways and derived their political claims from it. For some, pan-Islamic symbols stood in the foreground, like the Caliphate. Others rejected them. Again, others had no difficulty in bringing pan-Islam and ethno-nationalism down to the lowest common denominator. These cleavages were the same in Bosnia-Herzegovina and India. Such subjective self-ascriptions weaken the argument of a unified 'Islamic emotion' of any kind. Robinson's view is too undifferentiated and disregards the above-mentioned cleavages within the Muslim population. Nor does it say anything about how the Muslims who were syncretically or, as in Bosnia-Herzegovina, secularly oriented actually 'felt'. Of course, Brass's argument does not say anything in detail about how Muslims 'felt'. But his thesis does not claim in the first place to be able to give an answer to these questions. It evades the non-verifiable parameter of an 'Islamic emotion' and approaches the problem with external, visible factors (like symbols, political cleavages, etc.).

It cannot be denied, of course, that 'ethnic'—particularly religious—characteristics played a role in the formation of political interest groups, and not economic and social ones alone. If 'Muslim parties' had not been there, for example, some political processes would have looked different. This covers the prevention of land reforms in Bosnia-Herzegovina, the introduction of quotas in India, up to the forms of violence and territorial changes. Such an influence, in turn, was only possible in interaction and in competition with other actors who competed on the same level.

Thus, if the fact of an 'ethnic conflict' is denied, it refers to the factor of 'ethnicity' as a dependent variable. If this factor is investigated as an independent variable, one can speak of an 'ethnicized' or ethno-national conflict—namely of a dispute, into which the interests of action groups entered and who, in turn, legitimated their existence through the postulate of 'ethnic' differences.

For this *political* representation is decisive. The formation of political parties can be regarded as a catalyst. So Robinson alludes to the founding of the Muslim League in 1906 and to the system of separate electorates three years later: 'By 1909, a Muslim identity was firmly established in Indian politics. The first stage in the process had been the creation of a Muslim political organization [. . .] The second stage was the winning of a separate Muslim electorate [. . .].'[329] Similarly, this observation also applies in the case of Bosnia-Herzegovina. A Muslim political group representing Muslim interests made itself heard around the turn of the century, presenting memoranda to the Austro-Hungarian administration. Babuna describes this phase as a 'politicization of Muslim ethnicity' and as a new period in Bosnian politics.[330]

Many historians see a turning point already in the Austro-Hungarian administration in Bosnia-Herzegovina from 1878 onwards, although this is not reflected in the activities of the Bosnian-Muslim spokesmen (only around twenty years later). Dzaja speaks of an 'epochal turning point' from the Orient to Occident.[331] But this woolly cultural generalization is of little help. For (a) some Muslims cooperated with the occupants, while others did not,[332] (b) economic backwardness influenced nation-building more strongly than cultural differences, and (c) *even though* the Muslims presumably belonged to the 'Orient', it was the 'Occident' that specifically promoted the Bosnian-Muslim culture.

It is certain, however, that from 1878 on the Muslim elite had to struggle harder for posts than before when their faith had been a competitive advantage *a priori*. Their economic decline continued rapidly in communist Yugoslavia. This situation can be compared to that in India from 1857 onwards. After the Mughal era many Muslims experienced an economic and social decline. Simultaneously, the 'Hindu competition' moved up. This is why strong emphasis was laid on the struggle over social and economic positions as an argument for the necessity of political protection for 'the Muslims'. Nevertheless, their position considerably varied from region to region. Of all places the

Muslim elite did quite well in northern India, which was the breeding ground of ethno-nationalism. Therefore, the rhetoric of pity used by the spokesmen was often only a political instrument. The following poem voices for the well-cultivated Muslim inferiority complex:

> The Englishman is happy, he owns the aeroplane,
> The Hindu's gratified that he controls all trade,
> 'Tis we who're empty drums, subsisting on God's Grace,
> A heap of biscuit crumbs, the froth of lemonade.[333]

Such an attitude served both the Muslim Urdu-speaking elite of north India and the *beys* of Bosnia-Herzegovina as a means to mobilize their political constituencies.

The years 1878 and 1857 have another thing in common: they marked the beginnings of administrative and social modernization. This also gave an impetus to the modern phenomenon of nation-building. At the same time, the right of free religious practice remained as well, and the administration divided the social groups into rigid categories. In principle, the occupants did not rule by force but by integrating the different elites and by striving for political balance. This created competition among these—legitimized and categorized—groups.

In this way the conflicts in Bosnia-Herzegovina and India continued to simmer, and the labels 'ethnic'/religious/communal could gain importance. However, it must also be emphasized that different identity features existed and 'functioned' as demarcations. Many Bosnian Muslims effectively resisted the appropriation attempts by Serb and Croatian nationalists, even though religion lost its profile as a means of contrast. Similarly, Hinduism could not integrate Islam in its world view and way of life, unlike it had absorbed many other influences on the subcontinent earlier.

But these religious features could not automatically be transformed into a pattern of political behaviour. Their existence alone does not clarify why exactly *these* differences, among many others, could determine the arguments in political debates. Supplementary factors were also required. Some of them have been examined in the first part of this book. Now the next step must be looked at: why, of all things, could the religious features be turned into the demand for a 'nation state'—an idea which most Muslims did not support?

NOTES

1. Malcolm (1996), p. 12. See also pp. 199-200; Karpat (1997), in: *IS*, p. 344.
2. Fine, in: Pinson (1996), pp. 19-20.
3. Silber/Little (1995), p. 229.
4. Thus Thorvald Stoltenberg created a commotion with his ignorant thesis. See Chapter V.5.1.2. 'The Poker of External Powers: Clientelism'.
5. In Yugoslavia the term 'nationality' has been used in an inflationary way. With such a label a political-emancipatory intention was mostly postulated from the beginning. Often the term is only a euphemism for 'ethnic group' or 'ethnic minority'. See also: Perry (1994), in: *SOE*.
6. For a discussion on nationalism in the case of Serbs and Croats see, for example, the very clear and systematic work of Behschnitt (1980). For a discussion on the nation-building of the peoples in comparison to south-eastern Europe, see, among others: Berend and Ranki (1982).
7. Zulfikarpasic was a founder member of the Party of Democratic Action (SDA); he belonged to the secular wing, and, in September 1991, he was expelled from the party by its hardliners (among others by Izetbegovic). The quote appears in the Polish magazine *Wprost*, 21 March 1993. See: Oschlies (1993), in: *APuZ*, p. 8.
8. Malcolm (1996), p. 126. The same pattern can be found all over. So Vilfan (1988), p. 17-18 reports that, in 1887, a politically active and nationally-minded Catholic vicar came into the Slovenian city of Vitanje. Only then did problems arise in the German-Slovenian community. The dichotomy of 'we' and 'them' emerged, and mixed marriages were sabotaged.
9. Dzaja (1994), p. 192.
10. Dzaja (1994), p. 193.
11. In a 'genetic logic' Radovan Karadzic refers to Vuk Karadzic's double chin which he claims to have directly inherited from him. In addition, a Serb documentary film has a scene in which R. Karadzic stands in front of the portrait of the old Karadzic (Colovic, in: Stefanov and Werz (1994), pp. 94-5).
12. Banac (1984), p. 80. For a discussion on Karadzic's definitions, see, above all: Behschnitt (1980), p. 78. Karadzic considered the Cakavian-speaking people as Croats only. He regarded Serbs with scepticism, seeing them as people who either did not speak or who did not want to speak Iyekavian. See also: Chapter IV.3.1 'The "Ethnicization" of Language in Bosnia-Herzegovina'.
13. Dzaja (1994), pp. 193-4.
14. Dzaja (1994), p. 199; Banac (1984), p. 108.
15. Behschnitt (1980), p. 142.

16. Hobsbawm (1990), pp. 54-5.
17. The Illyrians settled in the north-western Balkans in the eighth and seventh centuries BC. Malcolm (1996), p. 4 establishes the connection to the South Slavic theories of recent times: '[. . . T]he romantic theory of some nineteenth-century Yugoslav ideologists, who argued that the Serbs and Croats were "really" Illyrians (and therefore a single, special, age-old racial unit), tells us more about modern Yugoslav politics than about early Balkan history.'
18. For a detailed discussion on Croatian South Slavism, see: Schödl (1990b); also: Behschnitt (1980); Dzaja (1994); Kessler (1981).
19. Kaplan (1994), p. 36.
20. Schödl (1990b), p. 77.
21. Malcolm (1996), p. 160.
22. See, for example, Schödl, in: Winkler and Kaelble (1993), p. 137; Schödl (1990a), p. 11.
23. Sundhaussen (1993), p. 36.
24. Banac, in: Pinson (1996), p. 141.
25. Balic (1992), p. 6.
26. See also: Höpken, in: Kappeler, Simon and Brunner (1989), pp. 190ff; Malcolm (1996), pp. 181ff; Banac, in: Pinson (1996), pp. 141ff; Steindorff (1997), in: *SOEM*, pp. 284-5; Manoschek (1993), pp. 114ff.
27. For a discussion on the respective state structures of Yugoslavia and its constitutional principles, see: Mayer, in: Grothusen (1975).
28. Tudjman (1981), p. 113.
29. Tudjman (1981), pp. 113-14.
30. 'Franjo Tudjman, Ex-Communist General Who Led Croatia's Secession, Is Dead at 77', in: *New York Times* (11 December 1999), see also: Internet bulletin 'Bosnet' (11 December 1999).
31. 'Das kroatisch-serbische Pulverfaß', Claudia Lepping, in: *Der Tagesspiegel* (26 April 1998). The sketch on the napkin is depicted in: Gervasi (1995): in: *konkret*, p. 36.
32. Oschlies (1993), in: *APuZ*, p. 8.
33. Colovic (1994), p. 92.
34. Silber and Little (1995), pp. 233-4. This conversation was confirmed by the political scientist Zagreb Ivan Zvonimir Cicak in an interview with *Der Spiegel* (28 June 1993). Besides, it was recorded by the military secret service. See: Oschlies (1993), in: *APuZ*, p. 8; Krizan, in: *OE* (1998), p. 60.
35. Pandey (1990), p. 83.
36. Horowitz (1985), pp. 149ff holds the same opinion about the effect of colonial policy in Africa and Asia in general. For a discussion on the western view of the orient and its consequences, see also: Said (1994), (1995).
37. Lelyveld (1996), p. 14; see also: Cohn (1997), pp. 3ff.

38. Pandey (1990), p. 83.
39. Thapar (1992a), p. 72
40. Pandey (1990), pp. 32ff, 40, 66ff, 84ff.
41. Thursby (1975), pp. 174-5.
42. Lelyveld (1996), p. 8. The same criticism was expressed by Veer (1989), p. 269.
43. Cohn (1997), p. 3.
44. See also, for example: Engineer (1995), pp. xiiff. Mill (1918) wrote the first pioneering and comprehensive history of India from the British point of view.
45. B. Chandra, in: Thapar, Mukhia and Chandra (1969), p. 50.
46. A strong plea for more social and economic history can be found in B. Chandra (1993), pp. 207-11.
47. Bakshi, Vol. V (1997), p. 6.
48. Aziz, Vol. I (1986), p. 11.
49. Sharma (1996), p. 20.
50. Nanda (1989), p. 7.
51. A.S. Ahmed (1997), p. 91.
52. Sharma (1996), pp. 416, 418.
53. For an introduction to Hinduism, see: Flood (1996).
54. For a detailed discussion see in particular the excellent book by Jaffrelot (1996), pp. 4ff.
55. A standard work on the Hindu Renaissance with its impacts until the movement of independence was written by Heimsath (1964). An introductory overview on Rammohun Roy is provided by: Flood (1996), pp. 251ff. A detailed discussion: Joshi (1975), K.N. Panikkar (1973). For a discussion on the Hindu Renaissance and its influence on Indian politics, also: Rothermund (1965), pp. 20ff; Kothari (1995), pp. 42ff. More on nationalization of Hindu traditions in: Dalmia (1997); K.N. Panikkar (1991), pp. 8ff (1997), pp. 73ff.
56. Mehta (1996), pp. 158ff. Above all, the influential nationalistic ideologue and philosopher Sri Aurobindo (1872-1950) was convinced of Herder's concept of an awakening of national culture. See also: Mehta (1996), pp. 187ff; Appadorai (1992), pp. 219ff. For a discussion on western-minded Indian intellectuals, and their contact with the European Renaissance, Reformation and Enlightenment, see: Tangi (1961), in: *CSSH*, pp. 368ff.
57. Panikkar (1995), pp. 32, 114.
58. Flood (1996), p. 254.
59. Robinson (1993), p. 68.
60. For an account of Savarkar's ideology, see, among others: Savarkar and Joshi (1967); Khilnani (1997), pp. 161ff; Flood (1996), pp. 262ff.
61. Savarkar and Joshi (1967), pp. 1, 203-4.

62. Savarkar and Joshi (1967), p. 64.
63. Khilnani (1997), p. 160.
64. Jaffrelot (1996), pp. 32, 53ff.
65. Jaffrelot (1996), p. 51.
66. Savarkar in his speech at the party conference of the Hindu Mahasabha in Lahore on 21 October 1936 [Aziz, Vol. 2 (1986), p. 125]. The same threat was uttered by Golwalkar [K.N. Panikkar (1997), p. 93].
67. Veer, in: Brass (1996a), p. 164.
68. Jaffrelot (1996), p. 26.
69. Jaffrelot (1996), p. 22.
70. Mandelbaum (1972), p. 401; also in: Veer, in: Brass (1996a), p. 156.
71. Mehta (1996), p. 178.
72. The Shiv Sena ('Shiva's Army') governed in Maharashtra and formed a coalition with the BJP at the centre. Shiv Sena's president, Bal Thackeray, likes to compare himself with Hitler.
73. Veer, in: Brass (1996a), pp. 164-5. More on the cow protection movements, see Chapter IV.2.2.2. 'The "Cow Deal" and the Caliphate'.
74. Jaffrelot (1996), p. 78 (original italics).
75. Panikkar (1991), p. 22; (1997), p. 116.
76. Savarkar and Joshi (1967), p. 207.
77. Bakshi, Vol. III (1997), p. 142.
78. Appadorai (1992), p. 209. See also: Mehta (1996), p. 219.
79. R. Duncan (1990), p. 168.
80. A. Ahmed (1997), pp. 104-5.
81. A. Rashid, in: M.A. Khan (1985), pp. 76-7.
82. Panikkar (1991), p. 16; (1997), p. 111.
83. The village in which Gandhi lived and weaved was called Wardha. The name was its programme. Muslim spokesmen expressed their rage at Gandhi's plans, and thereby at the Congress, in the so-called Pirpur Report. The Muslim League had commissioned it to collect details on 'Muslim' discontentment and criticism against the Congress. Detailed reports on violent riots of Hindu activists against Muslims can also be found there.

    The report is printed in: Aziz, Vol. 1 (1986), pp. 307ff. For criticism on the Wardha Scheme, see also Vol. 2, pp. 82-6. The Pirpur Report also plays a role in Chapter V.3.3.2. 'Hunt with Penis and Pistol'. An early discussion on the Wardha Scheme is found in: Shrimali (1949).
84. The complete text of the poem is printed in: Aziz, Vol. 1 (1986), pp. 118-19.
85. Parekh (1989b), p. 42. His work can be recommended in general for a good overview of Gandhi's philosophy.
86. Seervai (1994), p. xiv; A. Rashid, in: M.A. Khan (1985), p. 77.
87. Kaura, in: Grover and Arora, Vol. I (1997b), p. 118.

88. M.A. Jinnah in his speech iat the party conference of the Muslim League in December 1938 in Patna [Aziz, Vol. I (1986), p. 169].
89. Malcolm (1996), pp. 5, 189.
90. Mainly dependent Christian peasants.
91. Malcolm (1996), pp. 89, 105-6.
92. Malcolm (1996), p. 106.
93. Malcolm (1996), p. 131.
94. Malcolm (1996), p. 132.
95. Babuna (1996), p. 144, fn. 4.
96. Also later emigration waves always had a concrete reason: 1881-2 the introduction of compulsory military service by Austria-Hungary; 1901-2 the revolts; 1908 the formal annexation of Bosnia-Herzegovina. Altogether some 140,000 Muslims are supposed to have emigrated between 1878 and 1918 (Pinson, in: Pinson (1996), p. 94).
97. This judgement can often be found in the literature. See, for example: Babuna (1996), pp. 147ff; Pinson, in: Pinson (1996), p. 96, who describes the Habsburg era as an 'incubation period' of Muslim nation-building; also: Purivata, in: Blagojevic (1974), pp. 309-10.
98. Schödl (1990a), pp. 13ff.
99. The *kmets* (independent peasants) had to hand in a fixed quota of their harvest, independent of the yield, mostly one-third. The right of ownership, of first refusal and succession were often the causes of dispute. Besides, many *kmets* tried to evade the taxes by unprofitable cultivation and stock farming. See: Schödl (1990a), p. 17. For a detailed discussion on the agrarian relationships, see: Babuna (1996), pp. 61ff.
100. Babuna (1996), p. 61.
101. Babuna (1996), p. 288.
102. See Chapter III.1.2.1. 'The Social Structure of Muslims in Early Bosnia-Herzegovina'.
103. Babuna (1996), p. 56. For a discussion on the revolt of 1882, see pp. 53ff; Kapidzic (1972).
104. See also: Babuna (1996), p. 71.
105. Babuna (1996), p. 273.
106. Babuna (1996), p. 126; Dzaja (1994), p. 212.
107. Dzaja (1994), pp. 212-13.
108. Babuna (1996), p. 146.
109. Islamic teachings do strongly condemn conversions and provide the death penalty, yet, in the ethnically and religiously mixed Bosnia-Herzegovina this practice has not been punished so strictly until today. The Ottoman administration reduced the penalty to exile in the mid nineteenth century (Babuna (1996), p. 146). The new quality is that conversions now got a political-agitative implication which they did not have before.

110. The case is mentioned by: Babuna (1996), pp. 105ff; Dzaja (1994), p. 61. For a discussion on problems of conversions, see also: Pinson, in: Pinson (1996), pp. 99ff.
111. *Vakufs* are Islamic endowment properties (mosques, charitable institutions, pieces of land, etc.). In 1883 Austria-Hungary nationalized the administration of *vakufs*.
112. The case is described by Freitag, in: Burke/Lapidus (1988), pp. 119ff. See also: Yanuck (1974), in: *MW*.
113. Freitag, in: Burke and Lapidus (1988), p. 120.
114. Freitag, in: Burke and Lapidus (1988), p. 122.
115. The case is described by Freitag, in: Burke and Lapidus (1988), pp. 128ff.
116. Freitag, in: Burke and Lapidus (1988), p. 139. This was an India-wide phenomenon.
117. Gilmartin, in: Burke and Lapidus (1988), pp. 156ff. See also: Lapidus (1988), p. 734.
118. Examples documented in: Aziz, Vol. I (1986), pp. 348-9, 365, 374-5.
119. See also: Yang (1980), in: *CSSH*, p. 585.
120. Yang (1980), in: *CSSH*, p. 585 describes how the protests were directed against the British.
121. Yang (1980), in: *CSSH*, p. 580.
122. Freitag (1980), in: *CSSH*, p. 624. See also: Yang (1980), in: *CSSH*, pp. 585ff; Veer, in: Brass (1996a), pp. 164ff.
123. As a background, see, for example: Grunebaum (1990); Glasneck (1971).
124. For a discussion on the history of the Caliphate since Mohammed, and the dogmatic issues, see: Halm (1988), pp. 10ff, 17ff, 661. For the political history: Schulze (1990), pp. 446ff, (1994), pp. 88ff. See also Schimmel (1983), pp. 119ff. She points to the fact that the Caliphate is not included in Islam, instead it represented an ex-post fiction. For an account of the contradictions of the caliphate and the past history in the Indian context, see: Alavi, in: Hasan (1998), pp. 25ff.
125. For a discussion on the Khilafat movement, see in detail: Minault (1982); Nanda (1989), pp. 104ff; Islahi, in: Grover and Arora, Vol. I (1997b), pp. 49ff.
126. Islahi, in: Grover and Arora, Vol. I (1997b), p. 50.
127. Seervai (1994), p. 13 (original italics).
128. Dixit (1974), p. 67.
129. Rothermund (1997), p. 133.
130. Dixit (1974), p. 67. However, he himself was extremely inconsistent in his statements. As described in Chapter I.6.2. '"Nation State" Against *Umma*?', he found himself in a quandary between Indian nationalism and pan-Islamism.

131. Antes (1991a), p. 131. With such an extention of the caliphate concept to a role comparable to the papacy, it was possible for Muslims to consider countries under 'foreign rule' as a *dar al salam* as well.
132. Minault (1982), pp. 5, 10; Nanda (1989), p. 107.
133. Nanda (1989), pp. 104-5.
134. Minault (1982), p. 52.
135. Islahi, in: Grover and Arora, Vol. I (1997b), p. 50; Minault (1982), p. 6.
136. This is shown on coin mintings. Akbar carried the title 'The Exalted Khalifa'. Nanda (1989), p. 104.
137. Minault (1982), pp. 2, 11.
138. Nanda (1989), p. 108. More on Khan's philosophy, which was based on the teachings of Shaikh Ahmed Sirhindi of the seventeenth century, in: Ruthven (2000), pp. 274ff, 296ff.
139. Nanda (1989), p. 372. More on Iqbal's philosophy in: Ruthven (2000), pp. 323ff.
140. Seervai (1994), p. 13 (original italics). This quote is taken from a diary entry of the governor of Bengal, Richard Casey, dated 6 December 1945.
141. Engineer (1995), p. xv; Jalal (1985), p. 14.
142. Minault (1982), p. 68.
143. Islahi, in: Grover and Arora, Vol. I (1997b), p. 52.
144. A. Rashid, in: M.A. Khan (1985), p. 77.
145. Jaffrelot (1996), p. 25.
146. Aziz, Vol. I (1986), p. 171.
147. Hans Koschnik in an interview, 'Der Balkan braucht Zeit für Frieden', in: *Das Beste* (February 1998).
148. Thomas, in: Thomas and Friman (1996), p. 36. He refers to: Ignatieff (1993).
149. Horowitz (1985), p. 222.
150. Katicic, in: Lauer and Lehfeld (1995), p. 24.
151. For Herder's theories, see: Herder (1806-7).
152. More on Herder's reception in the Balkans, see, for example: Sundhaussen (1973); also: Behschnitt (1980), p. 66; Reiter (1984), pp. 283, 386ff; For a discussion on his reception in India, see: Mehta (1996), pp. 158ff, 187ff; Appadorai (1992), pp. 219ff.
153. Reiter (1984), p. 284. See also Chapter I.2.1. 'Crumbling Components'.
154. Sundhaussen, in: Elvert (1997), pp. 82-3.
155. Das Gupta (1970), p. 16.
156. Katicic, in: Lauer and Lehfeld, p. 25.
157. A few grammatical examples from Serbo-Croatian are provided by: Hamm, in: Hannik (1987), pp. 65-6.
158. Brozovic, in: Clyne (1992), pp. 347ff, above all p. 364. Besides, a detailed

discussion on linguistic differences in former Yugoslavia can also be found in this article.

159. Riedel, in: Elvert (1997), pp. 54-5.
160. Milovan Djilas (*1911), former Yugoslav Vice-President and later dissident and critic of Tito. Quoted according to: Oschlies, in: Tod . . . (1995), p. 195; See also: Oschlies (1993), in: *APuZ*, p. 7.
161. The names originate from the interrogative pronoun 'what', which means 'sto', 'kay' or 'ca' respectively.
162. The pronunciation depends on the original Slavic sound yat (e).
163. The details of the language conflict are highly interesting. Unfortunately, they would go beyond the scope of this work. Good accounts on this topic can be found in: Behschnitt (1980), pp. 67ff (esp. for Vuk Karadzic); and in: Hamm, in: Hannick (1987), pp. 65ff; Katicic, in: Lauer and Lehfeld (1995) (both sift out well the Serbo-Croatian dualism); Dzambo (1985), pp. 90ff.
164. More on Vuk Karadzic and his times in Lauer (1987).
165. Here, yet another irony comes up: Most Serbs in Bosnia-Herzegovina speak Iyekavian, as almost all Bosnians do. In this way, they differenciate themselves from the 'motherland'-Serbs who speak Ekavian (however, they again lie quite close to each other grammatically and lexically). Thus, in the logic of this language nationalism these would be two nations, too—a consequence which Serb nationalists ignore till today or try to prevent through the official introduction of Ekavian in the 'Republika Srpska'. This is indicative of the fact that other factors than language play the most important role in the nation-building in the Balkans. For a discussion on internal Serb language differences, see: Birnbaum (1987), in: *WS*, p. 2.
166. Quoted according to: Behschnitt (1980), pp. 70-1.
167. See also: Thomas, in: Thomas and Friman (1996), p. 36.
168. The phonetic modifications include: The frequent use of the letter 'h', 'æ' becomes 'è'; emphasis on the second syllable, ommission of 'd' in front of vowels. For a more detailed account, see: Dyker (1972), in: *SEER*, p. 243; Birnbaum (1987), in: *WS*, p. 18.
169. Hadzijahic (1962), in: *SOF*, pp.183-4; Babuna (1996), p. 33.
170. The quote is taken from a self-projection of communist Bosnian Muslims, which was addressed to the Muslims in India. Sarac (1947), p. 3.
171. Steindorff (1997), in: *SOEM*, p. 288.
172. Balic, in: IS (1997), p. 138.
173. Holbrooke (1998), pp. 358-9.
174. Mikic, in: Bernhard and Kandler-Pálsson (1986), p. 332.
175. The following comments are based in particular on: Shackle and Snell

(1990); Dua, in: Clyne (1992); Das Gupta (1970); Robinson (1974); Brass (1974).

176. The term 'Hindu-Urdu' is used mainly by Dua, in: Clyne (1992). Other terms used were Hindawi, Dehlvi and Dakani.
177. Brass (1974), p. 128.
178. Dua, in: Clyne (1992), p. 382.
179. Das Gupta (1970), p. 51.
180. Ethno-nationalists pointed to the fact that a divergence of Hindi and Urdu had already begun before the arrival of the British. In this regard, they were right. However, Hindi and Urdu were by far not as irreversibly associated with the 'Hindu' and 'Muslim' nation as they wanted to make believe.
181. Scholars agree that Hindi and Urdu are not *Abstandssprachen*. For a discussion on their linguistic differentiation, see: Dua, in: Clyne (1992), pp. 390ff; Shackle and Snell (1990), pp. 17ff; Das Gupta (1970), p. 52.
182. See among others: K.N. Panikkar (1995), p. 128; Dalmia (1997), p. 150. This concurs with the arguments of Anderson (1991).
183. Brass (1974), pp. 130ff describes the conflict in a detailed and systematic manner.
184. The influential British orientalist William Jones had received Herder (Dalmia (1997), pp.161-2).
185. M.A. Khan (1985), p. 73 holds a similar view. However, he falsely refers to 'ethnic' bonds of the Muslims beyond India's boundaries, which were to be weakened by Urdu. As described above, however, most Indian Muslims were converted locals.
186. Savarkar and Joshi (1967), p. 172.
187. Savarkar and Joshi (1967), p. 172.
188. Lakhi, in: Grover and Arora, Vol. II (1997b), p. 192 (original italics).
189. Lakhi, in: Grover and Arora, Vol. II (1997b), p. 191.
190. Lakhi, in: Grover and Arora, Vol. II (1997b), p. 194.
191. For a discussion on the inner Pakistani struggle of elites, see: Maniruzzaman (1988); Bhattacharjee (1973). For a discussion on the separation of Bangladesh, see also: Sisson and Rose (1990), and on Bengali nationalism: Zaheer (1995).
192. Regional identities in the south have become partly stronger against the 'Hindi dominance' of the north. This is observed by Gore (1996), in: *SS*, p. 41 for Tamil Nadu.
193. Das Gupta (1970), p. 124.
194. Das Gupta (1970), p. 53.
195. A. Rashid, in: M.A. Khan (1985), p. 74.
196. Examples, see among others: Khilnani (1997), pp. 175-7.

197. For a discussion on the cleavages in Sri Lanka, see: Das Gupta (1979), pp. 24-5; Roberts (1993), in: *ERS*; a detailed discussion in: Kearney (1967). However, a small minority of Tamils is also Muslim. But they do not have any political influence worth mentioning.
198. Khaliq-uz-Zaman (1961); Malik (1963); Aziz (1967a); Zakaria (1970). Also Aziz (1987), p. 13 writes that Khan was shocked at the demands of the Hindi activists and had since then abandoned the path of Hindu-Muslim unity.
199. Das Gupta (1970); Jain (1965).
200. Brass (1974), p. 137. The above mentioned discussion can also be found there.
201. Hindustani by itself is no ideological construction, of course, but a regional dialect. However, its sudden and surprising elevation to a 'national language' equals the ethno-national practice, only with contrary aims.
202. Clyne, in: Clyne (1992), p. 458. Thomas, in: Thomas and Friman (1996), pp. 37-8 also makes a brief comparison.
203. The Ottoman Tanzimat as a central administrative state is also compared with the British administration. Burke, in: Burke and Lapidus (1988), p. 25.
204. For the Serbs the magazines *Prosvjeta* and *Napredák* took over a similar function. They supported a loyal line towards the Habsburg Empire [Babuna (1996), pp. 148-9]. However, there had been an independent Bosnian press since 1866 [see also: Dzambo (1985); S. Ramet (1990), in: *SSJ*, p. 9].
205. For a detailed discussion on Kállays policy, see, for example: Babuna (1996), pp. 203ff; also: Malcolm (1996), pp. 147ff; Dzaja (1994), pp. 62ff, 208ff.
206. Head of the *ulema*.
207. Dzaja, in: Lauer and Lehfeld (1995), p. 98; Dzaja (1994), p. 236.
208. Dzaja (1994), p. 210.
209. Dzaja (1994), p. 211.
210. Dzaja, in: Lauer and Lehfeld (1995), p. 100; Babuna (1996), p. 237.
211. Dzaja (1994), p. 183.
212. Babuna (1996), p. 173. For a discussion on the economic situation of Bosnia-Herzegovina during the Habsburg period, see also: Hauptmann (1983).
213. Golant (1975), p. 66.
214. See Chapter IV.5.2. 'The Majority Trap in India' and Chapter V.5.2. 'The Communal Card: The British Game With Congress and Muslim League'.
215. Counter arguments against the 'divide and rule'—thesis in its absolute form can be found in: Robinson (1993), p. 164.

216. Dufferin in an interview with *The Pioneer*. Robinson (1993), p. 131, fn. 2.
217. Quote of Sir Charles Wood. Johari, Vol. I (1993), p. 342.
218. Wasti, in: Grover and Arora, Vol. I (1997), p. 28.
219. Lelyveld (1996), p. 103.
220. Robinson (1993), p. 110. Among others, the maharajas of Patiala, Benares, and Vizianagram lent support.
221. See also Aziz (1987), pp. 728-9. Starting from this 'legacy', he also describes the strong standing of the north Indian Muslims, but he comes to another conclusion than Brass (see below). For Aziz the fact to be a minority as such was decisive for the justification of Muslim claims, and not the economically strong standing of this minority. Aziz's explanation therefore does not reach beyond a diffuse psychological assumption.
222. Brass in particular points to this [Brass (1974), pp. 120-2, 138ff]. Examples for historians of a general Muslim theory of discrimination are W.C. Smith (1946), M.T. Titus (1959), K.B. Sayeed (1967) (with some exceptions) and, as a Pakistani myth maker, M. Husain (1961).
223. It mainly concerned the control of the *vakufs*. In Bosnia-Herzegovina like in India these religious endowment properties were administered by the occupants.
224. Muslimanska Narodna Organizacija (MNO).
225. Bosnia-Herzegovina: Babuna (1996), p. 71; India: Das Gupta (1970), p. 101; Robinson (1993), p. 131.
226. Popovic (1994), pp. 270ff. also: Babuna (1996), pp. 263ff.
227. This is the above-mentioned MNO.
228. See also in particular: Popovic (1994), p. 273.
229. From the Serb and Croatian points of view the ethno-national cleavages had become firmer, while Serb nationalism was stronger than the Croatian one. See also: Babuna (1996), p. 143.
230. After the revolt of *kmets* in 1910, the parlamentarians of the MNO signed an agreement with the Croatian delegates against the 'solution' of the agrarian question. In return, the Muslims supported the Croatian position in the language policy. See: Babuna (1996), p. 284. For a discussion on the tactics of the MNO, see also: Pinson, in: Pinson (1996), pp. 110ff; Malcolm (1996), pp. 151-2.
231. Jugoslavenska Muslimanska Organisacija, founded in 1919. It merged in 1935 with the Yugoslav Radical Party to form the Yugoslav Radical Community.
232. Banac, in: Pinson (1996), p. 375.
233. For a discussion on Spaho's tactics, see, among others: Malcolm (1996), pp. 164ff; Banac, in: Pinson (1996), pp. 135ff.

234. Malcolm (1996), p. 166.
235. Examples: The big landowner Serif Arnautovic from Mostar initially demanded a Croatian identity for the Bosnian Muslims in Croatian newspapers in the early 1890s. After the Habsburgers had twice refused him a promotion, he deserted to the Serbs in 1898, and began to stir up Serb nationalism. By contrast, Suljaga Salihagic changed from Serb nationalism to the view that he was actually a Bosnian Muslim with a basically independent identity. The Bosnian literary figure Musa Cazim Catic began his life also as a Serb, led it as a Muslim 'Bosnjak' in between, and terminated it as a Croat [S. Ramet (1990), in: *SSJ*, p. 10].
236. Malcolm (1996), p. 160.
237. Babuna (1996), p. 288.
238. In an overview in: Popovic (1994), pp. 273-6. He often refers to Purivata (1974).
239. Balic (1992), p. 5.
240. Yugoslav Muslim officials denied this. They wrote in 1947: 'Muslim peasants have won land, not only in Bosnia but throughout Yugoslavia. inspired by the common Yugoslav patriotism the Muslims are. now wholeheartedly engaged in achieveing their own economic, cultural and political regeneration for which all roads are open to them as never before' [Sarac (1947), p. 5]. However, the Muslim communities experienced an economic upswing not until the 1960s and 1970s [Meier (1995), p. 46].
241. More on this topic, see Chapter V.1. 'The Cage Breaks Open'.
242. Quoted according to: Burg and Shoup (1999), p. 270.
243. A good overview is offered by: Johari, Vol. I (1993), pp. 43ff, however from an Indian-nationalistic point of view.
244. See also: Kothari (1995), p. 65.
245. Frykenberg, in: *JCCP* (1987), p. 272.
246. Grover, in: Grover and Arora, Vol. I (1997b), p. 179.
247. Kothari (1995), p. 68.
248. For instance: Basu (1995), p. 5; Johari, Vol. I (1993), pp. 44-5. See also: Page (1982).
249. Johari, Vol. I (1993), pp. 45, 111.
250. Johari, Vol. I (1993), pp. 44-5.
251. Klennert (1995), p. 36; Hasan (1997b), pp. 73, 75ff; Inder Singh (1987), p. 3; Brass (1974), p. 161.
252. Wasti, in: Grover and Arora, Vol. I (1997b), p. 25.
253. Hasan (1997b), pp. 71-3.
254. Wasti, in: Grover and Arora, Vol. I (1997b), p. 24.
255. On this topic and for the following, see the excellent research with primary sources by Inder Singh (1987), pp. 2ff.

256. The franchise was extended from 7 to 35 million voters [Philips (1967), p. 4].
257. Further discussions on the competition between the NAP and the League in: Brass (1974), pp. 173ff.
258. A detailed report on the election results of 1937 can be found in: Aziz, Vol. I (1986), p. 58.
259. Inder Singh (1987), p. 13.
260. Rothermund (1997), p. 371.
261. Kaura, in: Grover and Arora, Vol. I (1997b), p. 110.
262. Aziz, Vol. 2 (1986), p. 108. In principle, the party of National Liberal Federation also shared this criticism. Its president, P.N. Sapru, said in Bombay in 1938: 'There is [a] tendency on the part of the leading spokesmen of the Congress to identify it with the nation [...] But we are thinking in democratic and not totalitarian terms' (ibid., p. 16).
263. Aziz, Vol. 2 (1986), p. 108.
264. Like Inder Singh (1987) and Seervai (1994). As early as in 1947 the magazine The Economist adopted this view (22 March 1947) [Aziz, Vol. 2 (1986), p. 99].
265. Parekh (1989b), p. 174.
266. The correspondence can be followed in: Aziz, Vol. I (1986), pp. 198ff.
267. See also: Popovic (1994), p. 270. Babuna speaks of a 'personal network' of the Bosnian Muslims to Istanbul: Babuna (1996), pp. 140, 190ff. See also: Donia and Lockwood (1978), p. 194.
268. Babuna (1996), p. 145.
269. Dzaja (1994), p. 66.
270. See also: Ramet, in: Kappeler, Simon and Brunner (1989), p. 108.
271. 'Holy war'. This term was literally used by the Mladi Muslimani (Young Muslims): Bougarel (1997), in: *IS*, p. 539.
272. Brunner, in: Kappeler, Simon and Brunner (1989), pp. 165, 167. See also: Kornrumpf (1984), in: *SA*.
273. Bougarel (1997), in: *IS*, p. 539.
274. See: Ramet (1984), p. 154; Popovic (1994), p. 231.
275. Quoted according to: Ramet (1984), pp. 153-4.
276. Irwin (1984), in: *EEQ*, p. 450.
277. Balic (1992), p. 9. He refers to: Cimic (1965), in: *Pregled*.
278. Calic (1996a), p. 30.
279. Quote of Purivata [Irwin (1984), in: *EEQ*, p. 445]. Another historian of this category was Hadzijahic. He was chairperson of the Commission for Nationality Issues at the same time. For a criticism on the works of both, see: Balic (1992), p. 39.
280. See, among others: Dzaja, in: Lauer and Lehfeld (1995), p. 103. Thus primordial arguments once again gained weight. This is a paradox because

from a Marxist modernization-theoretical point of view such cleavages were considered outdated (compare S. Ramet (1990), in: *SSJ*, pp. 8ff).

281. In 1963 the Muslims gained the status of a nation in the constitution of Bosnia-Herzegovina, in 1968 through the Federation of Communists of Yugoslavia, in 1971 in the Yugoslav constitution.
282. Meier (1995), p. 24.
283. Ramet (1984), pp. 6ff.
284. Compare S. Ramet (1990), in: *SSJ*, p. 3.
285. Balic (1994), p. 9.
286. Balic (1992), pp. 48-9 quotes a letter by Hadzijahic to the Muslim minister of the Bosinan government Sarac (20 May 1945): 'The term *Bosnian* did not reach the citizens' rights as, say, the terms *Macedonian* or *Montenegrinian*, although it does full justice to the understanding of a Bosnian composite state, and although it comprises all faiths of the country, and although it has at least an equally strong support in history as the terms *Serb* and *Croat*. I am in a position to prove this. If the Muslims in Serbia and those in Montenegro must rightly describe themselves as *Serbs* or *Montenegrinians*, then there should be no obstacles that also our Serb brothers of Orthodox faith and Croats of Catholic faith describe themselves as Bosnians. Thus Serbianism and Montenegrinism would be as little called into question as, for instance, it is denied to Montenegrinians to regard themselves as Serbs in view of all their Montenegrinism' (own translation, original italics).
287. In the assembly were Muslim members of the Bosnian parliament and other local Muslim dignitaries. If this circle, which met on 28 September 1993, spoke on behalf of the population, must be left open. See also: Wieland, in: *SOEM* (1995), p. 191.
288. In an interview with the author in Sarajevo (27 June 2000).
289. Höpken, in: Kappeler, Simon and Brunner (1989), p. 200.
290. S. Ramet (1990), in: *SSJ*, p. 12.
291. Höpken, in: Kappeler, Simon and Brunner (1989), p. 203.
292. Oschlies (1995), in: *DIALOG*: In this regard he refers to the assessment of Balic (1992), p. 49.
293. Miedlig (1994), p. 41.
294. Miedlig (1994), p. 41. Popovic differentiates also between: (a) Muslims, ideologues of the federation, who were associated with the Communist Party apparatus, and who forged history; (b) Muslim intellectuals, among them also party members, who spoke out in favour of the 'eternal values' of Islam and combined Islam and Marxism [Popovic (1994), p. 318]. Some intellectuals were enthusiastic about pan-Islamism and the 'socialism' of Ayatollah Khomenei in Iran. This also applied to Muslims in Kosovo [see: Irwin (1984), in: *EEQ*, pp. 450, 458].

295. Lapidus (1988), p. 732.
296. More on Maududi's philosophy in: Ruthven (2000), p. 327.
297. The Punjabi leader of the Ahmadiyya sect, Mirza Ghulam Ahmad (1839-1908), even saw himself as an incarnation of the prophets or divinites of Islam, Hinduism, Christianity and Buddhism at the same time. The Pakistani National Assembly in 1974 excluded the members of the Ahmadiyya from the religious community of Islam, although in rituals and religious practice they were by and large in agreement with the Islamic majority. For a discussion on the Islamic seminars, movements, and political groups in India, see: Reetz, in: Reetz and Liebau (1997); Weiss, in: Weiss (1986), pp. 6ff; Alavi, in: Weiss (1986), pp. 28ff.
298. Douglas (1993), pp. 193ff, 224.
299. For a further discussion on the ideologies of Gandhi and Nehru, look at Chapter V.4.2.2. 'The Alternatives to Jinnah'.
300. Hosseinbhoy A. Laljee at the All Parties Shia Conference in Lucknow (14 October 1945): 'No body can dispute that there exists amongst the Shia Muslims, the same feeling and desire as exist among other minorities for proper representation of their interests and legitimate rights' [Bakshi, Vol. III (1997b), p. 845].
301. In my opinion, Schimmel (1983) advocates a simplified arrangement of Muslim cleavages. She exclusively speaks of a dichotomy between a 'separatist', Mecca-oriented and a syncretic Islam rooted in the subcontinent. According to her, the partition of India is a direct result of these tensions (pp. 3-4, 137). This view might have arisen because of a consideration of purely dogmatic criteria. But since in Islam religion and political concepts are not easily separable, the political cleavages must also be taken into account. As said earlier, on the one hand, there are supporters of a consequent pan-Islamism, and, on the other hand, those of an own statehood. Those Muslims who clung to strongly syncretic customs and were thus rooted in the subcontinent were not those who demanded a Muslim state. It was more difficult to mobilize them for an ethno-national camp. Often they followed Gandhi's Indian nationalism.
302. See, for example, Tito's statements on Nehru, in: Zakaria (1989), pp. 95ff.
303. The first article of the pamphlet with the title 'Yugoslav Muslims' Message to India' was even written by an author with an Indian name, Mohan Kumaramangalam (who commits the usual Indian grammatical mistakes in English). His text is dated from 22 January 1947. The second article, dated 19 December 1946, carries the place name Sarajevo and contains a long list of signatories—first and foremost Dr Zajim Sarac, Minister of Commerce in the Yugoslav government. The brochure is also published in his name. Other signatories are the Bosnian Vice-President Sulejman

Filipovic, several Bosnian ministers, the chairperson of the Bosnian trade unions, a representative of the Yugoslav people's youth, a representative of the anti-fascist women's movement, a professor and chairperson of the Bosnian cultural organization 'Preporod', one artist, one author and one doctor.

304. Sarac (1947), p. 3.
305. Sarac (1947), p. 3.
306. Sarac (1947), p. 4.
307. Sarac (1947), p. 8.
308. Sarac (1947), p. 14.
309. Sarac (1947), p. 5.
310. Sarac (1947), p. 3.
311. 'Reports on conflicts between Hindus and Moslems reach us. That reminds us of our own grim past. We know that this is the work of English imperialists and reactionaries in the ranks of the Congress Party and the Moslem League' [Sarac (1947), pp. 13-14].
312. This thesis is advocated for Bosnia-Herzegovina by: Malcolm (1996), p. 166; Dzaja (1994), p. 218.
313. Reiter (1994), p. 183. See also Chapter I.2.1. 'Crumbling Components'.
314. Alavi, in: Weiss (1986), p. 22 (original italics).
315. Das Gupta (1970), p. 94. In this case, language and other cultural characteristics of the Muslim rural gentry became the standard for all other Muslims of the country [ibid. (p. 101)].
316. Reiter (1984), p. 183.
317. Dzaja (1994), p. 218 (original italics).
318. Dzaja argues that Reiter ignored the 'ethnic' demarcation of the Muslims towards Serbs and Croats, and viewed them only in the context of their religious affiliation. This argument does not hold good because many Muslims did just not demarcate themselves in an 'ethnic' way but ascribed themselves to the 'ethnic' competition.
319. Miedlig (1994), in: *SOE*, p. 42.
320. Miedlig (1994), in: *SOE*, p. 36.
321. Höpken, in: Kappeler, Simon and Brunner (1989), pp. 183-4; also in: Miedlig (1994), in: *SOE*, p. 38.
322. Höpken, in: Kappeler, Simon and Brunner (1989), p. 183; also in: Steindorff (1997), in: *SOEM*, p. 283.
323. Alavi, in: Weiss (1986), p. 22 (original italics).
324. Robinson (1993), p. 345.
325. Emerson (1960), p. 92.
326. Brass (1974), p. 125 (italics added).
327. Aziz (1987), p. 21.
328. For a discussion on this contradictory view, see: Brass, in: Taylor and

Yapp (1979), pp. 35ff and Robinson, in: Taylor and Yapp (1979), pp. 78ff. For a response to the debate, see Gilmartin, in: Burke and Lapidus (1988), p. 147 and A. Smith, in: A. Smith (1992), p. 72.

329. Robinson (1993), p. 173.
330. Babuna (1996), p. 125.
331. Dzaja (1994), p. 183.
332. Babuna concludes 'that the higher classes of the Muslim society accepted the occupation more easily than the lower classes. The poor Muslims from the cities and the countryside were most persistent and radical with their resistance' [Babuna (1996), pp. 44-5].
333. This poem was written by Akbar Illahabadi (1846-1921) [Freitag (1989b), p. 219].

V. An Own State Within Reach

1. THE CAGE BREAKS OPEN

The state-building in Bosnia-Herzegovina and India took place against the background of overriding crises. Both had a worldwide impact: colonialism and communism collapsed. The supra-levels of the British administration and the Yugoslav state ceased to exist. The future appeared in the paradigm of the 'nation state', and this gave rise to the problem of 'ethnic' minorities.

Now the Indian and Bosnian elites had to take political responsibility into their own hands. In this process they started to compete with each other. At the same time many politicians and officials who had already played a part in the old system turned up again in key positions of the new arrangement. So the independence of the states did not bring about a reshuffle in the political leadership.

All this, however, does not explain why the principle of ethnonationalism could prevail as a criterion for state-building. Three approaches compete with each other to explain such phenomena of social awakening: The 'freezer theory',[1] the 'pressure cooker theory' and the 'escape theory'.[2] The first one says that the higher bracket acted as a freezer and preserved the bad smell of the old era. Once the overriding authority is gone, 'the seed of the undigested past [...] bursts open in an unexpectedly bloody manner'.[3] The second theory argues that it is just under the lid that ethno-national conflicts really start seething in the first place. So the higher bracket acts as a catalyst for such developments. And, finally, the breakdown of the bracket itself is considered an impulse. Out of fear of the new freedom the people escape to a 'voluntary subservience'—into a new, ethno-national collectivism.

As always, a grain of truth can be found in each theory, of course. Unfortunately, here is no place to discuss all three theories in detail with regard to the case studies. But the arguments of this work tend to support the 'pressure cooker theory'. In other words, certain factors which emerge only under the cover of certain state structures favour the predominance of ethno-national cleavages above others. Some examples have already been mentioned in the first part of this book.

As far as the freezer argument is concerned, there is an important distinction between Bosnia-Herzegovina and India. English colonialism froze something different than Yugoslav communism. When the British tightened their control over India in 1857, Indian society was still largely rooted in traditional structures. National ideologies gained ground only gradually. The preconditions that they could be implemented came just into being (that is Gellner's criteria of central education, historiography, infrastructure, etc.). Besides, when the British took control in India, there were no clashes between the different 'religious camps' yet. Communalism is a modern concept from the age of nationalism and only possible under modern conditions.[4] Therefore it is not only too simple but also unrealistic to claim: 'The establishment of British power [transferred] the hatred formerly felt by Hindus for the Muslims to the English, as today with the disappearance of British rule the underlying hatred has again fastened itself on the Muslims.'[5]

When communism 'froze' Yugoslavia, Gellner's nation criteria were already far more developed. Above all, there was a history of cruel clashes between the ethno-national camps, the most recent one during the Second World War. Nevertheless, the all too popular claim that history had repeated itself does not hold water. It ignores decades of peaceful coexistence of millions of people and thoughtlessly implies a continuous subliminal hatred.[6]

It was just this approach which the British in India followed as well as the international protagonists who dealt with the Bosnian war. U.S. foreign secretary Warren Christopher maintained: 'The death of president Tito and the end of communist rule over the former Yugoslavia have lifted the lid from the seething kettle of the *age-old ethnic hatred*.'[7] The British Prime Minister John Major held the same view.[8]

Politicians have hardly ever made their mark as brilliant historians. But this time their prejudices were to cause serious disasters, too. With this approach they also veiled a clear look at the specific events which had favoured and provoked the ethno-national confrontations in both cases. This is why a lot of political options did not occur to them in the first place. US special envoy Richard Holbrooke, who negotiated the Dayton Agreement, criticizes this, too:

So the idea originated that 'historical hostilities'—a vague but useful term when history appears to outsiders as too complicated (or too trivial)—doomed to failure all external attempts to prevent the conflict. This theory played down and simplified the forces that made Yugoslavia drift apart in the early nineties.[9]

But Holbrooke partly succumbs to this freezer theory as well, when elsewhere he speaks of a 'deep-seated grudge' which the 'ethnic groups' haboured against each other. However, he qualifies: 'Of course, in Yugoslavia there were tensions between the ethnic groups but they existed in other parts of the world as well, and there the mutual hatred did not lead to mass murders and ethnic cleansings.'[10] Why this is so can be best explained by the 'pressure cooker theory'. With this approach one can investigate, for example, which *institutions* enhanced ethno-national confrontation in Yugoslavia and India.[11]

In the Indian case separate electorates and quota were introduced for the different 'ethnic' groups, as pointed out earlier. In general, British rule was no despotism but a practice of political accommodation. Negotiations took place in the triangle between the British, 'the Hindus' and 'the Muslims'. Also Nehru had the feeling that the British were trying to play both camps off against each other in order to weaken the Indian Independence movement.[12] The old question if the British ruled a divided country or divided the country while ruling it, can also be answered in a differentiated way with reference to British institutions: The British left behind a country *whose cleavages had gained a new quality*. They were more homogeneous, more institutionalized and ideologically more stable. This is just what speaks against the 'freezer theory'. But this view is very popular and often misused by nationalists as an argument of justification.[13]

Also in Yugoslavia one can determine institutions which prepared the way towards ethno-nationalism. The quota system had the same effect as in India. From 1969 on, all important public and party posts were filled through national proportion.[14] The communist party was split according to the constituing republics. Career chances depended on 'ethnic' criteria. Political and social conflicts were solved in terms of national interests. This brought about an 'ethnicization' of politics and strengthened national and confessional categories and interests.[15] Sekelj writes: 'The gradual emergence of a plurality of power centers since the 1960s was not an aspect of political but of *national pluralism* [...].'[16] And this, he says, in connection with missing democratic control, is the best precondition for (ethno-)nationalism.

The ailing economic system of the country gave another impetus. The strong regional centers considered each other as competitors. From 1988 they even waged a proper trade war against each other with special taxes and boycotts.[17] The domestic market of Yugoslavia was paralyzed long before the war. The federalist philosophy of solidarity shriveled amidst the ambitions of ethno-nationally orientated officials. Two years before his death, Tito admitted: His biggest failure was that he did not manage to bring the peoples of Yugoslavia together.[18] If he himself also contributed to the political division of the peoples by his state-model—this he had never asked himself.

Finally, the breaking open of the 'cage' in both cases caused a struggle for survival of the political elites in a new political arena which was characterized by democratic principles. In these uncertain circumstances the politicians relied on ethno-national constituencies.[19] In Yugoslavia as well as in India the argument of protection gained importance: The economic and social interests of the 'own' ethnic group were to be politically hedged against the predominance of the competitor who could now act freely. This argument was particularly used by the leaderships of Slovenia and Croatia, and by the Muslim League in India.

This 'escape-approach', however, catches on only with the interplay of the 'pressure cooker theory'. Otherwise the question remains open *why* the threatened elites did not fall back on other power bases. In fact, no other group was supported under this lid which was neither democratic nor dictatorial but accommodating. It directed the interests into particular channels. In these circumstances the different groups could not form a common *political* will. But at the same time they were in free *economic* competition. When the external control faded away, this tension became obvious. The political emancipation, says Kuper, 'raises the problem of finding some moral principle of superior validity to economic interest as a basis for consensus and integration'.[20] Yugoslavia and India disintegrated not because the religions and the 'ethnic groups' were incompatible but because their elites could not agree on common power sharing arrangements.[21]

2. THE MAJORITY TRAP SNAPS SHUT

The 'escape theory' gains support through the events in Bosnia-Herzegovina at the end of 1990 and in India in 1946—in each case about one year before independence and the beginning of 'ethnic' expulsions. Elections took place which had a sweeping effect in both cases. Surprisingly, the ethno-national parties performed very well. Their proportions came closer to those of the population segments which they claimed to represent. Hence, mockers spoke of a 'quasi census' in Bosnia-Herzegovina or of the entry into an 'ethnocracy'.[22] Nothing else provides better arguments for those who spot an 'ethnic conflict' in the cases of Bosnia-Herzegovina and Pakistan. What should otherwise be the measure of the will and attitude of the people if not their vote?

In 1991, the Bosnians had their first elections after the Second World War. In India, by contrast, elections had a tradition since 1909. Since then the number of those entitled to vote and the competences of government offices were constantly expanded. However, both the Indians and the Bosnians went to the polls under the crumbling roof of a common house and with the omens of a political awakening. The election campaign was characterized by clashes between the ethno-national camps and by the question of territorial reform. The programmes of the ethno-national parties were thin, in any case much thinner than those of the trans-'ethnic' alternatives.[23] But this took a back seat. Instead, the formula 'beating the drum of nationalism is one easy option [...] for leadership'[24] began to take effect.

Once the 'ethnic' voting pattern had established itself, it triggered a domino effect. As Horowitz describes, 'ethnic' parties distinguish themselves in the way that they represent limited objectives, and, due to their association with an exclusive group, scarcely receive any parliamentary support from another, just as exclusive, 'ethnic' party. This means that 'ethnic' parties must mobilize their own and only 'ethnic' constituency all the more. This, in turn, aggravates the rhetoric of hatred and the political cleavages along ethno-national boundaries.[25]

In this context some distinctions can be made between Bosnia-Herzegovina and India: After 1990 Bosnia-Herzegovina developed a strongly exclusive 'ethnic' party system, in which practically no voter seemed to crossvote. In India these boundaries were not so clearly drawn. The Congress was not as strongly 'Hindu' as the Muslim League 'Muslim'. So the main competitor of the League was not a distinctly ethno-national party. The radical Hindu Mahasabha played only a minor role. Besides, well-known Muslims contested on behalf of the Congress, too. In this light a second variation of the 'ethnic' voting pattern may have played a role: The voters give their vote to representatives of 'their' 'ethnic group' whichever party they may belong to.[26]

Both elections described here set a clear trend of a *political homogenization* along ethno-national cleavages.

2.1. Elections in Bosnia-Herzegovina in 1990

Surprisingly, an 'ethnic' voting pattern was nothing new in Bosnia-Herzegovina. In 1897 a (limited) electoral system was introduced for local parliaments. The confessional groups sat in the committees in proportion to the population groups.[27] The same applies to the Bosnian provincial parliament in 1910. The difference in 1990 lies in the fact that in 1897 and 1910 only the propertied class possessed the right to vote. The *beys* controlled political matters on the Muslim side, whereas in 1990 the entire population did. Thus, an 'ethnic' consciousness, which encompassed the entire 'ethnic group' and which manifested itself through the formation of a political will, cannot be proven for the early times.

By contrast, from 1990 onwards, the three big ethno-national parties could claim democratic legitimization (like all ethno-national leaders of the Balkans, by the way). Together they obtained 86 per cent of the votes. Out of 240 seats the party of 'the Muslims' (SDA)[28] got 86 seats, the party of 'the Serbs' (SDS)[29] 70, and the party of 'the Croats' (HDZ)[30] 45.[31] Interestingly, the SDS with its votes stood most clearly below 'its' share of the population.

Proportionally, Muslims voted for the left trans-'ethnic' parties to the greatest extent.[32] The Social Democrats (UBSD at that time)[33] achieved successes in Sarajevo and Tulza where they even put up the mayor. In Tuzla 70 per cent of the votes went to trans-'ethnic' parties. In the city centre of Sarajevo they gained an absolute majority altogether.[34] But this could not turn the overall picture. The Alliance of Reform Forces, the ex-communists under the last Yugoslav president Ante Markovic, was knocked out as well, though it was the only party which had presented a detailed economic programme. No one was interested in such questions any more. Not even the industrialists. Anyway they did not pay their taxes to the state anymore but to 'their' respective ethno-national parties.[35]

But, in spite of everything, what makes the claim refutable that this election was a blank cheque for ethno-national politics?

(1) The voting right fell to the citizens without the development of a civil and democratic tradition. So far, problems had never been solved through *political* programmes and alternatives but rather through the

balancing of *national* interests.[36] This thought pattern was reflected in the polling. The fact that presidential elections in the republics which took place simultaneously with the Yugoslav parliamentary elections favoured the ethno-national results even further, as Sekelj writes. Besides, the concept of 'ethno-democracy' was strengthened: '[P]opulus has been reduced to ethnos.'[37]

(2) It was the ethno-nationalists who, for the first time in the post-war history of the countries, created an active political public. Up to that point politics had taken place within the framework of an oligarchic party elite and its networks.[38]

(3) The crumbling of Yugoslavia happened in the whirlpool of a 'national awakening' in east and central Europe. German unification in 1990 and the first free elections in the ex-Soviet satellite states took place in the paradigm of national emancipation. In these countries the philosophy of ethno-nationalism still prevails today. The euphoria of those months seemed to confirm this concept all the more in the Balkans at that time.[39]

(4) The elections took place in a power vacuum. The time was too short to produce substantial debates. In this turbulent phase political alternatives could not develop either. New parties did not have any infrastructure. The HDZ and the SDS were supported by their home-lands logistically and with personnel. The young SDA could flourish easily as a counterpart on the same programmatic level.

(5) In the party spectrum the labels 'left' and trans-'ethnic' merged. Since the socialist forces had discredited themselves with the disintegration of the country, they now got the democratic revenge—and the trans-'ethnic' concept with it.

Sekelj aptly summarizes the consequences of the Yugoslav system for the party scene:

> Actually, in the absence of competing ideological systems either on the socialist or on the liberal side, there is nobody to oppose this new ideological manipulation: on the socialist side, because the League of Communists of Yugoslavia has so completely discredited socialism and communism, and on the liberal side, because the dominant ideological apparatus have in the last forty years so successfully curbed the emergence of liberal (in the political sense) ideological systems and liberal intelligentsia, that therefore *now the banner of liberalism in Yugoslavia bred conservative nationalists instead of liberal democrats.*[40]

Milosevic also recognized this for the retention of his power: 'From now on, he judged the situation correctly, in Serbia politics could only be played with the nationalistic card', Meier writes.[41]

There are two more arguments which make the election appear in a different light. First, it cannot be automatically equated with a national movement of the respective groups with a 'nation state' as their goal. Before the election no 'national enthusiasm' could be felt, so that there can be no talk of a 'political spring'.[42] Moreover, the election took place *prior to* the decision on the independence of Bosnia-Herzegovina. On this question the opinion polls showed different figures: 86 per cent of the Croats, 55 per cent of the Muslims, and 43 per cent of the Serbs wanted an independent Bosnia-Herzegovina.[43] This is much less than the relative strength of the ethno-national parties.

Secondly, all three ethno-national parties joined forces to form a coalition against the common enemy, the left-oriented parties. This means that, at this point of time, hardly anyone could have foreseen an open war between these parties. The people did not cast their votes to legitimize an ethno-national military conflict. Only *after* the failure of this coalition and *after* the referendum on the independence of the country did the SDS under Karadzic leave the parliament and proclaim the 'Republika Srpska'. The former partners in parliament became enemies on the battlefield. The Social Democrat Sejfudin Tokic explains this paradox situation:

> In 1990 the people voted for the nationalist parties because in them they saw an exit out of the communist system. At this time, the nationalist parties worked in a coalition. Today, many people don't want to hear this any more. Izetbegovic even suggested that the Muslim inhabitants of Srebrenica should vote for Karadzic.[44]

So the election was no more than a snapshot. Its result may be seen as a contribution to the subsequent escalation because it determined the political protagonists. But it does not automatically imply that the voters had anticipated this, and that they also supported the subsequent policy of military escalation. Tokic is convinced that the ethno-national parties would have suffered a 'disastrous defeat' a few years later after the sad consequences of their policies had become clear.[45] Indeed, in April 1992 (at the outset of the war) demonstrators gathered in front of the parliament in Sarajevo and reviled the leaders of the three ethno-national parties. They demanded new elections.[46]

2.2. Elections in India in 1946

Since the 1930s Jinnah had unbendingly insisted that the Muslim League were the exclusive mouthpiece of *all* Muslims and had to be treated as such by the British and the Congress. For a long time it had remained sheer rhetoric (though it had already obstructed certain political solutions). The election victories in 1945 and 1946 finally gave Jinnah a democratic legitimization. The Muslim League won 76 per cent of the 'Muslim' votes throughout India. It was by far not all, but, in any case, more than it was in 1937 when the League hovered around 4.8 per cent.[47]

It is particularly striking that Jinnah managed to bring the 'deviationists' in the Muslim-majority provinces back on track. The Unionists in Punjab were no longer able to convert their economic achievements into votes. The Krishak Praja Party in Bengal plunged into insignificance, too. In addition, the Muslim landowners from the north withdrew their support from the multi-'ethnic' NAP and rushed to Jinnah's side, almost unanimously. The League suffered a setback only in the NWFP.

The surprising success of the League was chiefly due to a well-aimed mass mobilization programme launched since 1937. Ironically, it was the Congress which had kicked it off. After its moderate performance with 'the Muslims' in the 1937 elections, it had started the 'Mass Contact' programme with the aim to win Muslim voters. As a counter-reaction the Muslim League did the same thing—and mutated from a withdrawn elite circle into a party with mass appeal. The membership fee was reduced considerably. Moreover, the League activists used Islamic symbols like the green flag, the crescent, and the Koran as symbols to identify the party. One vote for the League was one vote for the Prophet, as the demagogue Firoz Khan Noon preached.[48] Jinnah dubbed the Congress as a Hindu party.[49] The Bengal Muslim League distributed a leaflet with a synopsis of religious and 'ethnic' distinctions between Hindus and Muslims.[50] The League promised to liberate 'the Muslims' from Hindu moneylenders and to revive the faded glory of the 'Muslim past'. In particular, the emotional poetry of Muhammad Iqbal on the 'Golden Age' appealed to large target groups.[51]

The successful performance of the League makes three things clear: (1) 'The Muslims' turned away from provincial interests and oriented themselves more and more towards issues concerning the whole of India. They became politically more homogeneous. (2) The slogan 'Pakistan' went down well as the central campaign slogan for the League. Economic and social interests were pushed into the background in favour of ethno-national ones. (3) Political power was also divided territorially into the continuing dominance of the Congress throughout India and into most of the provinces with a Muslim majority which voted in favour of 'Pakistan'.

In spite of all, this election cannot be automatically declared a mass-supported national movement for a Muslim state.

(1) Only a small fraction of the Indian population was eligible to vote. The figures for the provincial elections in 1946 lie between 10[52] and 28[53] per cent. Much less (not even 1 per cent) were allowed to elect the Central Assembly in Delhi.[54] The masses were excluded from voting because they had to prove that they were able to read and write, by census and other barriers. Moreover, the voting lists were confusing, incomplete, and outdated, as Nehru criticized, too.[55]

The British-sponsored tradition of separate electorates had already favoured an ethno-national voting pattern. The strictly limited voting right strengthened this effect further. Most workers and peasants continued to be excluded. Instead, the ethno-nationally-oriented Muslim middle classes and landowners influenced the election results in disproportionate numbers. The lower Muslim strata were more pro-Congress because it had (at least) promised social and economic reforms.[56] Therefore, the most severe critics of this limited voting right were the Indian communists. Of course, they feared for their potential votes.[57] Sarkar considers it the biggest mistake of the Congress to have given up the demand for a general voting right and leaving the communists in the lurch. Thus, the Muslim League's claim to represent all Muslims remained democratically untested.[58] In this context, the so-called 76 per cent 'Muslim' votes for the League appear very relative.

(2) The Pakistan option was still in the stars. As late as 1947 not even Jinnah was sure if such a state would and should come into being at all.[59] Neither he nor anyone else had a clear picture of what 'Pakistan' was actually supposed to mean. Different concepts, including ideas of a federal system, were being debated. Voices *against* the state of Pakistan could even be heard from the politicians of the Muslim League.[60] Jalal writes on the strategy of the League: '[I]f it were to spell out its demands in hard, clear constitutional terms, it would lose votes, certainly split its support, and divide the leaders.'[61]

(3) Jinnah had turned the Muslim League into a catch-all party. The

slogan 'Pakistan' served as blotting paper that absorbed many grievances and dissatisfactions. A.S. Ahmed calls Jinnah a 'feel-good, look-good factor', a 'superstar' for young people.[62] Jinnah's statement is revealing: '[V]ote for a Muslim League[r] even if it be a lamp post.'[63]

(4) 'Pakistan' was not only a political rallying point but was also a religious one. The League propaganda equated Pakistan with Islam, and even with the revival of the caliphate.[64] But a feeling of Muslim solidarity did not immediately imply a Muslim state for everyone.

(5) Some votes were gained by force. Parts of the *ulema* in Punjab, UP, Bengal and Sind threatened to excommunicate Muslims in case they did not vote for the League.[65]

Nonetheless, it cannot be denied that in 1946 the politicization of the Muslim population received a big thrust. The Pakistan strategy of the Muslim League had added up—no matter if Pakistan was a programme or merely a means of leverage in the negotiations designed to wrench as much as possible for 'the Muslims' and their demand for autonomy within an Indian federation later on, and thus to secure the influence of the League.

Comparative view

The long-term consequences of the elections in Bosnia-Herzegovina and India became clear only *after* the voting. At the time of the elections a breaking apart of the states could not be foreseen and indeed it was not the issue. *They were no referenda on a Muslim nation state.* However, the election campaign in India revolved more clearly around the demand for autonomy for the Muslims—of whatever kind—than it did in Bosnia-Herzegovina.

Despite all reservations, it is true that the years 1990 and 1946 are turning points. The politicization of the 'ethnic groups' was far advanced. For the first time, the developments came very close to the third stage of Hroch's model, particularly in India.

3. HARMONY AND HATRED IN THE POPULATION

The above-mentioned election results show that the rift between ethnonational elites and the population, i.e. between action group and postulated large group, had shrunk. Doubts have already been raised whether the elections alone were enough to discern a mass movement behind the notion of a Muslim nation state-building.

Important indicators therefore are also the views and attitudes of the people which manifested themselves not only through the ballot paper in this one snapshot. For example, in 1990 as many as 60 per cent of the Yugoslavs were in favour of preserving the federation.[66] To investigate this question we have much better source material for the Bosnian case. In India, however, it is the preceding elections that tell us a lot about the political commitment of Muslims. Especially against the background of the human suffering in Bosnia-Herzegovina and India the central question is: to what extent did the people themselves follow the ethno-national cleavages which were proclaimed by the political spokesmen?

3.1. The Dream of a Multi-'ethnic' Bosnia

More than once 'the Muslims' were given the honour to be at the 'centre' or 'heart' of a new concept. Yet it seemed that Yugoslavism was best designed for them. The census of 1961 provided an opportunity to declare oneself as 'Muslim in the ethnic sense'. But not all Muslims made use of it. Many continued to call themselves 'nationally undecided Yugoslavs'. 87 per cent of those who did this in 1961 were from Bosnia-Herzegovina, and most of them were Muslims. Though in the 1971 census one could declare oneself as Muslim 'in the national sense' for the first time. In this way the absolute number of Muslims rose sharply statistically. But already in 1981 it became clear that more and more of those called themselves 'Yugoslavs', in certain areas of Bosnia-Herzegovina even up to 20 per cent.[67] Apparently, many Muslims did not want to classify themselves nationally. Moreover, in the 1980s one third of the marriages were mixed.[68]

On the eve of the war 5.5 per cent of the population still called themselves 'Yugoslavs'. Almost 16 per cent of the children were from mixed marriages.[69] In Sarajevo this number was much higher.[70] In 'ethnically' mixed communities Muslims felt more as Yugoslavs than in areas where they formed the strongest group and where the *ulema* had a strong influence.[71] But also this influence declined: In 1965 as many as 60 per cent of Muslims considered themselves religious whereas in the 1980s it was merely 37 per cent.[72]

According to a survey conducted by sociologists in Bosnia-Herzegovina in 1991 nationality[73] did not play any role for the majority of the people when it came to friendship or partnership.[74] Still in 1990 some

90 per cent of the Bosnians described 'ethnic relationships' at their place of residence as good or very good. Thus they were above the average in Yugoslavia. Bosnian and Croatian refugees from mixed communities could hardly cite a concrete dispute. Only a few mentioned intolerance towards other 'ethnic groups'.[75] However, sociologists also documented that since the 1960s the inter-'ethnic' relationships deteriorated constantly—namely from the point of time when nationality in Yugoslavia started to play an increasingly important role also politically.[76]

Still, such developments did not automatically turn into hatred and violence. When in 1991 the first armed confrontations in Yugoslavia began, war weariness prevailed in the population.[77] Hundreds and thousands of Croatian and Serb soldiers deserted, although the war propaganda was in full swing in the media.[78] A Serb soldier withdrew his tank from the front line, drove it up to Belgrade and parked it in front of the federal parliament in protest.[79] The morale of the troops was pathetic. The war was no war of fanaticized masses.

This became especially clear in the multi-'ethnic' city of Sarajevo,[80] where in 1994 60,000 Serbs, 30,000 Croats and 10,000 Jews lived in the territory of the Bosnian government forces.[81] The independent radio station *Radio 99* successfully opposed the planned 'ethnic' separation of school lessons with public support. In addition, citizens of *all* ethnic groups signed an appeal by the circle of intellectuals (*Krug 99*) for a 'free, open and undivided Sarajevo'.[82] With this also Serb segments of the population opposed the plan of the Serb ethno-nationalists under Karadzic to divide the city according to the Berlin model—although with 'ethnic' sectors. According to *Radio 99* and *Krug 99*, 150,000 people—half of the population of Sarajevo—signed this appeal.[83]

The pamphlet (with the Serbo-Croatian title *Sarajevo – slobodno i jedinstveno*) is signed by 'The citizens of Sarajavo'. They declare:

> We are firmly convinced that our life of diversity and tolerance is a priceless inheritance from our past, and the only secure foundation, for a peaceful and happy future for all citizens of Sarajevo and Bosnia-Herzegovina.

and:

> We will permit no-one to partition our city for any reason, especially at a time when the entire world is tending toward[s] greater inter-cultural collaboration and integration.

Thus the citizens endorsed a declaration of the city council at the beginning of the war in 1992 which said: 'The City of Sarajevo with 500 years of history of joint life in [a] multicultural, multiconfessional and multinational community is INDIVISIBLE.'[84]

This image reached even the United Nations: The UN resolution 824 speaks of the 'uniqueness of the city of Sarajevo, which as a center of various cultures, groups and religions, illustrates that the coexistence of all groups of the population of the Republic of Bosnia-Herzegovina and relationships between them are possible'.[85]

Early in April thousands of Muslims, Serbs and Croats marched with portraits of Tito towards a barricade which Serb nationalists had put up to divide the city. Serb snipers dispersed them and left behind the first fatal casualty in the city.[86] Up to that point many inhabitants of Sarajevo had never believed that war could come to their city. Despite the violence many expressed their pride over the cultural diversity.[87] They were also proud of the mosques, the synagogue, the Catholic and the Orthodox churches which are located next to each other within a radius of a hundred meters in the old city. The *reis-ul-ulema*, Jakub Efendi Selimoski, referred to this in a fax to the World Council of Churches in Geneva on 23 September. He underlined that Bosnia-Herzegovina were a 'perfect example of harmony, tolerance and civilized multicultural life'.[88] Similar attitudes were reported from the industrial city of Tuzla. Bauer and Kimmig hold that 'the daily effort against the ethnic ascription of people of bourgeois, proletarian, subproletarian and especially urban origin who completely detested and still detest the subordination under any of the three national-religious groups' were characteristic of Bosnia-Herzegovina.[89]

Holbrooke reports from his mission: 'Many people told me that till the collapse of their country they had not known at all who of their friends was Serb and who was Muslim.'[90] Since in Bosnia-Herzegovina the 'ethnic' ascription took and still takes place in an increasingly objective way, people who neither can nor want to define themselves 'ethnically' run into difficulties. An editor of the daily newspaper *Oslobodenje*—a Russian with Serb ancestors and a Croatian wife—admitted to me: 'It would be a hard choice to decide which part of me is politically acceptable and which part is not.'[91] The editorial staff itself was an example of a functioning cooperation of Serbs, Croats, Jews and Muslims even during the hardest days of war.[92]

Since most people do not differ from each other the name serves as a criterion. The second editor-in-chief of *Radio 99*, Asim Abdurahmanovic, said dejectedly: 'Our children are Bosnians but people divide people by their names.'[93] The young journalist Sanela Hadzihasanovic, who already had her say at the beginning of this book, told me: 'I am Muslim. But religion is a private thing. I can drink beer and wear short skirts. I am Muslim because I have a Muslim name.'[94]

Indeed, Bosnian Islam is known for its secularity and tolerance. Even at the beginning of the 1990s hardly any women in the street could be seen with a veil. Alcohol consumption and mixed marriages were widespread.[95] 'In Sarajevo,' the editor of *Oslobodenje* said mockingly, 'you will find fewer women dressed in veils than in Paris.'[96]

3.2. The Dream of a United India

In the absence of sociological opinion polls it makes sense to climb down as low as possible in the (democratic) political structure. Here one can find most likely the developments which reflect the attitudes of the people. So it makes sense to look closely at developments in the regions. In the first provincial elections of 1919 local interests clearly dominated. The political alliances crosscut ethno-national cleavages. It was like this almost always until the elections in 1946.

As mentioned before, the heads of the provinces of Bengal and Punjab were the biggest trouble-makers for Jinnah. In Calcutta Fazlul Huq and his Krishak Praja Party represented the interests of poor peasants and small landowners. Thus, he virtually had the majority of Muslims behind him. His political alliances, however, were inter-communal (even with sections of the Congress and the Hindu Mahasabha). Huq persistently refused to cooperate with Jinnah even though he himself was Vice-President of the Bengali Muslim League. Later he was expelled from the League.[97]

The Unionists ruled in Punjab. They strongly advised Jinnah to keep 'his finger out of the Punjab pie'.[98] Until his death in 1942 Sikander Hyat Khan remained a thorn in the flesh of the Muslim League despite signing a pact with Jinnah.[99] Khan's government cooperated with Hindus and Sikhs. It organized readings on religious harmony, supported like-minded newspapers, and celebrated the birthdays of the founders of different religions.[100] The Unionists enjoyed broad approval among the people. Khan's successor, Khizar Hyat Khan Tiwana, became Jinnah's most fierce opponent. In his propaganda Jinnah tried to represent the Unionists as henchman of the Hindus. Tiwana was finally expelled from the Muslim League. But the majority of the Muslim Unionists continued to stand by him.

Muslims, Sikhs, and Hindus strongly opposed the demand for Pakistan and thus the division of India and Punjab. This province resembled Bosnia-Herzegovina as an 'ethnic' rag rug. The west was predominantly Muslim and the east Hindu. Besides, there were Sikhs whose holy shrines were scattered in both the east and the west. Wherever the boundary would be drawn, a large number of people would always find themselves on the wrong side. The division of Punjab with its wide network of irrigation channels was nonsense in economic terms, too. Even today, India and Pakistan fight over water rights. But the arguments of the Unionists were swept away by the superior of the League, by Jinnah's trips to Punjab, and by his propaganda.

In the extreme north-west of the country not everything went Jinnah's way. The local Muslim population was very tribal and had little understanding of pan-Indian politics. In the NWFP the Muslim landowners could maintain their economic position against the Hindus even after the Mutiny in 1857.[101] Unlike, for example, in UP and Bihar, Muslims were in the majority there and did not see themselves in an economic competition with Hindus. Cunningham reported: 'In their electoral propaganda the League had talked "about little but Pakistan" . . . not really an intelligible war cry to ninety per cent of their hearers since for the "average Pathan villager in these parts, the suggestion that there can be such a thing as Hindu domination is only laughable".'[102]

The Pathan leader from the NWFP and Congress member Abdul Ghaffar Khan supported Gandhi's movement of civil disobedience to such an extent that he ended up with the nick name 'Frontier Gandhi'.[103] Many Muslims continued to vote for the Congress party. But even during the two years when the League formed the government in the NWFP (1943-5) and 75 per cent of the seats in the provincial legislature were reserved for Muslims, it did not pass a single resolution in favour of the founding of Pakistan.[104]

Also, at an all-India level opinions were largely divided within the Muslim population. The strong focus on personalities in Indian politics made Muslims look up to charismatic leaders. Gandhi especially knew how to use this skillfully. Over and over again he managed that Hindus and Muslims fraternized ostentatiously. He succeeded once more in his mission as late as 1947 through his protest fast and his popular public sermons. When Hindus and Muslims finally hugged each other, prepared food for each other, and accompanied each other to temples and mosques, Gandhi always longed nostalgically for the days of the Khilafat movement.[105]

Comparative view

Neither in Bosnia-Herzegovina nor in India was there a broad national movement which strove for a Muslim state. Off the arena of the political actors, different views existed in the population on the future of their polity. Particularly in places where people traditionally lived in mixed neighbourhoods and where a territorial division was impending (like in Sarajevo and in Punjab), inhabitants of all the 'ethnic' groups resisted ethno-national concepts most vehemently. Until shortly before their realization any other outcome had still been possible. There were enough signs in the population which indicated that cooperation beyond ethno-national cleavages was a plausible option.

3.3. Tactics of Terror

How could it still happen that people of different 'ethnic groups' thrash away at each other in masses, tormented innocent people, that millions had to leave their homes, although the signs pointed in a quite different direction?

The political (election) victory of ethno-national forces and the political mobilization was *one* step. Another one had only little to do with politics and 'ethnic' concepts. It was well-aimed terror that was supposed to tear open the ethno-national cleavages in the population. The methods which polarized different sections of the population against each other in Bosnia-Herzegovina and India are incredibly similar.

3.3.1. *The Rioters and Their Strategies*

The violent criminals proceeded systematically. First step: a violent group of the 'ethnic group' A ('riot specialists'[106]) topples the moderate authorities. Second step: prominent members of the 'ethnic group' B are murdered. Third step: A's—especially those who are angry with B's for all kinds of reasons—are encouraged to set fire to a house of B, to expel a B-family, etc. Fourth step: the A-rioters play the protectors of 'their ethnic group', distribute arms to the A-population, and demand more murders of B's. Thus, local residents become jointly responsible for the crimes. The population becomes polarized. An ethno-national conflict is the *result* and *not* the *cause* of this process.[107]

However, a tense political situation and propagandistic smear campaigns can quickly create an atmosphere which encourages such acts. Engineer speaks of 'macro-factors' and 'micro-factors' in the case of communal riots. The higher circumstances are ideological and country-wide. Concrete riots, in contrast, have nothing to do with ideology. Their protagonists and scenes are of a local nature.[108] Indeed, most victims know the culprits. They were their immediate neighbours or from the neighbouring village.[109]

In the presence of unfavourable 'macro-factors' people become more credulous. When the propaganda machine is in full swing, many accusations are heard without anybody verifying them or even being willing to verify them. In the Bosnian war 'witnesses' recounted on television that they were tortured by the enemy or that Muslims had declared *jihad* against them. Many stories were invented.[110] In the face of the turmoil Hindus immediately believed that a Muslim had assassinated Gandhi although it was a Hindu.[111]

Trivial matters make the situation escalate. In Sarajevo on the day of the referendum on independence (1 March 1992) a criminal Muslim shot at a wedding reception and killed Serb guests. As a response, Serb ethno-nationalists erected the first barricades in the suburbs of the city.[112] Brawls at a Holi celebration in Benares in 1938 (initially only among Hindus) sparked off the most violent ethno-national riots in the city until then.[113]

Such situations are perfect playground for freaks, criminals, hooligans, perverts, and paranoids. Their acts appear only in a different light. Brass concludes: '[T]he interpretation of virtually any act of violence between persons identified as belonging to different ethnic groups itself becomes a political act.'[114] Every fifth voluntary fighter from Serbia had a criminal record. Many of them joined the paramilitary forces right after their imprisonment. Most of them were poorly educated or were refugees themselves. The most brutal tormentors of prisoners were mostly of lower military ranks.[115] Also, the worst riots against Hindus in Calcutta in August 1946 were the doing of 'all kinds of bandits' whom the rabble-rousing prime minister of Bengal had carted into the city for this purpose.[116]

In general, ethno-national rioters in Bosnia-Herzegovina and India came and still come from the lower strata of society or from the lower castes.[117]

3.3.2. *Sexuality and Warfare*

Once normal life is disrupted, some take the chance to live out perverse taboos. 'Normal people turn out to be beasts, as if you're watching a Frankenstein movie', an inhabitant of the Bosnian town of Zvornik said. 'They become monsters.'[118]

In India and in ex-Yugoslavia violence assumed a new dimension. It fused torture with sexuality. 'In areas such as Bosnia and Kashmir the modern soldier, it appears, marches with gun in the one hand and penis in the other', A.S. Ahmed illustrates.[119] Ignatieff notes: 'For some young European males, the chaos that resulted from [the collapse of the state and its monopoly of power] . . . offered the chance of entering an erotic paradise of the all-is-permitted. Hence the semi-sexual, semi-pornographic gun culture of the checkpoints.'[120] Warriors need 'fucking and killing', as the cultural anthropologist from Belgrade, Ivan Colovic, describes a common attitude.[121] Patriotic and male pride reinforce each other. In fact, the war experience itself was eroticized: 'When you remove a mine it is like undressing a woman', or, 'The best fuck is before battle.'[122] In Serbia and Croatia numerous comics suggested that 'war is sexy', and sometimes an outsized phallus even swelled to the symbol of 'ethnic' superiority.[123]

In India things did not go quite that far. There were no concentration camps as in Bosnia. Nonetheless, rapes were part of a cruel strategy in both cases.[124] They served as weapons against Muslims in particular. The anthropologist El Guindi writes with regard to Algeria:

> Women are the center of the sanctified family identity and the guardians of honour and reputation of the Arab family. Motherhood is considered sacred. The national unity is defined in terms like 'motherland'. To assault a Muslim woman means to hurt the core of the socio-moral system.[125]

This is just the reason why fanatics employ this 'weapon'. They want to break the will and resistance of Muslims, and deprive the tormented ones of their 'national identity'.[126] In Islamic law rape is considered one of the most serious crimes and is subject to the death penalty. The 'impure' women are often expelled from society. This can also happen to them when they are abducted and forcefully married to a member of another religion, as it often happened in India. This occures to Hindu women, too, and they also have to suffer social ostracism.[127] Hasan published a report of a contemporary witness in which a Hindu women tells the story how she worked in the field just on the 'wrong' side when the country was divided. She was abducted, raped and detained by Muslims. After her escape even her husband and her friends repudiated her.[128] On the other hand, far away from reality, Hindu women were often chauvinistically idealized and thus used as an instrument against 'the Muslims'. Hindu poets of the nineteenth and twentieth centuries accused the Muslim rulers of having robbed them of 'women, prosperity and religion'. They also stylized the image of the heroic wife who preferred the *sati* to falling into the hands of a Muslim after the death of her husband.[129]

The ideological and physical abuse of women plays a special role not only in ethno-national conflicts described here but in all other conflicts, too. Women are considered 'biological reproducers of members of ethnic collectivities'.[130] They assume a key function in an 'ethnic'-biological perception of culture. Their ability and will to reproduce is responsible for the extent to which the key resource of the ethno-national project is strengthened—namely the number of physical members of an 'ethnic group', the number of the 'right' type of human beings. An abuse of women—that means a restriction of their reproduction or a 'distortion' of the same through rape by members of another 'ethnic' group—not only brings about ideological consequences but challenges the attribute of 'honour' on the individual level, too. It causes an immediate dismay to each individual and is generally sanctioned by men. Personal humiliation or a humiliation which is felt personally often results in bloody vendetta and breaks free the process of polarization of the population along ethno-national cleavages. In India systematic rapes are part of the atrocity of communal riots even today. Sometimes the act is even filmed and sold in the bazaar to the utmost humiliation of the women.[131] Of course, this terror against the civilian population has nothing to do any more with political ideology.

Comparative view

It is important to keep the chronology and causality of the events in mind. In both cases violence in the population is not the *cause* but the *consequence* of a conflict which is being fought along ethno-national cleavages on the 'macro-level'.[132] Once hatred is evoked in this way, it grows on its own and plays into the hands of the ethno-national activists. The atrocities were recorded meticulously on all sides and presented as a political lever.[133]

However, one clear distinction must be pointed out in the cases of Bosnia-Herzegovina and India: The scale of *systematic* 'ethnic' expulsion and extermination was much larger in ex-Yugoslavia. In India hardly any ethno-national spokesman of top position was involved in stirring up or even committing ethno-national atrocities. What remained controversial was rather their role in the prevention of violence. In Bosnia-Herzegovina the war criminal[134] and the ideological arsonist came often in one person.

In both cases personal views radicalized through extremely emotional experiences. Some of those people were to play an important role in the conflicts. Ratko Mladic (*1943), commander of Bosnian-Serb activists, who became famous as the 'butcher of the Muslims', said that his Serb identity was strengthened after he had witnessed the burning down of his house in May 1992, and after his daughter, a medical student, had committed suicide during this time. In the census of 1991 Mladic had still declared himself as 'Yugoslav'.[135] In India and Pakistan three refugees from the respective other side were to become main actors of the confrontation: The Pakistani military dictator Zia-ul-Haq (1924-88) came from east Punjab. The Pakistani general Pervez Musharraf (*1941), who took power in October 1999 by a military coup, was born in New Delhi. He belongs to the leading heads of the Pakistani army who have demanded stricter action against India in the simmering Kashmir conflict. On the other hand, Lal Krishan Advani (*1927), an RSS activist for many years and president of the Hindu nationalist party BJP had fled from Sind.[136] Advani, who likes to compare himself with Hitler, became Home Minister in April 1998, Deputy Prime Minister in 2002, and is one of the leading ethno-national demagogues in the country.

Both Bosnia-Herzegovina and India have further in common that massacres took place in proportions unkown until then. Hobsbawm had also these atrocities in mind when in 1994 he spoke of a return of barbarism even to the once enlightened and secular societies.[137]

This barbarism in Bosnia and India developed an automatism and greatly influenced the political development. The traumatic war experience seems to have left behind deeper traces than a long period of peace. Ivekovic writes: 'War is much more efficient than any narrative, it is *the best narrative*.'[138] Inder Singh also considers the mass riots in 1947 as the final breaking point which made Pakistan sheer unavoidable.[139] A political reorganization which separated the 'hostile ethnic groups' spatially appeared to be the only plausible solution in Bosnia-Herzegovina as well. The ethno-national activists—consciously or unconsciously—achieved their goal through a heavy toll of lives.

4. THE PROTAGONISTS

4.1. THE MUSLIM LEADERS

> The tragedy in Yugoslavia was not predestined. It was the product of power-hungry, partly even criminal politicians who misuse ethnic tensions to their personal, political and financial advantage.[140]
>
> *Richard Holbrooke*

With these words Holbrooke expressed only a part of the reality. The politicians did not only use ethno-national tensions for their own ends but created them themselves through their politics. And they were not only power-hungry but also extraordinarily well educated. The partition of India and the war in ex-Yugoslavia have discredited Plato's ideal state.[141] Whether philosophers are the best kings, whether education creates political farsightedness—the one who looks at the protagonists of these conflicts starts to question all this.

In ex-Yugoslavia as in India historians, political scientists, lawyers and scientists were at the helm. Most of them had enjoyed their higher education in the 'West'.[142] Writers, philosophers and clerics actively influenced the political development or supported it indirectly.[143] Particularly in India the high intellectual level of the political debate is striking. The replies to the question 'How do I define a nation?' supply plenty of material for the work of political scientists. In Bosnia-Herzegovina not much time was left for discussions after the disintegration of Yugoslavia. What counted were rather day-to-day political rescue manoeuvers. Nevertheless, Izetbegovic contributed to the academic discussion on Muslim identity, especially in his early years. Quite different from Jinnah, who was more of a pragmatist than a visionary.

The two lawyers knew their opponents personally very well and started their political career as spokesmen of ethno-national harmony.

In 1989 Izetbegovic took part in the inaugural function of the Serb SDS as a guest of honour. His speech received the longest applause. In the summer of 1990 both Izetbegovic and Karadzic visited a commemorative function for Serb and Muslim victims of World War II. On this occasion Karadzic is reported to have said: '[O]ur Muslim brothers are much closer to us [the Bosnian Serbs] than many Christian people in Europe.' In Foca they walked over the Drina bridge and declared that never again should blood flow down this river.[144] A few years later its water turned red once again.

Till the 1930s Jinnah enjoyed the title 'Ambassador of Hindu-Muslim Unity'. As a member of the Congress party, he had repeatedly spoken out in favour of a co-existence of members of both religions. For Gandhi and other Congress members he was a great white hope.

Izetbegovic and Jinnah did not carry any ethno-national hatred in themselves unlike their extremist opponents (Karadzic, Mladic, Milosevic, Tudjman, Savarkar). Nonetheless, both contributed to the emergence of an atmosphere charged with hatred and, at times, let themselves being carried away. Therefore, Holbrooke saw in Izetbegovic an embittered person and hardliner: 'He found it extremely difficult to make any kind of compromise, even small conciliatory gestures towards those Serbs who did not want the war and were ready to re-establish some kind of of multi-ethnic community.'[145]

So far some external factors have been mentioned which helped to politicize the Muslims: The Serbo-Croatian sandwich and Hindu-nationalism; the disintegration of Yugoslavia along with Bosnia-Herzegovina and the withdrawal of the British; the element of democracy. A politicization of 'ethnic groups' was now finally followed by the 'ethnicization' of politics. The following parts examine which part Izetbegovic and Jinnah played *themselves* in this development.

4.1.1. *Izetbegovic*

> He is one of the most mysterious of all political personalities in the former Yugoslavia.[146]
>
> *Lord Owen*

The past haunted Izetbegovic until his death in October 2003: A document which he wrote in the 1960s rose to significance again during the Bosnian war. As a leading member of the Young Muslims he wrote the Islamic Declaration, which, by the way, was also printed in Pakistan. He formulated a coherent religious conviction and ideology—something which Jinnah never put on paper. Izetbegovic was the only non-ex-communist of all presidents of the ex-Yugoslav republics. Twice he was sent to prison because of his activities (1948 and 1983).

It is difficult to classify this man who contradicted himself several times in word and deed during the conflict. Here the Islamic Declaration is to serve as a point of departure—mainly because it was received most by his opponents and thus played a major political role. The document is clearly pan-Islamic and anti-nationalist. But at the same time Izetbegovic wished that the 'emotional community' of Islam finally organized itself *politically* as well—and in fact as a confederation 'from Marocco to Indonesia, from tropical Africa to Central Asia'.[147] For this entity 'Islam is [...] its ideology and pan-Islamism its politics'.[148] Sceptics of a pan-Islamic belt he described as 'weaklings'. For him the following was clear: 'A Moslem as a rule does not exist as an individual entity. If he wants to live and survive as a Moslem, he must create a milieu, a community, an order. He must change the world or else undergo change himself.'[149] This was a call to change the social and political conditions in the country in which the Muslim lives. Izetbegovic emphasized that Islam was not a mere religion but a political system which does not go well with other ones:[150]

> [There is an] incompatibility of Islam and non-Islamic systems. There can be no peace nor co-existence between the 'Islamic faith' and 'non-Islamic' social and political institutions. [...] Claiming for itself the right to regulate its own world, Islam clearly rules out any right or possibility of action of any foreign ideology on its turf.[151]

However, elsewhere he made clear that a political order according to Islam is only then necessarily valid when the Muslims form a majority. Muslims should protect minorities—if they are loyal—and grant them freedom of worship. This is the same what Muslim minorities would expect in a non-Muslim society.[152]

For Bosnia-Herzegovina in the 1990s this resulted in a delicate twist: In Yugoslavia the Muslims were a minority without any doubt. But after its disintegration, with respect to Bosnia-Herzegovina, they formed a majority for the first time. As a logical consequence the Bosnian Muslims should strive for an Islamic social order. Indeed, Izetbegovic himself alluded to such a possibility when he said in 1990: 'At the moment' the building of an Islamic republic were out of question because the Bosnian Muslims did not form an absolute majority yet.[153] He had no illusions about the time schedule, though:

We are on the road to a national state, our only way out is towards a free civic union. This is the future. Some people may want that [to make Bosnia a Muslim state] but this is not a realistic wish. Even though the Muslims are the most numerous nation in the republic, there are not enough of them . . . they would have to comprise about seventy per cent of the population. (7 July 1990)[154]

Interestingly, Izetbegovic spoke of a 'nation state' but rejected a religious connotation as unrealistic. Thus he had an all-comprising Bosnian state in mind and not a Muslim 'nation state'.

The reference to 'ethnic' or religious population ratios strongly reminds of Jinnah's argument—only the other way round. This becomes even more obvious in September 1990. At that time, Izetbegovic announced that the next government would be determined by *one man–one vote* and no more by an equal representation of all three 'nations'. This would automatically make the SDA the strongest party—in case of an 'ethnic' voting pattern. Naturally the SDS and HDZ protested. Besides, it was against the constitution of Bosnia-Herzegovina in which all three 'nations' were mentioned as constitutive elements. Despite the fight all three parties worked things out with each other and formed an alliance against the common enemy—the communists.[155]

Izetbegovic built up a political cleavage between 'the Muslim brothers' and 'the others'. This is just what makes his approach so delicate in view of the Bosnian war in which particularly religion was used to legitimize ethno-national projects and draw borders against 'the others'. Moreover, many Bosnian Muslims, as shown, oscillated between pan-Islam and 'Bosnian' Islam. Izetbegovic and his SDA had to win over both.

During the foundation of his party Izetbegovic did distance himself from the programme of the former Young Muslims, who led pan-Islam and nationalism in one breath.[156] But the old contradictions have emerged again. The SDA referred and still refers to a feeling of religious solidarity and has done without a detailed party manifesto, like all other ethno-national parties as well. In this way it strengthened ethno-national Muslim forces. In 1997, Bougarel calls the election victory an irony of history: '[I]t was only by leaning on Bosnian Muslim nationalism that the pan-Islamist current of Bosnia-Herzegovina could emerge from its marginality', and, 'Izetbegovic found himself carried to the head of Bosnia-Herzegovina by the most secularized people of this republic'.[157]

This is why Izetbegovic can be placed in a row with the competing ethno-national actors in the Bosnian conflict. A vote for the SDA was an equally ethno-nationalistic one as for the SDS or the HDZ.

But this man was full of contradictions and subtleties. In his Islamic Declaration he did not mention Bosnia-Herzegovina or Yugoslavia even once. He also used this to justify himself in front of the tribunal in 1983.[158] He said he did not call for nationalism. Indeed, he rejected nationalism as a Western import which stood against the values of Islam. Izetbegovic considered its defeat as the biggest task of the century:

> The creation of the European Economic Community—although this claim may seem unacceptable at first sight—constitutes the most constructive event in 20th century European history. And the establishment of this supranational structure was the first real victory of the European peoples over nationalism. Nationalism has become a luxury, a thing too expensive for small and even for medium-sized nations.[159]

This quote puts Izetbegovic into a totally different light again. He was not an ethno-nationalist who aimed at a 'nation state' territory from the beginning. In a party congress of the SDA in late 1991 he said amidst applause: 'Serbia and Croatia are national states. Bosnia-Herzegovina is not this and it can only be a civil [*gradjanski*] republic.'[160]

These utterances explain his openness towards ideas of a confederation at the outset of the Balkan crisis. As late as 1991 he was the one who spoke out most persistently in favour of preserving Yugoslavia, along with the Macedonian President Kiro Gligorov. This is why Meier speaks of 'independence against will'[161] when he looks at the two new-born states. This attitude has contributed to the fact that in Bosnia-Herzegovina a Muslim nation state-building has not taken place till today. It is here where Izetbegovic distinguishes himself from his Serb and Croatian counterparts—especially from his former colleague Karadzic, who soon forgot the Drina episode and hissed: 'Serbs cannot live together with Muslims and Croats. I told Owen that it is equally impossible to put us in one bag as dogs and cats.'[162]

But Izetbegovic also blew hot and cold. In 1994 the Social Democrats (UBSD) quoted him with the words: A 'coexistence' in Bosnia-

Herzegovina was a 'lie'. The Bosnian army did not fight for a united and multi-'ethnic' state. Also the diplomatic corps of the Bosnian government consisted mainly of members who supported a Muslim nation state.[163] Besides, a small circle in the SDA controlled the army and the lucrative positions in economy and politics. In the end Izetbegovic also pushed through ethno-national recruitings at the top of the state (against the protest of Silajdzic): In case of his death a Muslim should succeed him.[164] This made Owen conclude for his negotiations: 'Basically, we had to deal with a Muslim government which catered the interests of a chiefly Muslim population.'[165]

The green flag of Islam with the crescent and Muslim greetings, which until then had almost been forgotten, became symbols of the SDA.[166] Someone composed a praising party-song on 'our leader Alija'. It emphasized the Muslim identity.[167] On the question if the SDA was a secular or a religious movement, Izetbegovic said in September 1990: '[N]either the one nor the other . . . it is a Muslim party, which resembles the nation from which it recruits its partisans. It is a religious nation [. . .].'[168]

In the schools and in the army, too, religious indoctrination prevailed. The soldiers sang Islamic songs and wore green head bands. One battalion even accepted the Sharia as its code of conduct.[169] After the war, most non-Muslims were expelled from the Bosnian army.[170] The most famous example was the highest-ranking Serb military in the 'Muslim'-Bosnian army and vice chief of staff, General Jovan Divjak. After having fought to defend Sarajevo and Bosnia for all 'ethnic groups', he was sacked in 1996 by Izetbegovic without personal notice. But Divjak's disappointment about the president is beyond personal nature. 'In the first two years of the war I still believed in Izetbegovic and in Bosnian multiculturalism', Divjak said in 2001. 'But I am convinced that he has quit this idea.'[171]

Moreover, Izetbegovic provided his Serb and Croatian opponents with political ammunition when, in 1991, he proposed that Bosnia-Herzegovina should join the Organization of Islamic States.[172] Such developments divided not only the population but also the Bosnian government and even the SDA itself.[173] Especially the then Bosnian prime minister, Haris Silajdic, and Izetbegovic were often at loggerheads with each other. Even though Silajdzic is an expert in Islam, he did not go along with the ethno-national U-turn of the president. He was considered as a representative of the liberal wing of the SDA and a spokesman for a pluralistic state. Holbrooke describes him as the most farsighted Bosnian politician. During the Dayton negotiations Izetbegovic, Sacirbey and Silajdzic had often fallen out with each other hopelessly.[174]

To what extent Silajdzic exerted a moderating influence on Izetbegovic during the war years has not yet been examined. But at least most of the president's statements indicate that he wanted to preserve a multi-'ethnic' state-structure in Bosnia-Herzegovina. In February of 1991 he said that for the intactness and sovereignty of Bosnia-Herzegovina he was even ready to make war. This was better than living under the Serb thumb, which is what the new Yugoslavia meant to him.[175] But at the beginning, he gave a naïve impression as if he could not quite assess the extent of his actions. The following quote shows in addition how difficult he found the balancing act between his role as the President of the republic and as the representative of 'the Muslims', as he saw himself. Faced with Karadzic's open threat that he would 'exterminate' the Bosnian Muslims, Izetbegovic reacted intimidatedly:

> I want to tell the citizens of Bosnia-Herzegovina not to be afraid, because there will be no war. . . . Therefore, sleep peacefully. . . . As President (of the presidency) of Bosnia-Herzegovina, I am sorry that in this situation I must talk for the Muslim people. I solemnly state that the Muslims will not attack anyone. However, just as solemnly I state that the Muslims will defend themselves with great determination and survive. They will not disappear as Karadzic said. They cannot disappear. (15 October 1991)[176]

On the following day the break-up of the coalition began, the break-up of the country, and finally outbreak of the war. The Bosnian-Serb nationalists blamed Izetbegovic for this, since 'the Serbs' did not want to live under Muslim dominance in an independent Bosnia-Herzegovina. Izetbegovic's stand often vacillated. But two standpoints became increasingly crystallized (1) He now wanted a *sovereign* Bosnia-Herzegovina, and (2) an *undivided* Bosnia-Herzegovina, which means no Muslim 'nation state'. By no means did he want an Islamic state: 'To be quite clear', said Izetbegovic, 'I don't want an Islamic Republic, but I want Islam to survive in this part of the world [if] somebody likes it or not.'[177]

In an interview with the magazine *Why* in Sarajevo he was more precise when he elaborated on a jointly launched platform of the (mixed) Bosnian state presidency:

Simply, the other side wanted to form separate Orthodox, Catholic and Muslim, or Islamic, States on the territory of Bosnia and Herzegovina. We said that we would not allow such a Bosnia and Herzegovina, that we wanted a normal, ordinary State like the other States of Europe. [...] I would say that [the Platform] rejects the idea of three theocratic States on the territory of Bosnia and Herzegovina, which would sooner or later attack each other, and which would provoke bad historical memories, national myths and so forth, and it that way set the peoples against each other. When I speak of a normal State, I mean, of course, one in which Islam and Orthodoxy and Catholicism would have every freedom to function as religions. Karadzic tried to impose three religious States on Bosnia and Herzegovina.[178]

In this interview the President also made it clear that he did not want peace at any cost. In the autumn of 1993 a Muslim 'nation state' was within reach—and the Bosnian government turned it down. The war parties had negotiated a referendum. It was supposed to take place two years later and decide whether the people wanted to live in seperate states or not. Silajdzic was the chief negotiator. But he got cold feet. The mediator Owen, who himself thought in terms of ethno-national cleavages, wondered:

Interestingly, it was Haris Silajdzic who had rejected a proposal which could have played a key function on the way to a separate Muslim state as he had closer formal connections with Islam than all other Muslim leaders: He had been adviser of the Reis-ul-Ulema.[179]

Owen interpreted this rejection in a tough way: 'The Muslims had clearly resolved to continue the war.'[180] He did not understand that they had tried not to make ethno-national cleavages the only basis of their politics. He stuck to this opinion when the Vance/Owen plan failed because of the Bosnian government. The envisaged Muslim rump state would not have been viable anyway. However, for a moment it appeared as if Izetbegovic would agree to an 'ethnic' division of the country into three parts. He said wearily:

This division will give Muslims a Bosnian state. For the moment the idea of a multi-ethnic Bosnia is dead. Future generations can hope for such a state. But only after they have sobered up from their state of drunkenness.[181]

But at the last minute he did a U-turn again. As a result the rift between the Bosnian Muslim leaders became unbridgeable. The war entered into a new round. Izetbegovic and Silajdzic had once again made it clear that they did not want a Muslim 'nation state'. But at the same time they hoped for territorial gains on the military side. In this context Izetbegovic's inconsistent view became clear once again. He criticized his adversary Fikret Abdic in the following words:

The Muslims have finally made it to become a people having a state and constitution. Abdic tries to throw us back by at least fifty years only to become the head of the state. He divides us into tribes, he wants to subjugate us to a feudal system, *he leaves our country at the mercy of the Serbs and Croats.*[182]

Somehow Izetbegovic did consider 'the Muslims' a superior people in Bosnia-Herzegovina: a people who experienced nation-building and who had a claim to a state and a territory of its own. Izetbegovic never talked about the 'citizens' of a state without ethno-national classification. Perhaps this statement was also a reaction to the increasing physical threat in a multifront war. For, in principle, Izetbegovic had not changed his view on a multi-'ethnic' state, although Bosnia-Herzegovina has more or less been divided into three parts under the Dayton Agreement. In an interview in January 1999 he said:

We have this rare project of a multinational Bosnia. More or less all peoples have a task to create their single-national states where minorities have rights, but we are trying to create a state out of three peoples, which had been drawn into a conflict from somebody else. This project is a sublime project. It is an experiment that will enter history if it succeeds. There are no such experiments, such projects, in the world. Bosnia is one of the rare examples where a state is tried to be made out of three peoples, three religions, three cultures, maybe even more.[183]

Izetbegovic always held a conservative religious concept of the Muslims (although, as already noted, he liked to use Muslim ethno-nationalism for his own ends). This is also evident from the fact that he refused to accept the name 'Bosnjak' as a synonym for the Bosnian Muslims. Thus, he did not want to alienate Serbs and Croats from this term.[184] In this way Izetbegovic rejected the secular Muslim concept of nation as it had prevailed under Tito.

But Izetbegovic's views on Islam were not at all fundamentalist. Croatian and Serb opponents are mostly responsible for such a classification. In a private get together Tudjman described the Bosnian head of state as 'an Algerian and fundamentalist'. For the public he toned down his words slightly: 'There are tendencies to create an

Islamic state in Europe, which is unacceptable to international sectors.'[185] Even some academic works classify Izetbegovic as an Islamic fundamentalist. Cohen writes: '[...] Alija Izetbegovic was a devout Muslim conservative [...], if not accurately described as a religious fundamentalist [...].'[186]

In reality Izetbegovic formed a clear contrast to fundamentalism. Already in the Islamic Declaration he spoke in favour of an openness towards science, towards modernization, efficiency, and education. Islam is supposed to be 'religion without mysticism and science without atheism'.[187] In this way religion could become attractive for all people. He spoke out clearly in favour of nonviolence, freedom, democracy, and the rule of law. Dictatorship did not go with the teachings and principles of Islam. On this point he further elaborated in more recent writings.[188]

4.1.2. *Jinnah*

> If I hadn't been a fanatic, there would never have been Pakistan.[189]
>
> *M.A. Jinnah*

Jinnah, the son of an ex-Hindu, went to a Christian high school, married a Parsee, as did his daughter (though against Jinnah's will). In his family several religions came together and different streams of Islam, too.[190] On the question of how religious the founder of Pakistan himself was, the opinions are divided—depending on whether the historian is from Pakistan, from India, or from the West. Contemporary witnesses and Muslim historians attribute to him a late transformation into a believing Muslim who oriented himself more and more towards the Koran.[191] At the end of his life he is even said to have spoken of a 'united front' of Islamic states.[192] This strongly reminds one of Izetbegovic's Islamic Declaration, although Jinnah had strictly rejected the pan-Islamic ideology all his life. Jinnah's statements are very contradictory. He never philosophized on them in such detail as Izetbegovic did. It is certain that because of his British education Jinnah was strongly influenced by British liberalism. His lifestyle and politics were secular and pragmatic.

Jinnah was not a founder member of the Muslim League. He joined only in 1913 and remained a member of the Congress at the same time. This was no contradiction. For at that time the Congress and the League worked together very closely. They even held their annual conferences at the same place simultaneously. The Lucknow Pact of 1916 symbolizes the climax of this rapprochement. Salman Rushdie even conjectures that Jinnah might not have accepted the leadership of the Muslim League in the first place if Gandhi's opponents had not hindered him in his ambition to become the president of the Congress.[193]

A religious fanaticization on both sides began only when Gandhi became involved with the conservative *ulema* and helped to carry out the Khilafat movement. Jinnah detested this. Since then the Congress and the Muslim League drifted apart.[194] The following circumstances furthered this estrangement: the increasingly aggressive rhetoric of the Hindu nationalist parties, the founding of the RSS, and—above all—the 'Hinduization' of the Congress and Jinnah's personal estrangement from Gandhi due to these reasons.[195]

This breaking-up is reflected in Jinnah's political career and political thinking. They indicate a turning point from the 1920s onwards, and particularly after 1937.[196] The former 'Ambassador of Hindu-Muslim Unity' and one-time Congress politician Jinnah now became the most bitter adversary of this unity, even to the point of demanding territorial separation. Gandhi could not understand the abrupt change. In 1938 he wrote to Jinnah in vague hope:

> Everybody spoke of you as one of the staunchest nationalists[197] and the hope of both the Hindus and Musulmans. Are you still the same Mr. Jinnah? If you say you are, in spite of your speeches, I shall accept your word.[198]

The idea of Pakistan stemmed neither from Jinnah nor from the Muslim League. As late as 1933 he turned down Pakistan as an 'impossible dream' when the Cambridge student Choudhary Rahmat Ali explained his proposal to him in the Waldorf Hotel in London.[199] For Ali the territorial division of the subcontinent represented more or less an act of nature:

> This supreme distinction between Pakistan and Hindoostan is ineffaceable, as it is based on eternal truths. Our constitution-makers must reckon with Nature's decrees. [. . .] This great cleavage . . . has existed from time immemorial, and must exist for ever.[200]

Jinnah soon took over this argumentation. Another model for him was the famous Urdu poet Muhammad Iqbal (1875-1938). He was the first person, in 1930, to have talked about an Islamic state as a Muslim homeland (composed of Punjab, NWFP, Sind, and Baluchistan). He justified the demand on the basis of cultural and religious arguments which correspond to the specific definition of 'ethnicity':

> Yet I love the communal group which is the source of my life and behaviour; and which has formed me what I am by giving me its religion, its literature, its thought, its culture, and thereby recreating its whole past, as a living operative factor, in my present consciousness.[201]

He also gave political reasons: 'The principle of European democracy cannot be applied to India without recognizing the fact of communal groups.'[202] Whether Iqbal propagated a sovereign 'nation state' even in 1930 is a contentious matter. His statements are contradictory. For instance, he spoke of an autonomous 'Muslim India within India' *inside or outside* of the British Commonwealth,[203] and denied it later in the British press—but also to pacify the British:

> I do not put forward a demand for a Muslim State, outside the British Empire, but only a guess at a possible outcome in the dim future of the mighty forces now shaping the destiny of the Indian sub-continent. No Indian Muslim with any pretence to sanity contemplates a Muslim State or series of States in North West India outside the British Commonwealth of Nations as a plan of practical politics.[204]

Jinnah also wavered. However, the Lahore Resolution of the Muslim League of 23 March 1940 is considered a political breakthrough (it is a Pakistani national holiday even today).[205] Later, to commemorate this event a monumental tower was built, the Minar-i-Pakistan, situated in the Iqbal Park right next to the Old Fort in Lahore. The resolution went down in history as the 'Pakistan Resolution' although it did not say a single word about Pakistan. Jinnah complained later that it was the British and the Hindus who imposed this name on the declaration.[206]

Nevertheless, in that party conference Jinnah made it clear where he wanted to go. Just as Iqbal, he also put forward political and 'ethnic' as well as religious and cultural arguments in favour of a Muslim state. On the one hand, he complained about what he saw as a poor representation of 'the Muslims' in the political arena. About Gandhi, who always addressed Jinnah as 'brother', he joked: 'The only difference is that brother Gandhi has three votes and I have one vote.'[207] With this he alluded to the numerical differences between the Hindu and Muslim populations. A democratic system in India would end in a 'Hindu Raj'.

On the other hand, he explained his Two-Nation Theory, which clearly came down to an 'ethnic' concept of nation:

The Hindus and Muslims belong to two religious philosophies, social customs, literatures. They neither intermarry, nor interdine together and, instead, they belong to two different civilizations which are based mainly on conflicting ideas and conceptions. Their aspects of life are different. It is quite clear that Hindus and Mussalmans derive their inspiration from different sources of history. They love different epics, their heroes are different, and different episodes. Very often the hero of one is a foe of the other, and likewise their victories and defeats overlap. To yoke together two such nations under a single state, one as a numerical minority and the other as a majority, must lead to growing discontent and final destruction of any fabric that may be so built up for the government of such a state.[208]

In particular, he cited everyday customs in order to suggest an irreconcilable contrast between Muslims and Hindus. In another speech Jinnah said:

India has never been a true nation. It only looks that way on the map. The cow I want to eat, the Hindu stops me from killing. Every time a Hindu shakes hands with me he has to wash his hands. The only thing the Moslem has in common with the Hindu is his slavery to the British.[209]

Elsewhere he listed how minorities can define themselves: by 'religion, culture, race, language, art, music and so on'. These features made them different 'units' in one state which needed political safety guarantees.[210] Exactly this point played an ever-increasing role in the course of Jinnah's campaign. Some of his statements refer to the sticking points over which political scientists argue till today regarding the nature of ethno-national conflicts. In a speech in 1941 Jinnah argued:

Majority rule in a single nation, in a single society, is understandable, although even there it has failed. Representative government in a single nation, harmonious, homogeneous and one is understandable. But you have only got to apply your mind for a few minutes to see the truth. Can such a system ever work or succeed when you have two different nations—indeed more than two different nations—in this sub-continent, when you have two totally different societies, the Muslim society and the Hindu society?[211]

For every ethno-nation defined this way, he demanded a sovereign 'nation state'. As an example for a Muslim Pakistan he mentioned the independence of Croatia in 1941 in which the Croatian 'nation' represented the majority.[212] As in the Balkans, Jinnah also took religious differences as the primary means of contrast and built on them the idea of separate societies and states. However, he never equated these states with a religious social order. For him, a Muslim state was not necessarily an Islamic state.

He mixed it only in his speeches during the hot phase of the 1940s. Before that he had strongly attacked the *ulema* in a speech in front of Aligarh students in 1938:

What the League has done is to set you free from the reactionary elements of Muslims and to create the opinion that those who play their selfish game are traitors. It has certainly freed you from that undesirable element of Maulvis and Maulanas.[213]

In a party conference of the Muslim League in 1943 he insisted on withdrawing a proposal which demanded a Pakistani state on the basis of Islamic doctrine.[214] In this context one is reminded once again of Jinnah's opposition to the Khilafat movement. Against this background his later slogans—such as 'Islam is in danger' or 'One God, one book, one prophet, and one nation'—were as much contradictory as superficial.[215] But they had the effect that the Pakistan movement did not remain a pure Aligarh action. Aligarh supporters even complained about 'unwanted and dubious persons' and 'soldiers of fortune' who went with the tide.[216]

The Pakistan movement used more and more Islamic rhetoric. External symbols were to homogenize 'the Muslims'. Hence the green (Islamic) flag fluttered for the Muslim League. From 1937 Jinnah no longer dressed in British suits but in a *sherwani*[217] which was given to him by—guess who—Aligarh students. In addition, he wore the famous *karakuli* cap like many Muslims in north India. Thus, Jinnah emphasized an important point. His clothes were trans-ethnically Muslim. Besides, they contrasted with Gandhi's 'Hindu' garments and 'Hindu' cap.[218]

Jinnah's talent was that he kept his idea of Pakistan under wraps. Thus, he prevented a division among the Muslim leaders and turned the Muslim League into a catch-all party. Only when he had achieved his goal did he make a swing again—to his old liberal views from the early Congress period. With his inaugural speech before Pakistan's Constitutional Assembly on 11 August 1947, he made himself many enemies among conservative Islamists. Today, many Pakistani ideologists and historians do not like to be reminded of this speech, they pass it off as an aberration in Jinnah's career, or they try to mitigate its impact through a new interpretation.[219] For suddenly Jinnah as head of state spoke in favour of a *secular civil society*:

You are free; you are free to go to your temples, you are free to go to your mosques or to any other places of worship in this States [*sic*] of Pakistan. You may belong to any religion or caste or creed—that has nothing to do with the business of the State. [...] Now I think we should keep that in front of us as our ideal and you will find that in course of time, Hindus would cease to be Hindus and Muslims would cease to be Muslims, not in the religious sense, because that is the personal faith of each individual, but in the political sense as citizens of the State.[220]

He even admitted the existence of the inner-Muslim and inner-Hindu cleavages and predicted that these 'corners and edges' would now wear away through the creation of the state of Pakistan.[221] On another occasion he went even further and said: 'I am going to constitute myself the Protector-General of the Hindu minority in Pakistan.'[222] In his first cabinet he appointed a Hindu minister.[223]

This shows that *political ideology* alone was the clip which held together the different groups of people in Pakistan. But had the situation not been similar in entire India? Had Nehru and Gandhi not made the same demand? For this, had it been necessary for 15 million people[224] to leave their homes—in both directions—and for many of them to die?

Jinnah did not ask these questions himself. In his inaugural speech he directed his view to the future and called on the Pakistanis to forget their past, and, in fact, to *change* it (!):

If you change your past and work together in a spirit that everyone of you, no matter to what community he belongs, no matter what relations he had with you in the past, no matter what his color, caste or creed, is first, second and last a citizen of this State with equal rights, privileges and obligations, there will be no end to the progress you will make.[225]

A few months later, Jinnah died of tuberculosis. The fatal disease was his best-kept secret. If one could have suspected it, said the British Viceroy Lord Mountbatten later, 'most probably' he would not have approved of the partition of India.[226]

Comparative view

Can Izetbegovic and Jinnah be compared at all? The stoic, religious visionary and the energetic, liberal pragmatist; the pan-Islamist and the secularist; the head of state who turns down a Muslim 'nation state' and the would-be head of state who finally achieves it after a hard political struggle; the one under military pressure and the other a persistent poker player at the green table?

Indeed, substantially both of them have little in common. Izetbegovic wanted—ideally—an *Islamic* state. Since the majority relations did not allow it (and in case they did allow it by drawing an 'ethnic' boundary, the amputated state structure would not be able to survive), he stood for a multi-'ethnic' or multi-religious state. Jinnah wanted a *Muslim* state in which Muslims were in the majority and had the say. For him the political *state structure* was important, whereas for Izetbegovic it was important to strengthen the (Muslim) *state's people*—in which state was a side issue for the moment. For Jinnah the form was important, for Izetbegovic the content. Jinnah argued politically in the first place, Izetbegovic religiously. Jinnah used Islam as a mobilizing instrument to attain a political goal. Izetbegovic considered Islam as the basis of all action which *per se* contains a political goal.

Nonetheless, both men saw in religion more than just belief. Jinnah associated it with cultural and 'ethnic' features, and from it derived political demands and consequences. Izetbegovic may have derived his demands *directly* from Islam. But he also made use of and supported the Muslim nationalistic forces which played politics with the help of the paradigm of 'ethnic' difference.

Not enough research material is available about Izetbegovic to clarify the question once and for all whether he himself combined 'ethnic' features with Islam, too. Against this presumption speaks the fact that he wanted to keep the term 'Bosnian' open for Serbs and Croats and preferred the term 'Muslim'. Izetbegovic seemed to anchor the Muslim identity in the *umma* and less in 'ethnic' features. Yet, with the 'Muslim people' he linked political ambitions during the Bosnian war. And this is crucial with the *political* conflicts talked about here.

Jinnah, too, wanted to overcome differences, though ethnic-regional ones. He wanted to homogenize the Islam ethno-nationally and thus attributed to it common 'ethnic' features which made it different from Hinduism. The idea of an 'ethnic'—India-wide—Islam had to be conceived at first, whereas in the tiny Bosnia-Herzegovina that of an 'ethnic'—Bosnia-wide—Islam already showed first contours in the early modern age, namely as a demarcation against Serb, Croatian and pan-Islamic projects.

In the historical context of the Indian colonial time and the crumbling of Yugoslavia it is important to know that Izetbegovic and Jinnah did not consider the people as citizens but as members of religious, and eventually ethno-national camps. They contributed to politicize the 'ethnic groups', and, above all, they 'ethnicized' politics. They represented an objective, ethno-national ascription of the people and made them the most important criterion of the political contest.

Initially, they both faced a vast majority of members of their identity feature who did *not* agree with their political objectives. However, both contributed to make the gap between the action group and the large group shrink. Both finally managed that, seen from the outside, their political objectives were equated with those of their ethno-national constituencies.

4.2. The Alternatives

4.2.1. *To Izetbegovic*

Already shortly after the foundation of the SDA in 1990 the Muslim politicians split up into a 'secular' and a 'religious' camp (under Izetbegovic). A group around the wealthy businessman Adil Zulfikarpasic left the party. They could not allow, the deviationists said, 'that the party be directed by eleven persons of conservative and generally religious orientation and conducted by a closed and privatized council held together by family ties'.[227] Their new party, the Bosnian Muslim Organization (MBO),[228] supported a liberal, democratic state without any emphasis on religious or 'ethnic' interests. But in the 1990 elections the MBO had almost no chance.

Zulfikarpasic also had an argument with Izetbegovic on the term *Bosnjak*. He wanted the Muslim identity to be understood in secular terms. Therefore, he said, Bosnian is the same as Muslim. He got support from the All-Bosnjak Assembly who said that the Muslims should be called *Bosnjaks* from now on.[229] This view has prevailed in Bosnia today.

Other Muslims struggled with Izetbegovic less ideologically than on every-day politics—first and foremost the agro-businessman Fikret Abdic. In the elections for the Bosnian state presidency he had gained more votes than Izetbegovic. Both always remained rivals for the highest state office. Abdic had good contacts with the Serb and Croatian ethno-nationalists. After the rejection of the Vance/Owen plan Abdic accused Izetbegovic of not having done enough to end the war.[230] He was convinced that there was no alternative to this plan.[231] Afterwards he marched with his private army against Bosnian government forces in the enclave around Bihac. Muslims fought against Muslims. At the latest by now there could be no more talk of an 'ethnic conflict'.

The Union of Bosnian Social Democrats (UBSD) denied this from the beginning. They had 10 per cent of the seats in the parliament and were the severest critics of ethno-national politics in Bosnia-Herzegovina. Their voters were mainly drawn from urban industrial areas. The alliance was largely formed by members of the Reformist Party which had been founded by the last president of Yugoslavia, Ante Markovic. In the so-called Tuzla Declaration of 1994 the UBSD called for '[p]reserving the territorial integrity of Bosnia-Herzegowina as a democratic, secular state of all its *citizens* and peoples with equal rights.'[232] Nationality and religion were private matters.

Its president, Seijfudin Tokic, insisted: 'There are also other ethnic members defending Bosnia and Herzegovina', and, 'The war was an attack of a whole population'. Nevertheless he also showed understanding of the view of 'the Muslims': 'The Muslims also wanted to become a political population, not only an ethnic group.'[233] In March 1997 Tokic founded an alternative ministry council as a shadow cabinet. He was supported by many non-governmental organizations as an alternative to nationalism. But 'ethnic' thinking also crept in here: The cabinet was elected according to an 'ethnic' key.[234]

The Social Democratic Party (SDP), where most of the well-known social democrats of the former UBSD are united now, seriously challenged the SDA in the 2000 elections and became the strongest political force with favourable election wind from the OHR.[235] It allied itself with a more recent alternative to Izetbegovic: The Party for Bosnia-Herzegovia (SBiH).[236] This trans-'ethnically'-oriented organization had been founded in 1996 by Izetbegovic's old companion Silajdzic. In that same year, however, it had disappointed many supporters because it had entered into a 'Coalition for a United and Democratic Bosnia' with its rival SDA and other parties.[237] But by founding the SBiH, Silajdzic cast his long simmering, fundamental differences with Izetbegovic into a party-political frame. These and similar political forces which rather focus on economic issues than national ones, like also the Party of Democratic

Prosperity (PDP), are evolving only gradually. The backlash for more moderate parties, especially the Social Democrats, in the 2002 elections shows that there is still a long way to go.

4.2.2. *To Jinnah*

The most prominent political alternative to Jinnah concentrated in the person of Nehru, although both of them had a lot in common when it comes to education and life philosophy.

Politically, Nehru thought in a cosmopolitan Marxist frame of history. For him only socio-economic issues counted. Critics consider this 'economic reductionism' a reason for his misjudgement of the situation.[238] His outlook made him deaf to Jinnah's arguments. Communalism, Nehru said in 1936: 'is, after all, a side issue, and it can have no meaning in the larger scheme of things'.[239]

This supposed side issue soon became his main problem, although the Congress supported a concept of nation which transcended primordial elements, and thus could find broad support. Heimsath writes: 'Having at its base an antitraditional, liberal-democratic, secular, and politically orientated concept of the nation, the nationalism of the early Congress could properly encompass all Indian cultures and religions.'[240] But the Congress could not integrate into this concept wide sections of the Muslim upper- and middle-class and their spokesmen.

Nehru was convinced that this 'bourgeoisie' (just as that of the Hindus) had nothing to do with the 'masses' on either side.[241] Therefore he neglected their political claims. Communalism, he concluded, was far away from the people of the communities: 'In political matters, religion has been displaced by what is called communalism, a narrow group mentality basing itself on a religious community but in reality concerned with political power and patronage for the interest group.'[242] Nehru had very well understood the principle. Yet he underestimated its practical effect. For the ethno-national protagonists he only spared contempt. He was diametrically opposed to Jinnah, also in his definition of minorities:

> Minorities in India, it must be remembered, are not racial or national minorities as in Europe; they are religious minorities. Racially, India is a patchwork and a curious mixture, but no racial questions have arisen or can arise in India. Religion transcends these racial differences, which fade into one another and are often hard to distinguish. Religious barriers are obviously not permanent, as conversions

can take place from one religion to another, and a person changing his religion does not thereby lose his racial background or his cultural and linguistic inheritance.[243]

Nehru tried to nail down Jinnah to a basic contradiction in his Two Nation Theory. But the latter avoided him over and over again. Nehru asked: 'Why only two I do not know, for if nationality was based on religion, then there were many nations in India.'[244] Why should the Sikhs, Parsis and Christians not get their own state? Each village comprised different 'proportions' of these 'nations'. Nehru considered all this to be deeply 'mediaeval':

> To think in terms of Pakistan when the modern trend is towards the establishment of a world federation is like thinking in terms of bows and arrows as weapons of war in the age of the atom bomb. The whole mentality behind this conception of bows and arrows and Pakistan is most dangerous and if we cling to such anachronisms, we shall never solve our problems.[245]

But Nehru could not prevent this 'bow-and-arrow'-mentality to creep into his own party, the Congress. Gandhi's conflicting attitude has already been mentioned.[246] Although Gandhi belonged to the big advocates of a pan-Indian nationalism, he did not have a secular civil society in mind, as Nehru did, where religion was irrelevant. He rather accepted the religious thinking in political camps but tried to overcome it dialectically by imploring the brotherhood of Hindus and Muslims and building a metaphysical, humanistic system of thought on top of it.[247] In practical life, the nation transcended religion for him: 'I find no parallel in history for a body of converts and their descendents claiming to be a nation apart from the parent stock. If India was one nation before the advent of Islam, it must remain one in spite of a change of the faith of a very large body of her children.'[248]

Gandhi's symbolic and often theatrical actions and words must not obscure his political acumen. Point by point he sounded out Jinnah's nation theory and, like Nehru, pushed him into an argumentative dead end: How could Jinnah take religion as a criterion when the Indian Islam differed considerably from the Islam outside India and had a lot in common with Hinduism? How could he use language as an argument when regional dialects predominated, and Muslims also spoke Hindi and Hindus Urdu? Why should some diverging customs lead to a division when other communities also lived peacefully in one state?

What did 'Islamic civilization' actually mean in the way Jinnah used it? Did he mean pan-Islam? Did he mean, when he talked about Muslims, the Muslims on the entire subcontinent or just those in the future Pakistan? Gandhi demanded from Jinnah 'facts and figures' on the Pakistan which he envisaged. He waited in vain.[249]

Not only the 'Muslim' votes for the Congress showed that with their critique Nehru and Gandhi appealed to a section of Muslims, too. Muslim politicians even offered themselves as an alternative to Jinnah. Congress President Azad considered the unity of India more important than the country's independence. He shared this opinion with many other Muslims who were organized in other parties. These Muslim spokesmen also had in common that they did reproduce the *religious*, and partly also the '*ethnic*' thinking in the political camps but did not consider it a *political* obstacle to the realization of a pan-Indian state. The following statement of Azad is typical of this approach:

> I am a Muslim and profoundly conscious of the fact that I have inherited Islam's glorious tradition of the last thirteen hundred years. I am not prepared to lose even a small part of that legacy. The history and teachings of Islam, its arts and letters, its culture and civilization are part of my duty to cherish and guard them. . . . But, with all these feelings, I have another equally deep realization, born out of my life's experience, which is strengthened and not hindered by the Islamic spirit. I am equally proud of the fact that I am an Indian, an essential part of the indivisible unity of Indian nationhood, a vital factor in its total make up, without which this noble edifice will remain incomplete. I can never give up this sincere claim.[250]

Just as the Congress, Muslim parties also understandably refused to accept the claim of the Muslim League to represent all Muslims. All Muslim and other parties—except the League—condemned the Pakistan plan until into the 1940s.[251]

Some examples: the Independent Muslim Conference described the Pakistan plan as 'absurd', 'detrimental', and 'dangerous'. It would lead to a strengthening of British rule. The Conference also pointed out that every Indian Muslim who went on a pilgrimage to Mecca was called a 'Hindu' by the Arabs. The Indian Muslims had just as much to do with the Dravidians and Aryans as the Hindus. In addition, the Conference defended separate electorates in a united India which encouraged the 'warm' and 'harmonious' relations between Hindus and Muslims.[252]

The South Indian Anti Separation Conference condemned the 'suicidal' founding of 'exclusive organizations' for Hindus and Muslims. India should be proud of Akbar's legacy and its capability to assimilate and absorb.[253] The Anti Communal Conference described the Pakistan plan as 'highly unpatriotic, anti-national and against the best interests of the country'. It clearly summarized the public sentiment in Punjab which was threatened by partition:

> Are we in the Punjab to be told that we, Hindus and Muslims, differ in culture and dress and speech? You may write down for Census, and communal purposes that your language is Urdu or Hindi but each one of you speaks Punjabi—your and my mother-tongue. Our mothers and grandmothers knew no other language. They wore and continue to wear the same dress, live in [a] similar style, eat practically the same food. Are we to be divided from one another in order to preserve the dignity, prestige and position of communal leaders? The masses do not appreciate or understand such cries which pass over their heads. Their concern is with the economic struggle which is common to the masses of all communities. There is no communalism in starvation.[254]

The Nationalist Muslim Conference also warned of the 'ruinous politics' of the Muslim League. In their eyes it was a through and through 'capitalist organization' which exploited the Muslims for their own ends.[255] This argument was similar to the one made by the Bosnian Muslims who supported Yugoslav socialism and warned the Indian Muslims against the bourgeois and separatist Muslim League.[256]

The All Parties Shia Conference had other reasons but the same goal: Pakistan must be prevented since it would lead to a Sunni social order (*Hanafi Shariat*).[257]

Hence there were plenty of arguments with quite contrasting approaches. But all of them rejected a separate Muslim state. Moreover, apart from Jinnah's Pakistan idea, a large number of suggestions circulated on how India might look after independence. Some of them supported a federation of various *culturally* 'homogeneous' states. Others (like Sikander Khan) had a federation in mind which was to be defined neither by religious/'ethnic' divisions nor by ethnic ones.[258]

The outcome is known. Unlike in Bosnia-Herzegovina, in India two opposing ideologies (ethno-national and civil-democratic) could be put into practice. A Muslim 'nation state' and a secular civil state faced each other in rivalry. However, both projects were soon to erode substantially.

Comparative view

The forces that had already been set in motion in the prehistory of nation-building continued in its final stage—only with party-political emphasis: 'the Muslims' did not speak with one voice. It is true that people were objectively classified in religions, 'ethnic groups', and 'nations'. But their spokesmen or action groups partly supported diametrically opposed objectives, and that on the core issue of an 'own' statehood.

Very few of them were consistently civil and secular. Some also slipped into the thinking of ethno-national camps. But they did not automatically support a territorial solution and an ethno-national exclusivism. The alternatives (particularly to Jinnah) represented a realistic political force, at least for a while. It should not be forgotten that it was external factors to which they succumbed in the end.

5. THE POKER OF EXTERNAL POWERS

> This is a country in which at least three religions and half a dozen ethnic groups have been *fighting with each other for centuries.*[259]
>
> *Warren Christopher* (1993)

> [W]e are confronted with the *age-old antagonism* of Hindu and Muhammadan, representatives not only of two religions but of two civilizations [...].[260]
>
> *Joint Committee of Indian Constitutional Reform* (1934)

The external powers had the same prejudices with respect to Bosnia-Herzegovina and India. They supported the 'freezer theory' and acted accordingly. Thus, they strengthened the ethno-national forces and weakened multi- and trans-'ethnic' alternatives in the country.

In India, British historiography and the political quota system reconstructed and reinforced ethno-national cleavages at an early stage. This continued up to the decisive crisis. The British accepted the Muslim League as the exclusive mouthpiece of 'the Muslims' during the negotiations for an independent India, and the Congress as that of 'the Hindus'. In Bosnia-Herzegovina, the UN, NATO, the EU, etc., treated the SDA as the equivalent of 'the Muslims', the SDS of 'the Bosnian Serbs', and the HDZ of 'the Bosnian Croats'. Even more important, they accepted the territorial claims of the ethno-national representatives in this way as a quasi logical consequence, although they resisted them initially. Kumar aptly describes the behaviour of the international actors in Bosnia-Herzegovina as *divide and quit* in allusion to the British policy in India.[261]

Afterwards, the only options left were all within the ethno-national paradigm. The side effects were the haggling over boundaries and territorial percentages as well as the demand for corridors and the digging of tunnels. 'Ethnic' expulsions and millions of refugees were the instrument and the result of this new reality.

5.1 The Ethno-national Card in Bosnia: Upgraded by the West

5.1.1. *The Temptation of International Law*

The Yugoslav crisis in 1991 brought the international main actors down to earth with a bump:

(1) The European Community was just in an early stage of developing a common foreign policy. In the course of the crisis these first attempts were thwarted by the national interests of the individual member states.

(2) The Soviet Union was in the process of disintegration.

(3) The Gulf War had absorbed the attention of the United States. In addition, a change of government took place, followed by a change in international priorities. The new US President Bill Clinton initially concentrated his attention on domestic affairs.

(4) The UN as well as the CSCE had not found their place yet in the new multipolar world order.

Simultaneously, in eastern Europe the end of the Warsaw Pact, the revolutions and reforms in its member states, and the German unification evoked the idea of a 'national awakening'. The 'nation' as a political reference point had gained significance while the supranational arrangements struggled for new concepts. The yet strong engagement of the international actors in Yugoslavia resulted in a short-breathed policy without concepts, which gave wrong impulses and legitimized ex-post the results of the ethno-nationalists.

The first decisive external influence on the conflict was the passivity of the US and the EU in the summer of 1991. Slovenia and Croatia had waited for a signal if the West would prevent a conflict by force or not.

Four days after US Foreign Secretary Baker had expressed his lack of interest, Slovenia and Croatia declared themselves independent. The war began.[262] The West was taken by surprise. Concepts and expertise were missing. 'President Bush asked me once a week to explain to him what it all was about over there', recalls his security adviser.[263]

By recognizing Slovenia and Croatia as sovereign states at the end of 1991, the West exercized decisive influence on the developments for the second time. Holbrooke considered this decision a mistake.[264] Shortly before that, for instance, the foreign affairs politicians of the US and the EU had firmly rejected such a possibility. In December 1990, the Italian foreign minister Gianni de Michelis still snubbed his Slovenian hosts:

> Gentlemen, in Europe there is no place for new states, there is no place for an independent Slovenia either, and you are not thinking to move to another continent, I suppose. Please understand, your place is in Yugoslavia. In this framework we will cooperate with you.[265]

One year later, everything looked completely different. After a German rush ahead the EU even accelerated the disintegration of Yugoslavia by an ultimatum.[266] The republics were asked to decide by 23 December 1991 if they wished international recognition.[267] Several factors made this decision problematic:

– In Slovenia and Croatia fighting had already broken out.

– The EU simultaneously maintained the diplomatic recognition of the existing state of Yugoslavia.

– Most of the new states did not meet the standards of the Montevideo Convention of 1933. It demands that states must have clear boundaries, a 'stable' or 'settled' population, and that governments must have control over their territory. Further, a state must be recognized by others.[268]

– The EC did not have any follow-up plan after this step. The German foreign minister Hans-Dietrich Genscher had hoped that with the plain trump-card of national sovereignty the new states were protected from further attacks of the Serb-Yugoslav federal army.[269]

– The recognition was rash and ignored the Badinter Commission.[270] It had been assigned by the EU to prepare an experts' report on the Yugoslav republics and, above all, to examine their guarantees vis-à-vis 'ethnic' minorities. The NATO member states also declared: 'The right of self-determination of all peoples in Yugoslavia cannot be exercised detached from the interests and rights of national or ethnic groups within the single republics.'[271] There were some reservations against Croatia, which, nevertheless, did not obstruct a recognition.[272] (In contrast, although Macedonia met all the requirements, the republic was not recognized initially.)[273] After that, the Serb minority immediately proclaimed the Krajina in east Croatia an autonomous mini-republic.[274] A territorialization of the ethno-national conflict had started. 'The West led by Germany and the United States,' writes Thomas, 'had set the stage for the "Balkanization" of the Balkans.'[275]

The message which emerged from such steps was clear: In spite of all contradictions, there was a big chance of recognition—also for the 'ethnic' rag rug Bosnia-Herzegovina which had never before existed as an independent state and which was impossible as a 'nation state'. In addition, the Badinter Commission interpreted all boundaries of the republics as unalterable state borders—and these had been quite arbitrary from old times on.[276] The Commission also defined Yugoslavia as a country 'in dissolution', rather than a country from which regions had seceded.[277] All these decisions weakened the pan-Yugoslav forces. The influence of the Serb ethno-nationalists on the rest of the republics grew.

It set off a domino effect. The Bosnian State Presidency stated with proper logic: 'Of course we're going to move ahead on recognition. With Croatia and Slovenia now gone, we can't consign Bosnia to a truncated Yugoslavia controlled by Serbia.'[278] Izetbegovic now felt encouraged to lead Bosnia-Herzegovina into independence although the Bosnian Serb nationalists threatened with war in such a case. He said: 'I must say here openly that if the threat that Croatia and Slovenia leave Yugoslavia is carried out, Bosnia will not remain in a truncated Yugoslavia. In other words, Bosnia will not tolerate staying in a greater Serbia and being part of it.'[279] The EC's position suggested its sympathy and support for the new states, which, however, remained a deceptive hope especially for the Bosnian government.[280]

The contrary took place. Several foreign affairs politicians distanced themselves from 'the Bosnian Muslims' with false arguments. For example, NATO General Secretary Willy Claes warned: 'Islamic fundamentalism is at least as dangerous as communism was. . . . Please do not underestimate it.'[281] With such misinterpretations the international community shed grist on the mills of Serb and Croatian nationalists. Claes sounded as if he had adopted Tudjman's opinion. The latter believed: 'They're dangerous fundamentalists, and they are using Bosnia as a beachhead to spread their ideology throughout Europe and even to the United States. The civilized nations should join together to repel this threat.'[282] The Serb ethno-nationalists also justified their war by playing the rescuer of occidental Europe from 'the virus of Islamic fundamentalism'.[283] Influential journalists (for example from the *New York Times*) parroted this.[284]

By devious means the Serb government obtained and bought influence on senior representatives of the British government through British lobbyists, and thus could prevent tougher action against the Serb side for a long time.[285] Also the Bosnian and Croatian governments paid heavy sums to American PR agencies in order to sell more effectively their views to politicians and the media. Owen writes with a touch of both irony and resignation: 'Perhaps we stand at the beginning of an era in which no UN package of sanctions is complete any more unless it includes a ban on engaging PR firms.'[286] The struggle had left the Yugoslav arena. Now it was a question of international acceptance and support.

5.1.2. *Clientelism*

The European states forgot their EC solidarity and played out the combatants against each other. The French president François Mitterand openly took the view in 1992 that it was only natural when each of the former European superpowers felt the obligation to support the former allies in the Balkans.[287] A French diplomat revealed: 'Our interests are much closer to the Serbs than you think. We worry more about the Muslims than about the Serbs.'[288] The constellation was a *déjà-vu* indeed: Great Britain, France, Russia and Greece were inclined to give in to the Serbs. Germany sided with the Croats. Still, the reasons for this constellation cannot be found in the past (only).[289]

And 'the Muslims'? For them Owen's speaker John Mills had a cynical advice: 'The Muslim side has only the choice to either negotiate or to perish.'[290] To top it all, the Norwegian UN mediator Thorvald Stoltenberg supported the Great Serb ideology and thus reduced the mediatorship of the United Nations to absurdity. On 31 May 1995, he said in an interview:

Ethnic war? I don't think one can say that. After all, they are all Serbs. The Serbs also call themselves like this, and there is nothing to be added. Then there are the Muslims. Actually they are Serbs who have converted to Islam. And quite a few of those who dress like Croats and present themselves as such, they are also Serbs.[291]

The Bosnian Muslims on their part got pan-Islamic support. But in the beginning it mostly remained limited to words only. In several statements the Organization of Islamic Countries (OIC) condemned the action of the Serbs in Bosnia-Herzegovina in particular and demanded an end to the international arms embargo against the Bosnian government forces. In practice, Pakistan was the only Islamic country which accommodated refugees from Bosnia-Herzegovina.[292] In July 1993 the OIC passed an 'action plan' in Islamabad, among other things for 'increased financial and material assistance' to Bosnia-Herzegovina. It restricted military help to soldiers for UN battalions.[293] However, in the later years the influence of especially Arab states on the military training and equipment of the Bosnian government forces has increased. Here they work together with the US 'so that the assistance which Bosnia gets from outside no longer comes from Islamic states only', as Holbrooke already emphasized in the early stage.[294] Meanwhile, the European states looked the other way.[295]

5.1.3. *'Ethnic' Labels and Enclosures*

It was not surprising that the ex-Yugoslav elites made ethno-national concepts the principle of their policy. But it was not natural at all that the international mediators accepted it and thus also lost sight of the possibility of a civil-democratic society.

As early as 1991 US Foreign Secretary James Baker had stated that the United States would never work together with 'self-proclaimed leaders'.[296] But soon the international actors gave them more legitimization than they themselves had dared to dream of. For example Karadzic: He was largely referred to as the 'Serb leader' and was made socially acceptable at international conferences at one level with elected heads of states. Karadzic was only president of a party and self-proclaimed president of an internationally not recognized 'Serb republic' with a self-appointed capital (village) Pale and a self-appointed 'parliament'. At the same time he was one of the main warmongers and war criminals. It was only the US special envoy Holbrooke who gave

Karadzic, Mladic and all Bosnian Serb politicians a brush-off. He did not speak to them and never shook hands with them.[297] This matched their behaviour and their political status.

The President of the Serb community in Sarajevo, Mirko Pejanovic, enumerated in November 1994 that out of 1.3 million Serbs of Bosnia-Herzegovina only 600,000 followed Karadzic. 'More than half of the Bosnian Serbs do not participate in the aggression', Pejanovic said.[298] Also the Serb General Divjak, who fought in Izetbegovic's army, said: 'It is nothing special that I stayed but that my Serb friends left.'[299]

This strengthens the thesis that a vote for the SDS cannot be equated with support for the later war acts and 'ethnic' expulsions.[300]

It is cynicism, said the Bosnian Foreign Minister, Muhamed Sacirbey (SDA), that those with the strongest military power who had committed widely known violations of human rights were awarded the right by the Western powers to represent all Serbs. The moderates remained left out. To support his argumentation he referred to the Bosnian Ambassador in Paris who is a Serb.[301]

The Social Democrat Seifudin Tokic was also incensed that 'suddenly it [became] self-evident that Mate Boban [president of the HDZ] speaks on behalf of all Croats in Bosnia, Karadzic is considered the unchallenged leader of all Serbs, Izetbegovic seems to be the only one who can represent the position of the Bosnian Muslims'. Even if this statement was certainly part of the UBSD's party politics, the following opinion of Tokic can hardly be contradicted: 'With its relationship with the Bosnian society the international community grants the nationalist leaders among Croats and Serbs or Izetbegovic as leader of the Muslim people far greater legitimacy than they objectively have in their society.'[302] He also complained that the international community wrongly associated the leftist reformists with communism, and therefore dumped them.[303]

So in addition to the internal struggle, the trans-"ethnic" forces found themselves compelled to defend their position vis-à-vis the foreign countries. Pejanovic was one of the signatories of a letter to mediator Owen, in which he criticized his division plan for Bosnia-Herzegovina:

> We will not accept the opinions or decisions of alleged impossibility of common life for the people of Bosnia and Herzegovina and we reject every possibility of any division of Bosnia and Herzegovina along ethnic principles. We remain loyal to our commitments for a united, sovereign Bosnia and Herzegovina, a State of equal people and all its citizens.[304]

The Vance/Owen plan intended to divide Bosnia-Herzegovina into ten 'autonomous provinces'. Each one was assigned to one of the three 'ethnic groups'. Sarajevo got a special status.[305] In this way the mediators accepted an ethno-national map—according to the longstanding wish of the Croatian and Serb ethno-nationalists. This is also the biggest reproach which has largely been made to this concept. However, it must be pointed out that *within* this paradigm attempts were made to preserve Bosnia-Herzegovina as one state and to revise military territorial gains and 'ethnic' expulsions. The plan was modeled on the 1991 census, i.e. on the census conducted before the war. But at the same time, it also means: The plan was based on an imaginary population structure which no longer existed.

The cantonization stirred up new fights. For each canton had its minorities in turn. The war took a new dimension when Tudjman's Defense Minister wanted to hoist the Croatian flag in the mainly Muslim city of Travnik. His justification: Travnik was now situated in a 'Croatian' canton.[306] From this moment on the Bosnian government forces were engaged in battles with the Bosnian-Croatian nationalists.

The failure of the Vance/Owen plan is also an example of foreign influence. Initially, all three ethno-national leaders had signed it. Karadzic's withdrawal had domestic political reasons.[307] But a sudden change in US foreign policy encouraged the Bosnian government and finally also Izetbegovic backed out.[308] The plan had no chance any more.

All the subsequent approaches were even more strongly tailored according to the ethno-national paradigm and re-enacted territorial gains of the parties. In view of this, the preceding statements of the EC foreign affairs politicians sounded cynical. On 28 October 1991 they still insisted: 'The Community and its member states point out once again that the use of violence and a policy aiming at the creation of *faits accomplis* for changing the boundaries are illusory and will never be accepted by them.'[309] But instead, they indirectly legitimized and encouraged 'ethnic' expulsions and accepted the concept of 'ethnically' homogeneous states.

The confederation model (Owen/Stoltenberg plan) triggered the haggle over territorial percentages beyond the decimal point.[310] This continued during all suggested solutions. During the Dayton negotiations the strongest outbursts of rage arose while debating about maps. The chief negotiators arbitrarily drew the internal boundaries of

Bosnia-Herzegovina on big drawing boards and with the joystick in computer cartographies.[311]

The details of the plans were equally absurd. The Owen/Stoltenberg plan intended to build a three-storey highway flyover over the so-called 'Serb corridor' near the north Bosnian city of Brcko. On the first level Serbs were supposed to drive, on the second Muslims, and on the third Croats. Also a 5 km. long bridge was to span 'foreign' territory so that 'the Muslims' could have access to the sea.[312]

Moreover, this model envisaged that the states could break away from the confederation to join other states. This would have been the dream of Serb and Croatian ethno-nationalists and the end of a united Bosnia-Herzegovina. This scenario was prevented, for the time being, by the 'Bosnian-Croatian Federation'[313] which was created through American pressure. This foiled just in time the (reluctant) foundation of the first Muslim state on European soil.

In this context two things are interesting: (1) Also on the political level the name 'Bosnian' became synonymous for 'Muslim'. For in the ethno-national paradigm of the negotiations the Federation was a marriage of convenience between 'the Croats' and 'the Muslims'. (2) A future confederation of this Bosnian-Croatian Federation with Croatia (which was the objective of Tudjman and the HDZ) was not very popular even among the Croatian population. Forty per cent of the people asked rejected it. They feared that they had to feed the poorer parts of Bosnia-Herzegovina.[314] In this example, a rift between action group and postulated large group becomes obvious once again: The population does not follow the ethno-national ambitions of their spokesmen. For them, economic matters were more important.

Until today the Federation is an empty husk—constitutionally and in practice.[315] To what extent Bosnia-Herzegovina exists as a state at all is an open question also after the Dayton Agreement of November 1995.[316] Bosnia-Herzegovina may sustain itself within its international borders. But the two 'entities' (the Bosnian-Croatian Federation and the 'Republika Srpska') have extensive competences. Among other things, they are allowed to grant separate citizenships, to sign treaties with international organizations, and to start 'parallel special relations' with their neighbours Serbia and Croatia.

Again, the homeland-thesis is wrapped up herein. The only ones who cannot engage in any kind of 'special relations' with anyone are 'the

Muslims', of course. They stick again in the Serbo-Croatian sandwich. Their territory has shrunk to such an extent and has become so little viable that some people compare it with a 'Balkan Bophuthatswana'.[317] The question remains open what would happen to them if this fragile, multilayered and contradictory state structure crumbles. So far, 'the Muslims' have scraped past an own 'nation state-building' by just an inch. But when everything breaks away around them again, perhaps they will be left with no other choice in the future.

The complex course of events and proposals during the Bosnian war could be broached only briefly here. But the following things have become clear:

(1) The ethno-national groups oriented themselves towards a higher political level. There they sought and found contact partners, helpers and international recognition.

(2) The international actors took over the ethno-national paradigm and acted as a catalyst (though not as the sole cause) of the Yugoslav disaster.

(3) This gave rise to a territorialization of the conflict with a multitude of new problems and contradictions.

(4) The smaller evil in view of the disastrous consequences—a reform of Yugoslavia and a civil society—was no longer up for discussion.

(5) Thus the multi-'ethnic' state approach of many politicians in the Bosnian government lost its meaning, too.

(6) Today more than ever, 'the Muslims' find themselves on the brink of an own nation state-building—simply because of the lack of alter-natives.

5.2. The Communal Card in India: The British Game with Congress and Muslim League

5.2.1. *The Temptation of Posts*

Similar to Bosnia-Herzegovina the foreign policy actors in India—here the British—were not in top form when the crisis approached:

(1) Great Britain had crossed the zenith of its colonial glamour. A 'graceful' withdrawal was often the last thing the naval power could still hope for.

(2) The Second World War absorbed the whole energy. Great Britain lost additional powers of self-assertion. India became a secondary arena and Indian soldiers functioned as objects of negotiation for the political actors.

(3) A surprising election victory of the rather anti-colonial Labour Party in London brought along a temporary confusion in the British India policy and finally led to an accelerated withdrawal.[318]

The Indian freedom movement and Gandhi's concept of civil disobedience gained dynamics, so that the independence of the country became a matter of time. The 'how' became the issue because a new state offers new posts and new resources. A political struggle for distribution started. This already took place in the provinces. Politicians of East Bengal and West Punjab were in favour of dividing the country and the provinces, because in this way they could expect cabinet posts.[319] At the top squad things were not very different: Nehru did not want to play the second fiddle under Jinnah, and Jinnah just as little under Nehru.[320]

Since the 1940s the British had committed themselves to the Muslim League as the representative of all Muslims. Nehru and Gandhi protested against this in vain. Thus the struggle for resources took place along the distorted line Congress ('Hindu') against League ('Muslim').

5.2.2. *Clientelism*

The many negotiations which were held before the independence of India always took place in the diplomatic triangle. The parties—British, Congress, Muslim League—tried to play themselves off against each other. This happened on a personal as well as on a substantive level.

For instance, Nehru got along well with Lord Mountbatten (and his wife).[321] On the other hand, Mountbatten—as viceroy the most important negotiating partner during the last months—considered Jinnah a 'psychotic case' and 'megalomaniac'. Pakistani authors took revenge with their opinion on Mountbatten as a 'Paki-basher'.[322] Ironically, Jinnah often was substantially much closer to the British than were the stubborn Gandhi and Nehru who were equally strongly determined for independence. Through political co-operation Jinnah tried to win the British over. He feared an alliance between the British and the Congress.

The Second World War helped Jinnah to wring concessions out of the British, although, at that time, he was particularly controversial in the Muslim League and among Muslims anyway. He pulled off his big coup with the issue of war support. On 3 September 1939 Viceroy Linlithgow declared India's entry into the World War. He wanted soldiers and money. For that, he had to win the support of the political representatives of India. But the Congress refused and even withdrew from the province governments. This was Jinnah's chance. He promised support on the condition that the British would take the representatives of the Muslim League 'into their confidence' and accept them as the sole spokesmen for the Indian Muslims. Moreover, Jinnah dissociated himself from the independence movement of the Congress.[323]

Thus a wedge was driven between the Indian parties. Jinnah had notched up a first success: The British agreed with him at least to the extent that they accepted him as the responsible person for the war support of all Indian Muslims. His loyalty was important since now Muslims formed the backbone of the British-Indian army.[324] Jinnah had also driven a wedge between the British and the Congress. The refusal of the Congress to actively support the war and the fact that now Indian politicians publicly spoke with split opinions reduced its negotiating power vis-à-vis the British. The latter were not willing to make any new constitutional concessions, also because of the war. The demands of the Congress for independence and for a national government with participation of all parties (!) fizzled out.[325] In the NWFP British authorities even ran anti-Congress propaganda together with the *ulema*.[326]

Hence, the Congress lost credibility as the mouthpiece of all Indians on the way to independence. London had never accepted this claim anyway. In particular Prime Minister Winston Churchill (1874-1965), who sympathized with the Muslim League, emphasized again and again the cleavages among the Hindus. He refused to revaluate the Congress that he considered an instrument of the Brahmans. In a confidential letter to Clement Attlee, Churchill wrote in 1942: 'The Indian troops are fighting splendidly, but it must be remembered that their allegiance is to the King Emperor, and that the rule of the Congress and Hindu Priesthood machine would never be tolerated by a fighting race.'[327] So he also had an understanding for the subjective perception of threat of many Muslims and other groups in an independent India. As an opposition leader he said in 1946:

> We must not allow British troops or British officers in the Indian Army to become agencies and instruments of enforcing caste Hindu domination upon 90 000 000 Muslims and 60 000 000 untouchables, nor must the prestige or authority of the British power in India, even in its sunset, be used in partnership on either side of these profound and awful cleavages.[328]

Churchill's distrust of the Congress was complemented by the policy of Viceroy Linlithgow, who wanted to strengthen the Muslim League. In order to prevent a rift among 'the Muslims', he had already dissuaded Jinnah's competitor Sikander Khan from negotiating with the Congress in the summer of 1940. Linlithgow considered it important to maintain the League as a 'solid political unit' and mouthpiece of 'the Muslims'. A division of the League could only strengthen the independence movement.[329] And a strong Quit India movement itself was a threat to the Muslim League. For if it was to compel the British to make concessions, the League would find itself marginalized.

Jinnah's only leverage in the negotiations was the threatening demand for an independent state. The Pakistan activists were in a belligerent mood. The Islamist Firoz Khan Noon even dreamed of new alliances: 'But if neither [the Hindus nor the British] give us Pakistan, then Russia will give it to us. We want our freedom and we shall have it.'[330] The spokesmen hoped for a nation state-building *from above*. They waited for someone to *give* them this state. From below their strength was not enough. For this endeavour the Muslim actors were too much divided. 'Up there' the British were wielding the baton. Actually, new impulses were to come from there, which made Pakistan come closer.

5.2.3. *'Ethnic' Labels and Enclosures*

After what has already been said about the British historiography and colonial politics, it is no wonder that the British thought in an ethno-national paradigm to solve their problems. Moreover, since the issue of war support at the latest Jinnah gained political importance more than he was actually entitled to through his party and his role among 'the Muslims'.

The British proposals at the end of their rule revolved mainly around the question of balancing out the interests between 'the Hindus' and 'the Muslims' because the colonial masters considered their dispute to be the biggest obstacle to an independence of the country. It had to be resolved for the British to leave the country 'gracefully'.

The first proposal which cast the ethno-national paradigm into territorial molds was that of the Cripps Mission in 1942. It envisaged a dominion status for India after the war. The provinces should be able to decide whether they wanted to join the union or not. Cripps made concessions to Jinnah who complained about the planned system of proportional representation. It would have implied that every minority had the right to demand a referendum. Even a simple majority would have been enough to form an independent state. Cripps remarked that Jinnah was 'quite surprised' about to what extent his ideas were matched.[331] The first secretary of the UP government replied: 'One permanent effect of the British Government's offer will probably be an increase in estrangement between the two major communities. Pakistan has advanced one stage further.'[332]

Both sides rejected the Cripps proposal for different reasons. But two years later it was Gandhi who came up with a big surprise: He himself made Pakistan the basis for negotiations and suggested to Jinnah to draw borders along the Muslim majority provinces in the northwest and east of India. With a referendum these provinces could go their own ways. This virtually took Jinnah's breath away. He was really glad that the negotiations failed because of minor details. The charismatic mass hero had almost taken the wind out of his sails.[333]

For the first time, it was also Gandhi who enhanced Jinnah's status enormously, not only the British. Jinnah could not even be sure of the support from the Muslim majority provinces, and yet he had become their spokesman.

Another poker of negotiations was the Simla conference (in June/ July 1945). At the foot of the Himalayas the diplomatic triangle argued over quota and representational rights at the green table for two months. The British Viceroy Wavell suggested to form an executive council of the Indian parties that was to form an interim government. But nothing came of it since Jinnah insisted on selecting all Muslim representatives himself. For him the Muslim nationalists and especially the Unionists from Punjab as representatives were out of question. Jinnah had to be careful that his role as the 'Muslim leader' did not slip out of his hand. Only the British could help him. Several times he implored Wavell: 'I am at the end of my tether; I ask you not to wreck the League.'[334] The British finally granted Jinnah a veto. The council did not come into being. It would have integrated 'the Muslims' into an all-Indian government and possibly subdued their call for Pakistan. This was

Jinnah's fear. He finally managed to emerge as the winner from the failed conference, thanks to his good contacts with the British conservatives in the House of Commons. Churchill admitted that he gave Wavell a free hand only because he knew that the conference would fail. The Congress was obviously enraged.[335]

When the Labour government, which was rather Congress-friendly, came to power in London, the way was finally paved for independence of India. Many Labour MP's saw it somehow as their 'moral duty' to release the colonies into freedom. The socialists supported a 'friendly handing-over of power'—especially in one of the most important colonies which the British Queen headed as 'Empress of India' since 1876.[336]

However, the Labour government did not really implement its plans more cleverly than its conservative predecessor. It declared elections in India straight away without any concept for the future of the country. Hence, the elections had to turn into a 'political freestyle wrestling', as Rothermund writes.[337] Above all, the election campaign and its results radicalized the political scene. From 1946 onwards there was virtually a two-party system which was more or less the equivalent of Jinnah's Two Nation Theory. The increasing riots between Hindus and Muslims seemed to confirm it, too. At some places they already took the form of 'ethnic' expulsions.

Against this background a solution beyond the ethno-national paradigm had become almost impossible. Nevertheless, time and again, there were moments when new compromises made a cooperation between Muslim League and Congress possible. But *all three* main actors—Nehru, Gandhi and Jinnah—blocked possible breakthroughs through their stubbornness or through provocations.[338]

The last straw was the Cabinet Mission Plan. It included a territorial division of India into 'groups' which the provinces could join. The plan reminds of the Dayton Agreement in Bosnia-Herzegovina. The central government was to keep only a few functions like the foreign policy. Here, too, the trans-'ethnic' forces were in favour of a stronger center. But, according to the plan, this center was to be occupied *on equal terms* by members of the Congress ('Hindu') and the Muslim League ('Muslim'). The Congress detested this suggestion more than the partition of the country. Because of these reasons, Jalal and Seervai come to the provocative conclusion: 'It was Congress that insisted on partition. It was Jinnah who was against partition.'[339]

Interestingly, Jinnah did not believe in a fully sovereign state until the end. He did not even want it if 'the Muslims' could continue to live under the British instead of under the governance of 'the Hindus'. Jinnah would have been most happy if the British had only implemented their 'group-plan' and had run the central government themselves for another fifteen years.[340] So if the British had not withdrawn, it would have delayed the formation of a Muslim 'nation state' or even prevented it.

However, the new Viceroy Lord Mountbatten saw this totally differently. He took the bull by the horns and accelerated the withdrawal of the British from the end of 1946 onwards. A 'clean division' of the country, Mountbatten concluded, came closest to the interests of all actors.[341] Finally, he forged a 'Balkan plan'. Each province—in form of its representatives—could decide independently what should happen with it. After a revision a constitution was formed for two dominions with the outline of the later India and Pakistan. Before that, the Congress—including Nehru—had brought down Gandhi's desperate surprise coup to make Jinnah the Prime Minister of entire India.

Mountbatten forced the parties to accept his plan. Jinnah made quite an unhappy impression, though. He had fought until the end to prevent the division of Punjab and Bengal. He wanted to see both provinces in Pakistan and struggled against an economically weak and 'moth-eaten' homeland. On the way he got caught up in a debate on identity with Mountbatten in which he called ethnic-regional features primary and religious ones secondary! Thus he delivered his own counterargument against his Two Nation Theory. The following dialogue between Jinnah and Mountbatten, as cited by Collins and Lapierre, is very enlightening:

> Jinnah protested. That would give him an economically unviable, 'moth-eaten Pakistan'. Mountbatten, who didn't want to give him any Pakistan at all, told the Moslem leader, that if he felt the nation he was to receive was as 'moth-eaten' as all that, he'd prefer he didn't take it.
>
> 'Ah', Jinnah would encounter, 'Your Excellency doesn't understand. A man is a Punjabi or Bengali before he is Hindu or Moslem. They share a common history, language, culture and economy. You must not divide them. You will cause endless bloodshed and trouble'.
>
> 'Mr. Jinnah, I entirely agree.'
>
> 'You do?'
>
> 'Of course', Mountbatten would continue. 'A man is only a Punjabi or Bengali before he is a Hindu or Moslem, he is an Indian before all else. You have presented the un- answerable argument for Indian unity.'

'But you don't understand at all', Jinnah would counter, and the discussions would start around the mulberry bush again.[342]

It is an irony of history that now it was rather the Congress that tended to accept Mountbatten's division plan. Gandhi did not go on a fast against the partition of the country unlike he had announced earlier.[343] He even advocated that the NWFP, where the Congress still governed, join the new Pakistan. Ghaffar Khan, the 'Frontier Gandhi' of the Pathans, boycotted a referendum on the annexation and left the field to the Muslim League without a fight.

What remained was the haggling over territory with all its grotesqueries. Jinnah demanded a 1,600 km. long corridor to connect West and East Pakistan.[344] It never materialized. But the drawing of the borders took place in such a make-shift manner that the British officer-in-charge Radcliff destroyed his documents with a bad conscience before he left India.[345] 'Never before was the destiny of so many millions of people at the mercy of the random pencil strokes of a single man', the later president of Pakistan, Ayub Khan, stated in a writing in 1960. 'Because Mr. Radcliff made a small indentation on the wrong side of the line by chance, four million inhabitants of Jammu and Kashmir have found themselves in a life-and-death struggle about the right of self-determination for long and dreadful thirteen years.'[346] Of course, the history of Kashmir is more complex than Khan's propaganda wants to make believe.[347] But the quote reflects the absurd dilemma which reminds so much of Bosnia-Herzegovina.

The influence of the British on the partition of India was considerable:

(1) They represented the higher political level through which alone political objectives could be achieved. A Muslim 'nation state' could come into being from above only.

(2) According to their thinking, they classified their contact persons in ethno-national camps. Thus they ignored the big rift between the postulated large group and the spokesmen. They raised the status of Jinnah and the Muslim League beyond their political legitimization.

(3) Thus trans-'ethnic' concepts lost ground, and other Muslim parties lost their role.

(4) They deliberately played off the selected spokesmen against each other, and, on the other hand, let themselves be used for their ends as well.

(5) For them the World War and a dignified exit was more important than a solution of the problems in India for which they were partly responsible. Behind the British tactics some see already a herald of the Cold War: Under Nehru India developed more and more sympathy for socialist ideas and approached the Soviet Union. If the British wanted to keep an ally in the region, it could only be Pakistan as a sovereign state.[348]

(6) They territorialized the conflict with different division plans, which legitimized the ethno-national principle despite all its contradictions. Thus they laid the foundations for long lasting border disputes.

At this point it must be emphasized that this chapter, like all other chapters of this book, can only present a part of the whole situation. A number of the points just mentioned hold true for Indian actors as well. They also pokered in the diplomatic triangle, drove wedges between their negotiating partners and manoeuvered back and forth in order to get as much as they could for themselves. Nevertheless, it was the British colonial system which set the stage and the rules for this game.

Comparative view

In the respective years of crisis the 'ethnicization' of politics in Bosnia-Herzegovina and India became obvious. Hardly any other issue played a role in the political confrontation except the resources of different 'ethnic groups'.[349] Those who distributed the resources to a large extent were the external powers. Their conduct sent out decisive signals as to how far the ethno-national spokesmen could dare to come forward with their demands or when they had to fear sanctions.

This is not to suggest a uni-dimensional conclusion that external forces *alone* were responsible for the disaster. But this sometimes direct, sometimes subtle influence should not be underestimated. Therefore I do not agree with the quasi primordial and monocausal explanation of Burg and Shoup: 'In the end, it was not external factors that brought Bosnia to ruin, but internal ones: the profound clash of perception and principle among the Bosnians themselves concerning the fate of their country that made compromise impossible.'[350] This eclipses the complex mechanisms that fostered the collapse. It was no pre-determined development, and compromises *were* possible, as the single incidents show.

In addition, the higher principle of order and a subjective sense of protection tempted the ethno-national actors to act more carelessly and to consider less the consequences of their actions. A cabinet paper of the Indian legation states (10 December 1946): 'The Cabinet felt that, however much the Indian politicians might abuse the British Raj, there was always at the back of their minds the sense that the Army was there and would be able to deal with civil disorder. This dulled their sense of responsibility for the consequences of their political policies.'[351] In the case of Bosnia-Herzegovina the same holds true with regard to the declaration of independence. Izetbegovic felt sure that the international powers would support his country as a subject of international law.[352] Kind, too, comes to the conclusion that the Bosnian-Muslim leadership let itself slide into a nationalistic track because it counted on foreign help.[353]

Lack of conception, overtaxed politicians, and prejudices on part of the external powers encouraged ethno-national efforts and weakened the alternatives. The tough struggle at negotiating tables and the tight results provoke the conclusion that, in the end, the creation of a Muslim state was decided by a downy feather on the scale—yet the background had been prepared by steps that are described in the first part of this book.

NOTES

1. This term is taken from Promitzer, in: Stevanov and Werz (1994), pp. 23-4.
2. The theory as such, although without this term, is also mentioned in Stevanov and Werz (1994), p. 23.
3. Sundhaussen (1993), p. 95. He uses the 'freezer theory' in this context.
4. See, for example: Dixit (1974), p. 1. This applies despite Bayly's reservation (1985), in: *MAS* (see Chapter III.1.2.2. 'Conversions and Social Structure in Early India').
5. N.C. Chaudhuri (1951), pp. 407-8. See also: Austin and Gupta, in: Janke (1994), p. 273.
6. Supporters of this theory like to quote works which describe the horror of ethno-national conflicts of early times, like the anti-Serb descriptions of Pilar (1943), or the novels of the Nobel Prize winner Ivo Andric. It is no coincidence either that books with these topics were newly published and released during the Second World War and the Bosnian war.
7. Christopher in a press release (Washington, 10 February 1993), in: *EA* (1993), p. D158 (italics added).

8. John Major: 'The biggest single element behind what has happened in Bosnia is the collapse of the Soviet Union and of the discipline that that exerted over the ancient hatreds in the old Yugoslavia. Once that discipline had disappeared, those ancient hatreds reappeared, and we began to see their consequences when the fighting occurred.' [Malcolm (1996), p. xx]. Malcolm criticizes Major particularly because he ignores the Serb nationalism under Milosevic which was virulent already *before* the collapse of the Soviet Union. Major's approach fails to explain this. By contrast, Wagner argues, in: *EA* (1992), p. 31: Ethno-national inhibitions in Yugoslavia did not fall with Tito's death but only with the collapse of the Soviet Union.
9. Holbrooke (1998), p. 40. He blames, among other factors, the Balkan literature which displays the conflict as unavoidable. Above all, Rebecca West's travel diary (Black Lamb and Grey Falcon, 1941) highly influenced and strengthened the friendliness towards Serbs. Kaplan (1993), in turn, quotes this book—and his own book had big influence on the Clinton government and its view on the Balkan.
10. Holbrooke (1998), p. 41.
11. Other fields of study would be the state of freedom of worship, freedom of press, forming of political opinions, etc. Unfortunately, this would go beyond the scope of this work. In these cases a comparison between Yugoslavia and India would be little fruitful. For the results are contradictory. Waardenburg says, in: *IS* (1997), pp. 387ff, the *suppression* of religion under the communists were responsible for the ethno-nationalism of eastern Europe. By contrast, Thursby (1975) p. 174, maintains that it was just the *freedom* of worship that caused communalism in India.
12. Nehru (1946a), p. 382.
13. The Ottoman Empire is also often described as a 'freezer' which preserved the nationalisms. Thus in: *The Economist* (24 January 1998), Balkan Survey, p. 17. The author refers to a comparison from: Unfinished Peace: Report of the International Commission on the Balkans, Aspen Institute and Carnegie Endowment for International Peace, 1996.
14. Here 'nation' is used in the Yugoslav sense.
15. See also, for example: Calic and Perthes (1995), in: *GP*, pp. 144ff. They compare this situation with Lebanon. See also the book by Sekelj (1993) which is very enlightening and systematic; moreover Goati, in: *NP* (1997); Remington, in: Thomas and Friman (1996), pp. 232ff; Schierup (1991), in: *NC*, pp. 122ff.
16. Sekelj (1993), p. xxiii (original italics).
17. See, for example: Reuter (1991), in: *EA*, p. 706; Todorovic, in: Thomas and Friman (1996), p. 183. The economic disintegration of Yugoslavia is best described and analysed by Sekelj (1993).

18. Meier (1995), p. 11.
19. This theory is used for Yugoslavia by Oschlies, in: Tod . . . (1994), p. 194. He calls this process 'ethnopoliticization'.
20. Kuper, in: *ISSJ* (1971), p. 597. Kuper refers to the research of Furnivall (1939). He had studied the economic life and co-existence of ethnic groups on the Indian coast under Dutch colonial rule.
21. A similar opinion on the Indian case is expressed by: Engineer (1995), in: *TSI*, pp. 90-1, and Freitag, in: Burke and Lapidus (1988), p. 141; on Yugoslavia: Farkas, in: Thomas and Friman (1996), p. 146.
22. Calic (1996a), pp. 85, 92. For a general idea on this phenomenon, see: Horowitz (1985), pp. 326ff.
23. On Bosnia-Herzegovina: Sekelj (1993), p. 250; Bougarel, in: *IS* (1997), p. 547; on India: Inder Singh (1986), p. 25. The Muslim League developed an economic programme only much later.
24. Farkas, in: Thomas and Friman (1996), p.150.
25. Horowitz (1985), pp. 318-19. See also Chapter I.8.1. 'Recipes for a Functioning Society'.
26. Horowitz (1985), p. 319.
27. Babuna (1996), p. 167.
28. Stranka Demokratske Akcije (Party of Democratic Action).
29. Srpska Demokratska Stranka (Serb Democratic Party).
30. Hrvatska Demokratska Zajednica (Croatian Democratic Union).
31. Calic (1996a), p. 85.
32. Babuna (1996), p. 298.
33. Unija Bosanskohercegovackih Socijal-Demokrata (Union of the Social Democrates of Bosnia-Herzegovina).
34. Tokic, in: Stefanov and Werz (1994), pp. 177-8.
35. Calic (1996a), p. 88.
36. Sundhaussen writes that this reason was already an argument for the communists not to hold elections: 'According to Kardelj's interpretation a multiparty system is out of question for Yugoslavia already because the differences which led to the revolution—and this includes, above all, the national question—"have not been eliminated through this revolution"' [Sundhaussen (1982), p. 205].
37. Sekelj (1993), p. 248.
38. For that see also: Sekelj (1993), pp. 207ff.
39. In this context stands the tendentious reporting of the *Frankfurter Allgemeine Zeitung (FAZ)*. It had used German unification as an occasion to actively support the 'national' freedom of Croatia and Slovenia. See also: Schloer, in: Thomas/Friman (1996), p. 324, and the books of *FAZ* publisher Reißmüller (1992), (1993).
40. Sekelj (1993), pp. 17-18 (italics added).

41. Meier (1995), p. 270.
42. Meier (1995), pp. 351-2. Meier had made this observation on the spot as a correspondent. He concludes: 'Basically, politicians and the population of all three nations would have preferred the further existence of a "habitable" Yugoslavia which would have covered up the national differences and would have made difficult decisions obsolete from the beginning.'
43. Calic (1996a), p. 88.
44. In an interview with the author in Sarajevo (30 June 2000).
45. Tokic, in: Stefanov/Werz (1994), p. 179.
46. Silber and Little (1995), p. 252.
47. Inder Singh (1987), p. 139. A detailed account of the election results in: Aziz, Vol. I (1986), p. 58.
48. Inder Singh (1987), p. 133.
49. But the Congress and Gandhi themselves delivered passes to Jinnah in this respect, too. See Chapter III.1.2.3 'From the Village God To *Hindutva*'.
50. The leaflet is printed in: Hasan (1997b), pp. 86-7 and Hasan (1997a), pp. 45-7.
51. Hasan (1997b), pp. 82ff; Inder Singh (1987), pp. 133-4.
52. Sarkar (1983), p. 427.
53. Kuwajima (1998), p. 47. According to him, a total of 41,075,839 persons were eligible to vote in the 1946 provincial elections. In 1945 the population of India was estimated at 299,621,000.
54. Sarkar (1983), p. 427.
55. Kuwajima (1998), pp. 37ff.
56. Sarkar (1983), p. 427.
57. Kuwajima (1998), p. 38.
58. Sarkar (1983), p. 427. He also points out that in East Pakistan the first elections on the basis of universal suffrage took place in 1954. The Muslim League lost.
59. Inder Singh (1987), p. 143; A.S. Ahmed (1997), p. 114.
60. Inder Singh (1987), p. 135.
61. Jalal (1985), p. 137; see also: Inder Singh (1987), p. 102.
62. A.S. Ahmed (1997), p. 87.
63. M.A. Khan (1985), p. 79; see also: Jalal (1985), p. 137; Hasan (1997b), p. 81; K.B. Sayeed (1967), pp. 54, 212.
64. Inder Singh (1987), p. 107.
65. Inder Singh (1987), p. 134.
66. Sekelj (1993), p. 277.
67. A detailed evaluation of the census in: Höpken, in: Kappeler, Simon and Brunner (1989), p. 197. See also: Balic (1992), pp. 10ff; Morokvasic, in: *DA* (1993), p.4.
68. Malcolm (1996), p. 222.

69. Calic (1996a), p. 45. *The Economist* (24 January 1998), Balkan Survey, p. 9, speaks of 6 per cent.
70. According to the editor-in-chief of the independent radio station *Radio 99*, Zoran Ilic, in Sarajevo 34 per cent of the marriages were mixed before the war; even during the war they were still 15 per cent [In an interview with the author in Sarajevo (10 November 1994)].
71. Höpken, in: Kappeler, Simon and Brunner (1989), p. 197.
72. Data from 1965: Dyker, in: *SEER* (1972), p. 243. In comparison, 74 per cent of the Catholics were religious, 39 per cent of the Orthodox. Data from the 1980s: Calic (1996a), p. 30; Calic, in: Seewann (1995), p. 157.
73. In the Yugoslav sense of an officially upgraded 'ethnic group'.
74. Calic (1996a), p. 58.
75. Calic (1996a), p. 59; Calic, in: Seewann (1995), p. 157; Calic refers to evaluations by Morokvasic, in: *DA* (1993), pp. 12-13.
76. Calic, in: Seewann (1995), p. 157.
77. In 1991 one-third of the people asked in Ljubljana, Zagreb, and Belgrad said that 'nothing can legitimate the war'. Only 16 per cent of the inhabitants of Zagreb, 6 per cent of Belgrad and no one in Ljubljana said that war was a 'means to protect the nation and its honour' [Morokvasic, in: *DA* (1993), p. 7].
78. At the end of 1991 some 100,000 Croatian deserters stayed in western Europe and 150,000 from the federal army (i.e. Serbs). In Belgrad, only 10 per cent of the persons liable for military service turned up for conscription! For the figures and the war fatigue, see: Morokvasic, in: *DA* (1993), pp. 7ff and Reuter, in: *EA* (1991), pp. 703ff.
79. Reuter, in: *EA* (1991), pp. 705-6.
80. Wieland, in: *SOEM* (1995), pp. 190ff.
81. According to Mirko Pejanovic in a discussion with the author in Sarajevo (9 November 1994). In entire Bosnia-Herzegovina 200,000 Serbs lived under the control of the Bosnian government forces (1996), p. 253).
82. This association of independent intellectuals (Krug = circle) consisted of professors, judges, ambassadors, writers, film producers, actors, journalists, businessmen and others.
83. Zoran Ilic in a discussion with the author in Sarajevo (9 November 1994).
84. Declaration from 19 April 1992, in: *Why*, 4/92, p. 3.
85. UN Resolution 824/1993, in: *EA* (18/1993), p. D372.
86. Silber and Little (1995), pp. 250-4. The demonstration took place on 5 April 1992, one day before the official recognition of Bosnia-Herzegovina by the European Community.
87. According to the unanimous opinion shared by independent journalists, politicians of different parties, and citizens of Sarajevo in discussions with the author (November 1994).

88. Balic (1994), p. 303.
89. Bauer and Kimmig, in: Stefanov and Werz (1994), p. 46.
90. Holbrooke (1998), p. 41. Haris Silajdzic also told him this.
91. Vlado Staka in a discussion with the author in Sarajevo (11 November 1994).
92. See, for example, a portrait of *Oslobodenje*: 'Zwischen den Fronten', Carsten Wieland, in: *journalist*, 4, 1995.
93. In a discussion with the author in Sarajevo (10 November 1994).
94. In a discussion with the author (10 November 1994). Hadzihasanovic finally emigrated to the United States.
95. Balic (1994), p. 288. The author did not notice any Islamic dress code in Sarajevo in 1994 either. Eicher, in: *SOEM* (1997) made the same observation in Mostar in 1996.
96. Vlado Staka in a discussion with the author in Sarajevo (11 November 1994).
97. Inder Singh (1987), pp. 5, 69.
98. Quote from Fazli Husain, Unionist Party Chief, of 1936. Inder Singh (1987), p. 4.
99. In 1938, Jinnah had finally also obtained the right from the Unionists to speak on behalf of *all* Muslims in India. In return, Khan got the assurance to have a free hand in Punjab [Inder Singh (1987), p. 29].
100. Inder Singh (1987), p. 65.
101. Lapidus (1988), p. 719.
102. Quoted from: Jalal (1985), p. 171.
103. Brown (1994), p. 279. For Khan's political biography and significance, see: Korejo (1994).
104. Inder Singh (1987), p. 107.
105. Bakshi, Vol. VI (1997b), pp. 394-5.
106. Brass, in: Brass (1996a), p. 14. Such types murder and plunder on contract.
107. For procedures and examples, see: Thomas, in: Thomas/Friman (1996), pp. 135-6; Calic (1996a), pp. 92ff; Morokvasic, in: *DA* (1993), p. 13; Silber and Little (1995), pp. 269ff; Malcolm (1996), pp. 216-17; Aziz, Vol. I (1986), pp. 349ff; Jalal (1985), p. 226.
108. Engineer (1995), p. 108.
109. Silber and Little (1995), p. 270. This was also told by raped Serb women who partly spoke of 'good aquaintances', in: Rape . . . (1993), pp. 13, 33 (this source which comes from the Serb ministry of information has been used despite all reservations. For reasons refer to the bibliography). Aziz, Vol. I (1986), p. 349, writes: In the Indian province of Bihar the people who attacked and harassed Muslims came from the neighbouring village.
110. Malcolm (1996), p. 237.

111. K.N. Panikkar in an interview with the author in New Delhi (27 September 1996).
112. Meier (1995), p. 375.
113. Aziz, Vol. I (1986), p. 331.
114. Brass, in: Brass (1996a), p. 1. Similarly in: Bowers, in: Janke (1994), pp. 30ff.
115. This becomes clear in several statements of Serb women who were raped. [Rape . . . (1993)]. The camp and prison commanders often brought soldiers back into line or called them to report. However, a systematic prosecution of offences is not discernible.
116. Rothermund (1997), p. 449.
117. K.N. Panikkar in an interview with the author in New Delhi (27 September 1996); Calic (1996a), p. 144; Brass, in: Brass (1996a), pp. 16-17; Jalal (1985), p. 226.
118. Quoted from the *New York Times* (24 May 1992) by: Moynihan (1993), p. 17.
119. A.S. Ahmed (1997), p. 160.
120. Ignatieff (1993), pp. 140-1. See also: Hobsbawm (1997), p. 254.
121. Colovic (1994), p. 68.
122. Colovic (1994), pp. 64, 63.
123. Colovic (1994), pp. 125ff.
124. The media worldwide reported on so-called mass rapes in Bosnia-Herzegovina, especially against Muslim women. The atrocities can be read, among others, in the book of the journalist and Pulizer Prize winner Gutman (1994) and in Rape . . . (1993). In north India rapes took place on a large scale in 1947, too. See: A.S. Ahmed (1997), p. 161.
125. Zerschnittene Kehlen, 'Fadwa El Guindi', in: *Die Zeit* (29 April 1998). See also: A.S. Ahmed (1997), p. 161. As background, see also: Bousquet (1966).
126. See also: Krizan, in: *OE* (1998), p. 72.
127. Aziz, Vol. I (1986), pp. 401, 451; Inder Singh (1985), pp. 195, 219.
128. Hasan, Vol. I (1997a), pp. 192-9.
129. Sudhir Chandra (1994), pp. 122, 132.
130. Walby, in: Smith (1992), p. 82. The article deals with the special role of women in 'ethnic' nation-building.
131. A.S. Ahmend (1997), p. 227ff. For the issue of systematic rapes in south Asia, see: Jayawardena (1996).
132. K.N. Panikkar also subscribed to this thesis in an interview with the author in New Delhi (27 September 1996). In reference to Yugoslavia the special envoy of the UN Human Rights Commission, Tadeusz Mazowiecki, also said: '[E]thnic cleansings [are] not the consequence of

this war but . . . the *objective* of this war.' [quoted from: Calic, in: Seewann (1995), p. 172 (original italics)].

133. For Bosnia-Herzegovina see, for example, the pamphlet Rape . . . (1993). In India the Muslim League had commissioned the so-called Pirpur Report at the end of 1938. It described the massacres and the inactivity of the authorties and Congress officials. The report can be looked up in: Aziz, Vol. I (1986), pp. 307ff.
134. This modern term, which came into being after the Second World War, and came back into use with the Bosnian war, was not used in India before independence.
135. Owen (1996), p. 243.
136. A.S. Ahmed (1997), p. 168.
137. Hobsbawm (1997), pp. 253-4. He defines 'barbarism' as follows: 'First, the disruption and breakdown of the systems of rules and moral behaviour by which *all* societies regulate the relations among their members and, to a lesser extent, between their members and those of other societoes. Second, I mean, more specifically, the reversal of what we may call the project of the eighteenth-century Enlightenment, namely the establishment of a *universal* system of such rules and standards of moral behaviour, embodied in the institutions of states dedicated to the rational progress of humanity: to Life, liberty and the Pursuit of Happiness, to Equality, Liberty and Fraternity or whatever.' (original italics).
138. Ivekovic, in: Hasan (1998), p. 487 (original italics).
139. Inder Singh (1985), p. 249.
140. Holbrooke (1998), p. 42.
141. Plato (1991).
142. Alija Izetbegovic (*1925) is a lawyer. Mohammed Ali Jinnah (1876-1948) studied law in England and was a successful lawyer in Bombay. Jawaharlal Nehru (1889-1964) studied, among other things, politcal science in England (partly in Cambridge). Mohandas Karamchand Gandhi (1869-1948) studied law in England und was a lawyer (even if a quite unsuccessful one). Franjo Tudjman (1922-99) was a historian and formerly a director of the Institute for the History of the Labour Movement in Zagreb. Slobodan Milosevic (*1941), son of an Orthodox priest, is an expert on the political system of the US; his wife is a professor in the faculty of mathematics and science in Belgrad. Radovan Karadzic (*1944) is a poet and psychiatrist; he studied in the US and worked in hospitals in several countries. Haris Silajdzic (*1945) also studied in the U.S. for a year, Arabic and Islamic studies.
143. For example, the Croatian nationalistic party HDZ was founded in the house of the Croatian association of writers in 1989 [Meier (1995), p. 258].

144. Thus they alluded to the Second World War. At that time the Drina was the scene of the worst atrocities. Andric (1962) made this the subject of his famous book *Die Brücke über die Drina* ('The Bridge Over the Drina'). Owen (1996), p. 253, describes the mentioned scene.
145. Holbrooke (1998), p. 158.
146. Owen (1996), p. 56.
147. Izetbegovic (1970), p. 49.
148. Izetbegovic (1970), p. 28.
149. Izetbegovic (1970), p. 20.
150. He elaborates on it also in: Izetbegovic (1984).
151. Izetbegovic (1970), p. 23.
152. Izetbegovic (1970), p. 40.
153. Cohen, in: *NP* (1997), pp. 486-7.
154. Silber and Little (1995), p. 230.
155. Silber and Little (1995), p. 231.
156. Bougarel (1997), in: *IS*, p. 546. See also Chapter IV.6.2. 'Delhi or Mecca?'.
157. Bougarel, in: *IS* (1997), p. 548.
158. Kind (1994), p. 124.
159. Izetbegovic (1970), p. 53.
160. Quoted according to: Burg and Shoup (1999), p. 127.
161. Meier (1995), p. 318. See also: Burg and Shoup (1999), p. 70. Gligorov and Izetbegovic argued for a 'Yugoslav state community'. In spring 1991 Izetbegovic also brought forward the idea of an 'assymmetric federation' with Bosnia-Herzegovina having closer ties to the federal government than Croatia and Serbia.
162. Owen (1996), p. 253.
163. 'What Hopes for Bosnian Multiculturalism', Seijfudin Tokic, in: *UBSD-Newsletter*, Sept.-Oct. 1994, p. 6. Izetbegovic said this at a party conference of the SDA in February and March 1994.
164. Tokic's accusations in: Krizan, in: *OE* (1998), p. 71; See also: Cohen, in: *NP* (1997), p. 495.
165. Owen (1996), p. 72.
166. Karcic, in: *IS* (1997), p. 574.
167. Colovic (1994), p. 92.
168. Cohen, in: *NP* (1997), p. 487.
169. Cohen, in: *NP* (1997), p. 494.
170. *The Economist* (24 January 1998), Balkan Survey, p. 7.
171. Divjak in an interview with the author in Sarajevo (12 July 2001).
172. Silber and Little (1995), p. 235.
173. For the domestic cleavages, see: Wieland, in: *SOEM* (1995), pp. 188ff.
174. This division within the Bosnian-Muslim leadership irritated the mediators (Holbrooke (1998), pp. 158, 296).

175. Silber and Little (1995), p. 233.
176. Silber and Little (1995), p. 237.
177. Karcic, in: *NP* (1997), p. 574.
178. Interview with Izetbegovic, in: *Why* (1992), p. 16. The interview must have been conducted in April 1992 or shortly before.
179. Owen (1996), p. 290.
180. Owen (1996), p. 295.
181. Silber and Little (1995), p. 337.
182. Owen (1996), p. 296 (italics added).
183. Internet bulletin *Bosnet* No. 1121 (5 February 1999). The interview was broadcast by Bosnian Radio TV from Tuzla on 31 October 1999.
184. Meier (1995), p. 361.
185. 'Franjo Tudjman, Ex-Communist General Who Led Croatia's Secession, Is Dead at 77', in: *New York Times* (11 December 1999), see also: Internet bulletin *Bosnet* (11 December 1999).
186. Cohen, in: *NP* (1997), p. 486.
187. Izetbegovic (1970), p. 24.
188. Izetbegovic (1970), pp. 30ff; Izetbegovic (1984), a review of the book from the conservative Islamic point of view in: Al-Ghazali, in: *IS* (1997), pp. 526-31; Izetbegovic, in: *Ogledalo* (1991), above all pp. 48-50 (partly translated in: Bougarel, in: *IS* (1997), p. 545).
189. A.S. Ahmed (1997), p. 32.
190. A.S. Ahmed (1997), pp. 3-4, 11; Golant (1975), pp. 119ff; Nehru (1946a), p. 390.
191. A.S. Ahmed (1997), pp. 194ff.
192. Sekhon, in: Grover/Arora, Vol. II (1997b), p. 235.
193. Salman Rushdie, 'Gandhi heute', in: *Die Zeit* (29 April 1998).
194. Alavi, in: Weiss (1986), pp. 37-8.
195. See, for example, A.S. Ahmed (1997), pp. 61ff; Khilnani (1997), pp. 163ff.
196. For the 1937 elections and their results, see Chapter IV. 5.2. 'The Majority Trap in India'.
197. In this case, what is meant is not ethno-nationalism but pan-Indian nationalism in the freedom movement of the country.
198. Gandhi's letter to Jinnah (3 February 1938). Aziz, Vol. I (1986), p. 198.
199. Kaushik and Kaushik, in: Grover and Arora, Vol. I (1997b), p. 42.
200. Aziz (1987), p. 357.
201. Aziz and Grunebaum (1970), p. 149.
202. Aziz and Grunebaum (1970), p. 149.
203. Aziz and Grunebaum (1970), pp. 149-50.
204. In an interview in *The Times* (20 October 1930), see: Aziz (1987), p. 285.

205. It is printed in: Bakshi, Vol. II (1997), pp. 75-6.
206. Brown (1994), p. 332.
207. Bakshi, Vol. II (1997), p. 16.
208. Bakshi, Vol. II (1997), pp. 20-1.
209. Collins and Lapierre (1976), p. 104; A.S. Ahmed (1997), p. 129.
210. Inder Singh (1987), p. 1.
211. Jinnah at a meeting of the Muslim League in Madras (April 1941). Bakshi, Vol. II (1997), p. 124.
212. Bakshi, Vol. II (1997), p. 127.
213. Alavi, in: Weiss (1986), p. 41. In this context Maulvis and Maulanas (religious scholars) are derogatory terms for the *ulema.*
214. Jalal (1985), p. 96.
215. Jinnah in a speech at a meeting of the Muslim League in Karachi (24 December 1943): 'It is the great book Quran that is the sheet-anchor of Muslim India. I am sure that as we go on and on, there will be more and more of oneness—one God, one book, one prophet, and one nation' [Bakshi, Vol. II (1997b), p. 315].
216. Hasan (1997b), p. 82.
217. Knee-long black coat.
218. A.S. Ahmed (1997), pp. 98-9; Rothermund (1997), p. 372.
219. The supporter of an *Islamic* state of Pakistan, Abbas Rashid, writesin: M.A. Khan (1985), p. 83, Jinnah perhaps exaggerated a bit in his statement and did not mean it like this.
220. The speech is printed, in: Grover and Arora, Vol. I (1997b), pp. 348-50. Here: p. 350.
221. '[I]n [the] course of time all these angularities of the majority and minority communities, the Hindu community and the Muslim community—because even as regards [the] Muslims you have Pathans, Punjabis, Shias, Sunnis and so on and among the Hindus you have Brahmins, Vashnavas, Khatris, also Bengalees, Madrasis, and so on—will vanish' [Grover and Arora, Vol. I (1997b), p. 349].
222. A.S. Ahmed (1997), p. 178.
223. Hoodbhoy and Nayyar, in: M.A. Khan (1985), p. 170.
224. Number in: A.S. Ahmed (1997), p. 1.
225. Grover and Arora, Vol. I (1997b), p. 349.
226. Inder Singh (1987), p. viii; A.S. Ahmed (1997), p. 129; Rothermund (1997), p. 460.
227. Bougarel, in: *IS* (1997), p. 546.
228. Muslimanska Bosnjacka Organizacija.
229. See also Chapter IV. 6.1.2. 'Nation Via Decree: The Bosnian Specialty'.
230. Silber and Little (1995), p. 339.
231. Quoted from a letter of the Permanent Representative of Croatia at the

United Nations addressed to the president of the UN Security Council (10 May 1993) [Trifunovska (1994), p. 939].

232. *UBSD newsletter* (1994), p. 1 (italics added). More on the UBSD in: Wieland, in: *SOEM* (1995), pp. 194ff.
233. In a discussion with the author in Sarajevo (9 November 1994).
234. Krizan, in: *OE* (1998), pp. 76-7
235. For more details, see Chapter VI.2.1. 'Bosnia-Herzegovina: In Search of the State'.
236. Stranka za Bosnia i Herzegovina.
237. The alliance 'Koalicija za jedinstvenu i demokratsku BiH' consists of the SDA, SBH, GDS (Civic-Democratic Party), LS (Liberal Party) and the MBO (Muslim Bosnian Organization).
238. B. Chandra (1993), p. 141.
239. Inder Singh (1987), p. 1.
240. Heimsath (1964), p. 139.
241. Nehru (1946a), p. 390; Pandey (1990), p. 241.
242. Nehru (1946a), p. 382.
243. Nehru (1946a), p. 382.
244. Nehru (1946a), p. 392.
245. Pandey (1990), pp. 241-2.
246. See Chapter IV.1.2.3. 'From the Village God to *Hindutva*'.
247. More on Gandhi's philosophy in: Mehta (1996), pp. 217ff; Rothermund (1997), pp. 495ff; Parekh (1989b).
248. Parekh (1989b), p. 178.
249. Bakshi, Vol. I (1997), pp. 415-16; Parekh (1989b), p. 179.
250. Douglas (1993), p. 275.
251. These include nationalists, regionalists, communists, liberals and parties of other minorities (like Shiites, Sikhs, Christians, Scheduled Castes etc.). See the party programmes and statements in: Bakshi, Vols. II and III (1997).
252. On a party conference in New Delhi (27 April 1940) [Bakshi, Vol. II (1997), pp. 29, 32, 38, 43, 35].
253. On a party conference in Kumbakonam (8 June 1941) (Bakshi, Vol. II (1997), p. 117).
254. Diwan Chamanlal, the president of the reception committee and member of parliament, in a speech on a party conference in Lahore (9 March 1941) [Bakshi, Vol. II (1997), p. 121].
255. On a party conference in New Delhi (18 September 1945) [Bakshi, Vol. III (1997), p. 851].
256. For the appeal see Chapter IV.6.3. 'A Warning to the Distant Brothers'. If there was an organizational link between them has not yet been examined.

257. On a party conference in Lucknow (14 October 1945) [Bakshi, Vol. III (1997), p. 848].
258. The first Indian president after independence, Rajendra Prasad, gives an overview of all contemporary plans in an article in 1940 [in: Grover and Arora, Vol. I (1997b), pp. 172ff].
259. The US Foreign Secretary in a press release (Washington, 10 February 1993), in: *EA* (1993), p. D158 (italics added). Elsewhere he is quoted with the words: 'The hatred between all three groups—the Bosnians and the Serbs and the Croatians—is almost unbelievable. It's almost terrifying, and it's centuries old. That really is a problem from hell' [S. Popovic, in: Thomas and Friman (1996), p. 300].
260. Report (meeting 1933-4), in: Aziz, Vol. 1 (1986), p. 13 (italics added).
261. Kumar, in: Hasan (1998), p. 426.
262. Holbrooke (1998), pp. 46-7.
263. The US security adviser Brent Scowcroft [Hobrooke (1998), p. 48].
264. Holbrooke (1998), p. 53.
265. Reuter, in: *SOE* (1/1991), p. 16. Jacques Delors, James Baker, George Bush and the entire CSCE group said similar things [Reuter, in: *SOE* (7-8/1991), p. 346].
266. About the recognition of the Yugoslav states and the friendly attitude of the German government and press towards Croatia, see: Axt, in: Volle and Wagner (1994); Giersch and Eisermann, in: *SOE* (1994); Goette, in: Elvert (1997), p. 232; Remington, in: Thomas and Friman (1996), pp. 237ff; Schloer, in: Thomas and Friman (1996), pp. 315ff; Holbrooke (1998), pp. 52ff, Burg and Shoup (1999), pp. 94ff.
267. 'Common standpoint' of the EC (Brussels, 16 December 1991), in: *EA* (3/1992), p. D121.
268. Thomas, in: Thomas and Friman (1996), pp. 200ff. According to him Slovenia came closest to it. Rump Yugoslavia initially did not get the recognition from outside.
269. Reuter, in: *SOE* (6/1993), p. 338.
270. More on the role of the commission that is named after the French justice minister, in: Radan, in: *NP* (1997), pp. 537ff; Goette, in: Elwert (1997), p. 231; Pellet (1992), in: *EJIL*, Burg and Shoup (1999), pp. 92ff.
271. Declaration of the summit conference of the NATO member states in Rome (8 November 1991), in: *EA* (2/1992), p. D72. The EC foreign ministers said the same thing on the 28 October 1991. Documents, in: *EA* (3/1992), p. D119.
272. However, Croatia made improvements soon afterwards and finally met the criteria [Goette, in: Elwert (1997), p. 231].

273. Hummer and Hipold (1992), in: *EA*, p. 93.
274. This took place on the same day of the recognition of Slovenia and Croatia on 19 December 1991 [Miedlig (1992), in: *SOE*, p. 120].
275. Thomas, in: Thomas and Friman (1996), p. 227.
276. The former confidant of Tito, Milovan Djilas, made no bones about the fact that after the Second World War these boundaries were drawn sometimes carelessly and without any consideration 'during a march' [Owen (1996), p. 51]. Owen considered the recognition of these lines as unalterable international borders as an even bigger stupidity than the hasty recognition of the states itself. The French president François Mitterand was against it but could not come out on top against Germany [Roberts, in: Thomas and Friman (1996), p. 370].
277. Burg and Shoup (1999), p. 93.
278. The Federation's vice president Ejup Ganic (SDA) to the last US Ambassador to Yugoslavia, Warren Zimmermann [Zimmermann, in: *FA* (1995), p. 16].
279. Quoted according to: Burg and Shoup (1999), p. 47. But already before the independence of Bosnia-Herzegovina the Bosnian Serb ethno-nationalists had splintered off and proclaimed the 'Republika Srpska' from the village of Pale.
280. See also: Zimmermann, in: *FA* (1995), pp. 16-17. The illusory hope of support was stirred up throughout the entire Bosnian war. See also: Lukic and Lynch, in: Thomas and Friman (1996), pp. 270-1.
281. M.R. Khan, in: *IS* (1997), p. 299.
282. Quoted from: Zimmermann, in: *FA* (1995), p. 15.
283. M.R. Khan, in: *IS* (1997), p. 298; See also the Serb propaganda document: The Violent Dissolution . . . (o.J.), p. 12.
284. Holbrooke (1998), p. 64.
285. See the enlightening book on the British-Serb connections behind the scenes by Leigh and Vulliamy (1997). The *FAZ* published excerpts of it: 'Handel mit dem Tod' (31 January 1997).
286. Owen (1996), p. 163.
287. Vollmer, in: *ER* (1996), p. 9.
288. M.R. Khan, in: *IS* (1997), p. 311. This quote stems from the New York journalist John Newhouse of the magazine *New Yorker*.
289. The German sympathy towards Croatia had many domestic motives and reasons which can be found in the public opinion and the press. See: Axt, in: Volle and Wagner (1994), pp. 96ff; Remington, in: Thomas and Friman (1996), pp. 237ff. Holbrooke does not see any reason either to explain Germany's behaviour with the past [Holbrooke (1998), p. 54]. However, the preferential treatment of the Croats by Germany encouraged

them in their aggressive policy. The EU-appointed mayor of Mostar, Hans Koschnik, complained about this [Eicher, in: *SOEM* (1997), p. 198].

290. Vollmer, in: *ER* (1996), p. 9
291. Quoted from: UN-Vermittler: 'Kroaten und Bosnier sind Serben', in: *Der Tagesspiegel* (28 June 1995).
292. Tibi, in: Volle and Wagner (1994), p. 111.
293. Action plan of the OIC (Islamabad, 13 July 1993). Trifunovska (1994), pp. 1011-16.
294. Holbrooke (1998), p. 84.
295. Reuter, in: *SOE* (3-4/1997), pp. 167ff; Giersch, in: *APuZ* (1997), p. 37.
296. Reuter, in: *SOE* (7-8/1991), p. 346.
297. Thus, at the same time, Holbrooke put Milosevic under pressure. Holbrooke posed conditions for the presence of Mladic und Karadzic during the negotiations. Among other things: '[T]hey must not tell us a pile of historical shit like to all others. They must be willing for serious discussions' [Holbrooke (1998), p. 236ff].
298. In a discussion with the author in Sarajevo (9 November 1994). See also: Wieland (1995), in: *SOEM*, pp. 190ff.
299. Divjak in an interview with the author in Sarajevo (12 July 2001).
300. See Chapter V.2.1. 'Elections in Bosnia-Herzegovina in 1990'.
301. 'What Hopes for Bosnian Multiculturalism?', Muhamed Sacirbey, in: *UBSD-Newsletter* (1994), p. 7.
302. Tokic, in: Stefanov and Werz (1994), pp. 175, 176.
303. In an interview with the author in Sarajevo (30 June 2000).
304. Declaration of members of the Bosnian state presidency on an invitation of Lord Owen to negotiations in Geneva (21 June 1993). Signatories: Dr Tarjana Ljuljic-Mijatovic, Dr Mirko Pejanovic, Miro Lazovic [Trfunovska (1994), p. 998].
305. The plan is printed and illustrated in: Documents, in: *EA* (18/1993), pp. D357ff. All plans of the international mediators are clearly described (including maps) in: Calic (1996a), pp. 188ff. See also: Burg and Shoup (1999), pp. 108ff, 189ff.
306. Remington, in: Thomas and Friman (1996), p. 244. In detail in: Owen (1996).
307. The Bosnian Serb parliament and a referendum of the Bosnian Serbs clearly rejected the plan and stabbed Karadzic in the back. The subsequent president of the Bosnian Serbs, Biljena Plavcic, made her mark as his main opponent. Still she was supported by the West later on.
308. For further details refer to: Lukic and Lynch, in: Thomas and Friman (1996), pp. 253ff; Kind (1994), p. 157.
309. Documents, in: *EA* (3/1992), p. D118.

310. Initially, 'the Serbs' were granted 52 per cent of the territory (!), 'the Muslims' 31 per cent and 'the Croats' 17 per cent. The plan is published in: Documents, in: *EA* (7/1994), pp. D211ff.
311. Holbrooke (1998), pp. 392ff.
312. Tokic, in: Stefanov and Werz (1994), p. 180.
313. The 'Croatian' part was called Herceg-Bosna where the Croatian flag and the acceptance of the Croatian currency etc. almost seemed to be a herald of a Croatian take-over. For details see: Reuter, in: *SOE* (3-4/1997), pp. 158ff; Hayden, in: *BF* (1994), pp. 77ff; Mappes-Niedeck, in: Calic (1996b), pp. 115ff.
314. Reuter, in: *SOE* (3-4/1997), p. 159.
315. This conclusion is made unanimously by: Reuter, in: *SOE* (3-4/1997), p. 160 and Hayden, in: *BF* (1994), pp. 78-9.
316. A description of the concept and an assestment in: Krizan, in: *OE* (1998), p. 58; Calic (1996a), pp. 249ff; Vollmer, in: *ER* (1996), pp. 1ff. A vivid description of the events leading to the Dayton Agreement in: Holbrooke (1998).
317. Silber and Little (1995), p. 386.
318. For the missed chances of the Labour government, see the brief overview in: Rothermund (1997), pp. 435-7. The indispensable adviser of the viceroy and future defence minister of India, V.P. Menon (1897-1974), described the negotiations in his book (Menon (1957)) first-hand. Here: p. 437. For the Labour government from 1945 to 1951 and its policy towards the colonies, see: Morgan (1984), for India pp. 218ff. See also: Kitchen (1996).
319. Jalal (1985), p. 266.
320. In his biography of Nehru Brecher (1959), p. 65 even claims that Nehru had agreed to the partition since he could not resist the temptation of power.
321. Allegedly, he did not only get along with her well but had more than a romance with her, too. At least, Pakistani authors like to claim this (A.S. Ahmed (1997), pp. 143ff).
322. A.S. Ahmed (1997), pp. 133-4.
323. Inder Singh (1987), pp. 48-9; Menon (1957), p. 437.
324. Golant (1975), p. 210.
325. Inder Singh (1987), pp. 62ff.
326. Inder Singh (1987) , p. 88.
327. Golant (1975), p. 205.
328. Churchill in a speech in December 1946 [Bakshi, Vol. V (1997), p. 738].
329. Inder Singh (1987), p. 66.
330. Bakshi, Vol. V (1997), p. 284.

331. Inder Singh (1987), p. 76. See also: Rothermund (1997), pp. 410ff. During the negotiations some British delegates must have acted quite ignorantly. The young Labour delegate and secretary of Cripps, Woodrow Wyatt, wrote 'that the struggle to get the Hindus and Muslims to agree was equalled only by the struggle to stop some of the members of the British delegation behaving idiotically' [Morgan (1984), p. 220].
332. Inder Singh (1987), p. 78.
333. Rothermund (1997), pp. 427ff; Inder Singh (1987), pp. 109ff.
334. Inder Singh (1987), p. 122.
335. Rothermund (1997), p. 434.
336. Morgan (1984), pp. 218-19, 223.
337. Rothermund (1997), p. 436. For the 1946 elections, see Chapter V.2.2. 'Elections in India in 1946'.
338. With his controversial book the Indian historian and lawyer Seervai (1994) displayed the roles of Nehru and Gandhi in a very critical light through well-founded argumentation. Thus he sparked many emotions and debates, especially in India, where the conventional wisdom tends to pin the blame for the partition of the country on Jinnah alone.
339. Jalal (1985), p. 262; Seervai (1994), p. 124.
340. Rothermund (1997), p. 445.
341. Jalal (1985), p. 262.
342. Collins and Lapierre (1976), pp. 104-5.
343. Sankhdher, in: Grover and Arora, Vol. I (1997b), p. 59 strongly criticizes Gandhi. Roy describes with convincing sources how leading Congress members (including Nehru, Gandhi and Patel) took the partition of the country willingly [Roy, in: Hasan (1994), p. 125ff].
344. Golant (1975), p. 244; Sankhdher, in: Grover and Arora, Vol. I (1997b), p. 65.
345. Khilnani (1997), p. 200. The report of the Boundary Commission is printed in: Grover and Arora, Vol. I (1997b), pp. 350-2.
346. Ayub Khan (1960), p. 5.
347. An up-to-date refletion on the Kashmir conflict, including the nuclear threat: Rothermund (2002). See also: Heimsath and Mansing (1971), pp. 146ff; Appadorai (1981), pp. 140ff; Dutt (1987), pp. 182ff; Ganjoo (1998); in a systematic description in comparison with other ethno-national problems of south Asia: Malik, in: Janke (1994), pp. 214ff.
348. M.K. Palat in an interview with the author in New Delhi (16 December 1998).
349. Here resources are to be understood in the broad sense of political science. In this context the term includes such varied elements like public offices, possibility of social and economic careers, size of territory, international recognition and prestige, etc.

350. Burg and Shoup (1999), p. 126.
351. Confidential attachment CAB 128/8, CM 104 (46) 3, in: Hyam (1992), p. 31.
352. Zimmermann, in: *FA* (1995), pp. 16-17.
353. Kind (1994), p. 145.

VI. A Muslim 'Nation State'?

This last section casts a glance at the present stage of Muslim nation-building in Bosnia-Herzegovina and Pakistan. On the subcontinent it has apparently passed its zenith. In the Balkans it may be still to come in the form of a Muslim 'nation state'. But since it is not a teleological development, the result is completely open—as open as it has always been in the past as well.

The following chapters make a small inventory, a momentary stock-taking, which attempts to compare postulates and realities. Thus, the circle is closed to the initial phase of this work: The ethno-national piracy of history has already seized those persons as well who were the protagonists of nation-building themselves. Their contemporaries and successors place them into the mythical chain of legitimacy. The former protagonists of nation-building become encrusted, mostly as a poor copy, as new components in the edifice of 'national history'.

1. THE APPROPRIATION OF THE HEROES

1.1. Izetbegovic Today

Izetbegovic has the makings of an Islamic martyr: He was very religious, he steadfastly saved himself and Islam from hostile regimes, defended 'his' people, defied stronger aggressors, was neglected by the West, and yet he united 'the Muslims' in common state structures for the first time.

Against the background of the Islamic Declaration it is not at all surprising that Izetbegovic has been stylized as the pan-Islamic champion. Knesevic calls him 'a fighter for the cause of Islam in the world'.[1] Just as such he was demonized by Serb and Croatian nationalists. Certainly, Izetbegovic cannot be classified easily. But had he been a pan-Islamic pioneer à la Young Muslims in the 1990s, he would have acted differently in the war, too. Not even because of tactical reasons he would have said: 'Europe and America must finally understand that it is not Bosnia but the principle of the Western civilisation which is being defended here',[2] and 'Iran is far, the enemy is near . . . America is our friend'.[3]

In Pakistan, the admiration for Izetbegovic is particularly deep-rooted. With satisfaction the ideologists have taken note of the fact that the Bosnian attributed to them a model role in his Islamic Declaration. Thus it is mainly conservative pan-Islamic and often fundamentalist intellectuals who appropriate Izetbegovic—people with whom the Bosnian did not agree on all issues and against whom he wanted, and was able to, dissociate himself also within the SDA. The Pakistani Al-Ghazali, who also regurgitates the Bogomil myth, bubbles over with enthusiasm for his hero:

> [Izetbegovic] is also a great *mujahid* who has devoted his life to a relentless and heroic struggle to preserve the Muslim identity of his people in Bosnia-Herzegovina. [...] He was also destined to assume the leadership of his people and guide them to independence in 1992. [...] He combined in himself the rare qualities of courage, valour, wisdom and sagacity that have been so typical of all the genuine successors of the Prophet Muhammad (peace be on him) throughout Islamic history. [...] The people of Bosnia-Herzegovina [...] also remained steadfast in trusting the singularity, sincere and sagacious leadership of Alija Izetbegovic throughout their struggle to preserve their leadership.[4]

With these words the author distorts the facts in a way that is dangerous for Bosnia-Herzegovina: 'The people of Bosnia-Herzegovina' were not 'his' (= Izetbegovic's) people but people from different faiths and ideologies. Izetbegovic had opponents among the Muslims as among other groups. Therefore, he was not the people's leader either—and, least of all, selected by destiny. He just won an election, that's all. Izetbegovic was a democrat and no Ayatollah. He was no religious warrior (*mujaheddin*) either. In the Islamic Declaration he pointed out: '[W]e must be preachers first and then soldiers.'[5] However, this by far does not make him a 'Yugoslav Gandhi' as some rather secular admirers call him.[6] Equally misleading is Tibi's label which describes Izetbegovic as a 'secular Muslim'.[7]

However, as mentioned above, it is the particularly conservative circles that appropriate Izetbegovic. Pakistani thinkers are stuck in an ideological dead end with their 'ethnic' concept of nation. Such a glorified Muslim leader from Bosnia exactly fits their purpose. Therefore, Al-Ghazali places him seamlessly into the 'galaxy of savants and intellectual masters of the Muslim scholarly tradition'. From one moment to the next, Izetbegovic becomes the successor of Muhammad Iqbal, the mentor of Pakistan.

The people that surrounded him also started glorifying the former president. In 1996, when Silajdzic founded a party of his own, a spokesman of the Bosnian foreign ministry criticized this with the following words: '[T]here is no replacing Izetbegovic. There is only one father of a nation.'[8]

Perhaps Izetbegovic himself strived to find a place among the mentioned traditions during his own lifetime in order to enter the Islamic history books with glory. It may also be, however, that after the death of the 'hero' a distorted historiography is taking root, no matter if he wanted it or not. This would not be the first time in the Balkans.

1.2. Jinnah Today

Unlike in Bosnia-Herzegovina, the history twisters in Pakistan had 50 years time to give Jinnah a new profile. His secular and pragmatic aspects are no more desired. Jinnah, who cared little about religion (except in his polemics and perhaps in the last few months of his life), has suddenly risen to the 'most blessed of all mortals'. He, who always vehemently rejected an Islamic social order, is supposed to have declared Islam the basis of Pakistani nationalism. Furthermore, ideologists announce a kind of eternal Khilafat movement which should be initiated by Pakistan.[9] As mentioned, however, Jinnah could not at all identify himself with pan-Islamism and the caliphate.

Already at Jinnah's funeral the Sheikh-al-Islam called him 'the greatest Muslim after Aurangzeb'.[10] This image has consolidated itself decades after his death. School books and state ideologists (the Jama'at-i-Islami in particular) describe Jinnah as an orthodox Muslim or a Muslim demigod.[11] One history book reads:

> The All-India Muslim League, and even the Quaid-i-Azam himself, said in the clearest possible terms that Pakistan would be an ideological state, the basis of whose laws would be the Qur'an and *Sunnah*, and whose ultimate destiny would be to provide a society in which Muslims could individually and collectively live according to the laws of Islam.[12]

This is absurd, since: (1) In Jinnah's lifetime the Jama'at-i-Islami had called him the great infidel (*quaid-i-kafir*). (2) The 'Pakistan-ideology' (= 'Islam') which occupies a central role in the history books since 1977 was 'invented' by the Jama'at-i-Islami itself only in 1962. Jinnah had never spoken of it.[13]

In his Islamic Declaration Izetbegovic also contributed to the distortion of Jinnah's image. Pakistan, he wrote, 'is the fruit of aspirations for the establishment of Islamic rule and [...] those who have envisaged it as well as those who have realized it were led by a clear Islamic idea'.[14] Izetbegovic described the country as a big hope: 'There is no Moslem heart that will not skip a beat when something so dear as Pakistan is mentioned [...].'[15] There are some more subtle forms to lift Jinnah to the status of a hero and founder of an Islamic social order: The Pakistani historian A.S. Ahmed associates Karachi, Jinnah's birthplace, at once with the Muslim conquerors in this area in 711.[16] Such suggestive historiography is common in Pakistan. Accordingly, on the Indian side, there are many demonizations against the 'divider of the nation'. Since this image is also reflected in Attenborough's screen epic 'Gandhi', the desire to produce a counter film has arisen in Pakistan. Jinnah has become the plaything of ethno-national ideologists.

Moreover, the founder of the state serves all political parties as a role model for all possible projects, as it could be seen with the nuclear tests in 1998. Jinnah has become a catch-all term for the people: 'Jinnah for Pakistanis is Washington, Lenin and Gandhi rolled into one', writes A.S. Ahmed.[17] But his new 'religious side' clearly predominates. It is the last straw of Pakistani ideologues to justify the legitimization of statehood. Divergent interpretations are a thorn in their eyes. For this reason they banned the famous book by Collins and Lapierre, *Freedom at Midnight*, in which the authors describe Jinnah as a man about town who drank alcohol and ate pork.[18]

Jinnah's daughter Dina, who after the partition remained in Bombay and presently lives in New York, also states resignedly about her father's religious appropriation: 'They don't respect Gandhi in India, so why should they respect my father in Pakistan where they are more ignorant. No man is a prophet in his own country.'[19]

2. OUTLOOK

2.1. BOSNIA-HERZEGOVINA: IN SEARCH OF THE STATE

> It was and is still, to a large extent, not possible to slice up Bosnia along ethnic lines, since the reality of Bosnia is not only an ethnically mixed country but also intermingled cities, neighbourhoods, businesses, marriages and bedrooms.[20]
>
> *Muhamed Sacirbey*

What the Bosnian foreign minister evoked in 1994 is more than only an idealized image of the past. But, at the same time, Bosnia-Herzegovina after the war is not what it used to be either. More than 1 million people have been displaced within the country, and more than 1.2 million have taken refuge abroad. This is more than half of the pre-war population. Till 1997 only about 0.5 per cent of the refugees settled in an area to which they do not 'belong' 'ethnically'.[21] The number of returnees has been below the target of the UN organizations since then. According to figures from the office of the High Representative, by the end of 1998, the total number of persons who were able to return to their homes in areas not under the control of their 'ethnic group' was estimated around 79,500.[22] Another example: Whereas before the war one third of the population of today's 'Republika Srpska' was Muslim, there were merely 1.7 per cent Muslims in 1996.[23] The structure of the population has come close to that of the former battlefield, even if a majority of refugees and displaced persons seem to be willing to return to their original homes.[24]

But it is not about territory only. Calic writes with reference to the Muslims: 'Ethnic expulsions combined with the systematic destruction of Islamic cultural monuments, mosques, libraries, and cities threaten the physical existence and the ethno-cultural identity of this people.'[25] The extent of the destruction was worse than after the Second World War. Most of the 200,000 war victims were Bosnian Muslims.[26]

On top of this, embittered refugees from the villages have shaken an open and tolerant city culture. Hans Koschnik, the former EU Governor of Mostar, reported from his own experience there:

> Just the people from the countryside often pushed this war and brought it into the cities—some of the key figures of the Balkan conflict come from these rural structures which are more characterized by legends of suffering in the extended family than by enlightment and humanism.[27]

A great number of multiculturally-minded intellectuals have left the country. Half of Sarajevo's inhabitants are Muslim refugees.[28] During the war the share of the Muslim population in the city had increased to a total of 70 per cent.[29] After the unification of the city through the Dayton Agreement once again 60,000 Serbs fled from the city.[30] (Many of them did this only because they had been pressurized by Bosnian Serb nationalists who also had set fire to their apartments. The inter-national peacekeeping forces did not interfere.[31]) Now the question is whether a Muslimization also goes hand in hand with an Islamization and/or the desire for a Muslim 'nation state'.

Signs of an Islamization of the country are clearly visible. During the war 'Islamic fighters' (*mujaheddin*) came to Bosnia-Herzegovina with different intentions, although all under the pretext to defend Bosnia-Herzegovina. Among others, Osama bin Laden's terror network Al-Qaida took advantage of the situation and collected funds to establish Islamist institutions in former Yugoslavia, especially in Bosnia-Herzegovina.

Yossef Bodansky, director of the US House of Representatives Task Force on Terrorism, estimates that between 4,000 to 6,000 'Islamist terrorists' from different Muslim states were operating there under the cover of about two dozen 'charities' and 'humanitarian projects'. According to Bodansky, bin Laden made at least one trip to Bosnia himself. The politicized Shia side of Islam became active in the region as well: Apart from supporting own charity organizations, Iran had shipped weapons and forces to Bosnia during the war and thus violated the arms embargo. Already in 1993 the Islamist leadership in Sudan (which had strong connections with bin Laden) issued a *fatwa* for a strategy of *jihad* in religiously mixed societies such as Kashmir, Palestine, and Bosnia. The US government was so afraid of a new Islamist hotbed in the Balkans that President Bill Clinton was even ready to sacrifice his old Egyptian ally Hosni Mubarak in favour of the establishment of an Islamist government in Cairo. In this horse trading, the Islamists were to promise to reduce the terrorist threat in Bosnia-Herzegovina. Al-Qaida constructed a base in Zenica from which operations that use weapons of mass destruction can be launched.[32]

The Bosnian government granted Bosnian citizenship to each Islamist fighter who came and helped during the war. But, although some of them got married to Bosnian Muslim girls many became disillusioned soon and took offence at the permissiveness of Bosnian Islam. In this they saw the reason why Allah had 'punished' the Bosnian Muslims in the war. The Muslims from outside also brought their own ways of prayer along with them which were unfamiliar to Bosnian Islam but are practiced in Bosnia-Herzegovina today. The fundamentalists exert influence especially on younger Bosnians. In December 1997 the 'Active Islamic Youth' distributed pamphlets in which Muslims were urged not to celebrate Christmas with Croats and Serbs. But not even the representatives of the Islamic community in Sarajevo complied with it. Instead, they protested against this letter.[33]

As far as strict Islamic dress codes are concerned, eye-witness accounts are inconsistent.[34] The journalist Michael Thumann fears, however, that 'the war of extermination by the Bosnian Serbs and the Hercegovinian Croats against the Muslims had much more effect than all Islamic preachers'.[35] Izetbegovic and the SDA have contributed to it considerably, and systematically excluded other 'ethnic groups'—also and especially in the open-minded city of Sarajevo. There, the selling of pork was hampered deliberately. The street signs have been painted in the colour of Islam (green on white background).[36]

But the *reis-ul-ulema* in Sarajevo, Mustafa Ceric, consistently opposes this tendency and warns against an Islamic fundamentalism. With regard to the *mujaheddin* he called out: 'I appeal to our youth to be careful and attentive and not to believe all those political activists who in the name of faith want to harm our unity.'[37] Elsewhere he said:

> At present no Islamic state exists anywhere in the world. But there are states where the Muslims are the majority and which call themselves 'Islamic states'. It is meant to justify certain things which evolve from the presence of Islam in every-day life. All these so-called Islamic states are secular and they have a legal system which is based on secular fundamentals. [...] We are neither Turks nor Arabs, we are Europeans.[38]

Ceric also took the initiative, along with the spiritual leaders of other religions, to visit places in Bosnia-Herzegovina where no freedom of movement for the population has yet been reached. His Serb-Orthodox, Catholic, and Jewish colleagues agreed. They also travelled together to European institutions.[39] This is a remarkable coalition of religious spokesmen if one takes into account that in the Balkans the politicization of the 'ethnic groups' was pushed mainly through the cleavage of religious ascription. The interests of official church representatives had often overlapped with those of the ethno-nationalists. The rift between the postulated large group and the spokesmen is once again evident—this time, however, the other way round. The gesture of reconciliation comes from above, whereas ethno-national antagonisms have gained ground in the large population.

By the way, the office of the *reis-ul-ulema* has meanwhile been 'nationalized' in the same way as the church posts in the neighbouring countries. Since 1995 he is no more called head of the Islamic

Community of Yugoslavia, but of Bosnia.[40] This is one step further towards a Bosnian 'ethnic' Islam, and stands in contrast to the pan-Islamic trends—an old strained relationship which has gained new dynamics through the war.

The progressive (official) *ulema* in Bosnia-Herzegovina does consider Islam an 'ethnic' feature but not necessarily the essence of a Muslim nation-building, and much less of a nation state-building. And if Islam plays a role, the focus is on a European type of its own. There is a saying in Bosnia: 'As much as the Bosnian plum would wither in the Arabian desert, the Arabian palm tree would be killed by the Bosnian frost.' A strong opposition against Arab-Islamist influences is also widespread in the Muslim *political* elite. The spokesman of the Bosnian foreign ministry, Amer Kapetanovic, told me: 'They [the *mujaheddin*] are Arabs and we are Europeans. We simply think in a much more progressive manner. They will never make Arabs out of us.'[41]

These attitudes follow a long tradition of self-definition by Bosnian-Muslim spokesmen. It also finds expression in the new national coat of arms of Bosnia-Herzegovina. It has nothing to do with Islamic symbols but with the Bosnian middle ages: six white lilies on a dark blue background. Pre-Islamic traditions serve as the godfather of Muslim self-consciousness and Muslim demarcation from their neighbours. Indirectly, this is a new edition of the Bogomil myth. In 1992, the periodical *Why* of the Peace Centrè in Sarajevo associated the lilies with mediaeval mythology, eroticism, purity, prosperity and the French kings[42]—by Balkan standards a rare and unaggressive form of modern, national creation of myths and symbols. Already during the referendum for independence in 1992 it turned out that many Bosnian Muslims got more friendly with the blue coat of arms than with the green colour of the prophet: The white lilies took public space on car bumper stickers.[43] This was an evidence for the fact that at least those drivers did not have an Islamic-Muslim 'nation state' in their mind when they went to the polling booth to cast their vote for independence.

This is why Muslim functionaries reject the anti-Islamic propoganda from outside: 'Now those are "fundamentalists"', complains the former imam of the Zagreb mosque, Darko Pavicic, 'who would have never believed that they could be such a thing, people who had not much to do with Islam except by virtue of birth and family.'[44] This shows that the *reis-ul-ulema* Ceric is not alone with his moderate opinion. Also

Fikret Karcic, who holds the chair of history of Islamic law in Sarajevo, supports an 'ethnic' Bosnian variant of Islam and a secular state that can integrate different religious ways of life. He mentions India as a model—not Pakistan (!):

The model how to regulate the interrelation between the political and religious authorities as provided by a secular state has turned out to be favourable in religiously and nationally mixed societies. The application of the model, however, does not automatically imply extinguishing the Sharia, i.e. of the general code of the Islamic rules of life, from the sphere of positive rights. The Indian example shows it clearly.[45]

The secular opinion of the official *ulema* stands in contrast to the ideas of Izetbegovic's Islamic Declaration. Also in practice, the former Bosnian president and the SDA have not been working into the direction that moderate Islamic scholars would have prefered. Fanatic supporters of Izetbegovic beat up Silajdzic in September 1997 when he spoke out in favour of a multi-'ethnic' Bosnia-Herzegovina in an election rally.[46] When at war, the whole cabinet went to Pakistan, Iran and other Islamic countries—and not, for instance, to India.[47] The SDA pursues an ethno-national homogenization of the state as described above. As a result, being in competition with the other ethno-nationalists, it complicates the cooperation between the authorities of the different Entities, to which they had to agree in the Dayton Agreement.

Meanwhile, the country disintegrates into ever new subdivisions of subdivisions. The Croatian administrators in Herzeg-Bosna have long insisted on using Croatian textbooks, police, flags, stamps and car plates. For Herzeg-Bosna the same telephone code applied as for Croatia.[48] The HDZ—for some time with open support from Zagreb—propogated an annexation to Croatia and treated the province as a Croatian colony.[49] In March 2001 the HDZ withdrew from Bosnian institutions and tried to set up a system of Croat self-government, and thus quasi a third entity in Bosnia. In the end, the High Representative intervened and some moderates quit the HDZ after an internal power struggle. Its relationship with the international authorities remains tense.[50]

The Serb spokesmen themselves fell out with each other hopelessly. Their 'Republika Srpska' practically split into two camps around Banja Luka and Pale and equally divided is the population. Moreover, the coalition with Milosevic of the Bosnian-Serb nationalists broke apart duing the war, which makes the idea of a Great Serbia absurd. In the peace talks Milosevic called the Bosnian-Serb politicians 'the idiots from Pale' and 'a pile of shit'.[51] Holbrooke recalls: 'In front of us he had repeatedly mentioned that the Bosnian Serbs were a particular tribe which differed from the 'civilized' Serbs in the big cities of Serbia. He often stated, '*They have more in common with the Bosnian Muslims than with us.*'[52]

Such statements do not really enhance the logic of this war, nor the prospect of an agreement among the current spokesmen. Let us now look at the 'Muslim side'. Do at least *their* political protagonists still want to save this country's unity? The question is not so simple (not any more).

In 1991, Muslim representatives from the parliament, from cultural institutions and were still sure that they wanted to safeguard a unified Bosnia-Herzegovina. In a declaration they described Bosnia-Herzegovina simultaneously as the 'home' of the Bosnian Muslims and the 'motherland' (that is: homeland) of all Yugoslav Muslims.[53] Therein lies a new claim which is difficult to convey to the other ethno-nationalists in Bosnia-Herzegovina. However, the Muslim representatives pointed out that they were ready to give up part of their national sovereignty in favour of a civil all-Bosnian sovereignty. This clearly distinguishes them from their ethno-national competitors.[54] Also in the population there are indications that Muslims are the most ready to make ethno-national concessions. In an opinion poll in 1997 a total of one-fourth of the Bosnian Muslims indicated that they wanted to vote for parties which stood for a co-existence of all the three 'ethnic' groups. This is little. But only one percent of each Bosnian Serbs and Croats said the same.[55]

During the Dayton negotiations even Silajdzic started to doubt about these splits between increased ethno-national consciousness and divided state sovereignty. He said he feared that by now it was too late for Bosnian multiculturalism in Bosnia-Herzegovina.[56] The teetering confederation, which Silajdzic describes as 'a house without walls and with a roof full of holes',[57] is filled with constitutional contradictions and daily traps.

The great number of different international institutions and organisations that romp around on the territory of Bosnia-Herzegovina and whose competences often crosscut do not ease the political work. Since they act within the ethno-national paradigm and strive for a balancing of 'ethnic' interests, they rather continue than end ethno-national pluralism in the former Yugoslavia.[58]

This also relieves the local actors from the pressure to agree on day-to-day issues. Had the High Representative of the OSCE for civil reconstruction (OHR) not the opportunity to govern by decree through the Dayton Agreement, the state would be paralysed. Only through coercive measure such decisions could be taken that entail symbols and history, like introducing uniform car plates and the motives of the new banknotes. People openly speak of a protectorate in Bosnia-Herzegovina which could not survive otherwise. The *Economist* calls Bosnia-Herzegovina a 'laboratory of sovereignty'.[59]

The spanner in the works are the ethno-national competititors who determine political decisions down to the local level. In such a situation the democratic elements have once again become a 'majority trap'. Elections legitimized and consolidated the ethno-national divisions. The local elections in September 1997 strengthened the radical nationalists, especially on the Bosnian-Serb side.[60] Only in Tuzla the social democratic Mayor could retain absolute majority. In September 1998, the presidential, parliamentary, and cantonal elections showed a similar trend. Still, some moderate candidates did win through, and the Social Democrats were highly satisfied this time and established themselves as an opposition to be reckoned with. But two radical representatives who wanted to tear apart Bosnia-Herzegovina into two states captured important posts: A Croat supported by Zagreb was elected into the Bosnian presidency, and a Karadzic supporter who strove for closer relationships with Belgrade became the new president of the 'Republika Srpska' (whom the then High Representative Carlos Westendorp dismissed again some months later).[61] This result was all the more surprising as this time the international community had intervened in the elections more intensively. Westendorp had banned some Great-Serb 'ultranationalists' from the election, crossed HDZ hotspurs off the electorates and silenced propoganda-'journalists'.[62]

The elections of 2000 showed a rather positive trend. The Social Democrats (SDP) proved victorious, although the HDZ and SDS scored better than expected. The three ethno-nationalist parties (SDA, HDZ, SDS) got only 19 of the 42 seats in the Bosnian House of Representatives. The SDP (9 seats) and Silajdzic's SBiH (Party for Bosnia-Herzegovina, 5 seats) formed a broad coalition (Alliance for Change), in which smaller Croat, Muslim, and other moderate parties agreed to participate. The first government was led by the Croat professor of economics Bozidar Matic, followed by the Muslim social democrat Zlatko Lagumdzija in 2001. Only in the 'Republika Srpska' did the ethno-nationalists triumph again. The SDS ousted the moderate government of Milorad Dodik. However, on the side of the Muslim-Croat Federation it was again the Muslims, as so often in Bosnia's young history, who proportionally supported the moderate parties most. The SDA suffered heavy losses.[63] In October 2000 Izetbegovic resigned from his post as the country's President, citing age as the main reason but also admitting 'some disappointments and misunderstandings' between him and the High Representative. Yet he also uttered disappointment about the low degree of Muslim nation-building in Bosnia! 'The Bosnjak people have not recovered their awareness to a sufficient degree,' he complained in a TV interview in June 2000, 'the Bosnjak people split easily, they are keen to argue amongst themselves, which is also one of the causes of my disappointment.' He dismissed any trans- or multi-'ethnic' efforts of the international community as 'propaganda and campaigning'.[64] In October 2001 he also stepped down as the SDA's President, although he remained an influencial figure.

The future path of the SDA remains uncertain. On the one hand, it makes an effort to present itself in much more moderate terms. Its Secretary-General Mirsad Ceman told me before the elections in June 2000: 'We feel like a democratic people's party in the modern European sense. [...] Our membership is open to all nationalities, although it is the reality that most of them are Muslims.' Ceman said that Izetbegovic had had no other chance than to focus on Muslims since 'our relations here are ethnically pre-determined'. He put the blame on the international community: 'It insisted on the parties to represent ethnic groups.'[65] The assessment of the SDA's opponents sounds different, of course: 'I don't believe in the transformation of the SDA', said Sejfudin Tokic (SDP). 'The SDA will end up as a pro-Islamic party with stronger connections to Iran and Saudi Arabia. [...] Its project will drown.'[66]

Where Tokic was right for the elections 2000, he proved to be quite mistaken for October 2002. In this polling the three ethno-nationalist parties scored high and sidelined the moderates, especially the trans-'ethnic' Social Democrats. The SDA was the big winner and gained 10 seats (8 in 2000) in the Bosnian House of Representatives, Silajdzic's SBiH 6, the HDZ and SDS 5 each, and the SDP fell back from 9 to 4.

Each of the three ethno-national competitors also won 'his' seat in the triple multi-'ethnic' presidency (although Silajdzic lost only scarcely to the SDA representative). The voter turnout was very low at 55 per cent, the lowest since the end of the war.[67]

However, analysts and political observers did not necessarily see an ethno-nationalist backlash. They regarded the results mainly as a protest against the poor economic record of the moderate 10-party coalition (Alliance for Change), not as a signal that Bosnians wanted to resume the hostilities of the 1992-5 conflict. Paddy Ashdown, the new High Representative, shared this view: 'Do not mistake the inevitable dissatisfaction with the last government with a desire to return to the nationalism of 10 years ago', he comforted. Nevertheless, Ashdown warned that the results could delay much needed changes: 'It does matter . . . a lot, because it is the pace [of reform] that matters.'[68] His worries were also founded on the fact, that this time the elected politicians were allowed to hold office for four years instead of two, as it used to be in the previous rounds.

The elections remain the biggest argument for sceptics of a multi-'ethnic' future of the country. Early in 1997 Holbrooke had still a convincing explanation for the disappointing outcome:

> The polling took place in an atmosphere poisened by the media—media which was still controlled by the same people who had pushed the country into the war. In the election campaign the whole field belonged almost exclusively to extremist views; the spokesmen of reconciliation were intimidiated by gangs of thugs in all three ethnic groups and forced onto the sidelines by the media which broadcast exclusively racist propaganda.[69]

But already a year later it had become more difficult to accept this monocausal view. Meanwhile, political alternatives got time to express themselves. Their moderate representatives were financially supported by the West.[70] In general, the election results make clear that the 'ethnic' way of thinking has still firm roots in the people's minds. Bosnia-Herzegovina is a united state on paper only. The expert on Europe of the US National Security Council, Ivo Daalder, said dejectedly: If the people themselves do not want any multi-'ethnic' Bosnia-Herzegovina, 'then who are *we* to tell them at all what they should do'.[71]

The elections bring up another problem: The option that refugees can choose if they want to register for the election at their old home place or at the place where they want to live in future (mostly in 'their' 'ethnic' area) again and again leads to manipulations with the aim to conquer cities and communities by the ballot.[72]

Since 'ethnicity' alone counts as the politically crucial factor, human beings on paper or in person become the most important resource in this politics of clientelism. It also means that returnees are systematically scared off or driven out of their villages by force.[73] Until now, hardly anyone of the leading spokesman of the three ethno-national camps has proven to be really helpful from the official side to settle refugees of another 'ethnic group' in their old homes. On the one hand, this is due to problem on the ground: If all the pre-war distributions of property were restored, a house-swapping of great scale would have to take place. Since the old and new refugees have settled in each other's houses, they all would have to move out simultaneously, which would come close to the game of musical chairs. The second reason is that an 'ethnically clean' region is still a valuable political resource in the present setting.

So an 'ethnically' adjusted map and hatred among some segments of the population are the most important results of the war. Given the economic plight,[74] and a weak state structure and an equally weak will to cooperate on the part of the *elected* spokesmen, the chances for a civil society, which could overcome the ethno-national cleavages in Bosnia-Herzegovina, are bleak in the overall picture.

However, there are a few hopeful indications, too. During the short term of the moderate government in Bosnia from 2000 to 2002 some important changes were made. Among others, the Constitutional Court took a landmark decision in July 2000 that the three main 'ethnic groups' represented in Bosnia—Muslims (or Bosnjaks), Croats, and Serbs—enjoy equal status throughout the whole country. Any form of discrimination is thus illegal.[75] The moderate parties embodied this principle of civil equality into Bosnia's constitution with the Mrakovica-Sarajevo-Agreement of March 2002. Since the three ethno-nationalist parties were obstructive once again, the High Representative Wolfgang Petritsch had to enact this principle by his own authority in April. In addition, Bosnia-Herzegovina, Serbia and Croatia signed a trilateral agreement that confirmed their international borders as inviolable. This gives optimists a boost who believe, like Solioz, 'that the state-building process and the political integration in Bosnia are finally on a good way'.[76]

The death of Franjo Tudjman, the internal power struggle of the HDZ hardliners in Croatia and Herzegovina, and the election victory of the Social Democrats under Stipe Mesic in Croatia at the beginning of 2000, who cutoff the funding to the Herzegovinian HDZ, provided favourable winds from the west. On Bosnia's eastern side, the peaceful revolution in Serbia led by Vojislav Kostunica and Zoran Djincic in October 2000, which toppled Slobodan Milosevic, sent cooling signals beyond Belgrade, too (although Kostunica still supported the Bosnian Serb hardliners).[77] Above all, these developments have one major impact: They have started diverting the domestic discourse away from the topic of ethno-nationalism towards different problems and cleavages, like economic and social issues, and, on the foreign policy level, a raproachement towards the European Union. The liberal Serb Prime Minister Djinjic, who was assassinated in March 2003, explicitly described his domestic aim as 'de-emotionalizing' political issues, and pushing through a 'change of priorities from nation and state to the economy'.[78]

There was also a glimpse of hope when it came to personal attitudes inside Bosnia-Herzegovina. In August 1998, Bosnian refugees mentioned trust in the local authorities as the most crucial factor for their return. Only 44 per cent gave importance to the fact that their neighbours belonged to the same 'ethnic group'. Among the Muslims most wanted to return to their old houses.[79] Some feel the urge to go back, even if it means to return to the site of horror where hardly anything has changed. In June 2000 I had a chance to witness an exceptional case: I met the first Muslim returnee in Srebrenica. The authorities of this city have long blocked its gates to any Muslim willing to return. But the then 86-year-old peasant Sacir Halilovic made it. When I spoke to him, he had a trowel in his hand and was constructing a new house from scratch, on the same hill where his previous home stood. His son is buried in the back garden. 'I am happy and proud that I am the first one who came back', he told me, and his 80-year-old wife nodded. It was just at this moment when an old Serb neighbour came along with a basketful of fruits and bread. 'I am happy that they are back,' said Stana Andric (60), 'He is a very good man and our children got along very well.' Down in the valley charred ruins still stood witness to the cruelest massacre in Europe after the Second World War.

A survey of mostly Bosnian-Muslim refugees from Tvornik as early as 1995 showed that almost everyone wanted to return to an undivided Bosnia-Herzegovina. Half of the respondents even approved a Bosnia-Herzegovina under long-term international administration. Despite heavy personal sacrifices the desire for a Muslim 'nation state' is not evident among most Muslim refugees. Interestingly, Muslim youngsters show a stronger feeling of Bosnian-Muslim 'national consciousness' than the Tito generation.[80]

A new body of ideas may also come from those Muslims who once used to live in today's 'Serb' and 'Croatian' parts of Bosnia-Herzegovina. They had to leave their home at high personal sacrifices and were often witnesses to atrocities. Mostly they came from rural areas where old thought patterns are more long-lived. Both factors could make them the biggest advocates of an Islamic state, the 'Bosnian *mohajirs*' like the Muslim refugees who moved from India to Pakistan.[81] Already at the beginning of the war the president of the Citizens' Forum of Sarajevo, Professor Seid Hukovic, predicted that a lot would change in the consciousness of 'the Muslims': 'We would become European Khurds [*sic*] or Palestinians, but without Arabic brothers because we have no reserve homeland or reserve brothers. After what happened to us, we will surely live in a new way.'[82]

This reminds of several historical parallels which have been addressed in this work: The ethno-national conciousness of 'the Muslims' is strengthened by external influences (this time by the consequences of war). In this context the question arises: 'Why did the Muslim population ignore the Bosnjak identification at that time [during the Habsburg Empire] and accept it hundred years later, so to say plebiscitarily, as dispersed refugees virtually all over Europe', as Dzaja writes.[83] One explanation lies in the described cross-cutting of political and dogmatic cleavages, and in the rift between the action group and the large group. Due to the physical threat of war these differences have dwindled today.

Nevertheless, the opinion polls conducted among refugess (the actual 'plebicitary elements') present a differentiated image, especially when it comes to the desire for an ethno-national state. Most Muslims are still hesitant unlike many of their spokesmen in the SDA. But what they have now, they do not know how to define even themselves. In any case, Serb and Croatian ethno-nationalists see in the Dayton Agreement not more than a stopover in the process of dividing the state into two, affiliating the parts with their respective homelands.[84] 'The Bosnian Muslims' are once again sandwiched in the pliers of Serb and Croat ethno-nationalists who are endowed with sovereign state structures this time.

The war in Bosnia-Herzegovina has led to a stronger demarcation of the ethno-national camps. This is true geographically, in the daily life of people, and at the level of political actors. The rift between the postulated large group and the ethno-national spokesmen in Bosnia-Herzegovina has dwindled due to well-directed media propoganda, a radicalizing war experience and a lack of basic alternatives. However, in the case of 'the Muslims' this, once again, does *not* go along with a clearly and widely articulated wish for an own 'nation state', although Izetbegovic's SDA strove for an Islamization and a poltical homogenization of 'the Muslims' at the same time. Yet Hroch's third phase of nation-building has not matured till today in case of 'the Bosnian Muslims' or Bosnjaks.

Instead, a new rift has developed between the Bosnian *ulema* on the one side and the political spokesmen and large parts of the Bosnjak electorate on the other. But it is doubtful if the Muslim population also identifies with the *religious* objectives of the political conservatives while voting in favour of the SDA. Yet the *ulema*, the (official) government policy, and the population have one thing in common: They mostly want to preserve Bosnia-Herzegovina as one state. At present, a real multi-'ethnic' approach can be found with the *ulema* and with parts of the political opposition.

2.2. Pakistan: In Search of the Nation

In Urdu *firquawarana fasad* means 'violent riots', and this especially between Hindus and Muslims (communal riots). Recently, this term has lost its original meaning in Pakistan. Now journalists use this term when they report on fights of Muslims against Muslims.[85] This semantic change tells a lot about the state of today's Pakistan.

'Islam' as the 'ethnic' cleavage has already been crumbling for a long time. Regional-ethnic and dogmatic cleavages have increasingly deepened in the last ten years. The fight between Sunnis and Shiites has broken out again since 1996. Parties and groups of different faiths battle against each other in the streets. The enmity began—only seemingly paradoxically—with the forced Islamization of the country. When in 1980 an obligatory welfare tax (*zakat*) was introduced, the Shiites protested against it. According to their view, *zakat* is a voluntary payment.[86]

Muslims not only of different faiths but also of different origins fight each other.[87] This took place in Karachi in a particular fanatic way in the last two decades. Already in 1985 at least one thousand people were killed there. In 1998, such scenes were repeated when one *mohajir* girl had eloped with a Pathan boy.[88]

The argument over the *mohajirs* has absurd traits.[89] This minority (5 per cent of the population[90]) has a difficult stand against the local ethnic groups of the country. *Mohajirs* are the former refugees from India. They come from the Urdu-speaking families of the north Indian Muslim minority provinces, i.e. from the hotbeds of the Pakistan movement. Today the personal sacrifices which they made to exchange their home for a homeland do not play a role any longer. The former Prime Minister Benazir Bhutto reportedly called them 'rats' and gave this ethnically varied group a homogeneous and racist connotation.[91] With this she triggered the riots in Karachi in the 1990s. A.S. Ahmed describes the destiny of the *mohajirs* as follows: 'They were being punished by both countries. They had become foreigners in a land they had dreamt of, their Pakistan, and strangers in their own land in India.'[92] M.A. Khan holds: 'They are, in fact, the true Pakistanis who gave up their homes to travel to their chosen land. They became Pakistanis by choice.'[93] Today *mohajirs* are represented by an organization of their own (MQM).[94] They strongly support the Islamists because for them Islam is the only link with this state.[95]

Bhutto's hatred against the *mohajirs* can be explained, among other things, by the simple reason that Bhutto's family comes from Sind. Many Sindhis consider the *mohajirs* economic rivals and feel discriminated against in their own province—above all in the port city of Karachi into which most of the refugees poured from India after Partition. 'The Sindhis', in turn, are again antagonists of 'the Punjabis', the strongest group in Pakistan. They hold most of the government and military posts. These ethnic cleavages have also become encrusted in party politics: Benazir Bhutto's People's Party[96] (Sind) fought against Nawaz Sharif's Muslim League (Punjab). The parties and persons are more than political opponents. The party spectrum fans out into ethnic cleavages although each government conjures the 'nation' Pakistan and the 'Pakistan ideology'. This competition of political parties, which had been distorted also by personal interests and power networks, suspended by the military coup in October 1999. Only after the parliamentary elections in October 2002—still under military rule—parties have come into the picture again.

Not only Sind and Punjab but other provinces as well express more and more regionalist interests. Their common—and not quite unjustified—accusation is: Punjabis and Sindhis exploit the country for themselves. The underdeveloped regions have no business in the national skirmish from Islamabad. The National Party (!) of Baluchistan condemned the nuclear tests.[97] On the other side, the NWFP was a clear outsider already before 1947. Strong tribal structures are preserved there till today, especially the tradition of secession attempts. During the presidential election in 1998 a provincial representative scribbled cheekily on his ballot paper: 'Down with Pakistan, up with Pakhtoonkhwa!'[98]

The old formula of Rahmat Ali, Pakistan's namegiver, symbolically stands for its fragmentation today: P = Punjab, A = Afghanistan, K = Kashmir, I (= and), S = Sind, TAN = Baluchistan.[99] Klennert speaks of a 'multinational state'.[100] Ziring concludes: 'The people of Pakistan, historically, are more or less what they were before they were Muslims, and long, long before they were Pakistanis.'[101] Astonishingly, in 1939 even the Muslim League had opposed the principle of a nation state for Pakistan. For these reasons it rejected a federalization of the state: 'Such a constitution is totally unsuited to the genius of the peoples of the country, which is composed of various nationalities and *does not constitute a national state.*'[102] This clearly contradicts the Muslim homeland thesis as Jinnah propagated it until 1947, and this contradiciton has supplied fuel for domestic conflicts in Pakistan since then.

Two other reasons contributed to this: (1) The Muslim League never had a mass base. When its leaders, Jinnah and Liaqat Ali Khan, died, it disintegrated into feuding feudal groups.[103] Huntington writes: 'In post-independence Pakistan the League lost both its constituency and its purposes.'[104] He claims that Pakistan has obtained its statehood 'too easily'. Therefore, a mass mobilization for the state turned out to be too weak and too little tenable. (2) Islamic groups have tried to whitewash the missing political persuasiveness of the Pakistan argument with an Islamization of the country. This provoked bad feelings among minorities. The Urdu-campaign in 1980 had an escalating effect when it replaced English in public life. 'To the extent the Islamization process disregards regional, lingusitic, and primordial ties, it only succeeds in hightening the national sentiments of a number of nationalities which constitute Pakistan', Hassan observes.[105]

Izetbegovic did not agree with this view in his Islamic Declaration, although he criticized an 'insufficient unity' among the Muslims: 'Soon after Pakistan was created, it became apparent that the Moslem League gathered very unequal elements who did not have uniform views on fundamental issues of social order and state organization.' But he called just for a stronger Islamization as the solution of the problems. This, he said, was a great chance for Islam which could now make use of a state that had been achieved with hard sacrifice: '[T]he struggle for Islamic order and the fundamental reconstruction of Moslem society can successfully be waged only by battle-tested and hardened individuals affiliated in a powerful and coherent organization.'[106]

Totally in tune with Izetbegovic's ideal, the influence of the Islamists has grown constantly. With a change of the constitution in 1962 Pakistan became the first 'Islamic republic' of the world. Its president must be a Muslim. In 1973 Islam was introduced as the state religion.[107] In August 1998 the then Prime Minister Sharif announced a constitutional amendment which was to make the Sharia the constitutional law.[108] Sharif and his predecessor Bhutto heavily supported Islamic fundamentalists inside and outside the country for their own political purposes. This has nothing to do any more with the principles of the state founders. The immediate successors of Jinnah had initially stuck to the secular and moderate character of the state and combined it with ideas of traditional Islam. Liaquat Ali Khan said in 1949:

> For us, there exists only one -ism, the Islamic socialism which in short means that in this country every human-being has an equal right to be provided with food, shelter, clothes, education and medical help. The economic programme that was given 1350 years ago still remains the best for us.[109]

Instead, the rising influence of Islamists today has marginalized social and economic arguments, and reduced any political discourse to emotionality. During the nuclear tests in May 1998 Sharif felt the power of the ghosts that he had called. The prime minister stated that the explosions were not a result of political rationality but a consequence of strong domestic pressure, especially by the Islamists, and of the high bubbling 'nationalist' atmosphere in the country[110] (officially, however, he justified the nuclear tests in view of the 'changed geo-strategic situation', that means, the threatening nuclear power of India).[111] With the decision to detonate the nuclear missiles Pakistan had also scared off foreign sponsors and aggravated its economic crisis. The country is heavily dependent on China and the United States. The three modern pillars of Pakistan are popularly seen as: Allah, Army, America.[112] The conscious renunciation of development opportunities in favour of the 'national pride' as a self-purpose indicated again that in Pakistan the ideology of an integral nationalism has spread (as certainly in India, too).

The tactics of Sharif's corrupt government to lean on the Islamists and, at the same time, to keep the US in good mood did not add up. In his two years in office the Punjabi tried too heavily to twist the institutions of the country—courts, press, military—according to his *gusto*. The generals had kept out of the civilian governments for 22 years. But in October 1999 their patience ran out. Once again it was the virulent legacy of Partition, the Kashmir conflict, which shook the domestic politics of Pakistan. In July 1999 Sharif had annoyed the army when he had ordered the withdrawal of Pakistani guerrillas from the Indian part of Kashmir under US pressure. The dispute escalated and led to the coup. The commander, the Western educated General Pervez Musharraf, was not considered an Islamist, which cast its shadow on domestic tensions with the radical Jama'at-i-Islami. Right in his first television address Musharraf clearly pointed the way: He delivered his speech in English, the language of the political and economic elite—and not in Urdu, the language of the *ulema*.[113]

When Musharraf staged his coup, he had no remote idea to what extent Pakistan's Islamization and its international consequences were to challenge his rule after September 11. For under his predecessors Pakistan had not only gone through a fundamentalist Islamization on the home front but had also exported it. In the Koran schools in western Pakistan the radical Sunni Taliban movement had come into being which ruled neighbouring Afghanistan with an iron fist from 1996 until it was toppled by an international force one month after Al-Qaida's terrorist attacks against the United States in 2001. The Taliban, who offered training grounds for bin Laden's terrorists, had, in turn, repercussions for Pakistan.

The 'Talibanization of Pakistan' started at the latest around 1998, when Sharif tried to divert public interest from the social, political and economic crisis (mostly due to his corrupt regime and to US sanctions after the nuclear tests) by trying to win over the Islamists with the introduction of the *Sharia*. The Westernized elite in the Pakistani secret service (Inter Services Intelligence, ISI) had to leave their posts and were replaced by Islamists who cooperated closely with the Taliban.[114] Bodansky concludes: 'By mid-September, Islamabad was arguing that

Islamization offered the only chance of holding Pakistan together. [...] By mid-October, Pakistan was formally an Islamist theocracy committed to the spread of militant Islam.'[115] Inspite of its own financial crisis, Pakistan supported the Taliban regime in Afghanistan with generous aid. Afghanistan even became part of Pakistan's domestic telephone network.[116]

This development again strained the Sunni-Shia relationship within Pakistan. According to the Pakistani journalist Ahmed Rashid, the Taliban armed the most violent Sunni extremist groups in Pakistan, who killed Pakistani Shiites.[117] The rise of the Taliban also affected the relations with India, which leads to an increased danger of a third major war over Kashmir. For bin Laden stressed his support for the Pakistani *mujaheddin* as part of the worldwide *jihad*, and added: 'We will support Pakistan in its war against India.'[118]

After the terrorist attacks on September 11th and the subsequent war in Afghanistan, Musharraf used the chance to crack down on many Islamists (albeit also under pressure from the US). He even sacked high-ranking members of the ISI who had cooperated with the Taliban as well as close personal aides, like the deputy chief of staff who favoured a less pro-American stance. He also clamped down on Islamist preachers and their followers in the streets.[119] In a speech on the 55th birthday of Pakistani independence, Musharraf warned against an 'insignificant minority' who blackmailed the country with its wrong understanding of Islam. He particularly condemned attacks on foreigners and Christians which, he said, gave Pakistan a bad image abroad.[120] In the 'war against terrorism' Musharraf has become a strong ally of the United States. This opens the doors for financial aid again. In early 2004 Washington even declared that Pakistan will be granted the same status of importance as Israel. This, of course, triggered fierce disputes in Pakistan, including assassination attempts against Musharraf.

In the long run, liberal elites will have a hard time to restrain ideologized Islam in Pakistan, not only because they have discredited their own reputation by corruption but also because Islam serves as a societal glue on which they equally depend. This could finally turn Pakistan into a theocratic state also in practice if Musharraf fails to counteract such attempts. Since a long time many Pakistani authors have regretted this politicization of Islam.[121] They point out that 'Islam' was already employed as a smoke grenade during the time of the

Pakistan movement in order to disguise material interests of the feudal land-owners. Until today, they criticise, nothing has changed.[122]

The ghosts whom the political elite called have proven hard to be re-bottled. Musharraf suffered a big setback in the parliamentary elections in October 2002 (which he called for under Western pressure only). The clear winners were the hard-core Islamists. From zero they became the third force in parliament. They declared that they wanted to stop the persecution of the Taliban and the terror network Al-Qaida, and to kick out US troops from Pakistani bases. The six strongest Islamist groups have tried to form an alliance under the leadership of Qazi Hussain Ahmed, chief of the biggest group Jama'at-i-Islami.[123] In the end, Mir Zafarullah Khan Jamali of the Muslim League became prime minister as Musharraf's puppet. It is questionable, however, if the General can withstand the Islamist forces, or if he will follow the footsteps of his predecessors and employ Islam as a political power tool again. There are first indications of such a development. Early in 2002 (before the elections) Musharraf quoted a verse from the Koran 'which implied that divine intervention had catapulted him to the top and had ensured him success in all his past, present and future endeavours'.[124]

All this suggests that the struggle between the two main streams featuring the theoretical debates of the country—the Islamists and the nationalists—is far from over.[125] The Islamists say: Pakistan is a state but not yet a nation. It only can and must become a nation by the supremacy of Islam. The nationalists say: Pakistan is a state *and* a nation. It has a 'national culture' which comprises Islam together with regional traditions. According to them, the foundation of Pakistan has religious *and* economic reasons. The state should not impose any religious rules. Socially speaking, the Islamists have gained the upper hand against the nationalists (especially against the military, landowners, trade unionists, educated classes, and urbanites).

Pakistan has always made up well for a big deficit of its own state legitimization with the help of the mere existence of the Indian arch-enemy. With military hardliners at the top of the state the hostile counterpart becomes all the more a cultivated power resource. The population, however, is generally more relaxed about the relationship with their neighbour. In 1997 an opinion poll conducted by the Pakistani newspaper *Herald* came to a surprising conclusion: Contrary to the policy of their leaders, a clear majority of Pakistanis spoke out in favour of a friendly relationship with India.[126] Anyhow, most Pakistanis enthusiastically watch movies from Bombay and sing their songs in the streets. Of course, strong family ties still exist between this side and that side of the once impermeable border. Since long, leftist parties on both sides have been supporting closer contacts.

However, as long as Pakistan sticks to Islamization as a compensation for its failed nation state ideology, religious-dogmatic and ethnic-regional rioting will remain the main problem of the country. As a vicious circle, Pakistan will remain in need of India as its lightening rod to divert attention from its own increasing destabilization. In this sense, the Indian columnist Pervez Hafeez, who noticed the semantic change of the term *firquawarana fasad* in Pakistan, concludes his article with the fitting sentence: 'In 1947 a nation was in search of a state. Today a state is in search of a nation.'[127]

Pakistan has not been able to realize its claim as a 'nation state' in the sense of a Muslim homeland because:

(1) More Muslims stayed on the Indian side.

(2) In 1971, East-Pakistan broke off to form Bangladesh which does not consider itself an Islamic state.

(3) Ethnic-regional and religious-dogmatic conflicts pervade the country.

To a great extent, these problems arise from counter-reactions against the attempts to homogenize the country linguistically and religiously. After Jinnah's main argument had become obsolete—that 'the Muslims' should decide their fate by themselves as a majority—the old intra-Muslim cleavages came up again. They were covered up only for a very short time of mass mobilization from the election campaign in 1945-6 till the foundation of the state by the Pakistan movement. The propogated Muslim ethno-nation as a demarcation against 'the Hindus' had lost its function and effect after the partition of the country. An orthodox and often pan-Islamically oriented Islam as an ideology is supposed to hold together Pakistan as a 'nation'—ex post.

Comparative view

In Bosnia-Herzegovina and Pakistan two opposing developments can be observed: the Bosnian Muslims are in a process of political and religious *homogenization*, the Pakistanis are in a process of *fragmentation* (which has been accelerated by the attempt of religious homogenization). Symbolical as it was, the two elections in each country in October 2002 stood for these developments. Most Bosnians, also Muslims this time, showed that they wanted to stick to their ethno-national spokesmen and strengthened them. Most Pakistanis proved to be determined to continue and reinforce the Islamization of the country, thus filling the legitimacy gap and, at the same time, fuelling intra-religious, inter-religious and inter-regional conflicts.

The postulate of the Muslim 'ethnicity' is crucial. In Bosnia-Herzegovina and Pakistan it is a *negative* concept, one which was mainly constructed to protect 'minority interests' and to ward off appropriations from the ethno-national competition. A massive effort of mobilization was necessary to implement this concept politically.

In Pakistan this Muslim ethno-nation collapsed as soon as statehood was achieved because the ethno-national competition as a stabilizing and homogenizing antithesis had thus broken away. Old and new cleavages broke out, finally leading to the fragmentation of the territory, which had actually been the biggest achievement of the ethno-national driving force. In Bosnia-Herzegovina a similar phenomenon can be observed on the Bosnian-Serb side.

In Bosnia the concept of Muslim 'ethnicity' was always strengthened in proportion to the 'threat' against it. Afterwards it subsided again. Through the extreme challenge of the war up to the danger of physical extermination the Muslim ethno-nation has entered into an advanced (however not yet final) stage of homogenization. But unlike in Pakistan the ethno-national spokesmen do not clearly link this development to the demand for 'nation state' of their 'own'. However, a break-up of the fragile Bosnia-Herzegovina could finally lead to it.

So in Pakistan one can speak of an *active* nation state-building in contrast to a rather *passive* one in Bosnia-Herzegovina. For in India the initiative and the mobilization for a 'nation state' came from the Muslim spokesmen themselves. The Bosnian-Muslim spokesmen, as a rule, acted in the opposite direction and followed an integrative approach. If a Muslim 'nation state' in Bosnia-Herzegovina finally does come to be, then it may even be *against* their will.

In this way Pakistan represents the case of an *active* nation state-building with the dynamics of a *negative* and *defensive* ethno-national concept. Bosnia-Herzegovina could become a case of a *passive* nation state-building also with a *negative* ethno-national concept.

NOTES

1. Knesevic, in: *IS* (1997), p. 500.
2. Vollmer, in: *ER* (1996), p. 18.
3. 'Der Kampf um die Seele Sarajevos', Michael Thumann, in: *Die Zeit* (12 April 1996). See also: Eicher, in: *SOME* (1997), p. 191.
4. Al-Ghazali, in: *IS* (1997), p. 524 (original italics).
5. Izetbegovic (1970), p. 45.
6. Like Balic (1994), p. 311.
7. Tibi, in: Volle and Wagner (1994), p. 109.
8. The spokesman was Mirza Hajric ['Bosnian Seeks Top Post With Call to 3 Religions', Stephen Kinzer, in: *New York Times* (5 March 1996)].
9. Jalal, in: *IJMES* (1995), p. 81.
10. A.S. Ahmed (1997), p. 36.
11. Hoodbhoy and Nayyar, in: M.A. Khan (1985), p. 165; Alavi, in: Weiss (1986), p. 37.
12. Hoodbhoy and Nayyar, in: M.A. Khan (1985), p. 170.
13. Even the former supreme judge of the Pakistani constitutional court confirms this, Mohammad Munir (1980), p. 26. See also: Hoodbhoy, Nayyar and Nayyar, in: M.A. Khan (1985), p. 166.
14. Izetbegovic (1970), p. 46.
15. Izetbegovic (1970), p. 48.
16. A.S. Ahmed (1997), p. 3.
17. A.S. Ahmed (1997), p. 28.
18. The following passage caused offence in particular: 'A more improbable leader of India's Moslem masses could hardly be imagined. The only thing Moslem about Mohammed Ali Jinnah was his parents' religion. He drank, ate pork, religiously shaved his beard each morning and just as religiously avoided the mosque each Friday. God and Koran had no place in Jinnah's vision of the world. His political foe, Gandhi, knew more verses of the Moslem Holy Book than he did' [Collins and Lapierre (1976), p. 102].
19. A.S. Ahmed (1997), p. 18. Dina symbolizes the conflict of many Indian Muslims. On the day of Partition she hoisted both the Indian and the Pakistani flag from her house in Bombay.
20. 'What Hopes for Bosnian Multiculturalism?', Muhamad Sacirbey, in: *UBSD-Newsletter* (1994), p. 7
21. 'Das reale und das virtuelle Bosnien', Xavier Bougarel, in: *Le monde diplomatique* (issue *taz*), September 1997. Reuter (1998), in: *SOE*, p. 97

points out that in 1998 Bosnia-Herzegovina had only 74.3 per cent of its pre-war population. The number of Croats decreased most (to 60.1 per cent), that of Muslims dropped to 66 per cent, that of Serbs only to 93 per cent. Reuter quotes the Bosnian demographer Vladimir Zerjavic.

22. Internet page of the OHR. Figures are from the OHR's Reconstruction and Return Task Force. UNHCR data suggests that the number has risen to 94,567 persons by mid 1999, although the Task Force holds the number to be higher due to returnees who do not register in the municipalities now run by the other 'ethnic group'. It is quite telling, however, that there are no more recent reports available from the OHR.
23. Figures in the 'Non-Paper' by: Bajrektarevic (1998). See also the maps in: *The Economist* (24.01.1998), Balkan Survey, p. 7.
24. According to a survey of 1999, 61 per cent of the more than 3,000 repondents declared that they wanted to return. 76 per cent of the respondents residing in the Federation and 34 per cent in the 'Republika Srpska' expressed this will. See: Joint press release of the CRPC and UNHCR, 22 November 1999.
25. Calic, in: Volle and Wagner (1994), p. 121. In November 1992, already 70 per cent of the Muslim historical buildings were destroyed [Weckbecker, in: Elvert (1997), p. 269].
26. Reuter (1998), in: *SOE*, p. 97. It is a very delicate matter to split the dead persons according to 'ethnic' camps, which makes sense only within the ethno-national paradigm.
27. Eicher (1997), in: *SOEM*, p. 186.
28. Calic (1996), p. 260.
29. According to Mirko Pejanovic in a discussion with the author in Sarajevo (9 November 1994).
30. 'Das reale und das virtuelle Bosnien', Xavier Bougarel, in: *Le monde diplomatique* (issue *taz*) (September 1997).
31. Holbrooke (1998), p. 514.
32. Bodansky (2001), pp. 44, 100, 111, 155-6, 211-12, 327.
33. Zdravko Ljubas in a letter to the author (26 September 1998). See also: 'Die Frau soll sich verhüllen', Alexandra Stiglmayer, in: *Das Sonntagsblatt* (7-13 February 1998).
34. Some report an increase of Islamic clothing in Sarajevo ([e.g.: 'Ein Land auf der Suche nach Balance', Peter Sartorius, in: *Süddeutsche Zeitung* (18 November 1994)]. However, Eicher reports the opposite from Mostar [Eicher (1997), in: *SOME*, p. 191]. The Bosnian journalist, Zdravko Ljubas, wrote to me from Sarajevo (26 September 1998): "There are many covered girls in Sarajevo, but not more than before the war. The thing is that before the war we didn't pay any attention to that, but after all terrible things happened here we are watching that with some different eyes and

mind. I can also explain that with the fact that the Faculty of Islamic Theology is situated in Sarajevo, as well as [the] Catholic and Franciscan Faculty of Theology, and all these were here before the war, too. As the students of [the] Christian faculty are obliged to wear collars as priests (since we haven't [a] civilian theology school), girls—students of [the] Islamic school—are obliged to wear long skirts and to be covered, so there is nothing new in that.'

35. 'Der Kampf um die Seelen Sarajevos', Michael Thumann, in: *Die Zeit* (12 April 1996).
36. Reuter (1998), in: *SOE*, p. 115.
37. 'Die Frau soll sich verhüllen', Alexandra Stiglmayer, in: *Das Sonntagsblatt* (7-13 February 1998).
38. The former imam of the Zagreb mosque, Darko Pavicic, quotes Ceric, in: *OEA* (1993), pp. A99-A100.
39. 'In Bosnien gehen die religiösen Führer voran', Bernhard Küppers, in: *Süddeutsche Zeitung* (25 February 1998). With him went the Serb-Orthodox metropolitan Nikolaj, the archbishop of Sarajevo, Cardinal Vinko Puljic, and the president of the Jewish community, Jakob Finci.
40. Karcic, in: *IS* (1997), p. 577.
41. In an interview with the author in Sarajevo, 24 June 2000.
42. 'A Golden Lillies', Ivica Pinjuh, in: *Why*, 4/1992, p. 14. She quotes an excerpt from: J. Chevalier and A. Gheerbrant: *The Dictionary of Symbols*, Zagreb, 1989.
43. Meier (1995), p. 374.
44. Pavicic, in: *OEA* (1993), p. A98.
45. Balic (1992), p. 352.
46. Holbrooke (1998), p. 528.
47. 'Ein Land auf der Suche nach Balance', Peter Sartorius, in: *Süddeutsche Zeitung* (18 November 1994).
48. Krizan, in: *OE* (1998), p. 63; *The Economist* (24 January 1998), Balkan Survey, p. 7.
49. See also, for example: Reuter (1998), in: *SOE*, pp. 104ff.
50. Bieber, in: Nations in Transit (2002), p. 109
51. Holbrooke (1998), p. 171, 394.
52. Holbrooke (1998), p. 394 (italics added).
53. However, at the latest since the escalated situation in Kosovo from 1998 onwards, the gap between theory and practice is glaring. Bosnian Muslim authorities and inhabitants complain about the 'filthy pigs' who come from Kosovo to Bosnia-Herzegovina as refugees and make the economic situation there even worse. The fact that the Kosovo Albanians are 'fellow believers' no longer plays any role ['Unerwünschte Brüder und Schwestern', Claudia Lepping, in: *Der Tagesspiegel* (10 November 1998)].

54. This declaration is printed in: Balic (1992), p. 371. See also: Steindorff (1997), in: *SOEM*, pp. 286-7.
55. Krizan (1998), in: *OE*, p. 65.
56. Holbrooke (1998), p. 428.
57. Holbrooke (1998), p. 245.
58. Calic (1996), in: *IP*, p. 25 and Eicher (1-2/1997), in: *SOE*, p. 9 also express this opinion.
59. *The Economist* (24 January 1998), Balkan Survey, p. 18.
60. Krizan (1998), in: *OE*, p. 65.
61. The Croat Ante Jelavic (HDZ) and the Serb Nikola Poplasen (SDS) came out on top against Kresimir Zubak (who had left the HDZ) and Biljana Plavcic (SDS), who were supported by the West ['Poplasen will eng mit Belgrad zusammenarbeiten', in: *Der Tagesspiegel* (27 September 1998)].
62. 'Meßlatte zur Umsetzung des Dayton-Abkommens', Claudia Lepping, in: *Der Tagesspiegel* (12 September 1998); 'Bloß weg von hier', Stephan Israel, in: *Der Tagesspiegel* (12 September 1998). From the beginning of the war *all three* war parties instrumentalized the media for their purposes, and partly put them under pressure. Examples in: Weckbecker, in: Elvert (1997), p. 27.
63. Bieber, in: Nations in Transit (2002), pp. 112-14. Izetbegovic said a few words about his reasons in an interview with TV BiH in 6 June 2000.
64. Interview with TV BiH in 6 June 2000.
65. In an interview with the author in Sarajevo (30 June 2000).
66. In an interview with the author in Sarajevo (30 June 2000).
67. Data from the Bosnian Institute, London (www.bosnia.org.uk).
68. 'Nationalists Take Lead in Bosnian Elections', Nicholas Wood, in: *Washington Post* (8 October 2002).
69. Holbrooke (1998), pp. 527-8.
70. Particularly the prime minister of the 'Republika Srpska', Milorad Dodik of the Independent Social Democratic Party, enjoyed sympathies from the West. He was elected into office with 18 *Muslim* votes in the parliament (more on Dodik and his administration: Reuter (1998), in: *SOE*, pp. 111ff). Dodik, who had trans-'ethnic' views, got Muslim support because Bosnians could caste their vote at the places where they had lived before the war. In the following, this provision of the Dayton Agreement is briefly discussed.
71. 'Bosnia vote sends US back to square one', David L. Marcus, in: *Boston Globe* (23 September 1998).
72. 'Das reale und das virtuelle Bosnien', Xavier Bougarel, in: *Le monde diplomatique* (issue *taz*) (September 1997).
73. See, for example: Eicher (1-2/1997), in: *SOE*, pp. 3-5.

74. The economic strength of Bosnia-Herzegovina after the war was at 7 per cent of the pre-war level [Reuter (1998), in: *SOE*, p. 97]. See also: Eicher (1-2/1997), in: *SOE*, p. 5. He speaks of 5-10 per cent in 1997. The monthly average wages amounted to about 22 Euro in the Bosnian-Croatian federation. In 2001 it had risen to a still moderate 223 Euro, but in the 'Republika Srpska' only to barely 11 Euro (1995) respectively 153 Euro (2001). In 2001 the unemployment rate was at more than 40 per cent. For more on the economic situation in post-war Bosnia, see also: Bojicic, in: *Eastern Europe . . .* (1997) and Bieber, in: *Nations in Transit* (2002), pp. 123-5.
75. Bieber, in: Nations in Transition (2002), p. 120.
76. Solioz (2002), in: *SOEM,* p. 43.
77. Bieber (2001), in: *ECMI Brief*, p. 7.
78. Djinjic (2002), in: *SOEM*, p. 32.
79. 'Heimkehr in die Fremde', Thomas Schmid, in: *Die Zeit* (20 August 1998).
80. Müller, in: *Südosteuropa* (1995), pp. 597ff.
81. Anis Bajrektarevic made this comparison in a discussion with the author (22 September 1998). For the *Mohajirs* see Chapter VI.2.2. 'Pakistan: In Search of the Nation'.
82. [Small article without title], Seid Hukovic, in: *Why* (April 1992), p. 4.
83. Dzaja (1998) in a book review on Babuna (1996), in: *SOE*.
84. Holbróoke (1998), p. 540; Reuter (1998), in: *SOE*, p. 113.
85. A well-known Indian columnist made this observation: 'Pakistan: A State in Search of a Nation', Pervez Hafeez, in: *The Asian Age* (29 January 1997).
86. For more background on this fight, see: Hassan, in: *MES* (1985), pp. 279ff; Mayer, in: Weiss (1986), pp. 71ff.
87. Background and history of the ethnic-regional conflicts in Pakistan in: Behera, in: Grover and Arora, Vol. II (1997b), pp. 153ff; F. Ahmed, in: M.A. Khan (1985), p. 229ff; Klennert, in: *PG* (1995), pp. 29ff; A. Feroz, in: M.A. Khan (1985), pp. 229ff; Hassan, in: *MES* (1985); Weiss (1986); Hyman, in: Janke (1994), pp. 171ff.
88. 'Love and Violence in Pakistan', in: *The Economist* (14 March 1998); 'Schleier und Schüsse', Gabriele Venzky, in: *Der Tagesspiegel* (15 March 1998).
89. More on the conflict, on the *mohajirs* and the illogicality of the Two Nation Theory in: Chitkara (1996).
90. Klennert, in: *PG* (1995), p. 29.
91. A.S. Ahmed (1997), p. 215.
92. A.S. Ahmed (1997), p. 215.
93. M.A. Khan, in: M.A. Khan (1985), p. 259.
94. Muhajir Qaumi Movement.

95. Wilder, in: M.A. Syed (1995), p. 45.
96. Bhutto had the Pakistan People's Party (PPP) 'renamed' for the election 2002 into PPPP (Pakistan People's Party Parliamentarians) in order to suggest a new start, after the PPP had been banned for corruption by Musharraf.
97. 'Schmerzliche Konsequenzen angedroht', in: *Der Tagesspiegel* (3 June 1998).
98. 'Sharif Country', in: *Economist* (10 January 1998). The voting took place to elect the new president, Rafiq Tarar. He was a minion of Sharif and equally stems from Punjab. The Pathan secessionists strive for an 'own state 'Pathanistan' (or 'Pakhtoonkhwa').
99. Pakistan can also be translated as 'land of the pure people'. Afghanistan was not integrated into the territory of Pakistan, of course.
100. Klennert (1995), in: *PG*, p. 29.
101. Ziring, in: M.A. Syed (1995), p. 90.
102. Resolution of the Muslim League (1939) (F. Ahmed, in: M.A. Khan (1985), p. 229 (italics added).
103. Klennert (1995), in: *PG*, p. 36.
104. Huntington (1968), p. 442.
105. Hassan (1985), in: *MES*, p. 280.
106. Izetbegovic (1970), p. 47.
107. Excerpts from the constitutions of Pakistan are printed in: Hassan (1985), in: *MES*, pp. 282-4. See also: Weiss, in: Weiss (1986), pp. 8ff.
108. 'Pakistan am Rande der Talibanisierung', Gabriele Venzky, in: *Der Tagesspiegel* (17 September 1998); 'The Crumbling of Pakistan', in: *Economist* (17 October 1998).
109. Schimmel, in: Italiaander (1987), p. 44.
110. 'Madam, I Was Hurt Very Much', Interview with Sharif, in: *Time* (8 June 1998).
111. 'Statement by the Prime Minister Mohammad Nawaz Sharif' (28 May 1998). Press release on the nuclear tests in Pakistan.
112. Hyman, in: Janke (1994), p. 171.
113. 'Oh, Pakistan', in: *Economist* (16 December 1999). Musharraf was partly educated in Great Britain, and, immediately after the coup, tried to calm down the foreign countries. Since Sharif's government was unpopular both at home and abroad, he succeeded to a great extent.
114. Rashid (2000), pp. 188ff.
115. Bodansky (2001), p. 338. He writes, according to Pakistani authorities, the nearly 4,000 religious schools registered had more than 540,000 Taliban students. Many more unofficial Taliban schools existed with a student body of about two million.

116. Rashid (2000), pp. 183, 185. For example, in 1997/8 Pakistan provided the Taliban with an estimated 30 million US dollars. Several infrastructure projects like road construction and water supply were financed by Pakistan.
117. Rashid (2000), pp. 187, 194.
118. Bodansky (2001), p. 251.
119. 'Not a pariah, a friend' (9 March 2002) and 'The worries of Musharraf' (8 June 2002), in: *Economist.* Musharraf fired, among others, General Mahmood Ahmad, chief of the Inter-Services Intelligence (ISI), and General Muzzafar, deputy chief of army staff, who helped Musharraf topple Sharif.
120. 'Warnung vor Islamismus', in *HAZ* (15 August 2002).
121. For example: A.S. Ahmed (1997); Alavi, in: Weiss (1986); the authors in M.A. Khan (1985).
122. O.A. Khan describes the alliance of feudal lords and the *ulema*, in: M.A. Khan (1985), pp. 133ff.
123. 'Islamisten in Pakistan erhalten Auftrieb', Gabriele Venzky, in: *HAZ* (15 October 2002).
124. 'Not a pariah, a friend', in: *Economist* (9 March 2002).
125. Hassan (1985), in: *MES*, pp. 271-2.
126. The wish for good relations varied in different cities. In Quetta 80 per cent of the respondents spoke out in favour, in Karachi 67.8 per cent, in Multan 61.7 per cent, in Lahore 52.2 per cent, in Peshawar 52.2 per cent, in Islamabad/Rawalpindi 50.6 per cent, and in Sukkur 43.9 per cent. However, the survey was conducted at a time of relative relaxation. In India governed the left oriented United Front under Prime Minister Inder Kumar Gujral. His approach towards Pakistan was a strategy of de-escalation ('Gujral Doctrine'). The data of the survey are taken from: 'Pakistanis favour friendly ties with India', in: *Times of India* (17 February 1997).
127. 'Pakistan: A State in Search of a Nation', Pervez Hafeez, in: *Asian Age* (29 January 1997).

VII. Résumé

The ones have a state but no nation (any more); the others have just about a nation but no state (yet). However different the temporary results for 'the Muslims' in Pakistan and Bosnia-Herzegovina may be, there were many parallels in their ethno-national development. This chapter summarizes them before it addresses the differences in the case studies and turns to other theoretical aspects.

SIMILARITIES

Bosnian and Pakistani/Indian Muslims do not show any natural differences vis-à-vis their respective fellow inhabitants who belong to another faith. Anthropological data proves this clearly. The 'difference' is based solely on what people believe.

The technique with which the differences between parts of the population were cobbled together is modelled along the concentric concept of 'ethnicity'. Religion was the starting point. But religion alone was not enough to make people understand themselves in such a different way that they acted accordingly, i.e. that they stood up for exclusive religious group interests, claimed resources, mobilized fellow believers against 'the others', etc. Two reasons were particularly responsible: (a) In the traditional sphere, faith did not have any offensive characteristics of its own. It was a private matter. (b) Religion was only one of many other social features and cleavages. People of different faiths lived at various places and in distributions of any possible form. The population structure in Bosnia-Herzegovina and India resembles a rag rug or a leopard skin of different religions, customs, traditions and—in the Indian case—also different languages *(Abstandsprachen)*. Bell-Fialkoff expresses the original rivalry of religion and any politicized form of 'ethnicity' in the following way:

> Although in many cases religion was incorporated into ethnic identity, it often clashed with nationalism because world religions such as Christianity or Islam,

with their message of inclusion of all the faithful, are anthithetical to nationalist pluralism on ideological grounds. Ultimately, religion cannot incorporate nationalism. But nationalism can and does appropriate religion and religious symbolism, which is why nationalism has almost invariably proved stronger than religion.[1]

Activists—initially from the widely diverse cultural spectrum, later with clear political objectives—sped up a homogenization of the religious communities. With the following ingredients they turned faith into something more than just religion, namely into an 'ethnic group' and eventually into an ethno-nation:

(1) *History.* The idea of a 'common' descent that dates back into the past as far as possible was a big solidarity factor. The past, viewed selectively through the rear view mirror, was to legitimize claims in the present. For this purpose myths were created. In Bosnia-Herzegovina and India the Bogomil myth and the Aryan myth had the same purpose: Religious communities should consider themselves communities of common descent whose common aspects are older than the religious element itself. The Pakistan myth works in a similar direction, although it is to anchor ex post already achieved ethno-national results in the dim and distant past. In this perception Pakistan is nothing but the state-encrusted Muslim community of common descent.

Until today, the collective feeling of self-esteem and the demarcation against 'the others' have been boosted by the fact that every ethno-national 'camp' looks back at its 'golden age', conjures up its heroes, and represents history as an 'eternal' confrontation with the religious enemy. In this process it is totally irrelevant (and also impossible to find out) whether the respective heroes actually counted themselves as members of this 'community of common descent' or even considered themselves as its rescuers.

(2) *Territory.* Closely related with history is the idea of a country as 'holy' as possible to which one religious community has a claim and the other one has not. So the Serb-Orthodox church consecrated the legend of the Field of the Black Birds in holy orders and supported the myth of a 'primevally Serb' soil. Bosnian Serbs and Croats derogatorily called the Muslims 'Turks', who, in their view, actually belonged to the Bosporus.[2] The Hindu nationalists laid claim to 'Mother India' as their

holy land, symbolized in the milk of the holy cow. The Muslims, they said, already had their holy land on the Arabian peninsula.

In turn, many Bosnian Muslims developed a territorial bond with Bosnia-Herzegovina as well. This might be simply because they have always lived there or because they were allowed to pass on their real estate and thus identified more strongly with their soil; or it might be because they had developed a specific form of Bosnian Islam. Similarly, it is true of Muslims in India. A sacralization of the soil, however, is not as prominent in the case of 'the Muslims' in Bosnia-Herzegovina and India as in the case of their rivals. Rather Muslims were constantly told that they actually did not belong at all to the place where they lived, or, at best, that they were guests, or that they were actually members of a different 'ethnic group'.

(3) *Language*. Someone who thinks differently must also speak differently. This is the argument for this 'ethnic' component as a supplement to religion. However, it is by far not given that the person in question does think differently in the first place, and, second, that he actually ends up speaking differently. Nevertheless: In Bosnia-Herzegovina and India ethno-nationalists strived and still strive to make the religious element overlap with language. Language is also a big solidarity factor. To be effective, the dialects of the members of the different religions must differ as much as possible. In Bosnia-Herzegovina and India the same problem occurred: no *Abstandsprachen* (different languages with regard to origin, grammar, etc.) were ascribed to 'ethnic groups'. Instead, in each case *one* language served as the raw material from which different *Ausbausprachen* (languages which were developed apart ex post for political reasons) were carved out. In and around Bosnia-Herzegovina there was no other language anyway. In India there was a wide selection of *Abstandsprachen* indeed, but the ethno-nationalists pounced upon the very same. This was due to the fact that the ethno-national movements of Hindu and Muslim activists were concentrated in the same region (north India). In both cases the 'ethnic' languages were cast in different scripts in order to demarcate them from the others. This left most people in front of the gates because they could neither read nor write, least of all the highly standardized literature which just created the differences and which served as a reservoir of arguments for the ethno-nationalists. It is no coincidence that, until

today, the most elusive thinkers of ethno-nationalism can be found among writers and poets.

The construction of language as a secondary medium of contrast makes the gap between the action group and the postulated category of identity particularly clear—not only because masses of illiterates had to take the rap for a fight over script but also because the oral participation was far from consequent, too. Only a fraction of the new Pakistanis spoke Urdu. Its cultural center remained in India, along with most of the speakers. The actual language of the masses in the eastern part of the two-winged state, Bengali, was the cause of a lot of reasons why the East Bengalis opted for a state of their own. Also in Bosnia-Herzegovina language and 'ethnicity' do not merge in the way as the language standardizers of the nineteenth century imagined. However, a drifting apart according to political, ethno-national criteria has gained new impetus after the Bosnian war. In both cases only a relatively costly political mobilization could and can obscure the contradictions and cracks in the religious language templates.

Thus in both cases religion had become more than a private matter of faith. The (postulated) members of a religion became part of an ideology. They were its carriers as well as its resource. Therefore, the religious ascription of each individual developed into a political asset. A conversion into the other camp amounted to desertion. The consistently objective ascription of human beings firmly drew the 'ethnic' boundaries. Ethno-national spokesmen increasingly developed political claims for 'their' constituency.

In both cases hostile nation projects faced each other. The homogenization of 'Serbism' and 'Croatianism' as well as 'Hinduism' had a strong influence on 'the Muslims'. Their spokesmen saw themselves as underdogs. They often reacted to the politicization of the 'ethnic' rivals and, above all, to their territorial claims. It is particularly noticeable in Bosnia-Herzegovina that 'the Muslims' lag behind the other nation projects. In India, too, an ethno-national fight between the camps would not have been possible without the homogenous concept of *Hindutva*.

Initially, cultural movements came up which claimed to represent the interests of 'their' group. In reality, however, they represented only a small fraction of the members of their category of identity. The Muslim spokesmen comprised big landowners and the urban upper classes. The cultural aspect increasingly lost significance. These movements developed more and more into political organizations. This means: (a) They put up concrete demands of everyday politics and pursued strategies accordingly. (b) Religion as a category of identity and contrast was watered down and served merely as a vehicle for political claims to power.

In this advanced stage of politicization additional factors could take effect that homogenized the 'ethnic groups' further and set their politically active followers against each other:

(1) *Banal conflicts*. In an atmosphere of distrust, incidents, which otherwise would never have been paid attention to, and/or which originally had a totally different reason, got worked up to fights between ethno-national camps. In both countries plenty of social and economic conflicts existed. It is hardly surprising that the interests of the farmers and the landowners lay far apart. But suddenly in Bosnia-Herzegovina it became significant that the majority of the landowners were Muslims and the farmers were mostly Serbs or Croats. Particularly in Bosnia-Herzegovina the social structure played into the hands of the ethno-nationalists. In India, too, socio-economic cleavages could more and more easily be turned into ethno-national conflicts, especially at places where they overlapped.

Since religion and its followers became a political asset, conflicts were mainly sparked off by religious symbols and conversions. Particularly in Bosnia-Herzegovina, Muslim activists reacted most sensitively to actual and alleged proselytizations. Thus they created new potential for conflict which led to an increased political mobilization. The same happened in India. There temples, mosques, religious symbols, and processions suddenly gained undreamt-of significance. Hindu activists rediscovered the sanctity of the cow, and Muslim provocateurs discovered how good it actually tasted. Immediately, they proclaimed their 'religious right' to slaughter cows. Such quarrels were starting points of political mobilizations and of new forms of organization of the rival camps.

(2) *Violence*. At the peak of the ethno-national conflicts cruel scenes unfolded in India and Bosnia-Herzegovina. The unavoidable objective ascription could mean life or death for each individual. Criminal gangs attacked villages and families, killed, tortured or kidnapped members

of the 'hostile' 'ethnic group'. People, who previously lived together peacefully, were pulled apart or were set at each other's throat. In both countries women suffered in particular. In the ethno-national ideology women reproduce the political asset of the 'right' human being. Rapes by the opponents prevent this, and, moreover, 'desecrate' the high religious and social status of the affected women, most of whom were Muslims. In Bosnia-Herzegovina and India such acts of violence were a systematic part of warfare for some ethno-national activists. In this way they suggested that the different 'ethnic groups' could not live together, and with this message to the outside world they were quite successful in both cases. In India the communal riots provided the last decisive argument for the British, who were keen on a dignified departure, to see the division of the country as the only way out. Those Indian nationalists who had stuck to the unity of the country till the end had to bow to the 'arguments' of violence too.

In the nineteenth century and towards the beginning of the twentieth century the ethno-national agitation in Bosnia-Herzegovina and India was carried from the cities into the rural areas. The above mentioned conflicts helped to connect both spheres—organizationally and personnel-related. In the later stages the power houses remained in the cities but riots in the rural areas did not lag behind the ones in the metropolis. Particularly in India an improved infrastructure helped a lot. In Bosnia-Herzegovina the image of the cities varied. Big tensions in Mostar contrasted with multi-'ethnic' communities of fate like in Sarajevo. The most horrific scenes often took place in the rural areas and in small cities.

War and separation gave rise to big streams of refugees in Bosnia-Herzegovina and India. Most people found an accommodation in the cities. This made the cities 'more rural'. Many refugees did not only bring frustrations and hatred with them but also ethno-national categories, which were partly not so prominent in the cities or had already been overcome. This applied especially to Sarajevo. This city shares with Delhi and Karachi the fate of a large population of refugees, which strongly changed the urban culture.

Throughout the leading ethno-nationalists had a higher (mostly 'Western') education and university degrees. The Muslim main figures at the time of crisis, Izetbegovic and Jinnah, were lawyers. Most of their models, followers and rivals were scholars of the humanities (historians, sociologists, poets, etc.). Therefore they strongly participated in the conceptual development of nationalism in the history of ideas, and tried to implement them according to the model of western and central Europe. Herder, the philosopher of history, had a particularly strong impact on the ethno-nationalists of the Balkans and India.

The fact that both countries remained under 'Western' rule for a long time made a networking of 'Western' and local ideas easier. Comparing the effects of the occupying powers, the following parallels can be drawn:

(1) They considered different religious groups as ethno-national blocks from the beginning and tried to play them off against each other.

(2) The British promoted the standardization of literatures, an ethno-national world view of history, and cultural and educational institutions where these approaches could unfold. The Habsburgers did the same, but, they supported 'the Muslims' against both the Serb and Croatian competitors from the beginning.

(3) Both powers allowed the formation of political parties, among them several Muslim ones. Those mostly pursued objectives of everyday politics and tended to cooperate with other ethno-national forces. Both in Bosnia-Herzegovina and India one party crystallized which could unite most Muslims behind it and/or was considered as the mouthpiece of 'the Muslims'.

(4) As a rule, the British and the Habsburgers tried to solve political conflicts by accomodation instead of using force of arms. Thus ethno-national actors could wangle political concessions.

The British rule had a similar function for India as the Habsburg rule, Tito-Yugoslavia, and the international state community of the 1990s for Bosnia-Herzegovina combined. Therefore the above-mentioned points have to be taken into consideration when the comparison proceeds chronologically. Between Tito-Yugoslavia and the British colonial power the following parallels exist: The meticulous categorization of 'ethnic groups' and censi increased the pressure on each individual to fit himself into an objective pattern. The formal criteria—which changed several times—promoted the homogenization of the groups on record, for with their formalization they obtained access to political resources. These include political quotas and, in some cases, even an officially awarded 'national status'.

In both cases 'the Muslims' were given a special role. In the British questionnaires and in the minds of the colonialists they were the only population group that was considered and treated as a homogenous unit. This contradicted the social facts. In Bosnia-Herzegovina, too, the ethnicentre religion was re-enacted as the main cleavage by the offical side after the socialists had thrown their trans-'ethnic' approach overboard.

Therefore, in India and Bosnia-Herzegovina a *national pluralism* developed instead of a *political-democratic* one. Separate electorates in India and a national proportional representation in the state structure of Yugoslavia made the task of the ethno-national actors easier and took away from multi- or trans-'ethnic' forces the basis of legitimacy and the political forum. In addition, democratic elements in both societies were weak. The result was that political cleavages could hardly develop beyond ethno-national ones. For other political issues depend more on factors like the building of public opinion, on debates, and on gaining political majorities, than ethno-national ones which can dock swiftly at primordial features and work affectively.

The mainly national pluralism and the lack of experience of democracy largely contributed to turn the election results in 1946 and 1990 into an 'ethnic' referendum. Moreover, in Bosnia-Herzegovina the leftist party spectrum was associated with the discredited Yugoslav socialism and thus ruled out as an alternative. With these elections both cases come very close to the third phase of Hroch's model of national movements. But, as a qualification, the special circumstances must be kept in mind, like the sudden democratization of Yugoslavia and the rash withdrawal of the British.

Above all, these elections cannot be judged as referenda on a Muslim 'nation state'. A thorough look at the chronology of events speaks against it. At the time of voting, a concrete state project was still a long way off. Although the Muslim League in India did run its election campaign with the slogan 'Pakistan', this hollow cliché was more a repository of Muslim dissatisfactions than a concrete secessionist project with a mass base. Moreover, a strictly limited franchise and separate electorates distorted the results in favour of ethno-national trends. In Bosnia-Herzegovina the ethno-national parties initially formed a coalition after the elections. It was only with the dispute over the independence of the country that the former coalition partners turned into wartime enemies on the battle field. Only *afterwards* a Muslim state became a practical option at all.

It was mainly due to the policy of the external actors that things could get to such a stage. After the collapse of Yugoslavia the international state community became the political reference point. It took over the same function as the British colonial masters in India. Both external actor groups orientated themselves at the ethno-national paradigm and acted accordingly. Not only did they take separate and irreconcilable 'ethnic groups', or even races, as a starting point but also the 'freezer theory' which claims that ancient conflicts unavoidably re-emerged. Their main concern was damage control. There was no political concept to solve the problems—and if at all, it was only within the ethno-national framework. In some form it made sense to the colonial British and to the state community of the 1990s when states were formed on an ethno-national basis. They referred to trans- or multi-'ethnic' alternatives only half-heartedly. Instead, they upgraded ethno-national spokesmen beyond their political legitimacy and thus encouraged them to pursue more and more risky goals, in whose fulfilment the activists had not even believed themselves.

Politics primarily revolved around the ethno-national distribution of resources. Those who distributed them as the highest authority carelessly gave away the highest price: International recognition for states whose weak legitimacy was an ethno-national ideology and homeland-building. Exception is made by Bosnia-Herzegovina (possibly Macedonia) and post-colonial India which followed this development reluctantly, and initially became the object of this development.

DIFFERENCES

Both case studies are different not only in their geographical setting at the point of time of the crisis, but also in their content. It starts with the piracy of history. Ethno-national Muslims themselves make use of the Bogomil myth in order to anchor their 'ethnic' tradition prior to the period of their conversion. On the other hand, the Aryan myth has been misused particularly by Hindu nationalists in order to exclude 'the Muslims' 'ethnically'. In the first case, conversions are not considered as a historic break but just as a transition from one chapter of the 'ethno-national' history to the next. In the second case, conversions are simply denied. The idea that the overwhelming number of Muslims are ex-Hindus does not fit into the picture. This comparison of myths does not imply that Muslim spokesmen in India remained historiographically passive. As in Bosnia-Herzegovina they also invented all possible historical anecdotes to 'ethnically' demarcate themselves from the others. Above all, their fantasy serves the purpose of tinkering myths of the state's foundation from which the homeland Pakistan is supposed to derive its legitimacy.

From a distance the conflicts in India seem to be more directly connected with religion than in the Balkans. The reason why it seems so—although in both cases the same construction of 'ethnicity' was used—may simply be that the politicized religious communities in the Balkans got new labels. Where this did not happen until recently—just with 'the Muslims'—it created big confusions and caused mis-interpretations. The name 'Bosnian' (or Bosnjak) could compensate for it. It has increasingly been appropriated by Muslim spokesmen for their constituency, and, in this sense, it is also used by external actors. In any case, despite the different labels, the conflicts in Bosnia-Herzegovina had just as much or rather just as little to do with religion as in India.

For a long time the 'missing' name for the Bosnian-Muslim nation also pointed to a substantive aspect: The Muslim nation-building clearly lagged behind the Serb and Croatian ones—until today. This may be responsible for the fact that one looks in vain for great (ethno-) national heroes in the Bosnian-Muslim historiography. Izetbegovic was pushed into this role only later. In India such posthumous supermen have been common on both sides for a long time, no matter from which century they were conjured up. Generally speaking, the historiography in India is more strongly personalized until today. This also shows that the Muslim nation-building in India was further advanced and thus closely coupled with the development of the Hindu competition—up to the point where it even overtook it. The Hindu nationalists in today's India are on the 'best' way to catch up and to finally put Nehru's secular version of nation out of the running. However, the surprising national victory of the Congress party in May 2004 could counterbalance this development.

The concept of Nehru and Gandhi once represented a strong alternative to the ethno-national efforts of Hindu and Muslim spokesmen. This did not happen in the Balkans. From this point of view we have a 'lop-sided synopsis' for the conflict in India: A party with a trans-'ethnic' claim (the Congress) was confronted with an ethno-national competitor (the Muslim League). In the Balkans, by contrast, almost exclusively ethno-national forces fought against each other. An 'ethnic' party system never existed in India either, unlike in the young Bosnia-Herzegovina. At the time of the formation of the respective states, the Indian Muslims were more fragmented in terms of party politics than the Bosnian ones.

This was also due to the fact that Muslim nationalism in India came from a regional hotbed, namely from the northern United Provinces, where the cultural 'heritage' of the Mughal period had maintained itself for the longest time. But the regional aspect of Muslim nation-building in India raises a big contradiction: The Muslim spokesmen justified their separatism with a feared political Hindu dominance and with the fact that 'the Muslims' were economically weaker than 'the Hindus'. However, in UP it was exactly the other way round (in the NWFP as well, by the way). There, the Muslim nationalists received the least support of their fellow believers, just because they had nothing to worry about any Hindu competition. Horowitz's thesis that a relative discrimination leads to separatism does not make any sense here. Between the economic situation and the pursuit of separatism there is a black-box that contains several intermediate steps, as described in this book.

The socio-economic position of the Muslim population in India was more differentiated than in Bosnia-Herzegovina, where a large number of Muslims were big landowners. Many of them lost their economic and, eventually, political dominance indeed with the land reform and the socialist division of church and state in Bosnia-Herzegovina. But this did not lead to a rebellion either. Instead, the Muslim spokesmen supported the supra-'ethnic' state project of Yugoslavia.

In this constellation they managed to 'rise' towards a national status. It was created from above by decree as a tactical counterbalance to the Serb and Croatian competition, although secular Muslim spokesmen themselves lobbied strongly for this purpose. In India there is no example of such a type of a formal definition of nation, combined with an upgrading of the concerned group in terms of everyday politics. There the political significance of the Muslim spokesmen grew gradually through separate electorates and the fact that the British accepted the claim of the Muslim League to be the exclusive representative of 'the Muslims'.

Accordingly, the League had pro-British leanings. Jinnah would even have appreciated it if the colonial masters had continued to play golf and polo on the subcontinent for a couple of years longer and thus had prevented an 'ethnic' dominance of the competition. This reveals a clear contrast to the early Muslim parties in Bosnia-Herzegovina. They mostly exercised persistent opposition against the Austro-Hungarian occupying power.

Jinnah's pro-British attitude was one reason for his firm rejection of the Khilafat movement which had an anti-British thrust. There is no parallel in the Balkans to this grotesque but mass appealing alliance of opportunity of the ethno-national opponents. It proves how much the interpretation of religious-political symbols lay in the hands of ethno-national activists. They could more or less reverse the bulk of public opinion to 'friendship', if they only wanted. A success of this movement might have eventually prevented an ethno-national state building. Its failure politicized both communities another step further .

This episode shows that a person like Gandhi could mobilize the Indian public across 'ethnic' boundaries. In this way he also brought Muslims into the Indian movement of independence. In contrast to the crumbling Yugoslavia, in India it was not merely ethno-national forces which, for the first time, created a wide political public. In ex-Yugoslavia it was almost exclusively ethno-nationalists who filled the young democratic arena, which helped them to achieve a clear election victory.

The comparison of the temporary state of Muslim nation-building in both countries brings up strong contrasts and contrary developments. In India, the Muslim action group itself was the driving force for an ethno-national state building. In Bosnia-Herzegovina, the Muslim spokesmen did not act with such dynamism. Therefore this book refers to a rather *active nation state building* with regard to the Indian Muslims in contrast to a rather *passive nation state building* with regard to the Bosnian Muslims, for whom there seems to be hardly any alternative in the present—national and international—environment.

With the formation of the state of Pakistan the Indian Muslim actors had achieved their main objective (even if not all territorial wishes were fulfilled). In that moment the politicization and homogenization of the Muslim 'ethnic group' was at its climax. But shortly after the ethnicentre religion lost its cementing effect. Many other old and new cleavages split the temporary interest group of Muslims loyal to the League. The ethnic, cultural, and political heterogeneity of the subcontinent could not be denied by the competition of two politicized 'ethnic groups'. When state boundaries kept away the hostile other, the old game began inside the new enclosure. On the one hand, Muslims in Pakistan fight among themselves. On the other hand, the original fight against 'the Hindus' now takes place on a bilateral level. Old but freshly refurbished weapons are used, like the ethnicenter religion, but also new weapons like atomic bombs with the names of medieval, ethno-nationally appropriated heroes.

By contrast, most Muslims in Bosnia-Herzegovina and in the diaspora feel more effectively united than ever. They are in the process of homogenization which could end with an ethno-national state. The state buildings of the rivals, the war experience, and the continuous appropriation attempts by Serb and, since Dayton, especially by Croatian ethno-nationalists, have propelled the Muslim nation-building into a new phase. But even today, most Bosnian Muslims do not want an independent state—be it for practical reasons because it would not be viable, or for the basic conviction that 'the Muslims' need not follow the same way as their neighbours.

CLEAVAGES

The study leads to the thesis that the actual and potential Muslim state formations in India and Bosnia-Herzegovina do not emerge from a widespread national movement of 'the Muslims' according to the theory of modernization, as exemplarily described by Hroch's third phase. The history of events proves this. A differentiated judgement of the elections in India in 1946 and Bosnia-Herzegovina in 1990 is of great importance here. Beyond that, this thesis is based on the basic observation which runs through the book like a red thread: The rift between action group and postulated large group.

This means, on the one hand, that the Muslim spokesmen always represented parts of the Muslim population only—from the point of view of their origin as well as of their political representation. On the other hand, Muslim spokesmen competed among themselves, partly with completely opposite objectives, especially with regard to an ethno-national state project. Moreover, those who claimed to represent 'the Muslims' politically in Bosnia-Herzegovina did not even regard themselves as Muslims but as Serbs or Croats at times. If this happened within the political elite, then it did all the more happen in the population where all possible variations of subjective ascription could be found. This is particularly true for India till today. In Pakistan, after the foundation of the state, the Shia-Sunni cleavage broke open in addition.

If one looks at the main contrasting feature religion in the dogmatic sense, various cleavages occur. Muslims, if spokesmen or not, follow different opinions which are shown in Table (c).

Two things link Islam closely to the political development: (1) Its doctrine is widely referred to postulate the inseparability of religion and politics. (2) In the concerned countries Islam is constructed as the ethnicenter. Therefore the dogmatic cleavages must not disappear from the focus of attention although Islam as a religion—as the religions of other ethno-national projects as well—faded in its original profile. Accordingly, Calic observes: 'The denominational "nation" (*Konfessions-nation*) (Emanuel Turczynski) can be [...] considered to be a meanwhile overcome intermediate stage on the way from a popular consciousness, which emphasizes religious characteristics, towards politically related

TABLE (C): DOGMATIC CLEAVAGES AMONG THE MUSLIMS

	orthodox	modern/ progressive	secular or syncretic
Bosnia-Herzegovina	partly Izetbegovic, parts of Mladi Muslimani, Muslim rural population, some early Muslim parties, early *ulema*	partly Izetbegovic, Muslim urbanites and upper class, present *ulema*	Muslim urbanites, Muslim communists (secular)
India	Deoband School, Jamiat-i-Ulema-i-Hind, Jama'at-i-Islami, other parts of the *ulema*	Jinnah, Muslim League, Aligarh School (esp. Iqbal, Khan), Muslim upper class in cities and rural areas	Congress-Muslims (esp. Azad), rural population (syncretic)

forms of group solidarity.'[3] This is true for the Bosnian Muslims, to whom Calic refers, as well as for the Indian, respectively Pakistani, Muslims.

Dogmatic cleavages influenced political ones. An orthodox approach slowed down the Muslim nation-building in the same way as secular forms in Bosnia-Herzegovina and syncretic ones in India. The Orthodox referred to the supra-national *umma* and lacked any political ambition. The numerous secularized Muslims in Bosnia-Herzegovina did not exactly provide a persuasive argument for pushing through a nation-building with religion as ethnicenter. It appears just as little plausible in the case of a long tradition of syncretic ways of life, like in India.

These differences come to light especially when the highest ethno-national goal of founding a state is concerned. It is striking that, on the one hand, some dogmatic cleavages become political ones—especially pan-Islamism. On the other hand, dogmatic approaches and political objectives wildly cross-çut. Political goals themselves also appear in fundamentally contradictory combinations, like ethno-nationalism plus pan-Islamism.

This work suggests that nation-building is not a deterministic concept but that there are many factors which can slow or accelerate it. Therefore it is important not to automatically lump together actors who follow an ethno-national approach with those who demand an ethno-national state. There were more and more Muslims in the course of their politicization who got the impression that they represented a nation of their own in demarcation against the competition. Those, however, who shouted and still shout from rooftops their slogan of a sovereign state can be almost counted with the fingers of one hand [Table (d), p. 382].

The classification of both main Muslim figures is interesting. Izetbegovic, the Muslim ideologue, was, above all, interested in the Islamization of society. Jinnah, the liberal pragmatist, had only one dogma: Pakistan. He pursued less religious than political goals. However, both thought along ethno-national lines. They helped politicize the 'ethnic groups' and added 'ethnic' ingredients to politics.

At the end of their career both followed separate paths again. When he took office, Jinnah declared that, from now on, Pakistan—as it now existed—would have a civil-democratic character. This was, in fact, a quite unconvincing idea after all the ethno-national trench wars but a turn to his early convictions. By contrast, Izetbegovic drifted more and

TABLE (D): POLITICAL CLEAVAGES AMONG THE MUSLIMS

	Pan-Islamism	Ethno-nationalism	For an ethno-national state	For a civic-democratic or a secular state
Bosnia-Herzegovina	Izetbegovic, Mladi Muslimani, some early Muslim parties, partly early *ulema*	Izetbegovic, SDA, some Muslim organizations after the Bosnian war, Mladi Muslimani	Radical wing of the SDA, Izetbegovic(?)	today's *ulema*, alternative parties like SBH, UBSD, MBO, early Muslim parties like MNO, JMO
India	large parts of the *ulema*, especially Deoband-School, Jama'at-i-Islami	Jinnah, Muslim League, Aligarh School, parts of Deoband School, partly other Muslim parties	Jinnah till Partition, Jinnah's close followers in the Muslim League	Jinnah's turned-round head of state, Congress Muslims, moderate Muslim parties (Liberals, Unionists), before Partition: Deoband School, Jama'at-i-Islami

more towards those who worked for a Muslim state. He preferred to fill it with Islamic contents, what Jinnah rejected but what his successors made up for all the more thoroughly.

FURTHER THEORETIC CONCLUSIONS

Ethnic conflicts do not exist. This is an important finding of this book. The fronts are by far not as clear-cut as that. And the contents of the conflicts have nothing to do with the descent of the people, neither with their faith, their language or their habits as such. These features serve only as docking stations for an accelerated political mobilization. Neither in India nor in the Balkans did ethnic groups fight each other, not even 'ethnic groups' or ethno-nations as such. The cleavages are complex, the interests numerous, the results open. The nation-building of the Bosnian and Indian Muslims was not a 'natural' awakening of a group with a 'natural' goal to become a state, as ethno-national historians would like to have it.

In the history of the Balkans and India there were several occasions when the points could have been set in a different direction. Bosnian Muslims did not show any interest in entering the stage as a nation for a long time, although they were encouraged to do so from above, by the occupants. Their parties advocated routine political objectives. Later the Muslim spokesmen and relatively many among the Muslim population supported the concept of a Yugoslav federation more than others. In India, in the beginning of the twentieth century, Congress and Muslim League displayed harmony. Hindus and Muslims found a common political goal in the Khilafat movement. This means: Even in the already politicized phase of the 'ethnic groups' there were possibilities of cooperation.

However, the politicization of the 'ethnic groups' was, at the same time, a precondition for making cooperation possible in the first place, and, second, for making it necessary. The cultural and religious homogenization, starting from the eighteenth, and especially from the nineteenth century, was the beginning of an ethno-national way of thinking and acting, be it aimed at confrontation or cooperation.

In Bosnia-Herzegovina and India the Muslim nation-building was reactively coupled with the national homogenization of the neighbours. In Bosnia-Herzegovina Muslim spokesmen refused—mildly at first, and then strongly—the ideological and territorial appropriation of Serb and Croatian ethno-nationalists. With each Balkan war this constellation became more and more delicate. Also in India 'the others' were initially stronger.

Religious activists modernized and standardized Hindudom. Gradually, integrative elements of Hinduism gave way to confrontational ones. Even Congress politicians like Gandhi accepted the ethno-national dualism and provoked it. These factors suddenly turned the numerical superiority of 'the Hindus' into a problem for the Muslim spokesmen, which is comparable with the Serbo-Croatian sandwich in Bosnia-Herzegovina. On the basis of the respective position of 'the Muslims' within the ethno-national constellation of their surrounding, the Muslim nation-buildings can be described as *negative* or *defensive*.

In this context, Muslim 'ethnicity' appears as a dependent variable first. However, with a progressive politicization of 'the Muslims', they influenced political events themselves, like other ethno-national spokesmen, too. In turn, they are supported by various factors. In India Muslim spokesmen took an *active* role in the buliding of the 'nation state'. In Bosnia-Herzegovina they have so far mostly remained *passive*. Table (e) shows the interaction of dependent and independent variables in a synopsis of several examples.

TABLE (E): MUSLIM ETHNO-NATION AS DEPENDENT AND AS INDEPENDENT VARIABLE

Muslim ethno-nation as dependent variable, influenced by independent variables:

- ideological construction of 'ethnicity' by cultural and political actors, European theories of nationalism
- advanced or ongoing ethno-national homogenization of the neighbours and their territorial ambitions, subjective feeling of threat
- stirring up of conflicts and violence with ethno-national intentions
- ethno-national approach of the higher political reference points (occupying powers etc.) at a time of incipient political mobilization; confusion of state and nation
- aimed support of the 'Muslim nation' by the higher reference points, formal categorization from above and thus homogenization of heterogeneous population groups, ways of life, etc.
- ethno-national pluralism through distorted elements of democracy and uneven allocation of resources (e.g. principles of recruitment)

Muslim ethno-nation as independent variable [represented by (party-)political spokesmen] influencing dependent variables:

- economic development (e.g. prevention of land reform in Bosnia-Herzegovina because of 'Muslim' land-owning interests)
- domestic political outcomes [e.g. by coalitions of Muslim parties with ethno-national or other parties. It also includes tensions which arise when coalitions are either not formed (India 1937) or break up (Bosnia-Herzegovina 1992)]
- allocation of resources (e.g. principles of recruitment, quota system)
- strengthening of an ethno-national character of institutions (from electoral procedures to state structures)
- secession, ethno-national state formation

The findings from both case studies suggest an ethno-national domino effect which deprives trans-'ethnic' options of resources. This means: If ethno-national agitation is cushioned with concessions (like separate electorates in India or ethno-national pluralism in Yugoslavia), representations of ethno-national interests can establish themselves as independent variables in the political process, which, in turn, leads again to 'ethnically' tailored consequences, and so on. At least in the cases of India and Yugoslavia multi-'ethnic' approaches did not lead to inter-'ethnic' cooperation. This contradicts the arguments of those political scientists who recommend the consensus model to accommodate ethno-national conflicts (e.g. Lijphart). The findings from the case studies rather recommend a model which does not lay itself open to any attack from ethno-national agitation, which does not promise any resources, or which does not allow the ethno-national momentum to start at all. The 'ethnic' alignment of political outputs cements ethno-national clientelism and plays in the hands of the radical forces.

The Indian subcontinent provides plenty of examples. In communal riots Hindu nationalists stylized the holy cow as a weapon against the Muslims. Rules for the slaughter of cattle are stricter in ethnically and 'ethnically' heterogeneous India than in Nepal, the only Hindu state of the world. There beef appears even on the menu cards of restaurants (but then it is not called *beef* but glossed over as *buff*). On the peaks of the Himalayas no Hindu has to prove to an ethno-national rival how devout a Hindu he is.

Similar things can be observed for Muslim practices in comparison of India and Pakistan. In general, the Muslim *ulema* in India is more conservative than in the hostile neighbouring country. The Sharia, which the Indian state has granted to Muslims for a long time as common law in family affairs (for matters relating to marriage, inheritance, etc.) carries more orthodox features than in the Muslim 'homeland' of Pakistan. This is not only because the *ulema* is keen to demarcate itself against the ethno-national competition—which Muslim scholars do not need any more in a Pakistan of their 'own'—but also because the conservative spokesmen in India could often prevail only because the Indian governments made specific concessions to them. Thus they gradually undermined Nehru's trans-'ethnic' approach. His successors and descendants courted Muslim voters and campaigned for ethno-national peace with politics of clientelism. This is a clear example of the negative effects of Lijpharts's consociational approach.[4]

None other than Nehru's grandson Rajiv Gandhi set off an ethno-national spiral when he snubbed liberal Muslims in 1986 and gave in to the conservative *ulema* in the dispute about the marriage act.[5] Thus he is believed to have secured his line of retreat in order to distribute, as a next step, a candy to 'the Hindus'. He opened the site of the Babri Masjid of Ayodhya, which the Hindu nationalists assume to be the birth temple of their 'national' god Ram (although Indian historians were able to show that nobody had regarded Ayodhya as the birthplace of Ram before the nineteenth century—and that Mughal emperors had no specific association with the mosque either.[6]) This concession to radical Hindus fueled the fights between the ethno-national camps, until, in 1992, a fanaticized Hindu mob finally demolished the mosque and provoked a chain reaction of violent ethno-national riots throughout the country.[7] The domino effect can be seen till today.

A closer look on recent communal riots in India, however, shows again, that Hindus and Muslims do not fight each other per se. Instead, the clashes are unequally distributed across India, and are not dependent on the number of Muslims living in the area. In Gujarat, which had most deaths (120) in such riots from 1950 to 1995 (and many more in 2001 and 2002) the Muslim population is only 8.1 per cent. By contrast, in Assam, with a third of deaths in riots, there are 25 per cent Muslims, and in Jammu & Kashmir, with 44.7 per cent Muslims, there were less than one fifth of deaths due to ethno-national riots.[8] This clearly shows that other factors are at play. There are corelations of low communal violence and high activity of cross-cutting non-governmental institutions or integrated business communities. In the case of Gujarat corrupt police and politicians, who exploit such riots for their gain, have contributed a lot to the tensions.

These examples parallel the same patterns that we have come across throughout India's and Bosnia's modern history. Unfortunately, they are very effective. Ethno-national activists can easily radicalize their constituency where the environment allows a free play. Islamization and politicization attempts of Bosnian Muslims, especially after the war, also fall in this category. Against this background, Konrád writes with resignation: 'The war has made the Serbs more Orthodox, the Bosnian Muslims more Islamic, the Croats more Catholic. Through religious-nationalistic separatism the linguistic-cultural-secular solidarity has lost acceptance.'[9] Although Konrád falls into a generalization here and ignores, among other things, the gap between action group and large group, he describes the ethno-national vicious circle which tends to drain off political resources from the secular concepts.

Support comes from the highest level. The 'ethnic' connotation of the term nation has gained acceptance worldwide which, in turn, has been carelessly associated with the concept of state. The international actors have succumbed to a confusion of state and nation. The United Nations comprises *states* which are far from being nations. This ethno-national state paradigm implies: The state level is the biggest distributor of ideological and material resources. Under the above mentioned preconditions, ethno-national spokesmen find the highest motivation and the best conditions to take hold of a state. Thus the ethno-national domino effect can easily reach the highest level where fights and insults of the 'ethno-egos' can finally spend themselves bilaterally. The advanced integration of the European Union crystallizes as the only counteracting force. At present, it is the only alternative to the concept of a nation state worldwide.[10]

In this book it became clear that the confusion of state and nation accelerated the nation-building and especially the nation-state-building on the Indian subcontinent and in the Balkans. In addition, the case of Pakistan indicates an ironic twist which reveals the substantial hollowness of the ethno-national-state paradigm. There are two observations: (1) Ethno-national ideologies are substantially meagre from the beginning. They are less complex, require—if at all—only a short process of public opinion building, hardly need any political discussion, and are inherently contradictory and illogical to the extreme. (2) They are victims of their own success. This means, ethno-national contents live from dynamism. They are good for mobilization but not for the preservation of the achieved status quo.

In the case of Pakistan this means, that as soon as new boundaries enclose the ethno-nation and homogenize it formally, the 'common' bond of 'ethnicity', breaksthrough which the state obtained its legitimacy. The idea of a Muslim state was a political construction without a mass base. In this vein Huntington concludes that Pakistan was able to come into being 'too easily'. The ethno-national paradigm of the distributors of resources helped in this process. Once the main goal was reached, the concept of 'ethnicity' turned out to be extremely short-lived and fragile. Only where ethno-national rivalry continues, it shows a continuous effect, as in the above mentioned examples of the orthodox *ulema* in India.

In its last consequence, this means: There cannot be any 'ethnically' homogeneous states at all—and if, then the category of 'ethnicity' becomes irrelevant. For the state is a political phenomenon. Primordial cleavages per se do not exist. And if they do, they are pre-politically ethnic (but highly improbable), and good neither for political mobilization nor for state-building. If political goals are to be achieved, 'ethnic groups' must be politicized, which means: wrapped into handy 'parcels of interests' and 'sold' politically. Once each 'ethnic group' has 'its' state, new and smaller parcels must be created since the paradigm of 'ethnicity' became too big and all-embracing, and thus unsuitable for political business. Political life is more complicated and multi-layered for the postulate of 'ethnic' solidarity to iron it out.

In other words, in those few countries that are considered to be 'ethnically homogeneous', like Japan, 'ethnicity' does not play any role as a political cleavage. With regard to the ambitions of ethno-national activists, this means: Not only are the contents which they transport terrible and terribly meagre, but they also make themselves superfluous through their own success. Or they desperately hold on to the obsolete ethnicentre, as in Pakistan, and must live with its contradictions and with new cleavages which they provoke day after day as a consequence.

Through such a distortion of political contents a stable democratic development with a pluralism of interests is unthinkable. Whether the Balkans succeed in breaking out of this vicious circle soon is doubtful, and whether on the other hand India can avoid drifting into it more and more deeply, too.

NOTES

1. Bell-Fialkoff (1999), pp. 75-6. When he speaks of nationalism here he means in the sense of ethno-nationalism.
2. Here it must be qualified that Bosnian Muslims also often described themselves as 'Turks'. With this they expressed their religious association with the Ottoman occupying power. However, here the emphasis is on 'derogatory'. Serb and Croatian ethno-nationalists use this word even today, although it has become obsolete long time ago as a Muslim self-given name.
3. Calic (1996a), p. 28.
4. A determined criticism is in Chapter I.8.1. 'Recipes for a Functioning Society'.
5. For a discussion on this case and on Islamic conservatism in India, see: Kerrin, in: Italiaander (1987), pp. 138-9; Jaffrelot (1996), pp. 370-1.

6. Hobsbawm (1997), p. 273.
7. For a discussion on the 'ethnicization' of modern Indian politics, see especially: Jaffrelot (1996), pp. 369ff.
8. 'After the Slaughter, What Hope?', in: *Economist* (9 March 2002), pp. 56-7. The magazine refers to findings of Ashutosh Varshney, professor at the University of Michigan.
9. Konrád (1997), p. 15.
10. Brubaker also holds this thesis (1996), pp. 1ff. At the same time, he discloses the schizophrenia of the developments while pointing out that, in 1992, the Maastricht Treaty with the European domestic market took shape, and in the same year the Bosnian war broke out.

Appendix

Periodicals and their acronyms quoted in the notes

ABS	*American Behavioral Scientist*
AP	*Anthropological Perspectives*
APSR	*American Political Science Review*
ApuZ	*Aus Politik und Zeitgeschichte (supplement of Das Parlament)*
AS	*Asian Survey*
BF	*Balkan Forum*
BSMESB	*British Society for Middle Eastern Studies Bulletin*
CSSH	*Comparative Studies in Society and History*
DA	*Demographie aktuell*
EA	*Europa-Archiv*
EE	*Ethnologia Europaea*
EF	*Ethnologie française*
EJIL	*European Journal of International Law*
ER	*Europäische Rundschau*
ERS	*Ethnic and Racial Studies*
FA	*Foreign Affairs*
GP	*Gesellschaft und Politik*
IA	*International Affairs*
IK	*Interkulturell*
IPSR	*International Political Science Review*
IS	*Islamic Studies*
ISSJ	*International Social Science Journal*
JEWS	*The Journal for East and West Studies*
KZSS	*Kölner Zeitschrift für Soziologie und Sozialpsychologie*
MAS	*Modern Asian Studies*
MES	*Middle Eastern Studies*
MW	*Muslim World*
NC	*New Community*
NP	*Nationalities Papers*
OE	*Osteuropa*

OEA	*Osteuropa-Archiv*
ÖZS	*Österreichische Zeitschrift für Soziologie*
ÖO	*Österreichische Osthefte*
PB	*Policy Brief (Institute on Global Conflict and Cooperation, IGCC)*
PC	*Problems of Communism*
PG	*Politik und Gesellschaft*
PSA	*Philosophy and Social Action*
SA	*Saeculum Augustum*
SEER	*Slavonic and East European Review*
Soc	*Sociologus*
SOE	*Südosteuropa*
SOEM	*Südosteuropa-Mitteilungen*
SOF	*Südost-Forschungen*
SS	*Social Scientist*
TSI	*Towards Secular India*
WS	*Welt der Slawen*
ZS	*Zeitschrift für Soziologie*

Bibliography

JOURNALISTIC NEWSPAPERS AND PERIODICALS USED

Asian Age
Das Beste von Reader's Digest (Das Beste)
Das Sonntagsblatt
der journalist
Der Tagesspiegel
Die Zeit
Frankfurter Allgemeine Zeitung (FAZ)
Hannoversche Allgemeine Zeitung (HAZ)
konkret
Le monde diplomatique (edition taz)
Newsweek
Süddeutsche Zeitung
The Boston Globe
The Economist
The New York Times
The Washington Post
Time Magazine (Time)
Times of India
Why (Sarajevo)

INTERNET

Internet-Bulletin 'Bosnet': owner-bosnet-digest@bosnet.org (not available any longer)
Office of the UN High Representative of Bosnia-Herzegovina: www.ohr.int
The Bosnian Institute, London: www.bosnia.org.uk

DISCUSSION PARTNERS AND EYE WITNESSES (PRIMARY SOURCES)*

Abdurahmanovic, Asim: Second editor-in-chief of the independent station *Radio 99* (Sarajevo).
Ceman, Mirsad: Secretary-general of Izetbegovic's SDA (Sarajevo).
Hadzihasanovic, Sanela: Journalist with *Radio 99* (Sarajevo).
Ilic, Zoran: Editor-in-chief of *Radio 99* (Sarajevo).
Kapetanovic, Amer: Muslim journalist and later spokesman of the Bosnian foreign ministry (Sarajevo).

* Positions of the partners refer to the posts which they held at the time of the interview. The city indicates where the interview took place.

Ljubas, Zdravko: Freelance journalist and correspondent for the German Press Agency (dpa) in Sarajevo.

Pejanovic, Mirko: President of the Civic Democratic Party of Bosnia-Hercegovina (Gradanska Demokratska Stranka, GDS) and chairman of the Serbian Community of Sarajevo (Sarajevo).

Pesic, Vesna: Serb opposition politician until Milosevic's fall, then ambassador to Mexico (Mexico City).

Purivata, Atif (†2001): Bosnian Muslim historian and President of the Council of the Congress of Bosnjak Intellectuals (Sarajevo).

Staka, Vlado: Editor of the independent daily newspaper *Oslobodenje* (Sarajevo).

Tokic, Sejfudin: Vice-president of the Union of the Bosnian Social Democrates (UBSD), later member of the SDP (Sarajevo).

OTHER QUOTED INTERLOCUTORS

Al-Azm, Sadiq: Professor of philosophy and controversial secular critic of the Arab world and Muslim societies (Damascus).

Bajrektarevic, Anis: Lawer, president of the Association of the Young Lawyers of Bosnia, law expert of the Bosnian OSCE embassy in Vienna and of the International Centre for Migration Policy (ICMP) (Vienna).

Palat, M.K.: Professor of history at Jawaharlal Nehru University and researcher at the Indira Gandhi National Centre for Arts (New Delhi).

Panikkar, K.N.: Professor of history and chairperson of the archive for contemporary history at Jawaharlal Nehru University (New Delhi).

Singh, Uma: Professor of international relations at Jawaharlal Nehru University (New Delhi).

OTHER ORAL SOURCES OF INFORMATION

Press spokesmen of the embassies of Bosnia-Hercegovina, India, and Pakistan in the Federal Republic of Germany (Bonn and Berlin).

LITERATURE ON BALKAN ISSUES

MONOGRAPHIES, ANTHOLOGIES, ARTICLES

Akadül, Deniz and Semih Vaner, 'Die Türkei und die neue Runde auf dem Balkan', in: *Europäische Rundschau*, 3, 1994.

Alexander, Stella: 'Croatia: The Catholic Church and Clergy 1919-1945', in: Richard J. Wolff and Jörg K. Hoensch (eds.), *Catholics, the State and the European Radical Right*, New York, 1987.

Algar, Hamid, 'The Hamzeviye: A Deviant Movement in Bosnian Sufism', in: *Islamic Studies*, 36 (1997), 2-3: Special Issue: *Islam in the Balkans* (Islamabad).

Al-Ghazali, Muhammad, 'Islam Between East and West: The Magnus Opus of Alija Izetbegovic', in: *Islamic Studies*, 36 (1997), 2-3: Special Issue: *Islam in the Balkans* (Islamabad).

Andric, Ivo, *Omer-Pascha Latas: Der Marschall des Sultans*, Frankfurt-M./Berlin/Vienna, 1983.

——, *Die Brücke über die Drina*, Munich, 1962.

Axt, Heinz-Jürgen, 'Kampf der Kulturen?: Europa nach dem Ende des Ost-West-Konflikts', in: *Europäische Rundschau*, 1, 1994.

——, 'Hat Genscher Jugoslawien entzweit?: Mythen und Fakten zur Außenpolitik des vereinten Deutschlands', in: *Europa-Archiv*, 48 (1993) 12 (also in: Angelika Volle and Wolfgang Wagner (eds.): *Der Krieg auf dem Balkan: Die Hilflosigkeit der Staatenwelt*, Bonn 1994).

——, 'Der "Islamische Bogen" vom Balkan bis Zentralasien: Die Türkei als neue Regionalmacht', in: *Südosteuropa*, 9, 1992.

Babuna, Aydin, Die nationale Entwicklung der bosnischen Muslime: Mit besonderer Berücksichtigung der österreichisch-ungarischen Periode, Frankfurt/M. et al., 1996.

Bajrektarevic, Anis, Bosnia and Herzegovina 1879-1998: Some Demographic Facts, 'Non-Paper', Vienna, 1998.

——, The Ethno-Structure: One View of the Former Yugoslavia, 'Non-Paper' (2nd edn.), Vienna, 1997.

Balic, Smail, 'The Cultural Achievements of Bosnian Muslims', *Islamic Studies*, 36 (1997) 2-3: Special Issue: *Islam in the Balkans* (Islamabad)

——, *Der Islam europakonform?*, Würzburg/Altenberge, 1994.

——, *Das unbekannte Bosnien: Europas Brücke zur islamischen Welt*, Cologne, 1992.

——, 'Der Islam in Jugoslawien: Eine Religion auf Sparflamme', in: Rolf Italiaander, *Die Herausforderung des Islam: Ein ökumenisches Lesebuch*, Göttingen, 1987.

Banac, Ivo, 'Bosnian Muslims: From Religious Community to Socialist Nationhood and Postcommunist Statehood, 1918-1992', in: Mark Pinson (ed.), *The Muslims of Bosnia-Hercegovina: Their Historic Development from the Middle Ages to the Dissolution of Yugoslavia*, Cambridge (Mass.), 1994.

——, *The National Question in Yugoslavia: Origins, History, Politics*, Ithaca/ New York, 1984.

Barany, Zoltan D., 'The Roots of Nationalism in Postcommunist Eastern Europe', in: *Balkan Forum*, 2 (1993), 2.

Basagic, Reuf and Domagoj Draskovic, 'Setzt Alija Izetbegovic Giftgas ein?', in: *Osteuropa-Archiv*, 10, 1993.

Bauer, Ernest: Zwischen Halbmond und Doppeladler: 40 Jahre österreichische Verwaltung in Bosnien-Herzegowina, Vienna, 1971.

Bauer, Harry and Thomas Kimmig, 'Frieden um jeden Preis?: Ein Diskussionsbeitrag zum Krieg in Bosnien und seiner Wahrnehmung in der Bundesrepublik', in: Nenad Stefanov and Michael Werz (eds), *Bosnien und Europa: Die Ethnisierung der Gesellschaft*, Frankfurt/M., 1994.

Bauer, Otto, *see Literature Theory.*

Bebler, Anton, 'Jugoslawiens Zukunftsperspektiven: Widerstreitende Konzeptionen zur Neuordnung des Staates', in: *Südosteuropa*, 1/ 1991.

Behschnitt, Wolf D., *Nationalismus bei Serben und Kroaten, 1830-1914: Analyse und Typologie der nationalen Ideologie*, Munich, 1980.

Benbassa, Esther and Aron Rodrigue, Juifs des Balkans: Espaces judéo-ibériques XIVe-XXe siecles, Paris, 1993.

Berend, Ivan, 'Agriculture', in: M.C. Kaser and E.A. Radice (eds.): *The Economic History of Eastern Europe 1919-1975*, Vol. 1, Oxford, 1985.

Berend, Ivan and Ranki, György, *The European Periphery and Industrialization 1780-1914*, Budapest, 1982.

Bernhard, Wolfram and Anneliese Kandler-Palsson, *Ethnogenese europäischer Völker*, Stuttgart/New York, 1986.

Bieber, Florian, 'Bosnia and Herzegovina', in: *Nations in Transit, Washington, D.C.*, et al., 2002 (annual report of Freedom House).

——, 'Croat Self-Government in Bosnia—a Challenge for Dayton?', in: *ECMI Brief*, May 2001 (European Centre for Minority Issues).

Binavince, Emilio S., 'Balkan Realities and the Constitution of a Polyethnic State', in: Raju G. Thomas and Richard H. Friman (eds.), *The South Slav Conflict: History, Ethnicity, and Nationalism*, New York, 1996.

Birke, Ernst, 'Herder und die Slawen', in: W. Hubatsch (ed.), *Schicksalswege deutscher Vergangenheit: Beiträge zur geschichtlichen Deutung der letzten hundertfünfzig Jahre*, Düsseldorf, 1950.

Birnbaum, Henrik, 'The Ethno-Linguistic Mosaic of Bosnia and Hercegovina', in: *Die Welt der Slaven* 32, 1987.

Bittner, Konrad, 'J.G. Herders "Ideen zur Philosophie der Geschichte der Menschheit" und ihre Auswirkungen bei den slawischen Hauptstämmen', in: *Germanoslavika*, 4, 1931-3.

——, *Herders Geschichtsphilosophie und die Slawen*, Reichenberg, 1929.

Bodansky, Yossef: *see Literature on Islam.*

Bojicic, Vesna, 'The Economy of Bosnia and Herzegovina', in: *Eastern Europe and the Commonwealth of Independent States 1997* (3rd edn.) London, 1997.

Bougarel, Xavier, 'From Young Muslims to Party of Democratic Action: The Emergence of a Pan-Islamist Trend in Bosnia-Herzegovina', in: *Islamic Studies*, 36 (1997), 2-3: Special Issue: *Islam in the Balkans* (Islamabad).

Bowers, Stephen R.: 'Ethnic Politics in Eastern Europe', in: Peter Janke, (ed.), *Ethnic and Religious Conflicts: Europe and Asia*, Aldershot et al., 1994.

Bowman, Glenn, 'Xenophobia, Fantasy and the Nation: The Logic of Ethnic Violence in Former Yugoslavia', in: *Balkan Forum*, 2 (1994) 2.

Braude, B. and Lewis B. (Hg:), *Christians and Jews in the Ottoman Empire*, New York, 1982.

Brey, Thomas, 'Der Vielvölkerstaat zerfällt, Teil I. und II.', in: *Osteuropa-Archiv*, Vols. 5 and 7, 1991.

Brozovic, Dalibor, 'Serbo-Croatian as a Pluricentric Language', in: Clyne, Michael (ed.), *Pluricentric Languages: Differing Norms in Different Nations*, Berlin/New York, 1992.

Brunkhorst, Hauke, 'Ungeordnete Hierarchien: Das alte Jugoslawien, die Intellektuellen und der Rückfall in den Naturzustand', in: Nenad Stefanov and Michael Werz (eds.), *Bosnien und Europa: Die Ethnisierung der Gesellschaft*, Frankfurt/M., 1994.

Brunner, Georg, 'Die Stellung der Muslime in den föderativen Systemen der Sowjetunion und Jugoslawiens', in: Andreas Kappeler, Gerhardt Simon and Georg Brunner (eds.), *Die Muslime in der Sowjetunion und in Jugoslawien: Identität, Politik, Widerstand*, Cologne, 1989.

Budding, Audrey H., 'Yugoslavs Into Serbs: Serbian National Identity 1961-1971', in: *Nationalities Papers*, 25 (1997), 3.

Bugajski, Janusz, 'Balkan Myths and Bosnian Massacres', in: Raju G. Thomas and Richard H. Friman (eds.), *The South Slav Conflict: History, Ethnicity, and Nationalism*, New York, 1996.

Burg, Steven L. and Paul S. Shoup, *The War in Bosnia-Herzegovina: Ethnic Conflict and International Intervention*, Armonk (N.Y.)/London, 1999.

Calic, Marie-Janine (ed.), *Friedenskonsolidierung im ehemaligen Jugoslawien: Sicherheitspolitische und zivile Aufgaben*, Ebenhausen/Isartal, 1996b.

——, *Der Krieg in Bosnien-Herzegowina: Ursachen, Konfliktstrukturen, Internationale Lösungsversuche* (2nd edn.), Frankfurt/M., 1996a.

——, 'Das Abkommen von Dayton: Chancen und Risiken des Friedensprozesses im ehemaligen Jugoslawien', in: *Stiftung Wissenschaft und Politik – IP 2948*, März, 1996.

——, 'Ethnische Konflikte in Bosnien-Herzegowina: Eine strukturelle Analyse', in: Gerhard Seewann (ed.), *Minderheiten als Konfliktpotential in Ostmittel-und Südosteuropa*, Munich, 1995.

——, 'Düstere Aussichten für Bosnien-Herzegowina', in: *Europa-Archiv*, 3, 1994 [also in: Angelika Volle and Wolfgang Wagner (eds.), *Der Krieg auf dem Balkan: Die Hilflosigkeit der Staatenwelt*, Bonn, 1994].

——, 'Jugoslawien-Politik am Wendepunkt', in: *Aus Politik und Zeitgeschichte*, B37, 1993.

Calic, Marie-Janine and Volker Perthes, 'Krieg und Konfliktlösung in Bosnien und Libanon: Ein Strukturvergleich', in: *Politik und Gesellschaft*, 2, 1995.

Castellan, Georges, *Histoire des Balkans XIVe-XXe siècle*, Saint-Amand-Montrond, 1991 (Paris, 1992 and 1993) (*History of the Balkans: From Mohammed the Conqueror to Stalin*, Boulder, 1992).

Cazacu, Matei, 'L'Eglise orthodoxe entre le renouveau et la tradition: Phanariotes et Anti-Phanariotes', in: Christian Hannick (ed.), *Sprachen und Nationen im Balkanraum: Die historischen Bedingungen der Entstehung der heutigen Nationalsprachen*, Vienna, 1987.

Cimic, Esad, 'Uticaj samoupravljanja na proces prevladavanja religije' (The impact of self-government on the process of overcoming religion), in: *Pregled*, 17 (1965), 7-8 (Sarajevo).

Claussen, Detlev, 'Mißglückte Befreiung: Zur ethnisierenden Auflösung des Realsozialismus', in: Nenad Stefanov and Michael Werz (eds.), *Bosnien und Europa: Die Ethnisierung der Gesellschaft*, Frankfurt/M, 1994.

Clayer, Nathalie and Alexandre Popovic, 'Muslim Identity in the Balkans in the post-Ottoman Period', in: Mushirul Hasan (ed.), *Islam, Communities and the Nation: Muslim Identities in South Asia and Beyond*, Delhi, 1998.

Cohen, Lenard J., 'Prelates and Politicians in Bosnia: The Role of Religion in Nationalist Mobilisation', in: *Nationalities Papers*, 25 (1997), 3.

Cohen, Philip J., 'The Ideology and Historical Continuity of Serbia's Anti-Islamic Policy', in: *Islamic Studies*, 36 (1997), 2-3: Special Issue: *Islam in the Balkans* (Islamabad).

Colovic, Ivan, *Bordell der Krieger*, Osnabrück, 1994.

——, 'Die Erneuerung des Vergangenen: Zeit und Raum in der zeitgenössischen politischen Mythologie', in: Nenad Stefanov and Michael Werz (eds.), *Bosnien und Europa: Die Ethnisierung der Gesellschaft*, Frankfurt/M., 1994.

Covic, Borivoj, 'Die Ethnogenese der Illyrer aus der Sicht der Vor- und Frühgeschichte', in: Wolfram Bernhard and Anneliese Kandler-Palsson, *Ethnogenese europäischer Völker*, Stuttgart/New York, 1986.

Cviic, Christopher, 'Kroatien ohne Reue', in: *Europäische Rundschau*, 4, 1994.

——, 'An Awful Warning: The War in Ex-Yugoslavia', in: *Balkan Forum*, 2 (1994), 3.

——, 'Das Ende Jugoslawiens', in: *Europa-Archiv*, 14, 1991.

Devetak, Silvo, *see Literature Theory.*

Dimitrijevic, Vojin, 'Usamljena zemlja: Spoljnopoliticki polozaj I spoljna politika Jugoslavije I Srbje' (The lonely country: The international situation and the foreign policy of Yugoslavia and Serbia), in: *Republika*, No. 164, 16-31 May 1997 (Belgrad) (German version in: *Osteuropa*, 1, 1998).

Djilas, Aleksa, 'Identities, Ideologies and the Yugoslav War', in: *Balkan Forum*, 2 (1994), 3.

Djinjic, Zoran, 'Serbien und seine Nachbarn', in: *Südosteuropa Mitteilungen* 42 (2002), 2.

Donia, Robert J. and William G. Lockwood, 'The Bosnian Muslims: Class, Ethnity, and Political Behavior in a European State', in: Joseph Suad and Barbara Pillsbury (eds.), *Muslim-Christian Conflicts: Economic, Political and Social Origins*, Boulder, 1978.

Dreschner, Karl-Heinz and Petrovic, Milan, *Weltkrieg der Religionen: Der ewige Kreuzzug auf dem Balkan*, Stuttgart/Vienna/Weitbrecht, 1995.

Dyke, Nancy B., 'The United States, International Organizations, and the Yugoslav Crisis', in: Raju G. Thomas and Richard H. Friman (eds.), *The South Slav Conflict: History, Ethnicity, and Nationalism*, New York, 1996.

Dyker, David A., 'The Ethnic Muslims of Bosnia: Some Basic Socio-Economic Data', in: *Slavonic and East European Review* 50, April 1972.

Dzaja, Srecko M., 'Book review on Babuna (1996)', in: *Südost-Europa*, 1-2, 1998.

——, 'Die bosnische Völkersymbiose: Genese und Verfall', in: Reinhard Lauer and Werner Lehfeld (eds.), *Das jugoslawische Desaster: Historische, sprachliche und ideologische Hintergründe*, Wiesbaden, 1995.

——, *Bosnien-Herzegowina in der österreichisch-ungarischen Epoche (1878-1918): Die Intelligentsia zwischen Tradition und Ideologie*, Munich, 1994.

——, 'Bosnien-Herzegowina', in: Weithmann, Michael: *Der ruhelose Balkan*, Munich (2nd edn.), 1994.

——, *Konfessionalität und Nationalität Bosniens und der Herzegowina: Voremanzipatorische Phase 1463-1804*, Munich, 1984.

——, *Die 'Bosnische Kirche' und das Islamisierungsproblem Bosniens und der Herzegowina in den Forschungen nach dem Zweiten Weltkrieg*, Munich, 1978.

Dzambo, Joso, *Buchwesen in Bosnien und der Herzegowina (1800-1878): Zum Problem der Lesersoziologie*, Frankfurt/M., 1985.

Eicher, Joachim, 'Die Wahlen in Bosnien-Herzegowina und ihre Durchführung', in: *Südosteuropa*, 3-4, 1997.

——, 'Kuda ides Mostar?: Mostar in der Ära Koschnik', in: *Südosteuropa-Mitteilungen*, 3, 1997.

——, 'Die Zukunftsperspektiven Bosnien-Herzegowinas', in: *Südosteuropa*, 1-2, 1997.

Elvert, Jürgen (ed.), *Der Balkan: Eine europäische Krisenregion in Geschichte und Gegenwart*, Stuttgart, 1997.

Farkas, Richard, 'Failure and Fantasy in the Yugoslav Successor States', in: Raju G. Thomas and Richard H. Friman (eds.), *The South Slav Conflict: History, Ethnicity, and Nationalism*, New York, 1996.

Fine, John V., 'The Medieval and Ottoman Roots of Modern Bosnian Society', in: Mark Pinson (ed.), *The Muslims of Bosnia-Hercegovina: Their Historic Development from the Middle Ages to the Dissolution of Yugoslavia*, Cambridge (Mass.), 1994.

——, *The Bosnian Church: A New Interpretation, A Study of the Bosnian Church and Its Place in State and Society from the 13th to the 15th Centuries*, New York/London, 1975.

See also: Donia

Freidenreich, Harriet P., *The Jews of Yugoslavia*, Philadelphia, 1979.

Geiss, Imanuel, 'Der Balkan als historische Konfliktregion', in: Jürgen Elvert (ed.), *Der Balkan: Eine europäische Krisenregion in Geschichte und Gegenwart*, Stuttgart, 1997.

——, 'Nation und Nationalismus in der modernen Welt', in: Dietrich Schlegel (ed.): *Der neue Nationalismus: Ursachen, Chancen, Gefahren*, Schwalbach/Ts., 1994.

Gervasi, Sean, 'Vietnam II: Die USA auf dem Balkan', in: *konkret*, 9, 1995.

Giersch, Carsten, 'Der Jugoslawien-Konflikt als Testfall europäischer Sicherheit', in: *Aus Politik und Zeitgeschichte*, 30-1, 1997.

Goati, Vladimir, 'The Disintegration of Yugoslavia: The Role of Political Elites', in: *Nationalities Papers*, 25 (1997), 3.

Goette, Julia, 'Von The Hague bis Dayton: Die internationale Staatengemeinschaft auf der Suche nach einer Lösung des dritten Balkankrieges (1991-1996)', in: Jürgen Elvert (ed.), *Der Balkan: Eine europäische Krisenregion in Geschichte und Gegenwart*, Stuttgart, 1997.

Golitzin, Alexander, 'Echoes of Another Christendom', in: Raju G. Thomas and Richard H. Friman (eds.), *The South Slav Conflict: History, Ethnicity, and Nationalism*, New York, 1996.

Gosztonyi, Kristof, 'Nationalitätenkonflikte in ehemalig sozialistischen Ländern: Ein spieltheoretisches Modell', in: *Osteuropa*, 43 (1993), 7.

Grothusen, Klaus-Dieter (ed.), *Südosteuropa-Handbuch*, Vol. 1, Jugoslawien, Göttingen, 1975.

Gumpel, Werner and Schönfeld, Roland (eds.), *Südosteuropa: Politik und Wirtschaft, Südosteuropa Jahrbuch*, Vol. 16, Munich, 1986.

Gutman, Roy, *Augenzeuge des Völkermords: Reportagen aus Bosnien*, Göttingen, 1994.

Haberl, Othmar N., 'Religion, Nationalismus und Bürgerkrieg in Bosnien', in: Dietrich Schlegel (ed.), *Der neue Nationalismus: Ursachen, Chancen*, Gefahren, Schwalbach/Ts., 1994.

Hadzijahic, Muhamed, 'Die Anfänge der nationalen Entwicklung in Bosnien und der Herzegowina', in: *Südost-Forschungen*, 21, 1962.

Hafner, Stanislaus, 'Kirche, Staatlichkeit, Sprache und Volkstum im Vielvölkerstaat und das Entstehen der slowenischen Nationalkultur', in: Christian Hannick (ed.), *Sprachen und Nationen im Balkanraum: Die historischen Bedingungen der Entstehung der heutigen Nationalsprachen*, Vienna, 1987.

Hamm, Josef, 'Randbemerkungen zur Entstehung und Entwicklung der serbokroatischen Schriftsprache', in: Christian Hannick (ed.), *Sprachen und Nationen im Balkanraum: Die historischen Bedingungen der Entstehung der heutigen Nationalsprachen*, Vienna, 1987.

Hannick, Christian (ed.), *Sprachen und Nationen im Balkanraum: Die historischen Bedingungen der Entstehung der heutigen Nationalsprachen*, Vienna, 1987.

Hauptmann, Ferdinand, *Die österreichisch-ungarische Herrschaft in Bosnien und Hercegowina, 1878-1918: Wirtschaftspolitik und Wirtschaftsentwicklung*, Graz, 1983.

Hayden, Robert M., 'The Constitution of the Federation of Bosnia and Herzegovina: An Imaginary Constitution for an Illusionary "Federation"', in: *Balkan Forum* 2 (1994), 3.

Heywood, Colin, 'Bosnia Under Ottoman Rule, 1463-1800', in: Mark Pinson (ed.), *The Muslims of Bosnia-Hercegovina: Their Historic Development from the Middle Ages to the Dissolution of Yugoslavia*, Cambridge (Mass.), 1994.

Höpken, Wolfgang, 'Die jugoslawischen Kommunisten und die bosnischen Muslime', in: Andreas Kappeler, Gerhardt Simon and Georg Brunner (eds.), *Die Muslime in der Sowjetunion und in Jugoslawien: Identität, Politik, Widerstand*, Cologne, 1989.

Hösch, Edgar, *Geschichte der Balkanländer: Von der Frühzeit bis zur Gegenwart*, Munich, 1995.

Hösch, Edgar and Seewann, Gerhard (eds.), *Aspekte ethnischer Identität*, Munich, 1991.

Holbrooke, Richard, *Meine Mission: Vom Krieg zum Frieden in Bosnien*, Munich/Zürich 1998 [orig.: *To End A War*, New York, 1998].

Hondius, Frits W., *The Yugoslav Community of Nations*, The Hague, 1968.

Hummer, Waldermar and Peter Hilpold, 'Die Jugoslawien-Krise als ethnischer Konflikt', in: *Europa-Archiv*, 4, 1992.

Ipsen, Gunther, 'Wachstum und Gliederung der Bevölkerung Jugoslawiens', in: Werner Markert (ed.), *Osteuropa-Handbuch: Jugoslawien*, Vol. I, Cologne/Graz, 1954.

Irwin, Zachary T., 'The Islamic Revival and the Muslims of Bosnia-Hercegovina', in: *East European Quarterly*, 17 (1984), 4.

Islamic Studies, 36 (1997), 2-3: Special Issue: *Islam in the Balkans* (Islamabad).

Ivekovic, Rada, 'The Bosnian Tangle: Is Bosnia-Herzegovina Multicultural?', in: Mushirul Hasan (ed.), *Islam, Communities and the Nation: Muslim Identities in South Asia and Beyond*, Delhi, 1998.

Ivanov, Andrei, 'Zweideutige Prioritäten: US-amerikanische Außenpolitik und der Krieg auf dem Balkan (bis Sommer 1993)', in: *Südosteuropa*, 3-4, 1994.

Izetbegovic, Alija, *Islam Between East and West*, New York, 1984.

——, *The Islamic Declaration*, n.p.; 1970 (*Islamska deklaracija*, Sarajevo, 1990).

Jacobson, Carl G., 'War Crimes in the Balkans: Media Manipulation, Historical Amnesia, and Subjective Morality', in: Raju G. Thomas, and Richard H. Friman (eds.), *The South Slav Conflict: History, Ethnicity, and Nationalism*, New York, 1996.

Janke, Peter (ed.), *Ethnic and Religious Conflicts: Europe and Asia*, Aldershot et al., 1994.

Kadritzke, Niels, 'Die überraschende Wiederkehr des Nationalismus in die Geschichte', in: *Prokla*, 87, 1992.

Kann, Robert A., *Geschichte des Habsburgerreiches 1526-1918* (3rd edn.), Vienna, 1993 (*History of the Habsburg Empire 1526-1918*, Berkeley/ Los Angeles, 1974).

Kapidzic, Hamdija, *Der Aufstand in der Hercegovina im Jahre 1882*, Graz, 1972.

Kaplan, Robert, *Die Geister des Balkan: Eine Reise durch die Geschichte und Politik eines Krisengebietes*, Düsseldorf/Vienna, 1994 (*Balkan Ghosts*, New York, 1993).

Kappeler, Andreas, Gerhardt Simon and Georg Brunner (eds.), *Die Muslime in der Sowjetunion und in Jugoslawien: Identität, Politik, Widerstand*, Cologne, 1989.

Karcic, Fikret, 'Islamic Revival in the Balkans 1970-1992', in: *Islamic Studies*, 36 (1997), 2-3: Special Issue: *Islam in the Balkans* (Islamabad).

Karger, Adolf, 'Der gescheiterte Vance-Owen-Plan und die ethnisch-geographischen Struk-turen von Bosnien-Herzegowina', in: *Osteuropa*, 43 (1993), 8.

Karic, Enes, 'Islam in Contemporary Bosnia: A Personal Statement', in: *Islamic Studies*, 36 (1997), 2-3: Special Issue: *Islam in the Balkans* (Islamabad).

Karpat, Kemal H., 'The Balkan National States and Nationalism: Image and Reality', in: *Islamic Studies*, 36 (1997), 2-3: Special Issue: *Islam in the Balkans* (Islamabad).

——, 'The Ottoman Ethnic and Confessional Legacy in the Middle East', in: Milton J. Esman and Itamar Rabinovich (eds.), *Ethnicity, Pluralism and the State in the Middle East*, Ithaca/London, 1988.

Katicic, Radoslav, 'Serbokroatische Sprache—Serbisch-kroatischer Sprachenstreit', in: Reinhard Lauer and Werner Lehfeld (eds.), *Das jugoslawische Desaster: Historische, sprachliche und ideologische Hintergründe*, Wiesbaden: 1995.

Kessler, Wolfgang, 'Jugoslawien—der erste Versuch: Vorgeschichte und Gründung des "Ersten Jugoslawien"', in: Jürgen Elvert (ed.), *Der Balkan: Eine europäische Krisenregion in Geschichte und Gegenwart*, Stuttgart, 1997.

——, *Politik, Kultur und Gesellschaft in Kroatien und Slawonien in der ersten Hälfte des 19. Jahrhundert*, Munich, 1981.

Kettani, M. Ali, 'Post-Ottoman Islamic Educational Institutions in the Balkans', in: *Islamic Studies*, 36 (1997), 2-3: Special Issue: *Islam in the Balkans* (Islamabad).

Khan, Mujeeb R., 'Bosnia-Herzegovina and the Politics of Religion and Genocide in the "New World Order"', in: *Islamic Studies*, 36 (1997), 2-3: Special Issue: *Islam in the Balkans* (Islamabad).

Kind, Christian, *Krieg auf dem Balkan: Geschichte—Hintergründe—Motive*, Zürich, 1994.

Klinar, Peter, 'Ethnic Conflicts in Postsocialist Societies in Europe: The Case of Yugoslavia and Slovenia', in: Silvo Devetak, Sergej Flere and Gerhard Seewann (eds.), *Kleine Nationen und Ethnische Minderheiten im Umbruch Europas* (*Small Nations and Ethnic Minorities in an Emerging Europe*), Munich, 1993.

——, 'National and Interethnic Conflicts in Yugoslavia', in: *Ethnicity and Nationalism in Central Europe*, Krakow, 1990.

Knezevic, Anto, 'Alija Izetbegovic's *Islamic Declaration*: Its Substance and Its Western Reception', in: *Islamic Studies*, 36 (1997), 2-3: Special Issue: *Islam in the Balkans* (Islamabad).

——, 'Social Background of a Hermeneutics of the Qur'an: The Case of Bosnia', in: *see above*; also in *Islamic Studies*, 36 (1997), 2-3.

Knesevic, Gordana, 'Why Bosnia Should Be Saved', in: *Why*, 4, 1992.

Komlosy, Andrea, Hannes Hofbauer and Jürgen Elsässer (eds.), *Krisenherd Europa: Nationalismus, Regionalismus, Krieg*, Göttingen, 1994.

Kornrumpf, Hans-Jürgen, 'Scheriat und christlicher Staat: Die Muslime in Bosnien und in den europäischen Nachfolgestaaten des Osmanischen Reiches', in: *Saeculum Augustum* (1984).

Koschnik, Hans and Jens Schneider, *Brücke über die Neretva: Der Wiederaufbau von Mostar*, Munich, 1995.

Krizan, Mojmir, 'Der widerspenstige "Friedensprozeß": Bosnien und Herzegowina zwei Jahre nach der Unterzeichnung des Friedensabkommens von Dayton', in: *Osteuropa*, 1, 1998.

——, 'Nationalismen in Jugoslawien: Von postkommunistischer, nationaler Emanzipation zum Krieg', in: *Osteuropa*, 2, 1992.

Kumar, Radha, 'Bosnia in the Annals of Partition: From Divide and Rule to Divide and Quit', in: Mushirul Hasan (ed.), *Islam, Communities and the Nation: Muslim Identities in South Asia and Beyond*, Delhi: 1998.

Kumin, Judith, 'Rückkehr der Flüchtlinge nach Bosnien-Herzegowina', in: *Südosteuropa-Mitteilungen,* 2, 1997.

Lauer, Reinhard, 'Das Wüten der Mythen: Kritische Anmerkungen zur serbischen heroischen Dichtung', in: Reinhard Lauer and Werner Lehfeld (eds.): *Das jugoslawische Desaster: Historische, sprachliche und ideologische Hintergründe*, Wiesbaden, 1995.

——, *Vuk Karadzic und seine Zeit*, Göttingen, 1987.

Lauer, Reinhard and Lehfeld, Werner (eds.), *Das jugoslawische Desaster: Historische, sprachliche und ideologische Hintergründe*, Wiesbaden, 1995.

Lazanski, Miroslav, 'Die Muslime haben gelernt, Krieg zu führen: Angaben über die Stärke der bosnischen Streitkräfte', in: *Osteuropa-Archiv*, 10, 1993.

Leigh, David and Ed Vulliamy, *Sleaze—The Corruption of Parliament*, London, 1997.

Lemberg, Hans, 'Ethnische Säuberung: Ein Mittel zur Lösung von Nationalitätenproblemen?', in: *Aus Politik und Zeitgeschichte*, B46, 1992.

Lendvai, Paul, 'Yugoslavia without Yugoslaves: The Roots of the Crisis', in: *International Affairs*, 67 (1991), 2 ('Jugoslawien ohne Jugoslawen: Die Wurzeln der Staatskrise', in: *Europa-Archiv*, 19, 1990).

Libal, Wolfgang, 'Glanz und Elend der Bosnien-Berichterstattung', in: *Europäische Rundschau*, 2, 1994.

——, *Das Ende Jugoslawiens: Chronik einer Selbstzerstörung*, Vienna/Zürich, 1991.

Lopasic, Alexander, 'Bosnian Muslims: A Search for Identity', in: *British Society for Middle Eastern Studies Bulletin*, 8 (1981), 2.

Lukic, Reneo and Allen Lynch, 'U.S. Policy Towards Yugoslavia: From Differentiation to Disintegration', in: Raju G. Thomas and Richard H. Friman (eds.), *The South Slav Conflict: History, Ethnicity, and Nationalism*, New York, 1996.

Malcolm, Noel, *Kosovo: A Short History*, New York, 1998.

——, *Bosnia: A Short History* (2nd edn.), London, 1996 (Geschichte Bosniens, Frankfurt/M., 1996).

Manoschek, Walter, *'Serbien ist judenfrei': Militärische Besatzungspolitik und Judenvernichtung in Serbien 1941/42*, Munich, 1993.

Markert, Werner (ed.), *Osteuropa-Handbuch: Jugoslawien*, Vol. I, Cologne/Graz, 1954.

McCarthy, Justin, 'Ottoman Bosnia, 1800-1878', in: Mark Pinson (ed.), *The Muslims of Bosnia-Hercegovina: Their Historic Development from the Middle Ages to the Dissolution of Yugoslavia*, Cambridge (Mass.), 1994.

Meier, Viktor, *Wie Jugoslawien verspielt wurde*, Munich, 1995.

——, 'Bosnien und seine Muslime als Sonderproblem des Vielvölkerstaates', in: Roland Schönfeld (ed.), *Nationalitätenprobleme in Südosteuropa*, Munich, 1987.

Miedlig, H.-Michael, 'Zur Frage der Identität der Muslime in Bosnien-Herzegowina', in: Südosteuropa im 19. und 20. Jahrhundert: Fremde Wege – *Eigene Wege (Berliner Jahrbuch für osteuropäische Geschichte)*, Berlin, 1994.

——, 'Gründe und Hintergründe der aktuellen Nationalitätenkonflikte in den jugoslawischen Ländern', in: *Südosteuropa*, 2, 1992.

Mikic, Zivko M., 'Die Ethnogenese der Slawen aus der Sicht der Anthropologie', in: Wolfram Bernhard and Anneliese Kandler-Palsson, *Ethnogenese europäischer Völker*, Stuttgart/New York, 1986.

——, 'Die Ethnogenese der Südslawen unter Berücksichtigung von West- und Ostslawen aus der Sicht der Anthropologie', in: *see above.*

Milojevic, Aleksa, 'National and Economic Development in Bosnia and Herzegovina', in: Silvo Devetak, Sergej Flere and Gerhard Seewann, (eds.), *Kleine Nationen und Ethnische Minderheiten im Umbruch Europas (Small Nations and Ethnic Minorities in an Emerging Europe)*, Munich, 1993.

Mønnesland, Svein, *Land ohne Wiederkehr: Ex-Jugoslawien, Die Wurzeln des Krieges*, Klagenfurt/Celovec, 1997.

Moreau, Odile, 'The Recruitment of Bosnian Soldiers During the 19th Century (1826-1876)', in: *Islamic Studies*, 36 (1997), 2-3: Special Issue: *Islam in the Balkans* (Islamabad).

Morokvasic, Mirjana, 'Krieg, Flucht und Vertreibung im ehemaligen Jugoslawien', in: *Demographie aktuell*, 2, 1993.

Müller, Stefan, 'Menschenrechte in Bosnien-Herzegowina: Die Situation in der Republika Srpska (RS) und das Verhalten der internationalen Staatengemeinschaft', in: *Südosteuropa*, 5-6, 1997.

——, 'Politische und gesellschaftliche Bedingungen einer Rückkehr nach Bosnien-Herzegowina', in: *Südosteuropa*, 9-10, 1995.

Neudeck, Rupert, 'Menschenrechtstragödien in Bosnien-Herzegowina', in: *Aus Politik und Zeitgeschichte*, 37, 1993.

Ocvirk, Drago, 'Les religions dans les relations interéthniques: Le cas Yougoslave', in: Silvo Devetak, Sergej Flere and Gerhard Seewann (eds.), *Kleine Nationen und Ethnische Minderheiten im Umbruch Europas (Small Nations and Ethnic Minorities in an Emerging Europe)*, Munich, 1993.

Oeter, Stefan, 'Bosnien und Europa: Ein Unfall der Völkerrechtsordnung?', in: Nenad Stefanov and Michael Werz (eds.), *Bosnien und Europa: Die Ethnisierung der Gesellschaft*, Frankfurt/M., 1994.

Okey, Robin, 'State, Church and Nation in the Serbo-Croat speaking Lands of the Habsburg Monarchy, 1850-1914', in: Donal A. Kerr, (Hg:): Religion, State and Ethnic Groups, Vol. II: *Comparative Studies on Governments and Non-dominant Ethnic Groups in Europe, 1850-1940,* New York, 1992.

Oschlies, Wolf, 'Unbefriedeter Balkan?: Mythen und Mächte, kämpfe und Komplexe in Europas Süden', in: Tod durch Bomben (Ergebnisse der internationalen State-of-Peace Konferenz); in: *DIALOG, Beiträge zur Friedensforschung*, Vol. 28, 1-2, 1995.

——, 'Ursachen des Krieges in Ex-Jugoslawien', in: *Aus Politik und Zeitgeschichte,* B37, 1993.

Owen, David, *Balkan-Odyssee,* Munich/Vienna, 1996.

Paasch, Rolf, 'Die halbherzige Intervention: Lektion aus dem Bosnien. Krieg', in: *Internationale Politik*, 7, 1997.

Parin, Paul, 'Das Lügenarsenal des Westens: Die Produktion falschen Bewußtseins zum Zweck der Legitimierung von Politik', in: Nenad Stefanov and Michael Werz (eds.), *Bosnien und Europa: Die Ethnisierung der Gesellschaft*, Frankfurt/M., 1994.

Pasic, Najdan, 'Factors in the Formation of Nations in the Balkans and Among the South Slavs', in: *International Social Science Journal*, 23, 1971.

Pavicic, Darko, 'Die schwerste Prüfung in unserer Geschichte', in: *Osteuropa-Archiv*, 2, 1993.

Pavkovic, Aleksandar, 'Anticipating the Disintegration', in: *Nationalities Papers*, 25 (1997), 3.

Pellet, Alain, 'The Opinions of the Badinter Arbitration Committee: A Second Breath for the Self-Determination of Peoples', in: *European Journal of International Law*, 3 (1992), 1.

Perry, Duncan M., 'Crisis in the Making? Macedonia and Its Neighbours', in: *Südost-europa*, 1-2, 1994.

Pinjuh, Ivica, 'A Golden Lillies', in: *Why*, 4, 1992.

Pinson, Mark (ed.), *The Muslims of Bosnia-Hercegovina: Their Historic Development from the Middle Ages to the Dissolution of Yugoslavia*, Cambridge (Mass.), 1994.

——, 'The Muslims of Bosnia-Herzegovina Under Austro-Hungarian Rule, 1878-1918', in: *see above.*

Popov, Nebojsa, 'Kriegerischer Frieden: Annäherung an ein Verständnis des Krieges in Bosnien-Herzegowina', in: Stefanov, Nenad and Werz, Michael (eds.), *Bosnien und Europa: Die Ethnisierung der Gesellschaft*, Frankfurt/M., 1994.

Popovic, Alexandar, 'The Muslim Culture in the Balkans (16th-18th Centuries)', in: *Islamic Studies*, 36 (1997), 2-3: Special Issue: *Islam in the Balkans* (Islamabad).

——, *Les Musulmans des Balkans à l'époque post-ottomane: Histoire et politique*, Istanbul, 1994.

——, *Les Musulmans yugoslaves (1945-89): Médiateurs et métaphores*, Lausanne, 1990.

See also: Clayer.

Popovic, Sanya, 'Debating Operation Quagmire Storm: U.S. Crisis Management in Bosnia', in: Raju G. Thomas and Richard H. Friman, (eds.), *The South Slav Conflict: History, Ethnicity, and Nationalism*, New York, 1996.

Poulton, Hugh, *The Balkans: Minorities and States in Conflict*, London, 1991.

Promitzer, Christian, 'Die Einebnung der Vielfalt: Nationen und Nationalismus in Bosnien-Herzegowina und im ehemaligen Jugolsa Vienna', in: Nenad Stefanov and Michael Werz (eds.), *Bosnien und Europa: Die Ethnisierung der Gesellschaft*, Frankfurt/M., 1994.

Purivata, Atif, 'On the National Phenomenon of the Moslems of Bosnia-Hercegovina', in: Dusan Blagojevic (ed.), *Nations and Nationalities of Yugoslavia*, Belgrad, 1974.

——, *Jugoslavenska muslimanska organizacija u politickom zivotu Kraljevine Srba, Hrvata I Slovenaca*, Sarajevo, 1974.

Radan, Peter, 'The Badinter Arbitration Commission and the Partition of Yugoslavia', in: *Nationalities Papers*, 25 (1997), 3.

Ramet, Pedro, 'Die Muslime Bosniens als Nation', in: Andreas Kappeler, Gerhardt Simon and Georg Brunner (eds.), *Die Muslime in der Sowjetunion und in Jugoslawien: Identität, Politik, Widerstand*, Cologne, 1989.

——, *Nationalism and Federalism in Yugoslavia, 1963-1983*, Bloomington, 1984.

Ramet, Sabrina P., 'Primordial Ethnicity or Modern Nationalism: The Case of Yugoslavia's Muslims Reconsidered', in: *South Slav Journal*, 13 (1990), 1-2.

Reißmüller, Johan-Georg, *Die bosnische Tragödie*, Stuttgart, 1993.

——, *Der Krieg vor unserer Haustür: Hintergründe der kroatischen Tragödie*, Stuttgart, 1992.

Reiter, Norbert, *see Literature Theory.*

Reljic, Dusan, 'A Mediator Between the Mass and the Power: Media and National Chauvinism', in: *Balkan Forum*, 2 (1994), 3.

Remington, Robin A., 'Yugoslavia and the Internationalization of the Balkan Conflict', in: Raju G. Thomas and Richard H. Friman (eds.), *The South Slav Conflict: History, Ethnicity, and Nationalism*, New York, 1996.

Reuter, Jens, 'Die politische Entwicklung in Bosnien-Herzegowina: Zusammenwachsen der Entitäten oder nationale Abkapselung?', in: *Südosteuropa*, 3-4, 1998.

——, 'Die Bosnisch-Kroatische Föderation: Künstliches Gebilde oder lebensfähiger Staat?', in: *Südosteuropa*, 3-4, 1997.

——, 'Bosnien nach der Wahl', in: *Südosteuropa Mitteilungen*, 36, 1996.

——, 'Interessenlage und Kriegsziele der Konfliktparteien im ehemaligen Jugoslawien', in: *Südosteuropa*, 1, 1996.

——, 'Jugoslawien: Versagen der internationalen Gemeinschaft?', in: *Südosteuropa*, 6, 1993.

——, 'Jugoslawien im Umbruch', in: *Aus Politik und Zeitgeschichte*, B14, 1992.

——, 'Die politische Entwicklung in Bosnien-Herzegowina', in: *Südosteuropa*, 41, 1992.

——, 'Der Bürgerkrieg in Jugoslawien: Kriegsmüdigkeit, Kriegspsychose und Wirtschaftsverfall', in: *Europa-Archiv*, 24, 1991.

——, 'Die Entstehung der jugoslawischen Krise und ihre Internationalisierung', in: *Südosteuropa*, 7-8, 1991.

——, 'Prioritäten der jugoslawischen Außenpolitik: EFTA und/oder EG?', in: *Südosteuropa*, 1, 1991.

Reuter-Hendrichs, Irena, *Der Islam in Jugoslawien*, Ebenhausen, 1988.

Riedel, Sabine, 'Die Politisierung Islamischer Geschichte und Kultur', in: *Südosteuropa*, 11/1997.

——, 'Sprach- und Nationalbewußtsein in den Balkanländern im 19 und 20 Jahrhundert', in: Jürgen Elvert (ed.), *Der Balkan: Eine europäische Krisenregion in Geschichte und Gegenwart*, Stuttgart, 1997.

Roberts, Walter R., 'The Tragedy in Yugoslavia Could Have Been Averted', in: Raju G. Thomas and Richard H. Friman (eds.), *The South Slav Conflict: History, Ethnicity, and Nationalism*, New York, 1996.

Roger, V. Paxton, 'Identity and Consciousness: Culture and Politics Among the Habsburg Serbs in the 18th Century', in: Banac Ivo, Ackermann G. John and Szporluk Roman (eds.), *Nation and Ideology: Essays in Honor of Wayne S. Vucinich*, Boulder/New York, 1981.

Rütten, Ursula, 'Die Stadt spiegelt sich im Menschen wie Wasser: Notizen zur Entwicklung und Vernichtung urbaner Lebensräume und zur Litanei des Hasses in Jugoslawien', in: Nenad Stefanov and Michael Werz (eds.), *Bosnien und Europa: Die Ethnisierung der Gesellschaft*, Frankfurt/M., 1994.

Sacirbey, Muhamed, 'What Hopes for Bosnian Multiculturalism?', in: *UBSD-Newsletter*, Sept.-Oct. 1994.

Salihagic, Suljaga, *Mi bos. herc. muslimani u krilu jugoslovenske zajednice*, Banja Luka, 1940.

Sarac, Zajim, *Yugoslav Muslims' Message to India*, Bombay, 1947.

Schissel, Gregory A., 'Contemporary Roman Catholic-Muslim Relations', in: Raju G. Thomas and Richard H. Friman (eds.), *The South Slav Conflict: History, Ethnicity, and Nationalism*, New York, 1996.

Schloer, Wolfgang F., 'Germany and the Breakup of Yugoslavia', in: Raju G. Thomas and Richard H. Friman (eds.), *The South Slav Conflict: History, Ethnicity, and Nationalism*, New York, 1996.

Schödl, Günter, 'Südosteuropa im 19. und 20. Jahrhundert: Fremde Wege – Eigene Wege', in: *Berliner Jahrbuch für osteuropäische Geschichte*, Berlin, 1994.

——, 'Die Dauer des Nationalen: Zur Entwicklungsgeschichte des "neuen" Nationalismus im östlichen Europa', in: Heinrich-August Winkler and Hartmut Kaelble (eds.), *Nationalismus–Nationalitäten–Supranationalität*, Stuttgart, 1993.

——, 'Nationsbildung und Minderheitenexistenz', in: Edgar Hösch and Gerhard Seewann (eds.), *Aspekte ethnischer Identität: Ergebnisse des Forschungsprojekts 'Deutsche und Magyaren als nationale Minderheiten im Donauraum'*, Munich, 1991.

——, *Kroatische Nationalpolitik und 'Jugoslavenstvo': Studien zu nationaler Integration und regionaler Politik in Kroatien-Dalmatien am Beginn des 20 Jahrhunderts*, Munich, 1990b.

——, *Formen und Grenzen des Nationalen: Beiträge zu nationaler Integration und Nationalismus im östlichen Europa*, Erlangen, 1990a.

Schönfeld, Roland (ed.), *Nationalitätenprobleme in Südosteuropa*, Munich, 1987.

Seewann, Gerhard (ed.), *Minderheiten als Konfliktpotential in Ostmittel- und Südosteuropa*, Munich, 1995.

——, Prologue, in: *see above*.

——, 'Die Ethnostruktur der Länder Südosteuropas aufgrund der beiden letzten Volkszählungen im Zeitraum 1977-1992', in: *Südosteuropa*, 1, 1993.

—— (ed.), *Minderheitenfragen in Südosteuropa*, Munich, 1992.

See also: Hösch.

Sekelj, Laslo, *Yugoslavia: The Process of Disintegration*, Boulder/New York, 1993.

Sergij, Vilfan (ed.), *Ethnic Group Studies*, Ljubliana, 1988.

Seton-Watson, Robert W., *see Literature Theory.*

Shaw, Stanford J. and Ezel K. Shaw, *History of the Ottoman Empire and Modern Turkey*, 2 vols., Cambridge et al., 1977.

Silber, Laura and Alan Little, *The Death of Yugoslavia*, London, 1995.

Solioz, Christoph, 'Bosnien und Herzegowina zwischen Abhängigkeit und Selbstverantwortung', in: *Südosteuropa Mitteilungen*, 42 (2002), 4.

Somel, Selcuk A., 'Ottoman Islamic Education in the Balkans in the Ninteenth Century', in: *Islamic Studies*, 36 (1997), 2-3: Special Issue: *Islam in the Balkans* (Islamabad).

Spahic, Ibrahim, 'Declaration: City Assembly of Sarajevo (Sarajevo 19.04.1992)', in: *Why*, 4, 1992.

Stavrianos, L.S., *The Balkans since 1453*, New York, 1958.

Stefanov, Nenad and Michael Werz (eds.), *Bosnien und Europa: Die Ethnisierung der Gesellschaft*, Frankfurt/M., 1994.

Steindorff, Ludwig, 'Von der Konfession zur Nation: Die Muslime in Bosnien-Herzegowina', in: *Südosteuropa-Mitteilungen*, 4, 1997.

Stingl, Josef, 'Südosteuropa ist heute überall', in: Werner Gumpel and Roland Schönfeld (eds.), *Südosteuropa: Politik und Wirtschaft, Südosteuropa Jahrbuch*, Vol. 16, Munich, 1986.

Stloukal, Milan, 'Die Ethnogenese der Westslawen aus der Sicht der Anthropologie', in: Wolfram Bernhard and Anneliese Kandler-Palsson, *Ethnogenese europäischer Völker*, Stuttgart/New York, 1986.

Struve, Karl W., 'Die Ethnogenese der Slawen aus der Sicht der Vor- und Frühgeschichte', in: Wolfram Bernhard and Anneliese Kandler-Palsson, *Ethnogenese europäischer Völker*, Stuttgart/New York, 1986.

Sugar, Peter F. (ed.), *Ethnic Diversity and Conflict in Eastern Europe*, Santa Barbara, 1980.

——, *Southeastern Europe under Ottoman Rule 1354-1804*, Seattle/London, 1977.

Sundhaussen, Holm, 'Nation und Nationalstaat auf dem Balkan: Konzepte und Konsequenzen im 19 und 20 Jahrhundert', in: Jürgen Elvert (ed.), *Der Balkan*, Stuttgart, 1997.

——, *Experiment Jugoslawien: Von der Staatsgründung bis zum Staatszerfall*, Mannheim, 1993.

——, *Geschichte Jugoslawiens 1918-1980*, Stuttgart, 1982.

——, *Der Einfluß der Herderschen Ideen auf die Nationsbildung bei den Völkern der Habsburger Monarchie*, Munich, 1973.

Suttner, Ernst C., 'Das religiöse Moment in seiner Bedeutung für Gesellschaft, Nationsbildung und Kultur Südosteuropas', in: *Südosteuropa-Mitteilungen*, 1, 1997.

Tapie, V.-L., *Die Völker unter dem Doppeladler*, Graz/Vienna/Cologne, 1975.

Taylor, John B., 'Religious Ideology and National Identity in the Balkans', in: *Islamic Studies*, 36 (1997), 2-3: Special Issue: *Islam in the Balkans* (Islamabad).

Thomas, Raju, 'History, Religion and National Identity', in: Raju G. Thomas and Richard H. Friman (eds.), *The South Slav Conflict: History, Ethnicity, and Nationalism*, New York, 1996.

——, 'Nations, States, and War', in: *see above.*

Thomas, Raju G. and Richard H. Friman (eds.), *The South Slav Conflict: History, Ethnicity, and Nationalism*, New York, 1996.

Thumann, Michael, 'Between Ambition and Paralysis: Germany's Role Towards Yugoslavia', in: *Nationalities Papers*, 25 (1997), 3.

Tibi, Bassam, *see Literature on Islam.*

Tito, Josip B., 'Sur le nationalisme et l'internationalisme', Belgrad, 1948 [excerpts in: Peter Alter (ed.), *Nationalismus*, Munich, 1994].

——, 'A Fighter for Peace', in: Rafiq Zakaria (ed.), *A Study of Nehru*, Calcutta, et al., 1997 (1989).

'Tod durch Bomben (Ergebnisse der internationalen State-of-Peace Konferenz)', in: *DIALOG, Beiträge zur Friedensforschung*, Vol. 28, 1-2, 1995.

Todorovic, Ilija I., 'Regional Economic Nationalism in the Former Yugoslavia', in: Raju G. Thomas and Richard H. Friman (eds.), *The South Slav Conflict: History, Ethnicity, and Nationalism*, New York, 1996.

Tokic, Seifudin, 'Ethnische Ideologie und Eroberungskrieg: Zur Kritik der Aufteilung Bosnien-Herzegowinas', in: Nenad Stefanov and Michael Werz (eds.), *Bosnien und Europa: Die Ethnisierung der Gesellschaft*, Frankfurt/M., 1994.

——, 'What Hopes for Bosnian Multiculturalism?', in: *UBSD Newsletter*, Sept.-Oct. 1994.

Tomac, Zdravko, 'Szenarien zur Entwicklung der politischen Lage im ehemaligen Jugoslawien', in: *Osteuropa-Archiv*, 2, 1993.

Tomasevic, George V., 'The Battle of Kosovo and the Serbian Church', in: Wayne S. Vucinich and Thomas Emmert (eds.), *Kosovo: Legacy of a Medieval Battle*, Minneapolis, 1989.

Tudjman, Franjo, *Irrwege der Geschichtswirklichkeit: Eine Abhandlung über die Geschichte und die Philosophie des Gewaltübels*, Zagreb, 1993.

——, *Die Nationalitätenfrage im heutigen Europa*, Bokatron, 1986 (*Nationalism in Contemporary Europe*, New York, 1981).

Trifunovska, Snezana, 'The International Involvement in the Former Yugoslavia's Dissolution and Peace Settlement', in: *Nationalities Papers*, 25 (1997), 3.

Turczynski, Emanuel, *Konfession und Nation: Zur Frühgeschichte der serbischen und rumänischen Nationsbildung*, Düsseldorf, 1976.

Ursinus, Michael, 'Zur Diskussion um "millet" im Osmanischen Reich', in: *Südosteuropa-Forschungen*, 48, 1989.

Veljak, Lino, 'The Collapse and Reconstruction of Legitimacy', in: *Nationalities Papers*, 25 (1997), 3.

Vickers, Miranda, *Serb and Albanian: A History of Kosovo*, New York, 1998.

Volle, Angelika and Wolfgang Wagner (eds.), *Der Krieg auf dem Balkan: Die Hilflosigkeit der Staatenwelt*, Bonn, 1994.

Vollmer, Johannes: 'Dayton–eine Pax Americana', in: *Europäische Rundschau*, 2, 1996.

Vucinich, Wayne S. and Thomas Emmert (eds.), *Kosovo: Legacy of a Medieval Battle*, Minneapolis, 1989.

Waardenburg, Jacques, 'Politics and Religion in the Balkans', in: *Islamic Studies*, 36 (1997), 2-3: Special Issue: *Islam in the Balkans* (Islamabad).

Wagner, Wolfgang, 'Acht Lehren aus dem Fall Jugoslawien', in: *Europa-Archiv*, 2, 1992.

Walters, Garrison, 'The Future of History in the Balkans', in: Raju G. Thomas and Richard H. Friman (eds.), *The South Slav Conflict: History, Ethnicity, and Nationalism*, New York, 1996.

Wandruszka, Adam and Peter Urbanitsch (eds.), *Die Habsburger Monarchie 1848-1918*, 6 vols., Vienna, 1973ff; Vol. 3: *Die Völker des Reiches*, 1980.

Weckbecker, Arno, 'Bye, bye Europe: Der jugoslawische Krieg in der öffentlichen Meinung der Anrainerstaaten. Oder: Zum Ansehen der internationalen Institutionen auf dem Balkan', in: Jürgen Elvert, (ed.), *Der Balkan: Eine europäische Krisenregion in Geschichte und Gegenwart*, Stuttgart, 1997.

——, 'Die politischen und ökonomischen Systeme der Nachfolgestaaten', in: *see above*.

Weithmann, Michael W. (ed.), *Balkan-Chronik: 2000 Jahre zwischen Orient und Okzident* (2nd edn.), Graz/Vienna/Cologne, 1997.

—— (ed.), *Der ruhelose Balkan: Die Konfliktregionen Südosteuropas* (2nd edn.), Munich, 1994.

——, *Der Balkan zwischen Ost und West*, in: *see above*.

'"Wenn die Kanonen donnern, schweigen die Musen": Gespräch über Intellektuelle, Bosnien und die Barbarei', in: Nenad Stefanov and Michael Werz (eds.), *Bosnien und Europa: Die Ethnisierung der Gesellschaft*, Frankfurt/M., 1994.

West, Rebecca, *Black Lamb and Grey Falcon*, Edinburgh, 1993 [1941].

Wieland, Carsten, *Syrien nach dem Irak-Krieg: Bastion gegen Islamisten oder Staat vor dem Kollaps*? Berlin, 2004 (*Syria After the Iraq War: Bastion Against Islamists or State at the Brink of Collapse*?, Seattle/London, forthcoming in 2005).

——, '"Ethnic Conflict" Undressed: Patterns of Contrast, Interests of Elites, and Clientelism of Foreign Powers in Comparative Perspective–Bosnia, India, Pakistan', in: *Nationalities Papers*, 29 (June 2001), 2.

——, Ethno-Nationalismus im neuen Europa, dpa-Sonderdienste Hintergrund, March 2001.

——, 'Vise od religije: Otimica historije i jezika radi oblikovanja "nacija" – Bosna i Indija' (More Than Religion: Hijacking History and Language to Shape "Ethnic Groups" – Bosnia and India), in: *Album* (Sarajevo), autumn edition, 2000.

——, 'Nationalstaat wider Willen: Ethnizität und Nation-building in Pakistan und Bosnien-Herzegowina', in: *iz3w*, Vol. 249, 2000 (Blätter des Informationszentrums 3. Welt).

——, 'Widersprüche auf dem Weg zum "Nationalstaat": Dogmatische und politische Spaltungslinien unter den Muslimen in Indien und Bosnien' (Contradictions on the Way to the "Nation-state": Dogmatic and Political Cleavages Among the Muslims in India and Bosnia), in: *Afrika, Asien, Lateinamerika*, No. 3, 2000.

——, *Nationalstaat wider Willen: Die Politisierung von Ethnien und die Ethnisierung der Politik, Bosnien, Indien, Pakistan*, Frankfurt-M./New York, 2000.

——, 'Izetbegovic und Jinnah: Die selektive Vereinnahmung zweier "Muslim-Führer"', in: *Südosteuropa-Mitteilungen*, 40 (2000), 2 (Izetbegovic and Jinnah: The Selective Appropriation of Two "Muslim-Leaders").

——, 'One Macedonia With Three Faces: Domestic Debates and Nation Concepts', in: *Intermarium* (internet-magazine of the Centre for

Eastern European Studies, Columbia University, New York), February 2000 [Ein Makedonien mit drei Gesichtern: Innenpolitische Debatten und Nationskonzepte, in: *Südosteuropa*, 46 (1997), 12].

——, 'Konvergenz der Kommunikationseliten oder "Kulturkonflikt"?' (Convergence of Communication Elites or "Clash of Civilizations"?), in: Ingrid Jonach (ed.), *Interkulturelle Kommunikation*, Munich, 1998.

——, 'Die aktuellen Konfliktlinien in Bosnien-Herzegowina', in: *Südosteuropa-Mitteilungen*, 35 (1995), 3.

——, 'Vielvölker-Föderation oder getrennte Schlafzimmer?', in: *Die politische Meinung*, 303 (Feb. 1995).

Wolff, Richard J. and Jörg K. Hoensch (eds.), *Catholics, the State and the European Radical Right*, New York, 1987.

Ziegengeist, Gerhard and Helmut Graßhoff (eds.), *Johann Gottfried Herder: Zur Herder-Rezeption in Ost- und Südosteuropa*, Berlin, 1978.

Zimmermann, Warren, 'The Last Ambassador: A Memoir of the Collapse of Yugoslavia', in: *Foreign Affairs*, 74 (1995), 2.

Zlatar, Zdenko, 'The Building of Yugoslavia: The Yugoslavian Idea and the First Common State of the South Slavs', in: *Nationalities Papers*, 25 (1997), 3.

Sources and Documents

'Action-Plan of the Organization of Islamic Countries Ministerial Meeting in Islamabad (13.07.1993)', in: Snezana Trifunovska (ed.), *Yugoslavia Through Documents: From its Creation to its Dissolution*, Dordrecht/Boston/London, 1994.

Christopher, Warren, 'Press Release on the Diplomatic Efforts of the United States in the Conflict in the Former Yugoslavia, Washington D.C. (Feb. 10th 1993)', in: *Europa-Archiv*, 7, 1993, D158-D161.

'Communiqué of the WEU in Bonn (Nov. 18th 1991)', in: *Europa-Archiv*, 2, 1992.

The Constitution of the Socialist Republic of Yugoslavia, Belgrad, 1974.

'Documentation of the Dayton Agreement from Nov. 21st 1995', in: *Internationale Politik*, 51 (1996), pp. 80ff.

'Declaration of the Summit Conference of the NATO Member States in Rome (Nov. 8th 1991)', in: *Europa-Archiv*, 2, 1992.

'Declaration of the Defense Ministers of the Euro-Group in the NATO in Brussels (Dec. 11th 1991)', in: *Europa-Archiv*, 2, 1992.

'EPZ (Europäische Politische Zusammenarbeit) Common Declaration (Oct. 28th 1991)', in: *Europa-Archiv*, 2, 1992.

'E.U.-Declaration on the Former Yugoslavia in Luxembourg (June 8th 1993)', in: Snezana Trifunovska (ed.), *Yugoslavia Through Documents: From its Creation to its Dissolution*, Dordrecht/Boston/London, 1994.

'Interview with Alija Izetbegovic', in: *Why*, 4, 1992.

'Interview with the Bosnian Croatian Foreign Minister Ljubijankic', in: *Südosteuropa*, 5, 1994.

'Letter from the Permanent Representative of Croatia to the United Nations Addressed to the President of the Security Council (May 10th 1993)', in: Snezana Trifunovska (ed.), *Yugoslavia Through Documents: From its Creation to its Dissolution*, Dordrecht/Boston/London, 1994.

'Overview of the Federal Constitution of Bosnia and Hercegovina', in: *Balkan Forum*, 2 (1994), 2.

Owen, David, Balkan-Odyssee, Munich/Vienna, 1996 [including CD-rom with documents on the process of the negotiations about Yugoslavia (Dayton-Agreement)].

'Owen/Stoltenberg-Plan', in: Dokumente, *Europa-Archiv*, 7, 1994.

Press release of the Commission for Real Property Claims of Displaced Persons and Refugees (CRPC) and the United Nations High Commissioner for Refugees (UNHCR) titled: '61% wish to return in Bosnia and Herzegovina, despite the obstacles', 22 November 1999.

'Rape and Sexual Abuse of Serb Women, Men and Children in Areas Controlled by Croatian and Moslem Armed Formations in Bosnia and Herzegovina and Croatia 1991-1993', Serbian Council Information Center, Belgrad, 15 January 1993 (*Documents of witness accounts in front of Serb authorities, published with the names of the minute-takers, of the victims and with the respective archive numbers*).

'Resolution of the Foreign Ministers of the Islamic Conference in Karachi (25th-29th April 1993)', in: Snezana Trifunovska (ed.), *Yugoslavia Through Documents: From Its Creation to Its Dissolution*, Dordrecht/Boston/London, 1994.

Roggemann, Herwig (ed.), *Die Verfassung der SFR Jugoslawien*, Berlin, 1980.

'Statement of the Members of the Presidency of Bosnia and Herzegowina Following a Joint Decision of the Presidency to Accept the Invitation of Lord Owen to Attend a Meeting in Geneva, Zagreb (June 21st 1993)', in: Snezana Trifunovska (ed.), *Yugoslavia Through Documents: From Its Creation to Its Dissolution*, Dordrecht/Boston/London, 1994.

Trifunovska, Snezana (ed.): *Yugoslavia Through Documents: From Its Creation to Its Dissolution*, Dordrecht/Boston/London, 1994.

UBSD Newsletter, Sept.-Oct. 1994 *(Organ of the Union of Bosnian Social Democrats).*

'U.N. Resolution 824 (1993) on the Establishment of Security Zones in Bosnia-Hercegovina (May 6th 1993)', in: *Europa-Archiv*, 18, 1993.

'Vance/Owen-Plan, Dokumentation', in: *Europa-Archiv*, 48, 1993.

'The Violent Dissolution of Yugoslavia: Truth and Deceit 1991-1994', San Francisco, n.d. *(Serb propaganda).*

Volle, Angelika and Wolfgang Wagner (eds.), *Der Krieg auf dem Balkan: Die Hilflosigkeit der Staatenwelt*, Bonn, 1994 (with documents on the conflict in Yugoslavia from October 1991 till March 1994, pp. 133-263).

Why: Publication for Human Rights and Peace, Ibrahim Spahic (ed.): International Peace Centre, Sarajevo.

BIBLIOGRAPHIES

Bernath, Mathias (ed.), *Historische Bücherkunde Südosteuropa*, 3 vols., Munich, 1978 (with comments).

Bestandskatalog der Bibliothek des Südost-Instituts München, Munich, 1990.

Bibliographie d'Études Balkaniques, Académie Bulgare des Sciences (ed.), Sofia, 1968ff.

Friedman, Francine (ed.), *Yugoslavia: A Comprehensive English-Language Bibliography*, Wilmington, 1993.

Horecky, Paul L. (ed.), *Southeastern Europe: A Guide to Basic Publications*, Chicago/London, 1969 (with comments).

Horton, John J., *Yugoslavia, World Bibliographical Series*, revised and expanded edition, Oxford/Santa Barbara/Denver, 1990 (with comments).

Katalog des Schrifttums über den Donauraum, Niedersächsische Landesbibliothek Hannover (ed.), 5 vols., Hannover, 1993.

Petrovich, Michael B., *Yugoslavia: A Bibliographical Guide*, Washington D.C., 1974.

Roth, Klaus and Gabriele Wolf (eds.), *Südslavische Volkskultur (South Slavic Folk Culture): Bibliographie zur Literatur in englischer, deutscher und französischer Sprache zur bosnisch-herzegowinischen, bulgarischen, mazedonischen, montenegrinischen und serbischen Volkskultur*, Columbus (Ohio), 1994.

Saradjan, Léon (ed.), *Bibliographie Balkanique 1920-1930*, 8 vols., Paris, 1931.

World bibliographical series, Vol. 1, Yugoslavia, Oxford, 1990.

LITERATURE ON THE INDIAN SUBCONTINENT

Monographies, Anthologies and Articles

Aggarwala, R.N., *National Movement and Constitutional Development of India 1857-1984*, Delhi, 1984.

Ahmad, Aziz and von Gustave E. Grunebaum (eds.), *Muslim Self-Statement in India and Pakistan 1857-1968*, Wiesbaden, 1970.

Ahmad, Mumtaz, 'Pakistan', in: John Esposito (ed.), *The Oxford Encyclopedia of the Modern Islam World*, Oxford, 1995.

Ahmed, Akbar S., *Jinnah, Pakistan and Islamic Identity: The Search for Saladin*, London/New York, 1997.

—— (ed.), *Pakistan: The Social Sciences' Perspective*, Karachi et al., 1990.

——, *Discovering Islam: Making Sense of Muslim History and Society*, London, 1988.

Ahmed, Eqbal, 'Islam and Politics', in: M. Ashgar Khan (ed.), *Islam, Politics and the State: The Pakistan Experience*, London, 1985.

Ahmed, Feroz, 'Pakistan's Problems of National Integration', in: M. Ashgar Khan (ed.), *Islam, Politics and the State: The Pakistan Experience*, London, 1985.

Ahmed, Zafaryab, 'Maudoodi's Islamic State', in: M. Ashgar Khan (ed.), *Islam, Politics and the State: The Pakistan Experience*, London, 1985.

Alavi, Hamza, 'Ironies of History: Contradictions of the Khilafat Movement', in: Mushirul Hasan (ed.), *Islam, Communities and the Nation: Muslim Identities in South Asia and Beyond*, Delhi, 1998.

——, 'Ethnicity, Muslim Society, and the Pakistan Identity', in: Anita S. Weiss (ed.), *Islamic Reassertion in Pakistan: The Application of Islam*, Syracuse (NY), 1986.

Ali, Chaudhry M., *The Emergence of Pakistan*, London/New York, 1967, (Lahore, 1973).

Ali, Tariq, *Die Nehrus und die Gandhis: Eine indische Dynastie*, Frankfurt-M./Berlin/Vienna, 1985 (*The Nehrus and the Gandhis*, London, 1985).

Allchin, Bridget and Raymond Allchin, *The Rise of Civilization in India and Pakistan*, Cambridge, 1996.

Appadorai, A., *Indian Political Thinking: Through the Ages*, Delhi, 1992.

Athar Ali, M., 'The Evolution of the Perception of India: Akbar and Abu'l Fazl', in: *Social Scientist*, 24 (1996), 1-3.

Austin, Dennis and Anirudha Gupta, 'The Politics of Violence in India and

South Asia', in: Peter Janke (ed.), *Ethnic and Religious Conflicts: Europe and Asia*, Aldershot et al., 1994.

Aziz, K.K. (ed.), *Public Life in Muslim India 1850-1947: A Compendium of Basic Information on Political, Social, Religious, Cultural and Educational Organizations Active in Pre-Partition India*, Delhi, 1993.

——, *A History of the Idea of Pakistan*, Lahore, 1987.

——, *Islamic Modernism in India and Pakistan 1857-1964*, London, 1967.

Baird, Robert D. (ed.), *Religion in Modern India* (2nd edn.), Delhi, 1991.

Basu, Durga D., *Introduction to the Constitution of India* (17th edn.), Delhi, 1995.

Bayly, C.A., 'The Pre-history of "Communalism"?, Religious Conflicts in India 1700-1860', in: *Modern Asian Studies*, 19 (1985), 2.

Behera, Ajay D., 'Separatist Insurgencies in Pakistan', in: Verinder Grover and Ranjana Arora (eds.), *Pakistan: Fifty Years of Independence*, Vol. II: *Independence and Beyond: The Fifty Years: 1947-1997*, Delhi, 1997b.

Bhambhri, C.P., *The Indian State 1947-1998*, Delhi, 1998.

——, *The Indian State: Fifty Years*, Delhi, 1997.

——, 'New Economic Policy: Indian State and Bureaucracy', in: *Social Scientist*, 24 (1996), 1-3.

Bhattacharjee, G.P., *Renaissance and Freedom Movement in Bangladesh*, Calcutta 1973.

Birnbaum, Erwin, 'Some Theoretical and Practical Aspects of the Islamic State of Pakistan', in: Verinder Grover and Ranjana Arora (eds.), *Pakistan: Fifty Years of Independence*, Vol. I: *Towards Independence: The Pre-1947 Period*, Delhi, 1997b.

Biswas, A.K., 'The Aryan Myth', in: A. Ray and S. Mukherjee (eds.), *Historical Archaeology of India*, Delhi, 1990.

Bodansky, Yossef, *see Literature on Islam.*

Brass, Paul R. (ed.), *Riots and Pogroms*, London et al., 1996a.

——, Introduction, in: *see above.*

——, *The Politics of India Since Independence* (2nd edn.), Cambridge, 1994.

——, *Ethnicity and Nationalism: Theory and Comparison*, Delhi et al., 1991.

——, *Ethnic Groups and the State*, London, 1985b.

——, *Caste, Faction and Party in Indian Politics*, Vol. I: *Faction and Party*, Vol. II: *Election Studies*, Delhi, 1984 and 1985a.

——, 'Elite Groups, Symbol Manipulation and Ethnic Identity among the Muslims of South Asia', in: Taylor David and Yapp Malcolm (eds.), *Political Identity in South Asia*, London, 1979.

——, *Language, Religion and Politics in North India*, Cambridge, 1974.

——, 'Coalition Politics in North India', in: *American Political Science Review*, 62 (1968), 4.

Brecher, Michael, *Jawaharlal Nehru: A Political Biography*, London, 1959.

Broomfield, John H., *Elite Conflict in a Plural Society: Twentieth Century Bengal*, Berkeley, 1968.

Brown, Judith M., *Modern India: The Origins of an Asian Democracy*, Oxford, 1994.

Burke, Edmund, *see Literature on Islam.*

Chakrabarti, Dilip K., *The Archeology of Ancient Indian Cities*, Calcutta/Madras/Bombay, 1997.

Chand, Tara, *Influence of Islam on Indian Culture*, Allahabad, 1954.

Chander, Sunil, 'Congress-Raj Conflict and the Rise of the Muslim League in the Ministry Period 1937-1939', in: *Modern Asian Studies*, 21 (1987), 2.

Chandra, Bipan, 'Fundamentalism and Communalism', in: Verinder Grover and Ranjana Arora (eds.), *Pakistan: Fifty Years of Independence*, Vol. II: *Independence and Beyond: The Fifty Years: 1947-1997*, Delhi, 1997.

——, *Essays on Contemporary India*, Delhi, 1993.

——, *Communalism in Modern India* (2nd edn.), 1987.

——, 'Historians of Modern India and Communalism', in: Romila Thapar, Harbans Mukhia and Bipan Chandra (eds.), *Communalism and the Writing of Indian History*, Delhi, 1969.

Chandra, Satish, 'History Writing in Pakistan and the Two-Nation Theory', in: Verinder Grover and Ranjana Arora (eds.), *Pakistan: Fifty Years of Independence*, Vol. II: *Independence and Beyond: The Fifty Years: 1947-1997*, Delhi, 1997b.

——, *Historiography, Religion and the State in Medieval India*, Delhi, 1996.

Chandra, Sudhir, *The Oppressive Present: Literature and Social Consciousness in Colonial India*, Delhi, 1992.

Chatterjee, Partha, *The Nation and Its Fragments: Colonial and Post-Colonial Histories*, Delhi, 1995.

Chaturvedi, Jayati and Gyaneshwar Chaturvedi, 'Dharma Yudh: Communal Violence, Riots and Public Space in Ayodhya and Agra City 1990 and 1992', in: Paul R. Brass (ed.), *Riots and Pogroms*, London et al., 1996.

Chaudhuri, K.N., *Trade and Civilization in the Indian Ocean: An Economic History from the Rise of Islam to 1750*, Cambridge, 1985.

Chaudhuri, Nirad C., *The Autobiography of an Unknown Indian*, London, 1951.

Chitkara, M.G., *Mohajir's Pakistan*, Delhi, 1996.

Chowdhury, P., *The Aryans: A Modern Myth. Part I: A Story of a Treacherous Theory that Concerns Every Indian*, Delhi, 1993.

Cohn, Bernhard S., *India: Colonialism and Its Form of Knowledge: The British in India*, Delhi, 1997.

Collins, Larry and Dominique Lapierre, *Freedom at Midnight*, Delhi et al., 1976 [1997].

Copley, Antony, *Religions in Conflict: Ideology, Cultural Contact and Conversion in Late Colonial India*, Delhi, 1997.

Dalmia, Vasudha, *The Nationalization of Hindu Traditions: Bharatendu Harischandra and Ninteenth-Century Benares*, Delhi et al., 1997.

Das, Veena (ed.), *Structure and Cognition: Aspects of Hindu Caste and Ritual* (2nd edn.), Delhi, 1992.

—— (ed.), *Mirrors of Violence: Communities, Riots and Survivers in South Asia*, Delhi, 1990.

Das Gupta, Jyotindra, *Language Conflict and National Development: Group Politics and National Language Policy in India*, Bombay/Calcutta/ Madras, 1970.

Dixit, Prabha, *Communalism: A Struggle for Power*, New Delhi, 1974.

Douglas, Ian H., *Abul Kalam Azad: An Intellectual and Religious Biography*, Delhi et al., 1993.

Dua, Hans R., 'Hindi-Urdu as a Pluricentric Language', in: Michael Clyne, (ed.), *Pluricentric Languages: Differing Norms in Different Nations*, Berlin/New York, 1992.

Dumont, Louis, *Religion, Politics and History in India*, Paris/The Hague/ Mouton, 1970b.

—— *Homo Hierarchicus: The Caste System and Its Implications*, London, 1970a.

——, 'Nationalism and Communalism', in: *Contributions to Indian Sociology*, 8, 1964.

Duncan, Ronald (ed.), *The Writings of Gandhi*, Delhi, 1990.

Dutt, V.P., *India's Foreign Policy* (2nd edn.), Delhi, 1997.

Dyke van, Virginia, 'The Anti-Sikh Riots of 1984 in Delhi: Politicians, Criminals, and the Discourse of Communalism', in: Paul R. Brass, (ed.), *Riots and Pogroms*, London et al., 1996a.

Elst, Koenraad, *Negationism in India: Concealing the Record of Islam*, Delhi, 1992.

Elvert, Jürgen and Michael Salewski (eds.), *Staatenbildung in Übersee: Die Staatenwelt Lateinamerikas und Asiens*, Stuttgart, 1992.

Embree, Ainslie T. and Friedrich Wilhelm (eds.), *Indien: Geschichte des Subkontinents von der Induskultur bis zum Beginn der englischen Herrschaft, Fischer-Weltgeschichte,* Vol. 17, Frankfurt/M., 1967.

Emerson, Rupert, *see Literature Theory.*

Engineer, Ashgar A, 'India at Fifty: Fault Lines in Two-nation Theory', in: Verinder Grover and Ranjana Arora (eds.), *Pakistan: Fifty Years of Independence* Vol. II: *Independence and Beyond: The Fifty Years: 1947-1997*, Delhi, 1997.

——, 'Communalism and Communal Violence in 1995', in: Grover, Verinder and Ranjana Arora (eds.), *Pakistan: Fifty Years of Independence*, Vol. II: *Independence and Beyond: The Fifty Years: 1947-1997*, Delhi, 1997.

——, *Communalism in India: A Historical and Empirical Study*, Delhi, 1995b.

——, *Ethnic Conflict in South Asia*, Delhi, 1987.

Erdosy, George (ed.), *The Indo-Aryans of Ancient South Asia: Language, Material Culture and Ethnicity*, Delhi, 1997 [Berlin, 1995].

——, 'Language, Material, Culture and Ethnicity: Theoretical Perspectives', in: *see above.*

——, 'Preface', in: *see above.*

Esposito, John L., *see Literature on Islam.*

Flood, Gavin, *An Introduction to Hinduism*, Cambridge, 1996.

Freitag, Sandria, *Collective Action and Community*, Berkeley, 1989b.

——, 'The Roots of Muslim Separatism in South Asia', in: Edmund Burke and Ira M. Lapidus (eds.), *Islam, Politics and Social Movements*, Berkeley, 1988.

——, 'Sacred Symbol as Mobilizing Ideology: The North Indian Search for a "Hindu Community"', in: *Comparative Studies in Society and History*, 22 (1980), 4.

Frykenberg, Robert E., 'The Concept of "Majority" as a Devilish Force in the Politics of Modern Asia', in: *Journal of Commonwealth and Comparative Studies*, 15 (1987), 3.

Furnivall, J.S., *Netherlands India: A Study of Plural Economy*, Cambridge, 1939.

Gandhi, M.K., *Collected Works,* 90 vols., Delhi, 1958-84.

——, *Selected Works*, Ahmedabad, 1966.

Gandhi, Rajmohan, *Understanding the Muslim Mind*, Delhi et al., 1987.

Ganjoo, S.K., *Kashmir: History and Politics*, Delhi, 1998.

Gidwani, N.N., 'Genesis and Growth of Pakistan: Weak Ideological Foundation', in: Verinder Grover and Ranjana Arora (eds.), *Pakistan: Fifty Years of Independence*, Vol. I: *Towards Independence: The Pre-1947 Period*, Delhi, 1997b.

Gilmartin, David, 'Democracy and Islam: The Colonial Context', in: Muhammad A. Syed (ed.), *Islam and Democracy in Pakistan*, Islamabad, 1995.

——, 'The Shahidganj Mosque Incident: A Prelude to Pakistan', in: Edmund Burke and Ira M. Lapidus (eds.), *Islam, Politics and Social Movements*, Berkeley, 1988.

Golant, William, *The Long Afternoon: British India 1601-1947*, London, 1975.

Golwalkar, M.S., *We or Our Nationahood Defined*, Bombay, 1938.

Gore, M.S., 'Unity in Diversity', in: *Social Scientist*, 24 (1996), 1-3 (Delhi).

Grover, Verinder, 'The Genesis of Pakistan', in: Verinder Grover and Ranjana Arora (eds.), *Pakistan: Fifty Years of Independence*, Vol. I: *Towards Independence: The Pre-1947 Period*, Delhi, 1997b.

——, 'Enigma of an Islamic State: The Case of Pakistan', in: Verinder Grover and Ranjana Arora (eds.), *Pakistan: Fifty Years of Independence*, Vol. II: *Independence and Beyond: The Fifty Years: 1947-1997*, Delhi, 1997b.

Grover, Verinder and Ranjana Arora (eds.), *Pakistan: Fifty Years of Independence*, Vol. I: *Towards Independence: The Pre-1947 Period*; Vol. II: *Independence and Beyond: The Fifty Years: 1947-1997*; Vol. III: *50 Years of Pakistan's Independence: A Chronology of Events 1947-1997*, Delhi, 1997b.

——, *India: Fifty Years of Independence*, Vol. I: *Towards Independence: The Pre-1947 Period*; Vol. II: *Independence and Beyond: The Fifty Years: 1947-1997*; Vol. III: *50 Years of India's Independence: A Chronology of Events 1947-1997*, Delhi, 1997a.

Gupta, Dipankar, *The Context of Ethnicity: Sikh Identity in a Comparative Perspective*, Oxford/Delhi, 1997.

Haq, Mushir U., *Muslim Politics in Modern India 1857-1947*, Meerut, 1970.

Haque, Ziaul, 'Islamization of Society in Pakistan', in: M. Ashgar Khan, (ed.), *Islam, Politics and the State: The Pakistan Experience*, London, 1985.

Hasan, Mushirul (ed.), *Islam, Communities and the Nation: Muslim Identities in South Asia and Beyond*, Delhi, 1998.

——, Introduction, in: *see above*.

——, 'My Life: Fragment: Mohammed Ali's Quest for Identity in Colonial India', in: *see above*.

——, *Legacy of a Divided Nation: India's Muslims from Independence to Ayodhya*, London, 1997b.

—— (ed.), *India Partitioned: The Other Face of Freedom*, 2 vols. (2nd edn.), Delhi, 1997a.

—— (ed.), *India's Partition: Process, Strategy and Mobilization*, Oxford/ Delhi, 1994.

Hassan, Riaz, 'Islamization: An Analysis of Religious, Political and Social Change in Pakistan', in: *Middle Eastern Studies,* 21 (1985), 3.

Hay, Stephen (ed.), *Sources of Indian Tradition,* Vol. II: *Modern India and Pakistan* (2nd edn.), Delhi, 1991.

Haynes, Douglas, *Rhetoric and Ritual in Colonial India: The Shaping of Public Culture in Surat City*, Berkeley, 1991.

Heimsath, Charles H., *Indian Nationalism and Hindu Social Reform*, Princeton, 1964.

Heimsath, Charles H. and Surjit Mansing, *A Diplomatic History of Modern India*, Calcutta et al., 1971.

Hoodbhoy, Pervez A. and Abdul H. Nayyar, 'Rewriting the History of Pakistan', in: M. Ashgar Khan (ed.), *Islam, Politics and the State: The Pakistan Experience*, London, 1985.

Husain, Mahmud et al. (eds.), *A History of the Freedom Movement*, Karachi, 1961.

Hussain, Akmal, 'Pakistan: The Crisis of the State', in: M. Ashgar Khan, (ed.), *Islam, Politics and the State: The Pakistan Experience,* London, 1985.

Hyman, Anthony, 'Pakistan: Towards a Modern Muslim State?', in: Peter Janke (ed.), *Ethnic and Religious Conflicts: Europe and Asia*, Aldershot et al., 1994.

Iftikar, H. Malik, 'The Continuing Conflict in Kashmir', in: Peter Janke, (ed.), *Ethnic and Religious Conflicts: Europe and Asia*, Aldershot et al., 1994.

Ikram, S.M., *Modern Muslim India and the Birth of Pakistan*, Lahore, 1965.

——, *Muslim Civilization in India*, New York, 1964.

——, *History of Muslim Civilization in India and Pakistan*, Lahore, 1961.

Inayatullah, 'The Weak Roots of Democracy in Pakistan', in: Muhammad A. Syed (ed.), *Islam and Democracy in Pakistan*, Islamabad, 1995.

Inder Singh, Anita, *The Origins of the Partition of India, 1936-1947*, Delhi et al., 1987.

Iqbal, Javid, 'Der Islam schuf Pakistan', in: Rolf: Italiaander, *Die Herausforderung des Islam: Ein ökumenisches Lesebuch*, Göttingen, 1987.

Irfani, Suroosh, 'The Progressive Islamic Movement', in: M. Ashgar Khan, (ed.), *Islam, Politics and the State: The Pakistan Experience*, London, 1985.

Islahi, M. Aslam, 'An Insight into the Khilafat Movement', in: Verinder Grover and Ranjana Arora (eds.), *Pakistan: Fifty Years of Independence*, Vol. I: *Towards Independence: The Pre-1947 Period*, Delhi, 1997b.

Jaffrelot, Christophe, *The Hindu Nationalist Movement and Indian Politics 1925-1990s: Strategies of Identity-Building, Implantation and Mobilization*, New Delhi, 1996 (enlarged edition of: *Les nationalistes hindoues: Idélogogie, implantation et mobilisation des années 1920 aux années 1990*, Paris, 1993).

Jain, M.S., *The Aligarh Movement: Its Origin and Development*, Agra, 1965.

Jalal, Ayesha, 'Conjuring Pakistan: History as Official Imagining', in: *International Journal of Middle East Studies*, 27 (1995), 1.

——, *The Sole Spokesman: Jinnah, the Muslim League and the Demand for Pakistan*, Cambridge, 1985.

——, 'Inheriting the Raj: Jinnah and the Governor-Generalship Issue', in: *Modern Asian Studies*, 19 (1985), 1.

Jayawardena, Kumari, *Embodied Violence: Communalising Female Sexuality in South Asia*, London, 1996.

Johari, J.C., *Indian Government and Politics*, 2 vols. (12th edn.), Delhi, 1993.

——, *Comparative Politics* (3rd edn.), Delhi, 1982.

Joshi, V.C. (ed.), *Rammohun Roy and the Process of Modernization in India*, Delhi, 1975.

Kakar, Sudhir, *The Colours of Violence*, Delhi, 1996.

——, 'Some Unconscious Aspects of Ethnic Violence in India', in: Veena Das (ed.), *Structure and Cognition: Aspects of Hindu Caste and Ritual*, (2nd edn.), Delhi, 1992.

Kaura, Uma, 'Provincial Autonomy and the Congress-League Rift 1937-1939', in: Verinder Grover and Ranjana Arora (eds.), *Pakistan: Fifty Years of Independence*, Vol. I: *Towards Independence: The Pre-1947 Period*, Delhi, 1997b.

Kaushik, Asha and Surendra N. Kaushik, 'Religion as Political Ideology: The Separatist Crusade of Jinnah', in: Verinder Grover and Ranjana Arora (eds.), *Pakistan: Fifty Years of Independence*, Vol. I: *Towards Independence: The Pre-1947 Period*, Delhi, 1997b.

Kearney, Robert N., *Communalism and Language in the Politics of Ceylon*, Durham, 1967.

Kedouri, Elie, *see literature Theory.*

Kennedy, Kenneth A.R., 'Have Aryans been Identified in the Prehistoric Skeletal Record from South Asia?: Biological Anthropology and Concepts of Ancient Races', in: George Erdosy (ed.), *The Indo-Aryans of Ancient South Asia: Language, Material Culture and Ethnicity*, Delhi, 1997 [Berlin: 1995].

Kerrin Gräfin von Schwerin, 'Die indischen Muslime nach der Unabhängigkeit', in: Rolf Italiaander, *Die Herausforderung des Islam: Ein ökumenisches Lesebuch*, Göttingen, 1987.

Khairi, Saad R., *Jinnah Reinterpreted: The Journey From Indian Nationalism to Muslim Statehood*, Karachi, 1995.

Khaliq-uz-Zaman, C., *Pathway to Pakistan*, Lahore, 1961.

Khan, M. Ashgar (ed.), *Islam, Politics and the State: The Pakistan Experience*, London, 1985.

——, 'Pakistan's Geopolitical Imperatives', in: *see above.*

Khan, Dominique-Sila, *Conversions and Shifting Identities: Ramdev Pir and the Ismails in Rajasthan*, Delhi, 1997.

Khan, Omar A., 'Political and Economic Aspects of Islamization', in: M. Ashgar Khan (ed.), *Islam, Politics and the State: The Pakistan Experience*, London, 1985.

Khilnani, Sunil, *The Idea of India*, London, 1997.

Khubchandani, Lachman M., *Language, Culture and Nation-Building: Challenges of Modernization*, Shimla/Delhi, 1991.

Kitchen, Martin, *The Bristish Empire and Commonwealth: A Short History*, Basingstroke/London, 1996.

Klennert, Klaus, Oligarchische Gesellschaft und demokratischer Staat?: Der Fall Pakistan, in: *Politik und Gesellschaft*, 1, 1995.

Korejo, M.S., *The Frontier Gandhi: His Place in History*, Karachi, 1994.

Kothari, Rajni, *Politics in India*, Delhi, 1995 [Boston, 1970].

Kumar, Radha, 'Bosnia in the Annals of Partition: From Divide and Rule to Divide and Quit', in: Mushirul Hasan (ed.), *Islam, Communities and the Nation: Muslim Identities in South Asia and Beyond*, Delhi, 1998.

Kuwajima, Sho, *Muslims, Nationalism and the Partition: 1946 Provincial Elections in India*, Delhi, 1998.

Lakhi, M.V., 'Language and Regionalism in Pakistan', in: Verinder Grover and Ranjana Arora (eds.), *Pakistan: Fifty Years of Independence*, Vol. II: *Independence and Beyond, The Fifty Years: 1947-1997*, Delhi, 1997b.

Lapidus, Ira M., *see Literature on Islam.*

Lelyveld, David, *Aligarh's First Generation: Muslim Solidarity in British India*, Delhi et al., 1996.

Majumdar, R.C., *History of the Freedom Movement in India*, Calcutta, 1963.

——, *Three Phases of India's Struggle for Freedom*, Bombay, 1961.

Malik, Hafeez, *Moslem Nationalism in India and Pakistan*, Washington, 1963.

Mallory, J.P., *In Search of the Indo-Europeans, Language, Archeology and Myth*, London, 1989.

Mandelbaum, David, *Society in India*, Bombay, 1972.

Maniruzzaman, Talukder, *The Bangladesh Revolution and its Aftermath*, (2nd edn.), Dhaka, 1988.

Manor, James, '"Ethnicity" and Politics in India', in: *International Affairs*, 72 (1996), 3.

Maududi, Abdul A'la, 'Psychological Basis of Separate Electorates', in: Verinder Grover and Ranjana Arora (eds.), *Pakistan: Fifty Years of Independence*, Vol. II: *Independence and Beyond: The Fifty Years: 1947-1997*, Delhi, 1997b.

Mayer, Elizabeth, 'Islamization and Taxation in Pakistan', in: Anita S. Weiss (ed.), *Islamic Reassertion in Pakistan: The Application of Islam*, Syracuse (NY), 1986.

Mehta, V.R., *Foundations of Indian Political Thought* (2nd edn.), Delhi, 1996.

Menon, V.P., *The Transfer of Power in India*, Calcutta, 1957 [Madras, 1968].

Metcalf, Barbara D., 'Nationalist Muslims in British India: The Case of Hakim Ajmal Khan', in: *Modern Asian Studies*, 19 (1985), 1.

——, *Islamic Revival in British India: Deoband, 1860-1900*, Princeton, 1982.

Mill, James, *History of British India*, London, 1918.

Minault, Gail, *The Khilafat Movement: Religious Symbolism and Political Mobilization in India*, New York/Delhi, 1982.

Morgan, Kenneth O., *Labour in Power 1945-1951*, Oxford, 1984.

Müller, Friedrich Max, *Lectures on the Science of Language*, London, 1861.

——, *History of the Sanskrit Literature*, London, 1859.

Mukhia, Harbans, 'Medieval Indian History and the Communal Approach', in: Romila Thapar, Harbans Mukhia and Bipan Chandra (eds.), *Communalism and the Writing of Indian History*, Delhi, 1969.

Munir, Mohammad, *From Jinnah to Zia*, Lahore, 1980.

Nag, Sajal, 'The Forth Dimension of Indian National Movement', in: Verinder Grover and Ranjana Arora (eds.), *India: Fifty Years of Independence*, Vol. I: *Towards Independence: The Pre-1947 Period*, Delhi, 1997a.

Nanda, B.R., *Gandhi, Pan-Islamism, Imperialism and Nationalism*, Bombay et al., 1989.

Nayar, Kuldip, 'Birth of Muslim League', in: Verinder Grover and Ranjana Arora (eds.), *Pakistan: Fifty Years of Independence*, Vol. I: *Towards Independence: The Pre-1947 Period*, Delhi, 1997b.

Nehru, Jawaharlal, 'The Testament', in: Rafiq Zakaria (ed.), *A Study of Nehru*, Calcutta et al., 1997 [1989].

——, 'Secularism and Unity', in: Rafiq Zakaria (ed.), *A Study of Nehru*, Calcutta et al., 1997 [1989].

——, 'Indiens Weg zur Freiheit', Zürich, 1946b (excerpts on the term of nation in: Peter Alter (ed.), *Nationalismus*, Munich, 1994).

——, *The Discovery of India*, Delhi, 1946a.

Noorani, A.G., 'Muslim Identity: Self-Image and Political Aspirations', in: Mushirul Hasan (ed.), *Islam, Communities and the Nation: Muslim Identities in South Asia and Beyond*, Delhi, 1998.

Oddie, Geoffrey A. (ed.), *Religious Traditions in South Asia: Interaction and Change*, Richmond, 1998.

—— (ed.), *Religion in South Asia: Religious Conversion Movements in South Asia in Medieval and Modern Times* (2nd edn.), Delhi, 1991.

Page, David, *Prelude to Partition: The Indian Muslims and the Imperial System of Control 1920-1932*, Delhi, 1982.

Pandey, Gyanendra, *The Construction of Communalism in Colonial North India*, Delhi, 1990.

——, 'The Colonial Construction of "Communalism": British Writings on Banaras in the Ninteenth Century', in: Veena Das (ed.), *Mirrors of Violence: Communities, Riots and Survivers in South Asia*, Delhi, 1990.

Panikkar, K.N., *Communal Threat and Challenge*, Madras, 1997.

——, *Culture, Ideology, Hegemony: Intellectuals and Social Consciousness in Colonial India*, Delhi, 1995.

——, 'Culture and Communalism', in: *Social Scientist*, Vol. 21, Nos. 3-4, March-April 1993.

—— (ed.), *Communalism in India: History, Politics and Culture*, Delhi, 1991.

——, *Communalism in India: A Perspective for Intervention*, Delhi, 1991.

——, *Culture and Consciousness in Modern India*, Delhi, 1990.

——, 'Rationalism in the Religious Thought of Rammohun Roy', in: *Indian History Congress Proceedings*, 1973.

Panikkar, K.N. et al., *India's Struggle for Independence 1857-1947*, New York, 1989.

Parekh, Bhikhu, *Colonialism, Tradition and Reform: An Analysis of Gandhi's Political Discourse*, New Delhi/Newsbury Park/London, 1989b.

——, *Gandhi's Political Philosophy: A Critical Examination*, London et al., 1989a.

Parekh, Bhikhu and Nederveen-Pieterse (eds.), *The Decolonization of Imagination: Culture, Knowledge and Power*, London, 1995.

Phadnis, Urmila, *Ethnicity and Nation-building in South Asia*, Delhi, 1990.

Philips, C.H. (ed.), *The Partition of India 1947*, Leeds, 1967.

Philips, C.H. and M.D. Wainwright (eds.), *The Partition of India*, London, 1970.

Poliakov, Leon, *The Aryan Myth*, New York, 1974.

Prakash, Karat, *Language and Nationality Politics in India*, Bombay et al., 1973.

Prasad, Rajendra, 'Pakistan' [orig. 1940], in: Verinder Grover and Ranjana Arora (eds.), *India: Fifty Years of Independence*, Vol. I: *Towards Independence: The Pre-1947 Period*, Delhi, 1997a.

Qureshi, I.H., 'The Founder of Pakistan', in: Verinder Grover and Ranjana Arora (eds.), *Pakistan: Fifty Years of Independence*, Vol. I: *Towards Independence: The Pre-1947 Period*, Delhi, 1997b.

——, *The Struggle for Pakistan*, Karachi, 1965.

——, *The Muslim Community of the Indo-Pakistan Sub-Continent (610-1947): A Brief Historical Analysis*, The Hague, 1962.

Rashid, Abbas, 'Pakistan: The Ideological Dimension', in: M. Ashgar Khan (ed.), *Islam, Politics and the State: The Pakistan Experience*, London, 1985.

Rashid, Ahmed, *Taliban: Militant Islam, Oil and Fundamentalism in Central Asia*, New Haven/London, 2000.

Redfield, Robert, *see Literature Theory.*

Reetz, Dietrich, 'Islamische Bewegungen im kolonialen Indien: Konzepte und Quellen', in: Dietrich Reetz and Heike Liebau (eds.), *Globale Prozesse und "Akteure des Wandels": Quellen und Methoden ihrer Untersuchung*, Berlin, 1997.

Renfrew, Colin, *Archeology and Language: The Puzzle of Indo-European Origins*, London, 1987.

Richter, Justus, 'Hindunationalismus und islamischer Fundamentalismus in Südasien', in: *Aus Politik und Zeitgeschichte*, 4 July 1997.

Richter, William L., 'The Political Meaning of Islamization in Pakistan: Prognosis, Implications and Questions', in: Anita S. Weiss (ed.), *Islamic Reassertion in Pakistan: The Application of Islam*, Syracuse (NY), 1986.

Robinson, Francis, *Separatism Among Indian Muslims: The Politics of the United Provinces Muslims 1860-1923*, Delhi et al., 1993.

——, 'Islam and Muslim Separatism', in: David Taylor and Malcolm Yapp (eds.), *Political Identity in South Asia*, London, 1979.

Rothermund, Dietmar, *Krisenherd Kaschmir: Der Konflikt der Atommächte Indien und Pakistan*, Munich, 2002.

——, *Mahatma Gandhi: Eine politische Biographie* (2nd edn.), Munich, 1997.

——, *Indien: Kultur, Geschcihte, Politik, Wissenschaft, Umwelt*, Munich, 1995.

——, *Staat und Gesellschaft in Indien*, Mannheim et al., 1993.

——, *An Economic History of India: From Pre-Colonial Times to 1991* (2nd edn.), London et al., 1993.

——, *Mahatma Gandhi: An Essay in Political Biography*, Delhi, 1991.

——, *The German Intellectual Quest for India*, Delhi, 1986b.

——, *Die politische Willensbildung in Indien 1900-1960*, Wiesbaden, 1965.

Rothermund, D. and H. Kulke, *Geschichte Indiens*, Munich, 1998 (*A History of India*, London, 1986).

Roy, Asim, 'Islamization in South Asia with Special Reference to the Bengali-Speaking Region: A Conceptual and Historical Re-evaluation', in: Geoffrey A. Oddie (ed.), *Religious Traditions in South Asia: Interaction and Change*, Richmond, 1998.

——, 'The High Politics of India's Partition: The Revisionist Perspective', in: Mushirul Hasan (ed.), *India's Partition: Process, Strategy and Mobilization*, Oxford/Delhi, 1994.

Said, Edward, *see Literature Theory.*

Sankhder, M.M., 'Gandhi and the Partition of India', in: Verinder Grover, and Ranjana Arora (eds.), *India: Fifty Years of Independence*, Vol. I: *Towards Independence: The Pre-1947 Period*, Delhi, 1997a.

Sarkar, Sumit, *Modern India 1885-1947*, Madras, 1983.

Savarkar, S.S. and G.M. Joshi (eds.), *Historic Statements: V.D. Savarkar*, Bombay, 1967.

Savarkar, V.D., *Hindutva: Who is Hindu?, geschrieben und verteilt*, Delhi, 1922, 1969.

Sayeed, Khalid B., *The Political System of Pakistan*, Boston, 1967.

Seal, Anil, *The Emergence of Indian Nationalism: Competition and Collaboration in the Late Ninteenth Century*, Cambridge, 1971.

See also: Gallagher.

Seervai, H.M., *Partition of India: Legend and Reality* (2nd edn.), Bombay, 1994.

Sekhon, J.S., 'Islamic Content in Pakistan's Foreign Policy', in: Verinder Grover and Ranjana Arora (eds.), *Pakistan: Fifty Years of Independence.* Vol. II: *Independence and Beyond: The Fifty Years: 1947-1997*, Delhi, 1997b.

Shackle, Christopher and Rupert Snell, *Hindi and Urdu Since 1800: A Common Reader*, Delhi, 1990.

Sharma, L.P., *History of Medieval India, 1000-1740* (3rd edn.), Delhi, 1996.

Shrimali, Kalulal, *The Wardha Scheme: The Gandhian Plan of Education for Rural India*, Udaipur, 1949.

Singh, Karan, *Prophet of Indian Nationalism: Study of the Political Thought of Sri Aurobindo Gosh 1893-1910*, London, 1963.

Singh, Yogendra, *Modernization of Indian Tradition: A Sytemic Study of Social Change*, Jaipur/Delhi, 1996.

See also: Unnithan.

Sisson, Richard and Leo E. Rose, *War and Secession: Pakistan, India and the Creation of Bangladesh*, Delhi, 1990.

Smith, Anthony D., *see Literature Theory.*

Smith, Vincent A., *The Oxford History of India*, added and edited by Percival Spear, Oxford, 1990 [orig. 1958, from manuscripts of Smith 1919].

Smith, Wilfred C., *Modern Islam in India: A Social Analysis*, London/ Lahore, 1946.

See also: Vincent A. Smith

Syed, Muhammad A. (ed.), *Islam and Democracy in Pakistan*, Islamabad, 1995.

Talageri, Shrikant G., *Aryan Invasion Theory and Indian Nationalism*, Delhi, 1993.

Tangi, Shanti S., 'Intellectuals and Society in Ninteenth-Century India', in: *Comparative Studies in Society and History*, 4, 1961.

Taylor, David and Malcom Yapp (eds.), *Pakistan*, Oxford/Santa Barbara/Denver, 1990.

—— (ed.), *Political Identity in South Asia*, London, 1979.

Taylor, P.J.O., *What Really Happened During the Mutiny: A Day-by-Day Account of the Major Events of 1857-1859 in India*, Calcutta/Madras/Bombay, 1997.

Thapar, Romila, 'The Theory of Aryan Race and India: History and Politics', in: *Social Scientist*, 24 (1996), 1-3.

——, *Interpreting Early India*, Oxford/New York/ Delhi, 1992.

——, 'Imagined Religious Communities?: Ancient History and the Modern Search for a Hindu Identity', in: *Modern Asian Studies*, 23 (2) 1989 [also in: Thapar (1992)].

——, *The Past and Prejudice*, Delhi, 1975.

——, 'Communalism and Ancient Indian History', in: Romila Thapar, Harbans Mukhia and Bipan Chandra (eds.), *Communalism and the Writing of Indian History*, Delhi, 1969.

Thapar, Romila, Harbans Mukhia and Bipan Chandra (eds.), *Communalism and the Writing of Indian History*, Delhi, 1969.

Thursby, G.R., *Hindu-Muslim Relations in British India: A Study of Controversy, Conflict and Communal Movements in Northern India 1923-1928*, Leiden, 1975.

Tibi, Bassam, *see Literature on Islam.*

Titus, Murray T., *Islam in India and Pakistan*, Calcutta, 1959.

Veer, Peter van der, 'Riots and Rituals: The Construction of Violence and Public Space in Hindu Nationalism', in: Paul R. Brass (ed.), *Riots and Pogroms*, London et al., 1996a.

——, *Gods on Earth: The Management of Religious Experience and Identity in a North Indian Pilgrimage Centre*, Delhi/Oxford, 1989.

——, 'God Must be Liberated', in: *Modern Asian Studies*, 21 (1987), 2.

Wasti, S. Razi, 'Early Years of the All India Muslim League (1906-1910)', in: Verinder Grover and Ranjana Arora (eds.), *Pakistan: Fifty Years of Independence*, Vol. I: *Towards Independence: The Pre-1947 Period*, Delhi, 1997b.

Weiss, Anita S. (ed.), *Islamic Reassertion in Pakistan: The Application of Islam*, Syracuse (NY), 1986.

——, 'The Historical Debate on Islam and the State in South Asia', in: *see above.*

Wilder, Andrew, 'Islam and Political Legitimacy in Pakistan', in: Muhammad A. Syed (ed.), *Islam and Democracy in Pakistan*, Islamabad, 1995.

Wilkinson, Steven I., *see Literature Theory.*

Witzel, Michael, 'Early Indian History: Linguistic and Textual Parameters', in: George Erdosy (ed.), *The Indo-Aryans of Ancient South Asia: Language, Material Culture and Ethnicity*, Delhi, 1997 [Berlin, 1995].

Wolpert, Stanley A., *Jinnah of Pakistan*, New York/Oxford, 1984.

Yang, Anand, 'Sacred Symbol and Sacred Space in Rural India: Community Mobilization in the "Anti-Cow Killing" Riot of 1893', in: *Comparative Studies in Society and History*, 22 (1980), 4.

Yanuck, Martin, 'The Kanpur Mosque Affair of 1913', in: *Muslim World*, 64 (1974), 4.

Zaheer, Hasan, *The Separation of East Pakistan: The Rise and Realization of Bengal Muslim Nationalism*, Karachi, 1995.

Zakaria, Rafiq (ed.), *A Study of Nehru*, Calcutta et al., 1997 [1989].

——, 'A Many-Splendoured Life: An Essay in Biography', in: *see above.*

——, *Rise of Muslims in Indian Politics: An Analysis of Developments from 1885 to 1906*, Bombay, 1970.

Zaman, Waheed uz and M. Saleem Akhtar (eds.), *Islam in South Asia*, Islamabad, 1993.

Zia, Hussein K., 'Mountbattan and Partition', in: Verinder Grover and Ranjana Arora (eds.), *Pakistan: Fifty Years of Independence*, Vol. I: *Towards Independence: The Pre-1947 Period*, Delhi, 1997b.

Ziring, Lawrence,'Islam and Ethnicity', in: Muhammad A. Syed (ed.), *Islam and Democracy in Pakistan*, Islamabad, 1995.

Ziring, Lawrence et al. (eds.), *Pakistan: The Long View*, Durham, 1977.

Sources and Documents

Aziz, K.K. (ed.), *Muslims under Congress Rule 1937-39: A Documentary Record*, 2 vols., Delhi, 1986.

Bakshi, S.R. (ed.), *The Making of India and Pakistan: Select Documents*: Vol. I: *Congress and its Ideology*; Vol. II: *Muslim League and its Ideology*; Vol. III: *Ideology of Hindu Mahasabha and Other Political Parties*; Vol. IV: *British Policy in India*; Vol. V: *Congress, Muslim League and British Cabinet*; Vol. VI: *Partition of India*, Delhi, 1997.

Hyam, Ronald (ed.), *British Documents on the End of Empire: The Labour Government and the End of Empire, 1945-1951*, Vols. I and II, London, 1992.

'Jinnah's Inaugural Speech to the Pakistan Constituent Assembly 11.08.1947 as First President', in: Verinder Grover and Ranjana Arora (eds.), *Pakistan: Fifty Years of Independence*, Vol. II: *Independence and Beyond: The Fifty Years: 1947-1997*, Delhi, 1997b.

Statement by the Prime Minister Mohammad Nawaz Sharif (28.05.1998), Pressemitteilung zu den Atomtests Pakistans (edited by the embassy of Pakistan in the Federal Republic of Germany, Bonn).

BIBLIOGRAPHIES

Ahmad Khan, Muinuddin (ed.), *A Bibliographical Introduction to Modern Islamic Development in India and Pakistan 1700-1955*, Dacca, 1959.

Ahmed, Uta (ed.), *Bibliographie des deutschen Pakistan-Schrifttums bis 1974* (Bibliography of German Literature on Pakistan up to 1974), Hamburg, 1975.

Brechmann, Nicole (ed.), *Ethnische und religiöse Konflikte in Südasien*, Hamburg, 1995.

Satyaprakash (ed.), *Pakistan: A Bibliography 1962-1974*, Gurgaon/Delhi, 1975.

Vir, Dharma (ed.), *Gandhi Bibliography*, Chandigarh, 1967.

LITERATURE ON ISLAM AND RELATED ISSUES

MONOGRAPHS, ANTHOLOGIES, AND ARTICLES

Ahmad, Mumtaz, 'Pakistan', in: John L. Esposito (ed.), *The Oxford Encyclopedia of the Modern Islamic World*, Vol. 3, New York/London, 1995.

Ahmed, Eqbal, *see Literature on the Subcontinent.*

Antes, Peter, *Der Islam als politischer Faktor*, Bonn, 1991b.

Antes, Peter, et al., *Der Islam: Religion – Ethik – Politik*, Stuttgart/Berlin/Cologne, 1991a.

Bani-Sadr, Abol-Hassan, *Human Rights in Islam* (Arab Encyclopedia House), n.p., n.y.

Bodansky, Yossef, *Bin Laden: The Man Who Declared War on America*, New York et al., 2001.

Burke, Edmund, 'Islam and Social Movements: Methodological Reflections', in: Edmund Burke and Ira M. Lapidus (ed.), *Islam, Politics and Social Movements*, Berkeley, 1988.

Burke, Edmund and Ira M. Lapidus (eds.), *Islam, Politics and Social Movements*, Berkeley, 1988.

Caesar, F. Farah, 'Islamic Fundamentalism as an Alternative to Nationalism', in: Ivo Banac, John G. Ackermann and Roman Szporluk (eds.), *Nation and Ideology: Essays in Honor of Wayne S. Vucinich*, Boulder/New York, 1981.

Cahen, C., *Der Islam*, Vol. I: *Vom Ursprung bis zu den Anfängen des Osmanenreiches*, Fischer Weltgeschichte, Vol. XIV, Frankfurt/M., 1991.

'Der', *Der Islam*, Fischer-Weltgeschichte, Vol. XV, Frankfurt/M., 1984.

Esposito, John L. (ed.), *The Oxford Encyclopedia of the Modern Islam World*, Oxford, 1995.

Geertz, Clifford, *see Literature Theory.*

Gellner, Ernest, *see Literature Theory.*

Glasnek, J., *Kemal Atatürk und die moderne Türkei*, Berlin, 1971.

Grunebaum, Gustave E. von (ed.), *Der Islam*, Vol. II.: *Die islamischen Reiche nach dem Fall von Konstantinopel*, Fischer Weltgeschichte, Vol. XV, Frankfurt/M., 1971.

See also, Aziz Ahmad, *in the literature on India.*

Halm, Heinz., *Die Schia*, Darmstadt, 1988.

Heine, Peter and Reinhold Stipek, *Ethnizität und Islam: Differenzierung und Integration muslimischer Bevölkerungsgruppen*, Gelsenkirchen, 1984.

Italiaander, Rolf, *Die Herausforderung des Islam: Ein ökumenisches Lesebuch*, Göttingen, 1987.

Khaldun, Ibn, *The Muqaddimah, translated into English by F. Rosenthal*, London, 1958.

Khoury, Adel T., Ludwig Hagemann and Peter Heine (eds.), *Islam-Lexikon*, Freiburg/Basel/Vienna, 1991.

Lapidus, Ira M., *A History of Islamic Societies*, Cambridge et al., 1988.

——, 'Islamic Political Movements: Patterns of Historical Change', in: Edmund Burke and Ira M. Lapidus (eds.), *Islam, Politics and Social Movements*, Berkeley, 1988.

Lewis, Bernard, *Kaiser und Kalifen: Christentum und Islam im Ringen um Macht und Vorherrschaft*, Munich, 1996 (*Islam and the West*, New York, 1993).

——, 'Die vielfältigen Ebenen der Identität im Nahen Osten', in: Michalski, Krzystof (ed.), *Identität im Wandel*, Stuttgart, 1995.

——, *The Political Language of Islam*, Chicago/London, 1988.

——, *Istanbul and the Civilization of the Ottoman Empire*, Oklahoma, 1963.

See also Braude in the *Literature on the Balkans.*

Nagel, T., *Staat und Glaubensgemeinschaft im Islam*, 2 vols., Zürich, 1981.

Piscatori, James P., *Islam in a World of Nation-States*, Cambridge/New York, 1986.

—— (ed.), *Islam in the Political Process*, Cambridge/New York, 1983.

Rosenthal, Erwin I., *Islam and the Modern National State*, Cambridge, 1965.

Ruthven, Malise, *Islam in the World* (2nd edn.), Oxford, 2000.

Schimmel, Annemarie, 'Der Islam in unserer Zeit', in: Rolf Italiaander (ed.), *Die Herausforderung des Islam: Ein ökumenisches Lesebuch*, Göttingen, 1987.

——, *Der Islam im indischen Subkontinent*, Darmstadt, 1983.

Schulze, Reinhard, *Geschichte der Islamischen Welt im 20 Jahrhundert*, Munich, 1994.

——, *Islamischer Internationalismus im 20. Jahrhundert: Untersuchungen zur Geschichte der Islamischen Weltliga*, Leiden et al., 1990.

Steinbach, Udo, *Der Islam im Nahen Osten, Informationen zur politischen Bildung*, Vol. 238, Bonn, 1993.

Tibi, Bassam, 'Die Spannung zwischen islamischen Universalismus und säkularem Nationalismus im Schatten der fundamentalistischen Herausforderung', in: Dietrich Schlegel (ed.), *Der neue Nationalismus: Ursachen, Chancen, Gefahren*, Schwalbach/Ts., 1994.

——, 'Die islamische Dimension des Balkan-Krieges', in: *Europa-Archiv*, 22, 1993 (also in: Angelika Volle and Wolfgang Wagner (eds.), *Der Krieg auf dem Balkan: Die Hilflosigkeit der Staatenwelt*, Bonn, 1994).

——, *Die Krise des modernen Islams: Eine vorindustrielle Kultur im wissenschaftlich-technischen Zeitalter*, Frankfurt/M., 1991.

——, *Vom Gottesreich zum Nationalstaat: Islam und panarabischer Nationalismus*, Frankfurt/M., 1987.

——, 'Islam and Modern European Ideologies', in: *International Journal of Middle East Studies*, 81, 1986.

——, *Nationalismus in der Dritten Welt am arabischen Beispiel*, Frankfurt/M., 1971.

Documents

Koran: Interpretation of the Meanings of the Noble Qur'an in the English Language (Arabic-English edition, translated by Muhammad Taqi-ud-Din Al-Hilali and Muhammad Muhsin Khan) (4th edn.), Riyadh, 1994.

LITERATURE ON THEORY

Monographs, Anthologies, and Articles

Almond, Gabriel and Sidney Verba, *The Civic Culture Revisited*, Boston, 1982.

——, *The Civic Culture: Political Attitudes and Democracy in Five Nations*, Princeton, 1963.

Alter, Peter (ed.), *Nationalismus: Dokumente zur Geschichte und Gegenwart eines Phänomens*, Munich/Zürich, 1994.

——, *Nationalismus*, Frankfurt/M., 1985.

American Behavioral Scientist, Special Issue on Ethnicity, 38, 1995.

Anderson, Benedict R., *Imagined Communities: Reflections on the Origin and Spread of Nationalism*, London/New York, 1991 (*Die Erfindung der Nation: Zur Karriere eines folgenreichen Konzepts*, Frankfurt/M., 1993, 2nd edn. 1996).

Armstrong, J.A., *Nations Before Nationalism*, Chapel Hill (N.C.), 1982.

Balakrishnan, Gopal (ed.) *Mapping the Nation*, London/New York, 1996.

Banac, Ivo, John G. Ackermann and Roman Szporluk (eds.), *Nation and Ideology: Essays in Honor of Wayne S. Vucinich*, Boulder/New York, 1981.

Banton, Michael, 'Rational Choice Theories', in: *American Behavioral Scientist*, 38, 1995.

Barber, Benjamin R., *Jihad vs. McWorld*, New York, 1995.

Barth, Frederik (ed.), *Ethnic Groups and Boundaries: The Social Organization of Culture Difference*, Oslo/London, 1969.

Bates, Robert H. and Barry R. Weingast, 'A New Comparative Politics: Integrating Rational Choice and Interpretivist Perspectives', paper presented at Duke University, Durham (N.C.), März, 1995.

Bauer, Otto, *Die Nationalitätenfrage und die Sozialdemokratie* (2nd edn.) Vienna, 1924 [1908].

Beck, Ulrich, 'Das Demokratie-Dilemma im Zeitalter der Globalisierung', in: *Aus Politik und Zeitgeschichte*, 38, 1998.

Bell, D., 'Ethnicity and Social Change', in: Nathan Glazer and Daniel P. Moynihan (eds.), *Ethnicity: Theory and Experience*, Cambridge (Mass.), 1975.

Bell, W. and W.E. Freeman (eds.), *Ethnicity and Nation-Building: Comparative, International, and Historical Perspectives*, Beverly Hills/London, 1974.

Bell-Fialkoff, Andrew, *Ethnic Cleansing*, New York, 1999.

Berend, Ivan, *see Literature on the Balkans.*

Berghe van den, Pierre L., *The Ethnic Phenomenon*, New York et al., 1981.

——, 'Race and Ethnicity: A Sociobiological Perspective', in: *Ethnic and Racial Studies*, 1, 1978.

See also Brass, Paul.

Bertsch, Gary K., 'The Revival of Nationalisms', in: *Problems of Communism* 22, Nov.-Dec. 1973.

Beyme, Klaus von, *Systemwechsel in Osteuropa*, Frankfurt/M., 1994.

Bhambhri, C.P., *see Literature on the Subcontinent.*

Blasco, P.G., 'Modern Nationalism in Old Nations as a Consequence of Earlier State-Building: The Case of Basque-Spain', in: W. Bell and W.E. Freeman (eds.), *Ethnicity and Nation-Building: Comparative, International, and Historical Perspectives*, Beverly Hills/London, 1974.

Brass, Paul, *see Literature on the Subcontinent.*

Breuilly, John, *Nationalism and the State*, Chicago, 1993.

——, 'Reflections on Nationalism', in: *Philosophy of Social Science*, 15, 1985.

Brubaker, Rogers, *Nationalism Reframed: Nationhood and the National Question in the New Europe*, Cambridge, 1996.

Clyne, Michael (ed.), *Pluricentric Languages: Differing Norms in Different Nations*, Berlin/New York, 1992.

——, Introduction, in: *see above.*

——, Epilogue, in: *see above.*

Coakley, John, 'The Resolution of Ethnic Conflict: Towards a Typology', in: *International Political Science Review*, 13 (1992), 4.

Cohen, Anthony P., *The Symbolic Construction of Community*, London/New York, 1985.

Comparative Studies on Governments and Non-Dominant Ethnic Groups in Europe, 1850-1940, European Science Foundation (ed.), 8 vols., New York, 1992.

Connor, Walker, *Ethnonationalism: The Quest for Understanding*, Princeton, 1994.

——, 'The Nation and its Myth', in: Anthony D. Smith (ed.), *Ethnicity and Nationalism*, Leiden/New York/Cologne, 1992.

——, 'The Impact of Homelands Upon Diasporas', in: Gabriel Sheffer (ed.), *Modern Diasporas in International Politics*, London/Sidney, 1986.

—— (ed.), *Mexican Americans in Contemporary Perspective*, Washington, 1985.

Coulton, G.C., 'Nationalism in the Middle-Ages', in: *Cambridge Historical Journal*, 5, 1935.

Dann, Otto, *Nation und Nationalismus in Deutschland 1770-1990* (3rd edn.), Munich, 1996.

Deutsch, Karl W., 'Nation und Welt', in: Winkler, Heinrich-August (ed.), *Nationalismus* (2nd edn.), Königstein/Ts., 1985.

——, 'Space and Freedom: Conditions for the Temporary Separation of Incompatible Groups', in: *International Political Science Review*, 5 (1984), 2.

——, 'On Nationalism, World Regions and the Nature of the West', in: Per Torsvik (ed.), *Mobilization, Centre-Periphery Structures, and Nation-building: In Commemoration of Stein Rokkan*, Bergen/Oslo/Tromsø, 1981.

——, *Der Nationslismus und seine Alternativen*, Munich, 1972b.

——, *Nationenbildung – Nationalstaat – Integration*, Düsseldorf, 1972a.

——, *Nationalism and Social Communication: An Inquiry into the Foundations of Nationality* (2nd edn.), Cambridge (Mass.)/London, 1966.

——, 'Social Mobilization and Political Development', in: *American Political Science Review*, 55, 1961.

Diner, Dan, 'Die jüdisch-israelische Nationalität: Über die Dialektik der Anerkennung', in: Wolfgang Benz and Hermann Graml (eds.), *Weltprobleme zwischen den Machtblöcken: Das 20 Jahrhundert III* (Weltbild Weltgeschichte, Vol. 36), Augsburg, 1998.

——, *Israel in Palästina: Über Tausch und Gewalt im Vorderen Orient*, Königstein/Ts., 1980.

Dipankar, Gupta, *The Context of Ethnicity: Sikh Identity in a Comparative Perspective*, Delhi et al., 1997.

Dock, Adolf, *Revolution und Restauration über die Suveränität*, Aalen, 1972 [1900].

Camilleri, Joseph A., 'Rethinking Sovereignty in a Shrinking, Fragmented World', in: R.B.J. Walker and Saul H. Mendlovitz (edn.), *Contending Sovereignties: Redefining Political Community*, Boulder/London, 1990.

Cassirer, Ernst, *Wesen und Wirken des Symbolbegriffs*, Darmstadt, 1994b.

——, *Philosophie der symbolischen Formen*, Vol. II: *Das mythische Denken*, Darmstadt, 1994a [1924].

——, *Der Mythos des Staates: Philosophische Grundlagen politisches Verhaltens*, Frankfurt/M., 1985 [1949].

Devetak, Silvo, 'The Right to Self-Determination as the Basis of Stability and Integration in Europe', in: Silvo Devetak, Sergej Flere and Gerhard Seewann (eds.), *Kleine Nationen und Ethnische Minderheiten im Umbruch Europas* (*Small Nations and Ethnic Minorities in an Emerging Europe*), Munich, 1993.

——, 'Ethnic Minorities and State-Nation: Equality or Subjugation'?, in: Gerhard Seewann (ed.), *Minderheitenfragen in Südosteuropa*, Munich, 1992.

Devetak, Silvo, Sergej Flere and Gerhard Seewann (eds.), *Kleine Nationen und Ethnische Minderheiten im Umbruch Europas* (*Small Nations and Ethnic Minorities in an Emerging Europe*), Munich, 1993.

Dörner, Andreas, *Politischer Mythos und symbolische Politik*, Opladen, 1995.

Edelstein, J.C., 'Pluralist and Marxist Perspectives on Ethnicity and Nation Building', in: W. Bell and W.E. Freeman (eds.), *Ethnicity and Nation-Building: Comparative, International, and Historical Perspectives*, Beverly Hills/London, 1974.

Elster, Jon, *Nuts and Bolts for the Social Sciences*, Cambridge, 1989.

Elwert, Georg, 'Nationalismus und Ethnizität: Über die Bildung von Wir-Gruppen', in: *Kölner Zeitschrift für Soziologie und Sozialpsychologie*, 41, 1989.

Emerson, Rupert, *From Empire to Nation: The Rise to Self-Assertion of Asian and African Peoples*, Cambridge (Mass.), 1960.

Enloe, Cynthia, 'Religion and Ethnicity', in: Peter F. Sugar (ed.), *Ethnic Diversity and Conflict in Eastern Europe*, Santa Barbara, 1980.

Eriksen, Thomas H., 'Ethnicity and Nationalism', in: *Anthropological Perspectives*, London/Boulder, 1993.

Esser, H., 'Ethnische Differenzierung und moderne Gesellschaft', in: *Zeitschrift für Soziologie*, 1988.

Estel, Bernd, 'Nation als Mythos', in: Wolfgang Frindte and Harald Pätzold, (eds.), *Mythen der Deutschen*, Opladen, 1994.

Fishman, Joshua A., *Language and Nationalism*, Rowley (Mass.), 1972.

Flere, Sergej, 'Tolerance as a Requirement for Ethnic Conflict Resolution', in: Silvo Devetak, Sergej Flere and Gerhard Seewann (eds.), *Kleine Nationen und Ethnische Minderheiten im Umbruch Europas* (*Small Nations and Ethnic Minorities in an Emerging Europe*), Munich, 1993.

Fraenkel, Ernst, *Völkerrecht und Internationale Beziehungen*, Munich/Vienna, 1994.

Friedman, Thomas L., *The Lexus and the Olive Tree: Understanding Globalization*, New York 2000.

Frindte, Wolfgang and Pätzold Harald (eds.), *Mythen der Deutschen*, Opladen, 1994.

Ganzer, Burkhard, 'Zur Bestimmung des Begriffs der ethnischen Gruppe', in: *Sociologus*, 40, 1990.

Geiss, Imanuel, *see Literature on the Balkans.*

Geertz, Clifford, 'The Integrative Revolution: Primordial Sentiments and Civic Politics in the New States', in: Welch, C.E. Jr., *Political Modernization* (2nd edn.), Belmont, 1971.

—— (ed.), *Old Societies and New States: The Quest for Modernity in Asia and Africa*, New York, 1963.

Gellner, Ernest, *Encounters with Nationalism*, Oxford/Cambridge (Mass.), 1994.

——, *Nations and Nationalism*, Ithaca/New York, 1983 (*Nationalismus und Moderne*, Berlin, 1991).

——, 'Nationalism', in: George Weidenfeld and Nigel Nicholson (eds.), *Thought and Change*, London, 1964.

Giles, Howard and Saint-Jacques Bernard (eds.), *Language and Ethnic Relations*, Oxford, 1979.

Glazer, Nathan and Daniel P. Moynihan (eds.), *Ethnicity: Theory and Experience*, Cambridge (Mass.), 1975.

Gosztony, Kristóf, 'Nationalitätenkonflikte in ehemals sozialistischen Ländern: Ein spieltheoretisches Modell', in: *Osteuropa*, 43 (1993), 7.

Grothusen, Klaus-Detlev, *see Literature on the Balkans.*

Gurr, Ted R., 'Why Minorities Rebel: A Global Analysis of Communal Mobilization and Conflict Since, 1945', in: *International Political Science Review*, 14 (1993), 2.

Habermas, Jürgen, 'The European Nation-state: Its Achievements and Its Limits. On the Past and Future of Souvereignty and Citizenship', in: Gopal Balakrishnan (ed.), *Mapping the Nation*, London/New York, 1996.

——, 'Anerkennungskämpfe im demokratischen Rechtsstaat', in: Taylor, Charles (ed.), *Multikulturalismus und die Politik der Anerkennung*, Frankfurt/M., 1993.

Hackstein, Katharina and Erwin Orywal, 'Ethnizität: Die Konstruktion ethnischer Wirklichkeiten', in: Thomas Schweizer, Margarethe Schweizer and Waltraud Kokot (eds.), *Handbuch der Ethnologie*, Berlin, 1993.

Hall, John A. (ed.), *The State of the Nation: Ernest Gellner and the Theory of Nationalism*, Cambridge, 1998.

——, 'Introduction', in: *see above.*

Haller, Max, 'New Societies or Social Anomie – Or Where Will the Awakening of Ethnic and National Consciousness in Europe Lead?', in: Silvo Devetak, Sergej Flere and Gerhard Seewann (eds.), *Kleine Nationen und Ethnische Minderheiten im Umbruch Europas* (*Small Nations and Ethnic Minorities in an Emerging Europe*), Munich, 1993.

Handelman, Don, *Models and Mirrors: Towards an Anthropology of Public Events*, Cambridge et al., 1990.

Hardtwig, Wolfgang, *Nationalismus und Bürgerkultur in Deutschland 1500-1914*, Göttingen, 1994.

Hebeisen, Michael W., *Souveränität in Frage gestellt: Die Souveränitätslehren von Hans Kelsen, Carl Schmitt und Hermann Heller im Vergleich*, Baden-Baden, 1995.

Hechter, Michael, *Principles of Group Solidarity*, Berkeley, 1987.

Heckmann, Friedrich, 'Ethnische Vorurteile', in: Gerhard Seewann (ed.), *Minderheiten als Konfliktpotential in Ostmittel- und Südosteuropa*, Munich, 1995.

——, *Ethnische Minderheiten, Volk und Nation: Soziologie interethnischer Beziehungen*, Stuttgart, 1992.

——, 'Ethnos, Demos und Nation, oder: Woher stammt die Intoleranz des Nationalstaates gegenüber ethnischen Minderheiten?', in: Gerhard Seewann (ed.), *Minderheitenfragen in Südosteuropa*, Munich, 1992.

——, 'Volk, Nation, ethnische Gruppe und ethnische Minderheiten: Zu einigen Grundkategorien von Ethnizität', in: *Österreichische Zeitschrift für Soziologie*, 3, 1988, pp. 16-31.

Hegel, Georg W.F., *Grundlinien der Philosophie des Rechts*, Stuttgart, 1970 [1821].

Held, David, *Models of Democracy*, Stanford (CA), 1987.

See also: McLennan, Gregor.

Henkin, Louis, 'The Mythology of Sovereignty', in: R.S. Macdonald (ed.), *Essays in Honour of Wang Tieya*, London, 1993.

Herder, Johann Gottfried von, *Ideen zur Philosophie der Geschichte der Menschheit*, 4 vols., Tübingen, 1806-7 (new edition: Berlin/Weimar, 1965).

——, 'Über den Ursprung der Sprache, Tübingen 1769', in: Regine Otto (ed.), *Herders Werke*, Vol. II, Berlin/Weimar, 1982.

Hobsbawm, Eric J., *On History*, New York, 1997.

——, *Age of Extremes: The Short Twentieth Century, 1914-1991*, London, 1994.

——, *Nations and Nationalism since 1780: Programme, Myth, Reality*, Cambridge, 1990 (*Nationen und Nationalismus: Mythos und Realität seit 1780*, Frankfurt-M./New York, 1991).

Hobsbawm, Eric J. and Terence Ranger (eds.), *The Invention of Tradition*, Cambridge, 1983.

Hösch, Edgar, *see Literature on the Balkans.*

Horowitz, Donald L., 'Irredentas and Secessions: Adjacent Phenomena, Neglected Connections', in: Anthony D. Smith (ed.), *Ethnicity and Nationalism*, Leiden/New York/Cologne, 1992.

——, *Ethnic Groups in Conflict*, Berkeley, 1985.

Hroch, Miroslav, 'Das Bürgertum in den nationalen Bewegungen des 19 Jahrhunderts: Ein europäischer Vergleich', in: Jürgen Kocka (ed.), *Bürgertum im 19. Jahrhundert: Deutschland im europäischen Vergleich*, Vol. 3, Munich, 1988.

——, *Social Preconditions of National Revival in Europe: A Comparative Analysis of the Social Composition of Patriotic Groups among the Smaller European Nations*, Cambridge, 1985.

——, 'Das Erwachen kleiner Nationen als Problem der komparativen sozialgeschichtlichen Forschung', in: Theodor Schiedler (ed.), *Sozialstruktur und Organisation europäischer Nationalbewegungen*, Munich, 1971; and in: Heinrich-August Winkler (ed.), *Nationalismus*, Königstein/Ts., 1985.

——, *Die Vorkämpfer der nationalen Bewegung bei den kleinen Völkern Europas: Eine vergleichende Analyse zur gesellschaftlichen Schichtung patriotischer Gruppen*, Prag, 1968.

Huntington, Samuel P., *The Clash of Civilizations*, New York, 1996 (*Kampf der Kulturen*, Munich/Vienna, 1996).

——, 'The Clash of Civilizations', in: *Foreign Affairs*, 72 (1993), 3.

——, *The Third Wave: Democratization in the Late Twentieth Century*, Oklahoma, 1991.

——, *Political Order in Changing Societies*, New Haven/London, 1968.

Hutchinson, John, 'Moral Innovators and the Politics of Regeneration: The Distinct Role of Cultural Nationalists in Nation-Building', in: Anthony D. Smith (ed.), *Ethnicity and Nationalism*, Leiden/New York/Cologne, 1992.

——, 'A Nation is a Nation, is a State, is an Ethnic Group, is a . . .', in: *Ethnic and Racial Studies*, 1 (1978), 4.

Hutchinson, John and Anthony D. Smith (eds.), *Nationalism*, Oxford, 1994.

Ignatieff, Michael, *Blood and Belonging: Journeys to the New Nationalism*, London, 1993.

Inglehart, Ronald, *Culture Shift in Advanced Industrial Society*, Princeton (NJ), 1990.

Johari, J.C., *see Literature on the Subcontinent.*

Kant, Immanuel, *Political Writings*, ed. Hans Reiss, Cambridge et al., 1991.

——, *Die Metaphysik der Sitten*, Stuttgart, 1990 [1797].

——, 'Idee zu einer allgemeinen Geschichte in weltbürgerlicher Absicht', in *Schriften zur Geschichtsphilosophie*, Stuttgart, 1985 [1784].

——, *Zum ewigen Frieden*, Stuttgart, 1984 [1795].

Kaschuba, Wolfgang, 'Identité, altérité et mythe ethnique', in: *Ethnologie française*, 27 (1997), 4.

—— (ed.), *Kulturen – Identitäten – Diskurse: Perspektiven Europäischer Ethnologie*, Berlin, 1995.

Kedourie, Elie, *Nationalism in Asia and Africa*, London, 1971.

——, *Nationalism* (4th edn.), London, 1993 [1960] (*Nationalismus*, Munich, 1971).

Kerr, Donal A. (Hg:), 'Religion, State and Ethnic Groups', in: *Comparative Studies on Governments and Non-dominant Ethnic Groups in Europe, 1850-1940*, Vol. II, New York, 1992.

——, *Religion, State and Ethnic Identity*, in: *see above.*

Kiliánová, Gabriela, 'Ethnicity, Culture and Boundaries: The Central European Case', in: *Ethnologia Europaea*, 16 (1995) 2.

Kimminich, Otto, *Einführung in das Völkerrecht* (6th edn.), Tübingen/Basel, 1997.

King, Gary, Robert O. Keohane and Sidney Verba, *Designing Social Enquiry: Scientific Inference in Qualitative Research*, Princeton (NJ), 1994.

Klinar, Peter, 'Ethnic Conflicts in Postsocialist Societies in Europe: The Case of Yugoslavia and Slovenia', in: Silvo Devetak, Sergej Flere and Gerhard Seewann (eds.), *Kleine Nationen und Ethnische Minderheiten im Umbruch Europas* (*Small Nations and Ethnic Minorities in an Emerging Europe*), Munich, 1993.

Kocka, Jürgen (ed.), *Bürgertum im 19 Jahrhundert: Deutschland im europäischen Vergleich*, 3 vols., Munich, 1988.

Köstlin, Konrad, 'Das ethnographische Paradigma und die Ethnologia Europaea', in: *Ethnologia Europaea*, 16 (1995), 2.

Kohn, Hans, *Prelude to Nation-States: The French and German Experience 1789-1815*, New York, 1967.

——, *Die Idee des Nationalismus: Ursprung und Geschichte bis zur Französischen Revolution*, Frankfurt/M., 1962 [*The Idea of Nationalism, Toronto*, 1969 (New York (1944)].

——, *Nationalism: Its Meaning and History*, Princeton, 1955.

——, *Geschichte der nationalen Bewegungen im Orient*, Berlin, 1928.

Konrád, György, *Vor den Toren des Reichs*, Frankfurt/M., 1997.

Kratochwil, Gabi, *Die Berber in der Entwicklung Algeriens, 1949-1990: Zur Konstruktion einer ethnischen Identität*, Berlin, 1996.

Kreile, Renate, 'Politisierung von Ethnizität in Afrika', in: *Aus Politik und Zeitgeschichte*, 9, 1997.

Kuper, Leo, 'Political Change in Plural Societies: Problems in Racial Pluralism', in: *International Social Science Journal*, 23 (1971), 4.

Lake, David A., 'Ethnic Conflict and International Intervention', in: *Policy Brief (IGCC)*, 3, 1995.

Lal, Barbara B., 'Symbolic Interactionist Theories', in: *American Behavioral Scientist*, 38, 1995.

Lemberg, Hans, '"Ethnische Säuberung": Ein Mittel zur Lösung von Nationalitätenproblemen?', in: *Aus Politik und Zeitgeschichte*, 46, 1992.

Lepsius, Rainer M., *Interessen, Ideen und Institutionen*, Opladen, 1990.

Lessing, Gotthold Ephraim, *Nathan der Weise*, Stuttgart, 1987 [orig. 1779].

Lévi-Strauss, Claude, *Mythos und Bedeutung*, Frankfurt/M., 1996.

Lijphart, Arend, 'Prospects for Power-sharing in the New South Africa', in: Andrew Reynolds (ed.), *Election '94 South Africa*, London/Cape Town/New York, 1994.

——, *Democracies: Patterns of Majoritarian and Consensus Government in Twenty-One Countries*, New Haven/London, 1984.

——, *Democracy in Plural Societies: A Comparative Exploration* (2nd edn.), New Haven, 1980.

Linz, Juan J., 'From Primordialism to Nationalism', in: Edward A. Tiryakian and Ronald Rogowski, *New Nationalisms of the Developed West*, Boston, 1985.

Lipschutz, Ronnie and Beverly Crawford, 'Ethnic Conflict Isn't', in: *Policy Brief (IGCC)*, 2, 1995.

Manor, James, *see Literature on the Subcontinent.*

Mayall, James, *Nationalism and International Society*, Cambridge, 1990.

Mayall, James and Mark Simpson, 'Ethnicity is not Enough: Reflections on Protracted Secessionsism in the Third World', in: Anthony D. Smith (ed.), *Ethnicity and Nationalism*, Leiden/New York/Cologne, 1992.

McKay, James and Frank Lewis, 'An Exploratory Synthesis of Primordial and Mobilizationalist Approaches to Ethnic Phenomena', in: *Ethnic and Racial Studies*, 5, 1982.

Meinecke, Friedrich, *Weltbürgertum und Nationalstaat: Studien zur Genesis des deutschen Nationalstaates* (4th edn.), Munich/Berlin, 1917.

Mickey, Robert and Adam Albion Smith, 'Resolving Ethnic Conflict: A Rethorical Intervention', in: Silvo Devetak, Sergej Flere and Gerhard Seewann (eds.), *Kleine Nationen und Ethnische Minderheiten im Umbruch Europas* (*Small Nations and Ethnic Minorities in an Emerging Europe*), Munich, 1993.

Mill, John Stuart, *On Liberty and Other Essays*, ed. John Gray, London/New York, 1991 (esp.: Considerations on Representative Government, Kap. XVI: Of Nationality, as Connected with Representative Government [1861]).

Mlinar, Zdravko, 'Small Nations and European Integration', in: Silvo Devetak, Sergej Flere and Gerhard Seewann (eds.), *Kleine Nationen und Ethnische Minderheiten im Umbruch Europas* (*Small Nations and Ethnic Minorities in an Emerging Europe*), Munich, 1993.

Moynihan, Daniel P., *Pandaemonium: Ethnicity in International Politics*, New York, 1993.

See also: Glazer.

Münkler, Herfried, 'Nationale Mythen im Europa der frühen Neuzeit: Die Relevanz mythischer Narrationen bei der Nationalisierung Europas', in: Jürgen Habermas, *Ernst Cassirer und die Bibliothek Wartburg*, Berlin, 1997.

——, 'Politische Mythen und nationale Identität: Überlegungen zu einer Theorie politischer Mythen', in: Wolfgang Frindte and Harald Pätzold (eds.), *Mythen der Deutschen*, Opladen, 1994.

Münkler, Herfried, Hans Grünberger and Kathrin Mayer, *Nationenbildung: Die Nationalisierung Europas im Diskurs humanistischer Intellektueller: Italien und Deutschland*, Berlin, 1998.

Münkler, Herfried and Wolfgang Storch, *Siegfrieden: Politik mit einem deutschen Mythos*, Berlin, 1988.

Nagel, Joanne, 'Resource Competition Theories', in: *American Behavioral Scientist*, 38, 1995.

Nielsson, Gunnar P., 'States and "Nation-Groups": A Global Taxanomy', in: Edward A. Tiryakian and Ronald Rogowski, *New Nationalisms of the Developed West*, Boston, 1985.

Okamura, J.Y., 'Situational Ethnicity', in: *Ethnic and Racial Studies*, 4, 1981.

Okey, Robin, *see Literature on the Balkans.*

Olzak, Susan, *The Dynamics of Ethnic Competition and Conflict*, Stanford, 1992.

Oommen, T.K., *Alien Concepts and South Asian Reality: Responses and Reformulations*, Delhi/Thousand Oaks/London, 1995.

Othmar, Nikola H., 'Religion, Nationalismus und Bürgerkrieg in Bosnien', in: Dietrich Schlegel (ed.), *Der neue Nationalismus, Ursachen, Chancen, Gefahren*, Schwalbach/Ts., 1994.

Paech, Norman, 'Minderheitenpolitik und Völkerrecht', in: *Aus Politik und Zeitgeschichte*, 6 Nov. 1998.

Pasquino, Pascale, 'Le concept de nation et les fondéments du droit public de la Révolution: Sieyès', in: François Furet (ed.), *Héritage de la Révolution Française*, Paris, 1989.

Patterson, O., 'Context and Choice in Ethnic Allegiance: A Theoretical Framework and a Caribbean Casestudy', in: Nathan Glazer and Daniel P. Moynihan (eds.), *Ethnicity: Theory and Experience*, Cambridge (Mass.), 1975.

Platon, *Der Staat (Politeia)*, Munich, 1991.

Preuß, Ulrich K. (ed.), *Zum Begriff der Verfassung: Die Ordnung des Politischen*, Frankfurt/M., 1994.

——, Introduction, in: *see above.*

Ragin, Charles C., *The Comparative Method: Moving Beyond Qualitative and Quatitative Strategies*, Berkeley/Los Angeles/London, 1987.

Ránki, György, *see Literature on the Balkans.*

Redfield, Robert, *Peasant Society and Culture*, Chicago, 1956.

Reiter, Norbert, *Gruppe, Sprache, Nation*, Wiesbaden/Berlin, 1984.

—— (ed.), *Nationalbewegungen auf dem Balkan*, Berlin, 1983.

—— 'Sprache und nationale Funktion', in: Klaus-Detlev Grothusen (ed.), *Ethnogenese und Staatsbildung in Südosteuropa*, Göttingen, 1974.

Reiterer, Albert F., 'Die politische Konstitution von Ethnizität', in: Gerhard Seewann (ed.), *Minderheitenfragen in Südosteuropa*, Munich, 1992.

——, *Die unvermeidbare Nation: Ethnizität, Nationalität und nachnationale*, Gesellschaft, Frankfurt/M., 1988.

Renan, Ernest, *Qu'est-ce qu'une nation?: Discours et conférences*, Paris, 1887 [1882] ('What is a Nation?', in: Homi Bhabha (ed.), *Nation and Narration*, London, 1990).

Rhoodie, Nic, 'Ethnicity: Some Major Conceptional Problems Regarding its Basic Behavioural Manifestations', in: Silvo Devetak, Sergej Flere and Gerhard Seewann (eds.), *Kleine Nationen und Ethnische Minderheiten im Umbruch Europas* (*Small Nations and Ethnic Minorities in an Emerging Europe*), Munich, 1993.

Rizman, Rudolf, 'The Sociological Dimension of Conflicts Between Ethnonationalisms', in: Silvo Devetak, Sergej Flere and Gerhard Seewann (eds.), *Kleine Nationen und Ethnische Minderheiten im Umbruch Europas* (*Small Nations and Ethnic Minorities in an Emerging Europe*), Munich, 1993.

Rösel, Jakob, 'Ethnic Nationalism and Ethnic Conflict', in: *Politik und Gesellschaft*, 2, 1995.

Rogowski, Ronald, 'Causes and Varieties of Nationalism: A Rationalist Account', in: Edward A. Tiryakian and Ronald Rogowski, *New Nationalisms of the Developed West*, Boston, 1985.

——, Conclusion, in: *see above.*

Rogowski, Ronald and Edward A. Tiryakian (eds.), *New Nationalisms of the Developed West*, Boston, 1985.

Said, Edward, *Orientalism*, London, 1995 [1978].

——, *Kultur und Imperialismus: Einbildungskraft und Politik im Zeitalter der Macht*, Frankfurt/M., 1994.

Schad, Ute, 'Wenn Kultur zur Falle wird: Entwicklungt und Gefahren einer kulturalisierenden Sichtweise in Gesellschaft und interkultureller Praxis', in: *Interkulturell*, 2-3, 2001.

Scheffler, Thomas, 'Ethnoradikalismus: Zum Verhältnis von Ethnopolitik und Gewalt', in: Gerhard Seewann (eds.), *Minderheiten als Konflikt-potential in Ostmittel- und Südosteuropa*, Munich, 1995.

Schieder, Theodor, *Nationalismus und Nationalstaat: Studien zum nationalen Problem im modernen Europa*, Göttingen, 1991.

Schlegel, Dietrich (ed.), *Der neue Nationalismus: Ursachen, Chancen, Gefahren*, Schwalbach/Ts., 1994.

Schmitt, Carl, *Der Begriff des Politischen*, Berlin, 1991 [1932].

Schödl, Günter, *see Literature on the Balkans.*

Schulze, Hagen, *Staat und Nation in der europäischen Geschichte*, Munich, 1999.

Schweizer, Thomas, Margarethe Schweizer and Waltraud Kokot (eds.), *Handbuch der Ethnologie*, Berlin, 1993.

Seewann, Gerhard, *see Literature on the Balkans.*

Seton-Watson, Hugh, *Nations and States: An Enquiry into the Origins of Nations and the Politics of Nationalism*, London, 1977.

Sharma, C.L., 'Ethnicity, National Integration, and Education in Japan', in: *The Journal of East and West Studies*, 25 (1996), 1.

Shils, S.E. (ed.), *Center and Periphery: Essay in Macrosociology*, Chicago/London, 1975.

——, 'Primordial, Personal, Sacred and Civil Ties (Aufsatz erstmals, 1957 veröffentlicht)', in: *see above.*

Shoup, Paul, 'The Evolution of a System', in: *Problems of Communism* 18, July-October 1969.

Smith, Anthony D., 'Culture, Community and Territory: The Politics of Ethnicity and Nationalism', in: *International Affairs*, 72 (1996), 3.

——, *Nations and Nationalism in a Global Era*, Cambridge, 1995.

—— (ed.), *Ethnicity and Nationalism*, Leiden/New York/Cologne, 1992.

——, 'Nationalism and the Historians', in: *see above.*

Smith, Donald E. (ed.), *Religion and Political Modernization*, New Haven/ London, 1974.

——, *Religion, Politics and Social Change in the Third World*, New York, 1971.

Smooha, Sammy and Theodor Hanf, 'The Diverse Modes of Conflict Regulation in Deeply Divided Societies', in: Anthony D. Smith (ed.), *Ethnicity and Nationalism*, Leiden/New York/Cologne, 1992.

Solomos, John and Les Back, 'Marxism, Racism and Ethnicity', in: *American Behavioral Scientist*, 38, 1995.

Stalin, J.V., *Marxism and the National Question*, New York, 1942.

Stanovcic, Vojislav, 'Problems and Options in Institutionalizing Ethnic Relations', in: *International Political Science Review*, 13 (1992), 4.

Steinberg, James B., 'International Involvement in the Yugoslav Conflict', in: Lori F. Damrosch (ed.), *Enforcing Restraint: Collective Intervention in Internal Conflicts*, New York, 1993.

Sterbling, Anton, 'Ethnische Strukturen und ethnische Parteien in Südosteuropa', in: *Südosteuropa*, 8, 1996.

Stone, John, 'Race, Ethnicity, and the Weberian Legacy', in: *American Behavioral Scientist*, 38, 1995.

Sulzbach, Walter, *Die Zufälligkeit der Nationen und die Inhaltslosigkeit der internationalen Politik*, Berlin, 1969.

Sundhaussen, Holm, *see Literature on the Balkans.*

Tagore, Rabindranath N., *Nationalism*, London, 1950 (*Nationalismus*, Munich, 1921).

Tarrow, Sidney, *Power in Movement: Social Movements, Collective Action and Politics*, Cambridge (Mass.), 1994.

Tiryakian, Edward, *see:* Ronald Rogowski.

Tiryakian, Edward and Neil Nevitte, 'Nationalism and Modernity', in: Edward A. Tiryakian and Ronald Rogowski, *New Nationalisms of the Developed West*, Boston, 1985.

Tönnies, Ferdinand, *Gemeinschaft und Gesellschaft*, Darmstadt, 1972 (acc. to edn. 1935) [1887] (*Community and Association*, London, 1955).

Tomuschat, Christian, 'Staatsvolk ohne Staat?', in: Staats- und Völkerrechtsordnung – Festschrift für Karl Doehring, Berlin, 1989.

Torsvik, Per (ed.), Mobilization, Centre-Periphery Structures, and Nation-building', in: *Commemoration of Stein Rokkan*, Bergen/Oslo/Tromsø, 1981.

Treffer, Gerd, *Israels Identitätskrise: Israel zwischen Judaismus, Zionismus und Israelismus*, Munich, 1975.

Varshney, Ashutosh, 'Ethnic Conflict and Rational Choice', paper presented at the meeting of the American Political Science Association in Chicago, 1995.

Voigt, Rüdiger (ed.), *Symbol der Politik – Politik der Symbole*, Opladen, 1989.

Walby, Sylvia, 'Women and Nation', in: Anthony D. Smith (ed.), *Ethnicity and Nationalism*, Leiden/New York/Cologne, 1992.

Walker, R.B.J. and Saul H. Mendlovitz (eds.), *Contending Sovereignties: Redefining Political Community*, Boulder/London, 1990.

Weber, Max, *Wirtschaft und Gesellschaft*, Tübingen, 1972 [1921].

Wehler, Hans-Ulrich, *Modernisierungstheorie und Geschichte*, Göttingen, 1975.

Wieland, Carsten, *see Literature on the Balkans.*

Wilkinson, Steven I., 'India, Consociational Theory, and Ethnic Violence', in: *Asian Survey* 40 (2000), 5.

Winkler, Heinrich-August (ed.), *Nationalismus* (2nd edn.), Königstein/Ts., 1985.

—— (ed.), *Nationalismus in der Welt von heute*, Göttingen, 1982.

Winkler, Heinrich-August and Hartmut Kaelble (eds.), *Nationalismus – Nationalitäten – Supranationalität*, Stuttgart, 1993.

Young, Crawford, *The Politics of Cultural Pluralism*, Madison, 1976. *See also:* Lipschutz, Ronnie.

Zimmermann, Moshe, *Wende in Israel: Zwischen Nation und Religion*, Berlin, 1996.

Sources and Documents

Charter of the United Nations and Statute of the International Court of Justice, United Nations Department of Public Information (ed.), New York, 1993.

Padover, Saul K. (ed.), *Wilson's Ideals*, Washington, D.C., 1942.

Universal Declaration of Human Rights, United Nations Department of Public Information (ed.), New York, 1993.

Bibliographies

Bentley, G. Carter, *Ethnicity and Nationality: A Bibliographical Guide*, Seattle/London, 1981.

Deutsch, Karl W. and L. Merritt (eds.), *Nationalism and National Development: An Interdisciplinary Bibliography on Nationalism 1935-1965*, Cambridge (Mass.), 1970.

Winkler, H.A. and T. Schnabel (eds.), *Bibliographie zum Nationalismus*, Göttingen, 1979

Index